THE PRE-OCCUPATION

OF POSTCOLONIAL STUDIES

THE

PRE-OCCUPATION

OF POSTCOLONIAL

STUDIES

EDITED BY FAWZIA AFZAL-KHAN

AND KALPANA SESHADRI-CROOKS

DUKE UNIVERSITY PRESS

Durham & London 2000

© 2000 Duke University Press
All rights reserved
Printed in the United States of America on acid-free paper ⊗
Typeset in Octavian by Tseng Information Systems, Inc.
Library of Congress Cataloging-in-Publication Data
appear on the last printed page of this book.
Permission to reprint previously published material appears on page 413.

CONTENTS

ACKNOWLEDGMENTS

We thank the many people who over the long and arduous years that this project has taken to complete have helped enormously with advice and suggestions. We are particularly grateful to Ken Wissoker. He has been an inspiring and exemplary editor. We thank him for his faith in this project and for his unerring advice through the years. Thanks to Richard Morrison for guiding us through the final stages of the production process, Ben Robertson for helping with the index, and to all our contributors for staying with us to the finish.

INTRODUCTION

At the Margins of Postcolonial Studies: Part 1

KALPANA SESHADRI-CROOKS

Postcoloniality is the condition of what we might ungenerously call a comprador intelligentsia: of a relatively small, Western-style, Western-trained group of writers and thinkers who mediate the trade in cultural commodities of world capitalism at the periphery. —Anthony Appiah, "The Postcolonial and the Postmodern"

As soon as any radically innovative thought becomes an -ism, its specific groundbreaking force diminishes, its historical notoriety increases, and its disciples tend to become more simplistic, more dogmatic, and ultimately more conservative, at which time its power becomes institutional rather than analytical. —Barbara Johnson, "Nothing Fails Like Success"

In the third world no one gets off on being third world. —Gayatri Spivak, "What Is It For?"

As the epigraphs to this essay suggest, the field of postcolonial studies is at present beset by a melancholia induced paradoxically by its new-found authority and incorporation into institutions of higher learning. As some of the essays in this volume attest (Larsen, Shohat), this melancholic condition derives not only from postcolonial scholars' apprehension that institutionalizing the critique of imperialism may render it conciliatory, but from other significant factors such as their own (First World) place of speaking (which implicates them in the problematic of neocolonialism), their criteria for political self-legitimation (i.e., the impossibility of representing the Third World as an anti-imperialist constituency, especially in the face of the retreat of socialism), and their peculiar immobility as an effective oppositional force for curricular change within the (American and British) academies. It is especially in the last sense that postcolonial studies differs from ethnic studies: for instance, unlike African or Asian American studies, it cannot commit itself to canon revision, which is essentially a minoritarian project. And, although it is often associated with the impossible category *Third World literature*, as a specific form of cultural criticism it continually questions such totalizing concepts and thus maintains a critical if not hostile relation to multiculturalism. The melancholia of postcolonialism also derives from the fact that today it faces its major criticisms and attacks against its very legitimacy and political viability from within its own ranks.[1] The term itself has become suspect: a catchall phrase for a post- (read fashionable) Third Worldism (see Ella Shohat's essay in this volume).

While postcolonial studies has not pervaded every arena of scholarly inquiry in the humanities today, it is not far-fetched to suggest that it has certainly acquired, if not power, a certain institutional cachet, or, to use Arif Dirlik's term, an *aura*, of innovativeness. Evidence of this newfound cachet or mystique is lodged, for instance, in a note in Naomi Schor's peculiar defense mounted on behalf of French departments in the United States. She says: "Commenting on the interest in postcolonialism, an eminent and respected colleague recently opined that Europe was dead. The statement seems astonishing in view of current (political) and future (economic) developments in that part of the world, which represents a population of 325 million and constitutes the second largest economic block in the world."[2] What is interesting here is that a scholar of such perspicuity as Schor asserts the importance of Europe instead of noting, for instance, the imbrication of Europe and postcolonial states or her colleague's peculiar disengagement of Europe from its others. This is to say that she seems aware of the growing influence of a so-called postcolonial studies but seems unclear about its scholarly foci, be it the critique of the continuing economic, political, and linguistic power of Europe and North America over the Third World (as the work of Edward Said and Samir Amin would testify) or of its institutional place—that it is not a parallel discipline to English or French literary studies but offers a critique of national literatures as such. It is inevitable that this sense of the postcolonial mystique renders the field incoherent, if not totally *bankrupt* (to use Emily Apter's term), to most area- or period-based scholars.[3] While there is no doubt that the field has grown rapidly in the past few years, producing its own journals, conferences, book-publishing series, and jobs (the recent spate of readers and anthologies, of which this volume is a part, bears testimony to the phenomenon), the field itself remains undefinable and amorphous in its outlines.[4] While it is possible to valorize rather than lament specific aspects of this amorphousness, much of the melancholia from within and the mystification from without emerges, I would argue, from an inadequately enunciated notion of the margin. The largely mechanical connection, even conflation, of postcolonialism with American multiculturalism, despite its perceived difference, even distance, from the latter, has meant that the relation between postcolonial studies and other minority studies has remained undertheorized (see Powell, Boyarin, and Afzal-Kahn in this volume). What we compromise by neglecting to articulate the linkages between these two (largely academic) initiatives is not only a more textured or nuanced notion of the margin, but the particularity and possibility of a postcolonial critique. In the following, I briefly consider the ideological thrust of multiculturalism and postcolonialism through a reading of Charles Taylor and Iain Chambers, respectively, not so much to rehearse their differences as to show how both discourses share a notion of the margin (as a spatial category) and thus once more overlook the possibilities of a postcolonial critique.

In the following, I focus on Charles Taylor as he represents one of the more popular and commonsense arguments in favor of multiculturalism, which I acknowledge is neither a consensual nor a monolithic practice or discourse. In "The Politics of Recognition," Taylor argues that multiculturalism is based on the recognition of the dialogic nature of identity.[5] As he defines it, the politics of recognition is based not so much on the admission of historical injustice (as with affirmative action) as on contemporary coevality.[6] According to Taylor, insofar as identity is constituted in our relations with others, being ignored or being negatively represented could have a detrimental effect on one's sense of self. Thus, the right of the powerless or of people in the minority to agitate for proper recognition (through inclusion of their cultural contributions in the curriculum) is deemed consistent with our notions of authenticity and dignity. As Taylor puts it:

> The reason for these proposed changes is not, or not mainly, that all students may be missing something important through the exclusion of a certain gender or certain races or cultures, but rather that women and students from the excluded groups are given, either directly or by omission, a demeaning picture of themselves, as though all creativity and worth inhered in males of European provenance. Enlarging and changing the curriculum is therefore essential not so much in the name of a broader culture for everyone as in order to give due recognition to the hitherto excluded. The background premise of these demands is that recognition forges identity. (pp. 65–66)

The key terms in Taylor's analysis of multiculturalism are *recognition* and *respect,* or the equal right to dignity. Taylor locates the concept of multiculturalism squarely in Western liberalism, and much of his characterization of multiculturalism as the quest for recognition is undergirded by a subjectivist notion of authenticity: "Being true to myself means being true to my own originality, which is something only I can articulate and discover. In articulating it, I am also defining myself. I am realizing a potentiality that is properly my own. This is the background understanding to the modern ideal of authenticity, and to the goals of self-fulfillment and self-realization in which the ideal is usually couched" (p. 31).

This sense of authenticity, Taylor says, quoting Herder, can be extended to "the people" as well, which idea then inaugurates the modern form of nationalism. Decolonization, according to Taylor, is "to give the peoples of what we now call the Third World their chance to be themselves unimpeded" (p. 31); in other words, it is a way of returning them to their authentic selves. It is obvious from this emphasis on authenticity that Taylor will privilege traditional and integrated societies. But the key issue in his argument, apropos multiculturalism, is judgment. No society, he argues, can be judged (as worthy or worthless) before it has been studied with respect. Taylor deplores the form of multiculturalism that demands not just respect and recognition but equal worth before study as hypocritical at worst and condescending at best. As a presumption he will allow "that it is reasonable to suppose that cultures that have provided the horizon of meaning for large numbers of human beings, of diverse characters and temperaments, over a long period of time—that have, in other words, articulated their sense of the good, the holy, the admirable—are almost certain to have something that deserves our admiration and respect, even if it is accompanied by much that we have to abhor and reject" (pp. 72–73).

But *real* judgments of worth, he suggests, must be reserved until after study, a study that will transform our standards of judgment and achieve "a fusion of horizons" in Gadamer's sense of the phrase. We will then be able to form judgments of worth on a comparative basis, for judgments of value and worth "cannot be dictated by a principle of ethics" says Taylor. They "are ultimately a question of the human will" (p. 69). Of course, the fact that, in studying a given culture, a transformation of one's standards of judgment may make comparative study logically impossible does not seem to trouble Taylor too much, invested as he is in the core authentic self that can apparently alter its perceptions of a culture without changing its fundamental vision of global cultural differences.

To sum up, in Taylor's notion of multiculturalism, hierarchy between groups can be redressed through recognition and respect for the other's authenticity. Marginalized people must be dealt with fairly, and all cultures must be given the right to survive in their authenticity. Such a formulation then necessarily assumes the following: integrated cultures; traditional, long-surviving cultures; stable national, ethnic, and cultural identities; the possibility of studying and completely comprehending the other; comparative studies; and, finally, "authentic" judgments of others based, not on ethics, but on human will. Taylor's multiculturalism is thus an epistemology of the other that can make sense only within the Christian liberal tradition that he invokes as its proper context. For our purposes, his analysis is useful as a reminder of two aspects of multiculturalism as it is practiced in the United States: (*a*) As a reinforcement of Western liberalism, it is essentially supplicatory: it asks to partake in the privileges of the center. (*b*) Despite its professed revisionism, it seeks to extend the bourgeois sphere of influence.

On a more mundane level, we see these claims borne out in Peter Brooks's 19 December 1994 letter to the editor of the *New York Times*. Addressing Yale's albatross, the $20 million gift from Lee Bass (which has since been returned) to establish a Western civilization program, Brooks says most trenchantly: "Western civilization versus multiculturalism is a false opposition." As Roger Rouse argues in his analysis of the bourgeois management of the crisis of the nation-state in the age of transnationalism: "The greatest significance of conservative monoculturalism [which argues for 'a single culture and identity' for the United States] and corporate liberal-multiculturalism [which appropriates the radicalism of Left/liberal arguments] lies in their relationship of complimentary opposition. Always offering at least the illusion of significant choice, they have seemed to fully exhaust the field of imaginable alternatives and, in doing so, they have endowed their commonalities [emphasis on bourgeois class positions, nationalism, and educational and political reform] with a powerfully constraining force."[7] We would do well to remember that, in our discussions of the alliance between postcolonialism and multiculturalism, far from undermining the hegemony of Western modernity as emblematized by the bourgeoisie, multiculturalism merely expands its frontiers both geographically (world culture itself is appended to the United States) and pedagogically, as the universal system of knowledge in terms of both method and ideology.

The discipline of postcolonial studies, however, is a much more ambiguous one pedagogically, given that it is not really a minority studies. Rather than enhancing the girth of Western liberalism, postcolonial studies, if it is possible to speak of it as a unity or generalize its political impulse, would work to examine the conditions by which a group arrogates to itself the function of granting or denying recognition and respect. Furthermore, it would seriously call into question Taylor's advocacy of studying the other for comparative purposes as another form of imperialism or Orientalism: one that reinscribes the Western bourgeois cultural relativist as universal subject with the other serving as informant.[8] However, I would argue that it is the critique of the discourses of modernity (of rationalism, even of humanism, and values of radical transformation), which, when undertaken by postcolonial studies, positions it awkwardly as neither liberalism nor Marxism, that has generated the crisis within this subdiscipline. In other words, it is at this point of differentiation from liberal multiculturalism (which characterizes itself as marginality studies) that postcolonial discourse becomes politically vulnerable. But, before I take up this theme with reference to Aijaz Ahmad's influential Marxist denunciation of the field on the grounds of its postmodern biases (see also Larsen in this volume), it is imperative to see how the agenda of postmodern criticism misappropriates postcoloniality by characterizing it yet again as the discourse of the margin (as the space of otherness) and placing it at the vanguard of cultural and political critique.

Affirmative action and multiculturalism in their liberal mode conceptualize the margin spatially, as the excluded and unintegrated other. In some ways, these initiatives posit a utopian moment when the marginal as such will cease to exist, with power circulating freely and fluidly connecting and equalizing all points of being. In this conception, the marginal is the space of agitation, subversion, and thus theoretical innovation. But, if with George Yudice we reexamine the notion of marginality as an essentially innovative space, we realize the futility of such a claim, which can be made only through an evasion of material history: "There was a time when to be 'marginal' meant to be excluded, forgotten, overlooked. Gradually, throughout this century, first in the discourses of anthropology, sociology, and psychoanalysis, 'marginality' became a focus of interest through which 'we' (Western culture) discovered otherness and our own ethnocentric perspectives. Today, it is declared, the 'marginal' is no longer peripheral but central to all thought." [9]

What is worth noting here is the way the spatial margin, that is, the margin as subject position, becomes also the source of rejuvenation of the center, where knowledge as positive knowing is made possible. The academic industry of postcolonial studies has gained the status of a phenomenon within this paradigm. Thus, despite its contrary political impulses (as I show in my reading of Iain Chambers), it is uncritically aligned (by liberalism and postmodernism) in an analogical relation with multiculturalism and thus faces the consequence of melancholia or debilitation. To elaborate: what this subdiscipline is perceived to offer today that ostensibly no other minority or ethnic studies does is not so much a revolutionary method, inventive theories, or even new fields of inquiry, but quite literally (and perhaps crudely) an exotic new frontier, a hitherto unaccounted for margin that must be tamed or theorized: it is here, we tell ourselves, that a theory will be made that will express in dazzling synchronicity and relationality the disparate and incorrigible issues of race, ethnicity, gender, nation, class, and Eurocentrism as well as the conditions of marginality, migration, and minoritization. For many scholars situated outside the field, postcolonial studies seems to or is exhorted to offer the possibility of a radically revised history: a relentlessly dissident method of reading that will alter the way business is done in and out of the academy. An excellent and particularly compelling example of this kind of exhortation is Iain Chambers's in many ways exemplary *Migrancy, Culture, Identity*.[10]

In the chapter "The Broken World," Chambers argues that the presence of increasingly vocal postcolonials in the metropolis not only challenges the univocity of European thought construed as reason, logic, universal, and objective but further confounds the comfortable binarisms of self and other, margin and periphery, English and native. The significant consequence of this disruption of categories is, however, according to Chambers, the exposure of the notion of authenticity: its fascist potential when deployed as Europeanness or Englishness and its derivativeness when deployed simplistically as Negritude (pace Leopold Senghor) or nativism. For Chambers, unlike Taylor, authenticity is not a subjective category but a structural one, positioning actors outside modernity. "To relinquish such a perspective" of authenticity or of returning to the roots, says Chambers, "leads us to recognise a post-colonial and post-European context in which historical and cultural differences, while moving to different rhythms, are coeval, are bound to a common time. 'Communication is, ultimately, about creating shared Time' " (p. 74).[11] In other words, insofar as (that suspect category of) authenticity, either of the self or of the objectifiable other, is enabled by the imperialist logic of modernity that positions others as occupying another temporality, the recognition of coevality in the postcolonial world means that claiming authenticity is no longer feasible: "Post-colonialism is perhaps the sign of an increasing awareness that it is not feasible to subtract a culture, a history, a language, an identity, from the wider, transforming currents of the increasingly metropolitan world. It is impossible to 'go home' again" (p. 74). For Chambers, the poetics of postmodernism best expresses this condition of homelessness and inevitable hybridity. Naming the cultural fusions in world music and other art forms the *metropolitan vernacular,* he interestingly circumvents the Marxist problematic of postmodern aesthetics as a symptom of late capitalism by citing a passage from Roland Robertson (see pp. 76–77) on the notion of local market demands versus the totalizing agency of capitalism without commenting adequately on it.[12] Further, he asks whether phenomena such as world music are not engaging in

> a movement of historical decentering in which the very axis of center and periphery, together with its economic, political and cultural traffic, has, as a minimum, begun to be interrogated from elsewhere, from other places and positions? For is it not possible to glimpse in recent musical contaminations, hybrid languages and cultural mixtures an opening on to other worlds, experiences, histories, in which not only does the 'Empire write back to the center,' as Salman Rushdie puts it, but also 'sounds off' against it? . . . The master's language is transformed into creole . . . and all varieties of local cultural refashioning, as it moves to a different tempo in a 'reversal of colonial history.' (pp. 84–85)

What is most commendable about Chambers's analysis is his insistence that the margin/center dichotomy be thoroughly dispersed. From within this productive confusion, he suggests, may arise two consequences: the exposure of the state apparatus in all its repressive and ideological operations and a recognition of the implication of the citizenry in all forms of repression: "Previous margins — ethnic, gendered, sexual — now reappear at the center. No longer restricted to the category of a 'special issue' (e.g. 'race relations'), or 'problem' (e.g. 'ethnic minorities,' 'sexual deviancy'), such differences become central to our very sense of time, place and identity" (p. 86).

But, despite (or perhaps because of) his utopian futurism, there are several logical problems in Chambers's argument. First is his inadvertent totalization of the postcolonial subject. In his single-minded determination to blow up the center, the postcolonial construed as the logical agent of sedition is made to carry the bomb. Less metaphorically: it is Chambers's assumption that all migrant subjects inevitably constitute a subculture that is untenable. It is this unstated assumption that enables him to construct pantheons of black artists and postcolonial discourse theorists as collectively (even consensually) engaged in the critique of the Occident in a manner that elides serious differences between these writers and ignores these writers as occupying (academically and performatively) an internally conflictual space.[13] As Stuart Hall puts it with reference to black British cinema:

> Films are not necessarily good because black people make them. They are not necessarily "right-on" by virtue of the fact that they deal with the black experience. Once you enter the politics of the end of the black subject you are plunged headlong into the maelstrom of a continuously contingent, unguaranteed, political argument and debate: a critical politics, a politics of criticism. You can no longer conduct black politics through the strategy of a simple set of reversals, putting in the place of the bad old essential white subject, the new essentially good black subject. Now, that formulation may seem to threaten the collapse of an entire political world.[14]

In other words, Chambers's vision of resistance does not enter into that phase of political engagement that Hall has rightly characterized as the shift from a "relations of representation," which involves counterracist narratives and a struggle over access to representation, to a "politics of representation," which not only involves theorizing the differences of race, ethnicity, and culture but is a "struggle around positionalities" itself: "There is another position, one which locates itself *inside* a continuous struggle and politics around black representation, but which then is able to open up a continuous critical discourse about themes, about the forms of representation, the subjects of representations, above all, the regimes of representation. Once you abandon essential categories, there is no place to go apart from the politics of criticism and to enter the politics of criticism in black culture is to grow up, to leave the age of critical innocence."[15]

Second, in his critique of authenticity secured by the argument about temporal noncoevality, Chambers elides Fabian's recommendation to create coevality for proper communication with a recognition of coevality given the condition of postcolonialism. Thus, coevality or the lack of it then becomes merely false consciousness; what is important, Chambers seems to suggest, is that we recognize that we are really, that is to say authentically, coeval. The problem with this logic is twofold: First, the situating of authenticity as a spatial category and that of hybridity as a temporal one effectively locates authenticity (insofar as space is conceived nonhistorically) on another temporal register outside the transforming currents of time. Second, authenticity is somehow made to depend on disjunct temporalities, and vice versa, and thus the absolute pronouncement—that one can never go home again. Thus, the postcolonial is not only always already hybrid but is so always in reference to the West. What Chambers is unable to visualize in his delineation of postcolonial ontology, which is really an idealization of the migrant as postcolonial paradigm, are forms of cultural practice—musical or otherwise—that adapt to and march in step with Western hegemony but do define themselves as authentic insofar as they continue indifferent to the West for purposes of validation, perpetuation, and aesthetic evaluation. This form of authenticity must, however, be distinguished from Taylor's more subjectivist and essentialist notion. In other words, authenticity can be understood more in performative than in ontological terms. The vigorous state of classical art music in North and South India is an example of this form of authenticity, and its practitioners not only presuppose the possibility of going home but would probably argue (despite their itinerant lifestyles) that they never left in the first place.[16] In other words, I am suggesting that Chambers's implication of authenticity in noncoevality is a non sequitur and has the curious effect of recasting the erstwhile dead native as hybrid. The overall effect, as I implied earlier, is the construction of the postcolonial as an authentically dissident or marginal subject. It is in response to this interpellation that postcolonial studies falls into melancholia and sometimes political disarray.

While it may appear that Taylor's liberal multiculturalism and Chambers's dissonant politics of no respect are aversive, what is interesting in both their analyses is the way in which the terms *authenticity, hierarchy,* and *margin* carry enormous burdens of significance. Briefly: while for Taylor (the recognition of) authenticity as "a vital human need" (p. 26) is an individualist category that directly impinges on one's self-esteem and sense of well-being, for Chambers authenticity is a structural notion, a subject position—an impossibility in the modern world because it implies hierarchy: "Subordinate subjects have invariably been ordained to the stereotyped immobilism of an essential 'authenticity,' in which they are expected to play out roles, designated for them by others ... for ever" (p. 38). Hierarchy for Taylor, however, means nonreciprocal "other dependence" (see pp. 44–51); for Chambers it means temporal noncoevality. Hierarchy can be undone for Taylor with respect and recognition (temporality and modernity being nonfactors in his analysis); for Chambers, on the other hand, hierarchy can be undone only through hybridity and confusion of categories. Modernity as Chambers construes it is univocal and imperialist and cannot accommodate authentic differences.[17] Both Taylor and Chambers agree, then, that equality and difference are contradictory and inevitably based on a notion of sameness. But Taylor is willing to let the contradiction lie, while Chambers wants to create equality where difference becomes a basis for identity rather than alienation. For Taylor, the margin is "them," the others who must be dealt with and managed: "The challenge is to deal with their sense of marginalization without compromising our basic political principles" (p. 63). The West, he implies, is guilty and can redress the problem. The margin for Chambers is the site of subversion; it must be made to arrive at the center and disrupt it. For both Taylor and Chambers, however, as I mentioned earlier, the margin is a source of rejuvenation. A future moment must be posited when it will be either incorporated or dissolved and hierarchy undone.

Gayatri Chakravorty Spivak has addressed the profound contradictions of this liberal/postmodern demand most notably in her "Who Claims Alterity?" Regarding the position of marginality (construed as a potentially subversive space) sometimes claimed by but often imposed on postcolonial subjects, Spivak says of this ideological entrapment:

> The stories of the postcolonial world are not necessarily the same as the stories coming from "internal colonization," the way the metropolitan countries discriminate against disenfranchised groups in their midst. The diasporic postcolonial can take advantage (most often unknowingly, I hasten to add) of the tendency to conflate the two in the metropolis. Thus this frequently innocent informant, identified and welcomed as the agent of an alternative history, may indeed be the site of a chiasmas, the crossing of a double contradiction: the system of production of the national bourgeoisie at home, and abroad, the tendency to represent neocolonialism by the semiotic of "internal colonization."[18]

The consequence of this poorly analyzed double contradiction is that, by homogenizing and masking the contingent otherness of postcoloniality into an undifferentiated margin, the political efficaciousness of a postcolonial critique is considerably weakened. However, it is actually in its points of differentiation from such homogenizing notions of the margin, more precisely in its critique of positive knowledge alluded to earlier, that postcolonial studies faces its greatest challenges. It is not simply that being marginal is no longer a possibility but that some of the ways in which the margin as sign and standard (as a measure of value and as political cause) gets deployed produce some of the impasses in our field.

We can conceive of margin/marginality in two ways. On the one hand, the margin can be conceived as the subject position — the excluded other that must be coaxed into the center through incorporation, inversion, hybridization, revolution. On the other hand, the margin can be conceived as the irreducible remainder — that which is necessarily excluded by every regime of power/knowledge, including that of the discourse of rights. In other words, the margin can be conceived, not so much as that which is external to the power structure, but rather as its constitutive outside, an intimate alterity that marks the limit of power. The margin or marginal, then, need not necessarily be tied to an identity, group, or individual predicated on a proper privation. Such a margin is the province, I argue, of multiculturalism and ethnic studies. The postcolonial margin must be acknowledged as incommensurable and nonrecuperable; on the other hand, given its investment in the critique of the discourses of modernity, this margin produces the very condition for the production of knowledge as such. The margin here functions as the residue of representation, which is discerned when the other is presented as immediately available in its truth and essence. The former notion speaks the positive discourse of rights, the latter the negative discourse of limits.[19] With reference to the latter: in *The Order of Things*, Foucault characterizes modernity itself as marked by the emergence of man in his finite spatiality as the subject and object of his own knowledge:

> At the foundation of all the empirical positivities, and of everything that can indicate itself as a concrete limitation of man's existence, we discover a finitude — which is in a sense the same: it is marked by the spatiality of the body, the yawning of desire, and the time of language; and yet it is radically other: in this sense, the limitation is expressed not as a determination imposed upon man from outside (because he has a nature or a history), but as a fundamental finitude which rests on nothing but its own existence as fact, and opens upon the positivity of all concrete limitation.[20]

In other words, modernity is no longer a question of knowing the limits of knowledge, as with classical philosophy, but one of discerning the constitutive negativity, the otherness, the nonrecuperable, the "unthought" that makes positive knowing possible.[21] It is this notion and use of the margin, of course, that has enabled the most powerful critiques of anthropology, Orientalism, and comparative philology.[22] That such critiques are often implicit in the deconstruction of the metaphysics of presence or more explicitly channeled through Foucault's notions of the limit and of power/knowledge is attested by Said's *Orientalism*, which was the first significant attempt to disclose the constitutive function of this margin for Western knowledge. That many of the analyses of colonialism that have followed in the wake of Said's work have reiterated the shadow of this margin has been the precise bone of contention between so-called orthodox Marxists (most vocally represented by Aijaz Ahmad) and postcolonialists.[23] As we shall see, the charge, with reference to Ahmad, is that postcolonial studies has compromised itself by capitulating to the theoretical fashion of the day, namely, postmodernism (sic). But let us attend in greater detail, if briefly, to Ahmad's problems with a so-called postcolonial discourse.

In his "The Politics of Literary Postcoloniality," Ahmad characterizes postcolonial literature and cultural criticism as the offspring of a postmodernism that they disseminate zealously.[24] While what Ahmad means specifically by *postmodernism* (other than the untenable proposition that it is an anti-Marxism) and why the term should be self-evidently disparaging remain unspoken, he illustrates his thesis of postcolonialism as the progeny of postmodernism by fastening on brief passages by Gayatri Spivak and Homi Bhabha and performing close readings of these after the manner of deconstructive critics. While there is much in Ahmad's essay that merits close attention, I focus on his interpretation of Spivak and those themes that he designates as characteristic of postcolonial postmodernity — hybridity and contingency (ambivalence is mentioned but not analyzed) — to show that, despite his call for a return to a fundamental Marxism, his own critique is caught up in the contradictions that attend totalizations of any kind, whether Marxism or postcolonialism.

For instance, in his reading of the often-quoted passage in which Spivak asserts that the concept metaphors *nationhood, constitutionality, citizenship, democracy,* and *socialism* are "effectively reclaimed" in postcoloniality as "regulative political concepts," for which "no historically adequate referent may be advanced from postcolonial space," Ahmad mounts his polemic on what turns out to be contradictory ground.[25] In his quotation, he elides the following: Spivak says, "Within the historical frame of exploration, colonization, and decolonization, what is *effectively* reclaimed is a series of regulative political concepts, the supposedly authoritative narrative of whose production was written elsewhere, in the social formations of Western Europe."[26] By choosing to elide the question of ideological regulation, which invokes Althusser's notion of ideology (in general) as having no history, Ahmad can read the phrase "no historically adequate referent" literally as about "political history" (p. 4).[27] There are socialism and nationalism in India, he reminds us; we have only to remember the masses who vote for the Communist ticket and the fact that it was the nationalist struggle and not colonialism that invested India with nationhood. The literalism here is a consequence of what Ahmad marginalizes: Spivak's insistence that, insofar as socialism, nationalism, etc. function as regulative political concepts, they effectively resituate struggle within the frame of imperialism and that this is not a denial of history but a comment on the limits of historiography itself. But the literalism permits Ahmad to read ideological critique here as free-floating dehistoricizing postmodernism, thus reenacting, in the name of Marx, what Spivak problematizes: ideological regulation. But Ahmad is not consistently an orthodox Marxist, for, in his consideration that perhaps Spivak is speaking of these concepts in terms of "the European origin of these words," he expresses his consternation thus: "Even with regard to concepts, I did not know that mere origins ('myth of origins?') mattered all that much in postmodern discourse, nor does it seem appropriate that everything that originates in Europe should be consigned so unilaterally to the 'heritage of imperialism,' unless we subscribe to an essentialist notion of an undifferentiated Europe where everything and everyone is imperialist" (p. 5). Here, the problem with Spivak is that she is not being constructionist (read postmodern) enough for Ahmad and is slipping into a premodern, "dangerous" notion of origins and essences. Having at first charged Spivak with too much postmodernism, Ahmad now castigates her for not being postmodern enough.

Nevertheless, *postmodernism* continues to function as a peculiar catchall term of derision for Ahmad, usefully encapsulating poststructuralism, deconstruction, and, of course, colonial discourses. The most egregious example of this totalizing impulse is evident in his critique of Bhabha's notion of hybridity. What is peculiar in Ahmad's reading of Bhabha is that he attributes a "celebratory" tone to the latter, believing that the notion "partakes of a carnivalesque collapse and play of identities, and comes under a great many names" (p. 13). Now, while it may be beside the point to engage in an argument over the correct interpretation of *hybridity* (see the postscript to this volume), which I understand to mean not an arbitrary mixture of cultures and a surplus of pleasure, but the uncanny and undermining effect produced by the incompatibility of discourses in unequal power relations, it must be acknowledged that the notion of carnivalesque subversion is more evocative of Bakhtin than of Bhabha.[28] But Ahmad's real quarrel with Bhabha's notion of hybridity is (*a*) that it dispenses with "a sense of place, of belonging, of some stable commitment to one's class or gender or nation [that] may be useful for defining one's politics" and (*b*) that it is "posited as the negation of the 'organic intellectual' as Gramsci conceived of it" (p. 14). The point about stable identities is an old one; we have already encountered it in relation to Charles Taylor. The fact that such stability may not be easily available in this age of total capitalist penetration and that, in fact, such (commodified) commitment to one's class, at this historical moment, may produce fascisms of the sort Ahmad himself laments in India and elsewhere is not considered at all. This is because Ahmad is interested not so much in the question of the nature or grounds of political commitment as in the deployment of Marx and Gramsci as prophylactics of postmodernism. Thus, Bhabha's bracketing of the organic intellectual is again read as travesty rather than on its own terms. While I do not want to open a discussion of Gramsci's concepts or Bhabha's reading of them at this point, it would be salutary to recall Gramsci's declared view of intellectual orthodoxy in "The Study of Philosophy" with its particular attention to limits as such: "Who is to fix the 'rights of knowledge' and the limits of the pursuit of knowledge? And can these rights and limits indeed be fixed? It seems necessary to leave the task of researching after new truths and better, more coherent, clearer formulations of the truths themselves to the free initiative of individual specialists, even though they may continually question the very principles that seem most essential." [29] *Organic intellectual* is not a term that transparently signifies "social good." Like everything else, the possibilities of such leadership too need to be "elaborated," in the Gramscian sense of the term, in its contingent and specific historicity.

This leads us to the next point that Ahmad invokes as characteristic of postcolonial postmodernity — the theme of contingency as mediated once again through Bhabha's quotation of Veena Das. For Ahmad, the emphasis on the contingent nature of a given (caste or class) conflict is an act of dehistoricization and political passivity. It is dehistoricizing because it recommends that, "when it comes to caste conflicts, each historical moment must be treated as *sui generis* and as carrying within itself its own explanation . . . [and] that the understanding of each conflict be confined to the characteristics of that conflict. . . . What is denied . . . is that caste is a structural and not merely contingent feature in the distribution of powers and privileges." Furthermore, "when the theorist . . . denies the structural endurance of histories and calls upon us to think only of the contingent moment[,] we are in effect being called upon to overlook the position of class and caste privileges from which such theories emanate and such invocations issue." The consequence of such antistructuralist analysis for Ahmad is political passivity: "Such premises preclude . . . the very bases of political action. For the idea of collective human agent (e.g., organised groups of the exploited castes fighting for their rights against upper-caste privilege) presumes both what Habermas calls communicative rationality as well as the possibility of rational action as such; it presumes, in other words, that agencies are constituted not in flux and displacement but in given historical locations" (pp. 15–16).

There are at least two unexamined contradictions in Ahmad's argument: (a) the opposition that he sets up between the historicity of conflict and contingency and (b) the alliance that he presumes between a structural reading of history and rational action. Much of the problem has to do with Ahmad's untheorized notion of conflict and its relation to history in the first place. For Bhabha, as I understand it, the analysis of conflict as contingency is reliant on the notion of conflict as constitutive of history or historical change, rather than of conflict as a factor in an idealist progression of an objective and real history. In Ernesto Laclau's terms, insofar as "identities and their conditions of existence form an inseparable whole," "the conditions of existence of any objectivity that might exist must be sought at the level of a factual history." For instance, with a question such as, "Is the English revolution of the seventeenth century the bourgeois-democratic revolution?" Laclau says:

> The "bourgeois-democratic revolution," far from being an object to be identified in different latitudes (France, England, Italy) — an object that

would therefore establish relations of exteriority with its specific conditions of existence in different contexts — would instead be an object that is deformed and redefined by each of its contingent contexts. There would merely be "family resemblances" between the different "bourgeois-democratic revolutions." This allows the formulation of questions such as: how bourgeois was the democratic revolution in the country X?; or rather, how democratic was the bourgeoisie in context Y?

Thus, for Laclau, and for "postcolonials" such as Bhabha and Veena Das, the analysis of conflict requires that "the very categories of social analysis . . . be historicized" in a movement that "radically contextualizes" rather than de-historicizes conflict.[30]

Furthermore, when, because he has no structural understanding of history, Ahmad goes on to read the consequences of radical historicization or contingency as precluding *communicative action* in Habermas's sense of the term, he generates a further confusion by collapsing structuralist theories of history with the more consciousness-based theories of Habermas or even Lukács. The relation between Habermas's notion of communicative action (which is based on Enlightenment notions of progress) and the more structural notions of history (which one associates with Althusser and Etienne Balibar) does not seem self-evident or in any way a logical connection. Again, the problem here is Ahmad's refusal to engage the fundamental question of identity as such; thus, his analysis falls into a kind of idealism that Gramsci would characterize as *common sense.* In conclusion, Ahmad's denunciation of postcolonialism as anti-Marxism (owing to its association with postmodernism) seems highly dubious given that Marxism is not some sort of ready-made grid that can be imposed on social realities but is itself a highly conflictual discourse whose terms and concepts must be constantly negotiated to be made useful. The fact remains that, insofar as they must be negotiated and redefined in their contingency, issues of ideology, structure, and conflict or historical change do radically call into question our totalizations of knowledge. To dismiss such inquiry as ludic postmodernism because of its compatibility with Derrida's critiques of philosophy or of Foucault's interrogation of historicism seems hasty at best and authoritarian at worst. The problem with Ahmad's criticism of postcolonial discourse is that, at the fundamental level of political orientation, that is, the investment in class and race politics, he refuses to acknowledge the continuity between his own position and that which he repudiates as the brood of postmodernism.

But, returning to the question of postcolonial studies as marginality studies, one consequence of deploying an undifferentiated notion of the margin has meant that postcolonial studies has been stereotyped as an acceptable form of academic radicalism.[31] This has meant that scholars once intimately, even emblematically, associated with the term find themselves necessarily having to denounce it from within and to distance themselves from it. What it comes down to is an anxiety over the loss of the margin that results in the redrawing of lines and a struggle over the margin itself. As R. Radhakrishnan puts it, "The critic intellectual is divorced from the politics of solidarity and constituency. The critic is forever looking for that radical 'elsewhere' that will validate 'perennial readings against the grain,' and the intellectual is busy planning multiple transgressions to avoid being located ideologically and/or macropolitically." [32] The notion of the margin as the site of struggle for the outermost limit, then, takes on a new meaning as it gets fetishized and reified as the dislocated and authoritative *critical position* that then reveals the real stake in these battles: the margin as turf. [33]

My task here is not to ride out in defense of postcolonial studies, even if such an object existed for the purpose. Rather, I am interested in the consequences that attend the deployment of an undifferentiated notion of the margin. In this volume, we suggest that the exploration of postcoloniality from the point of view of the margin (as the excluded and as the limit) can be thought of as the realm of scholarship. While we cannot cease to uncover the politics of marginalization as that which provides the impetus to criticism, we must also conceive of the *politics of criticism* as elaborated by Stuart Hall as an ironic project. By that, I mean that postcolonialism must continually rehearse the conditions for the production of its own discourse or be doomed to fall into a form of anthropology. [34] As Barbara Johnson says in the context of deconstruction: "Any discourse that is based on the questioning of boundary lines must never stop questioning its own." [35] If postcolonial studies can be said to possess any pedagogical efficacy at all, then that energy arises from its indeterminate location and failure to recoup the margin. The conflationary (anti)critiques mentioned above, then, cannot be located outside the field and be made thereby to engender what Said terms a *politics of blame.* [36] It is undeniable that the debates generated by these critiques are not only salient to the project of postcolonial studies but themselves indicative of the merciful lack of triumphalism of the field — or so it seems as long as they do not divert discussion from the issues of larger material determinants to a skirmish over or at the margin. To quote Radhakrishnan again:

> Postcoloniality at best is a problematic field where heated debates and contestations are bound to take place for quite a while to come. My point here is that whoever joins the polemical dialogue should do so with a critical-sensitive awareness of the legitimacies of several other perspectives on the issue. In other words, it would be quite futile and divisive in the long run for any one perspective such as the diasporic, the indigenous, the orthodox Marxist, etc., to begin with the brazen assumption that it alone has the ethico-political right to speak representatively on behalf of

"postcoloniality." Such an assumption can only take the form of a pedagogical arrogance that is interested more in correcting other points of view rather than engaging with them in a spirit of reciprocity. No one historical angle can have a monopolistic hold over the possible elaborations of the "post-colony," especially during times when master discourses in general, e.g. modernity, nationalism, international Communism/Marxism, are deservedly in disarray.[37]

Another reason for the lack of triumphalism in postcolonial studies pertains to its institutional and theoretical amorphousness: it does not have a theory to speak of, concerned as it is with local cultural practices and political issues in the context of transnationalism. Unlike other area studies, postcolonial studies has no identifiable object; it would be impossible to suggest that it pertains to one or the other area of the world or that it is confined to a period, genre, or theme; nor can it name a stable First or Third World subject as its legitimate speaker (as can, e.g., women's studies, African American studies, or gay and lesbian studies). From this perspective, it may be acceptable to claim that postcolonial studies is concerned more with the analysis of the lived *condition* of unequal power sharing globally and the self-authorization of cultural, economic, and militaristic hegemony than with a particular historical phenomenon such as colonialism, which may be plotted as a stage of capitalist imperialism. It is interested above all in materialist critiques of power and how that power or ideology seeks to interpellate subjects within a discourse as subordinate and without agency. In some ways, it is this amorphousness that permits it to be simultaneously self-critical and oppositional. As well, it is this freeform aspect of postcolonial studies that makes it the target of both the Right and the so-called Left, but perhaps it is this shapelessness, this refusal to stay still, to define itself or defend itself, that makes postcolonial studies a particularly hospitable interstice from which to work out the paradoxes of history (the temporality of modernity) and colony (imperialism and nationalism).

As my parenthetical citations indicate, the range of the essays collected in this volume, drawn as they are from disparate contexts, testifies to the relentless self-scrutiny of postcolonial studies, which is often rigorously engaged in undoing its own temporal pretensions. Thus, this volume is not a courageous call to abandon the old religion for a new one; it is not a "beyond" to postcolonial studies, an attempt to demarcate the boundaries of postcolonial knowledge or a strictly limited view of its pedagogical uses. Rather, insofar as we believe that texts are produced by the historical and material conditions of the moment and are in themselves productive of history, this volume participates in the process of writing postcoloniality by dwelling on some of the salient issues that preoccupy postcolonial scholarship today. What organizes these issues into a pedagogical and scholarly coherence is their focus on the dynamic between the local and the global (the relations of power) as they are determined in what Mary Louise Pratt has called the *contact zone* of modern imperialism.[38] The essays are grouped into sections that deal with the politics of *post* scholarship and those that are more directly the scholarship of politics. The essays fall into informal pairs to produce the sense of a highly energetic conversation between them. It will perhaps prove effective to read the essays in clusters, for, despite their difference in methodology and critical orientation, what is shared is their interrogation of, on the one hand, Western modernity as the universal standard and, on the other, a certain self-reflexivity as discourses that reproduce postcolonial studies institutionally.

Notes

1 As R. Radhakrishnan points out, "The important thing to notice here is the overall *culturalist* mode of operation: in other words, we are not talking about postcolonial economies, histories, or politics. The obsessive focus is on postcoloniality as a cultural conjuncture" (751) ("Postcolonialism and the Boundaries of Identity," *Callaloo* 16, no. 4 [fall 1993]: 750–71).

2 See Naomi Schor, "The Righting of French Studies: Homosociality and the Killing of 'La pensée 68,' " *MLA Professions* (1992): 33.

3 "It seems that the theoretical and political categories of postcolonialism, even as they burgeon and become increasingly sophisticated, are also becoming more rapidly used up and, in many instances, altogether bankrupt. Preludes and prefaces that take great pains to situate the writer/viewer in a redemptive practice that is ultimately a reenactment of just what she or he is trying to avoid (the voyeurism of 'other-gazing'), all these verbal markers and narrative devices repeat the colonial gesture of self-authorization" (299) (Emily Apter, "Ethnographic Travesties: Colonial Realism, French Feminism, and the Case of Elissa Rhais," in *After Colonialism: Imperial Histories and Postcolonial Displacements*, ed. Gyan Prakash [Princeton, N.J.: Princeton University Press, 1995], 299–325).

4 In an essay written in 1991, Vijay Mishra and Bob Hodge argue that Bill Ashcroft, Gareth Griffiths, and Helen Tiffin's *The Empire Writes Back* (London: Routledge, 1989) represents the first attempt to substitute for the erstwhile category *Commonwealth literature* that of *postcolonial writing* ("What is Post(-)Colonialism?" *Textual Practice* 5, no. 3 [1991]): 399–414. Although *The Empire Writes Back* came out eleven years after Edward Said's *Orientalism* (New York: Vintage, 1979), which most scholars consider the inaugural text in the field, I agree with Hodge and Mishra that, for all its problems, *The Empire Writes Back* did perform an important pedagogical function: it made available a teachable text that summarized the limits and possibilities of this new field of inquiry. Hodge and Mishra's essay has itself been recently included in *Colonial Discourse and Postcolonial Theory*, ed. Patrick Williams and Laura Chrisman (New York: Columbia University Press, 1993), which reprints the seminal essays marking the debates and concerns of the field. Other notable anthologies of postcolonial theory include *Colonial Discourse/Postcolonial Theory*, ed. Francis Barker, Peter Hulme, and Margaret Iversen (Manchester: Manchester University Press, 1994); *Past the Last Post: Theorizing Post-Colonialism and Post-Modernism*, ed. Ian Adam and Helen Tiffin (Hemel Hempstead: Harvester Wheatsheaf, 1991); *After Europe: Critical Theory and Postcolonial Writing*, ed. Stephen Slemon and Helen Tiffin (Mundelstrup: Dangaroo, 1989); *Re-Siting the Queen's English: Text and Tradition in Post-Colonial Literatures*, ed. Gillian

Whitlock and Helen Tiffin (Atlanta: Rodopi, 1992); *The Postcolonial Studies Reader,* ed. Bill Ashcroft, Gareth Griffiths, and Helen Tiffin (London: Routledge, 1995); *De-Scribing Empire: Post-Coloniality and Textuality,* ed. Chris Tiffin and Alan Lawson (New York: Routledge, 1994); and *Recasting the World: Writing after Colonialism,* ed. Jonathan White (Baltimore: Johns Hopkins University Press, 1993). But see also *Scattered Hegemonies: Postmodernity and Transnational Feminist Practices,* ed. Inderpal Grewal and Caren Kaplan (Minneapolis: University of Minnesota Press, 1994); *After Colonialism: Imperial Histories and Postcolonial Displacements,* ed. Gyan Prakash (Princeton, N.J.: Princeton University Press, 1995); and *Third World Women and the Politics of Feminism,* ed. Chandra Mohanty et al. (Bloomington: Indiana University Press, 1991).

5 Charles Taylor, "The Politics of Recognition," in *Multiculturalism: Examining the Politics of Recognition,* ed. Amy Gutmann (New York: Routledge, 1994); page numbers for quotations will be given in the text.

6 For a characterization of affirmative action as a recognition of past historical injustice, see Shelby Steele's problematic but nevertheless important argument in *The Content of Our Character: A New Vision of Race in America* (New York: St. Martin's, 1990), chap. 7.

7 Roger Rouse, "Thinking through Transnationalism: Notes on the Cultural Politics of Class Relations in the Contemporary United States," *Public Culture* 7, no. 2 (winter 1995): 381, 385.

8 See also S. P. Mohanty, "Us and Them: On the Philosophical Bases of Political Criticism," *Yale Journal of Criticism* 2, no. 2 (spring 1989): 1–32; and Anthony Appiah, "The Postcolonial and the Postmodern," in *In My Father's House: Africa in the Philosophy of Culture* (New York: Oxford University Press, 1992).

9 Geroge Yudice, "Marginality and the Ethics of Survival," in *Universal Abandon? The Politics of Postmodernism* (Minneapolis: University of Minnesota Press, 1988), 214.

10 Iain Chambers, *Migrancy, Culture, Identity* (London: Routledge, 1994); page numbers for quotations will be given in the text.

11 Chambers is quoting Johannes Fabian.

12 On postmodern aesthetics as a symbol of late capitalism, see, e.g., David Harvey, *The Condition of Post-Modernity: An Inquiry into the Origins of Cultural Change* (Cambridge: Blackwell, 1990).

13 For instance: "Here, in the crisis of enunciation, we can also recognise a potential convergence between radical feminist theory—Luce Irigaray, Carla Lonzi, Hélène Cixous, Alice Jardine, Rosi Braidotti, Jane Flax, Susan Hekman, Judith Butler—with its sustained critique of the presumptions of occidental discourse: a convergence that is directly inscribed in the work of Gayatri Spivak, Trinh T. Minh-ha, bell hooks, Paul Gilroy and Homi Bhabha, for example, and which is destined for greater dialogue" (pp. 68–70).

14 Stuart Hall, "New Ethnicities," in *Black Film, British Cinema,* ed. Kobena Mercer (London: ICA, 1988), 28.

15 Ibid., 30.

16 For a discussion of this notion of authenticity, see James Clifford, "Travelling Theories," in *Cultural Studies,* ed. Lawrence Grossberg, Cary Nelson, and Paula Treichler (New York: Routledge, 1992), 96–116.

17 For an excellent reconsideration of the monological views of modernity, see Martin Fuchs's introduction to the special issue "India and Modernity: Decentering Western Perspectives," *Thesis Eleven,* no. 39 (1994): v–xiii.

18 Gayatri Chakravorty Spivak, "Who Claims Alterity?" in *Remaking History,* ed. Barbara Kruger and Phil Mariani (Seattle: Bay, 1989), 274–75.

19 I am indebted to Drucilla Cornell's monumental *The Philosophy of the Limit* (New York:

Routledge, 1992) for an understanding of this concept as a primarily ethical demarcation. See esp. chap. 3.

20 Michel Foucault, *The Order of Things: An Archaeology of the Human Sciences* (New York: Vintage, 1973), 315.

21 For a neo-Marxist formulation of negativity as the foundation of radical politics and history, see Ernesto Laclau's manifesto *New Reflections on the Revolution of Our Time* (London: Verso, 1990), 3–85. For a powerful critique of Foucault's notion of the limit, see Gayatri Chakravorty Spivak, "Can the Subaltern Speak?" in *Marxism and the Interpretation of Culture*, ed. Cary Nelson and Lawrence Grossberg (Urbana: University of Illinois Press, 1988), 271–313.

22 See James Clifford and George Marcus, *Writing Culture: The Poetics and Politics of Ethnography* (Berkeley and Los Angeles: University of California Press, 1986); and Martin Bernal, *Black Athena: The Afroasiatic Roots of Classical Civilization* (New Brunswick, N.J.: Rutgers University Press, 1987), vol. 1.

23 See Aijaz Ahmad's virulent dismissal of Said's *Orientalism* in *In Theory: Classes, Nations, Literatures* (New York: Verso, 1992).

24 "The term 'postcolonial' also comes to us as the name of a *discourse* about the condition of 'postcoloniality,' so that certain *kinds* of critics are 'postcolonial' and others not. . . . Following on which is the attendant assertion that only those critics, who believe not only that colonialism has more or less ended but who also subscribe to the idea of the end of Marxism, nationalism, collective historical subjects and revolutionary possibility as such, are the *true* postcolonials, while the rest of us, who do not quite accept this apocalyptic anti-Marxism, are not postcolonial at all . . . so that only those intellectuals can be truly *postcolonial* who are also *postmodern*" (Aijaz Ahmad, "The Politics of Literary Postcoloniality," *Race and Class* 36, no. 3 [1995]: p. 3; page numbers for subsequent quotations will be given in the text).

25 Gayatri Chakravorty Spivak, "Scattered Speculations on the Question of Cultural Studies," in *Outside in the Teaching Machine* (New York: Routledge, 1993), 281.

26 Ibid.

27 On Althusser's notion of ideology, see his "Ideology and Ideological State Apparatuses (Notes towards an Investigation)," in *Lenin and Philosophy and Other Essays by Louis Althusser*, trans. Ben Brewster (New York: Monthly Review Press, 1971), 127–86, esp. 159–61.

28 On hybridity, see "Signs Taken for Wonders" and "Articulating the Archaic," in Homi K. Bhabha, *The Location of Culture* (New York: Routledge, 1994).

29 Antonio Gramsci, *Selections from the Prison Notebooks*, trans. Quintin Hoare and Geoffrey Nowell Smith (New York: International, 1971), 341.

30 Laclau, *New Reflections on the Revolution of Our Time*, 21–22.

31 I allude here to Homi K. Bhabha's essay "The Other Question" in *The Location of Culture* for an understanding of this concept.

32 Radhakrishnan, "Postcoloniality and the Boundaries of Identity," 761.

33 It can be argued that the skirmish over the margin is not peculiar to postcolonial studies and that feminism in fact seems to be at the center of such battles. The besieging of a perceived orthodox feminism by an ostensibly radical feminist wing is a sign of such battles. However, what is distinctive about postcolonial battles over the margin is the way in which the very terms — indeed, the field of study itself — are contested, with the metaphor of the subaltern acting as the category of delegitimation.

34 For a sweeping, although provocative, critique of so-called postcolonial cultural studies' failure to conceive of colonialism in plural and local terms, see Nicholas Thomas, *Colonialism's Culture: Anthropology, Travel, Government* (Princeton, N.J.: Princeton University Press, 1994).

35 Barbara Johnson, "Nothing Fails Like Success," in *A World of Difference* (Baltimore: Johns Hopkins University Press, 1987), 14.

36 Edward Said, "Intellectuals in the Post-Colonial World," *Salmagundi* 70–71 (spring–summer 1986), 44–81.

37 Radhakrishnan, "Postcoloniality and the Boundaries of Identity," 762.

38 Mary Louise Pratt, *Imperial Eyes: Travel Writing and Transculturation* (London: Routledge, 1992).

At the Margins of Postcolonial Studies: Part 2

FAWZIA AFZAL-KHAN

We have divided the volume into two sections to highlight the double duty of postcolonial studies. The first section deals with institutional and academic issues pertaining to postcolonial studies as a scholarly occupation, while the second section deals with the specific thematics that preoccupy this field of inquiry. For reasons alluded to in the first part of this introduction, it is clear that the movement of postcolonial discourse from the political arena into the academy, its consequent packaging as a field to be mined, has itself become a cause of debate and a point for theorizing. As the conversation with Homi Bhabha attests, the incessant, self-reflexive analysis in which postcolonial theorists engage can be understood as a salient aspect of the field's discursive location. Insofar as such self-scrutiny is attended by research into more local and systemic issues, we can be certain that postcolonial discourse will always be productively split between the assertion of its political convictions and the critique of those very convictions. Bhabha's own theoretical method exemplifies such a critical procedure.

The first four essays turn the prism of postcolonial studies to generate various illuminating theses regarding the nature of postcolonial knowledge. The first essay, by R. Radhakrishnan, opens the salient question of knowledge production in the West and the dominance of the postmodern paradigm over the rest of the world. In the author's own words: Postmodernism is the expression of a profound contradiction: deterritorialization and a borderless world, on the one hand and, on the other, the return of nationalism and the exacerbation of the gap between the "developed" and the "underdeveloped" worlds. The freedom that is associated with postmodernism is in fact an abject surrender to the dominance of capitalism. This essay argues that the significance of postmodernism has to be determined globally and world historically and not merely within the confines of the metropolitan West. Secure in its dominance, postmodernism travels the world over in the name of knowledge, theory, and epistemology. The pervasive epistemics of the "post-" sanctions the domination of other knowledges by the knowledge of the West. In a world polarized into the West and the Rest, the rest of the world has the "ethicopolitical" responsibility as well as the authority to ensure that postmodernism does not mandate itself as *the* universal human condition.

Ali Behdad's essay borrows Althusser's view of Marxist philosophy as a *pratique sauvage* (wild practice) for a definition of *postcolonialism* as a belated practice that arrives after the moment of anticolonialism spearheaded by such figures as Fanon, Cesaire, Memmi, and others. Behdad sees in what he calls the *savage practices of postcolonialism* a renunciation of the "depoliticized, divided space of compartmentalized academy, by connecting the separate disciplinary boundaries in alternative ways through their critical interventions." Edward Said's *Orientalism* is an example of such a counterdisciplinary interventionary practice and mode of knowledge in that it brings "into contact cultural, historical, social, and textual issues that have traditionally been kept apart in an attempt to neutralize the very political concerns these issues raise." In this scenario, the postcolonial critic negotiates new oppositional possibilities by linking various discourses kept apart by the boundaries of traditional disciplinary research, in order, through such linkage, to unravel the complexities of Western cultural hegemony and to formulate resistances to it. However, Behdad is critical of the assumption that postcolonial theory/criticism can be oppositional simply by virtue of its belatedness — that is, by reading belatedly the "traces of colonial memory." For postcolonial discourse to be an effectively oppositional praxis, it must maintain "a coeval recognition of its own historicity, its own 'worldliness,'" and then make use of "its historical consciousness to critique the cultural conditions that continue to produce unequal relations of power today." Thus, the *post* in *postcolonial* must not only recognize and articulate its connectedness to the past but see how the past impinges on the present in order to transform colonial archival knowledge into a politics of contemporaneity. It is only through such a continual rediscovery of colonialism/imperialism's "new traces today" that postcolonial criticism can "tactically use its knowledge against the reemergence of the science of imperialism in the United States today."

Walter Mignolo's essay argues that the subaltern discourses of post-Occidentalism, postcolonialism, and post-Orientalism are best understood as rational interrogations of the discourses of modernity. Mignolo develops the concept *subaltern reason* as a mode of critique that is characterized by its locus of enunciation at the margins of hegemonic knowledges. Sifting through the varied applications and geopolitical references of the term *postcolonial,* Mignolo proposes *post-Occidentalism* as the proper term germane to Latin American critical discourse on colonialism. *Subaltern reason* can be said to emerge from the different types of colonial legacies (hence the minority/postcolonial elision) that share the historical process and moment of "Western expansion identified as modernity." Such a distinction prompts Mignolo into mapping the shared histories of postcoloniality and postmodernity while acknowledging that what differentiates both theories — which he sees as countermodern moves — is the difference in their loci of enunciation. Both challenge the Western expansionist process of modernity, but from different sites. What such a theoretical move allows Mignolo is a way to challenge the essentialist, static notions of identity located in the us/them, the West and the rest binary while at the same time valorizing Bhabha's postcolonial appropriation of Fabian's theory, which marks ethnographic representation as the denial of coevality, as time lag. While all three essayists envision the postcolonial project as an oppositional one, they by no means see it as inherently or automatically so; they thus work within the two notions of the margin of postcoloniality — as the critique of the excluded and as autocritique or limit — without overvalorizing either pole. Each of these essays thus eschews a lapse into essentialist categorizing and opens up a space wherein a politics of criticism can emerge.

Ngugi Wa Thiongo's "Borders and Bridges" was originally delivered as the Tenth Krishna Memorial Lecture in February 1996 at Miranda House, University of Delhi. Here, in a surprising turn from his previous writings, in which he had advocated relinquishing colonial languages such as English as a necessary process of total decolonization, Ngugi recommends a revised pedagogy for teachers of English. His argument, shared by others in this volume, is for the interrogation of the binaries set up by colonial rule. Ngugi suggests, in tune with Walter Mignolo and with reference to his own novel, *The River Between*, that knowledge of culture and society must be produced about, in, and at the borders that ostensibly separate but in fact connect cultures. Challenging the notion of cultural purity and univocity as a Western colonial concept, Ngugi suggests that we learn to discern the connections between cultures and their inherent interdependency as a function of their identity and development. The bridges that he seeks to build are therefore between so-called Western modernity as a uniquely European achievement and the rest of the world that contributed to and sustained this modernity. Ngugi's perspective is unique in its assertion that such bridges make ecological as well as ideological sense. He reorients our thinking about knowledge and curricula by displacing the concept of identity and providing a new paradigm in the notion of interdependency that transcends multinational capitalism and the processes of globalization.

The next group of essays takes up the vexed issue of the status of postcolonial studies in the academy. The essays by Shohat and Larsen are particularly admonitory about the terminology and political pretensions of postcolonial studies. Ella Shohat warns against the "ahistorical and universalizing deployments" of the term *postcolonial*, which can potentially conflate, for example, the asymmetrical perspectives and locations of the "ex-colonized (Algerian), the ex-colonizer (French), the ex-colonial settler (Pied Noir), or the displaced hybrid in the First World (Algerian in France)." This can have the depoliticizing effect of neutralizing "significant geopolitical differences" between, for instance, France and Algeria, Britain and Iraq, colonizer and colonized. Further, the problematic temporality of the post in *postcolonial* suggests (falsely) that colonialism is over, hence inhibiting "forceful articulations of what one might call 'neocoloniality.'" The unified temporality of postcoloniality also prevents the articulation of political linkages and coalitions between contemporary anticolonial and national liberation struggles and those that are considered the proper purview of postcolonialism—"the all-too familiar discourses of the 1950s and 1960s." And, finally, the problematic spatiotemporality of the term has led much postcolonial theory to dismiss as regressive and essentialist all searches for communitarian origins, in favor of an emphasis on hybrid identities. Yet, as Shohat notes, "A celebration of syncretism and hybridity per se, if not articulated in conjunction with questions of hegemony and neocolonial power relations, runs the risk of appearing to sanctify the fait accompli of colonial violence." Given all these problems that Shohat identifies with the term *postcolonial,* she herself seems to prefer the use of the term *Third World,* despite its acknowledged limitations, because it contains a sense of a "common project of (linked) resistances to neo/colonialisms" that she feels is missing from the discussions and theories of postcoloniality. What she eventually advocates, however, and what provides the necessary grounds for this volume's intervention in the field of so-called postcolonial discourse, is that "the concept of the postcolonial must be interrogated and contextualized historically, geopolitically, and culturally."

Neil Larsen's essay takes on most forcefully the question of class and ideology and the failure of postcolonial theory to confront these issues in any meaningful way. The reason for this failure, namely, the class blindness of postcolonial theorists, can, in Larsen's view, be ascribed to their adherence, by and large, to the tenets of poststructuralist thought. That postcolonial theorists should have an affinity for poststructuralism is, Larsen suggests, hardly surprising, given that these scholars, as a class, represent the bourgeoisie of the formerly colonized countries and are now themselves firmly ensconced within metropolitan institutions in which poststructuralist thought valorizes the revolutionary potential of discursive power over material or historical reality. According to Larsen, the problem with postcolonial theory as enunciated by its major practitioners, such as Gayatri Chakravorty Spivak, Homi K. Bhabha, and Edward Said, has been the evacuation of history and historicism, both of which have produced the tainted teleological narrative of nationalism. Although Larsen seems to be in sympathy with the postcolonial rejection of cultural nationalism, what disturbs him, as a Marxist, is the refusal of these same critics to locate the failure of nationalism in the class betrayal of nationalist promises by the indigenous, neocolonial elite. Here, Larsen makes common cause with Aijaz Ahmed's controversial critique of Third Worldist postcolonial criticism and critics. Although it may appear strange to couple Said with Bhabha as antihistoricist, Larsen is at pains to point out how even Said's supposedly historically based analysis of imperialism in *Culture and Imperialism* turns out to be strangely ahistorical and anachronistic. As to why this should be so, Larsen proffers the following response: "The answer, I think, is that, as with Bhabha's antihistoricist rewriting of the nation as narration, Said's resort to a preeconomic, geographic concept of imperialism reflects what is, in the final analysis, the latter's intellectual retreat before the historical crisis of cultural nationalism and of the politics of national liberation." Instead of utilizing their apprehension of the collapse or falseness of nationalism's binary oppositions, or, as Larsen states, "the disclosure of the nation's essential ambivalence and disunity as ground"—to move "forward" into a "new, historical unity of class"—both Bhabha and Said (and the rest who follow their lead) move laterally, as it were, "into new alignments across . . . nations, whose danger to imperialism," fears Larsen, is no more than to "challenge" a "notion." Registering the historical truth of crisis, then, has prompted postcolonial consciousness à la Said and Bhabha only "to create the historical fiction—the fantasmagoria—of an emancipatory agency." Strong words, these. But, if, indeed, we agree with Larsen's conclusion that, despite its disavowal of the "reactionary political logic of cultural nationalism," postcolonial theory has not been able to steer clear of cultural politics, resulting in our historical moment's contradictory reality of "cultural revolution without social revolution," then certainly we must take up the challenge of Marxism in more concrete, less idealist ways. On this front, we must also grapple with the question of communism's failure as praxis in a much more objective way than does Ahmad in his *In Theory*, an issue to which Larsen refers only fleetingly in his appraisal of the latter.

It will be of value to read Bruce Robbins's essay in conjunction with Larsen's, as it engages seriously many of the charges levied against postcolonial theory by such hard-line Marxists as Larsen, Arif Dirlik, and Aijaz Ahmad. Robbins's take on the nationalist and class questions in postcolonial studies focuses on the institutional debates within metropolitan locations about the legitimacy of postcolonial discourse (and of its practitioners) as a critique of elitist nationalist practices in the postcolonies themselves as well as about whether postcolonial theory as practiced by a handful of radical academics is a legitimate left-wing multicultural incursion into the American academic body politic. Setting himself in direct contrast to such neonationalist scholars as Richard Rorty who accuse postcolonial academics of being anti-American and such postcolonial critics as Arif Dirlik who view most postcolonial theorists as self-serving academicians who are not oppositional enough (they are too pro-West, like the French *oblates*), Robbins favors Said's secular approach whereby he can claim that postcolonial theory and theorists have enriched and transformed the center or the metropolis. For Robbins, postcolonial theory is best understood as positioning itself against the exclusionary and restrictive rhetoric of nationalism and promoting, instead, a healthier internationalism. Although Robbins cautions against adopting a too-glib faith in a cosmopolitan ideal, predicated on narratives of upward mobility of postcolonial intellectuals in the First World, as the solution to the rest of the world's problems, he nevertheless argues persuasively that "the transnational story of upward mobility is not just a claiming of authority but a redefinition of authority and a redefinition that can have many beneficiaries, for it means a recomposition as well as a redistribution of cultural capital."

In the next section of essays, some of the themes reviewed above such as the discourses of modernity, nationalism, decolonization, and the oddly elided category of sexuality are examined in a more historically and culturally grounded manner. Taking up these discourses in particular contexts, the essays trace the transformations of many of our theoretical suppositions and pieties when brought to bear on the nuances of local historical events.

The issue of other knowledges that must be recognized inevitably bears on the politics of representation and raises the specter of authenticity embedded in the very notion of *home*. Rather than jettison questions of authenticity and representation altogether, while Afzal-Khan's essay on Pakistani Punjabi street theater also participates in the enterprise of actually looking at particular cultural practices in a postcolonial nation-state, it questions more critically the coercive processes at work in creating authentic or constitutional subjects of such states, which have historically denied or ignored the rights of minorities and women. While street theater activists in Pakistani Punjab do see the need for critiquing and moving away from colonial cultural influences, they seem to feel that it is more important to question present repressive state policies. Hence the need, as postulated by Afzal-Khan's project, to turn the postcolonial gaze inward, a gesture that is both a counterhegemonic move against the dominance of postmodern metropolitan theory via its documentation and celebration of other knowledges and one that opens up a space within cultural politics for a self-critical discourse.

In a powerful reading of the 1994 hysterectomy scandal in Maharashtra, India, Rajeswari Sunder Rajan provides a brilliant example of the way in which our interpretations of local histories intersect with larger epistemological issues. Although the marking of such conjunctions and their critique is often acknowledged as a ruling tenet of postcolonial theory, it is rarely practiced with such rigor. The case, involving the forced hysterectomization of eleven women inmates of a home for the mentally retarded, is analyzed with reference to the various discourses that were produced around it: the expert medical opinion, the legal, and the governmental. Sunder Rajan takes up as well the rhetoric of feminist organizations that mobilized around the case to point out that, insofar as the language of protest is at some level inescapably leveled at the failures of the institution, such protest is ironically and inevitably complicit with the exertion of disciplinary and penal power entailed by institutionalization as such. The particularity of the case permits Sunder Rajan to interrogate the relation of the postcolonial welfare state to its needy citizens, the complicity of the family with the state, and the inadequacy of much abstract postcolonial theory, which sometimes programmatically adopts an antimodernity position that may have the effect of shoring up the status quo for women in Third World countries. Sunder Rajan's essay then takes up a major preoccupation of postcolonial studies, namely, the gendered aspect of power relations and the role of sexuality in the visibility or erasure of marginalized women in the postcolony, to show that such a theme cannot be discussed without attention to local histories.

If, according to Sunder Rajan, institutional reform in the contemporary Indian context is a fraught issue, Daniel Boyarin suggests that cultural reform is even more egregious in the context of the internal colonialism of Jews and the discourse pertaining to their emancipation in turn-of-the-century Europe. In a bold new reading of the ideology of Zionism, which for such prominent Jewish intellectuals of the period as Sigmund Freud and Theodore Herzl represented liberation, Boyarin sedulously reconstructs the peculiar and hybrid genealogy of Zionism. He traces its emergence in the reformist impulses of contemporary Jewish leaders who had internalized many of the anti-Semitic representations of Jews from the dominant culture and came to believe that Zionism was the path to achieving dignity and respect from the Germans. Boyarin shows how this dependence on German approval and the wish to assimilate into the dominant culture were ironically coded as the assertion of a certain masculinist and reformed Jewish identity. Zionism, he argues, was a way for the Jewish male to refute his feminized Jewish self and assume a more *Germanic* identity — but in difference. Boyarin's characterization of the establishment of the Jewish state as neither simply colonialist nor simply anticolonialist but rather a unique phenomenon that bears adjacencies to both poses a new problematic for scholars interested in colonialism and neocolonialism. Reading beyond the raw political binaries of oppression and opposition, emigration and colonialism, Boyarin asks us to consider the effects of unsanctioned political desire: namely, "the self-deceiving logic manifested in the Zionist will to transform colonial reality into decolonized space." In Boyarin's essay, then, decolonization, political emancipation, cultural reform, and national self-determination take on valences that help nuance the more settled meanings that these terms have acquired in most postcolonial theory. Yet one must ask — as does Joseph Massad in this volume — at what expense is such nuancing achieved?

Saree Makdisi's essay seeks to complicate our understanding of the grand narrative of modernity, rooted in a unilinear concept of history and progress that emerged in the post-Enlightenment West. The essay attempts this alteration in thought by analyzing the reception and consequent appropriation of this grand narrative by the Arab world in a way that challenges its basic assumptions. In shifting attention to the narrative of modernity that emerged in the postcolonial Arab nation-states under pressure to conform to Western concepts of rationality, modernity, and technological and social progress, Makdisi charts the emergence of an alternative definition of *modernism* — one that is applicable to Arab literary and cultural forms. Through their disruptions of both traditional Arabic literary forms and styles and modern European ones (of which Tayeb Salih's novel *Season of Migration to the North* is a classic example), and through different renderings of history, these latter interrogate, problematize, and challenge the dominance of unilinear Western narratives of development and modernization. This challenging of teleological narratives is crucial, Makdisi maintains, if the Arab world is to fashion any alternative to that of the modern Western-style nation-state. In suggesting that the questions of Palestine and Lebanon are the central crises confronting the Arab world today, emblematic of the neocolonial nature of nationalist thought that has thoughtlessly carved up the region (at one time united under the banner of Greater Syria), Makdisi suggests that a postcolonial state of affairs can come to pass only if the temporality of Western-derived nationalist thought (used, ironically, by the "Nahda" or modernizing tendency within Arab nationalist thought) is discarded in favor of new and different conceptual categories. The strategies needed, then, to address the contemporary crises facing the Arab world can no longer be derived from either the Nahda or the West. In rejecting the temporal frame of a perpetually deferred modernity, Makdisi also rejects the totalizing narrative of postmodernity as applicable to the Arab world via a postcolonial counterpart. In this sense, the post as a signified of temporality is a misnomer since there is no afterstate that supersedes that of colonialism. In Makdisi's opinion, "colonialism . . . cannot be understood or measured in units of time, just as we cannot point to some clearly defined moment 'before' the sudden arrival of colonialism; for to think in these terms is to reinvent the now outworn teleology of modernization itself." One of the unfortunate consequences of such a teleological imperative has been the binary choice that Arabs have had to face between choosing an identity on the basis of a state of future modernity and choosing one on the basis of traditionalism. In place of such impoverished imaginary dualistic projections, Arab modernism, as defined by Makdisi, insists on the "immediacy and historicity of an inescapable present and points to the need to map this present through the invention and creation of new and at least conceptually postcolonial systems and structures, which can then perhaps be used in nonteleological projects of transformation and even, we might say, 'improvement.' " Thus, to follow Makdisi's argument to its logical conclusion, one arrives at a point similar to that postulated in the essays by Radhakrish-nan and Robbins — that is, looking at postcolonialism's ethical burden as being one of imagining new spatial configurations for identities that would transcend national borders and boundaries. In terms of the Arab world, which, as Makdisi sees it, would benefit from seeing itself as united across artificially created bor-ders, the problematic of the Palestinian struggle for self-determination along national lines seems ironic. Makdisi is certainly aware of this irony but sees it as emblematic of the situation that he is describing — in this case, a struggle for an independent state (Palestine) helping "inspire the creation of a postnationalist Arab unity based on the transcendence of states as have been hitherto defined and institutionalized."

In "Self-Othering," Hamid Naficy outlines the history and politics of early cinema in Iran around the turn of the century, that body of working provid-ing, according to him, a model of the self-othering that occurs in societies that either are directly colonized or, as in Iran's case, come under the West's ubiq-uitous sphere of neocolonial and imperial hegemony (as in the case of Euro-pean Jews — the "internal others" of Europe). According to Naficy, *self-othering* refers to a process whereby the subject as spectator is constituted primarily through identification with an other — in this case the West — that is seen by Iranian spectators as superior in every way. However, as Naficy is careful to explain, this hailing of the native self is not unidirectional, nor does it proceed along simple binaries of unified self and other. Rather, the self-othering model contains within its ambit of ambivalence the seeds of haggling (or *counterinter-pellation*, in Althusserian terms), as well as other modes of resistance and slip-page, arising out of an originary alienation of the self. Once again, Bhabha's notions of colonial mimicry and native parody, as well as hybridity, prove to be useful postcolonial tools in challenging what Naficy calls the *hypodermic* or *injection theory of ideology* vis-à-vis cinema spectatorship as proffered by both traditional/religious detractors and secular proponents of cinema in Iran. Seen in this light, the cultural haggling that resulted in Iran as a response to the Westernizing influence of the cinema "energized the desire to want to re-turn to the native symbolic order," especially among the traditionalists. How-ever, all returns are always already impure and syncretistic since they all in-volve acts of reimagination and re-creation after coming into contact with the "other." Further, a microphysical examination of the overdetermined nature of self-othering in this context establishes that the Iranian self was never unified to begin with — rather, reimaginings of such a self occur in response to a variety of social and political pressures. A postcolonial analysis that teaches that "self-othering is neither uniform, nor monolithic, nor unidirectional," can lead to an acknowledgment of difference that does not have to mean conflict. Thus, in present-day postcolonial, post-Revolution Iran, the resurgence of cinema de-spite the official discourse, which is moralistic and anti-Western, shows that binary thinking stressing absolute difference between Islam and the West has, in reality, given way to a more accommodationist view that prefers to indigenize and Islamize the Western innovation of cinema.

In the light of Naficy's analysis, Joseph Massad's piece in our final section becomes, then, a fitting critique of Boyarin's essay. Like Boyarin, Massad is interested in discovering the limits, both discursive and material, of the designation *postcolonial* as a diachronic (i.e., temporal) marker suggesting the end of an era of colonialism. But, whereas Boyarin traces the origins of Israeli nationalism to argue a sui generic status for Zionism, Massad's focus is on the limits of the racialized and gendered Zionist discourse of liberation as it coalesced around the symbol of the circumcised Jewish male/penis. What is highlighted in Massad's reading of the masculinized discourse of Zionism is its construction, through the formation of the state of Israel, of a space-time continuum called *postcoloniality* that designated freedom for Ashkenazic Jews while simultaneously rendering the *same* space-time inhabited by Palestinians discursively and materially colonial. The appellation becomes even more problematic when applied to the Sephardic or Mizrahic Jews, who, as Massad points out, "have a more difficult task characterizing the nature of the space and time they inhabit owing to their dual status of being colonized vis-à-vis the Askenazim with colonizer privileges vis-à-vis the Palestinians." What, then, *is* "this space and time called Israel?" Although, as noted, there are several variant responses to this question, it seems to us that the central question raised here by Massad can elicit only one unambiguous answer. He asks, "Can one determine the coloniality of Palestine/Israel [for Palestinians] without noting its postcoloniality (in relation to what or whom?) for Ashkenazic Jews?" It is his parenthetical query that supplies the answer, for it is clear that the Zionist project was conceived as colonial in nature, aided and abetted by the colonial powers of the time, specifically Britain and France. It was only later, after the coming to fruition of the Zionist project, that the Zionist establishment began the diachronic process of transforming its explicitly colonial heritage into an anticolonial one, resulting in the postcolonial space called *Israel,* which exists, synchronically, at the expense of a colonized Palestine.

One of the cases in which Boyarin's thesis of the disarticulation of the discourse of anticolonial liberation and freedom occurring at the moment of articulation seems most applicable is that of the United States—a case amply demonstrated by Timothy Powell's analysis of postcolonial theory in an American context. Powell argues eloquently for the viability of postcolonial theory as a tool for unpacking the "role of empire in forming America's national identity and the psychological anguish of the internally colonized." Thus, Powell raises important questions about the points of contact and difference between postcolonial and minority discourses. One must, as Powell does, raise the question, "How, for example, can we even begin to define the basic binary of colonizer/colonized when everyone involved—in this case African Americans, Chicanos, and Anglo-Americans—insists on seeing themselves as *the colonized*?" Part of the problem to be addressed is the temporality of the post, which locates the beginning of the postcolonial period in the year 1776, when the American colonies ruptured their political relation to Great Britain. Although correct from a strictly linear perspective, what this usage of the term *postcolonial* denies or disavows is the internal colonialism that continued even after such a postcolonial rupture—that is, the "economic deprivation and entrenched segregation that keeps contemporary Chicano barrios and black ghettos isolated outside the cultural quotation marks of America," not to mention the status and treatment of Native Americans by white colonizers who nevertheless saw themselves as colonized vis-à-vis the British. Because (most) white Americans see the United States as a "former colony that came into being as a nation through an act of revolutionary independence," they have been reluctant to acknowledge their own colonizing treatment of culturally different groups within the United States as well as the colonizing role of America abroad. It is "this anxiety and the ability to conceal imperialist impulses in the guise of a commitment to anticolonial democratic freedom" that Powell delineates as a fundamental aspect of "the self-cloaking mechanism of American colonialist discourse." This self-cloaking or disavowal—which is at the heart of perhaps all nationalist historiography—is what Powell's essay tries to unmask, by giving a postcolonial reading of an African American text, Martin Delany's novel *Blake*, published in 1861. Indeed, the tension between self-cloaking and unmasking remains, perhaps, one of the most productive sites of conflict and inquiry within so-called postcolonial studies today. It is our hope that the essays that follow will inspire us to continue challenging and redefining our roles as postcolonial readers, teachers, critics, and activists living and working on the margins of the West *and* the rest.

1 THE OCCUPATION OF POSTCOLONIAL STUDIES: KNOWLEDGE AND INSTITUTIONAL POLITICS

Postmodernism and the Rest of the World

R. RADHAKRISHNAN

W hat is an essay about postmodernism and the rest of the world doing in a collection of essays on postcoloniality? I would merely respond, Why not? For one thing, I am interested in delineating postcoloniality as a form of double consciousness, not as an act of secession from the metropolitan regime. Not only is postcoloniality a historiography in its own terms, but it is also a critical perspective on metropolitan goings-on. Indeed, these two functions of postcoloniality are mutually constitutive. It seems to me that it is incumbent on the Third World, having been coercively interpellated by colonialism and modernity, to continue to have a crucial say in the further developments, *post* or otherwise, of modernity. The Third World, which is often and almost always choicelessly globalized by advanced capital, cannot afford to forfeit its capacity to intervene in matters transnational and postmodern. Unlike such theorists of the Third World as Aijaz Ahmad, I do not read ambivalence as a sign of postcolonial weakness or instability. Quite the contrary, I would argue that postcoloniality is always already marked by ambivalence and that the task is to politicize this given ambivalence and produce it agentially. This taking charge of ambivalence, this polemical production of double consciousness, is intended as an act of affirmation and as a substantive intervention in the business as usual of metropolitan temporality.

It might be argued that there are indigenous realities of the non-West that are not necessarily related to colonialism and modernity. While this is indeed true, the brute fact that every conceivable local-native-indigenous reality has been touched by the morphology of modernism and the dominance of nationalism and the nation-state (notice that the very efficacy of countless grassroots movements and NGOs must be mediated athwart the authority of regnant nationalisms) makes it imperative for postcoloniality to participate on more than one level, in more than one location. My purpose here is neither to realize a pure either/or relation between West and non-West nor to offer any one version of postcoloniality as exemplary or authentic. My assumption rather is that there is a place for the ethicopolitics of persuasion and that, within this space, postcoloniality or the "rest of the world" has much to say to the postmodern West. I am aware that there are sections where I might be guilty of conflating postmodernism and poststructuralism. It is well beyond my scope here to begin to differentiate postmodernism and poststructuralism, but suffice it to say that, for my present purposes, postmodernism is the object of address if for no other reason than that, more than poststructuralism, postmodernism has taken on the authority of a global umbrella. And, besides, the travel of postmodernism all over the world, on the wings of capital and virtual technologies, has been more insidious than that of poststructuralism, which in many ways can actually be articulated sympathetically with the concerns of postcoloniality.

I begin this essay with a naive and perhaps brazen world-historical observation. The peoples of the world are currently unevenly situated between two historiographic discourses: discourses of the post and the *trans*, whose objective seems to be to read historical meaning in terms of travel, displacement, deracination, and the transcendence of origins, and discourses motivated by the need to return to precolonial, premodern, and prenationalist traditions of indigeny. My intention here is to bridge the gap somewhat between these polar choices and to suggest that these two paths must be historicized relationally, not as two discrete and mutually exclusive options.

Having said this, I briefly analyze three recent happenings in the context of global postmodernity and the emerging new world order. First, the NAFTA agreement. Much has been written about this deal from both sides. The debates are over, and NAFTA is for real. Yet the real implications of the treaty are far from clear. If, on the one hand, NAFTA represents deterritorialization, the breaking down of international economic borders, and the celebration of a seamless spatiality achieved by the spread of capital, why, then, did the rhetoric of NAFTA advocacy resort to assurances that *American* jobs will not be lost and that *American* identity will remain intact, un-deterritorialized by NAFTA?[1] As Marx's elegant analysis of the contradictory logic of capitalism points out, the discourse of protectionism on behalf of the dominant order goes hand in hand with the dehistoricization of the periphery. The polemical focus on *American* jobs and *American* identity demonstrates that, despite all claims of free trade, clearly, there is a *home* and a *not-home*, an *inside* to be protected and an *outside* that is really not *our* concern. How do we distinguish between who is "us" and who is "them"? Of course, through the good old category *nationality*. Thus, the return of nationalism lies at the very heart of a despatializing postmodernity.

Second, the floundering of the General Agreement of Tariffs and Trade (GATT) on issues concerning cultural autonomy and specificity. The sticking point here was the exportation to Europe of American culture through videos and television programs. Unlike NAFTA, which pits two developed countries against a Third World country, here the transaction is all Western. Yet this particular instance dramatizes the disjuncture between cultural and political/economic interests. It was not just a question of taxes and tariffs. Surely, we are all aware that, in the age of late capitalism, culture itself is nothing but a commodity infiltrated irrevocably by exchange value. Still, Europe resists American cultural commodities in the name of its own separate identity. Falling back on the notion of organic cultural interpellation, Europe resists the logic of postmodern homogenization or dedifferentiation. Clearly, this confrontation is taking place on the all-too-familiar turf of identity, and we had thought that identity had been sent packing in the advanced postmodern world of simulacra and the hyperreal. Culture becomes the embattled rhetoric of home, authenticity, and one's-own-ness deployed strategically to resist the economic impulse toward sameness. Yes, we want to be part of the borderless economic continuum, but, at the same time, let us be who we are; our cultural identities are not up for sale or commercial influence. It would seem, then, that the economic terrain activates a pure process without a subject, whereas the cultural domain is anchored deeply in identity.[2]

Third, the case of the Puerto Rican referendum concerning possible statehood. Here, too, *culture* came up as a fraught term. Would Puerto Rico sacrifice its cultural/historical uniqueness as a consequence of economic/political unionization? Tax issues and citizenship questions apart, the question of culture was raised in all its resistant autonomy. Not unlike a number of non-Western ex-colonized nations that assimilate the West as part of their outer selves and cultivate their inner selves in response to indigenous imperatives, the people of Puerto Rico, too, chose to symbolize the cultural domain in opposition to a capitalist postmodernist integration with the "Nation of nations."[3]

I bring up these examples to show that the identity question in our own times is profoundly fissured along different and often mutually exclusive trajectories. Also, all these events are taking place in a progressively postmodern world, one that is also being seen as a postnationalist world. Why is it that identity and nationalism are celebrating their return under the postmodern aegis? Why is it that the ideology of postmodernism is unable to chase away or exorcise the ghosts of identity and nationalism? Is it possible that the identity question and a variety of nationalisms have become the political weapon of underdeveloped peoples in their battle against the phenomenon of unequal global development, a phenomenon that is being exacerbated by the spread of postmodernism?[4] But, before we can respond to these questions (questions that focus on the global effects of postmodernism), we must take a closer look at postmodernism as it has developed in the West.

What, then, are the origins of postmodernism? What is the extent of its geopolitical jurisdiction, and what is its statute of limitations? Let us keep in mind that the text that gave postmodernity its undeniable cognitive-epistemic status — Jean François Lyotard's *The Postmodern Condition* — made three important and binding gestures.[5] First, postmodernity was a condition. Second, it had to do with knowledge and epistemology. Third, it was taking place within the advanced capitalist, postindustrial computerized societies. The term *condition* (as in, say, *the human condition*) has a strong ontological appeal. Unlike such words as *crisis, predicament,* or *dilemma,* the term *condition* carries with it a semantics of finality and fully achieved meaning. It is in the form of a fait accompli. In other words, the condition is real, and it has been theorized into lexical significance within the First World well before the underdeveloped world could even take a look at, leave alone have a say in, its ideological determination. Well might one ask why the underdeveloped countries of the Third World should be allowed even a peek into what is after all exclusively a First World phenomenon. And here lies the ideological duplicity of postmodernity as an epistemic condition: its simultaneity as both a regional and a global phenomenon. Given the dominance of the West, the epistemic location of postmodernity has a *virtual* hold over the rest of the world also. If modernity functions as a structure in dominance that regulates and normativizes the relation between the West and the rest, then, despite the so-called break from modernity, postmodernism sustains and prolongs this relation.[6] Furthermore, given the avantgarde-ism of the West, it is only inevitable that the very regionality of Western forms will travel the world over as dominant-universal forms. In other words, Western realities have the power to realize themselves as general human conditions. The passage from a specific reality to a general condition is effected through the mediation of knowledge and epistemology.

It is the formulation of the postmodern condition as a matter of knowledge that paves the way for the uncontested spread of First World priorities across the world. It is the ability of the developed world to conceptualize and theorize its particular-organic empirical reality into a cognitive-epistemic formula on behalf of the entire world that poses a dire threat to other knowledges.[7] After all, how can knowledge be irrelevant, especially when accompanied by claims of universality? Thus, a report on epistemology elaborated in the metropolis either begins to speak for the human condition the world over or assumes a virtual reality to be devoutly wished for by the rest of the world. To put it differently, the theoretical need to take postmodernism seriously becomes an imperative even in places where postmodernity is not a lived reality, that is, has no historical roots. The Third World is, then, compulsorily interpellated by postmodernity even though its own realities are thoroughly out of sync with the temporarily of the postmodern.[8]

To what extent and in what specific ways does postmodernism problematize and deconstruct the ideology of modernity? To what extent is postmodernism a radical critique of, and perhaps a form of secession from, the authority of modernity? If, indeed, postmodernism is an effective interrogation of the legitimacy of modernity within the confines of the First World, then how useful or relevant is this interrogation to other geopolitical areas? Is there common cause between the interrogation of modernity within the developed world and Third World critiques of modernity? Are there issues, agendas, and objectives that can be shared between these two constituencies despite the fundamental asymmetry that sustains East-West relations? In other words, why should the rest of the world pay attention to the emergence of postmodernist politics if all it is is an intramural Occidental antagonism?

Before I examine the relevance of postmodernism to postcoloniality and to Third World cultural politics, I briefly and selectively look into the claims of postmodernism within its place of origin. Keep in mind that, even within the First World, the evaluation of postmodernism is far from complete. There are great resistances and differences within the First World. Whether postmodernism is good or bad, whether it is a progressive or a repressive development in complicity with the rationality of capitalist dominance, are issues that are part of an ongoing debate. My purpose here is not to rehearse the many by-now familiar attitudes toward postmodernism, both supportive and antagonistic, but rather to focus on a few issues that have to do with the generalization of the post and the implications of such a generalization in the context of First World–Third World relations.[9]

Postmodernism within the metropolitan context is often equated with the advocacy of local, regional, and specific politics in opposition to total, global, universal politics. Western authority is over, the process of decolonization is well afoot the world over, and the dominance of Eurocentrism is viable no more. There is the reality of the other, not just the abstract other turned by theory into a transhistorical form of alterity, but several determinate others with different histories, cultures, and political destinies. The postmodern choice that gets formulated in response to this crisis is quite stark: an illegitimate universalism or relativism. But what about a universalism based not on dominance or representational violence but on relationality and a dialogism based on multiple interlocking histories?[10] Confronted by its ideological embeddedness in Eurocentrism, that is, Eurocentrism masquerading as authentic universalism, postmodernism eschews universalism altogether in favor of a rigorous and uncompromising relativism. Given its relativist stance, postmodernism can have nothing to say about other cultures. Its narrative, used to being grand and totalizing, fails altogether.

If narrative in Conrad is either mystified or enraged to hatred by the darkness of the other, the postmodern withdrawal from narrative attests to the objective reality of the other while at the same time claiming the other as unknowable.[11] The other's reality to the self is postulated on the prior premise of the other's unknowability by the self. Withdrawing from its sorry history of knowing the other through dominance, a self-critical Eurocentrism abandons the other altogether in the name of noninterference. The epistemology of relativism justifies this denial of reciprocity and relationality among different knowledges of the world.

This failure of postmodern relativism at both the epistemological and the political levels is typically recuperated as a radical triumph through the practice of what has become a quintessential postmodernist/poststructuralist strategy, that is, the strategy of self-reflexivity as a catchall answer for cross-cultural crises and problems.[12] If canonical anthropology's message to premodern societies was, "I think, therefore you are," postmodern orthodoxy takes the form, "I think, therefore I am not. You are 'I am not.' " The other becomes the burden of the self's negativity, a negativity produced by the self through its own autocritical-deconstructive engagement with itself. As Edward Said has argued eloquently in his analysis of Albert Camus's political as well as epistemological orientation toward Algeria, the postmodern impulse furthers the modernist thesis by actively negating the other through knowledge.[13] I am not trivializing the significance of deconstructive self-reflexivity within the metropolitan theater, but the problem is that such a self-reflexivity *by itself* does not and cannot guarantee the knowability of other cultures and histories.

Perhaps a brief explanation is in order here: an explanation of how postmodernism functions predominantly as a critique that is derived oppositionally from the very order that is the object of the critique.[14] The very exteriority of the postmodern critique relies on the givens of modernity; hence, despite vociferous claims to the contrary, postmodernism enriches modernity in the very act of transgressing it. The putative break that is associated with postmodern rebellion in fact rests securely on the spoils of nationalism/modernism. Nowhere is this more visible than in the so-called postidentitarian, postnationalist formations. As my opening paragraphs attempt to demonstrate, postnationalist developments are never at the expense of nationalist securities; if anything, they *foundationalize* nation-based verities and privileges to the point of invisibility. The benefits of citizenship of developed nationalism are effectively sublated through postnational transcendence, just as the legacies of modernity are preserved in the postmodern critique. All I am saying is that postmodernism does not absolve itself of modernity, just as powerful post- and transnational developments do not forfeit the privileges of First World nationalism.

This entire discussion leads to an important question: How real and historical is the post? I would argue that critiques (such as the postmodern critique of modernity) that are paradigmatically homogeneous with their objects cannot be real alternatives.[15] What, then, is a paradigm, and how are its parameters recognized? How is a paradigm identified economically, politically, culturally, philosophically? My concern here, quite Marxist in its intention, is with the self-identification of any paradigm, both in its totality and through the relative autonomy of the many levels and spheres that account for the totality. Although the historical reality of any paradigm, such as modernity, is independent of the conscious theory or the epistemology of the paradigm, it is through the latter that the paradigm achieves self-awareness qua paradigm. I say this to make two points: first, that the relation between any paradigm and its epistemology is one of *identification* and, second, that the epistemology is not constitutive of the paradigm, that rather the paradigm as an interrelated set of practices is anterior to the epistemology. In other words, the epistemology of the paradigm is a function and a product of the paradigm even as it enjoys its relative autonomy as theory.

Given this, what does it mean to assert that postmodernism is an epistemological break from modernity in particular and from Western thought in general? Is it possible that postmodernism functions as a break in matters epistemological even as it remains complicit with the West in matters political and economic? If the break is merely epistemological and not accompanied by concomitant economic and political changes, what is the status of the break, and, indeed, what is the subject of the break? By and large, theories of postmodernity have focused exclusively and obsessively on theory and epistemology to claim that a break has actually occurred. In this sense, postmodernism has been a revolution *in theory,* in both senses of the term. It is a revolution that seems quite prepared to leave history behind in search of theoretical-virtual realities informed by the temporality of the post.[16] The decapitation of history by theory, the celebration of subjectlessness, and other such motifs have been the burden of epistemology's impatience with history.[17] It is significant that there exists a telling divide between Marxist postmodernists and pure postmodernists when it comes to the question of accounting for the political and the social. Marxist postmodernists such as Neil Smith, David Harvey, Fredric Jameson, and Nancy Fraser tend to see postmodernism as a symptom of late capitalism; the pure postmodernists, à la Jean Baudrillard, are happy to inhabit the world of postmodernist immanence, virtually and theoretically. Also, the former are able to raise such questions as, Is postmodernism good or bad, desirable or not? whereas the latter are happy to thematize postmodernism intransitively, that is, as an end in itself.[18]

The dangers of hypostatizing postmodern theory as its own autonomous content are as follows.[19] First, the so-called theoretical break takes the form of an innocent countermemory that chooses to forget an uncomfortable and often guilty past.[20] Radical theory begins to function as a form of forgetfulness, that is, as a way of justifying the nonaccountability of theory to history. The organic and representational connectedness of postmodernity to its past is deliberately and strategically overlooked so that gains in epistemology may be localized in all their micropolitical specificity and then legitimated as a successful politics of secession. It is important to keep in mind that what is passed off here, through the dubious reference to the transaggressive autonomy of epistemology, as an exclusively metropolitan course of events has in fact tremendous global repercussions. The minimalization of the grand narratives into the *récit* of postmodernism is an epistemological move that in a sense attempts to launder the guilt of Eurocentrism. Modernity, after all, was achieved as an effect of colonialism, affecting the colonizer and the colonized unequally. Much of the capital needed for industrialization came from the colonies (one obvious example being cotton from India for the mills in Lancashire), and it was the production of surplus value from the colonies that paved the way for the universal sovereignty of modernity. And, of course, in the process, other knowledges were wasted. If the dominance of modernity was the result of both the creation and the maintenance of the developed-underdeveloped divide, why then does postmodernism, suddenly and by the sheer occult power of high theory, finds itself absolved of its modernist past?

The epistemological *coupure* begins to function as an alibi. Unable to deal with the enormity of its modernist-colonialist past, postmodernism desiccates itself into a bodyless theory so that its accountability to a *global past* could just be forgotten. I am not denying the possibility that postmodernism can be, or even is, an authentic quarrel of the West with itself, but the valence of such a quarrel can hardly speak for the victims of modernity in Africa or Asia. The postmodern quarrel with modernity is much in the nature of a family squabble that takes place within a well-established domain of solidarity and shared economic and political interests. There is nothing in postmodern epistemology that disinherits the beneficial legacies of modernism, in particular, the riches of developmental progress built on piratical capital accumulation. The postidentitarian games of postmodernism are possible precisely because identity here is no more at stake.[21] Postnationalist postmodernism, for example, does not cancel such earlier identifications as German, American, French, British, etc. If anything, these identifications are the rich but ideologically invisible bases from which postmodernity is deployed as the politics of heterogeneity, hybridity, and difference.[22]

This calculated suppression of macropolitical global memory results in the provincialization of the metropolitan political imaginary. The call for specific intellectuality, the insistence on an isolationist subject-positional politics, the understanding of *location* in opposition to global relationality, the grand obituary notice regarding the death of representation and narrative voice: these themes that constitute the very essence of postmodernity highlight a certain failure, the failure of Eurocentric thought to confront with conscience the history of its own narrative.[23] Such a version of postmodernism has been severely questioned within the West by feminists who have sought to postmodernize their feminisms without at the same time conceding to postmodernity its master claims concerning knowledge and theory. (In a way, we could also understand this venture as the feminization of postmodernity.) [24] In what sense could postmodernism be seen as an ally of Western feminism, and how and for what reasons does such an alliance break down? [25] For my purposes here, I focus on areas where feminism has pressured postmodernism to acknowledge its short-comings, blind spots, and internal contradictions. The distinction to which I am drawing attention here (and here I am drawing on the distinguished work of such feminist postmodernists as Nancy Fraser, Linda Nicholson, Nancy Hart-sock, and Donna Haraway, to name just a few) is between *social* postmodern-isms, in the plural, and an unqualified *postmodernism as such*. In other words, the work of these intellectuals warns us that the social significance of postmod-ernism is not to be taken for granted. Nancy Fraser and Linda Nicholson were among the first theorists to conceptualize postmodernism as simultaneously exciting and problematic and to spell out a critique of postmodernism from a macropolitical perspective that is external to the epistemic space provided by postmodernism itself, that is, the agential political space of feminism. Their significant contribution was to demystify the immanence of postmodernism in terms of its undeclared ideology and to insist on the accountability of the episte-mics of postmodernism to its social conditions of production. It would be redun-dant to capture the overall direction of their well-known and much commented on essay (in particular, the sophisticated way in which they turn the tables on Lyotard), so I will take their critique for granted and proceed further. [26]

Fraser and Nicholson rightly point out that the radical valorization of postmodernism as an epistemological coupure in fact throws the baby out with the bathwater — unless, of course, the very denial of the *socius* by postmodern theory is to be construed perversely as the ultimate revolution, and that would indeed be a bizarre comment on the teleology for which Marx had devoutly wished. Nicholson and Fraser point out that the epistemological site is made into a pure *elsewhere* that connects neither with history nor with sociality — hence their diagnosis that postmodernism is very much a *philosophical* formu-lation authored by male theorists and thinkers. Their essay makes us see that what gets celebrated in postmodernist thought is the capacity of Eurocentric philosophy to master and own itself even during its periods of dark and men-acing crisis, its genius to launch its very negativity in the form of a persuasive philosophy. Its loss of privilege thus recuperated by theory, postmodernism be-gins to assume the function of a nonorganic, free-floating signifier with global epistemic ambitions. If the West is the home of progressive knowledge, and if the West itself has begun to question its own knowledge, then, clearly, knowl-edge must be in universal jeopardy. And who else is to come the rescue but the Western subject all over again, who can convert this loss of authority into a pure theory of subjectless knowledge?

The uncoupling of the post from postmodernity confers on the post a uni-versal sanction to be exercised the world over in the guise of knowledge. It is this philosophical autonomization of the epistemology of the post that has facilitated the production of such categories as *postfeminism, postcoloniality, postethnic, posthistorical, postpolitical,* etc.[27] Every other constituency is then constrained, for reasons of knowledge, to work under the post umbrella. Without a doubt, a strong distinction must be made between the indigenous claims of postmodernism and its traveling authority as a blank, generic imprimatur. After all, why should ethnicity go postmodern, or, for that matter, Islam? What if Islam and postmodernism, and ethnicity and postmodernism, are mutually exclusive and/or irrelevant? Why should these constituencies update themselves in the name of postmodern epistemology and theory? If the historical irrelevance to these constituencies of postmodernism can be demonstrated, why should they still find room for postmodernism as theory within their internal structures? Why hitch their interests to an alien knowledge and risk their solidarity with themselves?

My purpose here is to submit postmodernism to the relevance test. How relevant and how representative is the postmodern condition, both within the First World and in global terms? In adopting the postmodernist framework as a metaframework, is there not the real danger of distorting and misrepresenting other realities and other histories? As Fraser and Nicholson have argued, postmodernism is real as a crisis. To Fraser and others, the denial of globality by postmodern theory indicates a dire need for imagining a politics of connections, correlations, correspondences, and common ground; and, clearly, postmodernism is no help at all here. How postmodernism can be socialized and politicized is a question that Fraser and Nicholson take up in their work.[28] As Western feminists, they share with postmodern theory a common heritage: Eurocentrism and the history of Western dominance. But there the commonality stops, for, as feminists, they occupy a different ground from the one inhabited by male postmodern theorists. Although they take heed of a whole range of self-reflexive practices prescribed by postmodern theory, they articulate (Fraser in particular) quite programmatically their political difference from male, white postmodernism. As feminists of the Western world, they have a relation of difference in identity with postmodernism, and the difference is to be explained in terms of interests and polemical situatedness, not just in terms of pure knowledge or epistemology. It is, indeed, the notion of interestedness and perspective that separates postmodern feminists from their male counterparts. Furthermore, in sizing down postmodernism into adjectival significance (i.e., not postmodernism as its own plenary politics but rather *postmodern* feminism), theorists like Fraser reinvent the need for a macropolitics that will not shrink into either a narcissistic self-reflexivity or a technology-driven set of nonorganic, specialist practices.

There is yet another important historical context that differentiates postmodern feminism from male, white postmodernism. Unlike the latter, which is obsessed with self-reflexivity, postmodern feminism sees the postmodern epistemological condition as a problem. Why is it that an increase in epistemological complexity results in the lessening of knowledge, especially of the other? Why are knowledge and practice, knowledge and "worldliness," posited in terms of mutual incommensurability?[29] What helps them out of this aporia is not yet another pure epistemological nuance but rather a very real historical challenge: the challenge both from women of color in the First World and from Third World women.[30] Postmodern feminism is different precisely because it responds (although not always successfully) to the ethicopolitical authority of other worlds, other knowledges, and other histories. There is a real *hors-texte* to the history and the discourse of postmodernism, and, unless this outside is acknowledged in its own terms, there cannot be any meaningful coalitions or cross-cultural projects between white women and women of color. It is the reality of other knowledges (and not merely the realities of other histories, for classical anthropology flourished on the notion of "their histories" requiring "our theories") that makes postmodernism vulnerable and thus open to dialogue and cross-locational persuasion.[31]

The major issue that in some sense brings feminists together, despite the fundamental differences of race, class, sexuality, and nationality, is that of identity and, to be more specific, the issue of identity politics and its relation to the theoretical/epistemological critique of *identity as such*.[32] First World feminism found itself in critical double sessions both with male postmodernism and with the feminisms of women of color, with the two double sessions connected through a relation of asymmetry. With postmodernism there was the project of, on the one hand, deconstructing the claims of essentialism and the stranglehold of metaphysical thought and, on the other, spelling out assertively the difference of an agential feminist politics from a male critique of phallogocentric identity.[33] In the contexts of the feminisms of women of color, however, the double session had a different sense of historical direction. On the one hand, there was the solidarity of women the world over in their fight against an omnihistorical patriarchy (with individual historical differences and variations to be worked contextually), but, on the other hand, there were real race- and colonialism-based differences when it came to the identity question in its theoretical aspect. The battle against essentialism that is an integral component of postmodern feminism resonates very differently in the subaltern women's context since essentialism had a different ring in the Third World context.

Postmodern feminists have done an impressive job of pointing out the slippage, within postmodernist and poststructuralist theory, between the notions of agency and subjectivity. Unlike postmodern theory, which glorifies this slippage as a hallmark of its difference from itself, postmodern feminism wonders whether this slippage is in fact real and, if it is indeed real, whether such a condition is something to be ecstatic about or a cause for worry. The postmodern turn taking shape exclusively as critique would have us believe that a critique is subjectless and that identity is a bad essentialist habit to be discarded by a hardheaded theory. We have heard tall claims that the epistemology of the post is a daring and self-consuming process of thinking that puts itself at risk, defoundationalized perennially by its own radical momentum. The subject of knowledge is dissolved in the process of knowing, and what is left is the intransitive *jouissance* of epistemological play.[34]

There are at least two ways of questioning such claims: first, by way of Marxist ideology critique (interestingly, *ideology* is the neglected term in so much postmodernist critique), with which one could argue that postmodern pleasure is nothing but the most abject form of mystification by the commodity form; and, second, by a form of global reasoning that tells us that the so-called subject in peril of postmodern epistemology is in fact a hyperidentitarian subject so secure in its dominant identity regime that it can afford to play games without in any way endangering its politicoeconomic base. The decentered play that the early Jacques Derrida champions neither forswears Eurocentric privilege nor situates itself relationally vis à vis the other coeval histories and cultures of the world.[35] In all these critical operations, we find the negative ontology of Eurocentrism playing doctor to the rest of the world. This negative ontology would have us believe that narrative in general is devoid of epistemological validity, a belief with shattering consequences for narratives in the rest of the world.

The theme of themes in postmodern thought is the statement of a relation: identity-knowledge-narrative. To put it broadly, postmodernism eviscerates narrative and purports to be fiercely antiessentialist in its attitude toward identity. (In the final analysis, such an attitude also turns out to be anti-identity since postmodernism reads *identity* and *essentialism* as interchangeable and synonymous terms.) As we can see, these two operations are closely related. Why does postmodernism posit an adversarial relation between narrative and radical epistemology? If narrative is seen as an act of agential-ideological production with the purpose of anchoring identities in their proper, teleological homes, radical epistemology is understood as the celebration of the free and unbounded spatiality of *knowing* in all its verbal-processual and desubjectified flows and energies.[36] If narrative works within specific parameters, historical and political, and the constraints of solidarity that go with parameters, postmodern *knowing* is endorsed as the perennial breaking down of boundaries, barriers, and roots by the sheer will to knowledge. Knowledge is a mercurial form of restlessness that disdains the category *home.* In the choice between postmodernism as the champion of a freedom-seeking knowledge (or, better still, as a border-busting knowledge) and narrative as a conservative-protectionist policy, postmodernism comes off as the more liberating option.[37] After all, what right-minded individual can be *against* freedom and *for* censorship and repression through narrative interpellation, particularly during the times of NAFTA and a capital-centered world order where any threat to the free flow of capital is construed as an act of terrorism, a heinous crime against the cause of universal freedom?

My polemic here is not to deny the post its travel from the center to the periphery or to assert that Third World resistances are necessarily pure and uncontaminated by metropolitan influence.[38] My intention is rather to mark the metatheory of the post with the historical realities of its uneven spread across contesting terrains and cultures. How differentially is the politics of the post received and experienced in Third World locations, and, in particular, how are the identity politics of those locations pressured by the epistemology of postmodernism? Let us now take a critical look at the form in which the identity question is brought to the Third World on the postmodern platter. First, the identity question is presented as an unfashionable and backward preoccupation. The Third World, in other words, has to choose between a relevant but backward project and a cutting-edge subjectivity that is purely virtual and devoid of an experiential base. Second, the identity question as it affects the Third World is as urgent as it is chronic (for nowhere else does the "enjoy-the-symptom" syndrome find a better context than in the Third World body) since the underdeveloped world must seek an alien epistemology to understand itself better.[39] Third, identity is put forward as a necessary and desirable object for deconstruction. Fourth, identity is divorced from the agential authority of specific narrative projects and their hegemonizing strategies. Fifth, the quest for identity is separated from legitimation procedures since all legitimation is deemed by theory to be always-already repressive. And, finally, the discourse of subaltern identity is emptied epistemically, that is, alienated from its prerogative to make its own truth claims, for the truth claims would come from the self of the dominant West.

For the deconstructive attitude toward identity to attain universal purchase, postmodernism sets up something called *essentialism* as the ideal straw man. In spite of prolific scholarship in the areas of essentialism and strategic essentialism, it is still not clear what essentialism is precisely or why it holds such a dominant position in contemporary debates in theory, cultural studies, postcoloniality, and gender and ethnic studies.[40] Why is essentialism bad, why are essentialists naive, stupid, or evil, and why has antiessentialism secured a monopolistic hold over theoretical-moral virtue? I am not for a moment discrediting a number of feminist poststructuralists who have argued memorably on behalf of a constructed and deessentialized notion of identity (Judith Butler and Diana Fuss, to name two prominent theorists) without sacrificing the agential power of identity politics. My point is rather than, when it comes to questions of essence and legitimation, deconstructive theories that emanate from the metropolis egregiously misread the burden of essence as it falls on the Third World and thus fail to appreciate the nuance of the "risk of essence" about which Gayatri Spivak speaks so eloquently even as she advances the claims of poststructuralist epistemology.

I suggest that the exaltation of the essentialism debate as the "Debate of all debates" serves only to obfuscate our understanding of the term *essentialism* and its specific underpinnings in Western thought. First, essentialism is one pole of a binary interpellation peculiar to Western epistemology: the other pole could be variously termed *history, existence, the nonessential/the accidental/the adventitious.* Second, essentialism has been ideologically determined as a critical bone of contention, that is, prepared as the main battleground where the main event will be the deconstruction of Western ontology by itself. And, as Foucault would have it, this deontologizing project takes the perennial form of an anti-Platonism so that the genus *anti-Platonic* is canonized as the permanent form of the permanent revolution in thought and theory.[41] Third, the drama of essentialism is always played out with reference to the non-West, which is made to take on the dark and mysterious burden of essentialism, whereas the West is busy producing its own powerful history. The primitivism of the other (stranded forever in the quagmire of an ahistorical essence) is variously cultivated by the West either as an object of dread, to be kept at bay, or as a source of exoticism (the example of Gauguin comes to mind), to be used to rejuvenate the fading Western spirit. Fourth, the West, particularly during the period of high modernism, was in the habit of projecting its inner fissures, dreads, and hatreds onto the other so that the other was made to appear as the Manichaean counterpart of the dominant Western self. Africa in particular became the favorite dumping ground of all those atavistic drives and terrors for which conscious modernity could not account. Africa thus became the dark continent (the ideal theater in which the modern European self could encounter its primordial origins) that would absorb the detritus of the modernist process. The coimplication of the Thames and the Congo, for example, in Conrad's *Heart of Darkness* invokes not so much a common humanity as an unequal humanity, where the African brother is constrained forever to remain the younger brother.[42] The contemporaneity of the other is psychologized as the atavistic prehistory of the dominant self, and the way is paved for the creation of the Third World as a necessary backdrop for the history of modernity.[43]

This little *de tour* has been necessary to drive home the point that, whatever the valences might be of the debates over essentialism within the developed world, such debates would not have been possible unless essentialism had also been deployed as a powerful weapon against the histories of other cultures. No chapter in Western modernity can really be understood unless it is located in both contexts of the history of colonialism: that of the colonizer as well as that of the colonized.[44] I also emphasize that this cognitive-theoretical hang-up with essentialism is not a postmodern phenomenon. It is, in fact, a quintessential modernist theme (the modernist angst with history and origins) that has been bequeathed to postmodernism. The allegorization as well as the anthropologization of the native, the ascription of a timeless irrationality or a brute, unregenerate facticity to native cultures, the attribution of a phenomenological/perceptual immediacy devoid of cognitive import to native bodies and behavior, and the dark and menacing idealization of the other's geography as primordial earth, nature, etc., all have been thoroughly constitutive of modernity's schizophrenic obsession with itself. Postmodernism's advocacy of these very themes is therefore if anything a continuation of the *longue durée* of modernism, not a break from it. Postmodernism's sensitivity to the politics of difference and heterogeneity and its seeming solicitude for the other must be grounded in a history of mutual relationality. On the contrary, what has been happening under the postmodern aegis is that familiar phenomenon of high metropolitan theory repeatedly accusing Third World identity politics of essentialism.

This is hilariously ironic when we consider that this entire obsession with essences and the deconstruction of binarity have very little to do with a number of indigenous African and Asian knowledges that do not axiomatize binarity as the founding principle of all thought.[45] It is the hubris of Western thought that accommodates the belief that the West's antinomian struggle with itself is *the* universal form of all revolution and that other cultures should genuflect to the jurisdiction of Platonism and its alter ego. To vary Derrida's dictum, it is as though the world can never really step out of the pages of Western thought; the only alternative is to turn the pages in a certain way. What is even more alarming is the fact that the postmodern countermemory conveniently forgets the history of essentialism as it has been foisted on the non-West. It was during the modernist regime (in collusion with colonialism) that traditions were invented by the colonizer on behalf of the colonized and, as Lata Mani had demonstrated brilliantly in the context of suttee, that the so-called authority of indigenous traditions was created and constructed by the colonizer to legitimate and inferiorize indigenous traditions, all in one move.[46] This so-called authority was really not representative of indigenous practices and worldviews. As Dipesh Chakrabarty has argued powerfully (and here I am extending his insight somewhat), the native's obsession with history as well as with knowledge was produced in response to the colonizer's need to dominate, not in response to the native's need for self-knowledge and authentication.[47]

But this is not all. Even if the discussion of essentialism were restricted to the First World, there is still quite a bit of semantic fuzziness for which to account. Even within the discourse of Western metaphysical thought, I doubt that essences were ever considered empirically valid. In the attempt to construct and valorize the discourse of ideality, and in the effort to mediate the gap between what is and what ought to be, the category (the essence function, if you will) of the essence functioned as a kind of telos, as the positing of an a priori authority to direct and regulate the paths that history is to take on its way, not to any random resolution, but rather to a desired and willed denouement. Essences, therefore, belonged to the level of abstract, transhistorical categoriality, whereas the historical world of narrative was subject to error and misdirection. How to theorize ideality with reference to history is by no means an easy task; nor is it an unnecessary task. My point here is that both the real/the historical and the ideal are products of the human imagination and therefore historical through and through. As in Saussurean linguistics, where the signified itself is understood as a function of the linguistic sign and signifying practices, here, too, the ideal itself should be comprehended as a discursive effect. Ideality and the notion of essences that direct history toward a desirable and ideal resolution are themselves (for *essence* connotes completion and an ideal completion) historically motivated categories. Essences have no significance whatsoever except in relation to the changing world of history and circumstance.

The next step in my argument is to state that the term *strategic essentialism* is redundant, for essentialism has been nothing but strategic. To restate my earlier point, the recourse to essences is a matter of strategy to gain control over processes of history along agential lines. In this day and age, I find it difficult to believe that a Hindu, a Muslim, or a Jew subscribes to Hinduness, Muslimness, or Jewishness except as a form of authority to live by and realize one's already given objectives as a group.[48] The important issues here are (*a*) the extent to which the anterior givenness of teleological objectives is open to historical modifications and re-versions and (*b*) the political process of representation through which the teleological blueprint is endorsed (from the grass roots, not as top-down authority) and hegemonized in authentic response to the will of the members constituting the group.

There is yet another deployment of strategic essentialism, that is, the recourse by one group, in the context of multiple contradictory and competing historical claims, to the notion *ontological essence* with the purpose of elevating and prioritizing its claims over and above the merely historical claims of other competing groups.

To transfer this philosophic discussion of essence and ideality to the realm of identity, identity politics, and the role played by narrative in the construction of identity, one must ask how narratives are interpellated and how they are adjudged as failures or as successes. Before I undertake this analysis, I would like to make it very clear that my position on these issues is historical to the core and that I have undertaken this polemical excursion into essentialism only to show that essentialism itself has been an interested practice undertaken by human beings in search of specific goals, not a disembodied and disinterested body of knowledge separated from the world of historical praxis.

Why do human communities take recourse to the rhetoric of essences? Any community has a given identity that is sedimented by the imbrication of many histories. There is also the desire to produce from the given identity an ideal community that one can call one's own, and narrative as a socially symbolic act is the way from *here* to *there*.[49] Can narrative function as pure process, that is, without the authority of some form of ideological apriorism?[50] Which pre-scripts does and should narrative follow? If narrative is an act of self-fashioning, which pre-scripts are liberating and which ones repressive? Can the narrative function be divorced from the need for identity? Is narrative owned and operated by any agency, or is it external to the jurisdiction of agency? My position is that no narrative is possible without some tacit axiology, simply because narrative is neither a value-free nor a purely descriptive act. The value that legitimates the narrative project is in a sense anterior to the project itself, and, in another sense, it can be realized only as a function of the narrative process.[51] The success or failure of the narrative is to be measured in terms of its closeness to the intended trajectory; that is, the value produced must be read in terms of the value intended. The two of course will never totally coincide with each other, for that would amount to the preemption of history by pure presence. Value thus presides over the narrative project (also the identity project) both as an epistemological and as an ethicopolitical imperative. The imperative is epistemological, insofar as the subjects involved in the process must be able to think of their intended identity as a worthy object of knowledge, and ethicopolitical, since the value is also related to questions of representation, hegemony, authenticity, correctness, and fairness. In short, it is utterly meaningless to disconnect identity politics from questions concerning the truth claims as well as the legitimacy of identity. One cannot by definition entertain an identity that is truthless or illegitimate, for *identity* is both an epistemic and a politico-juridical regime.

Furthermore, the thematic securing of any identity within its own truth marks the powerful moment when the for-itself of that identity is in addition transformed to an in-itself that can be acknowledged and respected by other identities.[52] Without this passage from its *being-for-itself* to its *being-in-itself*, any identity is doomed to a history of ghettoization; that is, it will have a reality for itself within its own niche and no more. If identities are denied the legitimacy of their own truths (both in their own eyes and through the eyes of the "others"), they are bound to languish within their histories of inferiority, deprived of their relational-objective status vis-à-vis the objective conditions of other identities.[53] To put it concretely, the self-image of an African American must be acknowledged as objective knowledge by non–African Americans. The historical intelligibility of a subaltern/minority worldview is neither a matter of special interests epistemology nor a function of some mysterious and esoteric insiderism. For any identity to participate equally and meaningfully in a comity of identities, its knowledge must be accorded objective validity by all other parties at the very outset of the meeting. Without such a recognition, some identities are bound to be equal and more than equal, others less than equal, for lack of an evenly realized universality. It might be objected (and more of this later) that the self-identity of any identity is for the other, but my contention is that historical differentiations must be made between intra- and interidentitarian notions of alterity. Such distinctions may not be necessary in the context of a perfectly realized universality, but, clearly, no one will claim that such a state has been attained.

If my reading of the essentialism-narrative nexus is correct, then it would seem that there is something disingenuous about the polarized choice offered by postmodern theory: essentialism or a pure subjectless process. This binary choice seems like the only option possible because postmodern theory considers the identity question purely from a philosophic perspective and, in so doing, represses the programmatic and intentional connections between *interests* and identity. What is left out of the discussion is of course the politics of representation.[54] Epistemology, theory, and philosophy are reified as absolute sites of revolution, cleansed of political and representational partisanship. Such a celebration of epistemological revolutions at the expense of organicity and the solidarities of representational politics ill befits the needs of postcoloniality, yet why is it that theorists of postcoloniality (myself included) take postmodernist/poststructuralist lessons to heart in their attempts to delineate postcolonial subjectivity?[55] My focus here is on some of the significant contributions made by Homi Bhabha in the area of postcolonial narratology. These interventions have been as much postcolonial in their intent as they have been postmodernist/poststructuralist in their conviction. The cardinal question that comes up in Bhabha's case (and, by extension, in any theoretical work that uses poststructuralist epistemology to clarify issues in postcoloniality) is, Which is the tenor and which the vehicle? Which is the figure and which the ground? Which is the historical body and which the animating spirit: poststructuralism or postcoloniality? What does it mean to articulate the two posts together?

The deconstructive dissemination that Bhabha proposes as a resolution to the contemporary identity crisis works on two levels: on the political level, *dissemination* stands for the dissipation of the legitimacy of nationalist regimes and their *imagined communities*.[56] On a philosophical level, dissemination works as the radical postponement of *identity as such;* in the place of identity, we have the notion of displaced hybridities.[57] If radical theory deconstructs and defers identity, history rebukes and calls into question the sovereignty of nationalism. Interestingly enough, the figure that connects the two levels is narrative. In Bhabha's reading, the narration of the nation is a historical failure; but, more consequentially, it is an allegorical failure of the "always already" variety. But why is it a failure? Is it a failure for specific historical reasons, or is the failure intrinsic to the very form of the project such that historical circumstances do not really play a part in the determination of the outcome? Is the narrative failure of nationalism but another name for an omnihistorical cognitive failure? The question that Bhabha does not raise (and this is consistent with his own stated intention of dealing not so much with the histories of nationalism as with the temporality of identity in a general sense), one that Partha Chatterjee would raise with tremendous rigor and specificity, is the following: Which particular agent of nationalism failed, through its performative, to achieve pedagogical authority on behalf of the people? The failures of different agencies, such as the neocolonialist, the comprador, the indigenous elite, the subaltern, the nationalist male, the nationalist female, are all conflated into one monolithic failure. What then follows is an idealist refutation of all pedagogical authority, and, consequently, no account is provided of how certain intentions went awry in their performance or how certain intentions were not truly representative of the people. There is no way to read diagnostically and meaningfully into the gap between the performative and the pedagogical. Quite in keeping with the Lacanian thesis that the very possibility of meaning is grounded in the radical possibility of miscommunication and misrecognition, Bhabha's thesis capitalizes failure absolutely, overlooking in the process the ongoing historical tension involved in any specific act of knowing the omnihistorical horizon of failure and negativity. Bhabha's theoretical model (more psychoanalytic than historical) thus loses the ability to learn something from failure.[58] Learning from failure is possible only when failures are understood as relational phenomena that help in evaluating the distance between intentions and achievements. But the essentialization of failure by Bhabha trivializes the significance of specific failures as they occur during specific times for specific reasons.

It could be argued that there is some justification for launching an all-out global critique of nationalism, for is nationalism not in disrepute the world over, including the West? Besides, is it not unfair to talk about the West as though it were one undifferentiated bloc? First, nationalisms the world over are defunct only in theory, not in historical practice. And, as my opening to this essay argues, nationalism is hale and hearty in the First World, including the United States. Yes, indeed, the West is not one homogeneous formation (there are all kinds of differences within), but my point is that, during colonialism, the West was orchestrated as a unified effect with telling consequences for the non-West. But, more important, yes, there is an East-West divide, but this divide was not the doing of the Third World. On the contrary, discourses of modernity and nationalism found it convenient to play the East-West game as a way of dealing with other cultures.[59] It is galling for the Third World to be told that the West suddenly no longer exists just because the West has willed so: yet another example of the West's ability unilaterally to change the very name of the game whenever it chooses. The *West* is not just its localized name but also the history of its travels and pernicious effects on other histories, and, unless this aspect of the historical effects of the West on the rest is acknowledged as part of its identity, East-West cooperation, by way of the post, is bound to be entirely superficial.[60]

The problem not addressed by Bhabha is that, after their overthrow of colonialism, decolonized people are faced with the crisis of agency. Bhabha's theory of postcoloniality does not acknowledge the basic noncoincidence of postcolonial *interest* with poststructuralist epistemology. Although, through his elaboration of such concepts as *sly civility* and *mimicry*, Bhabha has helped us understand how the native is always in an antagonistic-deconstructive relation with colonialist discourse. He never goes beyond the strategy of playing the master's game against him or her.[61] Nor is he interested in ascertaining whether there are other knowledges besides the master discourse of the West. Bhabha does assert that he is interested in producing through theory a "third space," but, here again, as a movement of deconstructive displacement and "difference," the third space falls well within the epistemological jurisdiction of Western discourse. The third space in which I am interested is an emergent macropolitical space (complicit neither with the West nor with fundamentalisms that are, after all, reacting to the West) with its own independent knowledge claims. To Bhabha, however, it is enough to theorize postcoloniality as a lack that frustrates the plenitude of metropolitan theory. Take postmodernism/postconstructivism away from Bhabha's theory, and instantly postcoloniality disappears also. In other words, there is no sense of *constituency in the theory* apart from the *constituency of theory*.

One way to account for this excessive dependence on poststructuralist theory is to invoke Bhabha's diasporic location as explanation. Living in the West, and being an integral part of theoretical, cultural, and academic developments in the West, how can one's theory not be constituted by one's location as well as one's subject position? Not only is this explanation insufficient, but it also trivializes and vulgarizes the profound significance of the very term *politics of location*.[62] Clearly, by *location* we cannot mean something as impoverished and debilitating as one's actual and physical location. Locations are as factual as they are imaginary and imagined, as physical as they are psychic, and as open to direct experience as they are to empathic participation. Location and identity, and location and knowledge, are not mutually implosive but mutually ecstatic. Besides, locations are never simple but rather multilayered realities overdetermined by diverse cultural and political flows. In a postmodern world that is almost a virtual product of protean and multidirectional transfers and relays of information bites and knowledge chunks, it is just a little bit shabby to claim location as an alibi for one's nonpresence in other realities. The politics of location is productive, not because location immures people within their specific four walls, but because it makes one location vulnerable to the claims of another and enables multiple contested readings of the one reality from a variety of locations and positions. As Lata Mani develops this notion so thoughtfully in her essay "Multiple Mediations," location is a heavily mediated concept, and, unless the many mediations that interpellate location are studied in all their interconnectedness, locational analyses will be no more than exercises in defensive self-absorption.

Like any location, diasporic locations are characterized by both an "expressive totality" and the reality of uneven and relatively autonomous mediation that constitutes and accounts for the totality.[63] The provocative question always is, How is the totality spoken for or represented? How does the straddling-many-worlds experience result in a home, and how is the ethnoscape of such a home produced into knowledge?[64] To take a hypothetical example, my taste in music could be primarily Carnatic music and jazz; secondarily, Hindi and Tamil film music; and, at a tertiary level, contemporary rock and Western classical music. My affinities in literature could be primarily the contemporary multiethnic literature of the United States; secondarily, canonical British and American literary works; and, tertiarily, contemporary Tamil best-sellers. My lifestyle may privilege the two-career nuclear family ethic, but my values may well endorse the extended family system. I could be a fierce champion of individual rights and the right to privacy, but, on another level, I am an uncompromising opponent of capitalism and the privatization of morality. I could be a secular atheist who participates in Indian religious events for cultural and ethnic reasons. I might scoff at nationalist ways of denominating realities, and at the same time I could be a passionate Indian, but under the Third World umbrella. In other words, I could be hyphenated more than once and in more than one direction. In each of these configurations, the relation between experience and identity is differently achieved: in some, through physical intimacy and proximity and, in others, through psychic and emotional solidarity. Some realities are real in a physical sense and others imaginary. Different spaces get collocated through the logics of nearness and distance: there are multiple accents and patterns and, often, clashing priority agendas. As I have argued elsewhere, this profile of multihistorical hybridity operates hierarchically, some of the elements that constitute hybridity having a greater say than others in giving it a name.[65] Thus, if my culinary preferences were exclusively South Indian, my cultural identity generally Indian, but all my cognitive-rational-intellectual value systems secular Western, it is inevitable that, in an overall sense, I would be more Western than Indian or South Indian. This is simply because the domain in which I have chosen to be Western, the domain of cognition and rationality, is more determining in this last instance of my totality than any of the other domains are. My very awareness of my Indianness in those other areas will be the result of a cognitive production, itself not Indian in its mode of operation. Within such a conjunctural crosshatching, to use Gayatri Spivak's ringing phrase, epistemology plays the honored role of speaking for the hybridity. In

Bhabha's version of hybridity, the expressive historical totality is in the final analysis articulated by poststructuralist epistemology.

Bhabha's reading of a poem by Jussawalla is an interesting example of how metropolitan theory rereads a postcolonial dilemma as a poststructuralist aporia. In his analysis of the semantics of the letter/spiritual symbol *om* (a religious Hindu symbol that raises the further question, What is the significance of a Hindu symbol to different secular Indians, the Hindu Indian, the Christian Indian, the Parsi Indian, the Sikh Indian, etc.), Bhabha felicitously subsumes *om* within poststructuralist-deconstructive procedures without ever acknowledging, let along analyzing, the indigenous genealogy of that profound symbol.[66] My concern is not with the correctness or the insiderness of one genealogy and the incorrect alienness of the other but rather with the nonchalant manner in which Bhabha's reading denies the poem its intense double coding.[67] The rich symbolics of a different culture automatically become the pretext for metropolitan theoretical virtuosity. Could poststructuralism by any chance be a problem here? Is it conceivable that Derrida, Lacan, and Foucault may at best be distracting when applied to postcoloniality? Could there be other epistemic starting points for the elaboration of postcolonial complexity?

I do not want to be misunderstood as an ideologue who would resist at any cost the interruptions and readings against the grain of the kind advocated and practiced by Gayatri Spivak.[68] There is a great and urgent need for transnational and transcultural readings, but these readings must concede the reality of other knowledges. Transcultural readings are the very turf where the legitimacies of different knowledges should be contested, not an arena where readings take on a purely epiphenomenal significance long after the question of knowledge has been settled in favor of metropolitan knowledge.[69] Unless and until other worlds are recognized not merely as *other histories* but as *other knowledges* that question the legitimacy of metropolitan theory, no substantive common ground can be coordinated between postmodernism and postcoloniality. The postmodern concern and solicitude for the other must step beyond the pieties of deconstructive-psychoanalytic thought.[70]

The vexing issue facing postmodern epistemology is how to reconcile a radical incommensurability among multiple knowledges and knowledge games with the dire need for a politics of mutual recognition? Analogously, how to honor multiplicity and heterogeneity without an understanding of the very terrain of connectedness that makes heterogeneity visible in the first place? The category *recognition of the other* is posited at the level of cognition and epistemology: ironically, the very level at which *incommensurability* is also posited as a motif intrinsic to the postmodern condition. If there is radical incommensurability, then there can be no recognition. If recognition is to go beyond the mere phenomenal and/or empiricist acknowledgment of the mere facticity of the other, then a way must be found to transcend this incommensurability.

Without such a transcendence in the name of a potentially multilateral universalism, we cannot even begin to pose the problem of how to read one history in terms of another. Neither the relativist postmodernist impasse nor the liberalist invocation of multiculturalism in the name of the dominant One serves the postcolonial need for equitable transactions among different histories and different knowledges.

To repeat myself, it is at the level of knowledge that the postcolonial subject has sustained crucial damage. Caught between two knowledges (one not one's own, the other one's own but lacking in historical-political clout), the postcolonial subject remains a purely reactive subject: its *for-itself* rendered exclusively a function of its existence *for the other,* its *for-itself* hampered from producing its self-version as a form of a universal *in-itself.* Proponents of Lacan may well claim universal purchase for their theories of alterity, but, in the case of the postcolonial subject, we cannot afford to forget that the self-other conjuncture has been mediated by the structure in dominance of colonialism that is historical, not a mere matter for allegory. As Partha Chatterjee has convincingly argued, decolonization by way of secularism has been a poisoned remedy for postcolonial peoples.[71] To them, secularism represents political victory at the expense of epistemological self-esteem. The difficult and unenviable task facing Third World intellectuals is that of upholding secularism as a political ideology while at the same time critiquing it as a form of epistemological dominance. As Madhu Kishwar develops her thesis in essay after essay, it is not a question of denying Western influences, some of which are beneficial, but rather a question of affirming one's own knowledge base in a global context that views experiences as underdeveloped and Eastern whereas the epistemic categories that make sense of experiences are deemed to be of the West.[72] Furthermore, an unquestioning acceptance of secular modernity often comes in the way of Third World projects that return in a revisionist mode to their own past: a past that in fact was invented by modernity in Manichaean opposition to its own spirit. These projects of return to one's own traditions have become epistemologically unfashionable, thanks to the postmodern insistence on identity deconstruction. It must be stated that the revisionist return projects are characterized not necessarily by nostalgia or by a fundamentalist impulse but by the need to separate the truth of one's own traditions from the significances attributed to them by the colonizer. Are the truths of Islam and Hinduism no different from the form they have been given by Indologists and Orientalists? What are the realities of one's tradition, good and bad, when viewed from within the tradition? Are there traditions other than the ones set up by colonialism in its attempts to essentialize and inferiorize indigenous cultures? The fact of the matter has been that modernity had effectively delegitimated the Hindu critique of Hinduism and the Islamic critique of Islam. It is as though such critiques did not exist at all and the only critiques available were through the deracinating modernist theories of knowledge. As we have already seen, capitulation to modernist ideology preempts possibilities of one's own history and one's own knowledge: the center of one's reality is always made to lie elsewhere.

As we look at hybrid realities the world over during a period of increasing demographic and cultural overlaps, it seems to be that a sensible option is to question modernity's claim that it is *the Interpellation of all interpellations*. Can the claims of modernity be relativized and contextualized with reference to the criteria of relevance as experienced in the Third World? Can the travel of modernity to the Third World, to borrow from Said's notion *traveling theory*, be anything other than an epistemic violence of local theories and knowledges? This negotiation between the local and the global is an all-important issue that unfortunately receives no attention in postmodern theory that lives and dies by the logic of binary opposition: local *or* global. Controversial issues the world over raise this question over and over again: When is global/universal policy or law relevant, and when is it a violation of local traditions and laws?[73] On what grounds can intervention be justified morally and epistemologically? If global law is involved, on whose terms will the law be drawn up and promulgated? Should some areas be made available for global jurisdiction and others left to the authority of local norms and values? Given such a diversity of epistemic-juridical-moral spaces, how are events, situations, and experiences to be understood both *within* and *across* the legitimacies of discrete spaces? This problematic of space and spatiality has received, and rightly so, extraordinary attention in postmodernist theory.[74] And, as I attempt to conclude this essay, I turn to the politics of space as empowered by postmodernist theory.

Unlike such existential phenomenologists as Martin Heidegger and Jean-Paul Sartre, who invoked time and temporality as radical agents of change, postmodernist theory suggests that temporality is a spatial-discursive matter and that, when we say *time* or *temporality,* we signify not some raw, feral, and preconstituted force, but a very specific structuration of time (nationalist time, women's time, industrial or pastoral time, etc.) that is produced discursively into a binding episteme. Foucault's brilliant notion of *dans le vrai* sums up this notion of truth in history as a matter of spatial subjection. Ideological time is nothing but discursive epistemic space. Second, such a notion of spatialized time interrogates the unilinear teleology that underlies so much historicism. The sense of space, both in the sense of physical geopolitical space and in an epistemic sense, cuts across and fragments the idea of identity evolving through history into a plenitude. Heterotopic and disjuncted realities are as much history as the history of rooted locatedness.[75] As Foucault's early work attempted so bravely, it is the advocacy of *discontinuity as history* that pits postmodernism against traditional historiographies that privilege the inherence of identity in nonmoving origins. Postmodernism thus offers a dire threat to discourses of identity. If identity is nothing but a narrative effect, and if, furthermore, narratives themselves are instances of unavoidable cognitive failure, then surely identity is neither viable ontologically nor defensible epistemologically. Hence the need in Foucault to "think a different history" and to write the history of the present that requires different tools, different strategies, and a different sense of space. This spatial revolution could be valorized as an entirely formal project (and I would not endorse that option) or, better still, empowered as a historical project of imagining different spaces for different histories and knowledges that have been subjugated for too long: constrained to exist in darkness as gaps, wholes, and "ineffables" within the body of a dominant historiography.

It all depends on how and in what interests postmodern spaces are to be imagined and activated. In the name of what principles should postmodern spaces be coordinated? Postmodernism at its best champions the phenomenology of lived experiences and verities against the authority of top-down identity regimes and their deceitful historiographies. These realities must imagine their own discursive homes, homes that are not as yet real in history. These spaces must be imagined in excess of and in advance of (avant-garde in this sense) actual history in the name of experiences that are real but lacking in legitimacy. Each of these lived realities, such as the ethnic, the diasporic, the gay, the migrant, the subaltern, etc., must imagine its own discursive-epistemic space as a form of openness to one another's persuasion: neither totalized oppression, where, for example, nationalist time/history presumes to speak for all other times/histories, nor relativist isolation, whereby each history remains an island unto itself.

Given the aegis of the post, what kind of new spatiality is to be conceptualized so that different histories can, in and of their very being, be responsive to the realities of other histories? How can the decentered spatial politics of the post help us understand the representational identity politics of specific groups and their interconnectedness? By way of responding to these questions, I go to a novel by Amitav Ghosh, *The Shadow Lines*, a work that goes a long way toward developing such a dialogic cartographic imaginary.[76] It would be well beyond the scope of this essay to do justice to the complex perspectives on nationalism and the diaspora that are historicized in the novel. I merely sketch, in summary fashion, a few of the important formulations on the space-location-identity problematic that Ghosh develops through a strategy of polyvocality and heteroglossia that is much more multihistorical than the kind of metropolitan ventriloquism one finds in the works of Salman Rushdie. Here, then, in schematic fashion are some of the insights in the novel:

a) Spaces are real precisely because they are imagined.

b) The imagination of spaces acknowledges both the need for and the limitations of fixed spaces.

c) The transcendence of fixed spaces is motivated globally but executed locally.

d) One need not be an insider to understand the reality of any specific space; all spaces are reciprocally ecstatic/exotopic.

e) The meaning of history is a function of narrative.

f) All realities are versions in their epistemological grounding but all too real in their political effects, hence the need to have one's own version.

g) One can, through global empathy and the practice of a "precise imagination," understand and experience realities other than one's own.

h) Understanding history is a deeply interpretive procedure, not a matter for a fact-based empiricism.

i) Histories are never discrete, and, in fact, when any collectivity looks into a mirror to get a reflection of itself, the mirror operates both as a mirror into one's self and as a window into other selves.

j) Distinctions are to be made between a longing for the other's reality based on violence or exoticism and a genuine dialogic longing based on possibilities of reciprocal and equal transcendence.[77]

k) The deconstruction of the "shadow lines" of nationalist divides is to be achieved by a transnational populist force that calls into question the adequacy of nationalist regimes by way of the authority of lived experiences and reciprocal realities.

My brief focus here will be on the manner in which Ghosh's postnationalist, traveling text calls for a thoroughgoing critique of existing discourses and regimes of identity. But, unlike a Rushdie text, this very call for deterritorialization is located in multiple histories: colonialism, nationalism, and only then transnationalism or the diaspora. There is no joyous countermemory at work here; all three histories, each with its different but related center, is made to commingle with one another in a variety of relations. This substantive critique, to use Lacanian parlance, is interested in the overthrow of the mighty Symbolic by the Imaginary.[78] Ghosh's text demonstrates the utter poverty of the regime of the Symbolic and argues for the need for a different political Imaginary. In a historical sense, the Symbolic stands for the authority of nationalism as interpellated by the nation-state, which insists that all other a priori imaginary relations and identifications (be they gender or sexuality based or class, religion, ethnicity, or community specific) be mediated and alienated into knowledge by the symbolic authority of nationalism that, like the duplicitous Lacanian phallus, exercises total command precisely because it cannot be *had* by any one group yet can perform its representative-pedagogical function with seeming neutrality. Consequently, the symbolic of nationalism is thus turned into a perennial and incorrigible "lack" that can be critiqued perennially but never transcended in the name of a different alternative.[79]

Like a number of feminists who have refused the notion of such a total interpellation by the Symbolic (in the name of the father), Ghosh, too, rejects the attractions of the negative critique, which in the ultimate analysis prolongs the same and "enjoys the symptom." Ghosh's fiction suggests that there is a pressing need for imaginary self-identifications of peoples across the world and that such a need is by no means naive or pretheoretical. The imaginary compels us to rethink our existing affiliations that have been founded entirely on an epistemology of alienation: the alienation of the Imaginary by the Symbolic. Perhaps I must hasten here to point out a few things about imaginary self-identification so as to anticipate a number of canonical Lacanian objections. First, the act of self-identification through the mirror is imaginary, not real, and adulthood is all about the realization that identifications are indeed as imaginary as they are necessary. Second, the imaginary realm is necessary so that human beings may measure and evaluate the extent to which they have or have not attained their imaginary self-identity. Without the Imaginary, there is no way of appraising the distance between who we are and who we want to be: all that we would be left with is the fetishized authority of the Symbolic accountable to none other than itself. Finally, unlike the Symbolic, the Imaginary is a historically vulnerable mode of operation, not the "name of the law." As Ghosh develops it in his fictional world, where voices resonate off each other and different worlds "image" one another despite distances in time and space, the mirror avoids the error of a dominant universalism based on one's self-image as well as the perils of a chic relativism that uses the mirror as a form of self-enclosure. The mirror turned into window becomes a mirror-window dyad that does not allow the relational-historical structure of the self-other conjuncture as it operates both within and athwart cultures to ossify into one self-other configuration as warranted by the dominant world order. As a result, the self-other problematic is posed as a multi- and interhistorical issue, not as a philosophical issue rooted in the rectitude of the dominant world order. There are selves and others operating within and across cultures; there are innumerable comings and goings, arrivals and departures, that refuse to make sense within a single historiography.

The spatial vision offered in *The Shadow Lines* is as imaginary as it is experiential. Between events and their meaning, between peoples and their destinies, a gap has opened up, and it should be the ethic of new historiographies to imagine new spaces that will connect legitimately the world of experience with the language of meaning. These spaces are the spaces of the post that transform the status quo. This transformative imagining of relational spaces is equally an attempt to enfranchise different knowledges with historical reference to one another.

This way of imagining the post seems to me to be more worthwhile than the fashionable global regionalism/localism that is being promoted currently in the name of the universal commodity form. It is in the interests of a capital-driven postmodernism to cultivate and support localism in far-off places, only to reclaim these localisms as part of a universally vendible global localism. Given the asymmetry of power relations, we also cannot afford to forget that the West retains the power to decide when the other is like us and when not, with the result that the very cultivation of the politics of difference and heterogeneity is subservient to the dominant demand for difference and heterogeneity. It is access that postmodernism is after, and consumption is its basic premise. Localism and specificity should be available to the metropolitan gaze so that the remotest spot from the most underdeveloped sector of the Third World may begin to satisfy the epistemological thirst of the metropolitan center.

This entire essay has been a tentative effort to separate out the emancipatory possibilities of postmodernism from its colonizing potentialities and to articulate coalitions between East and West, between First and Third. I have also tried to argue that the valence of postmodernism cannot be decided on without reference to the accountability of postmodernism to the rest of the world. For postmodernism to have any kind of meaningful travel across the world, it must present itself to the world as a finite ideology based on specific interests, not as a value-neutral and ideologically free form of knowledge or human condition, and be prepared to face challenges from other knowledges from other parts of the world and consent to have its self-story narrativized by the others. This turning of tables (or what Gayatri Spivak has termed suggestively *the anthropologization of the West*) is historically necessary before the time spaces of the post can begin to reinvent and reimagine a truly equal and multilateral universality. Without a change of direction, the post will serve only to exacerbate existing asymmetries. Perhaps postmodernism is also post-Western in ways not available to the metropolitan consciousness.

In the words of Samir Amin as he imagines a more egalitarian universal society, such a "society will be superior to ours on all levels only if it is worldwide, and only if it establishes a genuine universalism, based on contributions of everyone, Westerners as well as those whose historical course has been different." [80] A universalism liberated from dominance and captive no more to the ventriloquism of the West. [81]

Notes

1   For a thorough analysis of the effect of capital on the time-space of global culture, see Karl Marx, *Grundrisse: Foundations of the Critique of Political Economy,* trans. Martin Nicolaus (New York: Random House, 1973). For a sensitive analysis of selected formulations from the *Grundrisse,* see Ranajit Guha, "Dominance without Hegemony and Its Historiography," in *Subaltern Studies,* vol. 6, ed. Ranajit Guha (Delhi: Oxford University Press, 1989), 210–309.

2   The category *process without Subject or goals* is elaborated by the French structuralist-Marxist Louis Althusser, who inflects the Leninist-Marxist concept *the motor of history* through the discourse of structuralism (see Louis Althusser, *Essays on Ideology,* trans. Ben Brewster [London: Verso, 1984]). My point is that, while, on the one hand, NAFTA would seem to have inaugurated the seamless transnational mobility of capital, the Zapatistas in Mexico were involved in a very different relation with Mexican nationalism. For more on the

Zapatista insurgence and the deleterious effects of NAFTA on the Zapatistas, see Alexander Cockburn, "Beat the Devil," *Nation*, 28 March 1994. Similarly, just when national borders are sought to be erased through economic transactions, Europe and the United States are engaged in such controversies as whether American whisky should have the right to call itself *Scotch* and whether *Bourbon* is a proper name for liquor produced in France.

3 Walt Whitman refers to America as a *nation of nations* or as a mosaic formation in search of effective cultural identification in his poem "Birds of Passage: Song of the Universal" (*Walt Whitman: The Complete Poems*, ed. Francis Murphy [London: Penguin, 1975], 255–57).

4 For a useful typology of a variety of nationalisms, see Ernest Gellner, *Nations and Nationalism* (Oxford: Blackwell, 1983).

  Samir Amin has theorized the notion *unequal development* memorably (see *Eurocentrism* [New York: Monthly Review Press, 1989]), and the work of the geographer Neil Smith constitutes *unevenness* as a unavoidable category in the study of global systems (Neil Smith, *Uneven Development: Nature, Capital, and the Production of Space* [Oxford: Basil Blackwell, 1984]).

5 Jean François Lyotard, *The Postmodern Condition*, trans. Geoff Bennington and Brian Massumi (Minneapolis: University of Minnesota Press, 1984).

6 Jurgen Habermas, for one, would argue that modernity has been an incomplete project and that postmodernity is but a telling symptom of that incompletion (see "Modernity — an Incomplete Project," in *The Anti-Aesthetic: Essays in Postmodern Culture*, ed. Hal Foster [Seattle, WA: Port Townsend Bay, 1983], 3–15). For different positions on the modernist-postmodernist debate, see the contributions of Frederic Jameson, *Postmodernism; or, The Cultural Logic of Late Capitalism* (Durham, N.C.: Duke University Press, 1991); Nancy Fraser, *Unruly Practices: Power, Discourse, and Gender in Contemporary Social Theory* (Minneapolis: University of Minnesota Press, 1989), and *Justice Interruptus: Critical Reflections on the Postsocialist Condition* (New York: Routledge, 1997); Linda Hutcheon, *A Poetics of Postmodernism: History, Theory, Fiction* (New York: Routledge, 1988); and Andreas Huyssen, "Mapping the Postmodern," *New German Critique* 33 (1984): 5–52.

7 The difference between dominating and dominated knowledges has been developed by a number of South Asian scholars. For a spirited, antagonistic engagement with the secularist episteme, see Ashis Nandy, ed., *Science, Hegemony, and Violence: A Requiem for Modernity* (Tokyo: UN University; Delhi, Oxford University Press, 1990).

8 For a careful differentiation of the post see Anthony Appiah, "Is the 'Post' in Postcoloniality the Same as the 'Post' in Postmodernism?" *Critical Inquiry* 17 (1991): 336–57.

9 In general, it has become customary to separate out two kinds of postmodernism: the postmodernism of play and pleasure and a more serious postmodernism interested in oppositionality and resistance. But here, too, the privileged site has been epistemology.

10 For an enabling articulation of universalism that functions as a critique both of Eurocentrism and Marxism, see Amin, *Eurocentrism*.

11 As an author canonized by modernism, Conrad is an interesting example of narrative practice that fails in the presence of the other. Whereas Chinua Achebe (*Things Fall Apart* [London: Heinemann, 1958]) would attribute to *Heart of Darkness* a conscious fear and hatred of the "unknowability" of Africa, Edward Said gives more credence to the ambivalence in Conrad's narrative even as he reads the text symptomatically in the context of Eurocentrism and colonialism (*Culture and Imperialism* [New York: Alfred Knopf, 1993], 19–31).

12 For a particularly mechanical and uninspiring application of poststructuralist self-reflexivity to Third World feminism, see Julie Stephens, "Feminist Fictions: A Critique of the Category 'Non-Western Woman in Feminist Writings on India,'" in Guha, ed., *Subaltern Studies*, 92–125. See also Susie Tharu, "Response to Julie Stephens," in ibid., 126–31.

13 See Edward W. Said, "Narrative, Geography, and Interpretation," *New Left Review* 180 (1990): 81–107. For further discussion of overlapping territories and relations between the center and the periphery, see also his *Culture and Imperialism* (New York: Knopf, 1993).

14 For more on the nature of the critique as a form of knowledge, see *Postmodernism/Jameson/Critique*, ed. Douglas Kellner (Washington, D.C.: Maisonneuve, 1989). Where does the critique come from? is a pertinent question that is raised and discussed by Ranajit Guha in his "Dominance without Hegemony and Its Historiography."

15 I refer here to the work of Raymond Williams, to whom alternatives for change were more important than mere systems building or a deterministic celebration of technology (see his *The Politics of Modernism* [London: Verso, 1989]).

16 See Ella Shohat, "Notes on the 'Post-Colonial,' " *Social Text* 31/32 (1992): 99–113; and also my "Ethnic Identity and Poststructuralist Difference," *Cultural Critique* (spring 1987), and "Postcoloniality and the Boundaries of Identity," *Callaloo*, special issue, 16, no. 4 (fall 1993): 16–24.

17 The notion of decapitation is discussed at length by Jacques Derrida as he discusses the nature of entitlement and disentitlement in the context of Mallarmé's poetry (see *Dissemination*, trans. Barbara Johnson [Chicago: University of Chicago Press, 1981]). For a discussion of the decapitation of history by theory, see my "The Changing Subject and the Politics of Theory," *Differences* 2, no. 2 (1990): 126–52, reprinted in *Diasporic Mediations: Between Home and Location* (Minneapolis: University of Minnesota Press, 1996).

This flying away from history could also be read as postmodernism's rejection of a Marxist dialectic.

18 Jean Baudrillard's treatment of America, e.g., is virtual and not historical (*America*, trans. Chris Turner [New York: Verso, 1989]).

19 For a critique of such a hypostasis of theory, see Williams, *The Politics of Modernism*. See also Tony Pinckney's introduction to *The Politics of Modernism*.

20 For a wide-ranging discussion of Western guilt in the context of global ecology and the Earth Summit held in Rio de Janeiro, June 1992, see Akhil Gupta, "Peasants and Global Environmentalism: Safeguarding the Future of 'Our World' or Initiating a New Form of Governmentality" (paper presented at the Agrarian Studies Seminar, Yale University, 25 March 1994). For an insightful exhortation to go beyond the politics of blame and guilt, see Edward W. Said, "Intellectuals in a Postcolonial World," *Salmagundi* (spring–summer 1986): 70–71.

21 I refer here to Jean François Lyotard and Jean-Loup Thébaud, *Just Gaming*, trans. Wlad Godzich (Minneapolis: University of Minnesota Press, 1985).

African American intellectuals like Cornel West and bell hooks have eloquently articulated the postmodern difference within the First World (see, e.g., the interview with Cornel West in *Universal Abandon: The Politics of Postmodernism*, ed. Andrew Ross [Minneapolis: University of Minnesota Press, 1988], 268–86).

22 For a polemical discussion of hybridity, see my "Postcoloniality and the Boundaries of Identity."

23 Nadine Gordimer thinks through this issue of conscience in the context of white relevance in postapartheid South Africa in her collection of essays *The Essential Gesture: Writing, Politics, and Places* (New York: Knopf, 1988). See also Stephen Clingman's introduction to *The Essential Gesture*.

On the narrative of Eurocentric thought, see Gayatri Chakravorty Spivak, "Can the Subaltern Speak?" in *Marxism and the Interpretation of Culture*, ed. Cary Nelson and Lawrence Grossberg (Urbana: University of Illinois Press, 1988), 271–313; and my "Towards an Effective Intellectual," in *Intellectuals: Aesthetics/Politics/Academics*, ed. Bruce Robbins (Minneapolis: University of Minnesota Press, 1990), reprinted in *Diasporic Mediations*.

24 By *feminization*, I mean the ethicopolitical authority of feminism that functions both as a special interest and as a general perspective with the capacity to influence the overall scheme of things. For a brilliant argument that advocates the generalization of feminist historiography, see Kumkum Sangari and Sudesh Vaid's introduction to *Recasting Women: Essays in Indian Colonial History* (New Brunswick, N.J.: Rutgers University Press, 1989), 1–26.

25 For a provocative conjunctural articulation of feminist-theoretical agendas, see Gayatri Chakravorty Spivak, "Feminism and Critical Theory," in *In Other Worlds: Essays in Cultural Politics* (London: Methuen, 1987), 77–92, 277–80.

26 Nancy Fraser and Linda Nicholson, "Social Criticism without Philosophy: An Encounter between Feminism and Philosophy," in *Feminism/Postmodernism*, ed. Linda Nicholson (New York: Routledge, 1990), 19–38.

27 For discussions of the post, see "Postcoloniality," *Social Text*, special issue, vols. 31/32 (1992); and "Post-Colonial Discourse," ed. Tejumola Olaniyan, *Callaloo*, special issue, vol. 16, no. 4 (fall 1993). See also Aijaz Ahmad, *In Theory* (London: Verso, 1992); and Arif Dirlik, "The Postcolonial Aura: Third World Criticism in the Age of Global Capitalism," *Critical Inquiry* 20, no. 2 (1994): 328–56.

28 See, e.g., *Feminism/Postmodernism*, ed. Linda Nicholson (New York: Routledge, 1990); and Fraser, *Unruly Practices*.

29 For a sustained advocacy of worldliness, see Edward W. Said, *The World, the Text, the Critic* (Cambridge, Mass.: Harvard University Press, 1983).

30 See, among others, *Third World Women and the Politics of Feminism*, ed. Chandra Mohanty, Ann Russo, and Lourdes Torres (Bloomington: Indiana University Press, 1991); *Feminist Genealogies, Colonial Legacies, Democratic Futures*, ed. Chandra Mohanty and M. Jacqui Alexander (New York: Routledge, 1997); and *This Bridge Called My Back: Writings by Radical Women of Color*, ed. Gloria Anzaldúa and Cherry Moraga (New York: Kitchen Table/ Women of Color, 1983).

31 Both Chandra Talpade Mohanty and Lata Mani have consistently addressed in their work the problematics as well as the potentialities of location (see Mohanty, Russo, and Torres, eds., *Third World Women and the Politics of Feminism;* and Lata Mani, "Multiple Mediations: Feminist Scholarship in the Age of Multinational Reception," *Inscriptions* 5 [1989]: 1–23).

32 Gayatri Chakravorty Spivak has undertaken this project of the epistemological critique of identity as such in conjunction with a strategic practice of essentialism for certain political ends (see *The Postcolonial Critic* [New York: Routledge, 1990]).

33 See the work of Peggy Kamuf, Naomi Schor, and others in this regard.

34 I refer here to Michel Foucault's essay "Nietzsche, Genealogy, History" (in *Language, Counter-Memory, Practice*, trans. Donald F. Bouchard and Shery Simon [Ithaca, N.Y.: Cornell University Press, 1977], 139–64), in which he reads Nietzsche radically in the name of present history.

35 The reference here is to Jacques Derrida, "Structure, Sign, and Play," in *Writing and Difference*, trans. Alan Bass (Chicago: University of Chicago Press, 1978), 278–93, 339.

36 Guilles Deleuze and Felix Guattari's *Anti-Oedipus: Capitalism and Schizophrenia* (trans. Robert Hurley, Mark Seem, and Helen R. Lane [New York: Seaver Penguin, 1977]) is written in the vein of flows and energies. See also Foucault's introduction to *Anti-Oedipus;* Gilles Deleuze and Michel Foucault, *The Foucault Phenomenon: The Problematics of Style*, trans. Sean Hand (Minneapolis: University of Minnesota Press, 1986); and Paul Bove's foreword to *The Foucault Phenomenon*.

37 In spite of all this brave "border busting" and the travel of commodities, we are witnessing virulent forms of racism and xenophobia in the West when it comes to the migration or

movement of people from the underdeveloped to the developed world. Even in the area of economics and trade, Western governments are constantly following an industrial policy, although their laissez-faire chauvinism will not let them identify their practices as policy (see Arjun Appadurai, "Patriotism and Its Futures," *Public Culture* 5, no. 3 [1993]: 411–25; and Bruce Babbitt, "Free Trade and Environmental Isolationism," *New Perspectives Quarterly* 9, no. 3 [1992]: 35–37).

38 See Anuradha Dinghwaney Needham, "Inhabiting the Metropole: C. L. R. James and the Postcolonial Intellectual of the African Diaspora," *Diaspora* 2, no. 3 (1993): 281–303. For a more exhaustive treatment of this theme, see the chapter on Edward Said in *In Theory*, where, in my reading, Ahmad thoroughly misreads the nature of Said's critical agency and constitutes *metropolitan ambivalence* as a cardinal sin against the Third World.

39 The reference here is to Slavoj Žižek's *Enjoy Your Symptom: Jacques Lacan in Hollywood and Out* (New York: Routledge, 1992). See also the interview with Žižek in *Found Object* 2 (1993): 93–110.

40 See Spivak, *The Postcolonial Critic*. See also Satya P. Mohanty, "The Epistemic Status of Cultural Identity: On *Beloved* and the Postcolonial Condition," *Cultural Critique* 24 (spring 1993): 41–80.

41 See Michel Foucault, "Theatrum Philosophicum," in *Language, Counter-Memory, Practice*.

42 In his celebrated essay on Conrad's *Heart of Darkness*, Chinua Achebe makes the point that, even when Marlow grants humanity to the African, the African is always perceived as a junior (*Things Fall Apart*).

43 In work after modernist work, Africa becomes the backdrop for the working out of the European psyche, and in a real way the forwardness as well as the complexity of the psychological enterprise is posited on the simple backwardness of Africa. For a critical reading of modernity in terms of gender, see Alice Jardine, *Gynesis: Configurations of Woman and Modernity*, (Ithaca, N.Y.: Cornell University Press, 1986).

44 Gauri Viswanathan's *The Masks of Conquest* (New York: Columbia University Press, 1989) and her "Raymond Williams and British Colonialism: The Limits of Metropolitan Cultural Theory" (in *Views from the Border Country: Raymond Williams and Cultural Politics*, ed. Dennis L. Dworkin and Leslie H. Roman [New York: Routledge, 1993], 217–30) demonstrate this thesis with clarity.

45 The point to be made here is that the axiomatic force of binarity has been coextensive with the authority of anthropological thought.

46 See *The Invention of Tradition*, ed. Terence Ranger and Eric Hobsbawm (Cambridge: Cambridge University Press, 1983); and Mani, "Multiple Mediations."

47 Dipesh Chakrabarty's essays "Postcoloniality and the Artifice of History: Who Speaks for 'Indian' Pasts?" (*Representations* 37 [winter 1992]: 1–25) and "The Death of History? Historical Consciousness and the Culture of Late Capitalism" (*Public Culture* 4, no. 2 [1992]: 47–65) take up the question of who is speaking for the Indian past as well as the native's obsession with colonialist historiography.

48 The vicious development of Hindutva in India today is a conscious political practice to other the Muslim and secure for Hindutva the legitimacy of nationalism. Madhu Kishwar and others have been compelled to question such an ideological fixing of the meaning of Hinduism and in the process call the bluff of the Hindu zealots.

49 Here, again, Jameson's work has been crucial, for, more than most other Marxists, he has accepted the cultural logic of postmodernism without at the same time relinquishing the ethicopolitical mandate of Marxist thought (see his *Postmodernism*).

50 Much of this problem with narrative can be subsumed under the general rubric *legitimation*

crisis. Lyotard's *The Postmodern Condition* discusses at some length the relation between narrative and the epistemic authority of knowledge.

51 For a postmodern interrogation of the a priori status of value, see Donald Barthelme, *The Dead Father* (New York: Farrar Straus Giroux, 1975).

52 Philosophical discussions of *en-soi* and *pour-soi* have been fundamental to Western thought. See, in particular, Jean-Paul Sartre's elaboration of these concepts in his *Being and Nothingness,* trans. Hazel E. Barnes (New York: Philosophical Library, 1956).

53 One of the most poignant delineations of the invisibility of the subaltern self has been Ralph Ellison's *Invisible Man* (New York: Random House, 1952). Fyodor Dostoevsky's *Notes from Underground* (trans. Mirra Ginsberg [New York: Bantam, 1974]) is a powerful forerunner.

54 Gayatri Spivak's distinction in "Can the Subaltern Speak?" between the two meanings of *representation* has been most illuminating.

55 Michael Ryan's *Marxism and Deconstruction: A Critical Articulation* (Baltimore: Johns Hopkins Press, 1984) faces the same problem of assigning priorities. Are Marxism and deconstruction coordinated in an equal relation, or is deconstruction to be instrumentalized in the service of Marxism?

56 See Homi K. Bhabha, "DissemiNation: Time, Narrative, and the Margins of the Modern Nation," in *Nation and Narration,* ed. Homi K. Bhabha (London: Routledge, 1990), 291–322; and Benedict Anderson, *Imagined Communities: Reflections on the Origins and Spread of Nationalism* (London: Verso, 1991).

57 See my "Postcoloniality and the Boundaries of Identity."

58 The Lacanian algebra completely preempts the specificity of a historically located semantics.

59 For a lucid discussion of the East-West divide via nationalism, see Partha Chatterjee, *Nationalist Thought and the Colonial World: A Derivative Discourse* (London: Zed, 1986), and *The Nation and Its Fragments* (Princeton, N.J.: Princeton University Press, 1993).

60 One of the characters in Salman Rushdie's *The Satanic Verses* (New York: Viking, 1988) expresses this idea succinctly: "The trouble with the English is that their history happened overseas, so they don't know what it means" (343).

61 On *sly civility* and *mimicry,* see Homi K. Bhabha, *The Location of Culture* (New York: Routledge, 1994). Audre Lorde develops and points out the limitations of this strategy of using the master's weapons to destroy the master's house ("The Master's Tools Will Never Dismantle the Master's House," in *Sister Outsider: Essays and Speeches* [Los Angeles: Crossing Press, 1984]).

62 The term *politics of location* goes back to Adrienne Rich's 1984 essay, "Notes toward a Politics of Location," in *Blood, Bread and Poetry — Selected Prose, 1979–1985* (New York: Norton, 1986).

63 I am using the term *totality* to reinvigorate it as a Marxist concept and to question the immanence of the fragment and its autonomy (see *Aesthetics and Politics,* trans. and ed. Ronald Taylor [New York: New Left, 1977]).

64 The notion *ethnoscape* is developed persuasively in Arjun Appadurai, "Disjuncture and Difference in the Global Cultural Economy," *Public Culture* 2, no. 2 (spring 1990): 1–24.

65 See my "Postcoloniality and the Boundaries of Identity."

66 See Homi K. Bhabha, "Interrogating Identity: The Postcolonial Prerogative," in *The Anatomy of Racism,* ed. D. T. Goldberg (Minneapolis: University of Minnesota Press, 1990), 183–209.

67 For a compelling elaboration of double coding, see Kumkum Sangari, "The Politics of the Possible," in *The Nature and Context of Minority Discourse,* ed. David Lloyd and Abdul JanMohamed (Oxford: Oxford University Press, 1990).

68   See Gayatri Chakravorty Spivak, *Outside in the Teaching Machine* (New York: Routledge, 1993), and *In Other Worlds*.

69   I would like to make an analogous connection between the question of language and the question of knowledge. We must not forget that Volosinov/Bakhtin emphasized the reality that language itself is the contested terrain, not a mere nonideological vehicle of meaning.

70   The beyond is to be conceived as a proactive seeking out of alternative knowledges, value systems, and worldviews.

71   Partha Chatterjee, *The Nation and Its Fragments: Colonial and Postcolonial Histories* (Princeton: Princeton UP, 1993), 109–13. See also such theoretical work as Vandana Shiva, *Staying Alive: Women, Ecology, and Development* (London: Zed, 1989); Nandy, ed., *Science, Hegemony, and Violence*; and Alok Yadav, "Nationalism and Contemporaneity: Political Economy of a Discourse," *Cultural Critique* 26 (1993–94): 191–229. For a hopeful and populist take on nationalism, see David Lloyd, *Anomalous States: Irish Writing and the Post-Colonial Moment* (Durham, N.C.: Duke University Press, 1993).

72   See, e.g., Madhu Kishwar, "Why I Do Not Call Myself a Feminist?" *Manushi* 62 (1990): 2–8.

73   See "Orientalism and Cultural Differences," ed. Mahmut Mutman and Meyda Yegenoglu, *Inscriptions*, special issue, vol. 6 (1992).

74   One of the most influential books in this area has been Edward Soja's *Postmodern Geographies* (London: Verso, 1989). Equally illuminating has been David Harvey's *The Condition of Postmodernity* (Oxford: Blackwell, 1989).

75   It is to Michel Foucault that we owe this notion of heterotopia (see "Heterotopias," *Diacritics* [spring 1986]: 22–27).

76   Amitav Ghosh, *The Shadow Lines* (London: Bloomsbury, 1988).

77   A. K. Ramanujan has identified and analyzed the mirror-window dyadic function in Tamil poetry (see the introduction to *Folktales from India*, ed. A. K. Ramanujan (New Delhi, India: Viking Penguin, 1993], xiii–xxxii).

78   In this context, I make a qualitative distinction between the need, a postcolonial one, for transcendence as delineated by Ghosh through the character of Tridib in *The Shadow Lines* and the colonialist cartography of Conrad.

79   The French feminists — Hélène Cixous and Catherine Clement in particular — have worked on strategies to empower the Imaginary against the Symbolic (see their *Newly Born Woman*, trans. Betsy Wing [Minneapolis: University of Minnesota Press, 1986]). Deleuze and Guattari have critiqued Freud and "the Oedipus" along similar lines in *Anti-Oedipus*. For a poignant rendition of an incurably oedipalized condition that has no direct access to the mother, see Kafka's *A Letter to His Father*.

80   Amin, *Eurocentrism*, 152.

81   The controversy over *Miss Saigon* is a case in point (see Yoko Yoshikawa, "The Heat Is on Miss Saigon Coalition: Organizing across Race and Sexuality," in *The State of Asian America: Activism and Resistance in the 1990s*, ed. Karin Aguilar-San Juan [Boston: South End, 1994], 275–94).

Une Pratique Sauvage: Postcolonial Belatedness and Cultural Politics

ALI BEHDAD

In "Lenin and Philosophy," Althusser defines Marxism as a "philosophy of praxis." This new practice, he goes on to argue, is a kind of *pratique sauvage*, which, like Freud's wild analysis, "does not provide the theoretical credentials for its operations and which raises screams from the philosophy of the 'interpretation' of the world which might be called the philosophy of *denegation*. A wild practice, if you will, but what did not begin by being wild?"[1] This last rhetorical question has provided the theoretical beginning for my reflections on the possibility of postcolonialism today as a belated praxis, coming after the anticolonial responses of Fanon, Césaire, Memmi, and other founders of postcolonial discursivity. While these founders of postcolonial oppositional discourse provided what one may call *the science of anti-imperialism*, contemporary postcolonial critics are introducing a new practice of philosophy to politicize the academic debates about race and gender. I return to the problematic temporal relation between the decolonizing era and our globalized world toward the end of this essay, but, for the moment, suffice it to say that neither is the prefix *post-* used here in a salutary way nor are the theoretical debates of postcolonial academics equated with the political interventions of such figures as Fanon or Césaire.[2] But, before I embark on the belated task of reading postcolonial critics reworking the perception of the colonial encounter, I reflect briefly on Althusser's discussion of the new Marxist philosophy by way of contextualizing his discussion and my uses of it here.

Althusser distinguishes two phases of Marxism, a scientific and a philosophical, pointing out that Lenin, a figure often marginalized in philosophical discussions, produced a philosophy of Marxism, lagging behind Marx's science of history. Marxist philosophy must necessarily lag behind the science of Marxism as Lenin reads Marx belatedly to produce a crucial *décalage* (dislocation) in its history — and here Althusser, of course, reading belatedly Lenin's marginalized philosophy to politicize the debates in the Société Française de Philosophie by outlining an interventionist, political philosophy. Reading is in each instance necessarily late, lagging behind what it transforms or writes beyond.

Lenin's reading of Marxist science of history is not merely an interpretation but a kind of epistemological dislocation (décalage), producing a new phase, a new consciousness, a new set of practices—and as such it is capable of transforming the material world, Althusser claims. Practicing philosophy is, in short, the "consciousness of the ruthless" that divides in order to produce new political practices—*dividing* here should be understood as a form of political contestation, not as a kind of disciplinary separation by which the philosophy of interpretation operates. Althusser's emphasis on the necessary *lag* of Marxist philosophy, coming after the science, draws attention to the issue of the belatedness of political philosophy that I address in the context of postcolonial readings of the colonial encounter.

Althusser also insists on the newness of this wild practice, "*new* in that it is a practice which has renounced denegration, and, knowing what it does, *acts according to what it is.*" *Dénégation* in French not only means the psychological notion of denial but also implies political attitudes and acts of repudiation, or the action of refutation. Althusser's point about the newness of Lenin's "practice of philosophy" underscores the political consciousness of such a belated —and new by virtue of its belatedness—reading. The belated practice of philosophy is therefore a mode of political intervention, and, having renounced denegation, this wild practice is *consciously* political and "*acts according to what it is.*" The new practice of philosophy is, Althusser insists, a "certain investment of politics, a certain continuation of politics, a certain rumination of politics."[3]

Such a philosophical practice recognizes, however, the limits of its interventionist politics and can only *assist* in transforming the material world— it can only mediate the possibilities of change—because, Althusser acknowledges, "it is not theoreticians, scientists or philosophers, nor is it 'men,' who make history—but the 'masses.'"[4] In short, new practices act as the catalyst that mediates the political struggle of the contingent communities—mediation is here the political component of belatedness, of reading *behind*.

In what follows, I reflect on postcolonialism as a *belated* praxis in the academy, considering the two components of this formulation—the belated condition of postcolonial theory and the academic context of its formation. I have been using the word *postcolonialism* without qualifying what is meant by the term. Is it, one may wonder, a *geohistorical* notion designating the ensemble of writings by those subjects whose identities have been shaped, if not constituted, by the colonial encounter? Or is *postcolonialism* an *ideological* term, defining a field of discursive and visual practices that are in opposition to the dominating power of European colonialism and its new forms of technocultural imperialism by the United States? Still, is it a material condition produced by a complex set of neocolonial economic relations between the decentered new "center" and its other worlds? I raise these unending questions, not to provide a definition for what postcolonialism is, but to acknowledge the very predicament of describing such a plural and divided field of theoretical practices as well as the problematic uses of the prefix *post-*. With the proliferation of postcolonial studies, there has also emerged a self-conscious critique of the term *postcolonial* among its practitioners, questioning its "ahistorical and universalizing deployments" as well as "its potentially depoliticizing implications."[5] Attentive to such critiques of the term *postcolonialism*, I use the word to designate a field of theoretical and cultural practices that address the issues surrounding the colonial encounter between the West and its others. I am interested, on the one hand, in the ways in which critics labeled *postcolonial* have invoked the memory of colonial power in order to carve out a field of interdisciplinary practices mapping the relation of aesthetic and literary representations with what Edward Said calls "the world of politics, power, domination, and struggle."[6] On the other hand, I wish to critique the problematic tendency of this field to address mostly nineteenth-century European colonialism by way of emphasizing the need for a shift in postcolonialism from historical studies of imperialism to contemporaneous critiques of neoimperial relations of power.

In "Orientalism Reconsidered," Edward Said views the interventionary nature of postcolonial practices as a function of their interdisciplinarity. The counter-systematic and contestatory nature of the field is what makes the practices of postcolonialism wild — wild in that they defy the boundaries of the disciplinary impulse that tries to name and compartmentalize them, to borrow Raymond Williams's word.[7] The problematics and politics of postcoloniality demand a counterdisciplinary mode of knowledge to rethink the relations and distinctions between ideology, history, culture, and theory. The savage practices of postcolonialism renounce disciplinary denegation, the depoliticized, divided space of the compartmentalized academy, by connecting the separate disciplinary boundaries in alternative ways through their critical interventions. The counterdisciplinary position of postcolonialism can be viewed as a practice in negotiation and exchange — both in ways in which different modes of knowledge intersect and in ways in which postcolonial critics negotiate with the academy to mediate new oppositional possibilities.

Postcolonial counterdisciplinarity depends also on a certain historical consciousness that constitutes it as necessarily beyond the boundaries of disciplinary formation. Because, as a modern discourse of power, the science of imperialism produces a plurality of subject and ideological positions, any critique of such a science can be accomplished only through interdisciplinary praxis. In his introduction to *Orientalism*, Edward Said describes how his study has been worked out of a "decentered consciousness," a formulation that he would later use to describe the praxes of postcolonial critics in general:

> I have written [*Orientalism*] with several audiences in mind. For students of literature and criticism, Orientalism offers a marvelous instance of interrelations between society, history, and textuality; moreover, the cultural role played by the Orient in the west connects Orientalism with ideology, politics, and the logic of power, matters of relevance, I think, to the literary community. For contemporary students of the Orient, from university scholars to policymakers, I have written with two ends in mind: one, to present their intellectual genealogy to them in a way that has not been done; two, to criticize — with the hope of stirring discussion — the often unquestioned assumptions on which their work for the most part depends. For the general reader, this study deals with matters that always compel attention, all of them connected not only with Western conceptions and treatments of the Other but also with the singularly important role played by Western culture in what Vico called the world of nations. Lastly, for readers in the so-called Third-World, this study proposes itself as a step toward an understanding not so much of Western politics and of the non-Western world in those politics as of the *strength* of Western cultural discourse, a strength too often mistaken as merely decorative or "superstructural."[8]

I have quoted Said at length because these remarks provide an interesting example of a postcolonial belated praxis, situating itself within a plurality of interests and audiences as a necessarily counterdisciplinary practice. The discourse of Orientalism is itself a plural field, bringing into contact cultural, historical, social, and textual issues that have traditionally been kept apart in an attempt to neutralize the very political concerns that these issues raise. The postcolonial critic works against such disciplinary research and links its various discourses to unravel the complexities of Western cultural hegemony and the hidden relations of power that are *always at work but always kept invisible in their working.*

Said describes in great detail how Orientalism is a geopolitical awareness distributed into aesthetic representations as well as within economic, sociological, historical, and philological texts, all of which elaborate a complex series of "interests" in Europe's others. Here, culture becomes an arena in which these interests are articulated and brought into contact with the kind of military, economic, and political rationales that produce the complex system of colonial power — they operate in a circular system of exchange. Following Foucault's discussion of power, postcolonial practices argue that relations of colonial power are immanent in economic relations, social and cultural processes, and epistemological questions but rendered invisible through the effects of differentiation, separation, and denial — denegation, in Althusser's words. The counter-disciplinarity of postcolonial practices exposes the internal conditions of these strategies of differentiation through a decentered consciousness that rejects the systematic, totalizing authority of any discipline as such.

Said's introductory remarks in *Orientalism* suggest also an oppositional consciousness that one encounters among the practitioners of postcolonialism — oppositional in that they read against the grain, as he points out. Said describes the aim of his study as a critique of the intellectual genealogy of mainstream studies of the Middle East. It remembers through archival work what is historically forgotten. Homi Bhabha has cogently remarked, "Said's work focused the need to quicken the half-light of western history with the *disturbing memory* of its colonial texts that bear witness to the trauma that accompanies the triumphal art of Empire" (my emphasis).[9] Postcolonial critics are on the side of memory, their oppositionality a function of anamnesia, as they expose the genealogy of the oppressed, the veiled political economy of oppressive powers, the imaginative geography that separates the Orient from the Occident, the black from the white. Postcolonial critiques are the belated return of the repressed, disrupting that structure of colonial amnesia that denied the colonized his or her history. In "Orientalism Reconsidered," Said points out, "What for the most part got left out of Orientalism was precisely the history that resisted its ideological as well as political encroachments, and that repressed or resistant history has returned in the various critiques and attacks upon Orientalism, which has uniformly and polemically been represented by these critiques as a science of imperialism."[10] Postcolonial practices are, in short, the belated return of the repressed histories of resistance.

Crucial to the understanding of this belated return of the repressed is the notion of temporal difference in the discourses that these practices critique. In his powerful *Time and the Other,* Johannes Fabian describes how the concept of time is a crucial "carrier of signficance," defining the unequal relation of self and other — the *primitive* here being a temporal concept. In a genealogical approach like Said's, Fabian argues that the epistemological conditions of ethnographic representations of the other depend on a "persistent and systematic tendency to place the referent(s) of anthropology in a Time other than the present of the producer of anthropological discourse."[11] In other words, in spite of sharing time with the other in order to produce the empirical data for his or her research, the anthropologist writes an ethnography that denies the other coevalness, placing the object in a different time than the Western present. This is accomplished through a whole series of methods and techniques, such as unilateral observation of the "natives," classification of their habits and practices, taxonomic descriptions, the use of maps, charts, and tables to visualize the other's culture, etc.

Postcolonial practices, I have been arguing, are exercises in remembering; they bring into consciousness the repressed time of the other. They question the hegemony of taxonomic and allochronic representational strategies of the discourse of power through recourse to the history they were denied. They work out of a demand for coevalness in their belated readings of the science of imperialism. Whereas the discourses of power circumvent the question of history through the uses of cultural relativism or taxonomic approaches, the wild praxes of postcolonialism produce the conditions of coevalness and contemporaneity for dialectical confrontations of cultures through remembering; they demystify the allochronic discourse of power while reclaiming the unrepresented history. These practices recognize that the geopolitics of imperialism had and continues to have its ideological foundations in what Fabian calls *chronopolitics,* the politics of time. As belated return of the repressed histories of resistance, they struggle for recognition of coevalness in their new histories of resistance.

Malek Alloula's provoking rereading of the colonial postcard in *The Colonial Harem* is one interesting example of what one may call anamnesiac praxes of postcolonial historicity:

> To map out, from under the plethora of images, the obsessive scheme that regulates the totality of the output of this enterprise [i.e., the production of colonial postcards] and endows it with meaning is to force the postcard to reveal what it holds back (the ideology of colonialism) and to expose what is repressed in it (the sexual phantasm).
>
> Behind this image of Algerian women, probably reproduced in the millions, there is visible the broad outline of one of the figures of the colonial perception of the native. This figure can be essentially defined as the practice of a right of (over)sight that the colonizer arrogates to himself and that is the bearer of multiform violence. The postcard fully partakes in such violence; it extends its effects; it is its accomplished expression, no less efficient for being symbolic.
>
> A reading of the sort that I propose to undertake would be entirely superfluous if there existed photographic traces of the gaze of the colonized upon the colonizer. In their absence, that is, in the absence of a confrontation of opposed gazes, I attempt here, lagging far behind History, to return this immense postcard to its sender. (my emphasis) [12]

The postcolonial reading of the memories of the colonial encounter always lags far behind history to produce the absent gaze, the unwritten historical text; it is an exercise in remembering, a recourse to a repressed memory that history has swept away — such remembering produces new histories of resistance through speaking about the lack of a returned gaze in the history it tells. Alloula describes his text as a personal "exorcism" that thwarts the desolate gaze of the colonizer.

Such an anamnesiac practice is the opposite of the nostalgic histories of colonialism that have been and are in vogue today — for example, the colonial nostalgia in such films as *The English Patient, Chocolat, Out of Africa, A Passage to India,* and *Ishtar* or the nostalgic republications of Orientalist works in France. In fact, the critical incentive behind postcolonial anamnesia is to counter the nostalgic forgetfulness that obscures the genealogy of the science of imperialism and so allows for its return in new forms. The anamnesiac reading is therefore a "symptomatic" reading, one that unveils what the object holds back and exposes what it represses in its consciousness. It is, in other words, a *prise de conscience* that fashions itself by bringing into postcolonial consciousness what it finds in its colonial memory.

Yet to read belatedly the traces of the colonial memory or to send the card back to a sender who may or may not happen to be there to receive it does not *necessarily* constitute an oppositional praxis. To be sure, a large number of what claim to be postcolonial readings are belated in a very conventional sense. Produced within the very limits of topical studies — for example, "Commonwealth" literary studies, Orientalism as a literary topic, etc. — these readings do in fact lag behind the politics of contemporaneity in their conventional claim to history. A case in point is Sander Gilman's otherwise interesting essay "Black Bodies, White Bodies." On the surface, Gilman's essay embodies everything one can expect to see in a postcolonial reading: an interdisciplinary bent, historical consciousness, and anticolonial rhetoric. The essay also accomplishes its task of describing the genealogical connections between the icons of the Hottentot female and the prostitute in the nineteenth century. But Gilman concludes the essay by turning the political into the psychological as he argues that these medical and artistic myths of race and gender are the result of the white man's "internal fear, the fear of loss of power," which he projects into the sexuality of the other.[13] The essay leaves out the effects and genealogical connections of such myths in current discourses of race and imperialism. Such topical practices are exercises in what Althusser calls *the philosophy of interpretation* or *the philosophy of denegation,* which works out of a profound denial of contemporaneity. Not only does Gilman's essay undermine the complexities of the discourses of power by relegating them to mere psychological projections of fear, but it also circumvents historicity in that it displaces the current politics of race and gender, which has its genealogical roots in the discourses he discusses, into a safe past. For Gilman, history seems to be what is past, forgetting that the critic lives in history, that genealogy is not merely an erudite knowledge of the past but, as Foucault points out, a kind of research activity that "allows us to establish a historical knowledge of struggles and to make use of this knowledge tactically *today*." [14] In other words, historicity can be meaningful only if it accomplishes a link between past phenomena and present events.

Postcolonial belatedness can be an oppositional praxis only if it maintains a coeval recognition of its own historicity, its own "worldliness," and makes use of its historical consciousness to critique the cultural conditions that continue to produce unequal relations of power today. Without such historical consciousness, the postcolonial reading of the colonial encounter is at best an informative ethnographic representation of colonial violence or, at worst, a displaced interpretation of archival materials.

An example of such worldly practice — that is, a practice that is politically conscious of what it does — is Said's critique of the racist and neocolonial effects of Orientalist discourse today. In *Orientalism*, having described the scope of his genealogical project, Said describes the political implications of his critique of Orientalism as follows:

> Anyone resident in the West since the 1950's, particularly in the United States, will have lived through an era of extraordinary turbulence in the relations of the East and West. No one will have failed to note how "East" has always signified danger and threat during this period. . . . In the universities a growing establishment of area-studies programs and institutes has made the scholarly study of the Orient a branch of national policy. Public affairs in this country include a healthy interest in the Orient, as much for its strategic and economic importance as for its traditional exoticism. If the world has become immediately accessible to a Western citizen living in the electronic age, the Orient too has drawn nearer to him, and is now less a myth perhaps than a place crisscrossed by Western, especially American, interests. One aspect of the electronic, postmodern world is that there has been a reinforcement of the stereotypes by which the Orient is viewed. . . . This is nowhere more true than in the ways by which the Near East is grasped. Three things have contributed to making even the simplest perception of the Arabs and Islam into a highly politicized, almost raucous matter; one, the history of popular anti-Arab and anti-Islamic prejudice in the West, which is immediately reflected in the history of Orientalism; two, the struggle between the Arabs and Israeli Zionism, and its effects upon American Jews as well as upon both the liberal culture and the population at large; three, the almost total absence of any cultural position making it possible either to identify with or dispassionately to discuss the Arabs or Islam. [15]

Through his archival work, Said restores to the science of colonialism its political significance in the current global setting. What emerges out of reading Orientalist archives is not a specialized, erudite knowledge of Europe's guilty past but the provoking rediscovery of its new traces *today*. Here, the recourse to colonial archives transforms its belatedness into a politics of contemporaneity. Said makes use of his readings of Orientalist representations in France and England to critique the current problems of racism and imperialism in the United States, whose genealogy he traces back to European Orientalism. He provides a sustained critique of the new institutional formation of American Orientalism in area-studies programs and schools of public policy, which have played a crucial role in advancing the science of imperialism through their depoliticized, compartmentalized research.

Said also makes a crucial connection here between erudite knowledge and popular knowledge, a link that points to the complexities of the globalizing discourses of race and imperialism. Said's argument, developed throughout the book, is a complex one, describing the ways in which cultural and symbolic productions produce the political effects of power. Rejecting the repressive hypothesis of culture, his reading suggests that our technoculture provides the affirmative and persuasive environment in which symbolic productions enter into a productive relation with the state apparatus to serve the new interests of neocolonial power. In such a productive arena, the myths of the cruel Oriental despot can be strategically rearticulated into the stereotypes of Muslims as degenerate terrorists so that the neocolonial violence of the United States in the Middle East could be fully supported and justified by the culture as a whole — the overwhelming support for the Gulf War in the United States is an indicator of American culture's productivity in producing new ideologies of domination. Said's attempt to present his readers with their intellectual genealogy is aimed at demystifying the seeming neutrality of Western assumptions about the Middle East that have helped perpetuate these ideologies. This is a kind of writing back to the center that tactically uses its knowledge against the reemergence of the science of imperialism in the United States today.

Needless to say, the institutional limits of postcolonial practices make them ultimately incapable of preventing the return of the science of imperialism. These counterhegemonic praxes can only act as the catalyst in producing new histories of resistance, not only because, as Althusser acknowledges, it is the "masses," not the theoreticians and philosophers, who make history, but also because, as I pointed out earlier, the critical range of such practices is virtually limited to the institutional space of the academy. No doubt, the academic discussions of race and identity have exerted some power in bringing about such pedagogical changes as multiculturalism, but these changes, I would still argue, have been produced as a result more of U.S. minorities' demand for the inclusion of their history in the curriculum than of the writing practices of the postcolonial critics. This is an obvious but crucial point to consider because it problematizes the utopian optimism one encounters among many, even sophisticated, postcolonial critics, who sometimes conflate the clearing of a "space for the 'other' question" with the needs and aspirations of the neocolonized constituencies in the so-called Third World or in Western metropolitan centers.[16]

Such a temporal and spatial disjuncture is partly the consequence of a certain amnesia toward the politics of contemporaneity. In spite of their anamnesiac readings of colonial history, culture, and subjectivity, many postcolonial critics have been forgetful of the neoimperial context in which their work has been produced and received, evading for the most part the contemporary issues of globalization, transnationalism, and immigration in their elaborate critiques of power. As I have suggested here, the historical rationale for postcolonial readings of the colonial encounter has been to produce the colonized's absent gaze and unwritten text, but these readings rarely theorize the historical juncture that makes the colonial encounter relevant to our postcolonial condition and consciousness. In fact, many postcolonial readings have been the site of a historical chiasmus, failing to bridge the temporal split between colonial and post- and/or neocolonial moments.

Part of this historicist problem, I would argue, stems from our reliance on a politics of marginality derived from colonialism's Manichaean allegory of the dominator and the victim. Abiola Irele's problematic, yet suggestive, claim that "the discourse of Africanism as elaborated by black intellectuals on both sides of the Atlantic must be seen as a reinscription of an antecedent Western monologue on Africa and the non-Western world, its displacement and transformation by a new assertive self-expression on the part of a subjugated and voiceless humanity," points to the predicament that I am posing here.[17] Although Edward Said has warned us against the "politics of blame," most discourses of identity have continued to position themselves, paradoxically, within the confining matrix of identification they strive to subvert—a matrix dominated by such colonialist binaries as dominator/dominated, exclusion/opposition, etc.

These discourses have been ineffectual, not only because they fall prey to a benevolent Third Worldism that excludes in the very gesture of its sympathy for the "victim," as I will discuss briefly, but also because they fail to account for the crucial differences in configurations of power due to globalization, a phenomenon that demands new thinking on questions of modernization and marginality. As Néstor García Canclini has cogently argued, "To study inequalities and differences today is not simply to see mechanisms of exclusion and opposition; it is also necessary to identify the processes that unequally articulate social positions, cognitive systems, and the tastes of diverse sectors. . . . The dense web of cultural and economic decisions leads to asymmetries between producers and consumers and between diverse publics. But these inequalities are almost never imposed from the top down, as is assumed by those who establish Manichaean oppositions between dominating and dominated classes, or between central and peripheral countries."[18]

If, as Roger Rouse has suggested, "we live in a confusing world, a world of crisscrossed economies, intersecting systems of meaning, and fragmented identities," we ought to think of more nuanced ways to articulate our positionality in relation to this "new social space."[19] As cultural practitioners, our projects need not be only the rereading and retextualizing of the cultural or political object—whether the object happens to be colonialism or globalism. Instead, we may consider the importance of such crucial loci as institutional techniques and strategies that maintain and transform our cultural practices. The challenge here is to find "more circumspect and circumstantial calculations about how and where knowledge needs to surface and emerge in order to be consequential," as Tony Bennett reminds us.[20] With the disappearance of the "universal intellectual," Foucault has suggested, "the university and the academic emerge, if not as principal elements, at least as 'exchangers' [and as] privileged points of intersection [in globalized relations of power]."[21] We must, therefore, address the "scandal" of our own production in the university by situating the particular relations and conditions in which knowledge is disseminated and produces unequal relations of power.

The question of the academic setting also points to a whole series of predicaments surrounding the politics of affiliation and disaffiliation in postcolonial praxes that I discuss by way of conclusion. Crucial to the understanding of the issue of affiliation is the construction of diasporic identities. The condition of postcolonial displacement and the critics' hybrid identities situate them at once in discrepant cultural contexts of belonging and exile. Interestingly, the condition of displacement has been viewed by most postcolonial practitioners as a salutary notion. James Clifford, Homi Bhabha, and Edward Said, for example, have argued that theory in our world of global contacts is necessarily the product of displacement and distance. "To theorize," Clifford claims that "one leaves home," "the more one is able to leave one's cultural home, the more easily is one able to judge it, and the whole world as well, with the spiritual detachment *and* generosity necessary for true vision."[22] Although these practitioners of diasporic consciousness are right in claiming that such modes of travel have problematized notions of home, belonging, center, and periphery, they have ignored two fundamental predicaments of postcolonial displacement: the uneven distribution of the production of knowledge/power and the misappropriation of victimhood in new claims to alterity by many postcolonial critics in the Western academy.

First, the problem of unequal distribution of knowledge and information, and therefore power, has been peculiarly evaded in postcolonial discussions. Mostly contained within the institutional boundaries of the First World, postcolonial critics have not addressed the ways in which their critical productions have been complicitous with the geopolitical divisions of the First and Third Worlds, especially as they concern differences between educational systems and access to knowledge and material in the First and Third Worlds. Not only has the metropolitan West maintained its cultural hegemony, but its symbolic and material power has forced the conditions of displacement and exile. Although it is true that, in the late twentieth century, the community loses its centrality as a "home" base, as Clifford argues, one must remain politically conscious of the fact that such a decentering project has nonetheless maintained crucial material and symbolic distinctions between *Gastarbeiter* and Western tourists in Southeast Asia, between American businessmen in Saudi Arabia and Pakistani immigrants in England, or, say, between Indian intellectuals in American universities and Mexican farmworkers in Texas. Even a cursory glance at the new particularities of globalism — such as the creation of an international division of labor, the busting of the manufacturing industry in the so-called First World and its replacement with high-technology fields or the transference of certain industries to Third World countries, the growth of informal and dispersed economies, the rise of an international debt economy, and the mass immigration of rural communities to the more prosperous metropolises — confirms the claim that the everyday conditions of living have actually deteriorated for most immigrants and the underclass. The changes heralded by globalization do not diminish the importance of identity and the unequal access to power and knowledge, but what has been eliminated, as Kenneth Surin suggests, is the "absolute spatial division between exploiters and exploited . . . the exploiters are everywhere and so are the exploited."[23]

The point that I am making here may seem obvious, but it is peculiarly forgotten in the salutary trope of writer as exile that we encounter among many postcolonial critics; they tend to valorize the experiences of a few intellectuals who happen to have gained access to the privileged institutions of the West by virtue of their class and/or academic background or sometimes even to conflate in their discourses of victimhood such privileged experiences with those of disenfranchised underclass immigrants in the metropolitan West. In view of such uneven relations of power between West and its others, it is crucial to raise the question as to what extent postcolonial praxes have contributed to that depressing form of intellectual neocolonialism in which the ex-colonies have provided yet again the "raw materials" for Western academic consumption — not to mention, of course, the familiar issue of brain drain from Third World to First.

Paul Rabinow is to the point when he criticizes the euphoric proclamations of anticolonialism — by critics of anthropology like Clifford — arguing that "these proclamations must be seen as political moves within the academic community." He goes on to explain that postcolonial critics have often displaced the "crisis of representation within the context of the rupture of decolonization," ignoring the obvious fact that they are not writing in the late 1950s. Rabinow suggests a reconsideration of the politics of interpretation in the academy today to problematize the "micropractices of the academy," through which strategies of cultural power are articulated.[24]

The predicatment of postcolonial claims to alterity should be addressed in the context of such academic micropractices. An effective strategy of containment in the academy has been what Gayatri Spivak cogently calls *ghettoization through tokenization*. The hegemonic discourse of neocolonialism in the academy has often forced postcolonial critics to occupy the tokenized position of spokespersons for their contingent communities. This strategy works out of both the critics' misappropriation of a generic alterity and the discourse of authenticity that the academy perpetuates. In "Who Claims Alterity?" Spivak cautions postcolonial critics against, precisely, such uncritical and false claims to alternative histories. Drawing attention to the "disenfranchised *female* in decolonized space," she criticizes the "indigenous elite woman abroad" who obliterates her difference with the doubly displaced figure of disempowered woman in the Third World. "The stories (or histories) of the post-colonial world," she goes on to argue, "are not necessarily the same as the stories coming from 'internal colonization,' the way the metropolitan countries discriminate against disenfranchised groups in their midst."[25]

This conflation has dangerous consequences, namely, the misrepresentation of neocolonial struggles and the ironic complicity with the benevolent Third Worldism of the Euro-American academy. Identified and welcomed as the native informant, the postcolonial elite, Spivak argues, are often the "site of a chiasmus, the crossing of a double contradiction: the system of production of the national bourgeoisie at home, and, abroad, the tendency to represent neocolonialism by the semiotic of 'internal colonization.' "[26] The intellectual elite abroad can become the victim of two kinds of ahistoricity: a misrepresentation of alternative histories of colonialism and a misconception of the neocolonial story (history).

The discourse of authenticity plays a crucial part in perpetuating the benevolent Third Worldism of the academy. Even a cursory glance at the MLA job list would demonstrate the academy's profound belief in authenticity; the positions in the so-called postcolonial and minority literatures have been consistently filled by "natives" while those same individuals are being excluded in other fields. Positioned as the native informants, postcolonials are forced to "speak *as*," to be representative *of* the contingent communities whose culture, literature, and history are to be "covered" by these native representatives — I use the verb *cover* in the sense of both treating a subject matter and concealing the object of knowledge. Authenticity is a kind of positionality of the investigating subject in a category that claims final determinacy — I mean in particular the ways in which the category *race* finally determines the content of what the "minority" critic has to say. In spite of poststructuralist "deconstruction" of subjectivity, the recuperative strategies of the academy have reinscribed the essentialist and transcendental categories *race* and *gender* as a gesture of benevolent pluralism. These are some of the problems that postcolonialism as a savage practice faces today.

In "The Politics of Knowledge," Said argues that "our [postcolonial] point . . . cannot be simply and obdurately to reaffirm the paramount importance of formerly suppressed or silenced forms of knowledge and leave it at that, nor can it be to surround ourselves with the sanctimonious piety of historical or cultural victimhood as a way of making our intellectual presence felt. . . . The whole effort to deconsecrate Eurocentrism cannot be interpreted, least of all by those who participate in the enterprise, as an effort to supplant Eurocentrism with, for instance, Afrocentric or Islamocentric approaches."[27] To be oppositional in the academy today, one must denounce the denegating strategies of containment in the academy, strategies that produce the relatively comfortable and depoliticized sites of alterity, strategies that work out of a benevolent Third Worldism that excludes through tokenized inclusion.

Although we inhabit the problematic space of the academy, new tactics of opposition must be continually articulated, tactics that take advantage of loopholes in the system — such as the recent interests in diversity, multiculturalism, and postcolonialism in the academy — to subvert its neocolonial strategies masked by its benevolent gestures of plurality. In this respect, Spivak's "practical politics of the open end" can be of great use to us. Spivak uses the analogy of cleaning to describe the need for a continual maintenance of opposition, one in which the critic is neither pessimistic about "fighting a losing battle against morality" nor idealistic about the outcome of these activities.[28] An *oppositional, savage* practice of postcolonialism must view itself as an interminable struggle and a perpetually revisionist project that constantly questions its theoretical assumptions, reconsiders its critical tactics, and remains vigilant to the conjunctural position of the speaking subject in its discourse. In short, the new direction of postcolonialism must be toward a return to the science of history — that is the history that brought us here and the history that returns us there.

Notes

1   Louis Althusser, "Lenin and Philosophy," in *Lenin and Philosophy and Other Essays*, trans. Ben Brewster (London: New Left, 1971), 65–66.

2   For a fascinating critique of postcolonial critics' inattention to temporal and geographic differences, see Jenny Sharpe, "Is the United States Postcolonial? Transnationalism, Immigration, and Race," *Diaspora* 4, no. 2 (1995): 181–200.

3   Althusser, "Lenin and Philosophy," 67, 67, 37.

4   Ibid., 67.

5   Ella Shohat, "Notes on the 'Post-Colonial,'" *Social Text* 31/32 (1992): 99–113. See also Anne

McClintock, "The Angel of Progress: Pitfalls of the Term 'Post-Colonialism,'" *Social Text* 31/32 (1992): 84–98.

6   Edward Said, interview, *Diacritics* 6, no. 3 (fall 1976): 35.

7   Edward Said, "Orientalism Reconsidered," in *Literature, Politics, and Theory*, ed. Francis Barker et al. (London: Methuen, 1986) 210–29.

8   Edward Said, *Orientalism* (New York: Vintage, 1979), 24. On Said's later description of the praxes of postcolonial critics, see his "Orientalism Reconsidered."

9   Homi Bhaba, "The Other Question: Difference, Discrimination and the Discourse of Colonialism," in Barker et al., eds., *Literature, Politics, and Theory*, 149.

10 Said, "Orientalism Reconsidered," 216.

11 Johannes Fabian, *Time and the Other* (New York: Columbia University Press, 1983), 31.

12 Malek Alloula, *The Colonial Harem*, trans. Myrna Godzich and Wald Godzich (Minneapolis: University of Minnesota Press, 1986), 4–5.

13 Sander Gilman, "Black Bodies, White Bodies: Toward an Iconography of Female Sexuality in Late Nineteenth-Century Art, Medicine, and Literature," in *"Race," Writing, and Difference*, ed. Henry Louis Gates Jr. (Chicago: University of Chicago Press, 1985), 256.

14 Michel Foucault, *Power/Knowledge*, ed. Colin Gordon (New York: Pantheon, 1972), 83.

15 Said, *Orientalism*, 26–27.

16 The words are Homi Bhabha's, but the idea they express can be traced in many postcolonial critics ("The Other Question: Stereotype, Discrimination, and the Discourse of Colonialism," in *The Location of Culture* [London: Routledge, 1994], 66–84). For a critique of the inflationary rhetoric of postcolonial critics see Aijaz Ahmad, *In Theory: Classes, Nations, Literatures* (London: Verso, 1992), 56–64.

17 Abiola Irele, "Dimensions of African Discourse," *College Literature* 19, no. 3/20, no. 1 (1992/93): 49.

18 Néstor García Canclini, "Cultural Reconversion," in *On Edge: The Crisis of Contemporary Latin American Literature*, ed. George Yúdice, Jean Franco, and Juan Flores (Minneapolis: University of Minnesota Press, 1992), 34.

19 Roger Rouse, "Mexican Migration and the Social Space Postmodernism," *Diaspora* 1, no. 1 (spring 1991): 8.

20 Tony Bennett, "Putting Policy into Cultural Studies," in *Cultural Studies*, ed. Lawrence Grossberg, Cary Nelson, and Paula Treichler (New York: Routledge, 1992), 32.

21 Foucault, *Power/Knowledge*, 127.

22 James Clifford, "Notes on Theory and Travel," *Inscriptions* 5 (1989): 177.

23 Kenneth Surin, "On Producing the Concept of a Global Culture," *South Atlantic Quarterly* 94, no. 4 (fall 1995): 1188.

24 Paul Rabinow, "Representations Are Social Facts: Modernity and Post-Modernity in Anthropology," in *Writing Culture*, ed. James Clifford and Goerge Marcus (Berkeley and Los Angeles: University of California Press, 1986), 252, 253.

25 Gayatri Chakravorty Spivak, "Who Claims Alterity?" in *Remaking History*, ed. Barbara Kruger and Phil Mariani (Seattle: Bay, 1989), 274. See also Samir Amin, *Unequal Development*, trans. Brian Pearce (New York: Monthly Review Press, 1976).

26 Ibid., 274–75.

27 Edward Said, "The Politics of Knowledge," *Raritan* 11, no. 1 (summer 1991): 26.

28 Gayatri Chakrovorty Spivak, *The Post Colonial Critic*, ed. Sarah Harasym (New York: Routledge, 1990), 105.

(Post)Occidentalism, (Post)Coloniality, and

(Post)Subaltern Rationality

WALTER MIGNOLO

T he aim of this essay is to explore the emergence of what I would like to call *subaltern reason,* which I will limit here to its historical articulation in the frame of colonial legacies and contemporary globalization. While subaltern forms of rationality are also emerging in the domain of gender and sexuality, I will address only ethnic/racial issues related to colonial legacies. By *subaltern forms of rationality,* I mean not only that subalternity is a social class phenomenon and an object of study but that subalternity is characteristically theorized by those who are implicated in the very forms of subalternity they are theorizing. These theorists enact a particular form of "border gnosis," in the sense that the particular disciplinary location from which they analyze subalternity is itself crossed over. Such a border gnosis is an attempt to incorporate knowledge of the personal and social body, to restore the body to reason, and to reason from the subaltern (social and personal) body.

Although local histories are ingrained in global designs, the latter appear as independent of any local history. From the perspective of the grand narratives of the West, although local histories deliver the particular, they are informed by the reason of the global or of the West. In a sense, local histories are always in a relation of subalternity to the discourse of global designs. The grand narratives of global designs that characterize the long modern/colonial period (1500–1990, approximately) were Christianity, the civilizing mission, development and modernization, and, finally, the global marketplace. It appears, however, that the last stage of globalization (particularly since 1970) has been creating the conditions for releasing the energies that are becoming "local critical histories" reversing their subaltern location in relation to global designs. This essay explores this process of reversal, focusing on historical categories and on the geopolitics of knowledge entrenched in colonial legacies: local forms of knowledge, like local histories, have been subalternized by universal forms of knowledge, either in their Christian-philosophical foundations during the Renaissance or in their Enlightenment version of universal reason.

From the sixteenth century on, global designs (in their various forms and from their various loci of enunciation — e.g., the absolutist liberal state) distributed, classified, and reclassified the world into geocultural categories. The classification of the world meant, at the same time, devising and implementing strategies for the subalternization of knowledge: the world was there to be known, conquered, converted, and used. The various forms of cultural critiques that have emerged recently, such as post-Occidentalism, postcolonialism, post-Orientalism, double critique, etc., are to be understood as particular exemplars of local critical knowledges working toward the reversal of the colonial relations, especially between local histories and global designs, and hegemonic and subaltern forms of knowledge. They aim, above all, toward the affirmation of new identities, which will result in the negation of subaltern relations. While one of the major strategies of global designs in creating geocultural categories and establishing subaltern relations was *the denial of coevalness*, the restitution of critical local histories and knowledges also have as their goal the *denial of coevalness.*[1] In this context, border gnosis is a form of subaltern rationality, a way of thinking from the spaces in between local histories and universal knowledges. That is, by incorporating the global into the local, critical local knowledges have the power of the border that is lacking in deterritorialized global designs. While local critical knowledges can be articulated at the same time *from* the experience of the local and *from* the conceptual of the global, global designs — by definition — do not have the privilege delivered by local knowledge and local interests. Border gnosis and subaltern rationalities are precisely located at the intersection of the local and the global, from the perspective of the local. *Postcolonialism* and *post-Occidentalism* are key words in which the reversal that I mentioned is taking place.

1

The *postcolonial* or *postcoloniality,* it has been observed, is an ambiguous expression, sometimes dangerous, other times confusing, and generally limited and unconsciously employed.[2] It is ambiguous when used to refer to sociohistorical situations linked to colonial expansion and decolonization across time and space. For example, Algeria, the nineteenth-century United States, and nineteenth-century Brazil are all referred to as *postcolonial countries.* The danger arises when this term is used as one more *post* theoretical direction in the academy and becomes a mainstream played against oppositional practices by "people of color," "Third World intellectuals," or "ethnic groups" in the academy. It is confusing when *hybridity, mestizaje, space in between,* and other equivalent expressions become the object of reflection and critique of postcolonial theories, for they suggest a discontinuity between the *colonial configuration* of the object or subject of study and the *postcolonial position* of the locus of theorizing. Postcoloniality is unconsciously employed when uprooted from the conditions of its emergence (e.g., as a substitute for "Commonwealth literature" in certain cases, as a proxy for "Third World literature" in others). Thus postcoloniality or the postcolonial becomes problematic when applied to either nineteenth- or twentieth-century cultural practices in Latin America.

Occidentalism rather than colonialism was the main concern, first, of the Spanish crown and men of letters during the sixteenth and seventeenth centuries and, second, of the state and intellectuals during the nation-building period, which defined the Latin American selfsame in its difference with Europe and the Occident. America, contrary to Asia and Africa, became during the eighteenth century the "daughter" and "inheritor" of Europe. *Post-Occidentalism* better describes Latin American critical discourse on colonialism. José Martí's compelling expression *Nuestra América* summarized the debate, among nineteenth-century Latin American intellectuals, at the moment when the force of the European Enlightenment, which inspired the revolutionaries of independence and subsequent nation builders, was being replaced by the fear of a new colonialism from the North during the second half of the nineteenth century. The three colonial legacies, of Spain/Portugal, France/Great Britain, and the United States, were clearly described, some thirty years after José Martí in Cuba, by José Carlos Mariátegui in Peru, who saw in the Peruvian school system the "herencia colonial" (Spanish colonial legacy) and the "influencia francesa y norteamericana" (French and U.S. influence).[3] Mariátegui's distinction between *herencia* and *influencia* (the past and the present) is based on the linear historicism of modernity that hides, even today, at the end of the twentieth century, the synchronic coexistence of different colonial legacies. The Cuban Revolution brought a new perspective to Latin American history and inspired Fernández Retamar in Cuba (following the path of Martí and Mariátegui) to write his canonical "Nuestra América y Occidente" (Our America and the Occident), in which he introduced the key word *post-Occidentalism.*[4]

I would submit that, in spite of the difficulties implied in the term *postcolonial* (mentioned above) and the less familiar *post-Occidentalism*, we should not forget that both discourses contribute to a radical epistemic/hermeneutic change in theoretical and intellectual production, which I have described as *border gnosis*, linked to *subalternity* and *subaltern reason*. It is not so much the historical postcolonial condition that should retain our attention as the postcolonial loci of enunciation as an emerging discursive formation and as a form of articulation of subaltern rationality. In this essay, I propose that the most fundamental transformation of intellectual space at the end of the twentieth century is taking place because of the configuration of critical subaltern thinking as both an oppositional practice in the public sphere and a theoretical and epistemological transformation of the academy.[5] In this context, I find compelling Ella Shohat's description of postcolonial theories (to which I add post-Occidental [theorizing]) as sites of enunciation and as a forceful space for critical thinking and new cultures of scholarship:

> The term 'post-colonial' [and 'post-occidental'] would be more precise, therefore, if articulated as 'post-First/Third Worlds theory,' or 'post-anti-colonial critique,' as a movement beyond a relatively binaristic, fixed and stable mapping of power relations between 'colonizer/colonized' and 'center/periphery.' Such rearticulations suggest a more nuanced discourse, which allows for movemnt, mobility and fluidity. Here, the prefix 'post' would make sense less as 'after' than as following, going beyond and commenting upon a certain intellectual movement — third worldist anti-colonial critique — rather than beyond a certain point in history — colonialism; for here 'neo-colonialism' would be a less passive form of addressing the situation of neo-colonized countries, and a politically more active mode of engagement.[6]

Postcolonial and post-Occidental theorizing are, in the last analysis, post-subaltern forms of knowledges and rationality. As diverse sets of theoretical practices emerging *from* and responding *to* colonial legacies at the intersection of Euro-American modern history, they represent a new accounting of modern colonial histories with a view to superseding subalternity and recasting subaltern knowledges. I will not go so far as to suggest that the postcolonial/post-Occidental is a new paradigm; rather, we must view it as part of a larger one (e.g., postsubaltern reason). As a border gnosis, it is a way of thinking from and beyond disciplines and the geopolitics of knowledge imbedded in Occidentalism, Orientalism, and area studies; from and beyond colonial legacies; from and beyond the gender divide and sexual prescriptions; and from and beyond ethnic identities and racial conflicts. Thus, border gnosis is a longing to overcome subalternity and a building block of postsubaltern ways of thinking. I insist that the post in postcolonial/post-Occidental is significantly different from other posts in contemporary cultural critiques. I further suggest that, there are two fundamental ways of critiquing modernity: one, from colonial histories and legacies (postcolonialism, post-Occidentalism, post-Orientalism); the other, the postmodern, from the limits of the hegemonic narratives of Western history. Let me expand on this latter point.

2

I begin by recounting what I understand by colonialism and Occidentalism. First, I limit my understanding of *colonialism* to the geopolitical and geohistorical constitution of Western European (in Hegel's conception) modernity in its double face: the economic and political configuration of the modern world as well as the theological and epistemological space (from philosophy to religion, from ancient history to the modern social sciences) justifying such a configuration. From the very beginning of colonial expansion, subaltern reason opened up a place of contention (e.g., Guaman Poma de Ayala's *Nueva corónica y buen gobierno*, finished around 1615), making it possible to contest the epistemological space of modernity and the inscription of a world order in which the West and the East, the same and the other, the civilized and the barbarian, were inscribed as natural entities. Since 1500, the process of consolidation of Western Europe as a geohistorical entity coincided with transatlantic travels and the expansion of the Spanish and Portuguese empires. During the sixteenth century and the first half of the seventeenth, Italy, Spain (or Castile), and Portugal were the "heart of Europe," to borrow an expression that Hegel eventually applied to England, France, and Germany toward the beginning of the nineteenth century. I limit my understanding of postcolonial situations/conditions to any sociohistorical configuration emerging from people gaining independence or emancipation from Western colonial and imperial powers (such as Europe until 1945 or the United States from the beginning of the twentieth century). In this context, *postcolonial* is synonymous with *neocolonial*. In both cases, what matters is the transformation of our "external colonialism" into an "internal" one characterizing the nation-building process in territories that have been controlled or managed by a colonial country. Neocolonialism is the political and economical context in which internal colonialism was enacted.[7] Subaltern forms of rationality, instead, precede and coexist with postcolonial/neocolonial situations/conditions.

One of the first difficulties that we encounter in this map of colonial legacies and subaltern rationalities is that the United States is not easily accepted as a postcolonial/neocolonial country and, consequently, as a reality for which we can account in terms of postcolonial theories.[8] Because the U.S. surface shows a (post)modern appearance, and because it is the United States where Third World intellectuals found a shelter and postcolonial theorizing arose, one can say that it all came together in the United States. However, difficulty arises not only because of the differences between colonial legacies in the United States and those in, say, Jamaica, but also because postcoloniality (in terms both of situation or condition and of discursive and theoretical production) tends to be linked mainly with Third World countries and experiences. The fact seems to be that, even if the United States does not have the same kind of colonial legacies as Peru or Indonesia, it is nonetheless a consequence of European colonialism and not just one more European country in itself. Owing to American leadership in the continuity of Western expansion, postmodern rather than post-Occidental/postcolonial criticism would be more easily linked to the history of the United States. One could even suggest that U.S. colonial history explains postmodern theories such as those formulated by Fredric Jameson, where the space of contestation comes from the legacies of capitalism rather than from the legacies of colonialism.[9] The already-classic discussion between Jameson and Ahmad could easily be reread in this context.[10]

As Dirlik noted, postcolonial theorizing in the United States found its house in the academy among intellectual immigrants from the Third World.[11] But, of course, postcolonial theorizing is not an invention of Third World intellectuals migrating to the United States, as Dirlik suggested. What Third World intellectuals and scholars in the United States contributed to was the marketing of postcoloniality among an array of available theories and a spectrum of *post-* possibilities. On the other hand, African American studies in the United States, whose emergence is parallel to postmodern and postcolonial theorizing, is deeply rooted in the African diaspora and, consequently, in the history of colonialism and slavery. Dirlik has a point if we interpret his dictum as the marketization of postcolonial theory within the American academy. His point loses its poise when we consider, for instance, Stuart Hall and Paul Gilroy in England or when one goes beyond the American academy and takes seriously Ruth Frankenberg's dictum that, in the United States, the question is not colonialism and postcolonialism (as it is in England and India, for e.g.), but civil rights and post–civil rights.[12] In other words, civil rights is the manifestation in the United States of a postcolonial/post-Occidental discourse responding to a particular configuration of colonial legacies in a particular local history. The bottom line is the emergence of subaltern forms of rationality that are being articulated differently in the geopolitical distribution of knowledge and could be explained by colonial legacies and local critical histories.

Subaltern rationality, or whatever you want to call it, nourishes and is nourished by a theoretical practice that was prompted by the movements of decolonization after World War II and that at its inception had little to do with academic enterprises (Césaire, Amilcar Cabral, Fanon) and had at its core the question of race. If Marxist thinking could be described as having class at its core, postcolonial/post-Occidental theorizing could be described as having race/ethnicity at its core. Two of the three major genocides of modernity (the Amerindian and the African diasporas in the early modern period; the Holocaust as closing European modernity and the crisis of the civilizing mission) are, in my understanding, at the root of colonial and imperial histories, which is to say that they are at the root of the very constitution of modern colonialism and colonial modernities. Subaltern rationality, linked to colonialism, arises as a response to the need to rethink and reconceptualize the stories that have been told to divide the world into Christians and pagans, blacks and whites, civilized and barbarian, modern and premodern, and developed and underdeveloped. *Modernization* and *development* have been the key words of colonial discourse and subalternization since the mid-1950s.

If one more example from U.S. intellectual history is needed to justify postmodernism in complementarity with subaltern criticism and to understand the subalternization of knowledge, one may take seriously Cornel West's argument about the American evasion of philosophy as a genealogy of pragmatism.[13] By reading Emerson, Pierce, Royce, Dewey, Du Bois, James, and Rorty (among others), West convincingly suggests that the American evasion of philosophy is precisely the outcome of a philosophizing out of place—that is to say, of practicing a philosophical reflection whose foundations were grounded, not in the needs of a breakaway settler colony, but rather in the needs of colonial countries. Thus, when West states, "Prophetic pragmatism emerges at a particular moment in the history of North Atlantic civilization—the moment of postmodernity," he further specifies that "postmodernity can be understood in light of three fundamental historical processes": (a) the end of the European age (1492–1945), which decimated European self-confidence and prompted self-criticism;[14] (b) the emergence of the United States as the world military and economic power, offering directions in the political arena and cultural production; and (c) the "first stage of decolonization of the Third World," enacted by political independence in Asia and in Africa.[15]

Notice that the three fundamental historical processes that West offers for understanding postmodernity could also be invoked to understand postcoloniality. One could say that postmodernity is the discourse of countermodernity emerging from the metropolitan centers and *settler colonies,* while postcoloniality is the discourse of countermodernity emerging from *deep-settler* colonies, where colonial power endured with particular brutality.[16] Notice, too, that if decolonization after 1945 is taken into account (which mainly places decolonization in relation to the British Empire and German and French colonies), then nineteenth-century Latin America (e.g., Hispanic and Luso America) would not be considered as an early process of decolonization, and its status as a set of Third World countries would not be easily accepted. This is another reason why the postcolonial question in Latin America only recently began to be discussed in academic circles in the United States, and is still mostly ignored in Latin American countries, while modernity and postmodernity already have an ample bibliography in Latin America, particularly in those countries with a large population of European descent (e.g., Brazil and the Southern Cone). However, as we shall see, postcolonial theorizing *in* Latin America has been enacted since the 1970s without naming it as such.

The map presented by West suggests a threefold division of colonial legacies: (a) settler colonies; (b) deep-settler colonies; and (c) colonialism/imperialism without settlements after 1945. Thus, West states, "It is no accident that American pragmatism once again rises to the surface of North Atlantic intellectual life at the present moment. . . . The distinctive appeal of American pragmatism in our postmodern moment is its unashamedly moral emphasis and its unequivocally ameliorative impulse." [17]

The emphasis on postmodernity (instead of postcolonialism/post-Occidentalism) in a settler colony that became a world power helps us understand the attention that postmodernity has received in Latin America, particularly in Atlantic Continental Coast countries close to Europe and far away from the Pacific Coast and dense Amerindian population. That we are beginning to see articles mixing postcolonialism/post-Occidentalism and Latin America seems to stem from the fact that postcolonialism/post-Occidentalism has become an important topic of discussion in academic circles in the same settler colony that rose to be a world power, although the distinction between the emergence and the uses of both postmodernity and postcolonialism/post-Occidentalism is not always made, nor are its consequences evaluated. When Dirlik, for instance, blatantly and provocatively states, "The postcolonial begins when Third World intellectuals have arrived in First World academy," two parallel issues should be addressed: when and where does the postmodern begin? [18] The answer, following Dirlik's statement, would be: when metropolitan (and settler-colony) intellectuals frame as postmodern the drastic changes in the logic of late capitalism (Jameson), in the condition of knowledge in the most highly technological societies (Lyotard), or in the continuation of the critique of modernity in Western metaphysics (Vattimo). On the other hand, we should be able to distinguish *postcolonial theories* as an academic commodity (in the same way that postmodern theories were and are commodified) from *postcolonial theorizing* as particular colonial critics subsumed under subaltern reason and border gnosis. The latter is a process of thought that people living under colonial domination enact in order to negotiate their life and subaltern condition. Postcolonial theorizing may have entered the academic market when Third World intellectuals arrived in the United States, but it certainly did not begin then. Postcolonial theorizing as a particular enactment of the subaltern reason coexists with colonialism itself as a constant move and force toward autonomy and liberation in every order of life, from economy to religion, from language to education, from memories to spatial order, and it is not limited to the academy, even less to the American academy!

3

Let us now turn more specifically to the post-Occidental question. If one looks back to the deep-settler colonies of Latin America with large indigenous populations, there was much concern, especially after the Russian Revolution, with issues that today would be identified as postcolonial/post-Occidental among Marxist intellectuals such as José Carlos Mariátegui in Peru (around 1920) and

Enrique Dussel in Argentina (from the 1970s on) as well as among philosophers such as Leopoldo Zea and Edmundo O'Gorman (from 1960 on) in Mexico.

In 1958, Zea published *América en la historia,* in which Occidentalism was at the core of his concerns.[19] Zea's problematic was rooted in a long-lasting tradition among Hispanic American intellectuals since the nineteenth century: the conflictual relation with Europe and, toward the end of the nineteenth century, with the United States; in other words, with Occidentalism. Zea portrayed both Spain and Russia as marginal to the West. Two chapters are called, significantly, "España al margen de Occidente" (Spain at the margin of the West) and "Rusia al margen de Occidente" (Russia at the margin of the West). One can surmise that deep-settler colonies (type *b*) in neocolonial situations in Latin America have some similarities with the transformation of Russia into the Soviet Union, although almost a century elapsed between Latin America decolonization and the Russian Revolution. One obvious similarity that Zea points out comes from the marginal modernity of Spain and Russia during the eighteenth and nineteenth centuries. There are, however, enormous differences because of the separate era in which each historical process occurred and because of the fact that, while in Latin America decolonization took place in former deep-settler Spanish and Portuguese colonies, some interacting with deep-indigenous cultures (e.g., the Andes [Bolivia, Peru, Ecuador, Colombia] and Meso-america [Mexico, Guatemala] dealing with slavery as forced migrations, the Russian Revolution took place at the very heart of the empire. Both Spain and Russia had a similar relation with "Eurocentrism," to which Zea devotes a chapter of his most recent book.[20] He locates them in the foundation and aftermath of Cartesian and Hegelian conceptualizations of reason as well as in Marx's and Engels's inverted Hegelianism as a socialist utopia materializing, not in Europe, but at its margins. Historical inheritances and their revolutionary implementations in the Soviet Union are not, however, linked to colonial legacies and post-colonial thinking, for reasons that I will soon describe.

During the same years that Zea was writing his *América en la historia,* Edmundo O'Gorman was dismantling five hundred years of colonial discourse building and manipulating the belief that America was discovered when, as he clearly demonstrates, there was no America to be discovered in the first place and, for those who were already living in the lands where Columbus arrived without knowing where he was, there was nothing to be discovered at all.[21] O'Gorman's book is titled *La invención de América: El universalismo de la cultura de Occidente.* Certainly, neither Zea nor O'Gorman paid much attention to the contribution of people from Amerindian descent to the constant process of decolonization. However, there is a common dictum today among indigenous social movements, in both the Americas and the Caribbean, that "Columbus did not discover us." While two key concepts for Zea and O'Gorman were *Occidentalism* and *Eurocentrism,* Mexican American scholar Jorge Klor de Alva critically examined the meaning of the term *colonialism* and its misapplication to Latin America:

> The first part of my thesis is simple: Given that the indigenous populations of the Americas began to suffer a devastating demographic collapse on contact with the Europeans; given that the indigenous population loss had the effect, by the late sixteenth century, of restricting those who identified themselves as natives to the periphery of the nascent national polities; given that the greater part of the mestizos who quickly began to replace them fashioned their selves primarily after European models; given that together with Euro-Americans (*criollos*) and some Europeans (*peninsulares*) these Westernized mestizos made up the forces that defeated Spain during the nineteenth-century wars of independence; and, finally, given that the new countries under criollo/mestizo leadership constructed their national identities overwhelmingly out of Euro-American practices, the Spanish language, and Christianity, it is misguided to present the pre-independence *non-native* sectors as colonized, it is inconsistent to explain the wars of independence as anti-colonial struggles, and it is misleading to characterize the Americas, following the civil wars of separation, as postcolonial. In short, the Americas were neither Asia nor Africa; Mexico is not India, Peru is not Indonesia, and Latinos in the U.S.—although tragically opposed by an exclusionary will—are not Algerians.[22]

Klor de Alva formulated this thesis, as he himself makes clear, on the basis of his inquiries into the construction of identities of contemporary U.S. Latinos and Mexican Americans. Furthermore, although he does not make this point as clear, his conception of *the Americas* excludes the Caribbean (English, French, Spanish), whose consideration would radically change the picture of the colonial and the postcolonial/post-Occidental since the French Caribbean and English Caribbean are not the same type of colonies as the Spanish Caribbean. Basically, Klor de Alva's idea of the Americas is purely Hispanic and Anglo America, by which I mean that Klor de Alva overlooks the constitution of Latin American intellectuals for whom colonialism was indeed Occidentalism. Nevertheless, his effort to detach the Spanish/Portuguese from the British/French/Dutch invasion of the Americas and the Caribbean looks to me like a sheer semantic game, similar to the argument that Spanish nationalists used to enact in order to save Spain from the brutalities of the conquest or to emphasize the civilizing (i.e., Christian) mission of the crown and the missionary orders. But even if *colonization* is misapplied to Latin America, we should not lose sight of the fact that we are talking about European and Western expansion (*Eurocentrism* and *Occidentalism*, in the terms of Zea and O'Gorman), and we should not lose sight of the internal colonial conflicts, mainly between

Spain, England, and Holland toward the end of the seventeenth century, when Seville was no longer the center of global commerce, Amsterdam having taken its place. The change of hands in colonial power should be kept in mind if we are to understand the transformations, and, at the same time, the continuities, from the early modern/colonial period (Spain, Portugal, Renaissance) to the modern/colonial period (Holland, England, France, Enlightenment).

Moreover, *colonialism* is a notion denoting and describing colonial experiences after the eighteenth century (the stages of mercantile capitalism and the Industrial Revolution, according to Darcy Ribeiro, and, consequently, the Spanish and Portuguese expansion toward the Atlantic and the Pacific, mainly during the sixteenth century and the first half of the seventeenth, cannot properly be considered as such.[23] Klor de Alva underlines the anachronism of colonialism applied to historical events and processes in an imprecise "Latin America" under Spanish and Portuguese banners. While I sympathize with Klor de Alva's effort to avoid academic colonialism by reframing Spanish and Portuguese in a conceptualization that mainly emerged from the experiences of the decolonization of British and French colonialism, I feel uncomfortable with his argument because it falls next to an unwritten and officialist discourse of postimperial Spain, one in which the term *viceroyalty* is used to avoid the political (and negative, from the Spanish perspective) implications of the term *colonialism.*

To echo Klor de Alva's concerns of avoiding academic colonialism, which he defines as the framing of Latin American colonial and cultural histories in the vocabulary of English and Commonwealth criticism, it would be necessary to regionalize colonial legacies and postcolonial/post-Occidental theorizing to avoid the trap of the epistemology of modernity, wherein colonial languages (such as English, French, or German), in complicity with theoretical and academic discourses, produce the effect of universal knowledge by the sheer power of their exportability. The commodification and exportability of knowledge is perhaps the reason for Klor de Alva's discomfort with using colonialism and postcolonialism in relation to Latin America.

What really remain as paradigmatic examples of emerging forms of subaltern/colonial criticism in Latin America since the 1970s are located in the Caribbean (part of it belonging to the Commonwealth), in Mesoamerica, and in the Andes. Although thinking in Mexico, Zea and O'Gorman were detached from these epistemological locations. The Caribbean contribution to postcolonial theorizing is already well known, basically because a good deal of writing is in English and French (e.g., that of George Lamming, Aimée Césaire, Frantz Fanon, Edouard Glissant, Raphael Confiant, etc.), the dominant languages of the modern/colonial period. The Spanish Caribbean contribution is less familiar (that of Fernández Retamar, José Luis González) since Spanish as the dominant language of the early modern/colonial period lost its prestige as a "thinking language" with the fall of Spain and the rise of England and France.[24] It should be remembered, however, that, while colonial legacies in the Caribbean are entrenched in the African diaspora, in Mesoamerica (mainly Mexico and Guatemala) and the Andes their profile is obtained from the long-lasting interaction between dense Amerindian populations and Spanish institutions and settlements.

In the late 1960s, two Mexican sociologists, Pablo González-Casanova and Rodolfo Stavenhagen, proposed the concept *internal colonialism* to account for the relation between the state and the Amerindian population since Mexico's independence from Spain in 1821. As one would expect, the concept was criticized from a scientific-oriented sociology, as if the needs to which González-Casanova and Stavenhagen were responding would have been solely disciplinary![25] The vigor of the concept should be situated in mapping the social configuration of nation building in the Spanish ex-colonies rather than in whether or not it fulfills the demands of a disciplinary system of control and punishment. However, since the concept has been criticized from the hegemonic disciplinary perspective, it vanished from the scene, and few will remember it as an early manifestation of postcolonial theorizing in Latin America. More precisely, *internal colonialism*, a concept introduced by Third World sociologists to account for the social realities of their country and region, carries the trace of a different rationality or subaltern reason.

Certainly, the need of further elucidation of *internal colonialism* should not be denied. For instance, when the concept is used in the context of U.S. history, the differences between North and South colonial legacies cannot be ignored. In fact, who are in U.S. national communities in subaltern positions: Native Americans, Asian Americans, Mexican Americans? And, in Argentina, are Italian communities in the same subaltern positions as Amerindian communities? Be that as it may, internal colonialism, as used by González-Casanova and Stavenhagen in Mexico and, more recently, by Silvia Rivera Cusicanqui in the Andes, is clearly applied to the double bind of the national state after independence: on the one hand, to enforce the colonial politics toward indigenous communities and, on the other, to establish alliances with metropolitan colonial powers.[26] Chiefly, in nineteenth-century Mesoamerica and the Andes, the question was to break the ties with Spanish colonialism and to build a nation with the support of England and France, and this is perhaps the main profile of neocolonialism in the ex-Spanish and -Portuguese colonies. Above all, internal colonialism is relevant in Rivera Cusicanqui's work (as well as in that of other Bolivian intellectuals, such as Xavier Albó) to understand a society in which more than 50 percent of the population is of Amerindian descent, speaks Aymara or Quechua, and maintains a socioeconomic organization inherited from Inca and Aymara legacies, which coexisted for five hundred years with Western people and institutions.[27] The concept *internal colonialism* also helps establish a balance between class and ethnicity. In Rivera Cusicanqui's conception, one explanation of the crisis in Andean social sciences attributed their failure to understand such social movements as the Shining Path mainly to their blindness to ethnicity, colonial legacies, and internal colonialism.[28]

Post-Occidentalism was introduced, as I already mentioned, by Cuban intellectual Roberto Fernández Retamar in 1976. In doing so, he was assuming that *Occidentalism* was the key word in Latin American cultural history. Unlike Orientalism, *Occidentalism* was from the very beginning the extension of Europe, not its otherness: *Indias Occidentales* (the legal expression used by the Spanish crown all through its possessions from the continent to the Philippines) set the stage for the relations between Europe and what would later become the Americas, the "extreme Occident." Thus, we find the constant tension between the extreme Occident, the empty continent where Europe extended itself, and the Amerindians, the paradoxical inhabitants of an empty continent. Thus, Fernández Retamar recognizes that, "far from being foreign bodies in 'our America' [e.g., Latin America] because they are not Western, Amerindians and blacks belong to it with full right, with more right than the foreign and outcast agents of the civilizing mission."[29]

Fernández Retamar links this observation and Marxism since Marxism emerged as the critical voice of capitalism, which, for Retamar, is equivalent to Occidentalism. For him, Marxism is no longer an Occidental ideology but a post-Occidental one. What is interesting to note here is his assumption — from the Cuban and Caribbean experience — that Marxism allows one to go beyond the Western world. In fact, Amerindians and blacks, crucial in the Caribbean experience, were not so in the European context in which Marxism originated. The crossing over of colonialism and capitalism in Latin America allows Retamar to propose *post-Occidentalism* as a Marxist category, although incorporated in the colonial history of Amerindian exploitation and the African slave trade. Postoccidentalism could have been linked to internal colonialism and to dependency theory. However, the isolation imposed by colonial geocultural distribution, complemented by the scientific distribution of knowledge located in the metropolitan centers, makes of local histories and knowledge a curious and sometime folkloric incident in the larger map of global designs.

4

At this point in the discussion, there are two issues that must be untangled. One is the distinction between neocolonial situations, the other that between neocolonial discourses and post-/Occidental/colonial criticism. My first inclination would be to define *neocolonial situations and discourses* as a configuration arising from the liberation of colonial rules and the different stages of the modern period; for example, the independence of Anglo and Hispanic America at the end of the eighteenth century and the beginning of the nineteenth, respectively, the decolonization of Indonesia and Algeria, and the Cuban Revolution; that is to say, neocolonial situations and discourses of types *a, b,* and *c,* respectively. This may be too schematic for certain tastes, but it helps sort out some of the confusion and ambiguity inherent in the expression.

Post-Occidental/colonial criticism, by contrast, emerges mainly in the aftermath of decolonization, after World War II and in parallel to new forms of neocolonialism and dictatorship. Furthermore, it is the critical consciousness of colonialism and neocolonialism that created the conditions for postcolonial/post-Occidental theorizing and emergence of postsubaltern rationality. Now, if postsubalternity (understood as theory building) emerges from different types of colonial and neocolonial legacies, then post-/Occidentalism/colonialism and postmodernism are countermodern moves responding to different kinds of colonial legacies and neocolonial states that have in common the process of Western expansion identified as modernity/colonialism/Occidentalism.

The reader could object, at this point, by saying that postmodernity is not a particularly Anglo American or even European phenomenon but that it belongs to the history of humankind. Using similar logic, one can argue that the same observation could be made about post-/Occidentalism/colonialism, that it is not just an issue of modernity and colonized countries between 1492 and 1945 but rather a global or transnational issue. Modernity is both the consolidation of empire and nation/empires in Europe, a discourse constructing the idea of Occidentalism, the subjugation of people and cultures, and the counterdiscourses and social movements resisting Euro American expansionism. Thus, if modernity consists of both the consolidation of European history (global design) and the silenced critical voices of peripheral colonies (local histories), modernity is indeed modern colonialisms and colonial modernities. Thus, postmodernism and post-/Occidentalism/colonialism are alternate processes of countering modernity from different colonial legacies and in different national or neocolonial situations: (*a*) legacies from/at the center of colonial empires (e.g., Lyotard); (*b*) colonial legacies in settler colonies (e.g., Jameson in the United States); and (*c*) colonial legacies in deep-settler colonies (e.g., Said, Cusicanqui, Spivak, Glissant, Albó, Bhabha, Quijano, etc.). In other words, postmodernity and post-/Occidentalism/colonialism are both parts of postsubaltern rationality as extended critiques of colonialism and subalternity.

It is my contention that post-/Occidental/colonial theorizing allows for a decentering of theoretical practices in terms of the politics of geocultural locations and that the distinction between post-/Occidental/colonial discourses and theories becomes difficult to trace.[30] Cultures of scholarship become part of a political domain of discourses and social concerns coupled with cultures of scholarship. Thus, it would have been difficult to conceive of Fanon as a post-/Occidental/colonial theoretician in the late 1950s. His discourse, attractive and seductive as it was (and still is), was not part of the conceptual framework that, at the time, was seen in terms of theoretical discourse in the academy. Theory in the humanities was conceived then mainly in terms of linguistic models and, in the social sciences, in terms of the covering law model. Fanon became a post-/Occidental/colonial theoretician once the academy conceptualized a new kind of theoretical practice, invented a name to distinguish it from others, and placed it within a specific academic battlefield.

Theory becomes necessary to distinguish between an inherited concept of theory (from the social sciences, linguistics, semiotics, and sometimes the transposition from the natural sciences to the social sciences and the humanities) and a type of self-reflective and critical practice in the academy. There are two takes on the use of the term *theory* that I would like to point out, comparing *critical theory* with post-/Occidental/colonial theorizing and the emergence of subaltern reason.

a) Craig Calhoun described the use of critical theory by Frankfurt school philosophers as a displacement of the canonical concept of theory in philosophy, by adapting it to the social sciences:

> They challenged the presumed absolute identity of the individual as knower embodied famously in the Cartesian cogito ("I think, therefore I am"). Influenced by Freud, Romanticism, and thinkers of the "dark side" of Enlightenment like Nietzsche and Sade, they knew the individual person had to be more complex than that, especially if he or she was to be the subject of creative culture. They also saw the individual as social in a way most ordinary theory did not, constituted by intersubjective relations with others, all the more important where they furthered a sense of non-identity, of the complexity of multiple involvements with others, that enabled a person to reach beyond narrow self-identity.[31]

But perhaps more important to my purpose is Calhoun's observation that most of the early key Frankfurt theorists were Jews.[32] Here, we touch on a crucial issue in the formation of subaltern reason and post-/Occidental/colonial theorizing: the inscription of the colonial/subaltern experience of the theoretician in his or her theoretical practices, similar to the inscription of the Jewish experience in Frankfurt early critical theory (e.g., Adorno and Horkheimer's reading of the Jews' experience against the Enlightenment ideals).[33] Calhoun's reading of the connection between the ethnicity of the theoretician and the building of critical theory is the following:

> Most of the early key Frankfurt theorists were Jews. If this did not produce an acute enough interest in politics of identity to start with—most of them coming from highly assimilated families and assimilating further themselves in the course of their studies—the rise of Nazism and broader

anti-Semitic currents brought the issue home. Faced with the question why Jews were not just one minority group among many—for the Nazis certainly but also for most of modernity—Horkheimer and Adorno sought the answer in a characteristic way: Anti-Semitism represented the hatred of those who see themselves as civilized, but could not fulfill the promises of civilization for all those who reminded them of the failures of civilization.[34]

In a sense, then, critical theory as practiced by the Frankfurt school theo-retician is, like post-/Occidental/colonial theorizing, a kind of postsubaltern theorizing: a theoretical practice by those who oppose the clean and rational concept of knowledge and theory and theorize, precisely, from the situation into which they have been put, be they Jewish, Muslim, Amerindian, African, or some other Third World people, like Hispanics in today's United States. However, the link between theory and ethnicity in the early Frankfurt school detected by Calhoun is also similar to the awareness of being a Third World philosopher, like Zea or O'Gorman, who have to write from "marginalization and barbarism." Zea and O'Gorman placed themselves at the margin of the discipline, as historians and philosophers, although their own ethnic question did not reach their thinking. Frankfurt philosophers were at center stage disci-plinarily, epistemologically, and theoretically, although the ethnic question was inscribed in their thinking and transformed theoretical practices into critical theory. Zea and O'Gorman contributed, nonetheless, to value thinking from "marginalization and barbarism" or, as the controversial Argentinian philoso-pher Rodolfo Kusch would say, from the "philosophical location" where loca-tion is not only geographic but historical, political, and epistemological.[35] In other words, their contribution was to show the limits of civilization and the rise of "barbarian" theorizing (that of Jews, marginalized postcolonials, women, African Europeans, African Americans, Amerindians, gays, etc.).

b) Unlike Craig Calhoun, Mary John looks at the inscription of the sub-ject position in "doing theory" in France in the 1960s and also at the radical transformation of doing theory since the late 1970s.[36] That radical transforma-tion comes mainly from the awareness that theory is where you find it. There is no geographic or epistemological location that holds the property rights for theoretical practices but *the philosophical location,* in Kusch's terms, that is, the starting point and the road orienting our thinking with alterity constantly inter-vening, suggesting or showing at the same time the unthinkable.[37] Like Cal-houn, John looks for the inscription of subjectivity at the intersection of femi-nism and postcoloniality, in whatever form this intersection can manifest itself. The awareness and the inscription of feminism and postcoloniality in John's concept *doing theory* is equivalent to the awareness of Jewishness in the Frank-furt school's *critical theory.* But it is more: it is also an awareness that, linked to modern reason, the very concept of theory cannot be accepted, rehearsed, or applied to feminist concerns and postcolonial issues. John's disbelief in the dichotomy between linking theories to their context of origin or taking them in their universal scope and making them travel to illuminate alien contexts implies that the very concept of theory is interpellated. What I am arguing here is the need to unlink the concept of theory from its modern epistemological version (to explain or to make sense of unconnected facts or data) or its postmodern version (to deconstruct reified conceptual networks). One of the aims of post-/Occidental/colonial theorizing, in my understanding, is to reinscribe in the history of humankind what was repressed by modern reason, either in its version of the civilizing mission or in its version of theoretical thinking that was denied to the noncivilized, theorized by Gilroy through the concept of double consciousness in Frederick Douglass.[38] Post-/Occidental/colonial theorizing is leading the way to a new form of consciousness and new epistemological foundations. As such, one of the versions of theorizing that I envision and for which I argue is that of thinking from the borders and from the perspective of the subaltern. It is theorizing from the borders of modern theory and those unnamed ways of thinking that have been silenced by modern theory but have not been repressed. To think theoretically is a gift and a human ability, not just of those living in a certain period, in certain geographic locations, speaking a small set of languages, and assuming a hegemonic concept of reason and knowledge. If postcolonial/post-Occidental theorizing is not able to break away from the narrow concept linked to modern epistemology, it would become another version of modern epistemology with a different subject matter. It would be, in other words, a theory *about* a new subject matter but not the constitution of a new epistemological subject that thinks *from and about* the borders.

Postsubaltern rationality and border gnosis go beyond the Occidental/colonial and rejoin Frederick Douglass's inversion of the master/slave dialectic, analyzed by Paul Gilroy.[39] The allegorical relations of master and slave portraying independent and dependent self-consciousness in relation to consciousness and knowledge can be thought out (in Hegel) within a disembodied epistemology that assumes the locus of enunciation of the master as the universal one. Hegel's allegory is located within a Cartesian and disembodied concept of reason. As such, reason could be described and conceptualized with independence of gender and sexual relations, social hierarchies, national or religious beliefs, or ethnic prejudices. However, the silence implied in the disembodied (both individual and social) is at the same time the assumption of a universal position of power in relation to which sexual relations, social hierarchies, national or religious beliefs, and ethnic prejudices are subaltern categories. Hegel's allegorical speculations regarding master/slave relations shall be confronted constantly with the embodied reflection on consciousness and self-consciousness narrated and theorized by Douglass: "A few months of his discipline tamed me. Mr. Covey succeeded in breaking me. I was broken in body, soul and spirit. My natural elasticity was crushed; my intellect languished; the disposition to read departed; the cheerful spark that lingered about my eye died; the dark night of slavery closed in upon me; and behold a man transformed into a brute." [40]

At the moment that Douglass reflects on his experience and tells the story, he is no longer a slave, and one could say that he possesses a "consciousness that exists for itself," Covey becoming the representative of "a consciousness that is repressed within itself." [41] At this point, while Douglass is in a position to understand both the slave and the master from the perspective (and the experience) of the slave, Covey is not, lacking as he does the experience of the slave. Hegel's allegory is located on the side of Covey, not Douglass. Douglass thinks from the experience of the subaltern who has liberated himself from that position and can analyze slavery as a form of subalternity from that perspective. By so doing, Douglass introduces the perspective of the slave into the analysis of the master/slave relation. But now the questions asked and issues raised are no longer those of understanding an unincorporated consciousness and self-consciousness but those of understanding from the historical experiences made possible by the very concept of reason that Hegel was trying to elucidate in his *Phenomenology of the Spirit*. We all know that the concept of reason introduced by René Descartes had not only philosophical and metaphysical import but was a principle crucial to the development and management of the larger spectrum of society. [42] Consequently, one should expect that new forms of rationality, emerging from subaltern experiences made possible by the historical rationality articulated by Descartes and the philosophy of modernity, will affect not philosophy and social thought, but the reorganization of society. Thinking from subaltern experiences should affect both self-understanding and public policy, creating the condition for precluding subalternity. Thus, it seems that the possibilities of theorizing colonial legacies could be carried out in different directions: from a strictly disciplinary location, from the location of someone for whom colonial legacies are a historical but not a personal matter, and, finally, from the site of someone for whom colonial legacies are entrenched in his or her own history and sensibility, as slavery was for Douglass. Some of the confusion and ambiguity surrounding the term today is due, I believe, to the various possibilities of engaging oneself in postcolonial criticism. I am also convinced that the opposite prejudice is the common belief that persons who *are from* some place in the heart of the empire have the necessary competence to theorize, no matter where they *are at*, because theorizing is taken to be the universal practice of modern reason. This prejudice is anchored in the ideological distribution of knowledge in the social sciences and the humanities, parallel to the geopolitical distribution of the world into First, Second, and Third. Or, to put it another way, while *subaltern rationality* discloses a change of terrain regarding its very foundation as a cognitive, political, and theoretical practice, modern reason speaks for the foundation of the humanities and the social sciences during the nineteenth century, grounded in the Renaissance and the Enlightenment, rather than the colonial, legacies. In this sense, subaltern rationality as border gnosis is both postmodern *and* postcolonial/post-Occidental.

5

I owe this insight to Carl Pletsch.[43] Pletsch traced the parallel between the division of social scientific labor and the division of the First, Second, and Third Worlds between 1950 and 1975, a time during which social scientific labor was reorganized according to a new world order, and, coincidentally, the time in which the emergence of colonial discourses and the foundations of postcolonial theories are now being located. Colonial discourses and theories were not yet an issue at the time Pletsch wrote his article, which was mainly devoted to the social sciences. The period chosen by Pletsch is also relevant for the implied connections between decolonization and the emergence of the cold war, which brought Russia/the Soviet Union back into the picture on the fringes of Western modernity as the Second World. Pletsch's thesis is simple. Owing to the emergence of socialist nations and, above all, the Soviet Union, Western anxiety prompted the division of the world into three large categories: technologically and economically developed countries that are democratically organized; technologically and economically developed countries ruled by ideology; and technologically and economically underdeveloped countries. The foundation of such a distribution cannot necessarily be bonded to the properties of the objects classified but rather to the site of enunciation constructing the classification: the enunciation is located in the First World, not the Second or Third. Since the classification originated in democratically developed and capitalistic countries, it naturally became a First World decision and the measuring stick for subsequent classifications. My first assumption, in this context, is that postcolonial criticism strives for a displacement of the locus of theoretical enunciation from the First to the Third World, thus claiming legitimacy for the *philosophical location.*[44]

My assumption can be better understood if we pursue Pletsch a little further. The thrust of his argument lies in the fact that the academic redistribution of scientific labor is not parallel with the political and economical relocation of cultural worlds. Or, as Pletsch explains, "Terms evoking ethnocentrism, condescension, imperialism, and aggression were systematically replaced by apparently neutral and scientific terms—euphemisms. Not only did former colonies become 'developing nations' and primitive tribes become 'traditional people,' the War and Navy Departments of the United States Government were transformed into the 'Defense' Department. . . . It would have been simply impossible to explain the need for foreign aid and vast military expenditures in a time of peace with categories any more differentiated than those marshaled under the three worlds umbrella." [45]

From an epistemological location, the classic distinction between traditional and modern societies was relocated and redistributed. The modern world was divided in two: the First World was technologically advanced, free of ideological constraints and utilitarian thinking, and thus *natural;* the Second World was also technologically advanced but encumbered with an ideological elite that prevented utilitarian thinking and free access to science. The traditional Third World was economically and technologically underdeveloped, with a traditional mentality obscuring the possibility of utilitarian and scientific thinking. Thus, the epistemological distribution of labor was part and parcel of the ideological distribution of the world and the reconceptualization of science, ideology, and culture:

> Western social scientists have reserved the concept of culture for the mentalities of traditional societies in their pristine states. They have designated the socialist societies of the second world the province of ideology. And they have long assumed—not unanimously, to be sure—that the modern West is the natural haven of science and utilitarian thinking. Consistent with this scheme, one clan of social scientists is set apart to study the pristine societies of the third world (anthropologists). Other clans— economists, sociologists, and political scientists—study the third world only insofar as the process of modernization has already begun. The true province of these latter social sciences is the modern world, especially the natural societies of the West. But again, subclans of each of these sciences of the modern world are specially outfitted to make forays into the ideological regions of the second world. Much as their fellow economists, sociologists, and political scientists who study the process of modernization in the third world, these students of the second world are engaged in area studies. What distinguishes their area is the danger associated with ideology, as opposed to the now innocent otherness of traditional cultures. But the larger contrast is between all of these area specialists, whether of the second or third world, and the disciplinary generalists who study the natural societies of the first world.[46]

I quote Pletsch at length because of the substantial redistribution of the order of things and of the human sciences since the nineteenth century, described by Michel Foucault, and because doing so helps clarify the location of postcolonial and postmodern theoretical practices at the close of the twentieth century, following the collapse of the three worlds order and the end of the cold war.[47] One can surmise that a substantial characteristic of the postcolonial critique is the emergent voices and actions from Third World countries that are reversing the image of backwardness produced and sustained by a long colonial legacy until the redistribution of scientific labor. If, according to the distribution of scientific and cultural production in First, Second, and Third Worlds, someone is *from* an economically and technologically underdeveloped country, he or she cannot produce significant theoretical thought because theory is defined according to First World standards. Theory and sciences are produced, according to this logic, in First World countries where there are no ideological obstructions to scientific and theoretical thinking. Thus, the ideology of the civilizing mission was still at work in the distribution of scientific labor between the three worlds.

My second assumption is that the locus of postmodern theorizing (as articulated by Jameson) is in the First World, although in opposition to the epistemological configuration of the social sciences vis-à-vis the Third World analyzed by Pletsch.[48] One could argue that postmodern reason blends theoretical practices and training from the First World with the ideological underpinnings of the Second (not in terms of state policy but in terms of its Marxist-Leninist foundations). But, as such, it maintains its difference from postcolonial reason, in which the alliance is between the cultural production of the Third World and the theoretical imagination of the First — a powerful alliance in which the restitution of "secondary qualities" in theoretical production displaces and challenges the purity of modern reason, conceived as a logical operation without interference of sensibility and location. The restitution of sensibility and location is postcolonial theorizing empowering those who have been suppressed or marginalized from the production of knowledge and understanding.

There is no reference to literature in Pletsch's article. One must remember, however, the enormous impact of literary production (i.e., cultural rather than social scientific production) from Third World countries (e.g., García Márquez, Assia Djebar, Salman Rushdie, Naguib Mahfouz, Michelle Cliff) — which supports Pletsch's scheme of the distribution of knowledge. It also explains why magical realism became the imprint of the Third World's high cultural production. However, when literary narratives are also taken as theories in their own right, the distinction between the location of theoretical and that of cultural production begins to crumble.

Let us now rethink the distinction between *coming from, being at,* and *being from.*[49] If postcolonial discourses (including literature and theories) are associated with people (*coming*) *from* countries with colonial legacies, it is precisely due to the displacement of intellectual production from the First to the Third World. However, while literary output can easily be attributed to the cultural production of the Third World, theory is more difficult to justify because — according to the scientific distribution of labor analyzed by Pletsch —

the locus of theoretical production is the First rather than the Third World. My third assumption is that postcolonial theoretical practices are not just changing our vistas of colonial processes but also challenging the very foundations of the Western concept of knowledge and understanding by establishing epistemological links between geocultural locations and theoretical production.

By insisting on the links between the place of theorizing (*being from, coming from,* and *being at*) and the locus of enunciation, I am emphasizing that loci of enunciation are not given but enacted. I am not assuming that *only* people coming from such and such a place could do *x*. Let me insist that I am casting the argument, not in deterministic terms, but in the open realm of logical possibilities, of historical circumstances and personal sensibilities. I am suggesting that those for whom colonial legacies are real (i.e., those whom they hurt) are more (logically, historically, and emotionally) inclined to theorize the past in terms of coloniality. I am also suggesting that postcolonial theorizing relocates the boundaries between the known and the knowing subject (which was my reason for stressing the complicities of postcolonial theories with "minorities"). While I perceive the location of the knowing subject in the social economy of knowledge and understanding as the main contribution of postcolonial theorizing, I also believe that the description or explanation of the known is the main contribution of postmodern theories.

6

I move now to particular cases of countermodernity and differential loci of enunciation, where the differences are related to coming *from* different colonial legacies and being *at* different geocultural locations.

Enrique Dussel, an Argentinian philosopher associated with the philosophy of liberation, has been articulating a strong countermodern argument. I quote from the beginning of his Frankfurt lectures:

> Modernity is, for many (for Jurgen Habermas or Charles Taylor, for example), an essentially or exclusively European phenomenon. In these lectures, I will argue that modernity is, in fact, a European phenomenon, but one constituted in a dialectical relation with a non-European alterity that is its ultimate content. Modernity appears when Europe affirms itself as the "center" of a World history that it inaugurates; the "periphery" that surrounds this center is consequently part of its self-definition. The occlusion of this periphery (and of the role of Spain and Portugal in the formation of the modern world system from the late fifteenth to the midseventeenth centuries), leads the major contemporary thinkers of the "center" into a Eurocentric fallacy in their understanding of modernity. If

their understanding of the genealogy of modernity is thus partial and provincial, their attempts at a critique or defense of it are likewise unilateral and, in part, false.[50]

The construction of the idea of modernity linked to European expansion, as forged by European intellectuals, was powerful enough to last almost five hundred years. Postcolonial discourses and theories began effectively to challenge that hegemony, a challenge that was unthinkable (and perhaps unexpected) by those who constructed and presupposed the idea of modernity as a historical period and implicitly as *the* locus of enunciation — a locus of enunciation that, in the name of rationality, science, and philosophy, asserted its own privilege over other forms of rationality or over what, from the perspective of modern reason, was nonrational. I would submit, consequently, that postcolonial discourses and postcolonial theories are constructing a new concept of reason as differential loci of enunciation. What does *differential* mean? *Differential* here first means a displacement of the concept and practice of the notions of knowledge, science, theory, and understanding articulated during the modern period.[51] Thus, Dussel's regionalization of modernity could be compared with Homi Bhabha's, both speaking *from* different colonial legacies (Spanish and English, respectively): "Driven by the subaltern history of the margins of modernity — rather than by the failures of logocentrism — I have tried, in some small measure, *to revise the known, to rename the postmodern from the position of the postcolonial*" (my emphasis).[52]

I find a noteworthy coincidence between Dussel and Bhabha, albeit with some significant differences in accent. The coincidence lies in the very important fact that the task of postcolonial reasoning (i.e., theorizing) is linked not only to the immediate political needs of decolonization (in Asia, Africa, and the Caribbean) but also to the rereading of the paradigm of modern reason. This task is performed by Dussel and Bhabha in different, although complementary, ways.

After a detailed analysis of Kant's and Hegel's construction of the idea of enlightenment in European history, Dussel summarizes the elements that constitute the myth of modernity:

(1) Modern (European) civilization understands itself as the most developed, the superior, civilization; (2) This sense of superiority obliges it, in the form of a categorical imperative, as it were, to "develop" (civilize, uplift, educate) the more primitive, barbarous, underdeveloped civilizations; (3) The path of such development should be that followed by Europe in its own development out of antiquity and the Middle Ages; (4) Where the barbarians or the primitive opposes the civilizing process, the praxis of modernity must, in the last instance, have recourse to the violence neces-

sary to remove the obstacles to modernization; (5) This violence, which produces in many different ways, victims, takes on an almost ritualistic character: the civilizing hero invests his victims (the colonized, the slave, the woman, the ecological destruction of the earth, etc.) with the character of being participants in a process of redemptive sacrifice; (6) From the point of view of modernity, the barbarian or primitive is in a state of guilt (for, among other things, opposing the civilizing process). This allows modernity to present itself not only as innocent but also as a force that will emancipate or redeem its victims from their guilt; (7) Given this 'civilizing' and redemptive character of modernity, the suffering and sacrifices (the costs) of modernization imposed on "immature" peoples, slaves, races, the "weaker" sex, et cetera, are inevitable and necessary.[53]

The myth of modernity is laid out by Dussel to confront alternative interpretations. While Horkheimer and Adorno as well as such postmodernist thinkers as Lyotard, Rorty, or Vattimo all propose a critique of reason (a violent, coercive, and genocidal reason), Dussel proposes a critique of Enlightenment's irrational moments as sacrificial myth, not by negating reason, but by asserting the reason of the other—that is, by identifying postcolonial reason as a differential locus of enunciation. The intersection between the idea of a self-centered modernity grounded in its own appropriation of Greco-Roman (classical) legacies and an emerging idea of modernity from the margins (or countermodernity) makes clear that history does not begin in Greece and that different historical beginnings are, at the same time, anchored to diverse loci of enunciation. This simple axiom is, I submit, a fundamental one for and of postsubaltern reason. Finally, Bhabha's project to rename the postmodern from the position of the postcolonial also finds its niche in postsubaltern reason as a differential locus of enunciation.

While Dussel redraws the map of modernity by including in its geography the expansion of the Spanish and Portuguese empire after 1500 and revises the Enlightenment narrative by bringing in the phantom of colonial stories, Bhabha works toward the articulation of enunciative agencies. Dussel's programmatic suggestion that the accession of modernity lies today not necessarily in a process that will transcend modernity from inside (e.g., postmodernity), but rather in a *process of transmodernity* seems to concur with Bhabha's concerns. Let us read Dussel first: "Transmodernity (as a project of political, economic, ecological, erotic, pedagogical and religious liberation) is the co-realization of that which it is impossible for modernity to accomplish by itself: that is, of an incorporative solidarity, which I have called analeptic, between center/periphery, man/woman, different races, different ethnic groups, different classes, civilization/nature, Western culture/Third World cultures, et cetera."[54]

If, as Dussel claims, the overcoming of these dichotomies presupposes that the darker side of modernity (e.g., the colonial periphery) discovers itself as innocent, that very discovery will presuppose asserting loci of enunciation at the borders of colonial expansion and constructing postcolonial reason out of the debris of European modernity and the transformed legacies of world cultures and civilizations.

In my understanding, Bhabha's contribution to the articulation of postcolonial reason lies in the loci of enunciation taking ethical and political precedence over the rearticulation of the enunciated. Therefore, Bhabha must play enactment against epistemology and explore the politics of (enunciative) locations, which he does by introducing Charles Taylor's concept of *minimal rationality* in an effort to bring to the foreground human agency instead of representation: "Minimal rationality, as the activity of articulation, embodied in the language metaphor, alters the subject of culture from an epistemological function to an enunciative practice. If culture as epistemology focuses on function and intention, then culture as enunciation focuses on signification and institutionalization; if the epistemological tends towards a reflection of its empirical referent or object, the enunciative attempts repeatedly to reinscribe and relocate the political claim to cultural priority and hierarchy . . . in the social institution of the signifying activity."[55]

The postcolonial as the signpost of a differential locus of enunciation organizes Bhabha's discourse of countermodernity. These sites of enunciation are not, however, dialectical opposites to the locus of enunciation created by modernity (e.g., modern subject and subjectivity) in the constant invention and reconstruction of the self and of the monotopic concept of reason. They are, instead, places of interventions, interruptions of the self-invention of modernity. Bhabha is responding from the legacies of colonial British India to the same concerns expressed by Dussel from the legacies of colonial Hispanic America. Let us read Bhabha: "I am posing these questions from within the problematic of modernity because of a shift within contemporary critical traditions of postcolonial writings. There is no longer an influential separatist emphasis on simply elaborating an anti-imperialist or black nationalist tradition 'in itself.' There is an attempt to interrupt the Western discourses of modernity through these displacing, interrogative subaltern or postslavery narratives and the critical theoretical perspectives they engender." Furthermore, in the following paragraph: "The power of the postcolonial translation of modernity rests in its *performative, deformative* structure that does not simply revalue the contest of a cultural tradition, or transpose values 'cross-culturally.' "[56]

Bhabha's emphasis on agency over representation is reinforced by his concept *time lag*. In a revealing note in the conclusion to *The Location of Culture*, Bhabha reminds the reader that the term *time lag* was introduced and used in previous chapters and that he sees this concept as an expression that captures the "splitting" of colonial discourse.[57] Time lag becomes, then, a new form of colonial discourse and a new location of postcolonial theorizing. Postcolonial theorizing assumes both the splitting of the colonial subject (of study) and the splitting of postcolonial theorizing (the locus of enunciation). A similar epistemological quarrel is underlined by Norma Alarcón in the context of women's studies — of gender and ethnicity in particular — when she states, "The subject (and object) of knowledge is now a woman, but the inherited view of consciousness has not been questioned at all. As a result, some Anglo-American feminist subjects of consciousness have tended to become a parody of the masculine subject of consciousness, thus revealing their ethnocentric liberal underpinning." [58] The epistemological controversy in postcolonial theorizing is that the split subject of colonial discourse mirrors the split subject of postcolonial theorizing; likewise, women as understanding subjects mirror women as subjects to be understood. Because of this, an epistemological twist is in the making where enunciation as enactment takes precedence over enactment as representation. However, the location of postcolonial theorizing requires a temporal articulation. *Time lag* is for Bhabha the relevant concept to use to explore the decentered epistemology of postcolonial reason. The concept emerges from the intersection of two nonexplicit and disparate theoretical frameworks. One comes from the aftermath of the formal apparatus of enunciation (theorized by Benveniste in the early 1960s) and, independently, from Bakhtin's concept of hybridization and dialogism and — directly — the colonial bent introduced by Gayatri Spivak, who asked the influential question, Can the subaltern speak? The other resonates in Fabian's analysis of the denial of coevalness in colonial discourse.[59] When the denial of coevalness is not cast in terms of comparing cultures or stages of civilization on the basis of a presupposed idea of progress but applied to the locus of enunciation, time lag allows for a denial of enunciative coevalness and, therefore, for a violent denial of freedom, reason, and qualification for political and cultural intervention. It is through such concepts as *the denial of the denial of coevalness* and enunciative *time lag* that the restitution of the intellectual force emanating from colonial legacies could be enacted and the distribution of intellectual labor relocated.[60]

Bhabha's discussion of Foucault's colonial forgetting highlights a complex argument developed throughout *The Location of Culture*. Bhabha's interpretation of Foucault's statement that "there is a certain position in the Western ratio that was constituted in its history and provides a foundation for the relation it can have with all other societies, *even with the society in which it historically appeared*" points toward the fact that, by "disavowing the colonial moment as enunciative present in the historical and epistemological condition of Western modernity," Foucault closes the possibility of interpreting Western ratio in the conflictive dialogue between the West and the colonies. Even more, according to Bhabha, Foucault "disavows precisely the colonial text as the foundation for the relation the Western ratio can have, 'even with the society in which it historically appeared.' " The enunciative present, in other words, is the present of Western time and its locus of enunciation. Colonial loci of enunciation have been dissolved or absorbed by colonial discourse, including the production and distribution of knowledge for their lack of contemporaneity: colonies produced culture, while metropolitan centers produced intellectual discourse interpreting colonial cultural production and reinscribing themselves as the *only* loci of enunciation. Bhabha contributes to relocate — finally — the dialogue between modernity and postmodernity, on the one hand, and colonialism and postcolonial critical discourse and theorizing, on the other: "Reading from the transferential perspective, where the Western ratio returns to itself from the time-lag of the colonial relation, we see how modernity and postmodernity are themselves constituted from the marginal perspective of cultural difference. They encounter themselves contingently at the point at which the internal difference of their own society is reiterated in terms of the difference of the other, the alterity of the postcolonial site." [61]

By extending the concept *time lag* from the subject in psychoanalysis and its fracture between the sign and the symbol to cultural differences under colonialism, Bhabha is clearly underscoring Fanon's locus of enunciation: "He [Fanon] too speaks from the signifying time-lag of cultural difference that I have been attempting to develop as a structure for the representation of subaltern and postcolonial agency." [62] This is not the occasion to comment on *time lag* and its relation to *the representation of the subaltern*. I am more comfortable with time lag and postcolonial agency. In other words, the denial of coevalness that Fabian identified as a strategy by which colonial discourse can undermine other cultures, by locating them in a lower scale in the ascending march of (European) civilization and progress, is being contested (i.e., by denying the denial of coevalness) precisely by postcolonial agencies and postcolonial theorizing.

-      The aftermath of the Enlightenment project that Bhabha critiques in Foucault is also underlined by Paul Gilroy in his critique of Jurgen Habermas and Marshall Berman. Gilroy claims, in opposition to the belief in the unfulfilled promises of modernity, that the history of the African diaspora and, consequently, a reassessment of the role of slavery in the construction of modernity "require a more complete revision of the terms in which the modernity debates have been constructed than any of its academic participants may be willing to concede." The decentered and plural configuration of modern subjectivities and identities embraced by Gilroy runs against Berman's belief in the "intimate unity of the modern self and the modern environment." [63] Bhabha and Gilroy join Dussel in a critique of the construction of modernity in postmodern thinking. What differentiates their postcolonial theorizing is their colonial legacies: Spanish and Latin American for Dussel; African diaspora, French, German, and British Empires for Gilroy; British Empire and the colonization of India for Bhabha.

I conclude by opening up the discussion to emerging domains of subaltern metatheoretical inquiry. I have so far limited the discussion to loci of enunciation and geocultural categories. This is the terrain in which colonial legacies and postcolonial/post-Occidental theories have been mainly discussed in the recent past. Concepts such as *First* and *Third World, West* and *East, margin* and *periphery, Spanish* and *British colonialism,* etc. are all geocultural categories. When I elaborated on what I think is an epistemological breakthrough, I did so in terms of the politics of geocultural location, assuming that one of the motivations of postcolonial/post-Occidental theorizing is the geocultural location of the production and distribution of knowledge. The politics and sensibilities of geocultural location are comparable, in my argument, to the politics and sensibilities of gender, race, or class location. In all these cases, the production of knowledge and the need for theories are no longer driven by an abstract and rational will to tell the truth but also (perhaps mainly) by ethical and political concerns with the structure of domination and of human emancipation. It should be added that, if the production of knowledge was always driven toward human emancipation (as the Renaissance and Enlightenment projects claimed), one should make the qualification that the emancipation that postcolonial theories promote is from the categories of knowledge fabricated and established in Europe, which are part of modernity and partly in complicity with colonial expansion—and, we should add, not only for the emancipation of subjugated people but also for the self-emancipation of those who live and act within the structure of belief of modernity and colonialism, two sides of the same coin. Emancipation *as* liberation means not only the recognition of the subalterns but the erasure of the power structure that maintains hegemony and subalternity.

Thus, we have the important chronological distinction introduced by Sara Suleri that cuts across geocultural categories. By highlighting English India, she is able to bring the colonial and the postcolonial (situations, discourses) under a new light: "If English India represents a discursive field that includes both colonial and postcolonial narratives, it further represents an alternative to the troubled chronology of nationalism in the Indian subcontinent. As long as the concept of nation is interpreted as the colonizer's gift to its erstwhile colony, the unimaginable community produced by colonial encounter can never be sufficiently read."[64] What should retain our attention in this quotation is the fact that the chronological rearticulation of colonial/postcolonial is anchored in the connivance between language and empire. To say *English India* is similar to saying *Hispanic* or *Anglo America,* and the conceptualization of geocultural categories is very much connected to imperial languages.

Furthermore, Suleri brings to the foreground the connections between geocultural categories and gender, sexuality, and the politics and sensibilities of geocultural locations.[65] Suleri's arguments join those of other critics of gender and colonialism such as Trinh Minh-ha and Chandra Mohanty.[66] Their writings contribute very much to redirecting postcolonial theoretical practices toward the encounter with issues raised by women of color as well as with those theorizing borders.[67] From this perspective, Suleri sees two major issues haunting the future of cultural criticism and postcolonial theorizing: one is the realignment of the polarities (East-West, colonizer-colonized, us-them, etc.) in which early postcolonial theorizing was founded; the other is the question of the articulation of gender and the postcolonial condition:

> If the materiality of cultural criticism must now locate its idiom in the productive absence of alterity, it must realign its relation to the figure of gender. The figurative status of gender poses a somewhat uncritical discourse reliant on metaphors of sexuality, or does it merely reify the sorry biologism that dictates traditional decodings of the colonial encounter? Since the "femininity" of the colonized subcontinent has provided Orientalists' narratives with their most prevailing trope for the exoticism of the East, contemporary reading of such texts is obliged to exercise considerable cultural tact in the feminization of its own discourse. In other words, a simple correlation of gender with colonizer and colonized can lead only to interpretive intransigence of a different order, through which an attempt to recognize marginality leads to an opposite replication of the uncrossable distance between margin and center. The taut ambivalence of colonial complicity, however, demands a more nuanced reading of how equally ambivalently gender functions in the tropologies of both colonial and postcolonial narratives.[68]

What Suleri calls *cultural colonial studies* becomes in the hands of Silvia Rivera Cusicanqui and Rossana Barragan, in Bolivia, a network of colonial studies from a postcolonial perspective, a critique of Occidentalism in the Americas from a post-Occidental perspective, and, finally, a powerful academic and political statement recasting *internal colonialism* as a category critical in unraveling the hidden but always present colonial legacies in the Andes, at the crossroads of ethnic and gender studies. The legacies of Spanish colonialism are here at stake as the full-fledged ethic of the conquest (articulated in the debates of Valladolid between Las Casas and Sepulved and, later on, philosophically and theologically articulated in the School of Salamanca), rearticulated during the postindependence period when "les droits de l'homme et du citoyen" contributed to further marginalize women and indigenous people and, more so, indigenous women.[69] While Rossana Barragan has explored in detail the question of infamy and patriarchal hierarchy in building a national state (after 1831) and has showed how a Creole minority established the criminal code as the first founding law of the nation and, from there, installed a locus of judgment to form a minority of first-class citizens and a majority of second- and third-class citizens based on gender and ethnic criteria.[70] Finally, Rivera Cusicanqui has shown the intersections of gender and ethnicity as crucial categories in the articulation of postcolonial internal colonialism in Bolivia.[71] This serves as a particular and compelling way of bringing together internal colonialism and subaltern studies, beyond the local histories of British colonialism in India, and into the deep memories of sixteenth-century Spanish colonialism (early modern period), crossed and rearticulated with the colonial world order of the modern period (British, French) and the recent and emerging U.S. imperialism and the global colonialism enacted by transnational corporations.

Introducing gender and feminism into colonial cultural studies confirms the epistemological breakthrough being enacted by postcolonial/post-Occidental theorizing in at least two different and complementary directions: first, by discovering the complicities between modernity and the violence of reason and by recovering the suppressed secondary qualities from the domain of knowledge and, second, by opening up scholarly work and academic pursuit to the public sphere. The strength of postcolonial theorizing (as well as other theoretical practices transforming knowledge as representation into knowledges as enactment and erasing the subject/object destruction) resides in its capacity for epistemological as well as social and cultural transformation. It is, furthermore, helping redefine and relocate the task of the humanities and the cultures of scholarship in a transnational world; this will take the humanities and the cultures of scholarship beyond the realm of modernity and their complicity with national and imperial states.

Notes

1 See Johannes Fabian, *Time and the Other: How Anthropology Makes Its Objects* (New York: Columbia University Press, 1983); and Walter Mignolo, "Globalizacao, Processos de Civilizacão, Linguas e Culturas," *Centro De Recursos Humanos 22* (1995): 9–30 (an English version was published in Frederic Jameson and M. Miyoshi, eds., *Cultures of Globalization* [Durham, N.C.: Duke University Press, 1998] under the title "Globalization, Civilization Processes, and the Relocation of Languages and Cultures").

2 See, e.g., Anne McClintock, "The Angel of Progress: Pitfalls of the Term 'Post-Colonialism,' " *Social Text* 31/32 (1992): 84–98; R. Radhakrishnan, "Postcoloniality and the Boundaries of Identity," *Callaloo* 16, no. 4 (fall 1993): 750–71; Arif Dirlik, "The Postcolonial Aura: Third World Criticism in the Age of Global Capitalism," *Critical Inquiry* 20, no. 2. (1994): 328–56; and Ella Shohat, "Notes on the Postcolonial" (in this volume).

3 "American Latina," in Jose Carlos Mariátegui, *Textos Basicos: Selección, Pr'ologo y Nota Introductorias de Anibal Quijano* (Mexico: Fondo de Cultura Economica, 1996), 349–78.

4 Fernandez Roberto Retamar, "Nuestra América y Occidente," *Casa de las Americas* 98 (1976).

5   Gyan Prakash, "Subaltern Studies as Postcolonial Criticism," *American Historical Review* 99, no. 5 (1994): 1475–90.

6   Shohat, "Notes on the Postcolonial."

7   See Rodolfo Stavenhagen, "Classes, Colonialism, and Acculturation," *Studies in Comparative International Development* 1, no. 4 (1965): 000–000.

8   See McClintock, "The Angel of Progress"; and Ella Shohat, "Notes on the Post-Colonial," *Social Text* 31/32 (1992): 86–87, 102, respectively.

9   Frederic Jameson, *Postmodernism; or, The Cultural Logic of Late Capitalism* (Durham, N.C.: Duke University Press, 1991).

10 Frederic Jameson, "Third World Literature in the Era of Multinational Capital," *Social Text* 16 (fall 1986): 65–88; and Aijaz Ahmad, "Jameson's Rhetoric of Otherness and the 'National Allegory,' " *Social Text* 17 (fall 1987): 3–25.

11 Dirlik, "The Postcolonial Aura."

12 See Ruth Frankenberg and Lata Mani, "Crosscurrents, Crosstalk: Race, 'Postcoloniality,' and the Politics of Location," *Cultural Studies* 7, no. 2 (1993): 292–310.

13 Cornel West, *The American Evasion of Philosophy: A Genealogy of Pragmatism* (Madison: University of Wisconsin Press, 1989).

14 According to West, "This monumental decentering of Europe produced exemplary intellectual reflections such as the demystifying of European cultural hegemony, the destruction of the Western metaphysical traditions, and the deconstruction of North Atlantic philosophical systems" (Cornel West, *Race Matters* [New York: Vintage, 1993], 9–11).

15 Ibid., 9–11.

16 I am borrowing the distinction between *settler colonies* (e.g., the United States, Australia, New Zealand, etc.) and *deep-settler colonies* (Algeria, Peru, India, etc.) from McClintock (see "The Angel of Progress").

17 West, *The American Evasion of Philosophy*, 4.

18 Dirlik, "The Postcolonial Aura," 329.

19 Leopoldo Zea, *América en la historia* (Mexico: Fondo de Cultura Economica, 1958).

20 Leopoldo Zea, *Discurso desde la marginación y la barbarie* (Barcelona: Anthrops, 1988).

21 See Edmundo O'Gorman, *The Invention of America* (Bloomington: Indiana University Press, 1961); and also Walter D. Mignolo, "Colonial and Postcolonial Discourse: Cultural Critique or Academic Colonialism?" *Latin American Research Review* 28, no. 3 (1993).

22 Jorge Klor de Alva, *Colonial Latin American Review* 1, no. 1 (1992): 3.

23 Darcy Ribeiro, *O processo civilizatório etapas da evolucao socio-cultural* (1968; Petropolis: Editorial Vozes, 1978).

24 Mignolo, "Globalizacao, Processos de Civilizacão, Linguas e Culturas."

25 See Pablo González-Casanova, "Internal Colonialism and National Development," *Studies in Comparative International Development* 1, no. 4 (1965); and Stavenhagen, "Classes, Colonialism, and Acculturation."

26 Silvia Rivera Cusicanqui, "La raiz: Colonizadores y colonizados," in *Violencias encubiertas en Bolivia*, vol. 1, *Cultura y política*, ed. X. Albó et al. (La Paz: CIPCA-Aruwiyiri, 1993), and *Oprimidos pero no vencidos: Luchas del campesinado aymara y qhechwa de bolivia, 1990–1980* (La Paz: CSUTCB, 1984).

27 Xavier Albó, "And from Kataristas to MNRistas? The Surprising and Bold Alliance between Aymaras and Neoliberals in Bolivia," in *Indigenous Peoples and Democracy in Latin America*, ed. D. L. Van Cott (New York: St. Martin's, 1994).

28 See Silvia Rivera Cusicanqui, "Sendas y senderos de la ciencia social andina," *Autodeterminación: Análisis histórico político y teoría social* 10 (1992).

29 Retamar, "Nuestra América y Occidente," 52.

30 Walter Mignolo, "Globalization, Civilizing Processes, and the Relocation of Languages and Cultures," in *Cultures of Globalization Culture,* ed. F. Jameson and M. Miyoshi (Durham: Duke UP, 1998), 37–52.

31 Craig Calhoun, *Critical Social Theory* (New York: Blackwell, 1995), 16.

32 Ibid., 17.

33 Max Horkheimer and Theodor Adorno, *Dialectic of Enlightenment,* trans. John Cumming (New York: Continuum, 1994), esp. 168–208.

34 Calhoun, *Critical Social Theory,* 17.

35 Rodolfo Kusch, *Esbozo de una antropologia filosofica americana* (Buenos Aires: Editorial Castañeda, 1978), 107–14.

36 See John, *Discrepant Dislocations.*

37 Kusch, *Esbozo de una antropologia filosofica americana,* 109.

38 Paul Gilroy, *The Black Atlantic: Modernity and Double Consciousness* (Cambridge, Mass.: Harvard University Press, 1993).

39 See ibid., 58–64.

40 Douglass quoted in ibid., 61.

41 Ibid., 60.

42 Charles Taylor, *Sources of the Self: The Making of Modern Identity* (Cambridge, Mass.: Harvard University Press, 1989), 285–304.

43 Carl E. Pletsch, "The Three Worlds; or, The Division of Social Scientific Labor, circa 1950–1975," *Comparative Study of Society and History* 23, no. 4 (1981): 565–90.

44 On several occasions I have been told that I should not talk about First, Second, and Third Worlds because such entities never existed. I emphasize that I am talking not about the entity, but about a conceptual division of the world, which, as such, existed and still exists, even when the world is no longer so configured. I feel the need to apologize for introducing this note, but at the same time I cannot avoid it.

45 Pletsch, "The Three Worlds," 575.

46 Ibid., 579.

47 Michel Foucault, *L'archéologie du savoir* (Paris: Gallimard, 1969), and *Les mots et les choses: Une archéologie des sciences humaines* (Paris: Gallimard, 1966).

48 See Jameson, *Postmodernism.*

49 See Paul Gilroy, "It Ain't Where You're From, It's Where You're At . . . : The Dialectics of Diasporic Identification," *Third Text* 13 (1990/91): 3–16.

50 Enrique Dussel, "Eurocentrism and Modernity," *Boundary 2* 20, no. 3 (1993): 65.

51 A revealing example of what I am trying to articulate is Norma Alarcón's counterreading of Jean-Luc Nancy's theoretical allocating of meaning. While Nancy allocates meaning to Chicano culture by reading it from the space where ethnicity and language do not interfere with his own discourse (e.g., the total absence of reference to the Maghreb in French language and culture), Alarcón's discourse is a necessary relocation from the space in which ethnicity and language dislocate the production of knowledge and understanding (see Norma Alarcón, "Congugating Subjects: The Heteroglossia of Essence and Resistance," in *Another Tongue: Nation and Ethnicity in the Linguistic Borderland,* ed. A. Artega [Durham, N.C.: Duke University Press, 1994], 125–38; and Jean-Luc Nancy, "Cut Throat Sun," in ibid., 113–24).

52 Homi Bhabha, *The Location of Culture* (New York: Routledge, 1994), 175.

53 Dussel, "Eurocentrism and Modernity," 75.

54 Ibid., 76.

55 Bhabha, *The Location of Culture,* 177. Although Taylor does not elaborate the concept of

minimal rationality in *Sources of the Self,* the book quoted by Dussel, epistemological considerations emerging from colonial trajectories are not the paradigmatic examples of Taylor's arguments.

56 Bhabha, *The Location of Culture,* 241.
57 Ibid., 275, n. 15.
58 Norma Alarcón, "The Theoretical Subject(s) of *This Bridge Called My Back* and Anglo-American Feminism," in *Making Face/Make Soul,* ed. Gloria Anzaldúa (San Francisco: Aunt Lute, 1990), 357.
59 See Fabian, *Time and the Other.*
60 On the denial of the denial of coevalness, see Walter Mignolo, *The Darker Side of the Renaissance* (Ann Arbor: University of Michigan Press, 1995), 249–58, 329–30.
61 Bhabha, *The Location of Culture,* 196. Foucault is quoted on p. 195.
62 Ibid., 236. See also pp. 191–98.
63 Gilroy, *The Black Atlantic,* 46.
64 Sara Suleri, *The Rhetoric of English India* (Chicago: University of Chicago Press, 1992), 3.
65 Ibid. See also Sara Suleri, "Women Skin Deep: Feminism and the Postcolonial Condition," *Critical Inquiry* 18 (1992): 756–69.
66 See Trinh T. Minh-ha, *Women, Native, Other: Writing Postcoloniality and Feminism* (Bloomington: Indiana University Press, 1989); and Chandra Mohanty, "Under Western Eyes: Feminist Scholarship and Colonial Discourse," *Feminist Review* 30 (1988): 61–88.
67 See, e.g., Gloria Anzaldúa, *Borderlands/La frontera: The New Mestiza* (San Francisco: Spinster/Aunt Lute, 1987); José Saldivar, *The Dialectics of Our America* (Durham, N.C.: Duke University Press, 1992); and, on the African diaspora, Gilroy, *The Black Atlantic.*
68 Suleri, *The Rhetoric of English India,* 15.
69 See Silvia Rivera Cusicanqui, "Pro'logo: Los desafios para una demoracia e'tnica en los alnores del tercer milenio," in *Ser mujer ind'igena: Chola o birlocha en la Bolivia postcolonia anos 90,* compilador Silvia Rivera Cusicanqui (La Paz: Ministerio de Desarrollo Humano, 1996), 17–48.
70 Rossana Barragan, "The Spirit of Bolivian Modernity: Citizenship, Infamy, and Patriarchal Hierarchy," *Economic and Political Weekly* 32, no. 30 (1997).
71 Silvia Rivera Cusicanqui, "La nocion de 'derecho' o las paradojas de la modernidad postcolonial: Indigenas y mujeres en Bolivia," *Temas Sociales* 19 (1997).

Borders and Bridges:

Seeking Connections between Things

NGUGI WA THIONGO

I am only too aware that in the past I have been associated with a call for the abolition of English departments. But today I will not be calling for their abolition. It is rather curious: the more I call for the abolition of English departments, the more calls I get for lectures from departments of English! In 1969, I dropped my Christian name James and began receiving invitations from all kinds of Christian organizations, including one from the World Council of Churches.

Although I have spoken of the need to abolish certain things as they are, what I really seek is a way of studying in which we focus on the connections between various phenomena instead of seeing them in isolation from one another. Teaching English literature in India or in Africa ought to be a way of crossing borders. What has been wrong in the colonial context is that the act of interpreting the other culture that is far from us has, instead of clarifying real connections and each culture thereby illuminating the other, ended by making us captives of the foreign culture and alienating us from our own. In calling for abolition, therefore, I am primarily seeking a way to clarify connections between one culture and another, literature and politics, literature and economics, literature and the environment, literature and psychology, between the parts and the whole.

The first novel that I wrote (in 1960) — which was published as my second — had the title *The River Between*. It deals with two communities that live on two ridges that face one another. The two communities have always quarreled over one thing or another from time immemorial. The ancient rivalries are made worse after the coming of Christianity because one of the communities becomes identified with the new religion. Between the two ridges, and so between the two communities, flows the river. The river serves as the boundary between the two communities.

In the situation of the novel, the river may be viewed as a phenomenon that divides the two communities. But surely another way of looking at the river is as a way of uniting the two communities. After all, they both depend on the same river, water that is vital for life. When we think of borders, we think of divisions. But, if a border marks the outer edge of one region, it also marks the beginning of the next region. As the marker of an end, it also functions as the marker of a beginning. Without the end of one region, there can be no beginning of another. Depending on our starting point, the border is both the beginning and the outer edge. Each space is beyond the boundary of the other. The border in between serves as both the inner and the outer of the other. It is thus at once a boundary and a shared space.

The river between is also then the life between. But the key lies in whether the members of the two communities see it as a boundary or as a bridge. The connection is clearly there. But, to perceive it, they would have to educate themselves to see the links that bind them. They need teachers who can point out the links, who can point out that the identity of the river lies in its constant renewal through movement and, therefore, change. The river's function as a link depends on its constant renewal and change. A river that becomes stagnant is, in fact, no longer a river.

One of the inherited traditions of Western education in the last four hundred years is that of putting things in compartments, resulting in an incapacity to see the links that bind various categories. We are trained not to see connections between phenomena, and we become locked in Aristotelian categories. So the East becomes East, and the West becomes West, and never the twain shall meet! But is this really true in a world that ultimately is round? Nothing exemplifies this attitude better than our approach as teachers of literature to questions of art and aesthetics. What has aesthetics to do with the environment? With questions of wealth, power, and values in a society? What does it have to do with the question of poverty in a society? What does it have to do with the question of poverty in Africa, or of wealth in the West, or of Africa in the sixteenth century, or of the Africa of A.D. 2000, of the relations between Africa and the West in the year 2000? Literature, in particular, is often taught as if it had nothing to do with these "other" realms of our being. And you can see this in the current retreat into theory in the contemporary teaching of English. It is a retreat into what I term *modern scholasticism*. You get much argument on whether language has meaning at all. If you look at the 1950s, its literature was one of engagement, of commitment, as in the books of Sartre. Literature became very important, the basis of discussion for many vital issues. In the case of black writers, we had monumental meetings, for example, at Rome in 1956 and in Paris in 1959. All the debates in literature and aesthetics and culture were related to the anticolonial process.

What are the connections between phenomena? We start with human beings acting on the external world and changing it. Human beings as they act on the external world create a social environment. Very obviously, we start with the fact that we have to live, the fact that we have to work in the land in order to produce what we eat. In other words, we have to struggle with the outer elements in order to survive before we can do anything else. Thus, the first expression of a community may be said to be economic, a community in search of the means for its survival and sustenance. A community has different groups and individuals occupying different positions in organizations and in the management of wealth, whether you regard wealth in terms of what we extract from nature or in recent, more complicated forms.

So the first expression of society is a community based on economic relations. But in time it also becomes a community based on power relations. In eking a living from nature, even at the family level, at some point rules develop as to how to go about extracting those means from nature, rules about the division of work, and rules about what we have got from nature. At a more complicated level, the question of power in managing these relations develops — the question of who manages that power and for whom? So the community also becomes one of power relations. The community develops political structures for regulating the alignments in the economic sphere. In doing things in a certain way — sharing language, space, and temporality — the community evolves into one of cultural relations. Whatever we do, whether we are relating to nature or to one another, we develop certain ways of doing certain things, and we develop the means of passing on that knowledge to others.

We acquire not only information but knowledge and attitudes toward that information. We begin to develop structures for transmitting that information and those attitudes. And we therefore develop a community that is one of cultural relations. We develop forms of education, laws, religion, literature, art — in fact, all the intellectual, moral, and ideological forces that furnish an entire community of social relations with its distinctive character in a given historical phase. A culture embodies those values, those aesthetic and moral qualities, that determine their contact with one another and the universe. A community's structure of values is the basis of its world outlook; it is the basis of how its members see themselves and their place in the universe. And these values are the basis of a people's collective and individual image of themselves, their identity.

Note that our perception of who we are as individuals or as a community does affect how we look at our values, our cultural environment, our political environment, and so on. To complete the picture, remember that changes are taking place all the time at all the levels, as with the river in my novel. Profound changes in the economic and political spheres will eventually bring about changes in the cultural realm and hence in people's values and how they see themselves. In other words, what I have been describing is not a mechanical process. How people look at themselves, their values, their images of self, will affect their cultural, political, and economic universe. We should think of the whole as a dialectical process, with all things reacting with one another to produce the ever-changing complexity that goes under the name *society*. This is a somewhat simplified model, but think of the element of historicity, of the fact of change all the time!

For those of us who come from a colonial society, it would be easy to see this process in terms of those who are dominating and those who are dominated. For instance, you can see a situation in which a dominating section controls how the dominated people perceive themselves. We can see how our mental universe is connected with other realms when we put the structure in the context of those dominating and those who are dominated. If those dominating can in fact capture and control the self-perceptions of those who are being controlled, they will never in fact need police. One way of abolishing the police and the army would be the total enslavement of the mind by those who are ruling the economy, the power relations, and the values. If you control the mind of the people, you do not need the police to control them at any other level. You can also see how that control can change not only how people look at one another but how they look at their relationship to those controlling them. You can see this clearly in the colonial mode of education, which for many of us in Africa makes us look to Europe as the basis of everything, as the very center of the universe. We can see it in the way we are brought up to regard the English language as the basis of definition of our own identity. Instead of seeing English as just another language with a lot of books and literature available in it, we see it as a way of defining our own being. We become captives to this language, developing certain attitudes of positive identification with English (or French). We also develop attitudes of distancing ourselves from our own languages, our own cultures. It is not simply a question of acquiring another important tool; the acquisition of that intellectual tool becomes a process of alienating ourselves from our own languages and what they can in fact produce. Another way of looking at it, especially in Africa, is as the creation of an alienated elite. You can see the kind of communal investment that goes into producing these minds when these minds go to get their Ph.D.s from abroad and so on. They never, ever give anything back to the community by putting that knowledge into the languages available to the people themselves. They invest in us, and wherever we go — be it Miranda House, or Nairobi, or Yale — what we produce there we lock it with keys marked *English* or *French* or *Portuguese* or whatever the language of education.

Language is of the utmost importance. If you look at the area of cultural environment, language is the key. It is the means whereby we communicate with one another for the production of wealth. It is also what I have called elsewhere a *collective memory bank* of a people.

I have so far dwelt on one important form of connections, those that account for a society. Another kind of connection that I think is also important is that between one wholeness and another. Far too often, as humans, we see ourselves as distinct from plants and trees and animals. But in another sense we are, in fact, all connected. I can think of myself as Ngugi, Gary, Joseph, or whatever, as someone apart from others who has nothing to do with anyone else. If you study the aesthetics of the western, the cowboy films of America, you can see a deliberate and conscious placement of the individual as the one who defines humanity. The individual who has no connection with anybody else is the one who is victorious over those who are organized. So the single individual is able to overcome notions of organization. He is the anarchic individual whose own strength owes nothing to anyone else. He is often seen as being victorious over institutions, over masses of people.

But, if we look at it, who is this individual, the one who is not connected with anybody else? It should be self-evident that we are all connected to one another through the air we breathe. When we think of the air we breathe, it is recognizably something outside ourselves. If you ask me to talk about my own individual being, I would perhaps talk about my hands or my legs or my hair or the different parts that contribute to my wholeness as a single and individual human being. But, surely, the air I breathe is even more *me* than any of my limbs. If you cut off my finger, I can continue to live, but, if you cut off the air I breathe, I will not last a minute. So, although the air we breathe is a part of the external environment, it is central to my being and to that of all those who, like me, depend on it. We are, accordingly, ultimately all connected. When we think of ourselves as individuals, we see ourselves as completely free from all other individuals. But, even at the level of simple survival, this is just not true. We are, in fact, connected with our entire environment, yet it is the individual who is most often praised. For instance, when we pollute the environment or allow others to pollute it, we are actually polluting our own being. Again, you may think of a factory as being elsewhere and polluting *those* people, but, if you think of it very carefully, you will find that pollution affects our very being. If we are so connected with our natural environment, we have to keep a healthy balance between ourselves and the environment. But, if we are thus connected inextricably with our natural environment, we are even more connected with our social environment. It is that environment, whether one of oppression or nonoppression, equality or inequality, power used for the communal good or against it, that is of vital importance.

I am currently teaching at New York University as professor of comparative literature and performance. Before that, I taught at Yale University. Turning to the question of connections in the context of Western tradition, I recall how a billionaire gave a lot of money to Yale while I was there to promote the "undiluted" study of Western civilization. There was a general feeling that Western civilization was being eroded by the attention being given to postcolonial literatures and the call for multiculturalism. Two years ago, the billionaire withdrew his money because he felt that Yale was not doing what he set out for it to do. If *Western civilization* means the history, culture, literature, and arts associated only with Europe, how do you teach that portion of it that is Renaissance and post-Renaissance without going into the notions of, say, slavery and colonialism? We know that there is no post-Renaissance European economics, history, and culture without colonialism. If you look at history, you will find that all the wars fought between the European powers during the sixteenth, seventeenth, and eighteenth centuries were over colonial trade and colonial possessions. India, as we all know, is central to this, to the emergence of so many European nations. The discovery of so much of the New World had to do with the effort to discover a way to reach the riches of India. And how do you teach about slavery and the slave trade as integral to post-Renaissance Europe without talking about Africa? And, since Africans have been part and parcel of the founding settlements and growth of America, is slavery not integral to American civilization? How can one teach American literature and history and culture without seeing the centrality of Africa in their makeup? If there is any one continuous and unbroken centrality in American culture and life, it is surely the portion contributed by the economic and cultural inputs of the Africans or, shall we say, the African Americans. European and American studies that ignore the centrality of Africa and of coloniality are false.

Again, fostered by English departments, we see a lot of studies and comments on the notion of the *modern* and the *postmodern*. But they ignore what constitutes modernity. If you think of Western modernity in terms of Renaissance or post-Renaissance Europe, that modernity is bound up completely with colonialism. There is no way of extricating it from colonialism, and, in fact, in some cases it is directly reflected in the literature itself.

So the study of African, of Asian, or of Latin American literatures must be seen as part and parcel of teaching literature and culture in the West. The really important thing is to see connections. It is only when we see real connections that we can meaningfully talk about differences, similarities, and identities. So the border, seen as a bridge, is founded on the recognition that no culture is an island unto itself. It has been influenced by other cultures and other histories with which it has come into contract. This recognition is the basis of all the other bridges that we want to build across our various cultural borders. The bridges are already there, in fact. The challenge facing, say, teachers of English literature, of African or of Asian literature, is to recognize and find those bridges and build on them. That is why teaching literatures and teaching languages is a privilege that faces all of us — the challenge to see connections between literature and that wholeness that we call *society,* a wholeness constituted by all that comes under economics, politics, and the environment.

Note

This is the text of the Tenth Krishna Memorial Lecture delivered on 19 February 1996 at Miranda House, University of Delhi.

Notes on the "Post-Colonial"

ELLA SHOHAT

The academic opposition to the Gulf War mobilized a number of familiar terms — *imperialism, neocolonialism, neoimperialism* — in a verbal counterstrike against the new world order. But conspicuously absent from the discussion was the term *postcolonial*, even from speeches made by its otherwise prominent advocates. Given the extraordinary circulation of the term in recent academic conferences, publications, and curricular reformulations, this sudden invisibility was somewhat puzzling. Was this absence sheer coincidence? Or is there something abou the term *postcolonial* that does not lend itself to a geopolitical critique or to a critique of the dominant media's Gulf War macronarratives? When lines drawn in the sand still haunt Third World geographies, it is urgent to ask how we can chart the meaning of the postcolonial. It is from my particular position as an academic Arab-Jew whose cultural topographies are (dis)located in Iraq, Israel/Palestine, and the United States that I explore some of the theoretical and political ambiguities of the postcolonial.

Despite its dizzying multiplicity of positionalities, postcolonial theory has curiously not addressed the politics of location of the very term *postcolonial*. In what follows, I begin an interrogation of the term *postcolonial*, raising questions about its ahistorical and universalizing deployments and its potentially depoliticizing implications. The rising institutional endorsement of the term *postcolonial* and of postcolonial studies as an emergent discipline (evident in MLA job announcements calling for specialization in "postcolonial literature") is fraught with ambiguities. My recent experience as a member of the multicultural international studies committee at one of the CUNY branches illustrates some of these ambiguities. In response to our proposal, the generally conservative members of the college curriculum committee strongly resisted any language invoking issues such as "imperialism and Third Worldist critique," "neocolonialism and resisting cultural practices," and "the geopolitics of cultural exchange." They were visibly relieved, however, at the sight of the word *postcolonial*. Only the diplomatic gesture of relinquishing the terrorizing terms *imperialism* and *neocolonialism* in favor of the pastoral *postcolonial* guaranteed approval.

My intention here is not merely to anatomize the term *postcolonial* semantically but to situate it geographically, historically, and institutionally while raising doubts about its political agency. The question at stake is this: Which perspectives are being advanced in the postcolonial? For what purposes? And with what slippages? In this brief discussion, my point is neither to examine the variety of provocative writings produced under the rubric *postcolonial theory*, nor simply to essentialize the term *postcolonial*, but rather to unfold its slippery political significations, which occasionally escape the clearly oppositional intentions of its theoretical practitioners. Here, I argue for a more limited, historically and theoretically specific usage of the term *postcolonial*, one that situates it in a relational context vis-à-vis other (equally problematic) categories.

The postcolonial did not emerge to fill an empty space in the language of political-cultural analysis. On the contrary, its wide adaptation during the late 1980s was coincident with and dependent on the eclipse of an older paradigm, that of the Third World. The terminological shift indicates the professional prestige and theoretical aura that the issues have acquired, in contrast to the more activist aura once enjoyed by *Third World* within progressive academic circles. Coined in the 1950s in France by analogy to the third estate (the commoners, all those who were neither the nobility nor the clergy), the term *Third World* gained international currency in both academic and political contexts, particularly in reference to anticolonial nationalist movements from the 1950s through the 1970s as well as to the political-economic analysis of dependency theory and world system theory (Andre Gunder Frank, Immanuel Wallerstein, Samir Amin).

The last decade has witnessed a terminological crisis around the concept of the Third World. The three worlds theory is indeed, as many critics have suggested, highly problematic.[1] For one thing, the historical processes of the last three decades offered a number of very complex and politically ambiguous developments. The period of so-called Third World euphoria—a brief moment in which it seemed that First World leftists and Third World guerrillas would walk arm in arm toward global revolution—has given way to the collapse of the Soviet Communist model, the crisis of existing socialisms, the frustration of the hoped-for tricontinental revolution (with Ho Chi Minh, Frantz Fanon, and Che Guevara as talismanic figures), the realization that the wretched of the earth are not unanimously revolutionary (nor necessarily allied with one another), and the recognition that international geopolitics and the global economic system have obliged even socialist regimes to make some kind of peace with transnational capitalism. And, despite the broad patterns of geopolitical hegemony, power relations in the Third World are also dispersed and contradictory. The First World/Third World struggle, furthermore, takes place, not only between nations (India/Pakistan, Iraq/Kuwait), but also within nations, with the constantly changing relations between dominant and subaltern groups, settler and indigenous populations, as well as in a situation marked by waves of postindependence immigrations to First World countries (Britain, France, Germany, and the United States) and to more prosperous Third World countries (the Gulf states). The notion of the three worlds, in short, flattens heterogeneities, masks contradictions, and elides differences.

This crisis in Third World thinking helps explain the current enthusiasm for the term *postcolonial*, a new designation for critical discourses that thematize issues emerging from colonial relations and their aftermath, covering a long historical span (including the present). Dropping the suffix *-ism* from *postcolonialism*, the adjective *postcolonial* is frequently attached to the nouns *theory, space, condition*, and *intellectual*, while it often substitutes for the adjective *Third World* in relation to the noun *intellectual*. The qualifier *Third World*, by contrast, more frequently accompanies the nouns *nations, countries*, and *peoples*. More recently, the *postcolonial* has been transformed into a noun, used in both the singular and the plural (*postcolonials*), designating the subjects of the postcolonial condition.[2] The final consecration of the term came with the erasure of the hyphen. Often buttressed by the theoretically connoted substantive *postcoloniality*, the postcolonial is largely visible in Anglo American academic (cultural) studies in publications of discursive-cultural analyses inflected by poststructuralism.[3]

Echoing *postmodernity, postcoloniality* marks a contemporary state, situation, condition, or epoch.[4] The prefix *post-*, then, aligns postcolonialism with a series of other posts — *poststructuralism, postmodernism, post-Marxism, postfeminism, postdeconstructionism* — all sharing the notion of a movement beyond. Yet, while these posts refer largely to the supercession of outmoded philosophical, aesthetic, and political theories, the postcolonial implies both going beyond anticolonial nationalist theory and a movement beyond a specific point in history, that of colonialism and Third World nationalist struggles. In that sense, the prefix *post-* aligns the postcolonial with another genre of posts — *postwar, post-cold war, postindependence, postrevolution* — all of which underline a passage into a new period and a closure of a certain historical event or age, officially stamped with dates. Although periodizations and the relation between theories of an era and the practices that constitute that era always form contested terrains, it seems to me that the two genres of the post are nonetheless distinct in their referential emphasis, the former on disciplinary advances characteristic of intellectual history, the latter on the strict chronologies of history *tout court.* This unarticulated tension between the philosophical and the historical teleologies in the postcolonial, I would argue, partially underlies some of the conceptual ambiguities of the term.

Since the post in *postcolonial* suggests "after" the demise of colonialism, it is imbued, quite apart from its users' intentions, with an ambiguous spatio-temporality. Spreading from India into Anglo American academic contexts, the postcolonial tends to be associated with Third World countries that gained independence after World War II. However, it also refers to the Third World diasporic circumstances of the last four decades — from forced exile to "voluntary" immigration — within First World metropolises. In some postcolonial texts, such as *The Empire Writes Back,* the authors expand the term *postcolonial* to include all English literary productions by societies affected by colonialism:

> The literatures of African countries, Australia, Bangladesh, Canada, Caribbean countries, India, Malaysia, Malta, New Zealand, Pakistan, Singapore, South Pacific Island countries, and Sri Lanka are all post-colonial literatures. The literature of the USA should also be placed in this category. Perhaps because of its current position of power, and the neo-colonizing role it has played, its post-colonial nature has not been generally recognized. But its relationship with the metropolitan centre as it evolved over the last two centuries has been paradigmatic for post-colonial literature everywhere. What each of these literatures has in common beyond their special and distinctive regional characteristics is that they emerged in their present form out of the experience of colonization and asserted themselves by foregrounding the tension with the imperial power, and by emphasizing their differences from the assumptions of the imperial centre. It is this which makes them distinctively post-colonial.[5]

This problematic formulation collapses very different national-racial formations — the United States, Australia, and Canada, on the one hand, and Nigeria, Jamaica, and India, on the other — as equally postcolonial. Positioning Australia and India, for example, in relation to an imperial center simply because they were both colonies equates the relations of the colonized white settlers to the Europeans at the center with those of the colonized indigenous populations to the Europeans. It also assumes that white settler countries and emerging Third World nations broke away from the center in the same way. Similarly, white Australians and aboriginal Australians are placed in the same periphery, as though they were cohabitants vis-à-vis the center. The critical differences between Europe's genocidal oppression of aboriginals in Australia, indigenous peoples of the Americas, and African diasporic communities *and* Europe's domination of European elites in the colonies are leveled with an easy stroke of the post. The term *postcolonial,* in this sense, masks the white settlers' colonialist-racist policies toward indigenous peoples, not only before independence, but also after the official break from the imperial center, while also de-emphasizing neocolonial global positionings of First World settler states.

I am not suggesting that this expanded use of *postcolonial* is typical or paradigmatic.[6] The phrase *postcolonial society* might equally evoke Third World nation-states after independence. However, the disorienting space of the postcolonial generates odd couplings of the post and particular geographies, blurring the assignment of perspectives. Does the post indicate the perspective and location of the ex-colonized (Algerian), the ex-colonizer (French), the ex-colonial settler (Pied Noir), or the displaced hybrid in First World metropolitans (Algerian in France)? Since the experience of colonialism and imperialism is shared, albeit asymmetrically, by (ex-)colonizer and (ex-)colonized, it becomes an easy move to apply the post also to First World European countries. Since most of the world is now living after the period of colonialism, the postcolonial can easily become a universalizing category that neutralizes significant geopolitical differences between France and Algeria, Britain and Iraq, or the United States and Brazil since they are all living in a postcolonial epoch. This inadvertent effacement of perspectives, I should add, results in a curious ambiguity in scholarly work. While colonial discourse refers to the discourse produced by colonizers in both the colony and the motherland and, at times, to its contemporary discursive manifestations in literature and mass-mediated culture, *postcolonial discourse* does not refer to colonialist discourse after the end of colonialism. Rather, it evokes the contemporary theoretical writings, placed in both the First and the Third Worlds generally on the Left, that attempt to transcend the (presumed) binarisms of Third Worldist militancy.

Apart from its dubious spatiality, the postcolonial renders a problematic temporality. First, the lack of historical specificity in the post leads to a collapsing of diverse chronologies. Colonial settler states, such as those found in the Americas, Australia, New Zealand, and South Africa, gained their independence, for the most part, in the eighteenth and nineteenth centuries. Most countries in Africa and Asia, in contrast, gained independence in the twentieth century, some in the 1930s (Iraq), others in the 1940s (India, Lebanon), and still others in the 1960s (Algeria, Senegal) and the 1970s (Angola, Mozambique), while others have yet to achieve it. When exactly, then, does the postcolonial begin? Which region is privileged in such a beginning? What are the relations between these diverse beginnings? The vague starting point of the postcolonial makes certain differentiations difficult. It equates the early independence won by colonial settler states, in which Europeans formed their new nation-states in non-European territories at the expense of indigenous populations, with that of nation-states whose indigenous populations struggled for independence against Europe but won it, for the most part, with the twentieth-century collapse of European empires.

If one formulates the post in *postcolonial* in relation to Third Worldist nationalist struggles of the 1950s and 1960s, then what time frame would apply for contemporary anticolonial/antiracist struggle carried under the banner of national and racial oppression, for such Palestinian writers as, for example, Sahar Khalifeh and Mahmoud Darwish who write contemporaneously with postcolonial writers? Should one suggest that they are pre-postcolonial? The unified temporality of postcoloniality risks reproducing the colonial discourse of an allochronic other, living in another time, still lagging behind us, the genuine postcolonials. The globalizing gesture of the postcolonial condition, or postcoloniality, downplays multiplicities of location and temporality as well as the possible discursive and political linkages between postcolonial theories and contemporary anticolonial or anti-neocolonial struggles and discourses. In other words, contemporary anticolonial and anti-neocolonial resistant discourses from Central America and the Middle East to Southern Africa and the Philippines cannot be theoretically dismissed as epigons, as a mere repetition of the all-too-familiar discourses of the 1950s and 1960s. Despite their partly shared discourses with Third World nationalism, these contemporary struggles also must be historicized, analyzed in a present-day context, when the nonaligned discourse of revolutions is no longer in the air. Such an approach would transcend the implicit suggestion of a temporal gap between postcolonial and the pre-postcolonial discourses, as exemplified in the mélange of resistant discourses and struggles in the *intifada*.[7] What has to be negotiated, then, is the relation of difference and sameness, rupture and continuity.

Since, on one level, the post signifies "after," it potentially inhibits forceful articulations of what one might call *neocoloniality*. Formal independence for colonized countries has rarely meant the end of First World hegemony. Egypt's formal independence in 1923 did not prevent European, especially British, domination, which provoked the 1952 revolution. Anwar Sadat's opening to the Americans and the Camp David accords in the 1970s were perceived by Arab intellectuals as a reversion to pre-Nasser imperialism, as was Egyptian collaboration with the United States during the Gulf War.[8] The purpose of the Carter Doctrine was partially to protect perennial U.S. oil interests (our oil) in the Gulf, which, with the help of petro-Islamicist regimes, have sought the control of any force that might pose a threat.[9] In Latin America, similarly, formal "Creole" independence did not prevent Monroe Doctrine–style military interventions or Anglo American free-trade hegemony. This process sets the history of Central and South America and the Caribbean apart from the rest of the colonial settler states, for, despite shared historical origins with North America, including the genocide of the indigenous population, the enslavement of Africans, and a multiracial/multiethnic composition, these regions have been subjected to political and economic structural domination on some levels more severe, paradoxically, than that of recently independent Third World countries such as Libya and even India. Not accidentally, Mexican intellectuals and independent labor unions have excoriated the gringostroika of the recent Trade Liberalization Treaty.[10] Formal independence did not obviate the need for Cuban- or Nicaraguan-style revolutions or for the Independista movement in Puerto Rico. The term *revolution*, once popular in the Third World context, specifically assumed a postcolonial moment, initiated by official independence, but whose content had been a suffocating neocolonial hegemony.

The term *postcolonial* carries with it the implication that colonialism is now a matter of the past, undermining colonialism's economic, political, and cultural deformative traces in the present. The postcolonial inadvertently glosses over the fact that, even in the post–cold war era, global hegemony persists in forms other than overt colonial rule. As a signifier of a new historical epoch, when compared with *neocolonialism*, the term *postcolonial* comes equipped with little evocation of contemporary power relations; it lacks a political content that can account for the 1980s- and 1990s-style U.S. militaristic involvements in Granada, Panama, and Kuwait-Iraq and for the symbiotic links between U.S. political and economic interests and those of local elites. In certain contexts, furthermore, racial and national oppressions reflect clear colonial patterns, for example, the oppression of blacks by Anglo-Dutch Europeans in South Africa and in the Americas, the oppression of Palestinians and Middle Eastern Jews by Euro-Israel. The postcolonial leaves no space, finally, for the struggles of aboriginals in Australia and indigenous peoples throughout the Americas, in other words, of Fourth World peoples dominated by both First World multinational corporations and by Third World nation-states.

The hegemonic structures and conceptual frameworks generated over the last five hundred years cannot be vanquished by waving the magical wand of the postcolonial. The 1992 unification of Europe, for example, strengthens cooperation among ex-colonizing countries such as Britain, France, Germany, and Italy against illegal immigration, practicing stricter border patrol against infiltration by diverse Third World peoples: Algerians, Tunisians, Egyptians, Pakistanis, Sri Lankans, Indians, Turks, Senegalese, Malians, and Nigerians. The colonial master narrative, meanwhile, is being triumphantly restaged. Millions of dollars are poured into international events planned for the quincentenary of Columbus's so-called voyages of discovery, climaxing in the Grand Regatta, a fleet of tall ships from forty countries leaving from Spain and arriving in New York Harbor for U.S. Independence Day, the Fourth of July. At the same time, an anticolonial narrative is being performed via the view-from-the-shore projects, the Native American commemorations of annihilated communities throughout the United States and the American continent, and plans for setting up blockades at the arrival of the replicas of Columbus's caravels sailing into U.S. ports. What, then, is the meaning of *postcoloniality* when certain structural conflicts persist? Despite different historical contexts, the conflict between, on the one hand, the Native Americans' claim to their land as sacred and, on the other, communal trust and the Euro-American view of land as alienable property remains structurally the same. How, then, does one negotiate sameness and difference within the framework of a postcolonial whose post emphasizes rupture and deemphasizes sameness?

Contemporary cultures are marked by the tension between the official end of direct colonial rule and its presence and regeneration through hegemonizing neocolonialism within the First World and toward the Third World, often channeled through the nationalist patriarchal elites. The colonial in *postcolonial* tends to be relegated to the past and marked with closure — an implied temporal border that undermines a potential oppositional thrust. For, whatever the philosophical connotations of the post as an ambiguous locus of continuities and discontinuities, its denotation of "after" (the teleological lure of the post) — evokes a celebratory clearing of a conceptual space that on one level conflicts with the notion of neo.[11]

Like the postcolonial, the neocolonial also suggests continuities and discontinuities, but its emphasis is on the new modes and forms of the old colonialist practices, not on a "beyond." Although one can easily imagine the postcolonial traveling into Third World countries (more likely via the Anglo-American academy than via India), the postcolonial has little currency in African, Middle Eastern, and Latin American intellectual circles, except occasionally in the restricted historical sense of the period immediately following the end of colonial rule. Perhaps it is the less intense experience of neocolonialism, accompanied by the strong sense of relatively unthreatened multitudes of cultures, languages, and ethnicities in India, that allowed for the recurrent usage of the prefix *post-* over that of *neo-*. Now that debt-ridden India, where postcolonial discourse has flourished, has had to place itself under the tutelage of the International Monetary Fund, and now that its nonaligned foreign policy is giving way to political and economic cooperation with the United States, one wonders whether the term *neocolonial* will become more pervasive than *postcolonial*.[12]

The postcolonial also forms a critical locus for moving beyond anticolonial nationalist modernizing narratives that inscribe Europe as an object of critique, toward a discursive analysis and historiography addressing decentered multiplicities of power relations (e.g., between colonized women and men or between colonized peasantry and the bourgeoisie). The significance of such intellectual projects stands in ironic contrast to the term *postcolonial* itself, which linguistically reproduces, once again, the centrality of the colonial narrative. The postcolonial implies a narrative of progression in which colonialism remains the central point of reference, in a march of time neatly arranged from the pre to the post, but that leaves ambiguous its relation to new forms of colonialism, that is, neocolonialism.

Considering the term *postcolonial* in relation to such other terms as *neocolonial* and *postindependence* allows for mutual illumination of the concepts.

Although, like *postcolonial, neocolonial* implies a passage, it has the advantage of emphasizing a repetition with difference, a regeneration of colonialism through other means. The term *neocolonialism* usefully designates broad relations of geoeconomic hegemony. When examined in relation to *neocolonialism,* the term *postcolonial* undermines a critique of contemporary colonialist structures of domination, more available through the repetition and revival of the neo. The term *postindependence,* meanwhile, invokes an achieved history of resistance, shifting the analytic focus to the emergent nation-state. In this sense, precisely because it implies a nation-state telos, the term *postindependence* provides expanded analytic space for confronting such explosive issues as religion, ethnicity, patriarchy, gender, and sexual orientation, none of which can be reduced to epiphenomena of colonialism and neocolonialism. Whereas *postcolonial* suggests a distance from colonialism, *postindependence* celebrates the nation-state, but, by attributing power to the nation-state, it also makes Third World regimes accountable.

The operation of simultaneously privileging and distancing the colonial narrative, moving beyond it, structures the "in-between" framework of the postcolonial. This in-betweenness becomes evident through a kind of commutation test. While one can posit the duality between colonizer/colonized and even neocolonizer/neocolonized, it does not make much sense to speak of postcolonizer and postcolonized. *Colonialism* and *neocolonialism* imply both oppression and the possibility of resistance. Transcending such dichotomies, the term *postcolonial* posits no clear domination and calls for no clear opposition. It is this structured ambivalence of the postcolonial, of positing a simultaneously close and distant temporal relation to the colonial, that is appealing in a poststructuralist academic context. It is also this fleeting quality, however, that makes the *postcolonial* an uneasy term for a geopolitical critique of the centralized distribution of power in the world.

Postcolonial theory has dealt most significantly with cultural contradictions, ambiguities, and ambivalences.[13] Through a major shift in emphasis, it accounts for the experiences of displacement of Third World peoples in the metropolitan centers and the cultural syncretisms generated by First/Third Worlds intersections, issues less adequately addressed by Third World nationalist and world systems discourses, more rooted in the categories of political economy. The *beyond* of postcolonial theory, in this sense, seems most meaningful when placed in relation to Third World nationalist discourse. The term *postcolonial* would be more precise, therefore, if articulated as *post-First/Third Worlds theory* or *post-anticolonial critique,* as a movement beyond a relatively binaristic, fixed, and stable mapping of power relations between colonizer/colonized and center/periphery. Such rearticulations suggest a more nuanced discourse, which allows for movement, mobility, and fluidity. Here, the prefix *post-* would make sense less as "after" than as a following, going beyond, and commenting on a certain intellectual movement (Third Worldist anticolonial critique) rather than beyond a certain point in history (colonialism), for here *neocolonialism* would be a less passive form of addressing the situation of neocolonized countries and a politically more active mode of engagement.

Postcolonial theory has formed not only a vibrant space for critical, even resistant scholarship, but also a contested space, particularly since some practitioners of various ethnic studies feel somewhat displaced by the rise of postcolonial studies in North American English departments. If the rising institutional endorsement of the term *postcolonial* is, on the one hand, a success story for the PCs (politically correct), is it not also a partial containment of the POCs (people of color)? Before *poco* becomes the new academic buzzword, it is urgent to address such schisms, specifically in the North American context, where one has the impression that the postcolonial is privileged precisely because it seems safely distant from "the belly of the beast," the United States.[14] The recognition of these cracks and fissures is crucial if ethnic studies and postcolonial studies scholars are to forge more effective institutional alliances.

Having raised these questions about the term *postcolonial*, it remains to address some related concepts and to explore their spatiotemporal implications. The foregrounding of *hybridity* and *syncretism* in postcolonial studies calls attention to the mutual imbrication of "central" and "peripheral" cultures. Hybridity and syncretism allow the negotiation of the multiplicity of identities and subject positionings that result from displacements, immigrations, and exiles without policing the borders of identity along essentialist and originary lines. It is largely diasporic Third World intellectuals in the First World, hybrids themselves, not coincidentally, who elaborate a framework that situates the Third World intellectual within a multiplicity of cultural positionalities and perspectives. Nor is it a coincidence, by the same token, that in Latin America *syncretism* and *hybridity* had already been invoked decades ago by diverse Latin American modernisms, which spoke of neologistic culture, of *creolite*, of *mestizaje*, and of anthropophagy.[15] The culturally syncretic protagonists of the Brazilian modernists of the 1920s, the "heroes without character" coined by Mario de Andrade, might be seen as postcolonial hybrids *avant la lettre*. The cannibalist theories of the Brazilian modernists and their elaborations in the tropicalist movement of the late 1960s and early 1970s simply assumed that New Worlders were culturally mixed, a contentious amalgam of indigenous, African, European, Asian, and Arab identities.

At the same time, the problematic spatiotemporality implicit in the term *postcolonial* has repercussions for the conceptualization of the past in post-(anti)colonial theory. The rupture implicit in the *post-* has been reflected in the relation between past and present in postcolonial discourse, with particular reference to notions of hybridity. At times, the antiessentialist emphasis on hybrid identities comes dangerously close to dismissing all searches for communitarian origins as an archaeological excavation of an idealized, irretrievable past. Yet, on another level, while avoiding any nostalgia for a prelapsarian community or for any unitary and transparent identity predating the Fall, we must also ask whether it is possible to forge a collective resistance without inscribing a communal past. Rap music narratives and video representations that construct resistant invocations of Africa and slavery are a case in point. For communities that have undergone brutal ruptures, now in the process of forging a collective identity, no matter how hybrid that identity has been before, during, and after colonialism, the retrieval and reinscription of a fragmented past becomes a crucial contemporary site for forging a resistant collective identity. A notion of the past might thus be negotiated differently—not as a static fetishized phase to be literally reproduced, but as fragmented sets of narrated memories and experiences on the basis of which to mobilize contemporary communities. A celebration of syncretism and hybridity per se, if not articulated in conjunction with questions of hegemony and neocolonial power relations, runs the risk of appearing to sanctify the fait accompli of colonial violence.

The current metropolitan discursive privileging of palimpsestic syncretisms must also be negotiated vis-à-vis Fourth World peoples. It must account, for example, for the paradoxical situation of the indigenous Kayapo in the Amazon forest, who, on the one hand, use video cameras and thus demonstrate their cultural hybridity and their capacity for mimicry but who, on the other, use mimicry precisely in order to stage the urgency of *preserving* the essential practices and contours of their culture, including their relation to the rain forest and the communal possession of land. The de facto acceptance of hybridity as a product of colonial conquest and postindependence dislocations as well as the recognition of the impossibility of going back to an authentic past do not mean that the politicocultural movements of various racial-ethnic communities should stop researching and recycling their precolonial languages and cultures.[16] Postcolonial theory's celebration of hybridity risks an antiessentialist condescension toward those communities obliged by circumstances to assert, for their very survival, a lost and even irretrievable past. In such cases, the assertion of culture prior to conquest forms part of the fight against continuing forms of annihilation. If the logic of the poststructuralist/postcolonial argument were taken literally, then the Zuni in Mexico and the United States would be censured for their search for the traces of an original culture and the aborigines in Australia criticized for their turn to aboriginal language and culture as part of their own regeneration. The question, in other words, is not whether there is such a thing as an originary homogeneous past, and, if there is, whether it would be possible to return to it, or even whether the past is unjustifiably idealized. Rather, the question is who is mobilizing what in the articulation of the past, deploying what identities, identifications, and representations, and in the name of what political vision and goals.

Negotiating locations, identities, and positionalities in relation to the violence of neocolonialism is crucial if hybridity is not to become a figure for the consecration of hegemony. As a descriptive catchall term, *hybridity* per se fails to discriminate between the diverse modalities of hybridity, for example, forced assimilation, internalized self-rejection, political co-optation, social conformism, cultural mimicry, and creative transcendence. The reversal of biologically and religiously racist tropes—the hybrid, the syncretic—on the one hand, and the reversal of anticolonialist purist notions of identity, on the other, should not obscure the problematic agency of postcolonial hybridity. In such contexts as Latin America, nationhood was officially articulated in hybrid terms, through an integrationist ideology that glossed over institutional and discursive racism. At the same time, hybridity has also been used as part of resistant critique, for example, by the modernist and tropicalist movements in Latin America. As in the term *postcolonial*, the question of location and perspective must be addressed, that is, the differences between hybridities, or, more specifically, hybridities of Europeans and their offshoots around the world, and (ex-)colonized peoples. Furthermore, we must also address the differences among Third World diasporas, for example, between African American hybrids speaking English in the First World and those of Afro-Cubans and Afro-Brazilians speaking Spanish and Portuguese in the Third World.

Like *postcolonial, hybridity* is susceptible to a blurring of perspectives. *Hybridity* must be examined in a nonuniversalizing, differential manner, contextualized within present neocolonial hegemonies. The cultural inquiry generated by the hybridity/syncretism discourse needs relinking to geopolitical macrolevel analysis. It requires articulation with the ubiquity of Anglo-American informational media (CNN, BBC, AP) as well as with events of the magnitude of the Gulf War, with its massive and traumatic transfers of populations. The collapse of Second World socialism, it should be pointed out, has not altered neocolonial policies and, on some levels, has generated increased anxiety among such Third World communities as the Palestinians and South African blacks concerning their struggle for independence without a Second World counterbalance. The circulation of *postcolonial* as a theoretical frame tends to suggest a supersession of *neocolonialism* and *Third World* and *Fourth World* as unfashionable, even irrelevant categories. Yet, with all its problems, the term *Third World* still retains heuristic value as a convenient label for the imperialized formations, including those within the First World. The term *Third World* is most meaningful in broad politicoeconomic terms and becomes blurred when one addresses the differently modulated politics in the realm of culture, the overlapping contradictory spaces of intermingling identities. The concept *Third World* is schematically productive if it is placed under erasure, as it were, seen as provisional and ultimately inadequate.

At this point in time, replacing the term *Third World* with *postcolonial* is a liability. Despite differences and contradictions among and within Third World countries, the term *Third World* contains a common project of (linked) resistances to neocolonialisms. Within the North American context, more specifically, it has become a term of empowerment for intercommunal coalitions of various peoples of color.[17] Perhaps, it is this sense of a common project around which to mobilize that is missing from post(anti)colonial discussions. If the terms *postcolonial* and *postindependence* stress, in different ways, a rupture in relation to colonialism and *neocolonial* emphasizes continuities, *Third World* usefully evokes structural commonalities of struggles. The invocation of the Third World implies a belief that the shared history of neocolonialism and internal racism forms sufficient common ground for alliances among such diverse peoples. If one does not believe or envision such commonalities, then, indeed, the term *Third World* should be discarded. It is this difference of alliance and mobilization between the concepts *Third World* and *postcolonial* that suggests a relational usage of the terms. My assertion of the political relevance of such categories as *neocolonialism* and even that of the more problematic *Third* and *Fourth World peoples* is meant not to suggest a submission to intellectual inertia, but to point to a need to deploy all the concepts in differential and contingent manners.

In sum, the concept *postcolonial* must be interrogated and contextualized historically, geopolitically, and culturally. My argument is not necessarily that one conceptual frame is wrong and the other right but that each frame illuminates only partial aspects of systemic modes of domination, of overlapping collective identities, and of contemporary global relations. Each addresses specific and even contradictory dynamics between and within different world zones. There is a need for more flexible relations among the various conceptual frameworks — a mobile set of grids, a diverse set of disciplinary as well as cultural-geopolitical lenses — adequate to these complexities. Flexible yet critical usage that can address the politics of location is important, not only for pointing out historical and geographic contradictions and differences, but also for reaffirming historical and geographic links, structural analogies, and openings for agency and resistance.

Notes

1   See, e.g., Aijaz Ahmad, "Jameson's Rhetoric of Otherness and the 'National Allegory,'" *Social Text* 17 (fall 1987): 3–25; Arjun Appadurai, "Disjuncture and Difference in the Global Cultural Economy," *Public Culture* 2, no. 2 (1990): 1–24; and Chandra Talpade Mohanty, "Cartographies of Struggle: Third World Women and the Politics of Feminism," in *Third World Women and the Politics of Feminism*, ed. Chandra Talpade Mohanty, Ann Russo, and Lourdes Torres (Bloomington: Indiana University Press, 1991).

2   Does that condition echo the language of existentialism, or is it the echo of postmodernism?

3   The relations between *postcolonial, postcoloniality,* and *postcolonialism* have yet to be addressed more rigorously.

4   For a reading of the relations between postmodernism and postcolonialism, see Kwame Anthony Appiah, "Is the Post- in Postmodernism the Post- in Postcolonial?" *Critical Inquiry* 17 (winter 1991): 336–57.

5   Bill Ashcroft, Gareth Griffiths, and Helen Tiffin, eds., *The Empire Writes Back: Theory and Practice in Post-Colonial Literatures* (London: Routledge, 1989), 2.

6   For a radical formulation of the resistant postcolonial, see Gayatri Chakravorty Spivak, "Poststructuralism, Marginality, Postcoloniality, and Value," in *Literary Theory Today,* ed. Peter Collier and Helga Geyer-Ryan (London: Polity, 1990).

7   Read, e.g., Zachary Lockman and Joel Benin, eds., *Intifada: The Palestinian Uprising against Israeli Occupation* (Boston: South End, 1989), specifically Edward W. Said, "Intifada and Independence," 5–22; and Edward W. Said, *After the Last Sky* (Boston: Pantheon, 1985).

8   This perspective explains the harsh repression of movements in opposition to the alliance between the United States and Egypt during the war. In fact, the Camp David treaty is intimately linked to the open door economic policy with its dismantling of the Egyptian public sector. Referred to as the shadow government of Egypt, USAID is partly responsible for the positions that the Egyptian and most Arab governments took during the Gulf War.

9   The rigid imposition of Islamic law in Saudi Arabia is linked to efforts to mask the regime's antiregional collaboration with imperial interests.

10 *Gringostroika* is the coinage of Mexican multimedia artist Guillermo Gómez-Peña.

11 For discussions of the *post-,* see, e.g., Robert Young, "Poststructuralism: The End of Theory," *Oxford Literary Review* 5, nos. 1–2 (1982); R. Radhakrishnan, "The Postmodern Event and the End of Logocentrism," *Boundary 2* 12, no. 1 (fall 1983); and Geoffrey Bennington, "Postal Politics and the Institution of the Nation," in *Nation and Narration,* ed. Homi K. Bhabha (London: Routledge, 1990).

12 As these notes on the postcolonial were on their way to print, a relevant article appeared: Praful Bidwai, "India's Passage to Washington," *Nation,* 20 January 1992.

13 See, e.g., Homi K. Bhabha, "The Commitment to Theory," in *Questions of Third Cinema,* ed. Jim Pines and Paul Willemen (London: British Film Institute, 1989); and Trinh T. Minh-ha, *Woman, Native, Other* (Bloomington: Indiana University Press, 1989).

14 The replacement of *Third World* by *postcolonial* is ambiguous, especially when poststructuralist/postcolonial theories are confidently deployed with little understanding of the historical-material legacy of colonialism, neocolonialism, racism, and anticolonial resistance. These slippages have contributed to facile dismissals of Frantz Fanon's formulations as vulgar.

15 On the Brazilian modernists and the concept *anthropophagy,* see Robert Stam, *Subversive Pleasures: Bakhtin, Cultural Criticism, and Film* (Baltimore: Johns Hopkins University Press, 1989).

16 For another critical consideration of hybridity and memory, see Manthia Diawara, "The Nature of Mother in Dreaming Rivers," *Third Text* 13 (winter 1990/91): 73–84.

17 Aijaz Ahmad (" 'Third World Literature' and the Nationalist Ideology," *Journal of Arts and Ideas,* nos. 17–18 [June 1989]: 117–36) offers an important critique of the usages of *Third World* in the U.S. academy. Unfortunately, he ignores the crucial issue of empowerment taking place under the rubric *Third World* among diverse peoples of color in North American intellectual and academic communities.

DetermiNation: Postcolonialism, Poststructuralism, and the Problem of Ideology

NEIL LARSEN

What are the boundaries of postcolonial studies? And what are its theoretical and political dimensions? However one eventually answers these questions, at least one thing strikes me as certain: the questioner will have to consider very carefully what Aijaz Ahmad has had to say on the matter or be reduced either to intellectual irrelevance, to intellectual dishonesty, or to both. The essays constituting Ahmad's 1992 volume *In Theory*, including his already widely cited criticisms of Fredric Jameson's theory of Third World literature as national allegory, should, if nothing else, render the routine and unself-critical usage of such terms as *postcolonial, Third World*, etc. an embarrassment.[1] While in no sense denying the basic legitimacy and importance of studying the literature and culture of societies with a history of colonization, Ahmad has, to my mind, made it incontrovertibly clear that vital political questions already intrude as soon as one seeks to generalize these societies, or their literatures or cultures, under such categorical or abstract headings as *Third World, postcolonial*, etc. Principal among these is the question of *class*. As an "ideology of already constituted states" (p. 292), "three worlds" theory deemphasizes, even to the point of suppressing the reality of, class division and antagonism within social formations linked by their common subjugation within the global capitalist or imperialist system. Against the historical evidence that unfailingly discloses the complicity of these classes in reproducing the system's inequalities and brutalities, the emergent national bourgeoisie of the decolonized world are, in effect, vouchsafed by three worlds theory as the revolutionary opposition to imperialism. Third Worldism inflicts such a class blindness even on Marxists such as Fredric Jameson, who would scarcely allow themselves to lose sight of class division when assessing their own metropolitan social milieus. The category *postcolonial*, with its privileging of (de)colonization and the relation of colonizer to colonized as unifying factors qua a literary or cultural corpus, presents a similar risk, although here the overarching unity of colonialism or imperialism as *system* is at least logically entailed.

But the act of categorization prompts the class question in another sense as well: namely, vis-à-vis the *practitioner* of Third World or postcolonial studies. Ahmad here points with the utmost candor at the fact staring post-colonialism in the face, although rarely taken very seriously: that the category *Third World* or *postcolonial literature* is virtually a product of metropolitan or First World institutions. It is, as Ahmad puts it, in the metropolitan university or publishing house that a work of literature is "first designated a Third World text" (p. 45). And, in one of the more provocative essays of *In Theory* ("Languages of Class, Ideologies of Immigration"), Ahmad sketches a social history of postcolonial studies as a product of the increasing, although not un-complicated, integration of intellectuals from Asia, Africa, and Latin America into the North American and West European intellectual and academic estab-lishment. Despite the latent cultural chauvinism of the metropolitan univer-sity — or perhaps as a defensive response to it — there "arises" within it "a small academic elite" of immigrants "which knows it will not return, joins the fac-ulty . . . , frequents the circuits of conferences and the university presses, and develops, often with the greatest degree of personal innocence and missionary zeal, quite considerable stakes in overvalorizing what has already been desig-nated as 'Third World Literature' " (p. 85).

Ahmad, that is, has forcibly put the question to postcolonial studies of its possible service as an *ideology* in which particular class interests — those of the postcolonial national bourgeoisie, of an intellectual petty bourgeoisie en-sconced in metropolitan institutions, and, although perhaps in a less direct way, those of imperialism itself — may find ways to represent themselves as univer-sal and disinterested. While the question of postcolonialism and ideology in itself neither obviates the lateral questions of boundaries (i.e., what is the *object* of postcolonial studies?) or of the *method(s)* that such studies ought to utilize, it is clear that the effect of ignoring or suppressing it would only be to aid, even if unwittingly, in the reproduction of this (putative) ideology itself.

What makes a consideration of Ahmad's critique of postcolonialism even more compelling is the fact that he locates poststructuralism squarely within its ideological field.[2] Here, he confronts directly what must be one of the cru-cial issues in any critical or theoretical discussion of postcolonialism, namely, its demonstrable affinities for a philosophy that has declared itself the enemy of all notions of identity and fixed meaning, indeed — in its latest, postmod-ern strain — of any tendency for thought to ground itself in universal principles of whatever sort. This is not to suggest that all those who work in the area of postcolonialism necessarily adhere to such a philosophy. But the convergence here is surely more than an accidental one, and those who might be tempted to explain it as simply a mimicry of the field's more celebrated figures — Gayatri

Spivak, let us say, or Edward Said — would still have to account for this mimicry itself since there are other, and anything but poststructuralist, models to choose from: a Fanon, or a C. L. R. James, for example, or, among more contemporary figures, a Roberto Schwarz. As someone with a regional concentration on Latin America and the Caribbean, I can attest that even a gross familiarity with Derrida or Foucault, much less with Spivak or Said, is in no way a prerequisite for the general belief in what we might term the *incommensurability* of colonizer and colonized, of center and margin, North and South, First and Third Worlds, etc. I think that it is safe to say that broad variations of such a belief dominate the would-be cutting edge of postcolonial theory among Latin Americanists: witness the work of intellectuals otherwise as diverse as Roberto Fernández Retamar, Néstor García Canclini, Enrique Dussel, Mary Louise Pratt, Walter Mignolo, Rolena Adorno, Roberto González Echevarría, Antonio Benítez Rojo, and many others.

Ahmad proposes a historical explanation for this ideological affinity, centering on the decline of the Marxist wing of the anti-imperialist movement after the ascendant period punctuated by the Algerian and Vietnamese Revolutions: "When the degeneration of the Iranian state into clerical fascism became unmistakable, the last remaining illusion of Third Worldist cultural nationalism finally had to be abandoned. What, then, to replace it with? Socialism had already been renounced as the determinate name of imperialism's negation. Nationalism — the whole of it — also now went. This is the redoubled vacuum which, in the radicalized version of metropolitan literary theory, poststructuralism is now to fill" (p. 34). The insight expressed here — that of the redoubled vacuum — is, I think, crucial to a theoretical grasp of all contemporary cultural and intellectual developments, whether postcolonial or metropolitan. It is this insight that underlies Ahmad's sustained critique of Said's *Orientalism,* and of Saidian critical thought in general, and renders it, at least to my mind, essentially irrefutable. Observing how *Orientalism* effectively serves the metropolitan and postcolonial radical intelligentsia as the bridge between cultural nationalism and poststructuralist antinationalism, Ahmad connects the eclectic, self-divided quality of the work, its mythologizing fixation on that very West, the Orientalist myth-making of which it seeks to debunk, to what is in effect Said's captivity within a double bind of both antinationalism and post-Marxism.

But, as powerful as it is, I think that this historical insight into the evident ideological convergence of postcolonialism and poststructuralism is nevertheless a limited one. I see it as the starting point for an ideology critique that still faces the question of how and why, given the historical reality of the redoubled vacuum, it is poststructuralism in particular that rushes in to fill it. Ahmad explains this ideological shift as essentially a consequence of what poststructuralism is *not.* Since it is axiomatic that poststructuralism must pronounce against all principles of identity, totality, and universality, then, clearly enough, it will also pronounce against both nationalism and Marxism. What interests me, however, and what I mean to analyze in what follows, is how the poststructuralist strain of postcolonial theory discloses in the very course of its own conceptual procedures — that is, *immanently* — the material, historical determination exerted by the redoubled vacuum. I thus appeal to Marx's (and Engels's) theory of ideology, not merely as the false universalization of particular class interests (although this is an essential aspect of the theory as a whole), but as a false or inverted consciousness of the historical reality that, on another, more subjective plane, it desires simply to evade. To use Roberto Schwarz's marvelously succinct phrase (worth a thousand Althusserianisms), ideology is thus grasped as a "necessary illusion well grounded in appearances."[3] As such a necessary illusion, that is, as reflecting, in its own conceptual immanence, the redoubled vacuum, it seems to me that post(structuralist)colonialism reveals a more contradictory face than is suggested in Ahmad's exposé. I hasten to add that I share Ahmad's view of poststructuralism as ultimately "repressive and bourgeois" (p. 36). But what makes it truly pernicious in this sense — what makes it *ideological* rather than merely a doctrinal curiosity — is its apparent *correspondence* to an objective circumstance that it does not falsify or invert ab initio, but only as its final conceptual move. To cite, somewhat against the grain, Lenin's expression, postcolonialism takes "one step forward" so as to take "two steps back."

Before proceeding, however, I should clarify that to undertake such an ideology critique of postcolonialism is not to imply that theories of ideology are themselves necessarily unknown or extraneous to postcolonialism itself. It is sufficient to cite Spivak's now virtually canonical essay "Can the Subaltern Speak?" to refute any such implication.[4] Although the essay itself slightly predated the subsequent institutionalization of postcolonial studies, it continues to supply a forceful argument for adopting the postcolonial standpoint of the Third World subaltern as itself a site from which to undertake the critique of the most deep-seated ideologies of the European/colonizing subject. Indeed, it is the poststructuralist, antirepresentationalist politics of Foucault, Deleuze, and Guattari at which Spivak directs the initial brunt of her postcolonial ideology critique. This critique then leads her back to the Marx of the *18 Brumaire,* a text from which Spivak claims to draw a conceptual nuance with which to frame a critical standpoint as wary of naively representationalist epistemologies as it is of the naively spontaneist, and profoundly ideological claims of radical poststructuralist intellectuals to have dispensed with a *politics* of representation *tout court.*

To come to terms with "Can the Subaltern Speak?" would require that one do full justice to its painstaking if often rather refractory arguments, and that clearly cannot be the work of the present discussion. But, at the risk of overstatement, I would venture the observation that, notwithstanding the justice of its claims against the efforts of Foucault et al. to elide the contradictory relation of interest and desire, an elision abetted indeed by the latter's failure to consider its implications for the Third World, "Can the Subaltern Speak?" nevertheless returns, in the end, to the very same theoretical — and, as I hope to show, ideological — ground from which Foucault and Deleuze themselves set forth on their misguided quest for a politics without representation.

The missing link here is clearly Althusser, whose own deeply problematic, if frequently brandished, theory of ideology as an unconscious, presubjective mechanism of subject formation — what I have elsewhere termed its a priori and dogmatic "ban on consciousness" — informs Spivak's own formulations (see, e.g., her characterization of ideology as "subject-formations that micrologically and often erratically operate the interests that congeal the macrologies [of 'exploitation in economics' and 'domination in geopolitics']") and lends its characteristically tortured style of Marxological exegesis to Spivak's reading of the *Brumaire.*[5] Having posited ideology, or the famed ideological state apparatuses (ISAs), as a structure unavailable to consciousness, Althusser had to resort to philosophical subterfuges screened by grandiose invocations of the class struggle when pressed to explain how, then, one could ever hope or pretend to alter them. Spivak, for whom the nonspeaking, non-self-representing subaltern is finally to supply the Archimedean point from which the unfathomable rupture of the imperialist social text becomes theoretically possible, gives the initial impression of having sidestepped this problem. But thinking so hinges on an ability to credit the idea of a transrepresentational, transconscious subject of history that would have to make its entrance from the "other" side of the international division of labor in exactly the same way that Althusser's structurally unthinkable subject of class struggle is required to emerge full grown from the Jovian head of the unconscious. In the end, at least to my thinking, for all its genuine efforts to find the postcolonial locus from which to evade both ideology and consciousness/representation, "Can the Subaltern Speak?" walks backward into the core ideologeme of the colonial as the incommensurable that, as we shall see, governs the thinking of Bhabha and of other thinkers in every other respect Spivak's inferiors.

But, to demonstrate more concretely what I mean here by an *immanent* critique of postcolonialist ideology, I examine briefly the work of Homi K. Bhabha, in particular two essays, "Signs Taken for Wonders" and "DissemiNation."[6] I select these not because they can in any sense claim to initiate the postcolonial/poststructuralist convergence, or because they have necessarily provided theoretical models for other postcolonial critics and theorists, but rather because of their conceptual range and complexity. Such complexity often crosses the line into the willful obscurantism of Derridean jargon, making of Bhabha perhaps the less than ideal exhibit here. But it is also a sign of Bhabha's high degree of theoretical self-consciousness, of the fact that he remains aware of the many possible objections to what he is proposing and attempts to fend off such moves by introducing ever-subtler conceptual distinctions and nuances. In Bhabha, we thus have a sort of high-resolution moving picture of postcolonialist ideology in its immanent state.

In "Signs," Bhabha begins by stating what has become one of the standard aperçus of postcolonial theory, that it is the colonial relation as such — here the English colonization of India — that first elicits in the colonizing power the need for a symbolic image of itself as a stable, continuous *national* identity.[7] In "Signs," it is the "English book" that typifies this process of reverse symbolization: "As a signifier of authority the English book acquires its meaning *after* the traumatic scenario of colonial difference, cultural or racial, returns the eye of power to some prior, archaic image of identity. Paradoxically, however, such an image can neither be 'original' — by virtue of the act of repetition that constructs it — nor 'identical' — by virtue of the difference that defines it. Consequently, the colonial presence is always ambivalent, split between its appearance as original and authoritative and its articulation as repetition and difference" (pp. 168–69).

Ambivalence, here, becomes Bhabha's own substitute locution for the orthodox Derridean concept of prior displacement (*Entstellung*), or the *double inscription,* as formulated in "DissemiNation," a text to which Bhabha will repeatedly refer back. In bringing such a concept to bear on the colonial, however, Bhabha claims, not merely to be borrowing a conveniently descriptive terminology, but rather to have *discovered in the colonial relation itself* what is, as it were, a worldly and secular instance of *Entstellung* — an instance that, therefore, only Derridean or poststructuralist theory could adequately capture and convey. "It is this ambivalence that makes the boundaries of the colonial 'positionality' — the division of self/other — and the question of colonial power — the differentiation of colonizer/colonized — different from both the Hegelian master/slave dialectic or the phenomenological projection of Otherness" ("Signs," 169).

But here a problem arises. If the ambivalence of the colonial presence is, like Derrida's double inscription, the enabling condition for any possible act of meaning or placement (*Darstellung*), does this not confer on the colonial presence an a priori, transcendental necessity that, as worldly reality, it patently does not possess? Must we, in fact, be always already colonizer or colonized? Derrida might be content to have it so, but, for Bhabha, this seems an unacceptable conclusion. To the theorem of ambivalence, therefore, must be added a corollary: that of the possibility of *resisting* the ambivalent presence of the colonial by virtue of an effect of this ambivalence itself, an effect that Bhabha terms *hybridity.* It turns out that colonial power or domination can be maintained only through a process of disavowing its primordial *différance.* Such a power relies on rules of recognition and discriminatory identities by means of which this disavowal is enforced: "I am English; you are Indian." To be English is to be not-Indian, and vice versa. But what of the Indian who *reads* or even *rewrites* the English book, as in Bhabha's example of a group of Indian converts to Christianity who, to the horror of their English proselytizers, demand an "Indianized gospel"? (see "Signs," 177–83). Here, all at once, the discriminatory identities become crossed, the rules of recognition break down, and we are presented with a *hybrid*. And it is *then*, through the proliferation of such hybridity, that a "strategic reversal of the process of domination through disavowal" (p. 173) becomes possible. By exposing the originating ambivalence of colonial domination, hybridity "enables a form of *subversion* . . . that turns the discursive conditions of dominance into the grounds of intervention" (ibid.). Through hybridity, "other 'denied' knowledges [note the strategic entry of Foucault here] enter upon the dominant discourse and *estrange* the basis of its authority" (p. 175). "When the words of the master become the site of hybridity . . . then we may not only read between the lines, but even seek to *change* the often coercive reality that they so lucidly contain" (p. 181; my emphasis throughout).

It will not, I think, have escaped the attention of the careful reader how the danger of circularity creeps into the reasoning here: the colonial presence, it would appear, is to be resisted, subverted, estranged, and even, perhaps, changed entirely through a practice of exposing it for what it really is and always was. Colonialism exposed is colonialism overcome; its doing becomes its undoing. After all, what is the hybrid but an unsuspected reflection, or return, of ambivalence? Are these not, in actuality, synonymous terms, whose only difference lies in the fact that an act of disavowal, a veil rather than a transparency, has been, conveniently or inconveniently, placed between them?

These are questions that bear in important ways on the larger one of postcolonialist ideology, but, for the moment, I postpone that discussion and attempt a more generalized and abstract characterization of what Bhabha — and, I would suggest, a good deal of postcolonialist theory — is seeking to put forward here. There are, on analysis, two quite distinct and, it would seem, *logically* unrelated truth claims being advanced in "Signs." The first is that, although the relation of colonizer to colonized is manifestly unequal and transitive, it does not refer us back to some original equality or unity of terms but rather *hints* at a *primitive disunity*, an originating *incommensurability* as itself the prior condition of all existing relations of identity, including those internal to the nation itself as the supposed site of colonial power and authority. The first truth claim, that is, pertains to the question of the *ground* of the colonial relation. The second truth being claimed here, however, pertains to quite a different question — that of an emancipatory, anticolonial *agency*. According to "Signs," such agency resides in the spontaneous power of the *colonized* to make *visible* or *apparent* this same primitive disunity. Exposure of the ground is proposed as itself tantamount to, or at the very least as enabling, the undoing of its oppressive effects.

Thinking as a Marxist or even simply as a materialist, one's first instinct here is to reject the second of these truth claims as blatantly idealist. And such it surely is. Are we to believe that the mere act of turning the tables on a *discursive* authority will really liberate anyone from the coercive reality that stands behind it? All the many, excellent Marxist critics of poststructuralism, from Perry Anderson to Eagleton, Dews, Bhaskar, Meiksins Wood, and others, might be summoned here to good purpose.[8] But, to get at the ideological aspect of the postcolonialism/poststructuralism convergence here at its deepest level, one must, as I see it, look not only to the transparent fantasmagoria of its second proposition but to the tacit belief, clearly latent in "Signs," that the second proposition is *directly implied* in the first—that the ruptured ground *already*, somehow, in disclosing its own truth, works its own demise. We have just now remarked the fallacy involved in such reasoning. The crucial point qua ideology is that *it is this fallacy itself,* this peculiar circularity whereby *ambivalence* describes both the hidden *truth* of the colonial presence and—as the hybrid—the *power* to abolish it, that reflects the historical conjuncture described by Ahmad as the "redoubled vacuum." To try to spell this out more concretely, what I am suggesting is that the recourse of postcolonialist/poststructuralist theory to the first proposition—Bhabha's *ambivalence,* or what I have termed the *primitive disunity of identity relations*—reflects both the generalized, historical crisis of the cultural nationalism of the "Bandung era" set forth by Ahmad and the desire to move beyond it. The governing impulse of postcolonialism, to this extent, is clearly one of hostility to national*ism,* in implicit recognition of its betrayal of those who once saw in it the emancipatory alternative to colonialism and imperialism. Here, the postcolonial consciousness takes its one step forward.

But what should be the next step—namely, the *class* critique of Third Worldist cultural nationalism, leading to the principled and unambivalent repudiation of the postcolonial national bourgeoisie (even when self-proclaimed socialists) as either as leaders or allies in the struggle against imperialism—typically remains deferred.[9] Why? Clearly, a major factor here, and one to which Ahmad does not, perhaps, give quite its due, is the simultaneous and already well-advanced crisis of actually existing socialism itself, as marked, especially for postcolonial and Third World(ist) intellectuals, by the increasingly counter-revolutionary direction taken in China after the eventual defeat of the left-wing protagonists of the so-called Cultural Revolution in the early 1970s—what I have elsewhere referred to as the *ideological degeneration of class struggles.*[10] If, as Ahmad puts it, "socialism had already been renounced" by the apostates of cultural nationalism, this plainly reactionary renunciation was still not entirely without its objective historical basis. And no less of a factor in this deferral, to be sure, is the typically petty bourgeois origin and metropolitan location of the postcolonial intelligentsia itself as well as of its metropolitan sympathizers. With labor in general retreat, this intelligentsia, like others, knows with instinctive precision how far it can go before its own material interests become endangered. It is just here that Ahmad's sociological critique of the postcolonial intellectual comes most forcefully into play — as an explanation not so much of what this intellectual thinks as of what, for him or her, is unthinkable.[11]

Acknowledging the disunity of the nation(al) as ground of radical political identity and solidarity, but hesitant before the *unity of class* as the historically necessary alternative, the postcolonial consciousness then takes its two steps back into the second proposition, or the fantasmagoria of ambivalence as agency. To suppose, however, that poststructuralist doctrine somehow provokes or makes possible this move is, itself, to stand things on their heads. Poststructuralism's ideological role here is rather to furnish the postcolonial consciousness with the concepts it needs to, in effect, rethink the oppressive reality of the redoubled vacuum as the mock liberation of the double inscription — that is, in so many words, simply to equate the *historical crisis* of cultural nationalism with the fait accompli of its transcendence.

But this grows too abstract. Let us look again to Homi Bhabha, in "DissemiNation" this time, to see how this particular ideological process unfolds. Bhabha's argument here, reduced to its basic propositions, is roughly as follows. *First*, the nation, whatever may be its objective, sociohistorical determination, takes shape in the consciousness of its "citizens" as a discourse, even a narrative. Bhabha speaks of the "cultural constitution of nationness as a form of social and textual affiliation" (p. 292). (The casual conjunction of *social* and *textual*, implying equal ontological weight, is characteristic of the reasoning here.) *Second*, as this narrative construction, the nation exhibits a "disjuncture" or split "between the continuist, accumulative temporality of the pedagogical, and the repetitious, recursive strategy of the performative." (297) That is, as something narrat*ed* to its subjects — as pedagogical object — the nation remains constant and self-identical through a continuous, empty time, punctuating this time itself as both its origin and its telos. But, as an active process of narrat*ing*, the nation enters a different time, that of the subjective and performative — since, after all, the people must retell or perform the story of the nation for its affiliating powers to function. Bhabha's *third* proposition, finally, is that, within this disjunctive temporality, the time of "dissemiNation," the nation-space becomes a potential site for an emancipatory agency. Here, as one might expect, his reasoning becomes elusive. Referring to Raymond Williams's "crucial distinction between residual and emergent practices," Bhabha claims that "this disjunctive temporality of the nation would provide the appropriate time-frame for representing those residual and emergent meanings and practices that Williams locates in the margins of contemporary society" (p. 299). The disjuncture of national-narrative time, in other words, is said to enable the narrator (and social agent?) to disjoin the nation's emancipatory elements from its oppressive ones.

It will not be difficult to recognize here in the newer attire of the disjunctive our old friend ambivalence, as, indeed, in the conceptual movement of "DissemiNation," the underlying, dual propositional structure of "Signs." The obvious difference, of course, is that here it is the national rather than the colonial presence that, once disclosed as ambivalent, switches from oppressive ground of identity to the site from which to resist and even overcome all such oppressive power. The agency described as *hybridity* intrudes within the nation-space itself, whose "liminality" (i.e., "ambivalence," "disjuncture," etc.) "provides a place from which to speak both of, and as, the minority, the exilic, the marginal, and the emergent" (p. 300).

For a counterargument, one could do no better, here, than turn again to Ahmad, especially his relentless exposure of the myth of the exile as subversive in "Languages of Class" and in the long essay on Salman Rushdie.[12] But, given our speculative concern for the postcolonial consciousness as an inverse reflection of the historical crisis of cultural nationalism, what is particularly illuminating about the line of reasoning in "DissemiNation" is just the way in which Bhabha must first *explicitly* retract this space from the *integral* temporality of *history* in order to recast the nation-space as a site of internal, liberating displacement: "Historians transfixed on the event and origins of the nation never ask, and political theorists possessed of the 'modern' totalities of the nation . . . never pose [Bhabha appears to have Ernest Gellner specifically in mind here], the awkward question of the disjunctive representation of the social, in this double time of the nation" (p. 294). Against this, Bhabha's emphasis on disjuncture "serves to displace the historicism that has dominated discussions of the nation as a cultural force" (p. 292). But, turning the tables here, may we not likewise propose that the postcolonialist/poststructuralist critic, transfixed on the narrative, discursive aspects of the national, and possessed of the secrets of the national/colonial's amazing power to self-subvert, never asks, indeed, never poses, the awkward question of the nation and nationalism as the historical *product* (neither origin nor telos) of capitalism? Bhabha's polemical mise-en-scène here would lead us to suppose that, between the classical, orthodox, historicist *ideology* of nationalism per se and the antihistoricist discovery of the nation as the "liminality of cultural modernity" (p. 292), *tertium non datur.* Historical time — as opposed to narrative time — comes, by negative inference here, to be conceived as if foregrounded exclusively by the nation itself, hence as powerless to advance beyond — or retreat behind — this ground. To get free of nationalist ideology, one must first get free of history itself.

It is further revealing how, despite the customary deconstructionist invocation of difference (in whichever of its thousand and one alternative locutions) as the cure for all bad things, a foundational category does ultimately emerge in "DissemiNation" to supply the politically desirable alternative to historicity: that of *culture*, or even of the *ethnic*. "The nation," says Bhabha, "reveals in its ambivalent and vacillating representation, the *ethnography* of its own historicity and opens up the possibility of other narratives of the people and their difference" (p. 300). Or, again, even more suggestively: "Once the liminality of the nation-space is established, and its 'difference' is turned from the boundary 'outside' to its finitude 'within', the threat of cultural difference is no longer a problem of 'other' people. It becomes a question of the otherness of the people-as-one. The national subject splits in the ethnographic perspective of culture's contemporaneity and provides both a theoretical position and a narrative authority for marginal voices or minority discourse" (p. 301).

The otherness of the people as one—a better motto for the official, liberal version of multiculturalism would be difficult to imagine. The notion seems to be that, once we finally recognize that the *nation* is just a readymade construction, patched together out of the desires and voices of a variety of ethnographic subjects, then the oppressive logic of national*ism* will magically vanish. But, even assuming this to be true, how is this liminality to be established if it remains in the interest of the nation's pedagogues to keep it secret? And, if, somehow, we were to overthrow the pedagogues, what point would there be any longer in performing this nation, say, and not another? Or why not perform something entirely unlike the nation? Moreover, the question goes begging as to just why the ethnographic perspective is any less a narrative and a cultural construction (with its own pedagogical and performative temporalities) than the nation is. Thus, what good would it do us to split the national subject into ethnographic ones, unless there is something more benevolent about the narrative authority of the ethnographic over and against that of the national? (And that is a promise rather difficult to credit in the days of the warring micronationalities and ethnicities spilling all across the post-Soviet and postcolonial nation-spaces.) In any case, what Bhabha offers us here is, so to speak, not a historical alternative to cultural nationalism, but cultural nationalism as itself an alternative to history—cultural nationalism, only here with the national, or ethnographic, itself conveniently cleansed of its *historical* and hence of its *class* determination.

Let me try, now, to synthesize what has been said so far. If, as a theoretical consciousness, postcolonialism inverts the historical crisis of cultural nationalism, lifting the nation out of its historical determinateness altogether (and, as a possible final step, substituting a mechanism of *cultural* determination), then poststructuralism serves this ideological practice by supplying it with a set of conceptual moves (*play* or *game* might be the better words) with which to recast this indeterminacy (*ambivalence*, etc.) as an emancipatory drama with radical stakes and players. Agency, however, becomes a fiction if there is nothing determinate to act *on*, if the agenda is already determined in advance by the agent.

("Freedom" — to use Engels's more traditional vocabulary — "is the recognition of necessity.") What poststructuralism does is set the scene in such a way — by subtly or not so subtly rewriting the social as the textual, the practical as the discursive, etc. — that this fiction, for the naming of which it offers a vocabulary as limitless as it is pointless, can appear to be something real.

In Bhabha's case, this process of plotting out a semiotic, narrative, or simply cultural detour around the present historical impasse assumes a considerable degree of theoretical abstraction, requiring of the reader a patience for the aporias of high poststructuralism that he or she, of course, may not be able or willing to summon.[13] But, as noted earlier, while the postcolonial ideology is liable to such complication, it can take other, less rigorous, more traditional and accessible forms. Consider the example of Said himself, in one of his later works, *Culture and Imperialism*.[14] Here, we are presented with what appears, at least, to be a solidly historicist treatment of the postcolonial, a "history of the imperial adventure rendered in cultural terms" (p. xxiii). No escape into the disjunctive temporality of narrative here, but, rather, what itself promises to be the narrative of an objective, real-time set of events.

But this historical narrative itself turns out to be strangely impoverished and abstract, informed by none of the theoretical insights on which such a history of the imperial adventure might be expected to rely. Of course, *Culture and Imperialism* consists mainly of a series of textual commentaries, foregrounded more by a conventional sense of *literary* history than anything else, but, for a treatise that focuses so centrally on the nineteenth century, it is remarkable how *pre*-nineteenth century *Culture and Imperialism* seems, from a historicophilosophical point of view. Nothing, here, even of Hegel, much less of Marx. Listen, for example, to Said discussing the need to "set . . . art in the global, earthly context": "Territory and possessions are at stake, geography and power. Everything about human history is rooted in the earth, which has meant that we must think about habitation, but it has also meant that people have planned to *have* more territory and therefore must do something about its indigenous residents. At some very basic level, imperialism means thinking about, settling on, controlling land that you do not possess, that is distant, that is lived on and owned by others" (p. 7).

That, at some very basic level, imperialism concerns territory may surely be granted — but *Culture and Imperialism* never advances beyond this level. In an almost physiocratic reprise, Said commits the double anachronism here of projecting feudal and early capitalist notions of landed property both backward onto epochs that knew nothing of *territory* in the sense he gives it (the Taino/Arawak tribespeople encountered by Columbus at the time of his first American landfall would have been surprised indeed to know that they owned any territory at all) and forward onto a stage of historical development whose imperial elites have long since come to marshal their power for the possession, not of territory, but of an immense accumulation of commodities, labor power chief among them. The result is that imperialism — that entity, the cultural history of which Said has promised to tell — is emptied at the beginning of any historical concreteness. The class determination of territory and possession effectively drops out here. Instead, we are presented with a "focus on actual contests over land and the land's people," with a "kind of geographical inquiry into historical experience" (p. 7). This sounds intriguing, but, in practice, it reduces imperialism itself to a kind of geography, an unequal distribution of possession — or sovereignty — over a preexisting map of territories. It thus comes as no surprise that the history of this imperialism — and of the resistance to it — is virtually oblivious to both the Russian and the Chinese Revolutions, arguably the two most signal acts of resistance to imperialism in this century. In a book replete with invocations of Gramsci, Fanon, Nkrumah, C. L. R. James, etc., a book that claims repeatedly to stand on the shoulders of the great anticolonial leaders and visionaries of the Third World, it is to be noted that the name of Mao Tse-tung does not receive, unless I am mistaken, a single mention. And that, whatever one's sympathies or antipathies toward Maoism, is an omission that surely says as much about Said's view of imperialism as the entire text of *Culture and Imperialism* itself.

Given such an oddly anachronistic theory of imperialism, it becomes more difficult to be confident of what Said will have to say about its culture. To take just one brief example here, in the first chapter of *Culture and Imperialism*, Said sets out to illustrate how "the processes of imperialism occurred beyond the level of economic laws and political decisions" (p. 12) through a brief discussion of Dickens's *Dombey and Son*, a novel in which the latter satirizes the "world is my oyster" mentality of the British merchant class in the 1840s. Said notes how this very satirization itself "ultimately depends on the tried and true discourses of imperial trade" (p. 14). Dickens's criticism of this class may appear genuine, but "one must also ask, how *could* Dombey think that the universe, and the whole of time, was his to trade in?" (p. 13). Although Said is careful not to deny the value of novels such as *Dombey and Son* as works of art, the sense of his comment here is that Dickens, himself a product of British imperial culture, could not have been in a position to portray it in a genuinely critical light. If his character could think the whole world his, must not Dickens have at least entertained a similar thought? But how to explain, then, even just the *appearance* of criticism here? The truth that Said seems forced, by his own conceptual framework, to pass over is that Dickens could be profoundly critical of imperialist culture yet also reproduce key aspects of it at the same time. To grasp this, however, requires a *class* analysis of this imperialist culture — a grasp of its internal contradictions — as well as some notion of how the realist novel as a genre made possible this contradictory, limited, but nevertheless valid and historically progressive form of social criticism. To draw the full, theoretical connection between culture and imperialism, that is, one first needs a theory of imperialism that reflects it in its real, historically concrete dimensions and movement.[15] By basing his own theory of imperialism too narrowly on such concepts as *territory* and *overseas trade,* Said cannot adequately account for the contradictory aspects of a *Dombey and Son.* And, in a certain sense, his own critique of imperialism comes to seem more eclectic and morally abstract, even, than that of Dickens himself.

But the important question for us here is *why* this anachronism and theoretical impoverishment, affecting what is otherwise a work of stunning erudition and unassailable ethical convictions? The answer, I think, is that, as with Bhabha's antihistoricist rewriting of the nation as narration, Said's resort to a preeconomic, geographic concept of imperialism reflects what is, in the final analysis, the latter's intellectual retreat before the historical crisis of cultural nationalism and of the politics of national liberation. Let it be clearly stipulated here that, in *Culture and Imperialism,* Said is careful to disavow cultural nationalism on *ethical* grounds and that this disavowal is fully principled and sincere. Nor can it be denied that, on one level at least, *Culture and Imperialism* reasons out of an awareness of this crisis as historically inescapable. "Gone," writes Said, "are the binary oppositions dear to the nationalist and imperialist enterprises. Instead we begin to sense that old authority cannot simply be replaced by new authority, but that new alignments made across borders, types, nations, and essences are rapidly coming into view, and it is those new alignments that now provoke and challenge the fundamentally static notion of *identity* that has been the core of cultural thought during the epoch of imperialism" (pp. xxiv–xxv).

But note that the collapse of nationalism's binary oppositions—the disclosure of the nation's essential ambivalence and disunity as ground—still leads, not (forward) into a new, historical unity of *class,* but (as it were, laterally) into new alignments across nations, whose danger to imperialism is no more than to challenge a *notion.* Again, as with Bhabha, registering the historical *truth* of crisis can only prompt the postcolonial consciousness to create the historical *fiction*—the fantasmagoria—of an emancipatory agency.

Ahmad has pointed out how Said's loosely poststructuralist celebration of postcolonial difference and hybridity—what elsewhere in *Culture and Imperialism* he refers to as the *contrapuntal*—essentially becomes a celebration of the postcolonial intellectual him- or herself (fighting "behind the lines" in the metropolitan theater) as the true hero of cultural anti-imperialism. This becomes clear in such passages as the following: "In a totally new way in Western culture, the interventions of non-European artists and scholars cannot be dismissed or silenced, and these interventions are not only an integral part of a political movement, but in many ways the movement's *successfully* guiding imagination, intellectual and figurative energy reseeing and rethinking the terrain common to whites and non-whites" (p. 212).

The tendency for such pronouncements to become self-serving and elitist is transparent. But, if one may take issue with Ahmad to this very slight extent here, it does seem to me that there is something undeniably accurate in Said's observation of a cultural shift within the metropolis (the so-called voyage in). This even if, in classically ideological fashion, Said overinflates this new cultural and intellectual phenomenon with the power, *eo ipso,* to lead the masses into battle with imperialism. The underlying truth here, I would suggest, is that, although it has succumbed to a reflux of imperialism and has failed to deliver on its implicit promise of social emancipation for the masses on the imperialist periphery, many of whom now suffer greater oppression perhaps than at any point in the past, the historical epoch of national liberation struggles — the so-called Bandung era — *has* changed the cultural and intellectual landscape irrevocably for the better. Our own moment would seem to present us with the intensely contradictory reality of what might be termed *cultural revolution without social revolution.* As to how permanent this cultural revolution is, one cannot be sure. The widespread contemporary desire for multiculturalist reforms and for the rooting out of Eurocentric bias in metropolitan institutions, politically ambivalent though it often may be, suggests that the clock is not likely to be turned back without some resistance. Said exaggerates the importance of these cultural advances, but that does not mean that they should not be defended without compromise.

So soon, however, as these *cultural* advances substitute themselves for the *political* and *social* ends of anti-imperialism we enter the ideological thicket of what I would term *cultural politics,* with the emphasis on *cultural.* Much of contemporary postcolonial theory seems to me to fit this description. If it is to steer clear of cultural politics, postcolonial theory must not only disavow the reactionary political logic of cultural nationalism but break with it on its deeper, philosophical and theoretical levels as well. Poststructuralism cannot produce this break, only continuously defer it.

Notes

1   Aijaz Ahmad, *In Theory* (London: Verso, 1992); page numbers for quotation from *In Theory* will be given in the text.

   By way of circumstantial clarification, I should note that this essay was first drafted shortly after the appearance of *In Theory* and before the explosion of controversy touched off by the book, especially by its criticisms of Edward Said's *Orientalism,* had come to my knowledge. The reader should therefore avoid interpolating into the body of "DetermiNation" any direct or allusive engagements with Ahmad's many and vociferous detractors. This said, however, I also reaffirm my general and wholehearted agreement with the critical and theoretical core of *In Theory*. Having now read the bulk of its hostile reviews, I find nothing in them that would lead me to alter the substance of the present essay. For the most comprehensive record of the debate itself, see the special issue of *Public Culture* (vol. 6, no. 1 [fall 1993]) dedicated to *In Theory*, including Ahmad's own long response to critics ("A Response," 143–91).

2 Ahmad is not alone in this respect, although, owing to the notoriety of *In Theory*, he is unquestionably the most visible. Others who have taken up positions critical of poststructuralism within postcolonial studies include Arif Dirlik, Neil Lazarus, Timothy Brennan, and Benita Parry.

But, while many postcolonial theorists and critics engage poststructuralist theory with some degree of skepticism and caution, the result is not atypically a critical acceptance of certain aspects of, say, Foucault, Laclau/Mouffe, Deleuze/Guattari, etc., a rejection of others, but no sustained or rigorous posing of the ideological question as such. Thus, we are left, in the end, with a theoretical hybrid of sorts, in which, nevertheless, the basic premises of poststructuralist thought are grudgingly retained. In this respect, it is striking that, in the course of her long and painstaking rebuke to *In Theory*—a rebuke that also doubles as a defense of Said as well as of other, more orthodox poststructuralist critics of imperialism—Benita Parry ("A Mishandled Critique," *Social Text* 35 [summer 1993]: 121–33) consistently elides this issue. Parry, e.g., accuses Ahmad's critique of Said of having "distorted a narrative of how a field of textual representations naturalized political power and enabled the invasion of geographical and cultural space" (p. 125). That the thrust of Ahmad's critique is in any way to deny the role of representations in naturalizing political power is, in fact, entirely spurious. But note that the operant notion here—that of the capacity of textual representations to enable the invasion of not only cultural but *geographic* space, i.e., that certain discourses constitute, in and of themselves, an imperialist act against which other discourses could then, presumably, intervene as counteractions—is presented as a truth so obvious that *any* criticism, explicit or implicit, is self-evidently a distortion. *In Theory*, on the other hand, not only questions the tacitly accepted self-evidence of such poststructuralist tenets (for, whether Said is really an orthodox poststructuralist himself or not, the provenance of such truths is indisputably poststructuralist) but poses the question of their historical and social conditions of emergence and possibility, i.e., of ideology *strictu sensu*.

I myself, in fact, have sought to analyze the postcolonialism/poststructuralism nexus in the context of Latin American literary and cultural studies (see, e.g., my "Postmodernism and Imperialism: Theory and Politics in Latin America," in *Reading North by South: On Latin American Literature, Culture, and Politics* [Minneapolis: University of Minnesota Press 1995]). But, in the area of Latin Americanism, the really signal work on this question is that of the Brazilian critic Roberto Schwarz, especially the essay "Nationalism by Elimination" (in *Misplaced Ideas: Essays on Brazilian Culture*, trans. John Gledson et al. [London: Verso, 1992]), many of whose fundamental lines of critique bear a striking resemblance to Ahmad's.

3 See Roberto Schwartz, *Misplaced Ideas: Essays on Brazilian Culture*, trans. and ed. John Gledson (London: Verso, 1992).

4 Gayatri Chakravorty Spivak, "Can the Subaltern Speak?" in *Marxism and the Interpretation of Culture*, ed. Lawrence Grossberg and Cary Nelson (Urbana: University of Illinois Press, 1988), 271–313.

5 Neil Larsen, "Shades of Althusser; or, The Logic of Theoretical Retreat in Contemporary Radical Criticism," *Socialism and Democracy* 9, no. 2 (fall 1995). Spivak, "Can the Subaltern Speak?" 279.

6 Homi K. Bhabha, "Signs Taken for Wonders: Questions of Ambivalence and Authority under

a Tree outside Delhi, May 1817," in *"Race," Writing, and Difference,* ed. Henry Louis Gates Jr. (Chicago: University of Chicago Press, 1985), 163–84; and "DissemiNation Time, Narrative, and the Margins of the Modern Nation," in *Nation and Narration,* ed. Homi K. Bhabha (London: Routledge, 1990), 291–322; page numbers for both essays are hereafter given in the text. Both essays have since been republished as chaps. 6 and 8, respectively, of Bhabha's *The Location of Culture* (London: Routledge, 1994).

7 This historical irony has been explored at length in Gauri Viswanathan, *The Masks of Conquest* (New York: Columbia University Press, 1989).

8 See, e.g., Perry Anderson, *In the Tracks of Historical Materialism* (London: Verso, 1983); Terry Eagleton, "From *Polis* to Postmodernism," in *The Ideology of the Aesthetic* (Oxford: Blackwell, 1990); Peter Dews, *Logics of Disintegration: Poststructuralist Thought and the Claims of Critical Theory* (London: Verso, 1987); Roy Bhaskar, "What Is Critical Realism?" in *Reclaiming Reality* (London: Verso, 1989); and Ellen Meiksins Wood, *The Retreat from Class: A New "True" Socialism* (London: Verso, 1986).

9 I emphasize the word *typically.* There are exceptions, in fact, if we include under the rubric *postcolonial theory* not only the work of Ahmad himself but that of Ranajit Guha and the subaltern studies collective as well as, e.g., the more directly historical and politicoeconomical investigations of a Samir Amin. But here — with the possible exception of Guha at least — the poststructuralist nexus is either broken or absent, with the link to Marxism taking its place.

10 See Neil Larsen, "Marxism and Cultural Politics" (typescript, University of California, Davis).

11 The storm of anger and protest that this critique has elicited is now notorious, of course. As Ahmad remarks in his response to critics in *Public Culture,* "I seem to have said what must always remain unsaid" ("A Response," p. 174).

12 Aijaz Ahmad, "Languages of Class, Ideologies of Immigration" and "Salman Rushdie's *Shame:* Postmodern Migrancy and the Representation of Women," both in *In Theory: Classes, Nations, Literatures* (New York: Verso, 1992), 73–94, 123–58, respectively.

13 The term *impasse* is Samir Amin's (see *Eurocentrism,* trans. Russell Moore [New York: Monthly Review Press, 1989], esp. chap. 4).

14 Edward Said, *Culture and Imperialism* (New York: Knopf, 1993); page numbers for quotations will be given in the text.

15 To those who object here that Said incorporates certain aspects of Marxism and class analysis into *Culture and Imperialism,* I think the following remarks of Ahmad, here in sympathetic response to Michael Sprinker's criticisms, are sufficiently apposite: "That Said says a great many things in *Orientalism* that would be perfectly acceptable to a Marxist ought not to be elided into the claim that its methodological premises are the same as the ones that normally regulate Marxist analyses of imperialism's cultural domination, any more than Foucault's incorporating entire passages of Marx into his texts makes him a proponent of the labour theory of value" ("A Response," 186).

Secularism, Elitism, Progress, and Other Transgressions:

On Edward Said's "Voyage In"

BRUCE ROBBINS

In what has come to be called *colonial* and *postcolonial studies,* there seems to be a gathering consensus that the institutional rise of the field is somehow an anomaly and an embarrassment.[1] To judge from recent essays and conference presentations, the best thing to do with its success story, as perhaps with any success story, is to subject it to the most scathing critique possible. A certain sarcasm about the field's sociogeographic position, which seems irresistible even to observers who are otherwise quite opposed to each other, like Aijaz Ahmad and his many critics, takes the characteristic form of a more or less personal belittling of the field's practitioners, identified as upwardly mobile in terms of both their place of origin (Third World) and their class of destination (bourgeois). According to Kwame Anthony Appiah, "Postcoloniality is the condition of what we might ungenerously call a comprador intelligentsia: of a relatively small, Western-style, Western-trained group of writers and thinkers who mediate the trade in cultural commodities of western capitalism at the periphery."[2] According to Arif Dirlik, "Postcoloniality is the condition of the intelligentsia of global capitalism," and "the popularity that the term *postcoloniality* has achieved in the last few years has less to do with its rigorousness as a concept or with the new vistas it has opened up for critical inquiry than it does with the increased visibility of academic intellectuals of Third World origin as pacesetters in cultural criticism." For "Third World intellectuals who have arrived in First World academe," Dirlik argues, "postcolonial discourse is an expression not so much of agony over identity, as it often appears, but of newfound power."[3]

Such attacks on the field's metropolitan location and the power, privileges, and priorities that stem from that location raise one immediate tactical objection: they forget that the legitimacy and the institutional toehold enjoyed by such studies in the metropolis remain extremely fragile. It is often claimed that critical attention to the (post)colonial deviously serves the interests of neo-imperialism. Unfortunately, nothing obliges neoimperialism to agree that its interests are so served, and there are no guarantees that it will think or act accordingly. Indeed, there are many signs that post–cold war nationalism in the United States does *not* wish to recognize its supposed interest in sustaining all those left-wing critics, many of them originally from Third World countries, who are teaching unpatriotic lessons to American youths. And, if the tendency to delegitimate and defund continues, the ultra-Left paranoid view of the rise of postcolonial criticism will appear retrospectively to have been as misguided (to paraphrase Régis Debray) as Communist attacks on progressive French universities on the eve of the Nazi invasion.[4]

Still, it should be possible to admit the partial truth of observations like Dirlik's, it seems to me, without also endorsing the crushing conclusions that Dirlik draws from them about the illegitimacy and misguidedness of postcolonial studies generally — conclusions that offer comfort and consolation to the field's political opponents. Yes, the existence of (post)colonial discourse *does* express newfound power as well as agonies of identity on the part of its practitioners. So? Would this not be the case for any successful intellectual movement, any movement that wins provisional popular and/or institutional support for its terms and agendas, whatever the criteria of progressiveness by which it is judged? Or have we actually come to believe that any success in winning support is in itself a fatal sign of co-optation or evidence that the movement was never progressive to begin with? If not, then the failure to answer the many critiques like this, indeed, the seemingly masochistic tendency to repeat and delight in them, would seem to indicate an incoherence at the point where class and (inter)nationalism intersect that is rather mysterious. And this incoherence is also dangerous. For the lack of a vocabulary that would offer (post)colonial critics some other articulation between nationalism and class also means the inability to represent themselves and what they do in public. What (post)colonial studies needs, it seems to me, is not a political purge or purification (although, like everyone else, I have my own points of disagreement with various routine assumptions). It needs a different and impious view of its own authority (such as it is), some narrative of how it arrived at that authority, and some explanation of what that authority has to do with the transnational circle or sphere to which it holds itself newly accountable.

This is more than I am presently prepared to do myself. But it is with this task in mind that I make some remarks about the recent work of Edward Said and in particular about the distinctive version of internationalism that clusters around his favored phrases *secular criticism* and the *secular intellectual*.[5] Said is, of course, one of the few academic figures in the United States who have managed to give public voice both to serious criticism of American foreign policy and, with more difficulty, to solidarities that are not centered on or limited to the unquestioned priority of the American national interest.[6] Most remarkably, he has managed to defend the interests of the Palestinian national movement while maintaining an extremely skeptical view of nationalism as such. Indeed, perhaps the most crucial meaning of *secular,* in his usage, is as an opposing term, not to religion, but to nationalism. In the interview with Jennifer Wicke and Michael Sprinker published in Sprinker's *Edward Said: A Critical Reader,* Said sets the "ideal of secular interpretation and secular work" against "submerged feelings of identity, of tribal solidarity," of community that is "geographically and homogeneously defined." "The dense fabric of secular life," Said says, is what "can't be herded under the rubric of national identity or can't be made entirely to respond to this phony idea of a paranoid frontier separating 'us' from 'them'—which is a repetition of the old sort of orientalist model." "The politics of secular interpretation proposes a way . . . of avoiding the pitfalls of nationalism."[7]

Now, the word *secular* has usually served as a figure for the authority of a putatively universal reason or (narratively speaking) as the ideal end point of progress in the intellectual domain. In appropriating the word as a sort of insignia, then, Said clearly runs the risk of (in Tim Brennan's words) "assuming the nineteenth century mantle of progress and enlightenment."[8] Naturally enough, this usage has not gone uncontested among critics of Eurocentrism. R. Radhakrishnan, for example, objects to how " 'the secular' as a western norm is made to operate naturally and therefore namelessly."[9] "What we have to realize," Peter van der Veer writes in *Orientalism and the Postcolonial Predicament,* "is that the very distinction between religious and secular is a product of the Enlightenment that was used in orientalism to draw a sharp opposition between irrational, religious behavior of the Oriental and rational secularism, which enabled the westerner to rule the Oriental."[10] Meanwhile, the subaltern studies group has stressed the further connection between secularism and indigenous elites. Extending the argument from Western Orientalists to the secularism of Indian nationalist elites, Ranajit Guha argues, for instance, that the latter, "unable to grasp religiosity as the central modality of peasant consciousness in colonial India," necessarily fail "to conceptualize insurgent mentality except in terms of an unadulterated secularism."[11] Or, as Dipesh Chakrabarty puts it, secular nationalism in India has meant "an act of appropriation by elite (and elitist) Indians, on behalf of their project of building an Indian state, of diverse historical struggles of the subaltern classes."[12] The case against elites and the case against secularism seem to be the same case.[13]

Having seen a certain ressentiment directed at his professional renown and his privileged position in an elite metropolitan university, Said shows some bravery in standing together with so authoritative a term as *secularism.* And, at the same time, his descriptions of the intellectual also try to *evade* this authority. As he says in the Wicke/Sprinker interview, his version of secularism is an attempt to avoid nationalism's us/them without, on the contrary, espousing what he calls "universal values." If he speaks positively of "globalism" and "worldliness," he says a distinct no to "cosmopolitanism and intellectual tourism," to any internationalism that would express a "superior detachment . . . a general all-encompassing love for all of humanity." [14] In other words, the word *secular* seems to aim at a version of internationalism that would do without the direct authoritative backing either of a putatively universal class, as in the Marxist version, or of disinterested rationality. Is it, then, a sort of postmodern secularism that attempts to do without *any* authority? [15]

Here, another implication of secular is pertinent: the suggestion that the so-called clerisy must learn to work without the quasi-theological guarantees and quasi-theological self-conceptions that have served it in the past. At the end of his final Reith lecture in the summer of 1993, published in *Raritan* and in *Representations of the Intellectual,* Said declared, "The true intellectual is a secular being. However much intellectuals pretend that their representations are of higher things or ultimate values, morality begins with their activity in this secular world of ours — where it takes place, whose interests it serves." [16] Rather than some sort of exemplary otherworldliness, being a secular intellectual seems here to mean resigning oneself to an inevitable profane untidiness, an impurity, a political incorrectness. Yet it also seems to draw energy and authority from that refusal of virtue. And this is perhaps because, implicitly, it entails biting the not entirely bitter bullet of institutional privilege. According to the *Oxford English Dictionary,* secularism is "the doctrine that morality should be based solely in regard to the well-being of mankind in the present life to the exclusion of all considerations drawn from belief in God or in a future state." If intellectuals should be worldly or even profane, at least partially subdued to the untidiness of an unjust and hierarchical world, then perhaps they must do some strategic acquiescing in institutional or professional hierarchies.

The last lines of the last Reith lecture, "Gods That Always Fail," go as follows: "As an intellectual you are the one who can choose between actively representing the truth to the best of your ability, or passively allowing a patron or an authority to direct you. For the secular intellectual, *those* gods always fail." Add to this the refusal of all orthodoxy and dogma, of any "kind of absolute certainty" or any "total, seamless view of reality," and you get a secular intellectual who submits to *no* authority, even that of his or her own beliefs or findings.[17] Given this somewhat deconstructive thrust of the term *secular* — not just antinationalist, but against any grounding of intellectual mission and activity — one would imagine that Said would be quite harsh with Julien Benda's *La trahison des clercs,* a text that grounds its attractive antinationalism on a shamelessly sacred view of the intellectual. Surprisingly, he is not.[18] On the key issue of the clerics' betrayal, he comes down on Benda's side — which is to say that he implicitly endorses, here and throughout the Reith lectures, the sense of high vocation without which there could *be* no betrayal. This stubborn fidelity to an ideal of vocation is clearly one reason why his work is so moving to so many people. But it is all the more reason to ask on what grounds, on what secular authority, this sense of mission might be based. The question is absolutely crucial, for it seems to promise a *different difference* between intellectuals and nonintellectuals, an articulation between the two that does not demand that the first simply dissolve into the second, and at the same time an authority that is specifically and uncompromisingly internationalist.

The secular ideal of the intellectual who "speaks truth to power," which Said celebrates in Benda and elsewhere, pays no explicit attention to the decisive question — the same question in another form — of *why power would listen,* what might *make* it listen, what makes *anyone* listen. That is, it has nothing explicit to say about the source of *counterauthority* that intellectuals must be assumed to counterpose to "power." This absence of critical or countervailing authority is all the more evident given that the term *secular* functions elsewhere in Said to frustrate the usual answers to the authority question: the dogmatic authority of disinterested truth and the authority of an ethnically purified local or national community, as we have already seen, and also the borrowed sanctity of the *professional* community. In the introduction to *The World, the Text, and the Critic,* entitled "Secular Criticism," Said mobilizes the term *secular* in an attack on what he calls, again from the theological lexicon, the "*cult* of professional expertise," with its sense of "vocation" and its "quasi-religious quietism." [19]

What sorts of authority might there be, then? One hint comes from Said's most sympathetic words about Julien Benda, which suggest a sort of *economy* of authority. Intellectuals, Said says, have to be in a state of almost permanent opposition to the status quo. And this, he claims, is why Benda's intellectuals are perforce a small, highly visible group.[20] Here, intellectual authority would seem to come from the presumed rarity or scarcity of those willing to confront nonintellectual authority. It would come, that is, from a "rarefaction" of intellectuals — I borrow the term from Said's influential appreciation of Foucault — that formally resembles the dread concept *elitism* but that offers the restrictiveness of the group an ethicopolitical legitimacy (the unusual courage needed for opposition to the status quo) rather than a meritocratic one. Or perhaps it would be fairer to say that, rather than the profession deciding who is a competent scholar, it is power that decides who is a real intellectual, whose dissent is painful or threatening enough to be worthy of public expressions of dislike. The authority of the intellectual is a faithful inversion of the authority of power itself and is thus dependent on it. Here, the amoral connotations of secularism lie not far beneath the surface. Practically speaking, an *ethical* scarcity defined by opposition will be indistinguishable from a *social* scarcity that is a potential source of profit and prestige. An undesired visibility, resulting from the political hostility of the powers that be, can and perhaps must be exchanged for celebrity, the prized, often apolitical currency of honors and economic rewards.

This line of thought seems interestingly continuous with another answer to the question of where intellectuals get such authority as they possess, Anna Boschetti's analysis of the success of Sartre. For Boschetti, Sartre's trick was to manage a transfer to one domain of cultural capital accumulated in another domain; thus, Sartre brings the prestige of the École Normale Supérieure and the discipline of philosophy to literature, and he then brings that newly accumulated sum to his political activities, the government's dramatic reactions to which feed back into his literary and philosophical esteem.[21] For all its problems, the concept *cultural capital* makes a valuable stab at quantifying and mapping such transfers, translating an otherwise vague "guardianship of the archives" into a diversified and dynamic economy of cultural resources. And this import/export model brings out some distinctive features of—indeed, enables us to recognize as such—the authorizing story of the intellectual that Said calls, in *Culture and Imperialism,* "the voyage in," the movement of Third World writers, intellectuals, and texts into the metropolis and their successful integration there.

From one point of view, this movement could obviously be described as a form of upward mobility, and, to these, as to other such narratives, critics have reacted with various degrees of alarm. Can Third World fictions and careers that aim at and are embraced by the metropolis ultimately signify anything other than an opportunistic affirmation of the metropolis? Gayatri Chakravorty Spivak, for example, makes a pointed parallel between the current First World enthusiasm for Third World writers and the earlier divide-and-conquer strategy of colonialism, which simultaneously served the interests of the colonial power and of a native-born "aspiring elite." Do we see here again, she asks, "the old scenario of empowering a privileged group or a group susceptible to upward mobility as the authentic inhabitants of the margin"?[22]

Faced with the collective bildungsroman of Third World writers who have come to live and work in the metropolis, thereby repeating (with a transnational difference) the country-to-the-city journey so characteristic of the nineteenth-century European novel, Said in contrast is rather cheerful. You can see the cheerfulness, for example, in his innovative treatment of the novel of disillusionment. In an indirect reply to Franco Moretti's darkly Lukacsian view of the genre, Said appreciatively displays Third World reversals of *Heart of Darkness,* like Tayeb Salih's *Season of Migration to the North.* Moretti sees the genre dying when European men, losing faith in their own projects, have tired of it. Said's insistence on its continuing vitality in the hands of Third World men and women would appear on the contrary to express—in a wonderful corroboration of A. L. Morton's view of utopian and dystopian fiction—the intelligent optimism of a stratum or category that is still rising, energetic, confident of its powers.[23]

The grounds of this qualified optimism are clearly not that the story of an upwardly mobile elite can literally be everyone's story. It is hard to imagine that American readers would react so favorably to Jamaica Kincaid or Bharati Mukherjee, say, if they thought the entire Third World was being advised to emulate their upwardly mobile au pair heroines and head for the nearest international airport.[24] Said's point, rather, is that the center can be and has been changed. There has been what he calls "adversarial internationalization in an age of continued imperial structures."[25] Opposition has arisen in the modern metropolis — an opposition of which there was little sense in *Orientalism*. In the universities, the "impingement" of Third World intellectuals on metropolitan space has resulted in "the transformation of the very terrain of the disciplines." This implies, I would like to add, that the story of Third World intellectual migration has conferred a certain authority on oppositional intellectuals in and from the First World, including many for whom the work of representing colonial and postcolonial experience must unequivocally *be* work, that is, cannot even be misperceived as a matter of effortless identity. And all this has been possible — this is the key point — because of the risky and unstable fusion of personal mobility and impersonal representativeness: "Anti-imperialist intellectual and scholarly work done by writers from the peripheries who have immigrated to or are visiting the metropolis is usually an extension into the metropolis of large-scale mass movements."[26]

Let me offer a brief and schematic national contrast. In what I might call the *French model* of intellectual authority, as in Anna Boschetti and Pierre Bourdieu, the sole source of cultural capital is existing institutions. Bourdieu's model of the *oblate*, for example, describes the rewards given to a poor child, without social capital, whose upward mobility has depended entirely on the educational institution that elevated him and to which he responds with unconditional loyalty. Conservative reaction against disciplinary change often comes, Bourdieu writes in *Homo Academicus*, from "those I call 'oblates,' and who, consigned from childhood to the school institution (they are often children of the lower or middle classes or sons of teachers) are totally dedicated to it." "The 'oblates' are always inclined to think that without the church there is no salvation — especially when they become the high priests of an institution of cultural reproduction which, in consecrating them, consecrates their active and above all passive ignorance of any other cultural world. Victims of their elite status, these deserving, but miraculously lucky, 'survivors' present a curious mixture of arrogance and inadequacy which immediately strikes the foreign observer. . . . They offer to the academic institution which they have chosen because it chose them, and vice versa, a support which, being so totally conditioned, has something total, absolute, and unconditional about it."[27] In this model, no authority is ascribed to the place from which the mobile oblate sets out; all authority is imagined to flow from the institutional destination. There is no possibility that the protagonist's initial poverty might serve in any way the (legitimating) purposes of the institution or — more important — that the protagonist's rise from that origin might help change that destination in any way or change the composition of the cultural capital subsequently transmitted to others.

Said's "voyage in" narrative redistributes the emphasis radically. While it does not underestimate the continuing authority of metropolitan institutions, neither does it treat the composition of cultural capital as fixed once and for all or assume that to accept it is necessarily to offer the donor unconditional loyalty in return. National origin matters; transfers from the periphery to the center do not leave the center as it was. The transnational story of upward mobility is not just a claiming of authority; it is also a redefinition of authority, a redefinition that can have many beneficiaries, for it means a recomposition as well as a redistribution of cultural capital. In short, progress is by no means inevitable, but it is possible.

Ironically, critiques of postcolonial studies that declare their fidelity to Marxist orthodoxy also turn out to be those that, unlike Marx, seem to preclude the untidily dialectical existence of progress. Arif Dirlik, for example, agrees that success stories like this one must offer some answer to the crucial question of where the newfound authority comes from: "Merely pointing to the ascendant role that intellectuals of Third World origin have played in propagating *postcolonial* as a critical orientation within First World academia begs the question as to why they and their intellectual concerns and orientations have been accorded the respectability that they have." In Dirlik's view, the metropolitan success of Third World intellectuals that has given the term *postcolonial* its currency has been "dependent on the conceptual needs of the social, political, and cultural problems thrown up by [a] new world situation," that is, by changes in world capitalism. "In their very globalism, the cultural requirements of transnational corporations can no longer afford the cultural parochialism of an earlier day"; they have "a need to internationalize academic institutions (which often takes the form not of promoting scholarship in a conventional sense but of 'importing' and 'exporting' students and faculty)." [28]

The messiness of the word *secular* seems a necessary antidote to this invocation of world capitalism, an invocation that might be described as overtidy or theological. For Dirlik, global capitalism is assumed to be not only "organized" (a matter of dispute among Marxist economists) but ubiquitous and omnipotent; whatever happens expresses its will, a will that is undialectically unified and, in terms of its effects on Third World peoples, invariably malignant. There is no room here for a cunning of reason that, to cite Marx's famous discussion of the British in India, could bring forth a certain unintended political progress even from the worst horrors of colonialism. It is hard to see how, within this worldview, any progress is conceivable that would not, on its emergence, immediately demand to be reinterpreted as the result of capitalism's disguised but malevolent intentions.

The common assumption for all of us who begin, in the study of colonial and postcolonial culture, with the intolerable facts of global suffering and injustice ought surely to be, on the contrary, that progress is an absolute necessity. Of course, as Anne McClintock points out, the word itself is entangled with a history of racism and Eurocentric self-congratulation, and so too is *postcolonial*.[29] Of course, any historical instance of progress will obligatorily be compromised in any number of ways, as the rise of (post)colonial studies is compromised by its metropolitan and class location. But this does not mean that it is so contaminated as to be unsayable; we are not so rich in instances that we can afford to throw any out in the name of an ideal purity. Progress must be believed to be possible before it can be fought for, and narratives of progress, including narratives of upward mobility, do just this work. Thus, such narratives cannot be disposed of by the simple thought that, for most of the world's people, there has *been* no upward mobility. The incongruities between narratives of upward mobility and the static or declining state of the world cannot be corrected by some voluntary gesture of self-discipline whereby narrative would henceforth allow no image of fulfilled desire not statistically guaranteed by actual improvement on the part of however many thousands or millions of people. For narratives, including metanarratives, are obliged to make use of desire, and there is no politics without them. As Alan Sinfield has noted, the rise of British "Left culturism," including the careers of Raymond Williams, E. P. Thompson, and Richard Hoggart, was after all by no means an easy or inevitable fact of postwar cultural life; and their legitimation was secured in part by narratives of "upward mobility through education," which was "a story that society, or parts of it, wanted to tell itself, not a record of experience."[30] Anyone who sees (post)colonial studies as a ruse of world capitalism should be prepared to say that the cultural scene would have been better off without these figures or that the current scene would be better off without the equally contingent presence of figures like Said, Gayatri Spivak, and Stuart Hall.

In describing what he calls *the global cultural economy*, Arjun Appadurai has distinguished between *finanscapes*, or flows of capital, and *ideoscapes*, or flows of ideologies and images. His point is that there is a disjuncture between these flows; no one of them (he provisionally distinguishes five levels) is a mere effect of any other.[31] No account of global capitalism can afford to forget this disjuncture, which makes a space for redistributions of cultural capital that are neither simply metaphoric nor simply epiphenomena of the real thing. I am trying to suggest, a bit obliquely, that the new internationalism or multiculturalism of the academic Left can be seen as one effect of a recomposition of cultural capital—an effect that Said's "voyage in" narrative risks the charge of elitism in order to authorize and legitimate. The power of *anti*elitism, whether in Richard Rorty's denunciation of rootless cosmopolitans or elsewhere, does not, of course, depend on *refusing* narratives of upward mobility, only on *controlling* them. Said's "voyage in" can, I think, be seen as a courageous and well-timed effort to take back these narratives, to use them in a different sharing out of intellectual authority. It is more than incidental that, in so doing, it also offers an implicit answer to the enigma of where the postcolonial critic's secular authority comes from. The authority of internationalism, according to this narrative, comes from the national itself or even from nationalism — although not everyone's nationalism and not a nationalism that can itself be unchanged by taking part in the operation.

In the vocabulary of Abdul JanMohamed, we could perhaps say that the precarious but necessary authority that Said gives to secular internationalism is founded on an ambiguous border crossing: neither simply an exile (which privileges the place of origin), nor simply an immigration (which privileges the destination), but both an exile and an immigration at once.[32] It is tempting to stress the Americanness of the optimistic narrative that Said thus counterposes to the French oblation and even to allow for some legitimate pride that one might feel in belonging, in this somewhat modified version of John F. Kennedy's words, to "a nation of immigrants."[33] With all due gratitude, however, for the support that the United States thus offers to the multicultural project of changing the center, I prefer to express my affiliation internationally, with the many otherwise situated groups and individuals, in the United States and elsewhere, who take this secular, progressive project as their own.

Notes

1   In the interests of economy, I will henceforth combine the two into (post)colonial. On the development and limits of the term *postcolonial,* see Ella Shohat, "Notes on the 'Post-Colonial,' " *Social Text* 31/32 (1992): 99–113; and Anne McClintock, "The Angel of Progress: Pitfalls of the Term 'Post-Colonialism,' " *Social Text* 31/32 (1992): 84–98.

2   Kwame Anthony Appiah, *In My Father's House: Africa in the Philosophy of Culture* (New York: Oxford University Press, 1992), 149.

3   Arif Dirlik, "The Postcolonial Aura: Third World Criticism in the Age of Global Capitalism," *Critical Inquiry* 20, no. 2 (winter 1994): 356, 329, 339.

4   Régis Debray, *Teachers, Writers, Celebrities: The Intellectuals of Modern France,* trans. David Macey (London: Verso, 1981), 58–59.

5   It would also be interesting to consider at least two of Said's idiosyncratic uses of *secular,* which have to do especially with scholarship: (*a*) the association of the secular with a distinctively *slow* historical rhythm, the temporality of scholarship, and (*b*) its association with a sort of Weberian existential heroism of scholarship, one that does without the usual versions of transcendent reassurance.

6   See, more recently, Edward Said, *The Politics of Dispossession: The Struggle for Palestinian Self-Determination, 1969–1994* (New York: Pantheon, 1994).

7   Michael Sprinker, ed., *Edward W. Said: A Critical Reader* (London: Blackwell, 1992), 232–33.

8   Tim Brennan, "Places of Mind, Occupied Lands: Edward Said and Philology," in Sprinker, ed., *Edward W. Said*, 92.

9   R. Radhakrishnan, *Diasporic Mediations: Between Home and Location* (Minneapolis: University of Minnesota Press, 1996), 160. See also William Connolly, "Pluralism and Multiculturalism" (lecture delivered at the Bohen Foundation, February 1994): "But what if secularism remains, on points crucial to multiculturalism, too close to the partner it loves to struggle against? And what if these affinities make their own contribution to the periodic return of violent Christian and secular fundamentalisms in western states? . . . Both the celebration and the lament of the (precarious) victory of the secular underplay the degree to which the Christian sacred remains buried in it" (p. 25).

10 Peter van der Veer, "The Foreign Hand: Orientalist Discourse in Sociology and Communalism," in *Orientalism and the Postcolonial Predicament: Perspectives on South Asia*, ed. Carol A. Breckenridge and Peter van der Veer (Philadelphia: University of Pennsylvania Press, 1993), 39.

11 Ranajit Guha, "The Prose of Counter-Insurgency," in *Selected Subaltern Studies*, ed. Ranajit Guha and Gayatri Chakravorty Spivak (New York: Oxford University Press, 1988), 81.

12 Dipesh Chakrabarty, "The Death of History? Historical Consciousness and the Culture of Late Capitalism," *Public Culture* 4, no. 2 (spring 1992): 52–53. Again: "Nationalist history, in spite of its anti-imperialist stance and substance, shared a deeply embedded meta-narrative with imperialist accounts of British India. This was the meta-narrative of the modern state" (p. 52).

13 Another example comes from Faisal Fatehali Devji: "Ideologically, I think, Hindu nationalism has emerged as the only mode of resistance to the 'secular' state—indeed as the only credible, organized form of alternative politics in a country where the ruling elite has appropriated secular nationalism so completely as to allow no room for dispute in its terms. Even the Left collapses into secular-nationalist attitudes when faced with a 'communalism' it is incapable of understanding or dealing with apart from a largely irrelevant rhetoric of class conflict. Secular nationalism itself, in other words, has become a kind of state 'fundamentalism,' a sort of self-legitimizing mode of coercion that ends up generating its own nemesis in the 'communalism' it demonizes" ("Hindu/Muslim/Indian," *Public Culture* 5, no. 1 [fall 1992]: 5). Somewhat excessively, Devji blames secularists for the creation of communalism. Like Rorty's claim that the parochialism of the academic Left is responsible for the failure of a broader Left in the United States, this is a form of covert celebration of left-wing intellectuals, for it holds them responsible—i.e., credits their power and influence—for matters far beyond them, including the craziness of their enemies and critics (Richard Rorty, *Achieving Our Country: Leftist Thought in Twentieth-Century America* [Cambridge: Harvard University Press, 1998]).

14 Sprinker, ed., *Edward W. Said*, 235, 242, 242, 235. See, however, Partha Chatterjee, "Their Own Words? An Essay for Edward Said," in Sprinker, ed., *Edward W. Said*, which defends, within nationalism, the "many possibilities of authentic, creative, and plural development of social identities which were violently disrupted by the political history of the post-colonial state seeking to replicate the modular forms of the modern nation-state" (p. 216).

15 Note the uses of *authority* in *Beginnings*, vis-à-vis molestation: a coinage that is emphatically *not* antiauthoritarian (Edward W. Said, *Beginnings: Intention and Method* [New York: Basic, 1975]). But note also the pathos of Said's isolated, genuinely heroic critique of the Middle East "peace process" in his *Peace and Its Discontents: Essays on Palestine in the Middle East Peace Process* (New York: Vintage, 1996).

16 Edward W. Said, "Gods That Always Fail," *Raritan* 13, no. 4 (spring 1994): 13 (this essay has been reprinted in his *Representations of the Intellectual* [New York: Pantheon, 1994]; the quotation can be found on p. 120).

17 Said, *Representations*, 121, 120. One's own beliefs and findings, in Said's view, quickly and inevitably harden into authorities.

18 "Benda's examples, however, make it quite clear that he does not endorse the notion of totally disengaged, other-worldly, ivory-towered thinkers. . . . Real intellectuals are never more themselves than when, moved by metaphysical passion and disinterested principles of justice and truth, they denounce corruption, defend the weak, defy imperfect or oppressive authority" (ibid., 5–6). See also Julien Benda, *La trahison des clercs* (Paris: B. Grosset, 1975).

19 Edward W. Said, *The World, the Text, and the Critic* (Cambridge, Mass.: Harvard University Press, 1983), 2, 25.

20 Said, *The World, the Text, and the Critic.*

21 Anna Boschetti, *The Intellectual Enterprise: Sartre and "Les temps modernes,"* trans. Richard McCleary (Evanston, Ill.: Northwestern University Press, 1988).

22 Gayatri Chakravorty Spivak, "Poststructuralism, Marginality, Postcoloniality, and Value," in *Literary Theory Today*, ed. Peter Collier and Helga Geyer-Ryan (Ithaca, N.Y.: Cornell University Press, 1990), 222, 224.

23 Here, I borrow from my review of *Culture and Imperialism* in *Nineteenth-Century Contexts*, 18 (1994): 93–96.

24 See my "Upward Mobility in the Postcolonial Era: Kincaid, Mukherjee, and the Cosmopolitan Au Pair," *Modernism/Modernity* 1, no. 2 (April 1994): 133–51.

25 Edward Said, *Culture and Imperialism* (New York: Knopf, 1993), 244.

26 Said, *Culture and Imperialism*, 244.

27 Pierre Bourdieu, *Homo Academicus*, trans. Peter Collier (Stanford, Calif.: Stanford University Press, 1988), xxiv, 100–101. Note the irony that the secular scholar can hold to his institution only with a religious irrationality.

28 Dirlik, "The Postcolonial Aura," 330, 354–55. Note the repetition of the old charge against cosmopolitans, leveled equally by Nazism and Stalinism, of complicity with world capitalism.

29 McClintock, "The Angel of Progress."

30 Alan Sinfield, *Literature, Politics, and Culture in Postwar Britain* (Berkeley and Los Angeles: University of California Press, 1989), 234.

31 Arjun Appadurai, "Disjuncture and Difference in the Global Cultural Economy," in *The Phantom Public Sphere*, ed. Bruce Robbins (Minneapolis: University of Minnesota Press, 1993), 269–95.

32 Abdul JanMohamed, "Worldliness-without-World, Homelessness-as-Home," in Sprinker, ed., *Edward W. Said*, 96–120.

33 It is interesting to note the historical usefulness of *secular* as a qualifier of *multiculturalism*. William Connolly writes: "Eventually, of course, secularism emerges as a loose set of doctrines designed to prevent struggles between contending Christian sects from tearing the fabric of public life apart" ("Pluralism and Multiculturalism," 25).

2 THE PREOCCUPATIONS OF POSTCOLONIAL STUDIES: MODERNITY, SEXUALITY, NATION

Street Theater in Pakistani Punjab: The Case of
Ajoka, Lok Rehs, and the (So-Called) Woman Question

FAWZIA AFZAL-KHAN

This essay offers some observations and tentative conclusions about the nature and importance of the parallel theater movement, or *street theater*, as it is loosely called, in the province of the Punjab, Pakistan.[1] This form of theater, which emerged during General Zia-ul-Haque's repressive martial law regime (1979–89), raises several questions about the nature of the relation between the Pakistani "Islamic" state and society. The most pertinent of these for my project is the question of the state's coercive relation with its female citizenry. Related to this is the issue of relationships between men and women in the society and how these are complicated by class stratifications that inevitably affect the way gendered politics (and policies) actually get played out. There is also the increasingly vexed issue of national versus ethnic identity, which is reflected through the language politics of these groups; linguistic choices reveal these groups' conflicting and often self-contradictory ideological stands on this question.

In choosing to focus on such an area of inquiry for a (so-called) postcolonial project, I am seeking to resite the question, Who decolonizes? that Gayatri Spivak insists we confront. This question forces us to reevaluate "the task of the post-colonial," which, as Spivak sees it — and I agree — ought to involve a rigorous moving away from conflating "Eurocentric migrancy with post-coloniality."[2] In other words, let us, as postcolonial critics and scholars, turn our attention to "other sites of enunciation," as Walter Mignolo has urged.[3] This turning elsewhere is really a turning inward to the postcolonial nation-state, in order to cast a critical gaze at a decolonizing process that has simultaneously constructed a normative constitutional subject of the "new" nation: in Pakistan's case, middle-class urban and male or upper-class feudal and male.[4] Within the last decade or so, Ajoka (the major parallel theater group in Pakistan) as well as its other regional spin-offs, notably Lok Rehs, have cast a critical eye through their plays and performances on the way the state's coercive shaping of the constitutional subject of the new nation has had a repressive effect on the identities and rights of women, religious minorities, and the poor. At the same time, as subjects within conflicting ideologies themselves — nationalist, ethnic, secular humanist, feminist, socialist — these drama activists enact or rehearse the very conditions for performances of subjectivity that remain shot through with seemingly unresolvable contradictions — to be for or against a nationalist ethos or an ethnic one, for feminism or humanism, etc. — that will become apparent later in this essay.

The following discussion does not offer a historical overview of street theater in Pakistan with an eye to charting its development from its roots in precolonial indigenous theatrical traditions into the present times. Rather, what I outline here are some preliminary thoughts in the vein of a cultural studies project, initiated through personal involvement over the past decade with Punjab-based Ajoka. My project ultimately seeks to understand the effect that this type of theatrical activity has on various sectors and aspects of Pakistani society. My involvement with this activity began in the spring of 1987, when I was "home" in Lahore (the provincial capital of Punjab, still considered to be the hub of Pakistani culture) — having recently completed my Ph.D. (in English literature) in Massachussetts, and with a nine-month-old baby girl in tow. I was in my parents' house once again, looking forward to some respite from the pressures of academic life as well as from the hard living of the United States. Looking forward, that is (albeit semiguiltily, having lived among left-leaning liberal academics for the past eight years of my life), to a household run by servants, with the proverbial ayah to take over in the child-care department.

When I ran into an old friend, Madeeha Gauhar, and got invited to join her "alternative" theater group while I was in Lahore, I was pleasantly inundated with memories of Madeeha as Viola in Shakespeare's *Twelfth Night*, of Sara Suleri in her imperial grandeur as Anastasia, and of Fauzia Mustafa playing a most androgynous Prospero on the stage at Kinnaird College for Women, delighting elite audiences starved for more highbrow fare than the bawdy commercial theatrical productions around town could possibly provide. Well, was I in for a shock! While Sara, Fauzia, and I had followed a more predictable route from our English-medium schooling (i.e., the medium of instruction had been English) at elite institutions in Pakistan to pursuing doctorates in English abroad, Madeeha had stayed in Pakistan and, after completing her master's degree in English literature at a local institution, gone on to found a theater group whose performances were nothing like those I was reminiscing about. *Alternative theater*, as she and her group had begun to define it, not only set itself up in opposition to the commercial stage theatrical tradition of urban Punjab, but also saw its relation to the English-language productions of the Kinnaird College Drama Society as directly antagonistic.

My direct involvement with Madeeha's group as performer that spring has, in turn, led not only to an active interest in following the activities of Ajoka but to my becoming aware of the growth of similar groups all over Pakistan (such as Sanjh, which is Pindi based, or Saraike Lok Tamasha, a Multan-based group, or Baang, in Karachi), although so far I have witnessed the work of only one other group besides Ajoka, the Lahore-based Lok Rehs (which means "Folkways"). Nevertheless, it is my awareness that such groups have been increasing in number and influence over the last decade — performing in various outdoor locations (including street corners as well as the lawns of such cultural centers as the Goethe Institute of Lahore), in inner-city locations, as well as in factory sites and village *maidans* or open parks — that has led me to formulate the premise of my current project. I am convinced that the parallel theater movement in Pakistan constitutes a locus of cultural conflict where issues concerning women's rights, class conflicts, the rise of Islamic fundamentalism, and language politics are defined and contested in the evolving and often conflictual relation between the Pakistani state and Pakistani society. It is also my contention that the subject matter of Ajoka and its counterparts is "revolutionary" in the sense that it questions previous and current state policies that have curtailed the rights of women and secular individuals as well as of leftist intellectuals and writers like Faiz Ahmed Faiz. Furthermore, the very class composition of Ajoka has attempted something new and daring (Ajoka means "dawn of a new day" in Punjabi) in drawing its actor-activists from a wide range of classes — from the urban working class to upper-middle-class urban intelligentsia.

This type of class mingling is, however, not extraordinary, and neither is the questioning of repressive state policies in Pakistan or pre-Partition India. Certainly, much excellent historiographic work has been done in recent years chronicling the involvement of both Hindu and Muslim women in the nationalist political struggles against British occupation and, later, against the implementation of patriarchal state policies and laws.[5] Sumanta Banerjee, for example, has documented women's popular culture in Bengal, suggesting that, up until the late nineteenth century, popular culture generally, and women's popular cultural forms specifically, such as performances of *jatras*, songs and dances, etc., not only thrived, but created a space for the intermingling of elite and lower-class women in the *zenanas* where the performances often took place.[6]

However, as the research of Banerjee and others indicates, by the late nineteenth century, these forms died out or were superceded by elite, *bhadralok* cultural forms that took over the cultural terrain of Hindu Bengal under the express influence of British education and Victorian tastes, which shunned the "bawdy irreverence" of popular culture.[7] Certainly, many of the earlier folk traditions have been revived through the efforts of street theater activists of contemporary postcolonial India, such as the late Safdar Hashmi (murdered while performing in Delhi in 1989), the Bengali Badal Sircar and his Third Theatre group, and such other Indian urban and rural theater groups as Ankur, Alarippu, etc. Nevertheless, it is in the context of contemporary Pakistani society that the revolutionary nature of this type of cultural work makes itself felt in ways that are different than it would be in India. This difference is in large part due to the influence of Islamic ideology on the state, an ideology that is particularly inhospitable to the notion of women as performers and to any display of leftist ideas. The major difficulty continues to be the recruitment of women actors and activists — from any and all classes — in a society that frowns on the intermingling of the sexes, especially as part of public spectacles.

Street Theater and the Women's Movement

Undoubtedly, Ajoka has provided a space where men and women can intermingle in a setting where female actors do run the risk of being objectified as spectacle. It was ostensibly to counter such objectification that, in the mid-1980s, the government of Pakistan banned the publication of women's photographs in the press and introduced a series of measures for "eliminating the use of the fair sex for commercial purposes."[8] The leading women's rights organization at the time, the Women's Action Forum (WAF), found itself in an awkward position: from a "purely" feminist perspective, it could not disagree with the directives, but, seen in the context of a general tendency to equate women per se with obscenity and a move to reduce the public visibility of women, some women felt that the WAF was obliged to take a stand against the government directives. Confusion on the "proper" stand to take on such issues is, according to the authors of *Women of Pakistan,* a result of a general failure on the part of the women's movement to define feminist priorities in the context of Pakistan. On that score, Ajoka has taken an unambiguous stand. Not only do women perform in the plays, but the plays themselves are stamped in the mold of a strong, independent woman — Madeeha Gauhar — who is the group's founder as well as its artistic director to date. Of course, that fact alone does not make Ajoka a feminist group (in an interview with me in 1995, Madeeha herself denied that Ajoka is a feminist theater group; she defines it as interested in producing plays "with a conscience").

Nevertheless, it is interesting to note that Ajoka was formed in the same year that the leading women's rights organization in Pakistan came into being — 1983. Madeeha (who comes, as I do, from the urban middle class of Lahore) was one of the early members of the WAF, and she, along with other women activists, was beaten up and jailed in February 1983 when a women's demonstration against the antiwomen laws introduced in Parliament by the military dictator General Zia-ul-Haque was brutally suppressed by the police.

As one of Ajoka's manifestos points out, 1983 was a watershed for the

Fig. 1: Members of the Ajoka theater troupe: *extreme left:* Madeeha Gauhar, founding artistic director; *extreme right:* Shahid Mahmud Nadeem, in-house playwright.

Pakistani political scene in many ways. That was the year that saw the introduction of so-called Islamic (Shari'a) laws that significantly downgraded the position of women and religious minorities (and that, although contested, continue in force to this day). That was also the year when the opposition groups united for the first time to launch a movement for the restoration of democracy (MRD). These moves were brutally suppressed, and several thousand political workers were arrested and tortured all over Pakistan. Press censorship was strengthened, and all forms of political activity were banned under martial law.

Thus, perhaps, it was no coincidence after all that Ajoka was formed the same year, with the aim of providing not only good theater but also an opportunity for like-minded secular activists to express themselves culturally, if not politically. The linkage between the women's movement and alternative theater is not a mere coincidence. Both movements were manifestations of people's resistance to the antidemocratic and obscurantist thrust of General Zia's government. Both were democratic, secular, and cultural movements, unattached to any political parties as such — although, when pressed, most of their members would indicate a preference for the Pakistan People's Party, the party, with a woman, Benazir Bhutto, at its head.

With the changeover from martial law to democracy in the late 1980s, new challenges have arisen, while old ones, such as the twin legacies of feudalism and religious obscurantism, continue to exercise repressive sway. These challenges underscore the ongoing need for vigilant activity on the part of women's and other activist and cultural groups. To their credit, Ajoka and the WAF have maintained a close relation over the past decade, and other parallel theater groups have also joined in. For instance, every year, Ajoka organizes performances on the occasion of International Women's Day either in collaboration with a women's organization or independently. Apart from Ajoka's artistic director, Madeeha, many other women in the company are also active in the women's movement, and members of Lok Rehs seek the help of WAF activists to read their scripts and provide them with constructive criticism. On the tenth anniversary of the police action against women demonstrators in Lahore, WAF members and Ajoka joined hands to organize a commemorative event at which Ajoka presented its bold play on the theme of religious intolerance, *Dekh tamasha chalta ban*. More recently, International Women's Day 1993 was marked by the launching of *Khasman khanian* (The husband eaters), Shahid Nadeem's collection of feminist plays written for Ajoka. Interestingly, Ajoka's in-house feminist playwright is a man, a former Amnesty International employee who is married to Madeeha (this is her third and his second marriage).

Although the six plays in *Khasman khanian* are all written in Punjabi, it should be pointed out that an equal number of plays performed by Ajoka are written in Urdu, the national language, or have dialogues that utilize a mixture of Urdu and Punjabi. The primary theoretical influences that have shaped Madeeha's vision of Ajoka have been Bertolt Brecht and, to a lesser degree, Augusto Boal. In a director's note to the Punjabi-language adaptation of Brecht's *Threepenny Opera* (*Takay da tamasha*), Madeeha gives the following

Fig. 2: Ajoka's *Jaloos* (Protest march), written by Indian playwright Badal Sircar, first produced by Ajoka in 1984 on the front lawn of Madeeha Gauhar's mother's house and, later, in front of a village crowd (this photograph).

Fig. 3: Ajoka's *Dekh tamasha chalta ban,* a play on the theme of religious intolerance (first production, 1992). Here, it is being performed at a later date on a street corner in a low-income inner-city neighborhood.

explanation of the company's art and motivation: "Ajoka's current production has extended Brecht's technique of 'alienation' (the distancing of the actor from the character and of the audience from the actors) to the acting style used in Pakistani cinema, which is typified by larger-than-life characterization. As a backdrop to the theme and to the particular style employed in this production, Ajoka has tried to use popular visual images (truck art), which help create the ambience of a Lahore that we all know exists but that many of us would visit only under the cover of nightfall."

By focusing in its productions, on art forms outside the high art canon, on, for example, caricatures, cartoons, bawdy sayings, and garish decorations festooning the windows and sides of trucks and rickshas, Ajoka is attempting to deploy images and symbols as adversarial counterrepresentations to an elite worldview. Thus, in terms of both its language politics and its artistic credo, Ajoka seeks to deliver a populist, antihierarchical, anticolonial message. In the preface to an Urdu-language program copy of their first production, *Jaloos* (Demonstration), written by Badal Sircar and performed by Ajoka in February 1987, Shahid and Madeeha further elaborate their philosophy of theater:

> Commercial theater in Pakistan today [including stage and television productions] has become degraded and meaningless. We, the Ajoka Theater Workshop, wish to challenge the circulation of conventional theatrical forms and their pietistic content through the production of socially meaningful theater. We propose doing drama in which the distance be-

tween spectators and actors can be eliminated. The main purpose of our theater workshop is to raise critical consciousness in people, in order that it might lead to the creation of a more just society. Although we realize that such change cannot be brought about through progressive theater alone, we do believe that "the change in consciousness" [*Fiqr mey harqat*] that our type of theatrical activity aims to create is surely an important step in that direction.

In this early statement of philosophy, both the artistic director and the playwright of Ajoka seem to be espousing goals in keeping with a Brechtian poetics, in which, according to Augosto Boal, "the spectator delegates power to the character [to act] in his place but the spectator reserves the right to think for himself, often in opposition to the character." In contrast to Aristotelian poetics, wherein a passive spectator experiences a catharsis at the end of the dramatic action, the Brechtian spectator achieves a more activist, unsettling "critical awareness" of societal issues. In expressing the hope that such an increased awareness or "critical consciousness" will lead people to work for a more just society, Ajoka's artistic director and playwright are also gesturing toward the more radical "poetics of the oppressed" as espoused by Augusto Boal, the Latin American theater activist. In contradistinction to the poetics both of Aristotle and Brecht, the poetics of the oppressed, claims Boal, focuses on the action itself. The spectator delegates no power to the character (or actor) either to act or to think in his/her place; on the contrary, s/he himself assumes the role of the protagonist, changes the dramatic action, tries out solutions, discusses plans for change—in short, trains him/herself for real action. In this case, perhaps, theater is not revolutionary in itself, but it is surely a rehearsal for the revolution. The liberated spectator, as a whole person, launches into action. No matter that the action is fictional; what matters is that it is action![9]

Ajoka's overall method and philosophy are perhaps more in line with Brecht than Boal. Other theater groups, however, such as Lok Rehs, as well as those utilizing theatrical forms in community self-help organizations, seem to be moving in Boal's direction.

Class and Gender Issues

In keeping with Ajoka's antielitist and prowoman artistic and political credo, not only have Madeeha and Shahid chosen Urdu and Punjabi as their linguistic medium, but they have, by virtue of their choice to perform politicized plays in inner-city locations, village courtyards, and factory sites, defined themselves in opposition to other forms of popular theater, including commercial stage plays performed in state-run auditoriums or seen on state-owned television. Ajoka's performances also offer a populist alternative to the English-language productions staged for elite audiences at such locations as Kinnaird College for Women or the British Council (where, ironically enough, Madeeha first began her stage career, acting and directing plays in English).

Nevertheless, there are contradictions here—an obvious one being that Ajoka utilizes elite venues such as the Goethe Institute for some of its productions, although for the activist purpose of shocking elite audiences. I believe that some of these contradictions may pose serious obstacles to the articulation of a committed and consistent vision for social change. On one level, Madeeha's visible and influential presence as female founder and artistic director of Ajoka bodes well as signifier for articulating feminist priorities for change. Yet her strong personality, which has the force of class privilege on its side (hence her education at elite English-medium institutions such as Kinnaird College), makes the relationship between her and the nonelite members of Ajoka, male and female alike, somewhat one-sided. Only half jokingly referred to as *Medea* by those who know her, Madeeha is the child of an intriguing union between a loud, aggressively patriarchal army man of Pathan background and a soft-spoken, radically left-wing, South African–born activist-intellectual mother. No wonder Maddy Gauhar is herself a curious mixture of aggression and intellect—which often manifests itself as intellectual aggression! In any case, the complicated intersection of class, gender, and personality issues in Madeeha has meant that the very structure of Ajoka has remained hierarchical, with Madeeha (now together with Shahid Nadeem) very much in control of a theater group that espouses, in principle, an egalitarian and democratic philosophy.

Indeed, in the early years of its existence, the gender division of the group mirrored a class divide as well: the four female members (including myself) belonged to the (sub)urban middle-class bourgeoisie, while the male recruits hailed primarily from a lower-income, inner-city background. I want to make clear here that my critique of some of the contradictions in Ajoka's ideological stance as reflected through the positionalities of its founder and playwright is, thus, a form of autocritique—one that allows me to reflect on my own situatedness within this project. Thus, I am aware that my relationship with the group as a whole was complicated by the fact that I was "visiting" from the United States, where I had just completed my Ph.D. in—of all things—English literature! My commitment to political theater in Pakistan was seen by Madeeha and the others, then, as tenuous at best. Furthermore, I was—and remain—in a position of academic privilege in that I get to write about their (and other theater groups') activities for publication and circulation in prestigious North American journals and books. It therefore seems imperative that I continually interrogate my own imbrication within the complicated nexus of class, gender, and educational privilege that underwrites my commitment to social and political change "there," built as it is on my need to publish "here," in order to keep alive my reputation as "hybrid postcolonial scholar"! Not surprisingly, then, the source of distance between the men in the group and me seemed to be an awareness of class difference rather than one of gender difference. Nor was the relationship between the men and the other women in the group much different, although perhaps less complicated. It is only recently, with the recruitment of lower-middle-class urban women into the group, that the relationship between the sexes seems to have changed into one of a mutually respectful camaraderie. Clearly, this change suggests that class issues that profoundly affect one's mobility and access to institutional power must be looked at and considered as carefully as those of gender if a truly egalitarian feminist philosophy of change is to be articulated by this (or any other) group.

Content and Mise-en-Scène/Hudood Politics

In the next few pages, I analyze the following plays performed by Ajoka in the past decade: *Barri* (Acquittal), *Dhee rani* (Queenly daughter), and *Eik thi nani* (There was once a grandmother). It is worth keeping in mind that most of these plays are original, written on some burning topic of the day by Shahid. There are also a few adaptations of Brecht's plays in the group's repertoire. As Shahid spells out in the prefatory remarks to the collection of Punjabi street plays that he wrote for Ajoka during the 1980s, "*Street theater* is the name given to those plays that are written with the express purpose of conveying some information to the public, raising their consciousness about some injustice being perpetrated against them — such as the plight of the laborers, the passage of repressive laws against poor women, etc. The plays should be short and portable, able to be performed on street corners, in open courtyards, on factory grounds, etc." [10]

Many of the plays performed by Ajoka employ a mixture of idiomatic Urdu and a rich variety of Punjabi. The Punjabi language in the plays varies from the more commonly spoken and understood version used in (some) urban Lahori households, to the cruder idiom of street vendors, servants, and shopkeepers, to the more sophisticated variants spoken in rural parts of the Punjab and districts such as Multan and Shujabad from whence hail the Punjabi-language Sufi poets and philosophers of the seventeenth and eighteenth centuries Bulleh Shah and Khwaja Ghulam Farid.

Three of Ajoka's most interesting Punjabi-language plays — in terms of staging and aesthetic issues as well as their bold delineation of women's rights abuses — are *Barri, Jhali kithay jaavay* (Where should the madwoman go?), and *Dhee rani*. These plays draw their main characters and themes from the lives and experiences of the urban lower classes and rural peasantry, incorporating folk songs and dances and folk idioms into the production. In *Barri,* the

Fig. 4: Samia Mumtaz in Ajoka's *Jhalli kithay jaavey* (Where should the madwoman go?).

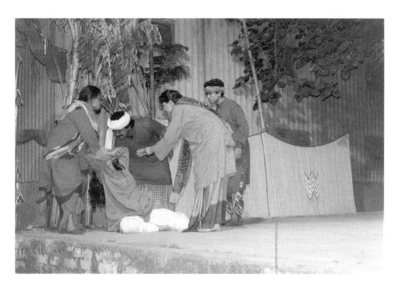

Fig. 5: Scene from *Jhalli kithay jaavey* (Where should the madwoman go?).

female narrator/activist/reporter, who functions in the capacity of a chorus, is the only character to be drawn from the urban upper-middle-class intelligensia and, as such, the only one who speaks in Urdu. The theme of madness is a pivotal one in the first two plays, which deal with state and familial injustices against women, a theme that stands in for a subversive carnivalesque subtext.[11]

Fig. 6: Cast members of first production of *Barri* (Acquittal), written by Shahid Nadeem. Performed at open-air stage on the lawns of the Goethe Institute of Lahore, March 1987. *Left to right:* Uzra Butt, Madeeha Gauhar, Fawzia Afzal-Khan, Sarwat Nawaz.

Barri

In *Barri,* the "madwoman" is an inmate in a Pakistani prison during the military dictatorship of General Zia-ul-Haque (whose rule lasted more than a decade, from 1977 to 17 August 1988, when a plane on which he was traveling exploded shortly after takeoff). At the time the play was first written and performed in 1987, Zia's regime, in cahoots with the conservative agenda of the Muslim fundamentalist parties, was trying to impose strict Islamic laws on the general populace, curtailing the rights of women and minorities. Regressive laws such as the Hudood Ordinances (passed by the *shariat* or religious courts in 1980) in most instances sanctioned violence against women through such bizarre moves as effectively equating the criminal offense of rape with that of adultery and fornication. Thus, women who brought charges of rape against men were in almost all cases assumed to be women of easy virtue and consequently guilty of the crime of adultery or fornication. The rapists were inevitably acquitted, it being extremely difficult to prove the rape in the absence of testimony from four adult male eyewitnesses to the act! [12] It should come as no surprise that, once arrested and imprisoned for the crime of *zina* (fornication), women were further harassed by the police and often sexually assaulted by them. The policemen realized that these women were helpless before the law.

This atmosphere of increasing repression against fundamentally poor and uneducated women was the backdrop for *Barri.* Women of elite classes rarely

Fig. 7: Fawzia Afzal-Khan in
Barri (Acquittal), 1987.

end up in prison, and, if they do, they are much more aware of their legal rights
as well as of how to manipulate the system through class privilege. Thus it is
that the poor and illiterate madwoman Miriam — a character based on a Sufi-
type dancer at the shrine of a local mystic saint (Madho Lal Husain) — is forbidden to continue her devotion through dance in accordance with the obscurantist fundamentalist bias rampant in society at the time. She is hauled off to
prison, where she is raped by several police officers. When we see her onstage,
she is one of four women cell mates in prison for a variety of "crimes." Two of the
other three are poor, illiterate women, one a peasant woman from a village who
has killed her husband, who abused her physically and verbally for years, the
second an old servant woman who is in prison for refusing to reveal the where-
abouts of her son, accused of stealing a tape recorder from the house where both
mother and son have been employed for many years. The fourth woman is of
a different socioeconomic background than these three: she is a middle-class
urban activist named Zahida, in jail as a political prisoner for having dared
to go on a hunger strike as a protest against the repressive Islamic laws being
pushed through Parliament during Zia-ul-Haque's regime. As the play begins,
Miriam is five months pregnant, and, during the course of the performance,
after her baby is forcibly aborted to remove all traces of her jailers' crime, she
becomes the catalyst for self-discovery on the part of the other women there.

She and the other "ignorant" women there have a profound effect on the consciousness of the educated activist. This character assumes that women's problems can be solved by a simple recourse to the law and is finally brought to the realization that not all women have such recourse. Justice, in any case, realizes that Zahida is neither blind nor impartial—the law can be and is manipulated by those in power to suit their purposes.

As Miriam retreats more and more into her "madness," symbolized by the hauntingly double-edged lyrics of Bulleh Shah, which she sings sitting in a trancelike state under the *peepal* tree, Zahida's eyes are opened for the first time to the depth and extent of oppression and injustice that the majority of women in Pakistani society suffer daily—and from which she, in the cocoon of upper-middle-class safety, is relatively immune. When, for instance, Jamila the murderess, sensing Zahida's disapproval of her actions, asks her what she ought to have done to end a lifetime of physical abuse, Zahida's first response is, "You should have asked for a divorce—a right that you and all women have had but that women like myself are fighting to preserve under this reactionary regime." Her "lawyerly"—not to mention self-aggrandizing—response is shown to be inadequate when Jamila scoffingly points out that she was a mere child of fourteen when she was married against her will, knowing nothing of how to ensure that the right to divorce got written into the marriage contract. As an illiterate peasant child, she did not know then that she had such a right under the law. When Zahida persists with, "You should nevertheless have pursued a legal path—why didn't you take your case to the village council?" Jamila bursts out with the sarcastic retort, "I did—only to find out that the chairman of the council was my husband's brother, who punched me in the face and dragged me back home! No, *memsahib,* my way was the only way."

With her difficult questions, Jamila continues to shake Zahida's faith in an abstract notion of the law, one that, secular or religious, remains cut off from the lived, complex realities of most women's lives. Why, she asks, should a woman like Miriam, who has never done any wrong to anyone, be imprisoned for a crime she did not commit? Who can save her? Why should Janat Bibi, the old servant woman, suffer imprisonment and worry ceaselessly about a son whose only crime was that he perhaps coveted a tape recorder that years of service did not allow him to obtain?

These are difficult questions, and, eventually, Zahida's easy answers run out. She and the urban middle-class audience of academic intellectuals, government servants, housewives, and urban professionals who constituted the first audience of the play when it was performed on the lawns of the Goethe Institute of Lahore in March 1987 were repeatedly made to confront their own culpability in perpetuating class and gender oppression. The Brechtian techniques used in the performance forced elite audiences in this setting to recognize, through the character of Zahida, their alienation from and collusion in perpetuating the

Fig. 8: Madeeha Gauhar in
Barri (Acquittal), 1987.

injustices faced on a daily basis by women like Miriam and the other two inmates. For instance, how many of the men and women in the audience could
look at the character of Janat Bibi and fail to recognize parallels between her
story and similar incidents involving their own servants? Servants — male and
female — are regarded as almost subhuman, not only in upper-class feudal, but
also in middle-class urban households, to be kept in their place through rough
treatment and the threat of the law. On being hired, they must always surrender
their identification cards to their employers, who make sure that the ID number is entered into the books at the local police station — as both deterrent and
tracking device should a theft be committed.

And what of the gap between rural and urban women of different classes?
Does their experience of domestic violence erase other barriers between them?
Can such shared abuse become the basis for elaborating a feminist coalitional
politics? One woman in the audience clearly saw the similarity between Jamila
and her own experience of being beaten by her husband for almost twenty
years before she sued for divorce. However, as a middle-class woman living in
an urban metropolis with a B.A. degree from an elite institution, she decided,
eventually, to exercise her individual right to divorce under Islamic law. Like
Zahida, she could conceptualize and execute such a course of action, however
socially unacceptable, because her class and educational background enabled
her to do so. But, as Jamila asks so poignantly in the play, how are women of

her class and background to exercise rights they do not even know they have? Furthermore, as her own as well as Miriam's and Janat's experiences demonstrate so clearly, the law itself is not just gender biased but class coded as well. Under such a legal system, poor, illiterate women such as Miriam, Jamila, and Janat, who are victims of criminal behavior (whether at the hands of family members, the police, or their employers), are treated as criminals in the eyes of the law.

When the play was performed for the first time, the mis-en-scène could not have been more perfect: a makeshift outdoor stage, consisting of a raised mud surface, extended outward from the servant quarters on the back lawn of the Goethe Institute, making a rectangular shape around a peepal tree that served, along with the barred skylight of the servant quarters in the background, as symbolic prop. The Brechtian technique employed by the playwright of having the play end inconclusively, with no resolution of Miriam's or Janat's fate but with Jamila's execution and the middle-class activist's acquittal imminent, allowed for some correspondence between Zahida's experience of alienation in trying to grapple with the political and moral meaning of her jailhouse experience and the alienation evoked in the audience at that particular outdoor location in the middle-class suburbs of Lahore. Indeed, as the play ends, we are left to gaze on the forlorn figure of Miriam sitting under the peepal tree, singing supplicatory lyrics (Bulleh Shah's "Spell") to the moon. Yet the lyrics of the folk songs that she continues to sing into the enveloping darkness (all stage lights are shut off one by one) hint at the subversive potential of Islamic Sufi thought — while simultaneously enabling the director to execute an audiovisually haunting scene, capitalizing on a South Asian audience's delight in song. These lyrics of Bulleh Shah celebrate the life force of a state of passionate rapture, embodied in song and dance, a passion that obliterates all obstacles in the path of true love, human and divine; it is, in fact, a state of being that allows for the redemptive power of love to heal one's wounds and assert one's desire — in this case, very clearly female desire: "I will cast a spell with my song, to get my lost love back.... Although I am neither married nor single, I will have an infant to love in my arms." In having Miriam represent a mystical version of Islam, which allows for the possibility of devotional practices rooted in song and dance, the playwright and director certainly seem to be hinting at the feminist possibilities of Sufi thought.

Dhee rani

Shifting performances to different sites with different audiences obviously complicates questions of communication, reception, and motive. One such location was a Muslim girls' school located in Shahdara, a lower-middle-class urban community on the outskirts of Lahore, where I accompanied Ajoka for a performance in March 1995. As one of the events organized around International

Women's Day, this was to be a performance of a short play, *Dhee rani,* on the theme of women's education.

The performance was going to take place in the central courtyard of the school, the audience consisting mainly of local housewives, who had been urged to attend via the efforts of area activists, as well as some of the older schoolgirls. ("We weren't sure the treatment of the subject matter would be appropriate for the girls to watch," said one of the teachers, in response to Madeeha's question as to why there were not more students there.) The four-room schoolhouse that we entered through a large steel gate was colorfully festooned with welcome banners in Urdu and had several other banners draped across its walls proclaiming the unity and oneness of God, the greatness of Islam, and the importance of following the "right path" as prescribed by Islam. Many of the women sitting in a circle around the courtyard were wearing black satin *burqas,* the Pakistani version of the *hijab* (veil); others were more "openly" clad, in colorful *shalwar kameezes,* with *dupattas* (scarves) drawn over their bosoms as a mark of their modesty. Most said that they were here because the performance provided them with a welcome excuse to suspend their daily chores and come out of their homes; they hoped that it was going to be "good entertainment." Yes, they knew Ajoka did issue-oriented theater or theater for social change, but, after all, it was theater, drama, music — spectacle!

This audience, seated all along the edges of the maidan or central courtyard of the schoolhouse on the dust-covered grass, was certainly in a good position to view the ritualized movements of the actors and hear the short, repetitive poetic refrains that punctuate the simple dialogue. The play opens with a young woman in the center of a rectangle formed by her father, brother, uncle, and mother surrounding her and chanting,

> Dhee Rani-ay, Dhee Rani-ay,
> Kee Chani-ay, kee chani-ay?

which, translated, means roughly, "Oh daughter/queen of the house, what do you desire?" When, in response to the question, the poor girl replies eagerly that she wishes to go to high school, she is severely reprimanded, first by her mother, who expresses astonishment at her daughter's nerve for thinking of attempting something "even your brother hasn't done!" The daughter challenges her mother's tradition-bound thinking by replying feistily, "but that is because he failed his class, and I didn't." Logic, however, does not persuade anyone since the brother lashes out with the age-old excuse, "My honor will be shamed if you pursue higher education," only to be seconded by his uncle's dictum, "A village lass has no business studying."

The rest of the play consists of rapidly changing scenes in which the mise-en-scène of the rectangle of family members surrounding the young woman becomes a symbolic prison hemming her in whenever she tries to express her autonomy. For example, when she tries to go out of the house to visit a friend, the chorus of four tells her she cannot; when she sits reading a book of poetry, they tell her she must get rid of it immediately, before it puts "unclean" thoughts in her head; when she tries to comb her hair and apply some *kohl* to her eyes, the gang of four upbraid her for her vanity, saying that she should attend to house-hold chores instead of wasting time and courting the devil by "prettifying" her-self like a prostitute. The chorus of nos builds to a terrifying crescendo that ends with the edict,

> Dee Rani-ay, Dhee Rani-ay,
> Mar jaani-ay, mar jaani-ay,

or, "Why don't you just die, oh daughter/queen."

The subversive or revolutionary potential of the play lies in the fact that, at each repressive moment, the young woman being browbeaten questions and protests the unfair treatment she is receiving in the name of family honor and tradition. The ritualized representation of convention also becomes a subversive theatrical technique in that it lays bare the life-killing nature of such convention. At the very end, when it appears as though her family/society has finally succeeded in crushing the very life out of her, the nameless Everywoman rises and comes forward to declaim, "In olden times, they used to bury new-born daughters alive; today, in our society, they want to see her buried within the four walls of a concept called *home.*" She goes on to point out the irony of the phrase *dhee rani,* which suggests that a daughter is to be treated as a queen, not a slave without rights. Her concluding statement insists that she, and other women, be treated as human beings rather than being put on false pedestals.

Those elements of the play that are rooted in traditional/indigenous popular forms — such as profane language and curses, certain folk gestures and crude mannerisms such as the twirling of humongous mustaches by the young woman's male relatives, who also direct lewd remarks and controlling gestures at her when she expresses her desire to pursue her education beyond the primary level — all fetched a lot of laughs from this all-female audience. The other aspect of folk tradition that Ajoka and other parallel theater groups have revived is the poetry of the mystical Punjabi-language poets set to popular folk music tunes. It is not surprising, given the secular bent of the street theater activists, that the poetry of someone like Bulleh Shah would prove so attractive and easily appropriable for their purposes, given his unremitting attacks on the priesthood. The antimullah songs of Bulleh Shah that Ajoka performed that day also proved to be immensely popular with the audience, especially those lyrics implying that a mullah's obsession with concepts of purity and filth have nothing to do with external objecs but rather reflect the unclean state of his own soul.

What is instructive here? Is the performance understood as the subversion that it is intended to be? Or is street theater (should it be?) more dialogic (hence less tied to an "instructive" mode) in its interventions in cultural politics? My question is prompted by the definition of a "poetics of the oppressed" as proposed by Augusto Boal in the context of Latin American street theatrical activity. He writes:

> In order to understand the poetics of the oppressed, one must keep in mind its main objective: to change the people — "spectators," passive beings in the theatrical phenomenon — into subjects, into actors, transformers of the dramatic action. . . . Aristotle proposes a poetics in which the spectator delegates power to the dramatic character so that the latter may act and think for him. Brecht proposes a poetics in which the spectator delegates power to the character who thus acts in his place but the spectator reserves the right to think for himself, often in opposition to the character. In the first case a "catharsis" occurs; in the second, an awakening of critical consciousness. But the poetics of the oppressed focuses on the action itself: the spectator delegates no power to the character (or actor) either to act or to think in his place; on the contrary, he himself assumes the protagonic role, changes the dramatic action, tries out solutions, discusses plans for change — in short, trains himself for real action. In this case, perhaps the theatre is not revolutionary in itself, but it is surely a rehearsal for the revolution. The liberated spectator, as a whole person, launches into action. No matter that the action is fictional; what matters is that it is action! [13]

Although it would appear that Ajoka's method is more in keeping with Brechtian poetics than those of Boal, the responses that I solicited from audience members after the performance defied any easy classification along such an axis. An old woman claimed that she thought that education and emancipation were worthy goals for women to strive for because then one could dispense with men — "What freedom!" Or, as an old woman only half joking put it, "So our daughters can be like you — very modern and fashionable, with short hair and lipstick!" Most of the women laughed at this. Several said that they already knew that it was important for women to be educated — that was why they were sending their daughters to this school. Many echoed the sentiment that most of the men they knew were not placing serious obstacles in the way of their sisters' or daughters' education, as the play implied. One of the women said to me in English inflected with a Punjabi-Cockney accent, "My problem isn't female education; it's culture shock!" Here was a woman from the urban lower middle class, raised in a working-class Pakistani family in Manchester, England, married off to "one of her own kind" from "back home," now herself a stranger in Shahadara, living in a joint-family system with in-laws she does not understand and who do not understand her. What/who speaks to her?

In yet another location, the play takes on a different resonance again. Sohail Waraich, a young man who has been with Ajoka since its inception and whose activism has led to his working for one of the earliest-formed women's rights NGOs, Shirkat Gah, explained how the play and its performance were regarded by the inhabitants of a village outside Lahore where the troupe had gone to perform it a year ago. According to him, when the troupe arrived at the village, they were first told by the village folk that there was no place they could go to perform the play. Some of the theater activists started going from house to house, asking if anyone would allow them to perform in their courtyard. Finally, a woman who was home alone at the time gave her permission. In this case, curiosity very nearly killed not only the cat but the performers as well. Apparently, while the performance was going on, most of the audience—comprising primarily men—started hurling invective and abuse at the Ajoka actors. However, more and more people did start turning out to watch the play, including women who began watching from their rooftops. Suddenly, one of the men who came into the compound realized that one of the few women in the audience was his wife; he grabbed her hair from behind, slapped her, and dragged her out. The man of the house where the play was being performed also returned and ordered everyone out when he realized that the play was advocating the right of women to an education and simultaneously undermining the authority of the men of the family. The Ajoka troupe departed ignominiously, amid derisive comments and angry invective. What had their performance achieved?

If the gender politics of *Dhee rani* can be said to be fairly straightforward in the advocacy of the right to education of women of all classes and sectors of society, it is the politics of reception that allows us to see that it will obviously have a different effect on different audiences; for some its message will be a threat, for others more of an entertaining spectacle, and sometimes a bit of both. However, a similar theme in a different play, performed in front of an upper-middle-class audience on the lawns of the Goethe Institute, creates rather different resonances because of its less cogent class politics as well as its simplistic antistate stance.

Eik thi nani

In the acclaimed comic production *Eik thi nani,* the central theme is that of women's emancipation in pre- and post-Partition India and Pakistan. We are shown, through the separate paths taken by two Muslim sisters, now in their seventies, how the one who opted to remain behind in Hindu-dominated India after the creation of the two nation-states has been able to lead a far more independent and creative life than the other, who married and moved to Pakistan with her husband and child. The latter—who had theater talent and aspirations like the sister she left behind—has repressed that side of her personality in her effort to become a model Pakistani Muslim woman, devoted to the ideology of home, hearth, and prayer.

Fig. 9: Ajoka's *Eik thi nani* (There was once a grandmother), April 1993, Lahore. Cast members (actual sisters and their grandniece), *left to right:* Uzra Butt, Samia Mumtaz, Zohra Sehgal.

The stage, bare save for an opulent dresser and a hidden harmonium, is the home of this Pakistani sister, where she is now raising her teenage grand-daughter. The girl's parents are busy making a comfortable living in one of the Gulf states but feel that their daughter's interests are best served living under the protective wing of her grandmother, attending "good" all-girl schools. The visit of the grandmother's sister from India, however, upsets all this "good girl" ideology, for the feisty old(er) woman's presence in a bright-colored sari be-comes a catalyst for the young woman's self-discovery, ending in her declara-tion that she, too, wants to become an actress. The play serves, then, as a secular critique of official Islamic doctrine that supposedly forces all women to accept its repressive regime; it also questions the very basis for the separate creation of the Pakistani nation-state as distinct from India. The message, loud and clear: What need of Pakistan when a Muslim woman actress could practice her art freely in India and not be hampered by enforced religious repression? Such a secular anti-Pakistan stance is simplistic in that it does not allow for a full-blown critique of nationalist ideology per se and inadvertently repeats Indian propaganda about its secular freedoms for all minorities — surely an untenable position in the aftermath of the Ayodhya incident, the Bombay riots, and the emergence of Hindu fundamentalist political parties in India within the past de-cade (which were voted into power in the 1996 national elections). What is even more interesting is that such an antistate stance is contradicted by a very jingoistic play on the Kashmir issue written by Shahid Nadeem for state-controlled television and performed in by Madeeha as recently as early 1995 — pointing to the occasionally opportunistic politics of Ajoka's playwright and director.

Furthermore, in plays like *Eik thi nani,* Ajoka's class politics also seem questionable. The coming-of-age-and-independence narrative that structures the play relates the story of a young, urban, upper-middle-class heroine from an educated household; the household employs a number of servants, including a young woman who functions primarily as an earthy, illiterate, hence comic foil to the heroine. When the grandaunt leaves to return to India in the last scene, having "liberated" her grandniece from thinking that she must acquiesce to such conventional pieties as an arranged marriage, home, and children, she hands out gifts to everyone in the house. Her gift to the servant girl is a piece of silk cloth, which she advises the blushing, grateful girl to "keep aside" for the day she must inevitably marry. Thus, the critiques leveled at Ajoka do point up some contradictions in its ideological stance.

Ajoka versus Lok Rehs on Language and Feminism

In using Urdu and Punjabi to replace/reconstruct a European idiom and language (this is especially true of their Urdu- and Punjabi-language adaptations of Brecht's plays), Madeeha and Shahid have very consciously formulated a practical resistance to linguistic imperialism rooted in a pre-Independence British colonial past. Madeeha has, in fact, called attention to this facet of her work in an interview published in 1991: "Stress should be laid on performing Urdu and Punjabi plays because every act of creation has its roots in its own reality. Moreover, it does not imply artificial situation, and you can more easily reach toward a greater number of audience [sic]."[14] Thus, Ajoka's language politics reflect more an anticolonial stance than an antinationalist one, even though some of their recent plays (such as *Eik thi nani*) have been viewed by Pakistani audiences as critiques of nationalist ideology.

Lok Rehs has taken a further step in analyzing the issue of linguistic imperialism by articulating a Punjabi-only policy for their productions. This is a means of countering Urdu-language hegemony, a stand that marks the members of Lok Rehs as proponents of (among other things) an ideology of cultural and artistic liberation based in ethnicity rather than in Pakistani nationalism. During an interview that I conducted with members of Lok Rehs in March 1995, several discussed the reasons behind their Punjabi-only stance. For Shafqat, the main singer in the group, the choice to perform in Punjabi is very much a gesture of resistance against state-mandated Urdu-language hegemony, which is rooted in British colonial policies of domination and control. According to Shafqat, Punjabi folk festivals, such as the various *melas* that were widespread in rural Punjab, where folk songs and collective dances such as *jhoomer,*

Fig. 10: Play in the round entitled *Saar* (Event), based on contemporary events involving familial restrictions on women's right to choose a marriage partner; performed in March 1999 by members of Punjab Lok Rehs.

bhangra, and *gidda* were performed and which allowed for a free intermingling and exchange of ideas among the people, were abolished by the British. Along with the institution of Urdu as the official language of the Punjab, official Western forms and concepts of theater and entertainment were introduced, such as proscenium-based drama. Punjabi folk theatrical forms (including song and dance) — which were collective in nature and noncathartic in affect — were abolished or suppressed. Hence, in trying to revive these forms — such as the Vaar, or epic theater; the Kafi tradition of Sufi poets; and Lok Geet, or the songs of the people — which naturally find expression in the Punjabi language, Lok Rehs is resisting the linguistic and cultural imperialism forced on the people of Punjab, not only by the British, but also by those who accepted and propagated the notion of Urdu as the culturally sanctioned language of the Pakistani state.

The language politics of Lok Rehs is also tied to its class politics, both of which are consistent with their self-definition as a nonhierarchical theater group. As Mohammed Wasim, one of the founding members of the group, explains,

> When this group was founded in 1985, none of us had any theatrical experience, and we all came from nonprivileged backgrounds. Hence, there was never any danger (or desire) for this group to devolve into a personality cult. From our inception, we have remained a collective enterprise, with everyone receiving equal respect and having an equal say in running

things. Since our aim, from the start, has been to use theater as a vehicle of communicating with the masses, it seemed to us not just desirable but essential that we use Punjabi as our linguistic medium since it is the language of the people in this province — spoken by 85 percent of the people. Urdu is the symbol of the state's success, spoken by an elite few — not the language spoken and understood by the majority of our people.

Hence, the question of audience, as well as of actors as a representative sampling of that audience, takes on ever more complex nuances — with those who identify as Pakistani citizens, on the one hand, and, on the other, an increasing number, critiquing all nationalist ideologies as coercive state mechanisms (as Ajoka does in *Eik thi nani*) and still others, such as members of the Lok Rehs troupe, looking to fashion and identity politics based in Punjabi and class-based ethnicity rather than a (male) gendered and elitist notion of Pakistani nationhood.

Despite the fact that Ajoka does not call itself a *feminist* street theater group, its agenda, according to Madeeha, being more broadly conceived in terms of human rights issues, the fact remains that the polemical nature of its plays and performances has lead to it being perceived as antagonistic to men, hence as deserving (certain) men's contempt and anger. Lok Rehs — the founding members of which originally started with Ajoka — has critiqued Ajoka for its undertheorized attacks on men in general as agents of women's oppression and for not paying sufficient attention to the oppression of both men and women of lower socioeconomic strata by men *and* women of higher/more powerful classes. Huma Safdar, a founding member of the Lok Rehs collective, voiced concern about what she perceived to be "a new trend" within the Pakistani women's movement, reflected in many of Ajoka's plays — to be "antimen." *Dhee rani* certainly bears the traces of the type of male bashing alluded to by Lok Rehs — hence, perhaps, the confrontation in the village. *Barri,* on the other hand, despite being an earlier play, is much more sophisticated in terms of its analysis of the class-based and class-biased oppression of women. In this respect, however, *Barri* does seem somewhat anomalous in the oeuvre of Ajoka since most of the other plays dealing specifically with women's issues do seem either to suffer from a certain class blindness or to reify male-female antagonism in a structural (fixed) account of gender relations, rather than locating them in a more fluid narrative of changing cultural, economic, and political realities.

The play that I witnessed being discussed and shaped collectively by members of the Lok Rehs troupe for performance on International Women's Day 1995 on the grounds of the Goethe Institute, and to be performed later at various other urban and rural sites, was not a play about Punjabi ethnicity per se despite the fact that it was performed entirely in Punjabi. Rather, it was a play that dealt head-on with the issue of the class-based oppression of women as well as the oppression of poor men in a class-structured society, who in turn often vent their frustrations on the women in their families. The play (performed on the same mud stage as *Barri* all those years ago, but now with a raised brick foundation outlining it) also presents conflicting viewpoints of women on men and of whether men ought to be included in the movement to fight for women's rights. One of the play's scenes shows a middle-class male householder abusing "his" woman by demanding that she submit to his boss's lecherous advances so that he can advance his career in the entertainment industry; another scene shows her resisting such abuse by questioning an unjust system that sets up women as objects of exchange and acquisition by men in a market economy. In yet another scene, a lower-class urban working woman accuses a woman from a higher socioeconomic class of using the women's movement to further her own class agenda — that of keeping the dominant status quo in place — with the following taunt: "How do you claim to be a leader of the women's movement when you can't tolerate being with us poor women for even a few minutes?" The next scene shows this "Begum" complaining to her feudal landlord husband about the increasing unruliness and "ingratitude" of the servant classes. He tells her to "keep them happy."

The play is essentially a collage of such thematically interrelated scenes that portray the contradictions and complexities facing the various classes and genders of Punjabi Pakistani society today. Antihierarchical and antielitist in its overall message, the play, as I said earlier, was itself a result of an antihierarchical process of collective creation. Huma Safdar and Mohammed Wasim, who appeared to me (and to whom I was directed) as the ostensible leaders of the group, themselves disavow such leadership. They are avid readers of the works of Paolo Freire and Boal. They believe in a "poetics of the people," a Pakistani version of Boal's concept of the theater of the oppressed.

Certainly, in the rehearsals that I witnessed, I saw an attempt to create a space for dialogue among all the participants in the play; several collective exercises were undertaken to aid actors in visualizing various happenings to which they were asked to respond in some way. A group of recent members to the collective were young women of lower-middle-class urban background, training to be paralegals. A portion of their performance on International Women's Day consisted of a response that they fashioned to a number of Punjabi folk songs usually sung at weddings. The lyrics to these songs are most often in service to sexist ideologies, extolling the virtues of the domestic sphere for women, relegation to which is what a wedding symbolizes. What the paralegals did was rewrite the lyrics so that, although the tunes remained the same, the words challenged everything the tunes embodied in the public imagination! For instance, one of the traditional lyrics goes something like this: "The train has pulled into the station; oh, pretty girl with the purple scarf, this boy is madly in love with you." The paralegals rewriting of it subverts the entire vision of gender relations and roles that the lyric encodes, by substituting political reality for romantic nonsense. "We will make our testimony count as equal to that of men," they sing. Thus, the rewritten and resung lyrics not only poke fun at romantic conventions that render the woman the passive object of the man's gaze but in fact insist on women's will to agency in the face of attempted repression.

Despite its revolutionary potential, Lok Rehs, like Ajoka, remains restricted in terms of its effectiveness as an agent for social change, albeit for different reasons. Whereas Ajoka's effectiveness is curtailed by its primary devotion to theater as an end in itself, Lok Rehs is restricted perhaps for the opposite reason. In the group's concern to stage aesthetically interesting plays that will please a variety of audiences, Ajoka's political and social message often gets lost in the spectacle: colorful costumes, hypnotic dances, increasingly elaborate sets. Lok Rehs, conversely, gets critiqued by both sophisticated urban and rural audiences, as well as its rival counterparts, for lacking enough action and spectacle. In other words, its productions are often perceived as being too preachy and underrehearsed. Eugene Van Erven quotes Shahid Nadeem's critique as typical in this regard: "They [Lok Rehs] think that political theatre means the message and the analysis. They don't think carefully enough about how to package it into attractive theatre." [15]

Thus, the gap between the political aims of these groups and their actual achievements so far, as judged by audiences' and critics' mixed reactions, begs questions about the effectiveness of street theater as a tool for social change. In 1994, a development that further complicated Ajoka's commitment to political theater, was that its playwright and Madeeha's husband, Shahid, was appointed Lahore Television's general manager. As a result, by 1996, several of Ajoka's plays were performed on television. What remains to be seen is whether Ajoka can maintain its politically subversive edge and independence or whether its politics will become seriously compromised as a result of this foray into government-sponsored territory. Interestingly in 1997, when Nawaz Sharif came to power after the dismissal of Benazir Bhutto's government on charges of corruption, Shahid Nadeem (perceived as a supporter of Bhutto) was summarily fired from his post.

Community Uses of Street Theater

Where Boal's insights into theater being used as a vehicle for the transformation of consciousness within local communities come into play most evidently is in the work of self-help community organizations such as the Awami (People's) Committee formed in Lahore in 1985. The president of its central executive committee is the manager of an Urdu-language Marxist bookstore in Lahore's inner city. While visiting him there, I noticed translated copies of Freire's *Pedagogy of the Oppressed* as well as Boal's *Theatre of the Oppressed*. The community-based organization that he heads — which has a women's wing that elects its own representatives to the central executive committee — has as its aim the creation of self-awareness in people regarding their political, economic, and social rights. It is also a self-help organization that tries to provide training for lower-middle-class urban youths in such fields as health and education as well as vocational training in such services as sewing and embroidery for women and electrical and mechanical skills for men.

The two *kachi abadis* (or slum areas) that have been primarily targeted for this type of community-based work so far are Garhi-Shahu (located in the inner city) and Pakistan Mint Colony (on the outskirts of the city, near the mint factory). The founding committee members are pretty much all leftists with past affiliations to the now defunct Pakistani Communist Party, which merged with the Mazdoor Kisan Party (the Laborers and Peasants Party) in 1971. Although the Mazdoor Kisan Party exists today, with labor-class affiliations to trade unions as well as to factions of the middle classes, it is hardly a viable political force. Thus, the project of these people is to focus on local, grassroots initiatives that could make some difference in the lives of the common people. The Garhi Shahu project, for example, started with offering adult education classes (the official literacy rate in Pakistan is 25 percent — a decrease of about 15–20 percent since Independence). It also started home schools for those children who cannot attend formal school either because their parents cannot afford the fees and the school supplies (even though the costs are generally minimal) or because they need the children at home for their labor. Currently, the entry point for committee-cadres into the community is through providing paramedical training; the lead in this project was taken by a woman doctor, Dr. Afshan, who started a seventy-lecture course for women in 1990. She used to go once a week to both community locations and saw her first batch of students yield nineteen successes in one year (out of seventy who started the program). These women paramedics then established a clinic in Garhi Shahu, where they continue to provide paramedical training to others and see patients for a fee of Rs 10.00 (approximately U.S. $0.50).

Many of these trained cadres, who not only provide training to others but also teach basic literacy skills to adults and children through home schools, are also committed to consciousness raising, and, to this end, some years ago they formed a drama group. On successful completion of their courses, young women started staging plays at award ceremonies, plays that were later performed on street corners within their communities. Their first performance was Shahid Nadeem's *Dhee rani*. In my earlier comments on the mixed reception of this play, I raised the question of Ajoka's effectiveness as theater for social change. Well, here was a more positive answer: Ajoka was contacted by the Awami Committee members at Garhi Shahu to provide training for the young women who formed the initial drama group. Now, this local group is in the process of evolving its own street theater troupe, one that also includes men. Just the idea of having a mixed-gender performing troupe is a revolutionary one to pursue at this location; for the women to obtain permission from their fathers and brothers to participate in it is a remarkable, even more revolutionary feat on their part. At their award ceremony on 15 January 1995, the Awami Committee Theater Troupe wrote and performed their own play, putting Boal's theory to work in this very different cultural location. *Odeek,* in Punjabi, explores the theme of women's right to divorce. Since most of the women of these communities do not even know that they have such a right under Islamic law, the practice of writing, performing, and viewing such a play becomes an act of revolutionary potential, through increasing individuals' awareness of their social and political rights.

To conclude, it is important to realize that the terrain of oppositional cultural praxis is messy, at the very least. Sorting through what constitutes an effective strategy of intervention in the field of cultural politics is no simple task since different practices seem appropriate at different junctures and in varying sites of cultural production, and even these are shot through with contradictions — including the contradictory politics and conflicting personalities of the cultural interpreters and producers.

Clearly, one of the needs, it seems to me, is for more grassroots, self-help-oriented organizations to emerge in ever more varied urban and rural locales, which might explore further the ways in which the concept and techniques of street theater might be put to most effective use in this particular Third World location. The Institute for Applied Socioeconomic Research (ASR) in Lahore, an NGO, has tried to aid such a process by sponsoring theater workshops that connect established theater groups such as Ajoka with community organizations such as Sindhiani Tehrik, a community initiative aimed at the uplifting of peasant women and based in rural Sindh. Cross-national dialogue between Indian and Pakistani street theater groups has also been encouraged by ASR's sponsorship of two theater conferences and festivals, held in 1988 and 1989, the latter in memory of Safdar Hashmi, who was killed in January 1989 by Indian Congress Party thugs while performing his play *Halla bol* (Attack) for workers in East Delhi. Since 1994, an Indo-Pak Forum of private citizens, many of whom are theater activists, has begun hosting meetings in both countries to encourage a cultural exchange of ideas. It will be interesting to see what types and degree of social and political change occur in the region in the coming years as a result of such initiatives.

Notes

I would like to thank John Brenkman for encouraging me to pursue this project. Thanks are also due to Kalpana Seshadri-Crooks and Carla Petievich for their careful readings of earlier drafts and to Rogelio Zapata for bringing important material to my attention. Unless otherwise indicated, all translations are mine.

1   I use the term *street theater* advisedly since not all the performances of the groups that practice this type of theatrical activity take place on urban street corners, as the term suggests. However, the concept *street theater* applies to more than just that type of venue of performance since it covers an entire philosophy of theater as a tool for social change that does constitute a central tenet of the beliefs and practices of most of the theater groups under discussion here.

2   See Gayatri Chakravorty Spivak, *Imaginary Maps: Three Stories by Mahasweta Devi* (New York: Routledge, 1995), 203.

3   Walter Mignolo, "Colonial and Postcolonial Discourse: Cultural Critique or Academic Colonialism?" *Latin American Research Review* 28, no. 3 (1993): 120.

4   On the "new" nation, see Spivak, *Imaginary Maps*, 203.

5   See, e.g., Ayesha Jalal, "The Convenience of Subservience: Women and the State of Pakistan," in *Women, Islam, and the State*, ed. Deniz Kandiyoti (Philadelphia: Temple University Press, 1991).

6   See Sumanta Banerjee, "Marginalization of Women's Popular Culture in Nineteenth Century Bengal," in *Recasting Women: Essays in Indian Colonial History*, ed. Kum Kum Sangari and Sudesh Vaid (New Brunswick, N.J.: Rutgers University Press, 1990).

7   See also Rustom Bharucha, *Rehearsals of Revolution: The Political Theatre of Bengal* (Honolulu: University of Hawaii Press, 1983); and Kathryn Hansen, *Grounds for Play: The Nautanki Theatre of North India* (Berkeley and Los Angeles: University of California Press, 1992).

8   Quoted in Khawar Mumtaz and Farida Shaheed, eds., *Women of Pakistan: Two Steps Forward, One Step Back?* (London: Zed, 1987), 149.

9   Augosto Boal, *Theatre of the Oppressed*, trans. Charles McBride and Maria McBride (New York: Theatre Communications Group, 1985), 122.

10 Preface to Shahid Nadeem *Khasman khanian* (The husband eaters) (Lahore: Maktaba Fiqro-Danish, 1992), 17.

11 See, e.g., Mikhail Bakhtin's discussion of the carnivalesque in his *Rabelais and His World*, trans. Helene Iswolsky (Bloomington: Indiana University Press, 1984).

12 See Asma Jehangir, *Legal Literacy Pamphlets: Violence against Women* (Lahore: AGHS Legal Aid Cell, n.d.).

13 Boal, *Theatre of the Oppressed*, 122.

14 Interview with Madeeha Gauhar, *Ravi* 68 (1991). The *Ravi* is a student publication at the Government College of Lahore.

15 Eugene Van Erven, *The Playful Revolution: Theatre and Liberation in Asia* (Bloomington: Indiana University Press, 1992), 172.

Beyond the Hysterectomies Scandal: Women, the Institution, Family, and State in India

RAJESWARI SUNDER RAJAN

y reflections on institutionalized women in relation to the family and state in India derive from and focus on the widely reported case of mass hysterectomies performed on women inmates of a state-run home for the mentally retarded in Pune, Maharashtra, in February 1994. The stated purposes of the operations were to maintain female hygiene during menstruation and to prevent unwarranted pregnancies.

It is important to clarify at the outset that I offer the following discussion of the hysterectomies scandal as a case study, not serving solely expository purposes, but also exemplifying a conjuncture of issues that I regard as useful and significant for an understanding of the postcolonial situation. Let me clarify further: I do not intend simply to rehearse the terms of the debate over the hysterectomies, much less resolve it by referring to some transcendent third term above the opposed ones that structure it. Nor is there much to be gained by shading in greater complexity to the issue; no one suggests that it is a simple one. Least of all is this intended as an exposé of Third World underdevelopment, followed by pleas for reform—although I shall suggest that reform is an inescapable, if insufficient, item on progressive agendas of change.

I am more interested in *extending* the implications of the issue. By placing it at the juncture of a number of lines of inquiry (which are suggested by the title), I hope to reveal their overlooked interconnections. Implicitly, I also hope to rebut the currently influential intellectual position that, in the name of cultural relativism, indigenous values, historical contingency, social heterogeneity, or communal libertarianism, seeks to rationalize, with reference to a certain *India,* various aspects of the status quo—and these include, needless to say, the position of women.

The news story reporting the hysterectomies was itself a brief one, but the debate in the press over pros and cons of the issue and feature articles on various aspects of it continued to appear for several weeks.[1]

On 5 February 1994, eleven women inmates of a home for the mentally retarded in Shirur had their wombs surgically removed at the Sasoon Hospital in nearby Pune City. The women were between the ages of fifteen and thirty-five, and their average mental age was younger than four. Activists from several women's groups in Maharashtra protested outside the hospital but did not succeed in having the operations canceled. A former member of Parliament from the Communist Party of India (Marxist), Ahalya Rangnekar, sought the intervention of the Maharashtra chief minister, who stayed the next batch of operations, scheduled for the following day, and ordered an inquiry. Subsequently, the ban was lifted, and these and similar procedures were permitted to continue. A writ petition questioning the legality of the operations was filed in the Bombay high court in June 1994.

The Shirur home had about fifty inmates of whom thirty were in the specified age group for the operation. Of these, only eighteen were found to be medically fit to undergo the procedure. The operations were performed free as a social service by a leading Bombay gynecologist, Dr. Shirish Seth, and his team, and, according to Seth and the director of the Department of Women, Child, and Handicapped Development of the Maharashtra State Government, Ms. Vandana Khullar, hysterectomies have been a standard procedure in the care and maintenance of mentally retarded women of reproductive age.[2] An organization of the parents and guardians of the mentally retarded in Pune, the Umed Parivar, came out in support of sterilization. The protests of women activists from such groups as the Sarva Mazdoor Sangh, Bombay, and the Forum against Oppression of Women and the Forum for Women's Help, Pune, were directed at the "fascist encroachment on the personal rights of the individual." Charnika Shah of the Forum for Women's Help held that "nobody has the right to decide on such a major intervention on the body when there is no reproductive health problem." Both the problem of managing menstruation and the fear of sexual assault, which the government offered as reasons for the hysterectomies, were unacceptable to the protestors. They pointed out that the removal of the uterus would in any case not protect the women against sexual attack or from sexually transmitted diseases but would only prevent pregnancy. "In fact, by doing away with evidence of assault, it will make them more vulnerable."

So much for what may be termed the *facts* of the event. The discussion that follows falls broadly into the following parts: the first identifies the discourses of "expert" knowledge generated by the hysterectomies scandal; the next two move into the larger implications of the controversy for questions of the family and the postcolonial state, respectively; the last is an analysis of "women in struggle" in this context.

The hysterectomies controversy, which at first sight appeared to be a straightforward issue of institutional expediency versus human rights, eventually became a battleground of conflicting "expert" views. The absence of unanimity among the experts involved was due partly to the real complexity of the issue, partly to their incomplete access to the facts of the case, but largely to differences of opinion among the participants. That prejudice and principle were operative in what is both an ethically and a politically fraught issue tended to be obfuscated by the claims or citations of expert knowledge advanced by all those involved. The victims' mental condition rendered them more than usually ciphers in the issue of their well-being, leaving the field clear for other "concerned" parties to battle it out.

The emergence of the acknowledged (or self-proclaimed) expert in any context is never entirely the natural procedure that it may appear to be; the intellectual's social formation, which Gramsci examined in terms of class/caste, is a complex one.[3] The appeal to the intellectual as expert, that is, as adjudicator and voice of truth, a function of our contemporary society's desire for certitude, is achieved primarily by the resources of the media. As will become apparent, the arguments in the hysterectomies debate would appeal to professional opinion, to precedent, to the practices and positions of the field in advanced Western societies, to tradition, to common sense, to the vox populi, endowing each with legitimacy, expertise, authenticity, and ethical validity while at the same time invalidating whoever and whatever lay outside these valorized sources of "truth." It is by such means that the layperson's faith in a singular truth is won even in the face of many and conflicting expert knowledges.[4]

I must draw attention here also to the intermittent instances of a "humanistic" perspective, which, drawing on clichéd and sentimental ideas and beliefs, developed from the attempt of several participants in the debate to enter into an empathetic understanding of the victims' subjectivity, in opposition to the prevalent appeal to experts. The regulation of the sexuality of the inmates of the Shirur home by means of sterilization brought to the fore the coexistence of physical maturity and mental underdevelopment in mentally retarded women, with the result that any understanding of their situation had to reconcile these two aspects of their plight. So, while, on the one hand, sympathetic activists argued that mentally retarded women's emotions could not be assumed to be gender neutral and that hence hysterectomy could conceivably lead to feelings of the "loss of womanhood,"[5] on the other hand, Vandana Khullar, the government director, could evoke the dismay of a "three-year-old" having to contend with the onset of the monthly menses or, worse, with motherhood: "If we look beyond their bodies into their minds, we will realise it is stupid to talk of their 'right' on par with normal women. They have no concept of motherhood."[6] If expert discourses pronounced on mentally retarded women's sexuality in terms of its problems and dangers, an attempted subjective understanding of female sexuality in a state of childhood was both inadequate and confused. In the overwhelming context of expert pronouncements and the nullity of the subjects of the issue — indeed, the comprehensive and frustrating impossibility, as it was deemed, of ascertaining their wishes, choices, and reasons, of reaching into their consciousness, as it were — these statements have a piquant theoretical and political interest.

In the ways and from the sources in which I read the expert discourse generated by the hysterectomies issue, it will become clear that it was essentially a *textual* production, where the text must be read in the sense that Macherey suggests, in the material contexts of reproduction, distribution, production of surplus value, circulation.[7] The textualization of the discourse points, too, to the social text of *literacy*. In a situation where those who represent the women — that is, speak of and for them — do so in the mode of literacy, the women themselves must be produced/represented as illiterate. While the scandal is circulated outside, the conditions of seclusion enhance the condition of illiteracy of those inside the institution: this becomes a constitutive definition of the situation of the institutionalized, even as it marks the limits of proposals for reform.

The politics of this issue was played out on the different sites of professional expertise that were invoked: chiefly, institutional functioning, law, and medicine. A more detailed consideration of each of these areas of expert discourse, necessary if the complex politics of the issue is to be fully understood, follows.

The Function(ing) of the Institution
The document prepared by seven women's organizations in India for the UN Conference for Women in Beijing in 1995 ("Women: Towards Beijing," henceforth Draft Report) begins the chapter on "Institutionalisation and Change" with the warning that an exclusive preoccupation with institutional *malfunctioning* and, following from this, proposals for its reform is likely to make us overlook the "normative structure" of the institution and fail to subject it to interrogation.[8] This reflexive comment derives from recently developed positions on reform that revise earlier progressive histories. These new theoretical premises are now well established in studies of disciplinary knowledges and institutional practices in the West. Revisionary explanatory/theoretical accounts, both Foucauldian/poststructuralist/European/anti-Enlightenment epistemic studies and Marxist/materialist/Anglo-American/anti-Whig historical analyses, are agreed that the segregation and incarceration of large sections of populations considered deviant and/or unproductive — the insane, the crimi-

nal, the poor, the sick — with a view not only to curing, reforming, rehabilitating, and tending them but also to disciplining and punishing them, is a historical innovation of modernity.[9]

The history of the development of the institution in the colony was linked to but not identical with its history in modern Europe. As David Garland notes, although the techniques and principles of the institution's development in the context of early European capitalism are "transferable and may be operated elsewhere and under different regimes," they do have a "special and interesting relationship to the development of democracy in the West, summed up in the aphorism that 'the "Enlightenment" which discovered the liberties, also invented the disciplines.' "[10] The first modern penal institutions, hospitals, and mental asylums in India were established by the British colonial government, although with peculiarities and differences that are only now beginning to be investigated by historians.[11] Many utilitarian Benthamite experiments for administrative efficiency were in fact introduced in the "laboratory" of the colony before they were either replicated, modified, or abandoned in Britain. Most existing institutional facilities in India are colonial legacies that have changed little in the years since Independence.

Thus, the rhetoric of reform in India is most likely to be couched in the language of modernization — in relation not only to institutional structures and practices but also to legal and medical provisions for those in institutions — invoked invariably with reference to the West. But, if this reflects an aspiration to a modern universality via equivalence to the West in matters of human rights and social development, there is also another and opposed tendency to stress the *differences* (read superiority) between traditional societies and the West, especially in the matter of the care of the needy. This argument is located within a broader antimodernist critique that harks back nostalgically to earlier social formations. In this view, the premodern community accommodated the deviant and the handicapped more easily than contemporary societies do, and the extended family uncomplainingly provided care and shelter to unproductive members. Whatever measure of truth there may be in such imaginings of the past, the suggested re-creation of such solutions in the present — given the beleagured condition of family and community in a rapidly changing society — is out of the question.

There are at least two major reasons why this should be so. The first would question the assumption that *family* and *community* are spaces that stand completely outside the modern state and therefore function as significant alternatives to it. The justification for and modalities of the confinement of the ill and handicapped — especially women — in institutions mark, on the contrary, the complicity between the family and the state in India in unambiguous terms, as I elaborate shortly.

Second, the significant *differences* between the family and the community, on the one hand, and the institution, on the other, in terms of structures, resources, and attitudes in the matter of the care of the handicapped, cannot be gainsaid. Mothers of mentally retarded girls interviewed in the wake of the hysterectomies scandal poignantly described the difficulties of caring for their daughters.[12] Suggestions that welfare programs for the care of the handicapped, sick, and aged be returned to the family must take into account the high likelihood that this task will once again fall to the women in the family. Social service activists are also quick to point out that destitute mentally handicapped women outside institutional care are not absorbed into adoptive families or communities, as is sentimentally claimed, but are, to the contrary, exposed to the most horrific threats of public abuse: stoning, jeering, stripping, and rape.[13] The logistics of special care would suggest that the institution is the more efficient custodian of those requiring special services, even if the more indifferent (i.e., impersonal).

The Indian state is of course indifferent in another sense as well: it simply fails to respond to this need. The most frequent explanation for this indifference is that of resource scarcity, combined with the administrative difficulty of adequately catering to the large numbers of those in need. The validity, and admissibility, if so, of this reasoning is not a matter that I will explore here. It is in any case, as I suggest later, coming to be less frequently offered by the government as an excuse under the new national economic programs of liberalization. But, like those of any developing country, the concerns of the Indian government are significantly statist, macroeconomic, and demographic in the administration of development-oriented programs—and these conflict with or simply override individual rights or community welfare. Examples are not hard to find: the displacement of tribal people in big dam projects, forced sterilization camps (especially notorious during Indira Gandhi's Emergency), batches of mentally retarded women undergoing sterilization simultaneously in institutions, all are justified by such priorities.[14] Institutional studies in developing nations are therefore obliged to take into account the state's neglect of and simple lack of interest in those of its population that need special services, rather than the systematic and intrusive forms of regulation that are read as the mark of the modern welfare state.[15] A Foucauldian study of the institution, in terms of intimate control and close surveillance of the inmates, would in this case be contradicted by the signs of neglect, inefficiency, and active exploitation that are everywhere evident in its functioning.

The Shirur home, for example, is the only government-run home for mentally retarded women in Maharashtra (the government gives aid to sixty-five other institutions run by NGOs). There are only twenty-two state-run institutions in Maharashtra, in addition to 252 state-aided institutions.[16] The allocation for social welfare in 1993–94 was Rs 35.00, crores, of which Rs 17.59 was intended for the welfare of the handicapped. The expenditure on social services fell in nominal as well as in real terms between 1989-90 and 1992-93, in both the union and the Maharashtra state budgets.[17]

Newspaper accounts of the Shirur government home describe it as a large building with few amenities. The living conditions of the inmates are appalling: no hot bathwater, inadequate change of clothes for the inmates, filthy surroundings. The staff is limited to a superintendent and a probationary officer ("who are there by virtue of a transfer they cannot wish away"!), a sweeper, a cook, and six caretakers. Three teachers' posts had not been filled since 1990-91.[18] All available accounts of state-run institutions — whether jails, homes for women, mental asylums, juvenile homes, or orphanages — have similar stories to tell.

Inadequate resources and bureaucratic apathy are the well-known and even widely accepted explanations for all official (mal)functioning. In this sense, the state's sins of omission, so to speak, are themselves likely to meet with indifference, if not apathy. Custodial institutions are further secured by outsiders' ignorance of what goes on on the inside, an ignorance made possible by the closed system in which they operate. The latter immunity leads to much more violent abuses than those caused simply by neglect. Women as well as juveniles in custody are routinely subjected to sexual harassment by their keepers, by other inmates, or by outsiders in connivance with their supervisors. A report on the pregnancy of a mentally retarded sixteen-year-old girl in Calcutta, which appeared shortly after the Shirur case, revealed that there were few officials and caretakers on the premises of the home for destitute women in Uttarpara where she had been lodged (the superintendent was "highly irregular in her duties," and other employees were absent). The husband of an employee of the home was therefore regularly able to let in "miscreants" in the afternoons, when the other inmates were at school. The discovery of the girl's pregnancy led to a police complaint, and all the "Class IV employees . . . were issued show cause notices." [19] Another recent report on the escape of twelve boys from a state remand home for juvenile delinquents in Ramnagar, near Benares, disclosed that they were frequently forced to "sexually gratify some of the officials." In response to this situation and to the sexual harassment of three women employees at the home, the boys went on a rampage, began a hunger strike, and demanded an inquiry.[20]

The exigencies of resource scarcity and the opportunistic corruption and abuse practised by its employees inhibit the institution's successful functioning — if by *success* in this instance we understand the effective incarceration and supervision of the inmates. The examples of resistance, escape, and rebellion by inmates of institutions suggest that their administration is barely effective in many cases. Reports of remand-home breaks periodically appear in the press — and it is from the escapee that information about the abysmal conditions in the institution is gleaned since the institutions are unwilling to give outsiders, and in particular journalists, permission to visit the homes.[21] Sex workers have also been organizing to resist rescue-and-rehabilitation operations by crusading government officials (since their relatives are forced to meet the demands of the police for money for their release from the institutions in which they are lodged following their so-called rescue).[22] The question of how one might read these instances of resistance by the institution's inmates — whether in the Foucauldian terms of a libertarian and populist politics and praxis or as the desperate revolt against intolerable circumstances to which even the most abject can be driven — is one to which I shall return.

It is the intermittent exposure in the press of aspects of state-run institutions that provokes large-scale public protest, or at least outrage. The name *scandal* — the form and dimension of public knowledge of the wrongs of the state and its functionaries — brings about, in more or less substantial and far-reaching ways, reform.[23] The government's responses range from disavowal, to explanation, to commissions of inquiry, to (in rare cases) actual acceptance of responsibility and the promise of change. It is largely these consequences that are responsible for a visible recent trend in institutionalization in India (the Shirur scandal is, of course, not singular): the state's increasing relegation of care functions to voluntary, that is, nongovernmental, organizations. These organizations might receive varying degrees of funding from the state government but are otherwise autonomous bodies.[24]

While one would need more factual data and research before pronouncing unequivocally favorable judgment on institutions run by voluntary organizations, there is no doubt that they are both motivated by greater commitment and informed by greater professionalization as regards the care of inmates than are state-run institutions.[25] The Draft Report, stressing the need for institutional options for women under difficult circumstances (such as those seeking to escape from family harassment, child laborers and other working women in cities needing residential hostels, prostitutes wishing to leave the profession, elderly women without family support), identifies a few such shelters and short-stay homes run by voluntary women's groups such as the Rajasthan University Women's organization in Jaipur and by Self-Employed Women's Association (SEWA) in Mithila, Bihar. These institutions are open in nature, and admission and discharge are voluntary, unlike, as they point out, state-run homes for women. The centers offer legal aid, counseling, and rehabilitation to women in need of them (Draft Report, 70). There are institutions for the care of the handicapped and rehabilitation centers for alcoholics and drug addicts, which are in some cases founded and run by the families of the afflicted: therefore, their interest in the proper functioning of the institution is guaranteed.[26] Further, they are called on to function with greater accountability, more especially in cases where their services may be paid for — and in such institutions, of course, the services are available only to those able to afford them, a limiting factor in comparison with free state-run homes. This limitation does not exist in missionary institutions, which are usually run as religious charities. Christian missionary organizations, usually foreign, were the earliest in India to offer institutional care to those traditionally outcast, such as lepers, orphans, the destitute, and the aged; and even today they remain a significant, if beleaguered, center of such charitable activities. There are also missionary organizations run by other religious denominations and by Gandhian social workers. I shall not enter into a discussion of the ideological aspects and the actual social implications of such charitable activities, although clearly these are complicated issues.[27]

This account of the institution has relied largely on description of its (mal)functioning, which, analytically, leads to reformist solutions. The call for reform — for both more and better institutions — is understandable, given the numbers and the needs of those requiring services. But, as the Draft Report began by insisting, equal attention must be paid to the *normative* structure of the institution. An examination in such terms uncovers the ideologies that underpin institutionalization and the control that the state wields by means of such confinement of sections of the population and hence, rather than respecting the obligation, more radically questions the right of the state in matters of institutional administration.

In the first place, the institutional defense became an expert discourse by virtue of the experience on which it claimed to rely — and that it denied to those who denounced the hysterectomies. The former was of course couched in the language of expediency, especially in defense of the performance of the hysterectomies in large batches (each operation took no more than an hour, the dean of Sasoon Hospital explained). Typically, state and institution define problems and seek solutions "in the gross" and by bureaucratic procedure, as I pointed out earlier. This conflict with the concept of individual human dignity remained unresolved even when the protestors could be persuaded that the hysterectomies were correct in other respects.[28] Undoubtedly, it was also the scale of this operation that brought it to the attention of the press in the first place. (The government's response concluded with a promise to be more discreet in the future!)

The opponents of the government — in this case, mainly activists in the women's movement — were held to be irresponsible, naive, or merely antigovernment.[29] (Subsequent research, however, showed that there are a number of institutions run by other agencies, even in Maharashtra, that, under similar circumstances, do not sterilize the women in their care).[30] The specific defenses of the authorities relied, as we saw, on arguments based on precedent, pragmatism, and procedural correctness — and support on these grounds was forthcoming from both the medical community and the families of retarded women. The prevention-of-pregnancy argument that the director of the Department of Women, Child, and Handicapped Development had advanced was withdrawn following accusations from protesters that the government was "rapist friendly," although the expert medical discourse kept it in view as a major reason for sterilization, the prevention of menstruation being (medically) viewed as a trivial reason for a major surgical intervention. The reality, however, is that women in custodial institutions, and in particular mentally retarded women, are extremely vulnerable to sexual abuse, as the Calcutta case made clear. But such an admission would obviously have been, as it had already proved, more damaging than exculpatory in this instance.

The reformist position is based on the expectation that the state provide care and security to those in need of them and attacks its failure adequately to do so. But the institution—and this is a further argument based on an understanding of its normative function (rather than only its malfunction)—is also a place of confinement and hence of control. So, while the government may divest itself of more and more of the actual responsibility of providing institutional *services,* especially as a response to scandals, it is unlikely to surrender or dilute the *authority* of its custodial powers—and here its targets are specifically women and juveniles—even when the very excess of this function may prove, as we have seen, to be self-defeating. In the next section, I turn to the specifically gendered aspect of the institutionalization of women in order to elaborate on this crucial aspect of the hysterectomies issue.

Women: In Custody

Custodial confinement has specific implications for women,[31] although the sweeping powers of arrest and confinement available to the police in India under draconian political laws affect people in several other categories as well.[32] Jails are filled with political detainees, those already on trial, and those arrested on suspicion as habitual offenders on the basis of such socioeconomic criteria as caste, (un)employment, etc. *Criminal* is an elastic and potent category that the state invokes to identify and punish antisocial elements, both men and women. Individuals in the state's care—the deviant, destitute, handicapped, ill—are also routinely lodged in jails. This is partly because of the inadequate number of other, more appropriate institutions in which to place them, partly because the distinction between crime and misfortune is legally as well as socially blurred, and to a great extent because the differences between penal and nonpenal institutions are in most cases not very significant. Nonpenal institutions such as health-care centers—that is, for the most part, mental asylums or leprosy asylums and remand homes, short-stay homes and shelters, and hostels for juveniles and working women run by the state—notoriously operate under jaillike conditions. Although legal remedies are repeatedly sought and legal strictures equally regularly passed to enforce these distinctions, the practice of jailing noncriminal men and women continues.[33]

Women placed in nonpenal institutions in particular—the destitute, the sick, or those accused of victimless crimes such as vagrancy or solicitation—are treated as if they were criminals. As the Draft Report points out, invariably such women are *forcibly* brought to institutions by their families or by the police. Families wishing to be rid of the social stigma of mentally ill, retarded, or leprosy-afflicted members commit them to asylums. The police (aided sometimes by social workers) pick up prostitutes, vagrants, and beggar women on grounds of soliciting and lodge them in custody—the argument being that a "single and especially poor woman, without any male support, must either already be working in prostitution or will soon be 'corrupted' into joining it." The state "completely overrides a woman's individual will and liberty by confining her within remand homes" (p. 69). As the Draft Report (pp. 72–73) makes clear, mentally ill women, or other problem members of a family or a community, end up in the care of the state primarily because they are rejected by the latter, and, in a reciprocal gesture, the institution will release them only to the care of the family. Moreover, it is the ideology of the family—the conviction that women's sexuality must be protected and controlled—that underpins the ideology of institutional confinement, making a vicious circle of the passage of women from family or community to the institution and back.

Given also that the processes of discharge/exit to which the report calls our attention are highly bureaucratic, the report questions "the legal procedures for the discharge of women inmates which allow release only if they had a family ready to receive them" when families are either reluctant or unfit to do so. Therefore, "while for men there is entry as well as exit from institutions," women are doomed to "a vicious and endless cycle of subsequent entries into other institutions" (p. 73).

The Draft Report outlines in general terms the bureaucratization and discipline that characterize the functioning of closed institutions for women. Disciplinary rules might require women inmates to give up all marks of personal identity, enforce the wearing of uniforms, the mandatory shaving of heads, etc., and insist on other forms of "deprivation" (p. 72). The dismal material conditions, the proneness to corruption, and the sexual abuse of inmates in institutions have already been described. There are other "genderized forms of brutality and bullying" (p. 72) that operate specifically among women inmates and between them and their wardens.

Why and how women enter institutional spaces, how and why they leave them (or fail to), what kinds of discipline and other forms of violence they are subjected to while in custody: the ideologies and modalities of these processes reveal the contradictions of as well as the profound complicities between the patriarchies of family and state. What is at stake, of course, is not, or at any rate not only, the protection of the victimized women but the putative protection of society *from them.* The anxieties produced by women's sexuality—the real and imagined fears about promiscuity, commercial sex, sexually transmitted disease, birth control, unregulated fertility, and deviant sexuality—are widely recognized as coexisting with the exploitation and regulation of aspects of woman's sexuality by social, religious, legal, communal, and state sanctions. The institutional confinement of certain women—usually, according to the Draft Report, "single women without obvious family" (p. 69) and therefore in need of support but therefore also potentially subversive—thereby serves the purpose of securing them: in the double sense of confinement and protection. As Rokeya Sakhawat Hossain ironically pointed out nearly a century ago in her fable *Sultana's Dream*, "Men, who do or at least are capable of doing no end of mischief, are let loose, and the innocent women shut up in the zenana!"[34] The logic of women's confinement has always been built on this paradox.

As a direct and pragmatic measure of care and discipline, the sterilization of the mentally retarded inmates of the Shirur asylum was clearly, then, a response to the prevalent beliefs about women's sexuality. The institution had little difficulty accepting the widespread cultural prejudice about menstruation as polluting and menstruating women as unclean and therefore respected the refusal of caretakers to attend to the women's hygiene. (Menstruating women in many societies, including those in most communities in India, are traditionally required to be set apart from other members of the family—an ostracism that links contemporary solutions for the "problem" with traditional religious, political, medical ritual practices). In institutional thinking, the feebleminded are promiscuous and/or vulnerable to sexual abuse—in any case, the authorities tacitly admitted, institutional lodging is no safeguard against rapists' attacks. Above all, there was the assured belief that pregnancy is undesirable not merely from the viewpoint of the women (as when it follows from forced intercourse or threatens health) but as a eugenic measure: and, following from this, that a uterus not useful for reproductive purposes is dispensable. The hysterectomies are an instance of advanced medical technology serving the ends of traditional patriarchal control, like the widespread use of aminocentesis for fetal sex detection, which serves as a prelude to female feticide.

Self, Subject, Citizen: The Mentally Retarded
and the Question of Identity
The institution, in this instance, perceived the problem and devised the solution in relation not only to the sexuality of the women inmates of the Shirur home but also to their mental condition. Rights and welfare in the democratic state are inevitably brought to crisis when liberal questions of individual choice and of entitlement are posed in relation to the mentally handicapped.

The legal provisions relating to the mentally retarded, which must ensure their rights, occupy at present a curious limbo. The mentally retarded are covered by the Indian Lunacy Act of 1912, whose definition of a *lunatic* as "a person who is an idiot or of unsound mind" has little scientific or medical basis, as Geetha Ramaseshan points out, "but simply reflects the bias that existed in society towards the mentally ill and the mentally retarded in the early twentieth century." The act, rightly considered outmoded and irrelevant given changes in the conception and treatment of mental illness, was replaced by the Mental Health Act of 1987, which came into effect in 1993. The new act, however, excludes retardation from the category *mental illness*, and there is as yet no legal statute on the books to safeguard the rights and regulate the treatment of the mentally retarded. However, the personal laws of different religious communities and certain uniform provisions pronounce on issues relating to them in various contexts. Ramaseshan provides a partial listing of these.

> Under "Hindu law" and "Special Marriages Act" (which governs inter-religious marriages), a party at the time of marriage should not be suffering from any mental disorder so as to be unfit for marriage and the procreation of children. . . . [M]ental retardation and mental illness are treated on par. The Indian Divorce Act, governing Christians, considers marriage with a "lunatic" or an "idiot" [*sic*] as a nullity. It is only under customary Islamic Law that a mentally retarded person is treated as a minor. The guardian can validly conduct a marriage on behalf of the mentally retarded under Islamic Law. The Indian Succession Act however treats the mentally retarded (though it uses the term lunatic) on par with a minor. Thus, a guardian of a mental retardate (either appointed under a Will or a court) will administer the property on behalf of the mentally retarded. . . . The Medical Termination of Pregnancy Act, 1971, permits the termination of pregnancy of a "lunatic" (as defined under the Lunacy Act and hence will include the mentally retarded) with the written consent of her guardian, provided the doctor is of the opinion that the pregnancy will cause injury to the woman's physical or mental health. The doctor can also take into account the woman's actual or reasonably foreseeable environment.[35]

The last, however, does not specify that sterilization may be legally performed on retarded women.

If certain personal laws define the mentally retarded, by analogy, as *minors,* thus entrusting decisions regarding their welfare to their guardians, Krishna Iyer demands their recognition as *minorities,* with a claim to the state's ameliorative measures, by analogy with economically disadvantaged and racially discriminated against groups.[36] The logic operative in these differing arguments by analogy highlights the conflict between welfare and rights legislation for the mentally ill.[37]

This conflict forms the basis for a discussion of the judiciary's role in the specific issue of civil and criminal commitment of the mentally ill in Amita Dhanda's "Law, Psychiatry, and Human Rights." The extension of the argument to the issue of the sterilization of mentally retarded women in the institutional custody of the state is one I undertake with reference to the conceptual issues that she highlights in this discussion. There is a double focus and a double demand that characterizes the jurisprudence concerning the rights of the mentally ill: on the one hand, the individual's "right to rational self-determination [free] from state interference," which the human rights approach privileges and seeks to protect, and, on the other, the "dysfunctional consequences" of mental disorders that affect the afflicted person's "logical reasoning and the capacity for independent judgement" and hence make state interference unavoidable. Therefore, the "concern for protecting their autonomy" must be balanced by the "need to alleviate their suffering." In the latter case—involving treatment, care, custody—the authority to decide on the "liberties" of the mentally ill is transferred to "another: whether state, professional or family."[38]

Recent judicial activism in the field of mental health has, however, Dhanda objects, privileged the suffering of the mentally ill over their right to autonomy since it has focused on the "unjust deprivation of liberty" (i.e., wrongful or overlong confinement in mental asylums) and "the dismal living conditions and treatment in mental hospitals." There has been insufficient emphasis on the "constitutional basis" of the various declarations that would have highlighted the constitutional *rights* of mentally ill persons. This latter is needed since often the mentally ill, necessarily dependent on surrogates, also need to be protected "*from* them" (this point is made with special reference to the need for accountability on the part of medical functionaries and psychiatric institutions).[39]

In a broad sense, therefore, the human rights perspective guarantees the mentally ill individual "an uninterrupted right to her psychosis" (unless her mental condition infringes on the rights of others), countering the "problem-centric" "interest-based perspective" that promotes programs for the alleviation of her condition.[40] Here, the nature and the degree of mental illness are obviously relevant in ways that would not apply to the mentally retarded, although any legislation relating to the latter would have to be discriminating about levels of retardation and competence in affected individuals and not homogenize them as a single category. Krishna Iyer would formulate the rights of the latter, in certain instances, as the right *not to be retarded* where it is "the adversities of poverty, medical neglect or environmental pollution" suffered by pregnant mothers that are responsible for the retardation of the child. If the retardation and any other disabilities are caused by accident, the victim must be adequately compensated.[41]

It will be clear that, in the debate over the hysterectomies, the government's most elevated defense of the practice was based on the alleviation of suffering, while the activists' opposition to it drew from the human rights defense of autonomy, liberty, integrity, and privacy extended and applied to mentally retarded women as to any citizen under the constitution. The question of the state's custodianship is itself, of course, defined by limits and safeguards, and whether these were observed in the decision to perform the hysterectomies is not easy to decide. The activist and media opposition to the hysterectomies began by denouncing the government as fascistic. But the government seemed at least to have followed the correct legal procedures by obtaining the permission of the families for the operations (only two of the women were, however, committed by their families; the others were destitute). The informal as well as the organized backing of the families of retarded women provided the government with important support. For the rest, it acted on behalf of the destitute women as their guardian.

Feminist activists pointed out that the state's decision to perform the sterilizations cannot be identical with a family's since the latter could be more unequivocally considered to have the interests of their daughters/sisters at heart and experienced greater difficulty in the care and protection of handicapped family members. The most forcible argument was that put forward by the feminist activist lawyer Indira Jaisingh, who clarified that, unlike the family, the state is only a *custodian,* not a guardian, of those in its care and as such "cannot appropriate the rights of a guardian." Using the Mental Health Act of 1993 as a guide, she pointed to the "elaborate" procedures, requiring judicial as well as medical clearance, for such appropriation.[42] The state becomes guardian only if the individual has been legally made its ward. In other countries, the sterilization of mentally retarded women requires the permission of the court and certification by medical practitioners, regardless of whether it is sought by the family or the state.[43] Since sterilization can be regarded either as a violation or as a boon, depending on the situation, those who are in no position take a decision about it can legally be said to be deprived of a right if the state does not act responsibly in either direction.[44] The state, either voluntarily or by unambiguous judicial direction, is called on to discharge the responsibility by entering into widespread consultations with medical experts, social workers, and the family. There is no indication that the hysterectomies performed on the inmates of the Shirur home were supported by any justification other than precedent, although the force of precedent as a legal and legitimizing argument must not be underestimated.

What is of interest and significance here is that, in a single stroke, the sterilization of the mentally retarded women wholly and comprehensively defined their identity in terms of the problems of women's sexuality (their identity as women) and in terms of the inability to make rational choices (their identity as mentally retarded). The individual's spaces of selfhood, subjectivity, and citizenship are entirely usurped by the state and the exigencies of institutional care.

Medical Perspectives
The opinions of the medical experts were, on the face of it, amazingly diverse on the different medical aspects of the issue as they related to mental retarda-

tion, to surgical and other procedures regulating menstruation and reproduction, and, more broadly, to the biomedical ethics of sterilization in the service of social engineering, especially as these applied to women.

Psychiatrists, psychotherapists, and other experts in mental health pointed out that there are varying degrees of mental retardation, that the IQs of most patients can show considerable improvement over time with proper stimulation, and that all but the most incompetent can be trained to some degree of self-sufficiency in their everyday lives, including in the observance of menstrual care—and even in parenthood. None of this was seriously disputed by others in the medical profession who, however, implicitly supported the institutional responses on the basis of the actual circumstances: that the mental age of the Shirur inmates was younger than four, the hygiene of the menstruating women was so poor that they were highly susceptible to infection, and in any case no facilities were available to train them in this matter or any other.[45] In other words, whatever may be the merits of the sterilization of mentally retarded women in the care of state-run institutions, in general and in the abstract, the particular circumstances of the case would determine the course of action to be followed. The major medical argument in favor of the practice consisted of denying any harm in an operation that at one stroke medically solved the problems of both menstruation and unwarranted pregnancy. (One doctor went so far as to suggest sewing up the vaginas of the women.)[46] The alternatives that were suggested—endometrial ablation of the bleeding surface of the uterus to prevent menstruation or tubectomies to prevent pregnancy—do not have this double advantage. Some doctors objected that hysterectomies involved a major surgical operation not free of the risks that any invasive procedure poses, that they required extensive postoperative care (of which there was no guarantee at the home), and that they could produce hormonal imbalances with long-term consequences if not properly followed up. However, the medical fitness of the inmates had been ascertained by the regulatory tests, and no doubts were raised about the competence of the Bombay gynecologist who led the surgical team.

The chief issue, therefore, was not so much the narrow or technical medical viability of the hysterectomies as the ethics of sterilization. The protest against sterilization was led by Dr. Sunil Pandya, founder of the Forum of Medical Ethics in Bombay: "Hysterectomy is an irreversible process. If a family does it, it is okay but it is not so for the State. Becuse it helps the State to set a precedent. Uncensured, it will lead the State to extend it to other areas to circumvent its own responsibilities."[47] This position was echoed by other doctors, including those in charge of institutions of mental health, like Dr. Sarada Menon, who had served as superintendent of the Madras Mental Hospital: "I think the operation is necessary. . . . But if you make it legal, then there is the possibility of people misusing it."[48] She therefore advocates using it extremely selectively.

Inevitably, reference was made to and clarification sought from the more advanced discourse on biomedical ethics in the West.[49] In short, while sterilization as such is not ruled out, as a measure either of protection or of eugenics, in the case of the mentally retarded, it is always treated as a last resort rather than a routine practice.

"Inside" the Family: Representations in Indian Film

The patriarchies of family and state combine, as we have seen, to enforce the distinction, in ideology and in practice, between women "in" the family and those "outside," in the institution. As the foregoing discussion has intermittently indicated, the distinction may be interrogated by both the organized women's movement and institutionalized "other" women in organized or spontaneous resistance. I consider the problems and possibilities of this politics at greater length in the concluding section of this essay. Here, I pursue the exploration of the complex ideology of family in relation to the institution, and, to do so, I turn to some recent Indian films that engage these issues. Film is a major ideological site for the shaping and reflection of public opinion and is particularly signficant in defining gender relations. In the films that I chose for discussion, Jabbar Patel's *Umbartha* and Rajkumar Santoshi's *Damini,* the representation of the middle-class female protagonist exemplifies as much as it explores the contradictions that underlie the "concerned"/activist woman's relationship to (her) family and to "other" women.[50]

Some preliminary clarifications are in order. First, it would be misleading to collapse the two films into mere thematic sameness. They belong to different and distinctive genres of Indian cinema, as I shall explain; further, the decade that separates them is responsible for the feminist consciousness that has now penetrated commercial cinema, although in the compromised forms of ideology that I have discussed elsewhere at length.[51] Nevertheless, their representation of women in institutions and their interest in relating the predicament of middle-class women's domesticity to that reality are rare enough preoccupations in Indian cinema: my choice of these films for discussion is therefore not arbitrary; and the common assumptions about family, women's politics, sexuality, and the state that they share despite their different genres and contexts make the point about ideology with which I began. Finally, although I do not connect them in any specific way to the hysterectomies issue, I do mean to suggest that the films partake of the latter's discursive, cultural, and political moment.

The earlier film, *Umbartha,* belongs to the Indian new wave or alternative cinema that, in the 1970s and 1980s, most significantly, made a conscious departure from the themes and conventions of mainstream commercial cinema by engaging social issues, using a stark neorealist idiom. Thus, *Umbartha* was offered as a bold and novel feminist statement about the middle-class woman's aspirations to career, her sympathetic understanding of fellow or destitute women, her recognition of widespread patriarchal double standards, and her growth to individualistic selfhood. Sulabha, the film's protagonist (played by Smita Patil, virtually an icon of the parallel cinema), leaves her home—her husband, child, and extended (in-law) family—to work as superintendent of a *mahilashram* (remand home for women) in a small town in Maharashtra. The film has an extended middle section that exposes the depraved conditions prevailing at the mahilashram. Sulabha is placed in the position of a bewildered mediator between the women inmates and the governing body of the institution. She fails in this situation and returns home, only to find that she is no longer needed there. She leaves home again, with determination and hope for a new life.[52]

The film places Sulabha's career in specific opposition to her mother-in-law's lifelong involvement in social work through various charitable organizations. Unlike her mother-in-law, Sulabha has been professionally trained for her work; she has special credentials for working with women, and she has progressive ideas about the administration of institutions for them. The mahilashram is a dumping ground for mentally ill, sexually deviant, abandoned, and vagrant women and prostitutes. The women are powerfully depicted, not only as pathetic, but as unruly and disobedient. Equally revelatory is the corrupt way in which the institution is run, the sexual exploitation of the inmates, and the ignorance and apathy as well as the authoritarianism of the governing body's members. Among the institutionalized are women who seek freedom as well as women who seek shelter, but the governing body does not take the women's own wishes into consideration when deciding their fate, acting instead "in their own best interests." This leads two of the women to commit suicide and a third to commit infanticide.

These are the film's strengths as a feminist statement. Its weakness lies in what we actually see of Sulabha's work at the institution—and its failures point not only to her limitations as custodian but also to the limits of the filmmaker's imaginative re-creation of the relationship between women of different classes. When Sulabha is not recoiling in horror from the women under her supervision, she is punishing them (shutting them up, scolding them) or enforcing discipline (prayer meetings, uniforms for the attendants, etc.). Her self-righteousness is in no way different from that of her mother-in-law, an observation that can only be ironic in the context of the film's message. A series of disasters take place, some due to her own bungling since there are major failures of sympathy and understanding on her part. But, more important, the film fails to undertake any *radical* reconceptualization of the functions of those institutional spaces meant to serve noncriminal women. Even as the mahilashram experience ostensibly moves Sulabha to the realization that she is one of them—as she progressively loses the privilege of marriage and familial security — it insists on her superior self-sufficiency, her resources in terms of education and professional prospects. At the same time, despite the (ironic) accompaniment of the voice-over lyric that celebrates love and springtime, the unremittingly bleak visual representation of the mahilashram marks her voluntary departure from the institution as an escape that is not available to the inmates.

The most ambivalent aspect of the film — and perhaps a necessary ambivalence given the power and appeal of the ideologies underpinning it, and an inescapable one given its formal resolution — is the attitude it expresses toward marriage and family, the alternative not only to the institution but also to women's independent careers. By making Sulabha's husband a sympathetic and attractive figure (a representation overdetermined by the choice of Girish Karnad for the role), Jabbar Patel makes out a fair case for the man's culminating infidelity: in terms of tolerance stretched to its limit by his wife's neglect and "natural" male sexual need.[53] The extended family — the mother-in-law fair, in spite of her harshness, the brother-in-law and his wife affectionate and supportive — is therefore not oppressive except in being *too* comfortable and well run. For most audiences, as for the characters in the film, Sulabha's decision to seek a career elsewhere can seem irrational, even perverse, and the situation then becomes one of choices that she must confront, of not being allowed to have one's cake and eat it too. Smita Patil gives the role of Sulabha a fine edge of hysteria cutting into brooding unhappiness: a rendering that enhances the imputation of blame, or at least ignorance, that attaches to her actions. Because of its commitment to a realistic representation, the film's criticism of patriarchal bourgeois values is not able to penetrate the strength of their ideological pervasiveness but remains fixated on them.

Paradoxically, it is the commercial cinema's melodramatic mode that achieves this unequivocal identification. Commercial or mainstream Indian cinema, in Hindi or one of the score of regional languages, commands a vast viewership as a popular cinema. It subscribes to the star system, relies on song-and-dance interludes, and is usually made on large budgets — all this in contrast to the parallel cinema. In *Damini*, a major success of the Bombay cinema, the eponymous heroine is played by the glamorous star/actress Meenakshi Seshadri. Like Sulabha, Damini is located within a love marriage and a comfortable extended family, and, although she too is responsible for her eventual ejection from the family, it is only because her principled integrity is in conflict with their wickedness. Damini is eyewitness to the rape of the family's servant girl by several drunken revelers, including her brother-in-law, at a Holi festival. She decides to speak out against them and files a police report, while supporting the raped woman, who is admitted to the hospital. The family hopes to cover up the incident and succeeds in doing so by throwing Damini out of the house, bribing the police, hiring a corrupt lawyer, and discrediting Damini as a madwoman and confining her in a mental asylum. Damini escapes from the asylum and is rescued by a lawyer who shelters her and takes up her case, ultimately vindicating her in court. She is then reconciled to her estranged husband.

The asylum interlude, phantasmagorically depicted, opens the film, which then moves to a flashback of the events that have led to Damini's incarceration. There is a certain horrific credibility about the swiftness with which the respectable, domestic bourgeois woman is pitched into the outer darkness of destitution and confinement. The asylum scenes are impressionistically rendered with all the stereotyped features of the popular cinema's conception of the mad. Nevertheless, Damini's reduction to one among many women who share her predicament does make a statement. After this point, the film works in the genre of the psychological thriller, as fear, excitement, and suspense build toward the triumph of good over evil.

Both Damini's mode of departure from her home—reluctant, bewildered, and clutching an idol of the goddess Lakshmi—and her reconciliation with her husband at the end—despite what might well have, but is never allowed to become, an involvement with the young lawyer—keep her actions at a safe distance from feminism. Her stand is attributed by the film's epigraph to a Gandhian adherence to "the truth of conscience." By thus keeping a personal feminist politics separate and different from a disinterested ethical praxis, the film manages the contradictions in Damini's behavior. Within this explanatory frame, there is thus no surprise in her unshaken allegiance to her husband and her return to the institution of marriage and family that has already been revealed as hollow and corrupt.

Both films show that, for women, the divide between safety and danger, freedom and confinement, sanity and insanity, respectability and criminality, is a tenuous one, secured only if they conform to the values of family and marriage. But, since these values are finally upheld, or at least held to be unshakable, solidarity among women across class and circumstances is never consolidated into a politics of gender. For the female protagonist of *Umbartha*, contact with fallen women is an episode on the way to feminist self-realization; for the heroine of *Damini*, the raped woman is a moral and sentimental cause. The limitations of these films, even with their broadly feminist pretensions, clue us in to the difficulties of women's struggle for gender equity and justice—whether regarded in terms of their solidarity with other women or in terms of a politics of rights—when the appeal (in both senses of the word) of the family divides their loyalties. While feminists hold that the family is a patriarchal *institution,* in the Shirur case, too, as we saw, the protesting women's groups were reluctant to condemn the *actual* families of patients for a number of reasons (delicacy about intrusion, the imputation of self-righteousness, the recognition of the burdens borne by women in the family in such situations, among others).

Another of the larger questions framed by the hysterectomies scandal relates to the welfare commitments of the developing nation in the Third World: what are the responsibilities acknowledged by the state toward such "victims" as the mentally retarded and other disabled individuals, and how does it fulfill them?

Barbara Harriss-White argues that the alleviation of disability in *all* countries, but particularly in the developing nations, is bound to be an issue of low priority in "public choice theoretic terms": for the state, the political and economic costs of such welfare measures are high and its benefits low.[54] But, in the constitution of India, the role of the state in the promotion of the people's welfare is recognized in unequivocal, if large and general, terms: first foreshadowed in the preamble, then included among the fundamental rights in the broad category *equalization of gender, caste, and class differences,* and, finally, explicitly identified in the directive principles.[55] It is article 41 of the directive principles that directs the state, "within the limits of [its] economic resources and capacity," to "ensure the right to work, to education and to public assistance in cases of unemployment, old age, sickness and disablement and in other cases of undeserved want." Justice Krishna Iyer praises these provisions as reflecting the Indian constitution's faith in "administrative engineering" and its "comprehensive backing for humanitarian jurisprudence in the area of retardates and handicapped classes." [56]

But a limiting factor is already indicated in article 41: "within the limits of its resources." Here, we come to the crucial question of government policy and the implementation of constitutional rights and directives. Developing nations of the Third World are constrained, not only by limited resources, but also by the overwhelming number of those in need of relief, the frequency and scale of disasters, and the limited and tardy means of legal recourse available to those denied their rights. *Victims,* in this context, would appear to be a category of political beings who do not have full citizenship rights.[57] They are at once less and more than the normative (tax-paying?) citizen: less because often denied the rights available to other citizens, subjected to further exploitation on account of their vulnerable status, and blamed for their misfortunes; more because, by the terms of a liberal democratic constitution, they are (arguably) entitled to the special provisions that actualize equality of opportunity.[58] Between social practice and legal entitlement, they become the paradox or the exception in our understanding of their political identity.

We might also include here, in a loose and admittedly speculative way, what are often adduced as "civilizational" aspects of the Indian polity that inhibit a fuller commitment to a concept of human rights: an indifference to the plight of others, a fatalistic acceptance of one's own and others' misfortune, and an entrenched acceptance of hierarchical differences based on age, caste, and gender. There is a basic (although not for that reason self-evident) argument to be made for the protection of the rights and welfare of the retarded and other handicapped individuals on the basis of humanitarianism, even civilizational decency, even while we admit, with Harriss-White, that definitions of disability are culturally relative. "The test of any civilised society lies in the way it looks after those who cannot look after themselves," insisted S. D. Sharma, director of the Institute of Human Behavior and Allied Sciences in Delhi, in a polemical response to the hysterectomies scandal.[59] Justice Krishna Iyer argues the case for the recognition of the disabled individual as a "human being" and a "full member of [any] society that does not subscribe to a project of the survival of only the fittest." Given the necessary accessories, training facilities, and milieu, he pleads, the "high human potential" of the handicapped can be realized, and they can be made contributing members of society.[60] A recent public interest advertisement on behalf of Tamana, a voluntary organization for the mentally impaired, is motivated by the same purpose of stressing their human identity: "They dream like we dream, they hope like we hope, they try like we try . . . the only difference is that they have to strive a lot harder than we do." It carries a picture of a student of the Tamana school, identifies him by name ("Vipin"), and describes him in glowing terms as a "responsible and friendly" young man.[61] This strategic pleading must be construed as a response to what, clearly, is perceived as popular skepticism in the Indian mind about the fully human stature of the mentally retarded. Translated into the language of state policy, this social apathy means, according to Harriss-White, that programs for achieving equality require "ab initio convincing justifications that the social health of disabled people is a necessary precondition not only for economic growth but also for social welfare" (p. 9).

But, above all, it is the degeneration of the powers exercised by the postcolonial state's functionaries—the police, army, elected bodies, and bureaucracy—into authoritarianism, abuse of power, and corruption that results in the worst forms of exploitation. The opportunistic use of armed and custodial powers by the state's functionaries is reflected in the notorious and widespread instances of army and police brutalities, custodial rape, and deaths in custody. Corruption at the administrative level ensures that funds from aid, developmental, and welfare programs are siphoned off at various levels before reaching the intended recipients. Even at less extreme levels, governmental functioning ensures inefficiency and bureaucratic slowness of process; and, as Harriss-White also points out, administration requires the "labelling, categorising, and prioritising" (p. 9) of the disabled, especially in conditions of scarce resources, leading to their further marginalization and segmentation. Although scarcity of resources is no longer the powerful pretext it once was for the Indian state's inability to meet basic needs, the issue of resource allocation remains an important one in defining the obligations and functions of the state in developing countries. Harriss-White's concluding indictment of the Indian state's welfare provisions for the disabled is uncompromising: "The state has failed to create a coherent agenda for disabled people, a legal frame of obligation, the institutional means whereby needs can be translated into practical claims and consistent trend of real decline in the resources devoted to alleviating disabilities [*sic*], to which a tiny fraction of those needing support actually gain access. The state also fails to regulate both the private sector and NGOs with any consistency. For the mass of disabled people, the state does not exist" (p. 19).

Ironically enough, it is the new regime of a liberalized economy, currently being shaped under various structural adjustment programs, that is likely to provide the greatest acceleration and stimulus to reform measures and welfare services such as literacy, environmental protection, health care, public health, free primary education, sanitation, public transportation, and institutional care. The reasons for this development are too many and too complex to go into here; they include the expansion of markets; the increase of funding from foreign agencies and the number of beneficiary NGOs working in these areas; pressure from the American and European governments to boycott goods produced by child labor; the recent establishment of human rights agendas covering the disabled and mentally retarded by the United Nations and other international bodies and the scrutiny of their observance by international human rights organizations; and the diffuse but real influence of the West as a model.[62] (The last is a persistent aspect of the discourse surrounding the hysterectomies issue.) It is another matter that the actual human rights record in the United States, for instance, will not stand up to scrutiny, that welfare is an area of considerable political-ideological conflict and compromise in advanced countries, and that the humanitarianism of Western governments' strictures on Third World market production dissimulates real commercial and political considerations.[63] Nor is there any real contradiction between this observation about piecemeal reform and improvements in specific social sectors, on the one hand, and the increase in gross levels of poverty under the new liberalization, on the other.[64]

It is simply that, if we are not to let the depressing realities of the functioning of the postcolonial state turn into a somber litany or become, simply, titillating exposés, thus foreclosing further discussion, we must acknowledge that the currents of economic liberalization reforms are likely — however incidentally — to effect social change. An aspect of this change is reflected in, as it is directed by, an increasing middle-class sensitivity to urban conditions, the environment, communal violence, and the more blatant social and economic disparities.[65]

But, in order to *direct* change toward desired goals, we are also called on to explore the available legal means as well as the strategies of protest that constitute the terrain of oppositional politics. The reminder that constitutional legal rights on the books are the necessary but insufficient condition for social justice prompts us to look at the means that can enable their actualization. Among these, in India in the present-day context, are a committed, even interventionary judiciary; a system of electoral politics that at least intermittently makes politicians accountable to the electorate; organized movements for social justice based on demands for civil liberties, on broad class, caste, and gender interests (trade unions, self-employed women's associations, peasant movements, student unions, urban women's groups), and on the solidarities forged from the shared experience of specific disasters (e.g., the Bhopal Gas Victims' Association, the Sikh Riots Victims' Association) or from spontaneous opposition to the state on such specific issues as price rise, liquor sales, power and water shortages, custodial death of a member of the community, etc. In other words, the voices of the victims are themselves beginning to be raised in protest and demand and beginning to be heard in the spaces available in a democratic civil society, predominantly, of course, in the press.[66] The combination of protest, media exposure, and judicial intervention that I am projecting here as an oppositional politics — the trajectory followed in the hysterectomies case — does not, of course, by any means guarantee success, in the sense of the restitution of rights or the correction of wrongs.[67] But a scenario in which such an oppositional politics is absent or even, simply, weaker would undoubtedly be one of unbridled social injustice. Within an ethical rationale of social struggle, we must consider the check on such absolute powers of state and elites as the sufficient sign of success.

In the next and final section of this essay, I turn to the lessons of the hysterectomies scandal for such a reading of oppositional struggle, locating its sites chiefly within the organized women's movement, but also addressing tangentially the possibilities of resistance by those within the institution.

Feminists, "Other" Women, and the State

Women's groups in Pune found themselves in a familiar situation: they were called on to define their relation to the women whose case they were supporting — here, the inmates of the Shirur asylum, whose sterilization they had tried to prevent — in order to justify their involvement. The situation was familiar since, in recent years, the intervention of women's groups in similar instances of perceived injustice and violence toward women, such as the Shahbano case, the Deorala suttee, and Banwari's rape, has met with resistance from the concerned parties — these being, generally, the religious or caste community to which the women belonged, their families and guardians, and the institutions of the state. Neither a concern for abstract justice nor a concern for the politics of feminism ("sisterhood," in a loose sense) has been considered sufficient justification or authentic motivation for feminist intervention.

The problem of *locus standii* has been met by women's groups at least partially and legally, by resorting to public interest litigation. Public interest litigation in India, in recent years, has been used as a means to transcend the traditional doctrine of locus standii, thus permitting "social action groups and individuals to agitate matters in the courts on behalf of the oppressed and weaker sections of society." [68] Most cases of public interest litigation involved, in the early years of the movement, issues of "violations of individual rights and liberties and state lawlessness." [69] While the general effectiveness or otherwise of judgments on public interest litigation is open to debate, there is no doubt that they have allowed people or groups of people with few resources access to legal remedies from the Supreme Court—and these have included those in custodial institutions, specifically mental asylums.[70] It is primarily activist women's and health-care groups that took the lead in the protest against the hysterectomies. Dr. Anant Phadke, founder of Paryaya, an organization promoting the welfare and rights of mentally handicapped women, and Jayshree Velankar of Forum for Women's Health, a society that engages issues of women's health, in particular reproductive technologies, have filed a writ petition in the Bombay high court against the state of Maharashtra, questioning its authority in ordering the hysterectomies.[71]

The women's movement has at all times had to negotiate with/within a major contradiction defining its relation to the state. The state's functionaries, on the one hand, are the major perpetrators of oppression, injustice, and violence against women, and, therefore, the state must be held accountable for the offenses committed; on the other hand, it is the state that must also provide the means for instituting and protecting the rights of women through its various mechanisms, especially, as we have seen, judicial redress. This situation is further complicated by the state's strategy—replicated in the agenda of most political parties—of constructing women as a *constituency* and addressing their interests with proposals for their "welfare," "development," or "upliftment" (as the titles of government departments or ministries indicate). This draws the support of urban middle-class women social workers for such programs, which also find favor among broad sections of the intelligentsia as being constructive in nature. It is hard to draw an absolute distinction between social work activism and feminist activism: clearly, the former has subversive and destabilizing potential even where it functions within the broad parameters of patriarchal reformism, while the latter may seize on the concessions and the opportunities made available by the state and society in order to wrest greater rights for women. It is largely the tag *feminism* itself, with its identification not merely with the activists' class/urban location but with Westernization, that calls forth social disapproval.

The charge of alienation directed at women's groups remains, therefore, a provocative one at the level of polemic and political expediency since feminists are definitionally not identical with victimized women, in this case, of course, not themselves the guardians of the mentally deficient. (In a letter to the editor that appeared in the *Hindu*, a prominent Madras neurosurgeon asked, with a rhetorical flourish: "Will the so-called activists make arrangements all over the country for the care of these retarded unfortunates?")[72] Women activists are also accused of being selective in the causes they espouse and the abuses they protest—hence hypocritical, interested, or reflexively antiestablishment. Above all, the activists' recourse to rights arguments—constitutional, human, gender equity—is anathema because those arguments are pitted against what are invariably described as complex situations, traditional values, the force of custom, or competing rights demands.

A piquant and, to my mind, by no means insignificant aspect of the Shirur case, one that illustrates this ideological divide, was the prominence that the subject of menstruation came to have in the discourse. Menstruation is still a largely forbidden or at least ignored topic in polite public discourse in India. In this instance, however, it allowed feminists to speak as women, in alliance with the women in the Shirur home, even as their no-nonsense demystification of the female body's functions marked them as alienated, once again, from prevalent social norms and conventions. Such openness and oppositionality are treated—negatively—as a mark of modernity by feminism's opponents, but their usefulness in asserting a politics of the female body was considerable. (The modern is, however, visible in other guises. Female hygiene products—marketed predominantly by multinational companies—have recently entered public advertising space; here the idiom of "freedom" and "confidence" produces even a dissimulation of feminist rhetoric).[73] In line with the feminist politics generated by the breaking of social taboo, a recent short story by Manjula Padmanabhan, "The Stain," ends in a sturdy, unapologetic assertion of feminist individualism when the (African American) female protagonist refuses to be cowed by her (Indian) fiancé and his mother into observing traditional Indian menstrual rituals. When asked by him, rhetorically, if she would compare "five thousand years of civilization to . . . feminine hygiene products," she answers, quite simply, "yes."[74] This unequivocal stand on priorities is as unexpected as it is stimulating. The story must be viewed as part of the discursive regime of the female body that Indian feminism has begun to construct.[75]

This, however, is only a tangential gain. Feminist arguments were appropriated by a government official, Vandana Khullar, to argue precisely the reasonableness of the solutions sought by the hysterectomization: "Is it not a gross invasion of a woman's privacy and independence to have someone else take care of her menstrual hygiene, to even change napkins for her?" Further: "Suddenly the 'wombs' of a few unfortunate women have become news, as if its [sic] removal will eliminate her femininity. In fact this operation does not even affect their capacity for sexual enjoyment. Why then are we equating womb with womanhood?"[76] Khullar blames feminists for projecting their own "preconceptions of what a woman must feel about her rights."[77] Such appropriation of feminism's arguments by its opponents is by no means rare in the contests over women's rights, and it must alert us to the limits of simply debating such issues.

Whether the publicity generated by the protests or even a favorable judgment in the public interest litigation pending in the Bombay high court will lead to radical reforms in the functioning of state-run institutions is open to question. The success of feminist interventions cannot be judged simply from the results. Rather, the struggle around specific issues has been the occasion for considerable introspection as well as conflict *within* women's groups in India and points to the need for the constant rethinking of feminist policy and strategy. Admittedly, there is at present a lack of political focus, which has meant that the women's movement has been reactive rather than sustained in its agenda of action. Protests are spontaneous, hence hasty and ill planned; the activities of urban women's groups—chiefly directed at dowry deaths—have been described as "fire-fighting" by one prominent activist; there is insufficient mobilization at the grassroots level among those whose causes are being fought.[78]

For instance, while rightly calling for institutional reforms and also for more institutional spaces for women in need, the Draft Report does not envisage the possibilities of a libertarian organizational politics initiated by the inmates of the institutions themselves. Lately, however, historical studies of the institution from a subaltern perspective have begun to address such a politics; Sanjiv Kakar attributes inmates' revolts against poor living conditions in asylums between 1860 and 1940 to a combination of factors, including the "relation between the agitating patients, the (medical) situation [medical advances in leprosy treatment], and the wider political climate."[79] It would be in cynical bad taste to raise the possibility of such organized resistance by the mentally retarded in custodial institutions.[80] (It is precisely the disagreement over who might most disinterestedly represent their interests that, as we saw, brought the state and women's groups into conflict with each other, with the family occupying an ambivalent position.) National development and social well-being, we are poignantly brought to realize, are not to be won by the unceasing struggle of the disadvantaged victim-citizens and their champions but require the establishment of ethical absolutes.

The foregoing discussion must be viewed as an attempt—difficult, but necessary in my view—to extend the implications of a women's issue to the fullest while at the same time grounding that issue in the specificity of gendered analysis. I have been concerned to raise questions about institutionalization in the postcolonial state (the extent of the state's responsibilities and the limits of its control in relation to dependent citizens) and to explore strategies of social protest and struggle (specifically, how feminists may strategically define their relationship to victimized women). In theoretical terms, the issue may be read, first, in the light of Rawlsian welfarist moral theory, that is, as a means to judge the "goodness of a state of affairs," in this case the contemporary Indian, in terms of the "utility level of the worst off individual in that state," in this case, of course, the hysterectomized women.[81] Second, since the issue concerns destitute mentally retarded women involuntarily sterilized while under the care of the state-run institution — women who inhabit, therefore, the intermediate ground between adult and child, women and not quite women, victim and citizen, social responsibility and social threat — it may be invoked as a *deconstructive* tool. It is the deconstructive method that has taught us to reconceptualize the center in relation to the margin, to interrogate the positivity with reference to the differenced, and to invoke the contingent and singular to bring the normative to crisis: a methodology for reflexive feminism. Above all, the ambiguities within and the overlaps between schemes for social *control* and social *welfare* that a feminist politics brought to light as the scandal of institutional care, in this instance, illustrate the intimate, indeed, constitutive, connections between (actual) violence and (ostensible) protection in the relation between women and the state.

Notes

This paper was originally prepared for the conference Violence against Women and Ideologies of Victimization, organized by the SSRC, New York, and the ICES, Colombo, in Colombo, March 1996. I am grateful for the responses that I received from the participants, especially Ritu Menon, my respondent. For their help, encouragement, and criticism of earlier drafts, thanks also to Daniel Moshenberg, You-me Park, Anupama Rao, and S. Subramanian. Finally, my gratitude to Aalochana and the Voluntary Health Association of India for providing material on file.

1   A report about the proposed operations first appeared in the *Indian Express,* 4 February 1994. I have relied on the subsequent coverage in the English national dailies (the *Hindu,* the *Indian Express,* the *Times of India,* the *Hindustan Times,* the *Telegraph,* the *Pioneer,* and the *Deccan Herald*), on reports by Nagmani Rao and Sarita Pungaliya, based on discussions with a cross section of people in Pune, that appeared in the *Economic and Political Weekly,* 12 March 1994, 601–2; and on K. Badrinath in *Frontline,* 11 March 1994. I have also had the benefit of access to a number of activist groups' reports: those of Action for the Rights of the Child; Stree Kuti, Shramjivika, Forum against Oppression of Women, Lokashahi hakk Sanghatana, and volunteers ("Butchers in the Guise of Saviours"); Parvay (c/o Aalochana); the Research Centre for Women's Studies, SNDT Women's University; the National Addiction Research Centre ("Hysterectomy and Mentally Retarded Women: Issues and Debates"); and the writ petition filed by Anant Phadke and others against the state of Maharashtra. These, and press reports, draw freely on each other. The coverage in the English-language press was extensive as well as exceptionally in-depth, and the activist reports provide invaluable background and research information.
    For a bare account of the facts of the case, on which the reports are fairly unanimous, I have not indicated specific borrowings. In subsequent discussion I do.

2   Dr. Seth said that he had operated on sixteen patients the previous year in association with the Rotary Club of Bombay (*Hindustan Times,* 9 February 1994).

3   Antonio Gramsci, *Selections from the Prison Notebooks*, ed. and trans. Quintin Hoare and Geoffrey Nowell Smith (London: Lawrence and Wishart, 1971), chap. 1, sec. 1.

4   As Foucault has argued, the production of knowledge is built on consensus over what counts as truth and also over what must be excluded from such a description.

5   Lakshmi Iyer, "Pune Operations: Some Ethical Questions," *Hindustan Times*, 14 February 1994, quoting Dr. Pandya.

6   Vandana Khullar, quoted in *Indian Express*, 14 February 1994.

7   Pierre Macherey, *A Theory of Literary Production*, trans. Geoffrey Wall (London: Routledge, 1978).

8   "Women: Towards Beijing," *Lokayan Bulletin* 12, nos. 1-2 (July–October 1995): 67-73, 67. The *Lokayan Bulletin* is produced by the Joint Women's Programme. Page numbers for all further quotations from this report will be given in parentheses in the text.

9   The differences between the two schools of thought, and other theories of social control, are discussed by Stanley Cohen and Andrew Scull in their introduction to *Social Control and the State: Historical and Comparative Essays* (Oxford: Martin Robertson, 1983). See also Michael Ignatieff, "State, Civil Society, and Total Institutions: A Critique of Recent Social Histories of Punishment," in ibid.

10 David Garland, *Punishment and Modern Society: A Study in Social Theory* (Oxford: Clarendon, 1990), 146-47.

11 Some examples of recent work, specifically related to institutions of medicine, are the essays in Roy Macleod and Milton Lewis, eds., *Imperial Health in British India, 1857–1900* (London: Routledge, 1988); David Arnold, *Colonizing the Body: State Medicine and Epidemic Disease in Nineteenth-Century India* (Berkeley and Los Angeles: University of California Press, 1993); and Sanjiv Kakar, "Medical Developments and Patient Unrest in the Leprosy Asylum, 1860–1940," *Social Scientist* 24, nos. 4–6 (April–June 1996): 62–81. Kakar points out that, in the case of leprosy, colonial administrators did not have views very different from or more progressive than native people and held to the same belief in the segregation of leprosy patients.

12 Rasheeda Bhagat, "Agony in the Asylum," *Indian Express*, 20 February 1994.

13 Ibid. Bhagat bases these accounts on an interview with S. Vidyakar, director of a voluntary organization, Udavum Karangal, in Madras.

14 Similarly, the Asiawatch human rights group reported that orphanages in Shanghai were letting children die of starvation as a means of population control.

15 For a careful and introspective essay on the administration of welfare, see the case study of "Mrs. G" in Lucie E. White, "Subordination, Rhetorical Survival Skills, and Sunday Shoes: Notes on the Hearing of Mrs. G," in *Feminist Legal Theory*, ed. Katherine T. Bartlett and Rosanne Kennedy (Boulder, Colo.: Westview, 1991). White stresses the need to replace the "bureaucratized normative vision of the New Deal regulatory state" with a "less holistic vision of power" (p. 422).

16 Iyer, "Pune Operations." There are fourteen hundred people in state homes and seventeen thousand in state-aided homes.

17 "Butchers in the Guise of Saviours," 8-11. Barbara Harriss-White ("Onto a Loser: Disability in India," in *Illfare in India*, ed. S. Subramanian and Barbara Harriss-White (forthcoming) points out that the sum of Rs 980 lakhs allotted by the union Ministry of Welfare for disability-related programs in 1988–89 is "less than what neighbouring Sri Lanka spends on a population under 2 percent that of India's." Of an estimated 4 million mentally retarded people requiring services, only eighteen thousand received any through institutions funded by the National Institute of Mental Health.

18 Alka Kshirsagar, "No Method in the Madness," *Times of India*, 20 February 1994.

19 *Telegraph,* 2 March 1994.

20 *Indian Express,* 9 January 1996. For a recent report on state juvenile homes, see Reeta Dutta Gupta, "Juvenile Homes Are Like Jails," *Times of India,* 11 January 1996. Stories of sexual abuse also figure in a newsmagazine's report on juvenile homes (see Lopamudra Bhattacharya, "Home Sickness," *Sunday,* 26 November–2 December 1995). The *Times of India* (5 March 1996) carried a report of an eleven-year-old boy in a Delhi remand home beaten to death by an older inmate; it turned out, on investigation, that such abuse is routine in the institution, the caretakers permitting and even encouraging various brutalities.

21 Bhattacharya, "Home Sickness."

22 J. Dey, "Prostitutes Oppose Khairnar's Rescue Bid," *Indian Express,* 13 January 1996.

23 Both the role of the media in such investigations and the genre of scandal—in the structure and function specific to the postcolony—call for a more detailed examination, one that lies beyond the scope of this essay. *Scandal,* from the Greek meaning "snare for an enemy, cause of moral stumbling, orig. trap," has grown in meaning from "a moral lapse" (1582), to "damage to reputation" (1590), to "a disgraceful reputation" (1622), to "a slander" (1814), to "offence to moral feeling or sense of decency," and, in a legal sense, "injurious report published concerning another which may be the foundation of legal action" (1838), according to *The Shorter Oxford English Dictionary. The Oxford English Reference Dictionary* gives us the several senses of the word in contemporary usage: "a. a thing or person causing general public outrage or indignation; b. the outrage so caused, especially as a subject of common talk; and c. malicious gossip or backbiting." The shift from the relatively simple "moral lapse" to "a slander" already marks *scandal*'s connotation of crisis; the sense of outrage that it causes—"the offence to moral feeling or sense of decency"—is not free of titillation or relish and concomitant feelings of self-righteousness. While the more playful sense of "faults and foibles" that the *OED* identifies continues to have currency, particularly with reference to sexual escapades, increasingly it is in the context of politics, and in particular the behavior of political personalities, that the word is most heard. Note, too, that scandalous reports never come to us as entirely new: there is a sense in which they have circulated for a long time in the subterranean streams of rumor or have been popular knowledge. The force of disclosure lies in the strength that rumors may gather and in the publicity (even the publication: cf. the 1838 definition) that they receive. In the case of government institutions, which are closed, access is closely guarded, and official information is of dubious value. There is a sense, therefore, in which the scandal would consist precisely of there being no scandal, i.e., in the repression of public knowledge of a state of affairs for a long period.

24 Lakshmi Iyer ("Pune Operations") writes that the Maharashtra government "hinted at the incapabilities" of the state-run institution to provide specialized care for the handicapped, quoting the secretary of the Maharashtra Women and Child Welfare Ministry. In Maharashtra, the majority of the institutions are already run by NGOs. By way of grants, the government pays the NGO 100 percent of staff salaries, rent, etc. and 66 percent of all other expenses but has few supervisory powers or control (see "Butchers in the Guise of Saviours," 9).

25 A negative appraisal of the capacities and performance of NGOs in offering institutional care to the handicapped is to be found in Harriss-White, "Onto a Loser." For a wider discussion of NGOs as an alternative to the state, see Andre Gunder Frank and Marta Fuentes, "Nine Theses on Social Movements," *Economic and Political Weekly,* 29 August 1987.

26 Some examples: the Spastics Society of India; Mentaid, in Calcutta, a school set up by parents of mentally handicapped children; the Naga Mothers' Association, which runs a detoxification and counseling center in Kohima, Nagaland.

27 Christopher Hitchens's book on Mother Theresa, *The Missionary Position* (London: Verso, 1995), expresses misgivings about many aspects of her activities among the Calcutta poor.

28 Ahalya Rangnekar (who had sought the stay on the operations), retracted: "On grounds of compassion and human dignity, these surgeries are okay. Our quarrel is over the manner in which the Rotary Club went about organizing it. We are against mass hysterectomy." Sharada Sathe of Stree Sanghatana expressed similar views. Both are quoted in Iyer, "Pune Operations."

29 See the remarks made by Vandana Khullar, director, WHCD, Maharashtra: "The Government is always an easy target for levelling accusations at" (*Indian Express*, 14 February, 1994). Also, D. B. Ramamurthy: "We seem to be going the U.S. way in holding meaningless agitations out of which nothing good can come" (quoted in Bhagat, "Agony in the Asylum").

30 Some of these are listed in "Butchers in the Guise of Saviours," 4–5, and include Mother Theresa's order's Asha Daan, in Bombay.

31 An incisive and comprehensive treatment of the topic of this section is to be found in Usha Ramanathan, "Women, Law, and Institutionalisation: A Manifestation of State Power," *Indian Journal of Gender Studies* 3, no. 2 (July–December 1996): 199–224. Since Ramanathan's essay appeared after mine was completed, I have not cited specific arguments in it but content myself with this general reference and recommendation. Ramanathan also provides a brief but useful list of references.

32 The Terrorist and Disruptive Activities (TADA) Act, which lapsed on 23 May 1995, is now succeeded by the Criminal Law Amendment Bill, which has many similar provisions. From the inception of TADA in 1985 to June 1994, there were 76,036 arrests (National Human Rights Commission). On TADA, see *Black Law, White Lies,* report of the People's Union for Democratic Rights (PUDR) (1995).

33 See the Draft Report; and Amita Dhanda, "Law, Psychiatry and Human Rights," *Seminar* 430 (June 1995): 22–25.

34 Rokeya Sakhawat Hossain, *Sultana's Dream* (1905), ed. and trans. Roushan Jahan and Hanna Papanek (New York: Feminist, 1988), 9.

35 Geeta Ramseshan, "What about Their Rights?" *Hindu,* 16 April 1994.

36 Krishna Iyer, *Justice and Beyond* (New Delhi: Deep and Deep, 1980), 196.

37 See, e.g., Norman Daniels, *Just Health Care* (Cambridge: Cambridge University Press, 1985). Daniels's position draws on John Rawls's *Theory of Justice* (Cambridge, Mass.: Harvard University Press, 1971). For the argument that charity and compassion must inform welfare measures (over and above rights) in the modern capitalist state, see Loren E. Lomasky, "Justice to Charity," *Social Philosophy and Policy* 12, no. 2 (summer 1995): 32–53.

38 Dhanda, "Law, Psychiatry, and Human Rights," 22–23.

39 Ibid., 25. For more on accountability, see the National Addiction Research Centre report.

40 Dhanda, "Law, Psychiatry, and Human Rights," 22–23.

41 Iyer, *Justice and Beyond,* 195, 202.

42 Indira Jaisingh quoted in Iyer, "Pune Operations."

43 See Nitya Jacob, "Ethics of Hysterectomy for the Retarded," *Pioneer,* 23 February 1994. Jacob specifies that, in South Africa, "the Abortion and Sterilisation Act of 1975 authorises sterilisation for severely retarded women provided the procedure is performed in a state hospital, certified by two medical practitioners and the parent or guardian gives informed consent." In Britain, the patient would first have to be made a ward of the court and a court order then obtained for the sterilization.

44 See, e.g., G. R. Sridhar, "A Beginning Must Be Made," *Hindu,* 20 March 1994. Sridhar cites some of the guidelines provided by the committee on Bioethics of the American Academy of Pediatrics.

45 The opinions of the medical community were widely canvassed by Rasheeda Bhagat ("Agony in the Asylum").

46 Dr. Suresh Deshpande, president of the Indian Medical Association, Pune, quoted in Arshia Sattar, "The Blood of Others," *Times of India Sunday Review,* 20 February 1994.

47 Dr. Sunil Pandya, quoted in Iyer, "Pune Operations."

48 Dr. Sarada Menon, quoted in Bhagat, "Agony in the Asylum."

49 I refer, in particular, to the use of Medline, Popline, and other global databases for this research by the National Addiction Research Centre (NARC).

50 *Umbartha* (Threshhold), dir. Jabbar Patel, color, 135 minutes (1982), in Marathi (also appeared in Hindi under the title *Subah*); *Damini,* dir. Raj Kumar Santoshi, color, 140 minutes (1993), in Hindi.

51 See Rajeswari Sunder Rajan, *Real and Imagined Women: Gender, Culture, and Postcolonialism* (London: Routledge, 1993), esp. the chapter "The Name of the Husband."

52 *Umbartha* inevitably calls to mind *Arth* ([The meaning], dir. Mahesh Bhatt, color, 140 minutes [1982], in Hindi), another contemporary feminist film, in which the betrayed wife leaves home, finds refuge in a women's hostel, and learns independence and achieves fulfillment in her single life. Also contemporary, but made in a different mode, that of satiric and carnivalesque fable, is *Mandi* ([Marketplace], dir. Shyam Benegal, color, 130 minutes [1983], in Hindi). Set in a city brothel, *Mandi* pits this lively community of women, with all their misery and brutality, against the deadening morality of the social worker's reformatory and the outside world in general.

53 Karnad is primarily a playwright, but he is also himself a director of alternative cinema, and he occasionally acts in film and television in dignified and sympathetic roles.

54 Harriss-White, "Onto a Loser," 1; page numbers for subsequent quotations will be given in the text.

55 I have relied on Vinay Kumar Malhotra, *Welfare State and Supreme Court in India* (New Delhi: Deep and Deep, 1986), 86–93. The preamble affirms the resolve to secure justice, liberty, equality, and fraternity for all citizens; the fundamental rights guarantee equality and freedom of speech, expression, and assembly; articles 23–30 are provisions against forced labor, child labor, and traffic in human beings and ensuring equal educational opportunity and the protection of minorities. Various articles of the directive principles of state policy (articles 30–51 of part 4) explicitly commit the nation to guaranteeing the "welfare of the people" and a "social order" that ensures social, economic, and political justice.

56 Iyer, *Justice and Beyond,* 193. Harriss-White points out, however, that, despite the commitment to creating a welfare state, there are critical limitations to achieving it: "The institution to preside over this, the Planning Commission, does not have a constitutional status, and many of the interventions required were under the jurisdiction not of the central government but of the states" ("Onto a Loser," 12). Directive principles also cannot be enforced under the law.

57 *Victims* is a term that prompts specificity: victims of what (whom)? Thus, although as a description *victim* always already fits those who by social status—class, caste, gender, minority identity—are traditionally underprivileged and those who—as a result of age, disease, or handicap—are naturally disadvantaged, it is also more specifically identified with the plight of individuals in exceptional crises: such as man-made and natural disasters (the Bhopal gas tragedy, e.g., or communal riots, caste wars, and periodic drought, flood, and famine), destitution, and gendered violence (rape, abduction, prostitution, forced labor, domestic brutality). Although contingencies of the latter sort may uniformly and democratically occur among any people—disasters, e.g., are often moralistically viewed as "levelers" —their victims invariably, and not coincidentally, are the traditionally underprivileged and naturally disadvantaged. Built into the definition of *victim,* further, is the notion of *blamelessness* (although blame can be a criterion that is ambivalently judged—victims often get

blamed for their misfortune either by the curious logic of divine justice or by the harsh one of existential responsibility or, more mundanely, simply for not being smart enough to avert it): the Indian constitution, e.g., guarantees the right to assistance of those suffering from "undeserved want" (article 41); and the UN Declaration of Human Rights (1948) specifies the right to security of a person in the event of lack of livelihood owing to "circumstances beyond his control."

58   This exists in India in the form of a "weak reservation policy" in the areas of education and the employment of the disabled (Harriss-White, "Onto a Loser," 15, 18).

59   S. D. Sharma quoted in Kalpana Jain, "The Mindless Matter," *Times of India*, 20 February, 1994. Dr. Sharma echoes Rawls's position that a society should be judged by how it treats its less fortunate members (John Rawls, *A Theory of Justice* (Cambridge: Harvard UP, 1971).

60   Iyer, *Justice and Beyond*, 189, 195.

61   The advertisement appeared in the *Indian Express* on 9 January 1996 and was created by Akshara Advertising.

62   Regarding the expansion of markets, Krishna Kumar argues that the "sustained official push for achievement of mass literacy has come at a time when the Indian economy is being speedily 'opened up' for penetration by the world capitalist system" and sees functional literacy as serving the purpose, in this context, only of propagating advertisements and pulp literature ("Market Economy and Mass Literacy," *Economic and Political Weekly*, 11 December 1993, 2727–34, esp. 2727, 2730).

63   On the welfare state in Britain and the debates with socialism and Marxism, see, e.g., Vic George and Paul Wilding, *Ideology and Social Welfare* (London: Routledge and Kegan Paul, 1985); Phil Lee and Colin Raban, *Welfare Theory and Social Policy: Reform or Revolution?* (London: Sage, 1988); Ramesh Mishra, *The Welfare State in Crisis: Social Thought and Social Change* (Brighton: Wheatsheaf, 1984). On the right to welfare, see S. N. Eisenstadt and Oha Ahimar, *The Welfare State and Its Aftermath* (London: Croom Helm, 1985). Eisenstadt and Ahimar describe the welfare recipient in the modern state as the very type of the citizen, making claims "in the name of either the universal right as citizen or in the name of some new overall criteria of distributive justice" (p. 310). For a provocative contrary view, see William Connolly, *Identity/Difference: Democratic Negotiations of Political Paradox* (Ithaca, N.J.: Cornell University Press, 1991). In the late capitalist state, welfare recipients, he argues, become the object of "generalized resentment." "The welfare class thus becomes a permanent demonstration project on the theatricality of power" (p. 208). I am grateful to Anantha Giri for bringing Connolly's argument to my notice.
     On the crisis of the welfare state or, more accurately, the beginning of the crisis, see Etienne Balibar, "What Is a Politics of the Rights of Man?" in *Masses, Classes, Ideas* (New York: Routledge, 1994). On the accreted ideological connotations of welfare dependence in the contemporary United States, see Nancy Fraser and Linda Gordon, "A Genealogy of Dependency: Tracing a Keyword of the U.S. Welfare State," *Signs: A Journal of Women and Culture* (winter 1994): 309–36.

64   On health-care issues in particular, see Arun Ghosh, "Health Care and Globalisation: Case for a Selective Approach," *Economic and Political Weekly*, February 24, 1996, 441–42. Ghosh quotes data taken from the *Sample Registration Bulletin* (January 1995) that reveal that, while infant mortality rates declined by 5.6 percent over the period 1987–90, they declined only 2.6 percent between 1990 and 1993 (1991 being the year of the onset of structural adjustment programs in India) (Fraser and Gordon, "A Genealogy of Dependency").

65   On the connections between reform and middle-class sensibilities, see Garland, *Punishment and Modern Society*.

66 For an analysis of the role of the press as both reformist and sensationalist, see my "Ameena: Gender, Crisis, and National Identity," *Oxford Literary Review* 16, nos. 1–2 (1994): 147–76.

67 The most notorious instance, of course, is the failure of the victims of the Bhopal gas tragedy still to receive compensation, or proper medical treatment even, thirteen years after the leak occurred, despite the worldwide publicity that activists have generated for their plight and the directives of the Supreme Court.

68 I rely on V. Suresh and D. Nagasila, "In Public Interest," *Seminar* 430 (June 1995): 37–41.

69 Suresh and Nagasila (ibid.) cite *Rakesh Chandra Narayan v. State of Bihar,* 1991 Supp. (2).

70 Ibid.

71 *Asian Age* (28 June 1994) also reported that a writ petition was filed by the director of the National Addiction Research Centre, Gabriel Britto.

72 *Hindu,* 14 February 1994. Other similar letters may be found in the columns of *Times of India,* 4 March 1994.

73 See the chapter "Real and Imagined Women" in my *Real and Imagined Women.*

74 Manjula Padmanabhan, "The Stain," in *Hot Death, Cold Soup* (New Delhi: Kali for Women, 1996), 229.

75 The report of the Fifth National Conference of Women's Movements, held in Tirupati, January 1994, gives an indication of the increase in attention to sexuality issues in many women's groups. The women's movement also strongly opposes unsafe contraceptive techniques propagated by the government.

76 See the remarks made by Vandana Khullar cited in n. 29 above.

77 See the remarks made by Vandana Khullar cited in n. 29 above.

78 The person quoted is Ruth Vanita (former coeditor of *Manushi*) in "Thinking Beyond Gender in India," *Seminar* 446 (October 1996): 66–71. Many of the other observations may be found in the report of the Fifth National Conference of Women's Movements.

79 Kakar, "Medical Developments and Patient Unrest," 78.

80 The organizing of children in bonded labor in unions is also criticized as exploitative. Harriss-White bemoans the fact that "disability has a weak constituency," and that there are severe constraints on disabled people as activists (19, 20).

81 Rawls, *A Theory of Justice.*

The Colonial Drag: Zionism, Gender, and Mimicry

DANIEL BOYARIN

*To Michel Warschavsky and Tikva Hoenig Parnas, tireless fighters
against the Zionist occupation in all Palestine*

After Sabina Spielrein, Jung's patient and mistress, having abandoned her dream of bearing a Jewish "Siegfried" to Jung, had informed him that she was pregnant by her Jewish husband, Freud wrote her: "I am, as you know, cured of the last shred of my predilection for the Aryan cause, and would like to take it that *if the child turned out to be a boy he will develop into a stalwart Zionist*. He or she must be dark in any case, no more towheads. Let us banish all these will-o'-the-wisps."[1] The racial aspects of Freud's prayer for the child are obvious, but the gender encoding is more mysterious.[2] The Zionist is gendered male for Freud. Why?

For Freud (*at the time that he wrote this letter*), the reason that Zionism is coded male is that it is essentially about masculinity.[3] The Spielrein letter was explicitly written in reaction to Freud's break with Jung and his acrimonious feelings toward Jung's anti-Semitic tendencies, as Yerushalmi has made clear. Jung had unambiguously ventilated the European topos of Jewish male "effeminacy."[4] Another way of saying this would be that Zionism had for Freud at this point in his life precisely the same function that Oedipality had for him at others. Both signify a masculinizing of the allegedly feminized — queer — Jewish male. As in the case of his relations with Fliess, in his letter to Spielrein, also, disavowed homoeroticism and Zionism are correlated.[5] Freud was quite frank about his homoerotic feelings toward Jung, having written Jones that a faint in Jung's presence had to do with "some unruly homosexual feeling," and interpreting this faint in terms of the "negative Oedipus complex."[6] Giving up the Aryan cause consists, then, of overcoming the unruly desire for the Aryan Jung.[7]

For Freud, Moses stands on a mountain looking yearningly at the Promised Land, not, however, at the land of Israel, but at Rome—the very heartland of the Aryan—like Hannibal at Lake Trasimeno.[8] Freud's Rome dreams and especially the dream known as "My Son the Myops" encode Rome as object of desire as well as being the site of the hated oppressor. This text—dream and interpretation in Freud's dream book—constitutes the most replete statement of an ambivalent wish somehow to remain Jewish in name but have this Jewishness transformed into a "manly" essence undistinguishable from Aryanness.[9] As we shall see, such ambivalence is emblematic of Zionism at the foundation of the movement.

It is, by now, famous that, when the child Freud heard from his father of his "passivity" in the face of anti-Semitic intimidation, his response was to fantasize about being Hannibal, whose brave father swore to seek revenge for his "Semitic" people against the Roman oppressors. Indeed, Moses seems almost to be merged with Hannibal in his mind. Moreover, one can add the not insignificant point that even Freud's "Semitic" hero Hannibal was hardly Jewish. From a traditional Jewish point of view, he was every bit as pagan in both religion and cultural identity as his Roman adversaries. As Bluma Goldstein has so keenly written: "And with what better model to wage battle against such antagonism and antisemitism than with a Semitic warrior! But with a Semitic warrior who is not a Jew?" Precisely! Freud's fantasies of Hannibal the Semite, and of Massena the allegedly Jewish war hero, and ultimately of Moses the Egyptian prince who founds the Jewish people, represent a wish to remain Jewish in name but be entirely transformed in such a way that the Jewishness would be invisible. Goldstein has shown how this Freudian fantasy applied to Freud's very Moses identification:

> In 1900 Freud characterized his own adventurous nature in terms of conquest: "I am actually not at all a man of science, not an observer, not an experimenter, not a thinker. I am by temperament nothing but a *conquistador*, an adventurer, if you wish to translate this term—with all the inquisitiveness, daring, and tenacity characteristic of such a man." Whether in the guise of *conquistador* or Semitic warrior, Freud apparently conceived of himself at that time as conquering Rome in the name of Jewry, which the Roman Church, in his view, had persecuted and continued to threaten. But what did happen when he finally reached Rome?[10]

According to Goldstein's brilliant reading of Freud's essay on Michelangelo's Moses, what happened was that Freud discovered a Moses that embodied all the values and traits of European Christians, indeed, was a central monument of European Christianity in the heart of Rome itself, like Hannibal, another *non-Jewish Jew* (to appropriate a term coined for an entirely different context).[11] The point is that Freud decided ultimately to remain Jewish but wanted to reconfigure Jews in the image of Romans (i.e., Christians).

The Jewish heroes, whether of the Bible or of modernity, are all transformed into mimics of gentile heroes. This point could use some further expansion because, as it stands, it sounds both essentialist — "War heroes could not possibly be *really* Jewish" — and counterfactual. What, after all, about Samson and the other biblical warriors? My point is not to deny that there was ever a Jewish martial tradition or to assert that being violent is un-Jewish, which would be at best a nonstrategic essentialism. As it developed historically, however, diasporic Jewish culture had little interest in Samson, and its Moses was a scholar. Even the Maccabees were deprived of their status as military heroes in the Talmud. What is significant, therefore, is that, as emancipated Jews became desperate to remake the Jewish male in the image of the Anglo-Saxon (in particular) as the ultimate white male of their world, they sought to discover such male models within something they could call Jewish — Hannibal, the Semite; a transformed Moses; Massena, an allegedly Jewish general; and ultimately the whole biblical tradition of sovereignty and war making understood precisely as the antithesis of the diasporic Jewish wont for passivity.

Zionism is thus for Freud a mode of repression, of overcoming, of his Jewish homosexual effeminacy.[12] Both this family romance — I am a direct descendant of the warrior Semites of old, not the child of passive, effeminate Ostjuden — and the Oedipus romance function in the same way to deny Freud's paternity as the son of the impotent — queer — Jew who picked up the hat that the gentile threw down, thus signifying his passivity in the face of the virile Aryan: "If he had to have a Jewish father, little Sigmund would at least have wanted him to be a man proud of his race, a bold warrior."[13] Similarly, and revealingly, early proto-Zionist Jewish gymnastic groups took the names of Jewish warriors like Bar Kochba and Maccabee (both quite marginalized and often disparaged in rabbinic Jewish tradition) as their icons.[14]

Seen in this light, Zionism is truly the most profound sort of assimilationism, one in which Jews become like all the nations, that is, like Aryans (Oedipus), but remain Jews in name (and complexion): Bar Kochba, warrior Moses, and Maccabee; not Tancred (Herzl's *nom-de-mensur*) or Siegfried (a *Jugendstil* representation of whom appeared on the souvenir card of the Second Zionist Congress held in Basel in 1898). Sabina Spielrein is not to give birth to a blonde Siegfried, but, again, if he is a boy he must be a stalwart Zionist. For Freud, it seems, it was not actually necessary to participate in the building of a Jewish national home in order to solve the Jewish problem; merely being a stalwart Zionist was enough to transform the Jewish man from his state of female degeneracy into the status of proper, that is — in spite of Freud's disclaimer — mock Aryan male.[15]

I propose that Freud's reading of Zionism was not as idiosyncratic as it might, at first glance, appear. As has been shown more than once, Zionism was considered by many to be as much a cure for the disease of Jewish gendering as a solution to economic and political problems of the Jewish people.[16] Exemplary in this regard is Max Nordau, cast by Berkowitz as "the second great embodiment of early Zionism." D. Biale writes that "Nordau's demand that the Jews reform their bodies was yet another attempt from witin the Jewish community to adapt the underlying structure of anti-Semitic rhetoric and use its strong, political message for other ends. Nordau's call for a 'new muscle Jew' was based on the degeneration of the Jew 'in the narrow confines of the ghetto.' . . . Zionism demanded that the new muscle Jews have healthy bodies and healthy minds."[17] George Mosse had already succinctly written, "Zionists and assimilationists shared the same ideal of manliness," which in my reading cashes out as an equivalence of Zionism and assimilation.[18]

Given the contemporary gendering of muscularity, it is hardly surprising, then, to find Freud encoding Zionism as male, as virile, and as the specific answer to Jung's anti-Semitic descriptions of Jewishness as effeminate.[19] Freud, like Nordau, had, on this reading, internalized the negative and pathologizing interpretation of Jewish manhood of the anti-Semites and saw Zionism as the solution. To a not inconsiderable extent, the project of these Zionists was precisely to transform Jewish men into the type of male that they admired, namely, the ideal Aryan male. If the political project of Zionism was to be a nation like all other nations, on the level of the reform of the Jewish psyche it was to be men like all other men. The Zionist catchphrase, *kexol haggoyim,* "like all the nations," thus has a double meaning since, in its popular acceptance, it would have meant rather "like all the (male) gentiles." It was this aspect of Zionism, I propose, that appealed to Freud. By identifying himself with Moses, conquistador, Freud was remasculating himself, undoing the unmanning of his Jewishness, but remaining nominally and affectively Jewish, just like the Austrian Jewish men who created the Jewish gymnastic clubs, Maccabee and Bar-Kochba. Berkowitz refers to the "Jewish gymnast's symbiosis of *Deutschtum, Judentum,* and liberalism" and remarks that this combination "was a critical transmitter of Zionist national culture."[20]

Herzl the German

I am a German-speaking Jew from Hungary and can never be anything but a German. At present I am not recognized as a German. But that will come once we are over there.

Through Zionism Jews will again be able to love this Germany to which, despite everything, our hearts have clung. — Theodor Herzl

I turn to the texts of Theodor Herzl, the father of the Jewish state. Rereading these texts with the critical categories of postcolonial theory in mind will be productive of a dramatic new take on Herzlian Zionism.[21] Zionism is presented by its adherents as antiassimilationism, a will to power in the face of oppression or as a nativism not entirely unlike the Negritude movement. The passages presented above, quoted from Herzl's diaries, need only be compared to the following statement by an exemplary assimilationist German Jew to show how mystified this picture is: "I have, and know no other, blood than German blood," wrote Walter Rathenau, "no other tribe, no other people than the German. Expel me from my German soil, I still remain German, nothing changes."[22] With somewhat greater insight, Herzl had realized that only by leaving German soil and founding a Jewish state would he ever be truly German, but his identification with the Germans and desire fully to be one were the same as Rathenau's. Zionism's opponents, on the other hand, see it as plain colonialism, a mere undiluted extension of European practices. My project is to describe how Zionism occupies a peculiar interstitial position, neither wholly nativist, in that there is only a partial assertion of difference, nor an univocal tributary of colonialism.

In order to follow the argument that I shall be making, it is crucial first to understand the ideology of Jewish emancipation as it was originally formulated by liberal European Christians. As opposed to racist anti-Semites who claimed that what was wrong with the Jews was biological and immutable, the liberals held that, in their eyes, everything despicable about Jews was a product of the material conditions within which Jews had to live and especially a result of the oppression that they suffered at the hands of Christians. A further cause of the degraded and decadent state of the Jews was their hanging on to a primitive and "Oriental" way of life. The solution to the "Jewish Problem," according to a liberal like Christian Wilhelm Dohm, then, was for Jews to give up their primitive, Oriental, distinctiveness and become "civilized."[23] Then they would show manly virtues and engage in such manly practices as dueling and soldiering, the civic duties and privileges of every citizen. Dohm's *Concerning the Amelioration of the Civil Status of the Jews* (1781) bears interesting analogies to Macaulay's "Minute on Indian Education," which set out infamously to produce a class of people "Indian in blood and colour, but English in taste, in opinions, in morals, and in intellect."[24] *The "emancipation" of the Jews is thus functionally akin to a colonization.*

This view of the Jewish condition was completely taken over by Herzl, who was more than prepared to be a member of the class of those who would civilize the Jewish masses. In 1882, he was prepared to agree with all the charges leveled against "the Jews" by the anti-Semite Eugen Dühring, charges of crookedness, lack of ethical seriousness, and parasitism. His only disagreement with Dühring was that, while the former considered these to be biological, Herzl considered them entirely the product of the environment in which the Jews found themselves. For Herzl, the Talmud and all that it contained and produced was but "the product of an unnatural, imposed isolation from the mainstream of humanity, the pathetic consolation of distressed spirits." There were other Jewish readings of the Jewish past; enlightened and learned rabbis of Vienna considered Jewish culture in Europe the product of a fertile interchange between talmudic textuality and practices and the European culture as it developed around the Jews and as they contributed to it, and, thus, "in emphasizing Judaism's Oriental character and foreignness to Europe, Herzl was closer to anti-Jewish polemicists." For Herzl explicitly, as I have suggested above, and for Freud when we read between the lines, that which distinguishes Jews from gentiles is a deformation: "For Herzl, Jewish distinctiveness and disfigurement were one and the same." [25]

Freud had expressed a desire in the Myops dream that his children would be educated in such a fashion that they would be able freely to cross the border into gentile society.[26] He stopped quite short, however, of desiring that they convert. He wished them, somehow, to remain loyal to some memory of Jewish identity, as long as it did not distinguish them in any way from gentiles. This was ultimately the solution that Herzl arrived at also, the solution known as Zionism, but, before getting there, he had tried thought experiments with other means of turning Jews into gentiles and thus of having the Jews disappear as an independent cultural entity.

Herzl wrote in his diaries of his plan (of 1893!) to save the Jews via mass conversion. This remarkable and bizarre text will repay extended quotation:

> About two years ago I wanted to solve the Jewish Question, at least in Austria, with the help of the Catholic Church. I wished to gain access to the Pope . . . and say to him: Help us against the anti-Semites and I will start a great movement for the free and honorable conversion of Jews to Christianity.
>
> Free and honorable by virtue of the fact that the leaders of this movement—myself in particular—would remain Jews and as such would propagate conversion to the faith of the majority. The conversion was to take place in broad daylight, Sundays at noon, in Saint Stephen's Cathedral, with festive processions and amidst the pealing of bells. Not in shame, as individuals have converted up to now, but with proud gestures.

And because the Jewish leaders would remain Jews, escorting the people only to the threshold of the church and themselves staying outside, the whole performance was to be elevated by a touch of great candor.

We, the steadfast men, would have constituted the last generation. We would still have adhered to the faith of our fathers. But we would have made Christians of our young sons before they reached the age of independent decision, after which conversion looks like an act of cowardice or careerism. . . . I could see myself dealing with the Archbishop of Vienna; in imagination I stood before the Pope — both of them were very sorry that I wished to do no more than remain part of the last generation of Jews — and sent this slogan of mingling of the races flying across the world.[27]

This text reveals brilliantly fundamental and critically significant elements in Herzl's thought world. The only problem with which he is concerned is the problem of Jewish honor and acceptance, obviously not the problem of cultural survival. In the very text that becomes the foundation stone of Zionism, *The Jewish State,* Herzl indeed wrote, "I referred previously to our 'assimilation.' I do not for a moment wish to imply that I desire such an end. Our national character is too glorious in history and, in spite of every degradation, too noble to make its annihilation desirable." On such statements is the myth of a Herzlian conversion back to Judaism founded, but, in the very next sentence, he writes: "Though perhaps we *could* succeed in vanishing without a trace into the surrounding peoples, if they would let us be for just two generations. But they will not let us be. . . . *Only* pressure drives us back to our own; *only* hostility stamps us ever again as strangers." To find a way to continue Jewish difference in a creative, vital manner was never in the program at all, not in the beginning, and not at the end. The scheme was ever to find a way for Jews to assume their proper status as proud, manly, warlike people — just like everybody else. Herzl's most stirring statement, "We are one people," carries its immediate disavowal: "Our enemies have made us one whether we will or not." The suggestion is clear that, if only allowed to, we would have disappeared long ago, and, indeed, Herzl says so explicitly.[28]

There is no more efficient mode of facilitating Jewish disappearance than actual conversion. As Kornberg shows, this "solution" to the Jewish problem had been a frequent one in the writings of assimilationist Jews who considered that "whatever differentiates men, also divides them." That being the case, the best solution would be for Jews to abandon that which differentiates them from other men since Judaism was now, as Theodor Gomperz put it, "worn-out and out of date."[29] Herzl had adopted such notions as early as 1883 and continues them here in his call for a "mingling of the races." In contrast to previous biographers of Herzl, who considered this idea of his as the swan song of his assimilationism, Kornberg shows how precisely it was preparatory to his Zionism.

Herzl had come to the conclusion that anti-Semitism was essentially justified by the behavior of the Jews, especially, of course, the despised Ostjuden, and that only a radical act of self-transformation would win the esteem of Christendom for his degenerate compatriots. As we have seen, his only argument was with the modern versions of anti-Semitism that considered the degradation of the Jews to be a biological characteristic and therefore unchangeable. With classic Christian anti-Judaism, which considered the Jewish Problem effectively a necessary product of the Jewish refusal to accept Christ, he was apparently quite comfortable. The bold act of mass conversion, carried out in a decorous way, bravely and openly was to be just such an act of Jewish self-transformation.

His curious notion that this project was somehow more honorable if the leaders remained Jewish is, in fact, of a piece with the whole affective and ideological endeavor because the entire point of this drastic exercise would be sacrificed if the Jews were to appear cowardly, to appear as if they were converting out of an unmanly and dishonorable fear or opportunism. By the leaders remaining faithful, and especially by enacting the conversion of children who have not yet reached the age of decision, somehow it is imagined that any imputation of cowardice or careerism would be entirely avoided. We have here the very essence of Herzl's cultural fix. Kornberg considers Herzl's dual impulses toward assimilation and toward Jewish self-assertion as symptoms of extreme ambivalence. I would suggest, rather, that they are symptomatic of a double-bind situation that he (and other colonials, mutatis mutandis) find themselves in without any easy breakout. The anti-Semitic charges that Herzl had internalized were of cowardice and opportunism, lack of principle in the face of external pressure. Kornberg himself documents such representations: "In one display of wit, a Viennese Jew claimed that it was his *Germanic* sense of loyalty and pride that prevented him from converting to Christianity," and another refers to baptism as Jewish nonsense.[30] By not converting, the Jew converts, but, by converting, he remains Jewish!

No wonder Herzl manifests a paradox. The dual impulses to transform Jews into gentiles and to be self-assertive in the face of anti-Semitism are thus both parts of the same answer to the same problem, one that leaves Jews damned if they do and damned if they don't. Conversion, which is by definition not self-assertion, would seem to be a sign of precisely such cowardice and careerism, while self-assertion without conversion would lead to a continuation of the same kind of anti-Semitic pressure that had led to the degradation in the first place. The problem was how to find a mode of becoming indistinguishable from gentiles without appearing cowardly. Herzl's initial solution was for the leaders to convert the simple people and children while they themselves remained tenaciously Jewish and presumably suffered the consequences bravely. The ultimate solution, however, was to be Zionism.

In 1894, again according to Herzl's own account, Jewish difference was for him only a negative and unwilled condition, imposed on Jews by anti-Semites: "I understand what anti-Semitism is about. We Jews have maintained ourself, even if through no fault of our own, as a foreign body among the various nations. In the ghetto we have taken on a number of anti-social qualities. Our character has been corrupted by oppression, *and it must be restored through some other kind of pressure.* . . . All these sufferings rendered us ugly and transformed our character which had in earlier times been proud and magnificent. After all, we once were *men* who knew how to defend the state in time of war." [31] By 1894, Herzl had become convinced that this "other kind of pressure" could not be conversion — not, however, because he had undergone a transformation and "returned to his people," but because Christian friends of the Jews had responded extremely negatively to the suggestion. The notion of what constituted a proud and magnificent *Volk* never changed. The tension here is palpable; once more, we are faced with the paradox that the very definitions of what constituted regaining *Jewish* honor for Herzl involved a virtual transformation into Germans. Such tensions are precisely what we have found in Freud and are to be found in Spinoza as well, who, in a fascinating passage, writes: "The mark of circumcision is also, I think, of great importance in this connexion; so much so that in my view it alone will preserve the Jewish people for all time; indeed, did not the principles of their religion make them effeminate [*effoeminarent*] I should be convinced that some day when the opportunity arises . . . they will establish their state once more, and that God will choose them afresh." [32] What a double bind! Precisely that which preserves the Jewish people is that which has emasculated them and prevents them from establishing their state. With ideas like this blowing in the wind, no wonder the Zionist Herzl did not have his own son circumcised. No wonder also that Freud, in search of a Jewish masculinity, an antidote to circumcision and its uncanniness, finds the erection of a state.

In 1894, Herzl wrote *Das neue Ghetto.* [33] Much of the plot turns around a cultural motive with which Herzl, like many other Austro-Hungarian Jews of his time, was obsessed, the duel. The protagonist, a thinly disguised representation of himself, has provoked a gentile cavalry officer and then refused to duel him because he was preoccupied at the time with a dying father. This incident had taken place five years before the opening of the play. To a gentile friend who dismisses the importance of the event, he says: "I haven't been able to forget it. Not I — you see, I'm a Jew. You and your kind can take that kind of thing in stride. When you, Franz Wurzlechner, settle such a run-in peaceably, that makes you a solid clear-headed chap. Me — me, Jacob Samuel — it makes a coward" (*DnG,* 163). An even more unsettling moment is provided by a scene in which the same Franz Wurzlechner has come to "break up" with his former best friend because the latter has married into a too-Jewish (in our parlance) family: "It's you — you've changed. Your environment is different — the company you keep. I don't belong there—with these Rheinbergs, Wassersteins, the whole lot of them—they rub me the wrong way. And since your marriage I'm likely to run into them at any time in your home—there's no escaping them. It's not your fault—they're your people" (p. 168). Samuel's response is to understand, thank his "friend" for his frankness, and detail what he had learned from him over the years: "I learned big things and little—inflections, gestures, how to bow without being obsequious, how to stand up without seeming defiant—all sorts of things" (p. 169). Jacob goes on to provide the usual Herzlian litany: Of course, you're right, we are despicable, but it's all your fault. There we have it, the perfect representation of the Austrian Jew, admiring and adapting gentile mores, and then hurt when it doesn't work, when it's not enough—in short, Theodor Herzl.

Wurzlechner is an allegory of liberal Austrian society, which had at first encouraged Jewish emancipation and now, in the 1890s, was becoming anti-Semitic again. In Jacob's response, although it is a full year before his "conversion," Herzl already reveals the affect—both pretty and ugly—that will be the motor for his Zionism: "Even if you had given me a choice between you and Wasserstein [an extremely unattractive Jewish speculator, a sort of Ostjude who even *Mauschels,* speaks with a Yiddish accent]—well I've already made it. My place is with Wasserstein, rich or poor. I can reproach him no more than I can praise you. You each stand where history has placed you" (*DnG,* 169).[34] This highly equivocal identification with Wasserstein is precisely what will reappear a year later as: "We are one people. Our enemies have made us one whether we will or not" in the Zionist manifesto. Moreover, it is this most contemptible Wasserstein, the Eastern Jew, who paradoxically "carries the germs of Jewish redemption," just as Herzl was to realize that Russian Jewry was the key to his Zionist plans.[35] Not only Jacob Samuel but other characters as well are made to voice sentiments that would reappear in *The Jewish State* as Herzl's own. Thus, Herzl has the rabbi in the play opine: "Antisemitism isn't all bad. As the movement gains force, I observe a return to religion. Antisemitism is a warning to us to stand together, not to abandon the God of our fathers, as many have done" (pp. 164–65). How far is this from Herzl's idea in his Zionist tract that Jews have remained Jews only because of anti-Semitism? The major difference is that the rabbi considers the result to have been desirable, while Herzl is at best very ambivalent.

Following the "breakup" with Wurzlechner, Jacob Samuel reaches for other ways to break out of the "new ghetto." His first turn is to support the striking workers in a coal mine in which his wealthy brother-in-law is investing. This move in the play parallels Herzl's second great scheme for achieving Jewish honor (and thus acceptance and disappearance), the plan for mass Jewish conversion to socialism. Kornberg writes: "In unpublished notes, he [Herzl] called socialism the answer to antisemitism in German, and baptism the answer in

Austria, evidence that he was thinking more of the method and style of Jewish action, rather than of its ideological content." Even more to the point, socialism was for Herzl more an issue of the expression of ressentiment than anything else. Jews and the workers were both oppressed; they would make common cause in promoting violence against the state. Herzl had seen the dignity that the oppressed workers achieved through their radical activity and devoutly wished for Jews to achieve that same self-transformation into proud fighters for a cause—almost any cause at all would do. If Jews were not to be allowed to defend the state, well, then, they could attack it: "In proposing that Jews turn to socialism he mentioned, indifferent to their goals, parties reformist in action and revolutionary in rhetoric, like the Austrian and German Social Democrats, and terrorist groups like the violent wing of French anarchism." [36]

Although Herzl himself was *not* a socialist (at the same time that he was advocating Jewish conversion to socialism in Germany, he was attacking the program of socialism itself), he was, it seems, from the characterization of Wasserstein and even Rheinberg, Jacob Samuel's relatively decent brother-in-law, as genuinely disgusted with parvenu Jewish capitalism as was Marx. The difference between them is that, where Marx was genuinely motivated by the plight of the workers, for Herzl it seems to have been ultimately the vulgarity of the Jews that was disturbing and the way that it prevented their full acceptance by the gentile elites.[37] Herzl, in a letter, described Jews as "harmless, contemptible fellow human beings, not to say fellow citizens, lacking honor and thus bent on profit, become crafty through prolonged oppression." [38] The case that I am trying to build is that, for Herzl (as for Freud in another key), it was primarily passivity that was the blemish that caused the degradation and degeneration. The very Slavic workers who, in the play, come to see Jacob and express their anger at the terrible conditions under which they labor can thus almost be read as a screen for the Ostjude whom radical *activity* would transform into a dignified, masculine human being. Carl Schorske has discovered a key issue when he points to Herzl's association between radical politics and sexuality. In a feuilleton, Herzl had written of the anarchist Ravachol, "The common murderer rushes to the brothel with his loot. Ravachol has discovered another kind of lust: the voluptuousness of a great idea and martyrdom," and Schorske sees that Herzl descries the same "voluptuousness" in socialist action that he had seen in the anarchist leader, the very same transformation from degraded passivity into virile activity.[39] Since the main—if not the only—meaning of the activity was activity itself and the masculinity that it conferred, it hardly mattered at all whether it was socialism, anarchism, or, finally, colonialism that composed the content, for it was the violence that was pivotal. Almost any respectable violence to which Jews would turn would restore their dignity and honor, their masculinity.

This harsh interpretation can be verified by a closer reading of the play.

The historical parable of Moses of Mainz, related by the rabbi at a crucial plot turn in the play, forms the central trope and motive force from thence until the end. Like Herzl and the assimilated Jews of Austria, Jacob Samuel has been rebuffed in his attempt to win simple acceptance from his friend, the aristocratic gentile, Franz Wurzlechner. And, we will remember, he had related his avoidance of a duel with the arrogant Count Von Schramm. Although Franz pooh-poohs this cowardice as grounds for shame, it is soon after that he renounces his friendship with the now too-Jewish Jacob, claiming that it is the association with the capitalists Wasserstein and Rheinberg that disturbs him.

In act 3, after Jacob has heard from the miners of their plight, gone there, supported their strike, and then witnessed a terrible mine collapse, he intends to confront his brother-in-law, who has invested in the mine. At first we would think that it is genuine leftist sentiment that moves Jacob, as he describes his horror at the scene of destruction:

> Indescribable, beyond words. When I got there, they were just bringing up the bodies. Outside the pit entrance the women stood weeping and moaning. Some of them never said a word. I could hardly look at them. I tell you, I'll remember the scene as long as I live. Everything black in black, as though in mourning. The tattered clothes, all black with coal dust, and a sharp autumn breeze making the thin bodies shiver under the rags. . . . And the children. . . . They'll ride down just like their fathers who were being brought up — they'll push the iron trolleys before they're in their teens, for forty-five kreuzer a day. . . . Later on, when they become pickmen, they'll lie on their sides in the holes, hacking at the seam in the dark. One slip with the lamp, and the firedamp comes crashing about their ears. This time it was the water. It was a holocaust! . . . Yet tomorrow, they'll go down again. If they don't they'll just starve to death up above. (*DnG*, 182)

In response, the rabbi recounts the story of Moses of Mainz as a cautionary tale. In 5143 (A.D. 1383), while studying the Talmud, a certain Moses ben Abraham hears a cry of distress from outside the walls of the ghetto. He goes out to help the gentile in distress: "When he failed to return, his mother grew more and more anxious until at last she went after him. She too did not return. The next morning Moses was found stabbed to death just outside the open gate of the Ghetto. By his side sat his mother, an unearthly smile on her lips. She had gone mad." Jacob's response to this moral tale of caution, this plea for Jews to stay within the ghetto, is, "I say my heart goes out to Moses of Mainz, that I am proud of him. All of us should take him as an example. The cry for help is sometimes genuine." The rabbi replies, "But we are too weak," and Jacob's final word is, "What merit is there when the strong show compassion?" (*DnG*, 183).

After this impassioned speech of radical indignation and Jacob's response to the parable, our expectation is that the resolution of the play will indeed be a socialist one, that the play will end with a glorious vision of workers and new Jews arising together to create a brave new world. The way out of the ghetto is through class solidarity between subaltern Jews and subaltern gentiles (Slavs and workers). That, however, is not Herzl's enterprise. Not only have the workers been harmed through the capitalists' manipulations, but so also has the old money been attacked. The hereditary owner of the mine, the same Count Von Schramm, has also been done out of his inheritance. Jacob has come, not to convince his brother-in-law to support the workers and ameliorate their conditions, but to convince him to make good the losses to the count for the sake of the honor of the Jews, of course. The brother-in-law cannot, even had he wanted to, because he has sold short and the real parvenu capitalist, Wasserstein, the Ostjude, has cornered the stock.

When Schramm comes to demand financial satisfaction from Rheinberg, who has left, Jacob decides to defend his brother-in-law. His motives are unclear since, a few minutes earlier, he had been condemning him. He attacks Schramm in the very terms that Rheinberg had proposed, namely, that it was his own incompetence in playing the market that defeated him, and, moreover, "While you indulged your aristocratic pastimes, your slaves drudged for you underground" (*DnG*, 187), in other words the socialist theme redivivus. The following exchange is astonishing:

> JACOB. I've seen them with my own eyes. I've seen the widows too, and the orphans, who must go hungry now, because their fathers died for the Honorable Count Von Schramm! I don't think you even attended the funeral!
> SCHRAMM. I know you did. I have it on good authority.
> JACOB. I was there.
> SCHRAMM. Yes, for the strike too! It was because the miners refused to go down that the water backed up. At first I didn't understand what you were after. What's the Jew up to, I asked myself?
> JACOB. The Jew was doing his Christian duty. (p. 188)

Of course, Schramm does not believe in Jacob's honor and accuses him of simply having been in league with his brother-in-law to make sure that the bottom fell out of the mine stock. Schramm calls Jacob a "dirty Jew" and says that, once more, as he had before, he will "crawl." However, this time is different. Jacob slaps him in the face. Jacob is certain that Schramm will challenge him to a duel, and the rabbi intones as the curtain falls, "Like Moses of Mainz!" Were Jacob going out to fight for the workers, the simile would make sense to me. The rabbi would be saying, "Don't worry about the goyim; don't save them," and Herzl-Jacob would be responding, "No, the Jew must be a man with common human *Mitleid und Ehre.*" As it is, with Jacob only going out to fight a duel, the semblance that Jacob and the rabbi — and Herzl — see entirely escapes me. There is no one in distress who is to be saved here, only a point of honor that must be rescued with violence. This is where Herzl's energy lies. Socialism has nothing to do with *Mitleid,* only with *Mannlichkeit.*

The denouement confirms this. In the fourth act, the duel finally takes place. Jacob Samuel has become a Jewish Siegfried.[40] Wurzlechner, reconciled with his friend, has brought the dying man home:

> JACOB. Where is Franz?
>
> WURZLECHNER. (*Moves to his side.*) Here I am.
>
> JACOB. Thank you. . . . Franz! I want to stay here . . . with my books. Remember what I wanted? . . . Fellowship!
>
> DR. BICHLER. Don't talk so much.
>
> JACOB. (*Caresses Franz's hand.*) Good old Franz! . . . Tell the Rabbi . . . like Moses of Mainz. (*Mumbles.*) And by the side of the body sat his mother, an unearthly smile on her lips. (*Lapses into unconsciousness.*) . . .
>
> JACOB. (*Comes to.*) Tell the Rabbi!
>
> WURZLECHNER. What does he want the Rabbi for? The last sacraments?
>
> WASSERSTEIN. No, we Jews die without sacraments. . . .
>
> JACOB. (*Cries out weakly.*) Father! Mother!
>
> HERR SAMUEL. Kobi, here we are.
>
> JACOB. Help me up! . . . (*Takes his mother's hand and kisses it.*) Forgive me this sorrow, Mother. . . . (*Kisses his father's hand.*) *You can understand, Father! You're a man!* . . . (*Raises his voice.*) O Jews, my brethren, they won't let you live again — until. . . . I want to — get — out! (*Louder.*) Out — of — the — Ghetto! (*DnG,* 178)

Just as for Freud, it is the duel that restores the Jew's honor and gets him out of the ghetto, not his willingness to take risks for the sake of downtrodden others. Gender is encoded right on the surface of this scene as well. The father will understand because he is a man, not a fearful, female Jew; he, too, would understand that his son has performed his "Christian duty" by engaging in a duel to the death with someone who has insulted him and his people. In the draft of the play, the continuation of the sentence, broken off after "until," is "you have learned how to die."[41] It was a commonplace of anti-Semites that Jews did not know how to die with honor.[42] The contempt that Zionists in Palestine had for the Jews killed by the Nazis in concentration camps is, I put forth, a direct descendant of this anti-Semitic representation, but those who died in the hopeless Warsaw ghetto "rebellion" were glorified as "New Jews," as the Polish branch of the "Palmach," the Zionist shock troops. They had "learned to die." Over and over again, Zionist writers of the 1940s wrote in near-fascist terms of the "beautiful death" of the Warsaw rebels and the "ugly death" of the martyrs of the camps. This represents identification with the oppressor in one of its most naked and obvious forms, and it has its effects in imitation of that oppressor as well.[43]

The New Ghetto was written only one year before The Jewish State was conceived, and, if we do not accept the myth of a sudden and total conversion of Pauline proportions, then the two texts must be seen in their contiguity. Contrary to later Zionist myths, Herzl himself wrote that the play was "the young fruit of The Jewish State."[44] We have seen, moreover, how compatible the two texts are. The play does also represent, no doubt, the psychic damage that Jews suffer through assimilation, and it does so in terms, moreover, that are not entirely different from those of Frantz Fanon's Black Skins, White Masks.[45] Kornberg has phrased it well: "Embracing the material culture, they had internalized its Jewish stereotypes. Assimilation had bred Jewish self-contempt and an idealization of gentiles, persuaded them that Jewishness carried a taint of materialism and cowardice, and robbed them of self-respect. For this reason, Jews themselves had to alter the terms of gentile acceptance."[46] Repeatedly in the play, Herzl identifies the very attempt to become one with the gentiles as yet another source of Jewish servility. After his rebuff by Wurzlechner, Jacob realizes that his friendship with the gentile had been based on servility, not civility, on gratitude at being thrown a crumb of acceptance. My point, however, is that this is not a new insight of Herzl's but only yet another rendition of the conversion paradox: How to become like them without being servile, ingratiating, and false. But not only, I argue, is it the case that this problematic as explored in The New Ghetto is exactly the same one that plagued Herzl at the time of the conversion scheme; I suggest as well that it remains the problem that his Zionism sets out to solve. Herzlian Zionism is the ultimate project for an honorable conversion of the Jews to Christianity, understood as it always was for Herzl as, not a religion, but Kultur itself, as civilization. When Herzl argued to the grand duke of Baden that Zionism was an extension of German Kultur, this was not, I fear, for diplomatic effect.[47] The only models that Herzl can mobilize for the very alteration "of the terms of gentile acceptance" still involve mimesis of gentile patterns of honor, that is, masculinity.

In this respect, I quite dissent from Kornberg, who seems to read Wasserstein as the hero of the play and the play as revealing that "the seeds of Jewish transformation existed in the Jewish character itself."[48] It seems to me, at best, that the Ostjuden, the Wassersteins, are to be admiring supporters and beneficiaries of Herzl's transformation of the Jewish character. I am convinced that, when Herzl has Wasserstein say, "Yes, I buy and I sell—everything revolves around money. But there is something else too—honor," this is almost Tartuffian and hardly an attempt to "underline Wasserstein's noble side."[49] Wasserstein supports whatever is winning, and, when honor seems to be successful, then it is honor that he shall have, too. It is true, as we have seen, that Jacob expresses solidarity with the not unredeemable Wasserstein—

a solidarity born, however, of the fact that gentiles simply will not *let him* differentiate himself from the Ostjude. That, indeed, Herzl had truly understood by 1894. But this solidarity cashes out as yet another version of the civilizing mission, directed this time by Western Jews at Eastern Jews. The problem continues to be, for Herzl, that the Jews have been released too precipitously and too late from the ghetto and are unable fully to assimilate. Their mimicry is too palpable and too pathetic.[50] Herzl had not here, and never did, escape the stereotype and self-contempt of the assimilated Jew. What he did eventually discover was a way for Jews to assimilate, while escaping from the painful need to seek gentile acceptance on a day-to-day basis, by rediscovering Jewish honor, not merely by stripping off the distorting effects of anti-Semitism in Europe — which was not going to happen so easily — but by going somewhere else. Actual return to the biblical glory days of Jewish independence — and imperialism — it was this that would cure the Jews of Jewishness, for Jewishness remained despised. Zionism is, then, only a logical extension of the liberal Dohm's solution to the Jewish problem. If Jews had, indeed, been courageous, warlike, manly, and patriotic in the golden age of the biblical kingdom, then the solution is to restore that kingdom itself, a Camelot in the desert or, rather, Vienna on the Mediterranean. At the end of the first draft of the play, the transformed Jacob reminds Wasserstein of a Maccabee.[51] We have already seen the assimilationist meaning of that appellation. It is merely a code word for *Judentum* converted into *Deutschtum*, almost identical to Freud's converted *Judentum*.

Herzlian Zionism, I suggest, is dueling carried on by other means, yet another desperate attempt to win Jewish honor and cultural disappearance as a deformed alterity by "doing our Christian duty." In fact, Zionism did not quite replace dueling for Herzl. In his diary entry for 9 June 1895, Herzl wrote of his Zionist state, "I need dueling in order to have real officers and to impart a tone of French refinement to good society." He did, however, allow for a possibility that, in certain circumstances, instead of a duel, the "dueling tribunal" would decree something that he called a *secret verdict* because, after all, "since only men of honor can fight a duel, the loser in any case would be the state, and for a long time to come it will need every able-bodied man. Therefore these duellers will be sent out on dangerous missions which the state happens to require. It may be cholera vaccination or at other times the fighting of a national enemy. *In this way the risk of death from the duel will be retained*" (emphasis added).[52] The contempt that traditional Jewry — including many in assimilated Vienna and Berlin such as Arthur Schnitzler and Stefan Zweig — would have manifested for such senseless adoration of the risk of death is palpable.[53]

Many of these same Jews understood the affective basis of Herzl's Zionism in contempt for Jews as well. Fifteen years after the production of *The New Ghetto,* Arthur Schnitzler has a Jewish character in his novel *The Road to the Open* say: "I myself have only succeeded up to the present in making the acquaintance of one genuine antisemite. I'm afraid I am bound to admit . . . that it was a well known Zionist leader." [54] Herzl was, indeed, an anti-Semite, as were many fin de siècle Viennese Jews. [55] He adopted all the most vicious stereotypes of Jew hatred but employed an almost classic psychological move, splitting, in order to separate himself from them. There were two kinds of Jews in the world. The "true Jews," the manly, honorable, dueling, fighting Jacob Samuels were the Zionists. The others were the *Mauschel,* crooked, "low and repugnant," frightened, unresponsive to beauty, passive, queer, effeminate, the very embodiment of Otto Weininger's description of what Jews were. Herzl himself realized the complicity of his plan with that of the anti-Semites. Both, after all, wanted to rid Europe of the Jews: "The anti-Semites will become our most dependable friends, the anti-Semitic countries our allies." [56] Fichte had already written that there was "only one way in which the tension between dominant orders and the Jewish 'state within a state' could end and the Jewish obstacle to human unity be overcome—namely, the conquest of a homeland for the Jews and the deportation of them all to it." [57] Within Europe, Fichte thought, the Jews presented a serious obstacle to "brotherhood," and, indeed, at the 1878 International Conference on Demography, "The Russian delegate, starting from the proposition that a 'certain race tended to multiply faster than others' and thus threatened the numerical dominance of the native populations of its host countries, had urged 'its deportation en masse [laughter] to Jerusalem in order to restore the ancient kingdom of the Jews.' " [58] The kaiser wrote in the margins of his Swiss consul's report on the First Zionist Congress: "I am all in favor of the *kikes* going to Palestine. The sooner they take off the better." [59] Herzl was capable of worrying that the gentiles left behind in Europe might, *quel horreur,* undergo a *Verjudung* (Jewification) after the Jews left, thus mobilizing one of the most vicious of all anti-Semitic terms. [60]

Even more appalling, in his essay "Mauschel," Herzl wrote that this Jewish essence had been produced racially, through an admixture: "The irreconcilable, inexplicable antitheses make it seem as though at some dark moment in our history some inferior human material got into our unfortunate people and blended with it. . . . Race! As if the *Jew* and *Mauschel* were of the same race." [61] This notorious anti-Semitic remark is the exact equivalent of Houston Chamberlain's charge that the Jewish race had an "admixture of negro blood" and thus doubly racist in import. [62] The title of Herzl's vulgar anti-Semitic screed says it all. *Mauschel*—Little Moses—is the German anti-Semitic equivalent of *kike* or *Ikey,* and Herzl opens his piece by stating, "Ikey is an antizionist." Mauschel, the Ostjude, who is not—even racially—a true Jew is an anti-Zionist. [63] Only a Zionist could be a Jew. Herzl even ended the essay with a threat (characteristically alluding to Wilhelm Tell): "Zionism's second arrow is aimed at Mauschel's heart." In fact, this vicious (in both senses of the word) sentence was carried out in the refusal of Zionist leaders in Jewish Palestine to engage in rescue operations of European Jews during the Nazi genocide unless these would contribute to the creation of the "new Jew" and the state. Ben-Gurion infamously wrote in 1938 after Kristallnacht: "If I knew that I could save all of the [Jewish] children of Germany by moving them to England, or only half of them by moving them to the Land of Israel, I would choose the second." [64]

The point of this exercise is not, of course, to condemn Herzl or Freud as individual Jewish anti-Semites or self-haters but rather to argue that, while such views held by Jews of themselves are clearly not the only ones available, they were enormously widespread, particularly among Viennese Jews of their generation. As Jenny Sharpe has written, it is not "useful to demand from authors what was historically impossible for them to represent." [65] Sander Gilman's *The Jew's Body*, with its repeated demonstrations of Jewish doctors who believed that the Jewish foot, the Jewish nose, the Jewish psyche, the Jewish libido, were deformed, is enough to argue this case. The reason for focusing on Freud and Herzl is to argue that these affects were crucial in the formation of two of the most fateful movements of modern times, psychoanalysis and Zionism — both founded in Berggasse (Herzl at no. 6, Freud at no. 19), Vienna, in the mid-1890s. Anti-Semitism was real, ubiquitous, and deadly, and, in his own way, each of these figures was searching for a way out of a terrible plight. Moreover, the internalization of both the stereotype and the evaluation of the dominant culture is a common phenomenon among dominated minorities — if not an inescapable one.[66] I am not so arrogant as to presume to know how I would have reacted to being a Jewish student in a university of which the official policy of the student government was the following: "Every son of a Jewish mother, every human being in whose veins flows Jewish blood, is from the day of his birth without honor and void of all the more refined emotions. He cannot differentiate between what is dirty and what is clean. He is ethically subhuman. Friendly intercourse with a Jew is therefore dishonorable; any association with him has to be avoided. It is impossible to insult a Jew; a Jew cannot therefore demand satisfaction for any suffered insult." [67]

To be sure, I might have responded as Herzl did, assimilating the negative stereotype and desiring only to escape it, but Schnitzler, for instance, who was obviously subject to exactly the same discourse, did not. If, from the vantage point of my world, I find Freud's, and especially Herzl's, solutions disastrously flawed in their political effects — on women, gay men, Jews, and Palestinians — this is not because I consider myself ethically superior to them. The question that I ask is not, Were Freud and Herzl good men? but rather, What can be learned from their mistakes that can help us now? It is clear — to me — that a solution to the Jewish Problem whose bedrock is a repudiation of Jewish male "femininity" will not provide a useful answer.

Of Mimicry and Mensur

Blond, moustached, dapper, the perfect lady-killer, Herzl's ideal of masculinity. — *Amos Elon*

I have argued that Zionism had for Freud replaced Greekishness ("the Aryan cause") as the means to manliness, honor, and civility. For Herzl, it was conversion to Christianity, radical politics, and dueling — another variety of the Aryan/Teutonic cause — that Zionism replaced as the means to Jewish masculinity, to Jewish assimilation.[68] Peter Loewenberg has, I think, captured this Herzlian countenance perfectly. Remarking that Herzl referred to Jews in the derogatory terms of the virulent anti-Semite Henrich von Treitschke and envisioned these "pants-peddling boys" transformed into knights, Loewenberg writes:

> This expressed a deliberate effort to forge a new heroic national character (or to recapture a mythical biblical racial character), create a flag and accessory symbols that would be honored and would win "respect in the eyes of the world." This fantasy of a nation peopled by proud militant "new men" is, in Herzl's case, what Anna Freud has defined as "identification with the aggressor." He shares with anti-Semites a negative stereotype of the Jew. Herzl's contempt for "pants-peddling boys" is an admission of hatred of the Jews of the ghetto — and of the self. . . . *In this sense Herzl was a Jewish anti-Semite.* . . . For the learned, humiliated, sensitive Jew of the ghetto, he would substitute the rigorous, heroic, healthy farmer in his own land. Yiddish, the language of suffering, would be replaced by any cultured language. *The exclusive nationalism of Europe which rejects Jews would be replaced by a chauvinistic nationalism of Zion.* The values of the dominant majority are internalized and via reaction formation would become the ego ideal of the persecuted minority. (emphasis added)[69]

Herzl is, then, an almost perfect example of that condition of the colonial subject so brilliantly anatomized in Frantz Fanon's *Black Skins, White Masks;* a book about Herzl and his compatriots could be called *Black Pates, Blond Wigs.*

We can now read the symbolic significance of Herzl's early determination that the Jewish state must be founded in Africa or South America. These were the privileged sites for colonialist performances of male gendering. My suggestion is that Herzlian Zionism imagined itself as colonialism because such a representation was pivotal to the entire project of becoming "white men."[70] What greater Christian duty could there be in the late nineteenth century than carrying on the civilizing mission, exporting manliness to the Eastern Jews and to darkest Palestine? Emblematic, perhaps, of this tendency was Herzl's plan to transform the wonder-working, mystical shaman, the Hassidic rebbe of Sadigora, into the bishop of Haifa. Herzlian Zionism is thus itself the civilizing mission, first and foremost directed by Jews at other Jews, and then at whatever natives there happen to be there, if, indeed, these natives are noticed at all. Herzl spun out his fantasies of a Jewish colony without any reference whatever to where it would be—the Argentine, Uganda, or Palestine—and thus without reference as well to the native natives of this no place. The only natives to whom he imagined directing his civilizing mission were those "Hottentot" Ostjuden, who, as we have already seen, were read by him as constituting another race. Like a Macaulay who could consider "a single shelf of a good European library worth the whole native literature of India and Arabia," Herzl has nothing but disdain for the two-thousand-year-old tradition of postbiblical Jewish literature and culture; the Bible and Goethe are more than worth the whole literature of the Jewish Diaspora.[71] Let it be said right here, however, that the failure to recognize the possibility and then the very existence of already existing natives in the place where the Jewish colony was to be founded did not mitigate its destructiveness with reference to those natives but exacerbated it.

After finally meeting Eastern European Jews, "formed by both modern European culture and their Jewish heritage," Herzl writes, "But we had always imagined them dependent on our intellectual help and guidance. . . . They are not Caliban but Prospero."[72] Herzl has then found some East European fellow Prosperos, but the Calibans of the world remain just that, whether Jewish or gentile. The Jews, as Zionists, constitute themselves both as natives and as colonizers. Indeed, it is through mimicry of colonization that the Zionists seek to escape the stigma of Jewish difference. If, one can almost hear Herzl thinking, being civilized means colonizing, then we, too, will be colonizers. If our choice is between being Caliban and being Prospero, then it is Prospero whom we shall be. Among the first acts of his enactment of Zionism was the foundation of "the Jewish Company"—precisely under that name and in London. Herzl had finally found a way for the Jews to become Europeans; they would have a little colony of their own.

Herzl's Mirror

Preemancipation Jewishness in Eastern Europe (and traditional Jewish identity in general), it could be argued, was formed via an abjection of the *goy*, as Ivan, a creature stereotyped as violent, aggressive, coarse, and drunk and given to such nonsense as dueling, seeking honor in war, and falling in romantic "love"—all referred to as *goyim naches* (games gentiles play).[73] For those Jews, it was abjection of manliness—itself, of course, a stereotype—that produced their identity. In the colonial/postcolonial moment, the stereotyped other becomes the object of desire, of introjection rather than abjection, and it is the stereotyped self that is abjected. Freud and Herzl imitated the discourse of colo-

nization itself as a prop — in both the theatrical and the architectural senses —
for their newfound Jewish masculinity: If he is a boy he must be a stalwart
Zionist.

The Zionist slogan that was the foundation of their movement, or, better,
the foundation of the state — "The Jewish people reentered history" — is testimony to this interpretation of Zionism. If the Jewish people have reentered history because of Zionism, then, the implication is clear, previously they were
a people without history, natives, Africans, Hottentots. This was, indeed, explicitly the way in which West European Jews experienced their East European
compatriots. Gilman evokes this moment brilliantly: "In the eyes of the formerly Yiddish-speaking convert [who had described the Hebrew words in Yiddish as so deformed as to appear 'Hottentot'!], Yiddish moved from being a
language of a 'nation within nations' to a language of the 'barbarian.' But for
the Jew, convert or not, these barbarians must be localized, like the Hottentot,
in some remote geographic place to separate them from the image of the German Jew. Their locus is the East." [74] This trope, I claim, finally provided Herzl
with the solution to his dilemma, how to make the Jews be like everybody else.
He had tried having them become Christians, duelers, socialists. [75] All these
had failed. Now the solution was at hand: Make the Jews into colonists, and
then they will turn white! Zionism is thus the ultimate version of that practice
dubbed *colonial mimicry* by Homi Bhabha. [76]

At the outset of his essay "Of Mimicry and Man," Bhabha reproduces the
following quotation:

> It is out of season to question at this time of day, the original policy of
> a conferring on every colony of the British Empire a mimic representa-
> tion of the British Constitution. But if the creature so endowed has some-
> times forgotten its real significance and under the fancied importance of
> speakers and maces, and all the paraphernalia and ceremonies of the im-
> perial legislature, has dared to defy the mother country, she has to thank
> herself for the folly of conferring such privileges on a condition of society
> that has no earthly claim to so exalted a position (Sir Edward Cust). [77]

Ultimately, however, the joke is on the colonized, for precisely what the British
were exporting was mimic representations of the British Constitution, the
French mimic representations of the land of the "rights of man." This colonial
project, like imperialist business, required native compradors. This was the role
that Herzl chose for the Jews; in Uganda, the Argentine, even Palestine, the
Jews were to turn into people "English in tastes, in opinions, in morals and
in intellect," but they would go even further, exceeding the intentions of their
British patrons, just like those mimic men with maces and parliaments, and
actually turn white in blood and color as well. There is thus an ambivalence at
the very site of such mimicry, just as there is at the very site of that other form of

mimicry, conversion to Christianity. Bhabha constantly points to the ways that the most apparent complicity with the colonizer turns into resistance.[78] I suggest, however, that it is also true that the seemingly most forceful resistance can turn into the most efficient complicity with the cultural project of the colonizer, by becoming just like him, sometimes even more than he is himself, and that this is what we need to understand about Zionism.[79] The socialist cocommander of the Warsaw revolt, the anti-Zionist Marek Edelman, who remains in Poland as a diasporic Jewish (Yiddish) nationalist and member of Solidarity, saw this very clearly: "This was a revolt!? The whole point was not to let them slaughter you when your turn came. The whole point was to choose your method of dying. All of humanity had already agreed that dying with a weapon in the hand is more beautiful than without a weapon. *So we surrendered to that consensus*" (emphasis added).[80] The Zionist leaders decided that Edelman was insane and silenced his voice. As late as 1981, his book could not find a publisher in Israel and had to be printed privately.

Bhabha writes, "What I have called mimicry is not the familiar exercise of *dependent* colonial relations through narcissistic identification so that, as Fanon has observed, the black man stops being an actional person for only the white man can represent his self-esteem."[81] For Fanon, then, mimicry is that which deprives the colonized subject of any claim to self, while, for Bhabha, it is the parodic performativity that deconstructs the very discourse of European civilization, in the way in which Judith Butler argues that butch-femme deconstructs the discourse of gender.[82] I am proposing that these two meanings of *mimicry* are two sides of the same coin, two moves in an inexorable oscillation or dialectic.[83] Ambivalence cuts both ways. Bhabha focuses on — indeed, uncovers — the former part of this dialectic, while I focus on the latter, perhaps more familiar aspect of mimicry; he on the systole (the syntonic), and I on the dystole. If Bhabha has produced an account of how the discourse of colonialism is disarticulated at the very point of its articulation, a parallel account of the disarticulation of the discourse of resistance, national liberation, at *its* point of articulation must also be assayed. And that disarticulation consists of a rearticulation of the civilizing mission in a moment that forgets its own mimicry.

The returned gaze, the shot/countershot, to use the cinematic conventions of contemporary theory, is partly (perhaps largely, but never entirely) lost for the colonial subject — not yet white, no longer wholly black/not white, not quite — precisely because she no longer looks at the colonizer but at herself with his eyes; the colonial subject indeed regards "himself" in the Lacanian mirror. This is the gaze from the black skin looking through the eyeholes of a white mask. Herzl's famous passion (shared by many German Jews) to achieve the honor of the dueling scar, the notorious *mensur,* is, in this sense, a mimicry of inscription of active, phallic, violent gentile masculinity on the literal body, to replace the inscription of passive Jewish femininity.[84] His ultimate remedy, however, was to lead to the inscription of this maleness on the body of Palestine — and Palestinians.[85]

Herzl's Zionism, I argue controversially, is *almost, but not quite,* colonialism. There are too many "striking features" that "betray its colored [Jewish] descent."[86] Zionism was not to produce wealth for a mother country. Just trying to figure out just what might be the mother country of Zionism immediately reveals the problem.[87] Zionism, moreover, was anything but the instrument of an attempt to spread Jewish culture or Judaism to other peoples. Yet, in its discursive forms and practices, Zionism is very *similar* to colonialism. The plan was not for Jewish Palestine to *be* a colony but for it to *have* colonies. When Herzl was offered Uganda for Jewish settlement, his notion was that it would be "a miniature England in reverse," that is, first the colony, then the "mother country."[88] We can now reread Herzl's fear of a Jewification of Europe on the Jews' departure. Herzl's Zionism as an assertion of partial difference was intended, as we have seen, to allow the true German essence of the German Jew to appear. The logic of such Zionism is that, if we can prove our manliness to the Germans by becoming colonizers, then they will see that we are the same. The ambivalence of Zionism thus comes to the fore most sharply in Herzl's fear of the *Verjudung* of Europe. On the one hand, as I have said, this involves an infamous anti-Semitic stereotype. On the other hand, in this fear there is acknowledgment that Germans may lose their Germanness in the absence of the other against whom hegemonic identity is constructed. So, if the Jews were to leave Germany, the Germans would have to acknowledge the integral Germanness of the Jews, but they would also become vulnerable to losing their identity, thus making the Zionists the true Germans. The insight on Herzl's part is that hegemonic identity can be constructed only in the mirror of the other — thus the necessity for colonialism. As François Hartog has written of quite another time and place: "How must the Athenians, who so insistently claimed to be of autochthonous birth, have represented this alien figure [the Scythian] whose whole being consisted in having no attachment to any place? It is not hard to foresee that the discourse of autochthony was bound to reflect on the representation of nomadism and that the Athenian, that imaginary autochthonous being, had need of an equally imaginary nomad."[89]

As much as it is a reterritorialization of Jewishness, then, Herzlian Zionism is a deterritorialization of Germanness. Thus, Jewish nationalists are really ardent Germanists, a peculiar trajectory wherein one ends up believing that, by having a colony, one can claim a nation, thus "a miniature England in reverse."[90]

This is masquerade colonialism, parodic mimesis of colonialism, Jews in colonialist drag. Jewish "women" dressed up like "men." Indeed, the very total destruction of Jewish difference that the liberal Zionist Herzl envisioned is the very point of such mimesis. Precisely by spreading *Bildung* to *Mauschel,* Herzl and his compatriots would reconfigure themselves as gentile men.

This should not be read as a trivialization of the disastrous effects of this discourse, especially with respect to its primary victims, the Palestinians. At the same time that Zionism subverts itself as discourse, it shores itself up even more frantically with the pseudoagency of the M16 rifle and racist legislation. Colonial mimicry in many of its practices can be a bloody business. The violence of Jewish hegemony in Palestine is a particularly egregious version (because of the transplantation in space) of the violence of national hegemony over separate ethnicities in many parts of the postcolonial world since that also frequently materializes as the violent political domination of one particular tribe over others.

Herzl's colonialism, however, was not intended to be of the violent kind. He was, as I have said, the ultimate mimic man of British liberalism, not of rapine and plunder, a John Stuart Mill, not a Cortez or a Salazar.[91] Answering a Palestinian leader who had written him with great sympathy for the cause of a Jewish state but had pointed out that Palestine was unfortunately already inhabited, Herzl wrote: "You see another difficulty in the existence of a non-Jewish population in Palestine. But who wishes to remove them from there? Their well-being and individual wealth will increase through the importation of ours. Do you believe that an Arab who owns land in Palestine, or a house worth three or four thousand francs, will be sorry to see their value rise five- and ten-fold? But this would most certainly happen with the coming of the Jews. And this is what one must bring the natives to comprehend."[92] In his novel, Herzl imagined a German Jewish doctor setting up an eye clinic in Jerusalem and defeating trachoma for all the Middle East.[93] In a speech in London on 26 June 1899, Herzl actually referred to Zionism as a "burden that the Jews were assuming for the wretched and poor of all mankind."[94]

For the Freud of the Spielrein letter and *Moses and Monotheism*, and for Herzl, it was the discourse of colonialism itself that caught them. The very inappropriateness of Jewish mimicry, that very ridiculousness that Herzl perceived finally in such mimic behavior as conversion, in the end tragically (d)eluded him with regard to violence: dueling, defending the homeland, and white-settler state making. The mimicry of the figures that Bhabha cites, from both sides of the imperialist power structure, "alienates the modality and normality of those dominant discourses in which they emerge." Like Macaulay's interpreters, the Zionists "are the parodists of history. Despite their intentions and invocations they inscribe the colonial text erratically, eccentrically across a body politic that refuses to be representative, in a narrative that refuses to be representational. The desire to emerge as 'authentic' through mimicry—through a process of writing and repetition—is the final irony of partial representation."[95] But the parodists too often do not themselves see how their mimicry disarticulates the colonialist text and thus find themselves trapped within the imaginary of its articulation.

Epilogue: Anti-Zionism as Postcolonial Mimicry?

In demonstrating that Herzl's decolonization of the Jews consisted of a neo-colonialism, I now must acknowledge how my discourse is implicated in that of Herzl. I am also in search of a Jewish political subject who will find a place in modernity. As a Jew, like other people who do not unproblematically belong in the metropolis, I find modernity a dilemma. We are always in a "derivative discourse." The very struggle against colonialism, homophobia, and sexism of which my project is borne is *structurally* identical with Herzl's struggle for manliness and its signifiers: colonialism, homophobia, and sexism. He lived in a colonial world; I live in a postcolonial one, but my people are involved in one of the last extant colonialist projects. Horrified by seemingly inescapable injustices committed by Jewish statehood, I react to this phase in Jewish historical practice with the same kind of nausea that motivated Herzl to write "Mauschel." Where Herzl argued that only a Zionist is a Jew — and his view has become hegemonic — I construct an antithetical — equally outrageous — strategic proposition that only an anti-Zionist is a Jew in order to reopen a space for non-Zionist Jewish political subjectivity, both in and out of Palestine.[96] I could not disavow Zionism as a Jewish practice without involving myself in an invidious and artificial essentialism cum triumphalism, something on the order of, "This isn't us; the goyim made us do it."[97] Zionism is what most Jews who identify strongly as Jews — not all — are doing now, but it is precisely there that I hope to intervene.[98] However, much of the very possibility of my own Jewish cultural continuance — including the absolutely critical ability to read Hebrew — is a product of the very Zionist entity that I struggle against. Spivak has articulated this dilemma as "saying an 'impossible "no" to a structure, which one critiques, yet inhabits intimately.' "[99]

Looking for a way of remaining Jewish, of preserving Jewish memory and being what I consider to be a politically moral human being, I construct moments and models in the Jewish past that seem to make this possible. This is intended not as a fantasized restoration of an ideal or idealized Jewish past, neither of the Talmud nor of Eastern Europe before the *hurban* of the Nazis, but as the critical deliverance of cultural materials and practices from that past and their resiting in a different modernity.[100] The crisis of Jewish identity bears important comparison to the sometimes seemingly intractable dilemmas faced by all people caught in the syncopated arhythmicalities of modernity that are the subject of postcolonial cultural studies.

I ask of myself, Is the very desire to be in the "postcolonial club," to grab as a Jew some bit of moral high ground, ultimately any different from Herzl's desire to be in the "colonial club," to grab a bit of literal territory? Still seeking acceptance as a Jew, am I a specimen of "white skin, black masks," a postcolonial mimic, a talmudic Jazzjew?

Undoubtedly, the answer is yes, but, then, that is precisely the crux. Postcolonial theory is productive of materially new ways of asking the Jewish Question. If the role of theory is "to bring to the surface the naturalized, concealed frames of intelligibility that enable cultural enunciation and also to produce new conceptual frames which, by providing new perspectives on the problem, enable (re)thinking in the service of social transformation," this is a project in the deployment of postcolonial theory to make visible the ideological processes by which Zionism has been naturalized as Jewish survival, in the service of a social transformation that may unsettle Zionism and lead us toward a binational Palestine/Israel in which two cultural/linguistic communities and three religions will learn to live and create together.[101]

Jewish cultural studies may have something, however, to offer postcolonial studies as well. Following a reading of Ella Shohat's "Notes on the 'Post-Colonial,' " I would wish to reserve this term for the study and theorization of cultural dilemmas in a world produced in the wake of colonial discourse and practice, retaining other terms—*neocolonial, postindependence*—for articulating highly variable political and economic situations. In this sense, cultural hybridity and complex negotiations between traditional and metropolitan or modern culture become the proper realm of postcolonial studies and *diaspora* one of its privileged terms. As Shohat notes, however, *hybridity* itself has many modalities, including "internalized self-rejection, political co-optation, social conformism, cultural mimicry, and creative transcendence."[102] Zionism seems to fit the first four of these but the last hardly at all. Prasad has written that "national culture in general is one of the representational machineries that serve to consolidate the nation-state."[103] Pre-Zionist Jewish culture suggests that this condition is not a necessary one. The long Jewish history of cultural survival in diaspora, with almost no even fantasized moment of precolonial purity, may provide, then, some useful data and models for a praxis of hybridity that will avoid "an anti-essentialist condescension toward those communities obliged by circumstances to assert, for their very survival, a lost and even irretrievable past."[104]

Notes

I wish to express gratitude to Homi K. Bhabha, who read a much earlier and a very recent version of this essay and whose influence is felt on every page, even where I have not been able to assimilate it completely. His critique is unfailingly rigorous and empowering at the same time. The essay began its life in his seminar at the School of Criticism and Theory at Dartmouth in the summer of 1993, a course as exhilarating and challenging as an Outward Bound for the mind. It was first delivered in the guest lecture series (cosponsored by the Geisel Chair) at that same school in the summer of 1994. Fawzia Afzal-Khan, Jonathan Boyarin, Sidra Dekoven Ezrahi, Yaron Ezrahi, Schlomo Fischer, Galit Hasan-Rokem, Hanan Hever, Martin Jay, Adi Ophir, Donald Pease, and Kalpana Seshadri-Crooks have also read drafts of this essay and provided much good advice. I am sure that none of them want to take responsibility for the final product.

1 Y. H. Yerushalmi, *Freud's Moses: Judaism Terminable and Interminable* (New Haven, Conn.: Yale University Press, 1991), 12–13.

2 Yerushalmi completely misses the gendered aspect of this wish. Gilman goes so far as to erase this point, arguing that "Freud did not articulate the difference in terms of gender — the imagined Jewish 'boy' can become a Zionist, a Jewish nationalist, and the Jewish 'girl' (Spielrein's daughter Renate) 'will speak for herself.' " But Freud articulates the difference precisely in terms of gender, as Gilman himself seems to have noticed earlier. Although he expresses somewhat parallel ambitions for the male Jewish infant and the female one, after all "speaking for oneself" is simply not the same as being a Zionist (see ibid., 33; and S. L. Gilman, *The Jew's Body* [London: Routledge, 1991], 195).

3 Freud's affect about Zionism was ever changing, as shown in W. J. McGrath, *Freud's Discovery of Psychoanalysis: The Politics of Hysteria* (Ithaca, N.Y.: Cornell University Press, 1986), 313–17.

4 Sander Gilman, *Freud, Race, and Gender* (Princeton, N.J.: Princeton University Press, 1993), 31.

5 On Freud's relations with Fliess, see Daniel Boyarin, "Freud's Baby; Fliess's Maybe: Male Hysteria, Homophobia, and the Invention of the Jewish Man," *GLQ* 2, no. 1 (1994).

6 E. Jones, *The Life and Work of Sigmund Freud* (New York: Basic, 1953), 348; H. P. Blum, "The Prototype of Preoedipal Reconstruction," in *Freud and His Self-Analysis*, ed. M. Kanzer and J. Glenn (New York: Jason Aronson, 1979), 155.

7 See Boyarin, "Freud's Baby, Fleiss's Maybe," 115–47.

8 S. Freud, "The Interpretation of Dreams (First Part)," in *The Standard Edition of the Complete Psychological Works of Sigmund Freud*, vol. 4, ed. and trans. J. Strachey and A. Freud, trans. A. Strachey and J. Strachey (London: Hogarth, 1955), 194–95. See also J. M. Masson, ed. and trans., *The Complete Letters of Sigmund Freud to Wilhelm Fliess, 1887–1904* (Cambridge, Mass.: Harvard University Press, 1985), 285.

9 See Daniel Boyarin, "Bitextuality, Psychoanalysis, Zionism: On the Ambivalence of the Jewish Phallus," in *Queer Diasporas*, ed. Cindy Patton and B. Sánchez-Eppler (Durham, N.C.: Duke University Press, in press).

10 Bluma Goldstein, *Reinscribing Moses: Heine, Kafka, Freud, and Schoenberg in a European Wilderness* (Cambridge, Mass.: Harvard University Press, 1992), 73, 76.

11 This may be an appropriate point to indicate that the ambition of my work is not to denounce Jews who choose the path of non-Jewishness, as did Deutscher. It is, rather, the aggressive combination of asserted Jewish identity and an emptying out of Jewish cultural creativity, a combination that usually issues in violence, that I am condemning. I find such a combination in much of Zionist and Holocaust discourse as well as in such groups as the Jewish Defense League.

12 Boyarin, "Freud's Baby, Fleiss's Maybe."

13 M. Robert, *From Oedipus to Moses: Freud's Jewish Identity*, trans. R. Manheim (Garden City, N.Y.: Anchor Doubleday, 1976), 112.

14 M. Berkowitz, *Zionist Culture and West European Jewry before the First World War* (Cambridge: Cambridge University Press, 1993), 108.

15 For this seeming paradox of the very site of assertion of cultural identity being as well the most intense locus of denial, one need only cite Herzl's comments on the writing of *The Jewish State:* "My only recreation was listening to Wagner's music in the evening, particularly to *Tannhäuser*, an opera which I attended as often as it was produced. Only on the evening when there was no opera did I have any doubts as to the truth of my ideas" (T. Herzl, *Zion-*

ist Writings: Essays and Addresses, trans. H. Zohn [New York: Herzl, 1973], 17). See also A. Elon, *Herzl* (New York: Schocken, 1986), 3. I thank Jonathan Boyarin for reminding me of this reference.

16 See Berkowitz, *Zionist Culture*, 18–19; and D. Biale, *Eros and the Jews: From Biblical Israel to Contemporary America* (New York: Basic, 1992), 176.

17 Berkowitz, *Zionist Culture*, 9; Biale, *Eros and the Jews*, 178–79. Max Nordau, "Jewry of Muscle," in *The Jew in the Modern World: A Documentary History*, ed. Paul Mendes-Flohr and Jehuda Reinharz (Oxford: Oxford University Press, 1980), originally published as "Muskeljudentum," in *Juedische Turnzeitung* (June 1903).

18 George Mosse, *Nationalism and Sexuality: Middle-Class Morality and Sexual Norms in Modern Europe* (Madison: University of Wisconsin Press, 1985), 42.

19 On Zionism as virile, see Biale, *Eros and the Jews*, 176–77.

20 Berkowitz, *Zionist Culture*, 108.

21 I will qualify the *Zionism* to which I refer here with the adjective *Herzlian* as there were/are different Zionisms. For all my disdain for Herzlian liberalism, religious Zionisms (those that combine statism with religion, whether Orthodox or not, e.g., blood and soil mysticism of the Right and Left) are even more problematic to me and, given the actual situation of the populations of Palestine/Israel today, more deleterious. It is a matter of controversy to what extent Herzl's ideas are actually carried out in the state of Israel. The best of them certainly are not. I try to indicate here some of the negative manifestations of Herzlian thought about Jewish history as they play themselves out in Israeli cultural performance. I would argue that much of the violence of contemporary Israeli cultural and political life is generated by inchoate anticolonial struggles on the part of Oriental and traditionalist Jews against the civilizing mission of the Western liberals, which unfortunately often enough (but not always) result in intensification of neocolonialism with respect to the Palestinians rather than in solidarity with their anticolonial struggle. The only variety of historical Zionism with which I can identify at all is that of Judah Magnes and the Covenant of Peace group, which did not seek Jewish political hegemony, a Jewish state, but quested rather for shared sovereignty together with Palestinians in a binational state. Today such a program is labeled *anti-Zionism*, so I am an anti-Zionist.

22 W. Rathenau to Wilhelm Schwaner, 23 January 1916, in *Schriften*, ed. A. Harttung (Berlin: Berlin Verlag, 1965).

23 J. Kornberg, *Theodor Herzl: From Assimilation to Zionism* (Bloomington: Indiana University Press, 1993), 16–19.

24 Quoted in Homi Bhabha, *The Location of Culture* (London: Routledge, 1994), 87.

25 Kornberg, *Theodor Herzl*, 20, 24.

26 Boyarin, "Bitextuality, Psychoanalysis, Zionism."

27 Theodor Herzl, *The Complete Diaries of Theodor Herzl*, ed. R. Patai, trans. H. Zohn (New York: Herzl, 1960), 7.

28 Theodor Herzl, "The Jewish State" in *Theodor Herzl: A Portrait for This Age*, ed. L. Lewisohn (Cleveland: World, 1955), 251, 238.

29 Theodor Gomperz. See Kornberg, *Theodor Herzl*, 115.

30 Ibid.

31 Herzl, *The Complete Diaries*.

32 J. Geller, "A Paleontological View of Freud's Study of Religion: Unearthing the *Leitfossil* Circumcision," *Modern Judaism* 13 (1993): 59, citing B. Spinoza, *The Political Works*, trans. A. G. Wernham (Oxford: Oxford University Press, 1958), 63. See also J. Boyarin and D. Boyarin, "Self-Exposure as Theory: The Double Mark of the Male Jew," in *Rhetorics of Self-Making*, ed. D. Battaglia (Berkeley and Los Angeles: University of California Press, 1995).

33 The text of *Das neue Ghetto* (*DnG*) that I will cite here is the slightly abridged version published in Lewisohn, ed., *Theodor Herzl*. Page numbers for quotations will be given in the text.

34 See Sander Gilman, *Jewish Self-Hatred: Anti-Semitism and the Hidden Language of the Jews* (Baltimore: Johns Hopkins University Press, 1986).

35 Kornberg, *Theodor Herzl*, 138.

36 Ibid., 122.

37 J. M. Cuddihy's claim that all Jewish socialism is a bourgeois Jewish response to the problem of the uncouth Eastern Jew (*The Ordeal of Civility: Freud, Marx, Lévi-Strauss, and the Jewish Struggle with Modernity* [Boston: Beacon, 1987], 5) fits Herzl much better than it does Marx. For a critical reading of Cuddihy, see Daniel Boyarin, "*Épater l'embourgeoisement:* Freud, Gender, and the (De)Colonized Psyche," *Diacritics* 24, no. 1 (spring 1994): 17–42. Herzl did, however, have a genuine concern for the safety of miners, as shown by his plan that all mines be nationalized in the state of the Jews, in order that "mine workers should not be subject to an entrepreneur's parsimony. The State will not economize on safety measures" (see Herzl, *The Complete Diaries*, 162). He also manifested a genuine liberalism in his proposal that the Jewish state enshrine the seven-hour workday even on its flag. My argument is not that Herzl was some sort of reactionary but that he was a liberal like John Stuart Mill, for e.g. Given the state of contemporary Israeli society, even a liberal colonialist vision would be preferable, but that is Cold Comfort Kibbutz, in my view. See also Elon, *Herzl*, 38, 118.

38 Kornberg, *Theodore Herzl*, 124.

39 Herzl's feuilleton appeared in the *Neue Freie Presse* of 29 April 1892, quoted in Elon, *Herzl*, 105. Carl Schorske, *Fin-de-Siècle Vienna: Politics and Culture* (New York: Knopf, 1980), 154.

40 Kornberg, *Theodore Herzl*, 171.

41 Ibid., 146.

42 Mosse, *Nationalism and Sexuality*, 149–50.

43 See also I. Zertal, "The Sacrificed and the Sanctified: The Construction of a National Martyrology," *Zemanim* 12, no. 48 (spring 1994): 35.

44 Herzl, *The Complete Diaries*, 2:612.

45 I am not the first who has sensed some affinity between Fanon and Herzl (see Elon, *Herzl*, 140); and Frantz Fanon, *Black Skin, White Masks*, trans. Charles Lam Markmann (London: MacGibbon and Kee, 1968).

46 Kornberg, *Theodor Herzl*, 131.

47 Elon, *Herzl*, 266.

48 Kornberg, *Theodor Herzl*, 145.

49 Pace Kornberg (ibid., 147).

50 On Jewish mimicry, particularly with reference to Herzl, see J. Geller, "Of Mice and Mensa: Anti-Semitism and the Jewish Genius," *Centennial Review* 38 (1994): 361–85. Geller, however, maintains the position that Herzl eventually dropped the mimicry solution to the Jewish Question, whereas I am arguing that he merely perfected it.

51 See Kornberg, *Theodor Herzl*, 146.

52 Herzl, *The Complete Diaries*, 1:58. See also the rich discussion in Kornberg, *Theodor Herzl*, 66–71.

53 Herzl, *The Complete Diaries*, 1:69. Obviously, cholera vaccinating and even war making under certain circumstances are not negative activities; it is the encoding of them as of value, not so much in themselves, but as signifiers of manliness, like dueling, to which I am pointing here. Cholera vaccinating is produced by Herzl as only a poor substitute for duel-

54 Kornberg, *Theodor Herzl*, 154.

55 My point is not, then, obviously, that Herzl was unusual in his self-hatred—indeed, the phenomenon was so well known as to merit a name—but only that his Zionism was a manifestation of this self-hatred, not an antithesis to it. Zionist writers consistently obscure this point by such circumlocutions as, "Some of his diatribes against Jewish scribes and businessmen echoed those of Herzl's, but in his hateful bitterness Kraus sounded like a precursor of Nazi propaganda" (Elon, *Herzl*, 306)—and Herzl's "Mauschel" does not sound like such a precursor? Sander Gilman's *Jewish Self-Hatred* is the classic study of this cultural practice, which, I suggest, is typical of the colonial situation.

56 Herzl, *Complete Diaries*, 1:84.

57 Jay Goldstein, "The Wandering Jew and the Problem of Psychiatric Anti-Semitism in Fin-de-Siècle France," *Journal of Contemporary History* 20 (1985): 528–29.

58 Ibid.

59 Elon, *Herzl*, 245.

60 Kornberg, *Theodor Herzl*.

61 Gilman, *Jewish Self-Hatred*, 238.

62 H. S. Chamberlain, *Foundations of the Nineteenth Century*, trans. J. Lees (New York: Howard Fertig, 1968). Note that the kaiser made no such inner-Jewish racial distinctions. Mosse's claim that "Jews never directed the weapon of racism at others in order to facilitate their own acceptance into society" (*Nationalism and Sexuality*, 42) is at least partially falsified by this moment in Herzl. Western Jews did sometimes direct the weapon of racism at Ostjuden for precisely this purpose.

63 The remarkable thing is that Herzl could also produce exactly opposite sentiments as well. After meeting actual Russian Jews for the first time at the First Zionist Congress in Basel (1897), he wrote: "How ashamed we felt, we who had thought that we were superior to them. Even more impressive was that they possess an inner integrity that most European Jews have lost. They feel like national Jews but without narrow and intolerant conceit" (Elon, *Herzl*, 246). "Mauschel," however, was written quite a bit later than these sensitive lines.

64 J. Tamir, "The March of the Coopted Historians," *Ha'aretz*, 20 May 1994.

65 Jenny Sharpe, *Allegories of Empire: The Figure of Woman in the Colonial Text* (Minneapolis: University of Minnesota Press, 1993), 29.

66 Mosse, *Nationalism and Sexuality*, 106–7.

67 A. Schnitzler, *My Youth in Vienna*, trans. C. Hutter (New York: Holt, Rinehart, and Winston, 1970), 128.

68 Elon, *Herzl*, 53.

69 P. Loewenberg, "Theodor Herzl: Nationalism and Politics," in *Decoding the Past: The Psychohistorical Approach* (Berkeley and Los Angeles: University of California Press, 1985), 120–21.

70 This gives us a new way of reading Herzl's notorious inability to "see" the Palestinians, for, as Sir Herman Merivale wrote in his 1839 lectures on colonialism, "The modern colonizing imagination conceives of its dependencies as a *territory*, never as a *people*" (Bhabha, *The Location of Culture*, 97).

71 Sharpe, *Allegories of Empire*, 21.

72 Kornberg, *Theodor Herzl*, 221; Herzl, *Zionist Writings*, 153.

73 Boyarin, "*Épater l'embourgeoisement.*"

74 Gilman, *Jewish Self-Hatred*.

75 " 'Nowadays one must be blond,' Herzl wrote in a revealing little note found among his

papers from that time. Was this irony? The evidence suggests that he may have meant it in all earnestness, manifesting in one short, casual line all the tortured convulsions of a sensitive secularized Jew's search for identity. One good way for a dark-haired Jew to appear blond, figuratively speaking, was to be active in one of the prestigious dueling fraternities" (Elon, *Herzl*, 54).

76   Bhabha, *The Location of Culture.*

77   Ibid., 85.

78   See ibid., 102–22.

79   Romans such as Virgil and Lucan admired those of their enemies who fought and died bravely — "like Romans" — but King Telesphorus, who preferred to live in prison because "while there's life there's hope" was branded an effeminate coward (C. A. Barton, *The Sorrows of the Ancient Romans: The Gladiator and the Monster* [Princeton, N.J.: Princeton University Press, 1993], 10).

80   Marek Edelman, quoted in Zertal, "The Sacrificed and the Sanctified," 38.

81   Bhabha, *The Location of Culture,* 88.

82   See Judith Butler, *Gender Trouble: Feminism and the Subversion of Identity* (London: Routledge, 1990).

83   See the very similar point made in D. Fuss, "Interior Colonies: Frantz Fanon and the Politics of Identification," *Diacritics* 24, nos. 2–3 (summer–fall 1994): 20–42.

84   On the dueling scar, see Peter Gay, *The Bourgeois Experience, Victoria to Freud,* vol. 3, *The Cultivation of Hatred* (New York: Norton, 1993), 11.

      As Jay Geller ("Of Mice and Mensa") points out in an extraordinary reading of Kafka's 1917 story "A Report to an Academy," his allegorized assimilated Jew, Red Peter, an ape aping humanness, has a scar on his cheek and one on his thigh. Geller associates the lower scar with circumcision, but I think that he misses the association of the upper one with the mensur. Although Geller's focus in that context is elsewhere, this point only strengthens his overall reading of the text.

85   The discourse of gender of the actual Zionist movement and its eventual practices of oppression both with regard to gender and with respect to the Palestinians are much more complex than any account of Herzl, for all his being the father/prophet of Zionism could possibly envision. I hope someday to return to this project in the form of a book to be entitled *Mentsh and Supermentsh in Jewish Palestine.*

86   Bhabha, *The Location of Culture,* 89. For a fascinating parallel discussion of the not white/not quite syndrome in Jewish decolonization, see Geller, "Of Mice and Mensa."

87   In this sense, it is difficult to fit Israel into a class that includes such "former" white-settler colonies as Australia, New Zealand, and Canada (P. Williams and L. Chrisman, eds., *Colonial Discourse and Post-Colonial Theory: A Reader* [New York: Columbia University Press, 1994], 4). The fact that Zionist theory and practice cannot be easily classified does not in any way constitute an apologetic for its effects, and little is gained politically for the Palestinian people by simply categorizing Israel as a *white-settler state.*

88   Elon, *Herzl,* 375.

89   François Hartog, *The Mirror of Herodotus: The Representation of the Other in the Writing of History,* trans. J. Lloyd (Berkeley and Los Angeles: University of California Press, 1988), 11.

90   K. Seshadri-Crooks, "The Primitive as Analyst: Postcolonial Feminism's Access to Psychoanalysis," *Cultural Critique,* no. 28 (fall 1994).

91   As such, there are versions of Zionist practice that are considerably more vicious than Herzl's liberalism, including some that are murderously assertive of Jewish difference. Liberalism has worse alternatives.

92 Elon, *Herzl*, 312.

93 Theodor Herzl, *Old-Newland (Altneuland)*, trans. L. Levensohn (New York: Bloch, 1941), 110–11.

94 Elon, *Herzl*, 312.

95 Bhabha, *The Location of Culture*, 88.

96 A. Raz-Krakotzkin, "Exile within Sovereignty: Toward a Critique of the 'Negation of Exile' in Israeli Culture," *Theory and Criticism: An Israeli Forum* 4 (autumn 1993) (an English summary is provided).

97 Kalpana Seshadri-Crooks made me aware of this danger in my text. Paradoxically, such an argument for an *Aryanization* of Jewish culture could end up analogous to the *Semiticization* interpretation of what happened to the peaceful, tolerant Hindus — a term to which I have, understandably I think, objected.

98 On 4 May 1994, the president of Palestine, Yasser Arafat, appointed Rabbi Moses Hirsch of the Neturei Karta, anti-Zionist Palestinian traditionalist Jews, as minister for Jewish affairs in the new Palestinian Autonomy.

99 Gayatri Chakravorty Spivak quoted in G. Prakash, "Postcolonial Criticism and Indian Historiography," *Social Text* 31/32 (1992): 8–19.

100 On the restoration of an ideal past, see M. Prasad, "A Theory of Third World Literature," *Social Text* 31/32 (1992): 59.

101 Ibid., 57–58.
    The two people whom I wish to honor by my dedication of this *essay* have dedicated their *lives* to that political project.

102 Shohat, "Notes on the 'Post-Colonial,' " *in The Pre-Occupation of Postcolonial Studies*, ed. Fawzia Afzal-Khan and Kalpana Seshadri-Crooks (Durham, N.C.: Duke University Press, 2000).

103 Prasad, "A Theory of Third World Literature," 72.

104 Shohat, "Notes on the 'Post-Colonial.' "

Postcolonial Literature in a Neocolonial World:
Modern Arabic Culture and the End of Modernity

SAREE MAKDISI

The objects on both banks of the river were semivisible, appearing and disappearing, shimmering and flickering between light and darkness. The river was flowing, making its old familiar sounds: flowing strongly and yet presenting the appearance of being motionless. There was no sound except for that of the river and the hammering of the nearby water pump. I began swimming toward the northern shore. . . . I kept swimming and swimming, determined to reach the northern bank. That was the goal. The bank in front of me rose and fell, just as the sounds and noises rhythmically increased and receded. Gradually I came to hear nothing but the sounds of the river. Then it was as if I were in a great echoing chamber. The bank steadily rose and fell, and, with it, the sounds of the river came and went. In front of me I saw the world in a semicircle. Then I hovered on the brink between vision and blindness. I was conscious and not conscious. Was I asleep or awake? Was I alive or dead? And yet I was still clinging to a thin, frail thread, and I felt that my goal was in front of me, not below me, and that I must move forward, not downward. But the thread was so frail that it threatened to break; and I reached a point where I felt that the forces of the riverbed were pulling me down to them. . . . Turning to the left and to the right, I realized that I was halfway between north and south. I was unable to continue and unable to return.[1]

In the eerie hush of the closing moments of the Sudanese novelist A Tayeb Salih's *Season of Migration to the North*, the narrator finds himself at a turning point in the Nile: a bend in the river, where the current's usual northerly flow is disrupted and cut off by a sudden swerve from west to east. It is here, in this geographically uncertain location, that the final scene takes place, in which the narrator is left screaming for help in the darkness and immensity of the Nile. Steadily weakening, having been stripped of the directional certainty normally provided by the river's unwavering northward flow, and having been cut off from the reassuring and familiar landmarks on its banks (not only because they rise and fall with the swells of the Nile but also because there are actually four banks at this bend, rather than two), the narrator is unable to situate himself in terms of a directional flow: he is unable either to continue his "migration" to the north or to return to his point of departure, which had vanished as soon as he entered the water. The summoned help never arrives, and a great darkness closes in on both the narrator and the narrative—a darkness in which *Season of Migration* comes to an ambiguous and uneasy close.

Ultimately, the migration referred to in the title (a quest whose failure the closing scene represents) never takes place; and one of its figurative vehicles, the Nile itself, appears in the end to be incapable of deliverance—incapable of steady progress toward a predefined goal or objective. The narrator's confusion in those closing lines thus replicates the confusion or ambiguity of the river's own flow: just as the Nile seems no longer to proceed evenly and directly from south to north, he is unable figuratively to use it as a "runway" on which to launch himself toward his "goals" (or, for that matter, on which to reverse or abort his takeoff and return to his point of departure). For it is precisely such unilinear narratives of possibility that *Season of Migration* seeks to contest; and, in this context, the narrator's perplexity and the diversion in the Nile's course are also, whatever else they may be, figurations of certain disruptions in other teleological narratives, courses, directions, and flows, which intrude on the novel's discursive space from a context that does not simply lie outside it. Saleh's novel chronicles such disruptions at once in its formal construction—an unstable mixture of modern European and traditional Arabic styles and forms—and in its narrative concerns, central to which are not only the inability of the traditional to become modern but also the self-violence (and violence to others) demanded by such a futile project of transformation and development as well as the illusory nature of this project, illusory precisely because neither of the dualistic categories implied by it, nor others, including the *native* and the *foreign*, the *Western* and the *Eastern*, is satisfactory, or even plausible, as such. *Season of Migration* questions not only such projects of transformation and development but their very ontological, epistemological, and ideological premises: it questions not only the direction of the "threads" pointing the way to development but also the very existence of such gossamer lines, such clues and markers supposedly left behind by those who have already progressed—*migrated*—to a modernity that they, these others, have defined.[2]

Written in the late 1960s, *Season of Migration to the North* grows out of, and indeed contributes to, a crisis in the Arab world, a crisis in which the all-too-easy evolutionary and Eurocentric narratives of modernization and de-

velopment (and others like them, including the narrative of national independence) began to be questioned and thrown into doubt by a new generation of
Arab writers. Such narratives had, in a sense, emerged from the shattered societies of a slowly modernizing Europe in the nineteenth century and were from
the beginning intertwined not only with the developing doctrines of evolution
(and its post-Darwinian, Spenserian derivative, progress) but also with a new
version of colonialism, in which modern Europe's cultural others — including
such peoples as the Scottish Highlanders, the Irish, the Sicilians, the urban poor
of various nightmarish cityscapes, such as Manchester and Birmingham —
gradually became seen as underdeveloped or as farther behind the various self-
proclaimed representatives of modernity on what Johannes Fabian has usefully described as the unilinear "stream" of evolutionary time.[3] According to
such narratives, for instance, Asia became seen, roughly from the time of Byron
on — although not by Byron himself during *his* first pilgrimage to the Orient —
as a space that needed to be raised and improved until it became identical to
modern Europe, as a sphere that needed to be propelled up the stream of time
to the shores and breakwaters of modernity. The problem here, of course, is not
that nineteenth- and twentieth-century *Europeans* gradually came to see Asia
as an underdeveloped relative to a Eurocentric standard but that many Arabs
(and other Asians) also came to see *themselves* in precisely such terms. And
even many of those who have refused to acknowledge such putative European
superiority have nevertheless established their challenges to it in the very narrative and discursive terms that it has itself proposed and invented; hence, such
challenges have more often than not been defused or negated by their participation in the very same conceptual and discursive system (of modernity) against
which they seek to define themselves as oppositional.[4]

Faced with what they perceived to be the overwhelming superiority of the
European empires and the mercantile and industrial structures of capital that
were imbricated with them, a number of Arab philosophers and writers in the
nineteenth century found themselves in a double bind as the Arab world was
gradually incorporated into what had by then become the dual structure of colonialism and capitalism. These Arab writers conceived of themselves (and their
societies) as trapped between, on the one hand, the residual cultural formations
represented by the great Arabic classical heritage and, on the other hand, the
appeals to modernity and modernization that European institutions and educa-
tions seemed to offer them. In what is by now a familiar story, some of these
thinkers (e.g., al-Afghani and Abduh, among others) held out the possibility of
a return to, or a revitalization of, the classical and traditional heritage, while
others, including the founders of a movement that came to be called the *Nahda*,
insisted that the only way out of this double bind was forward, in the direction of progress, development, modernization, and — ultimately — Europe.[5] The
advocates of both positions, however, accepted the premise of a dualistic oppo-

sition — between tradition and modernity, between evolution and involution —
as well as the historical assumption underlying it: namely, that to accept modernity as a goal implied entering into the flow of the river of evolutionary time,
which had already been charted by Europe, and that to reject this goal implied
trying to move backward against the powerful forward current of history, or at
least trying to defy that current by resituating indigenous structures within the
contemporary world. The debate between the advocates of these opposed positions was carried on through the nineteenth century and into the twentieth. By
the time of the Arab nationalist movements of the early twentieth century, however, those who called for a Nahda (or cultural and scientific renaissance) were
in the ascendancy, although, for the advocates of such a rebirth, modernity was,
from the beginning, not only inextricably associated with Europe but a goal that
one could define only as a *future* condition, a *future* location, a *future* possibility.
Modernity, in other words, is, on this account, always already displaced and
deferred: it is always on the other side of the river, or up the stream — or up in
the sky.

There are, of course, other cultural and political positions than these two
mutually reinforcing ones (modernity vs. tradition), and it is to some of these
that I will turn shortly for evidence not only of alternative Arab constructions of
history from those originally proposed by the Europeans but also of challenges
to both the Nahda and its traditionalist or fundamentalist opponents and, indeed, to the very concepts of modernity and tradition as they have hitherto been
formulated. I will tentatively refer to these alternative visions and constructions as embodying an Arab *modernism*, and, by way of conclusion, I will come
back to this term — which I use guardedly — and question its vexed relation to
the concepts of modernity and modernization with which I opened this essay,
its relevance to contemporary theorizations of postmodernism, and, finally, its
relevance to discussions of what some critics have (very problematically) referred to as the *postcolonial* and (even more problematically) *postcolonialism*.

By the late nineteenth and early twentieth centuries, the various Arab movements of renewal had become increasingly concerned with (and focused on) the
need to create an independent state as the appropriate vehicle for cultural, economic, and political development and modernization. "The idea of Europe as
the exemplar of modern civilization," as Albert Hourani has pointed out, "was
powerful in these national movements. To be independent was to be accepted by
European states on a level of equality, to have the Capitulations, the legal privileges of foreign citizens, abolished, to be admitted to the League of Nations. To
be modern was to have a political and social life similar to those of the countries
of western Europe."[6] From the secret societies established in Beirut in the 1880s,
to the Arab revolt during the First World War, to the declarations of the Syrian
Congress of 1919 and 1920, Arab nationalist struggles for various forms or

levels of independence from (successively) the Ottoman Empire and the European empires centered on the attempted creation of modern independent states, whether in all the Arab world, in greater Syria, in western Asia, or in other configurations or forms (Egypt, e.g., had its own nationalist movement, generally distinct from those to the east).[7] The various independence movements intensified following the First World War, when the Ottomans were forced to withdraw from the Arab lands of southwest Asia, which then fell into the hands of the two greatest European empires — the British and the French. At that crucial juncture, the political future of the region was open to question.[8] As Hourani has also observed, "the existence of the Arabs had not been questioned in the later Ottoman Empire, and the various Arab provinces had been thought of as a whole. The division of the postwar settlement called it in question, and threatened to set up the idea of a Syrian, a Lebanese, and an Iraqi nation as its rival, sometimes with the encouragement of the mandatory Power."[9]

Indeed, while the earliest Arab nationalist movements had called for the formation of one unified Arab state, such a call became more difficult to realize after the war, and the nationalist movements gradually shifted their claims to smaller units of the Arab world — Egypt, Arabia, Syria, Iraq, and so forth — more often than not as a result of the divisions and inscriptions imposed by European imperialism, which slowly divided the region into spheres of influence or into areas of greater or lesser control.[10] The Arab struggle for independence was particularly strong in greater (or geographic) Syria, and, despite various offshoots and splinter factions, it culminated in the General Syrian Congress, which focused largely on the creation of an independent state in all of what is now Syria, Lebanon, Israel, Palestine, and Jordan.

It is the fate of this particular area — greater Syria — on which I will briefly focus, for it is within this region that the struggle between Arab nationalism(s) and European colonialism(s) has had the most enduring effects. It is also in this region that the very principles of cultural, political, and economic modernization in the unit of the independent state (a program embodying the principles of the Nahda) were first implemented, following the demise of a postwar effort to maintain Syria's unity — just as it was here that that program (along with the principles of the Nahda) has been increasingly thrown into question in recent years. In other words, the future and possibilities of modernization in the terms originally devised by the advocates of the Nahda (and by its implicit adherents since then) have — implicitly or explicitly — been inextricably tied to the fate of greater Syria, where they were first put to the test, following the division of greater Syria into three or four (nominally) independent states.

The General Syrian Congress met in 1919 to plan the eventual independence of greater Syria. This congress, one of the earliest Arab anticolonial movements to emerge following the war, aligned itself explicitly against the rapidly unfolding European policies for the region and declared its democratic-secularist program in a series of resolutions in the summer of 1919, largely in an effort to preempt or circumvent European mandatory plans. "In view of the fact that the Arab inhabitants of Syria are not less fitted or gifted than were certain other nations (such as the Bulgarians, Serbs, Greeks, and Rumanians) when granted their independence," the Congress declared, "we protest against Article XXII of the Covenant of the League of Nations, which relegates us to the standing of insufficiently developed races requiring the tutelage of a mandatory power." Thus, the congress insisted on a strong "misreading" of the League of Nations' mandatory system (in actuality, a new version of colonial domination, with a built-in logic opposing developed and undeveloped races and nations) as "implying no more than the rendering of assistance in the technical and economic fields without impairment of our absolute independence."[11] And, in response to the European colonial attempts to carve greater Syria into different pieces, the congress affirmed Syria's historical and cultural unity—although it made no pretense at homogeneity or uniformity—and rejected both the proposal to allow the French greater control over what is today Lebanon and the European Zionist colonial project in Palestine (although it specifically added that "our Jewish fellow-citizens shall continue to enjoy the rights and to bear the responsibilities which are ours in common"). The congress's final claim was a demand "to be allowed to send a delegation to represent us at the Peace Conference, advocate our claims and secure the fulfillment of our aspirations."[12]

These claims and demands notwithstanding, the British and the French militarily parceled out greater Syria, as well as Iraq, according to the plans that they had drawn up in 1916, and, instead of one Arab state, there appeared a number of such states.

By the early 1920s, then, the Arab struggle for the formation of a single state gave way to a series of often conflicting struggles for the creation of a number of independent states along the fragmentary and arbitrary lines drawn up and militarily imposed by the great European empires. Yet each of these states (with the obvious exception of Palestine) has, since independence, tried to resuscitate the principles of the Nahda and embark on its own path to modernity. Thus, the Nahda's insistence on the importance of the independent state as the appropriate vehicle for modernization has been put into effect by the different Arab states. Since the states gained their independence (mostly in the 1940s and 1950s), however, the divisions separating each state from the next—divisions originally inscribed by the European empires when they carved the region into units of control—have been, for the most part, ruthlessly enforced by the Arab states themselves. There have been exceptions to this, of course, as with the United Arab Republic, which Gamal Abdel Nasser instituted in the late 1950s and early 1960s (and which was short-lived), and as more recently illustrated by the Iraqi invasion of Kuwait, which, whatever else it may have been, was also an attempt to erase just such an old colonial border, a line that was redrawn during the Gulf War — with the ample monetary blessings of the Saudis, Kuwaitis, and the other Arab principalities of the Gulf as well as the moral and material support of several other Arab states (Egypt, Syria, Morocco), all of which are eager for such boundaries to remain in place.

Thus, the Nahda-inspired goal of modernization has, since independence, been stressed in a drive to development constructed on, and restricted to, the scale of the nation-state, even if through a range in experiments in national development, from unbridled laissez-faire capitalism (as in Lebanon) to various kinds of socialism (as in Egypt, Syria, and Iraq), and through a variety of different state forms, from a (technically) parliamentary democracy (Lebanon, once again) to absolute monarchies or principalities (the Gulf) to single-party states (Syria and Iraq). Moreover, each Arab state has been integrated into the world economic system on its own, individually bound into a technologically and structurally dependent relation to the global economy. As a result, the Arab world has been divided into state-defined units (national economies) that bear little or no resemblance to the economic and political needs, or even the population distribution, of the Arab people; thus, for example, the oil-rich little states of the Gulf, with their minuscule populations, must import up to 80 or 90 percent of their skilled workforce, often from other Arab countries, while the bulk of their considerable capital outflow is directed, not at the Arab world, but at the more developed capital markets of Europe, East Asia, and the United States.[13] At the same time, other Arab states are in need of capital, suffer from weak economies and high unemployment rates, and are dependent on remittances from expatriate laborers. Overall, in other words, there is a grossly disproportionate distribution of wealth and resources within the Arab world and, consequently, not only a great deal of inefficiency (not to mention injustice) but an absurd lack of cooperation and cohesiveness and hence an often crippling self-inflicted weakness with regard to the rest of the global economy. With a few exceptions, attempts to facilitate and coordinate economic development among the Arab states — by instituting a pan-Arab monetary unit, for example — have ended in utter failure, as each state tries to achieve its own narrowly defined goals of modernization at the expense of the other Arab states and, if necessary, at the expense of the needs of its own people and of the Arab people in general.[14]

Throughout the various attempts at modernization since independence, in other words, many of the central ideological and conceptual categories that emerged from the Nahda have remained in the ascendancy (including a quasi-institutionalized bifurcation between the preservation of a certain religious traditionalism and the adoption of certain modern principles in science and technology).[15] In the meantime, and until very recently, those who called for a revitalization of traditional Islamic cultures remained in abeyance. Indeed, the current attraction of various so-called fundamentalist revolutionary movements (e.g., Hizballah in Lebanon, Hamas in the Israeli-occupied territories, the FIS in Algeria, the Gama'a al-islamiyya in Egypt—all movements that may usefully be considered first and foremost politically revolutionary and only in a secondary sense religiously fundamentalist) has very much to do with the all-too-apparent monumental failure of the advocates of modernization to achieve much beyond the loss of Palestine, the devastation of Lebanon, and the ever-increasing Arab humiliation and subordination to Israel, Europe, and the United States (as most recently illustrated by the ongoing events in the Gulf).

For what, indeed, has the drive toward modernization achieved in the Arab world? Better roads, bigger buildings, excellent hospitals, airports, banks, factories, refineries, universities, schools—to be sure. But *not* modernity as it was originally defined by the Europeans and by their uncritical admirers among the Arabs, for that modernity remains, as it has been from the beginning, a perpetually deferred future status rather than ever being, or becoming, an immediately apprehensible present one. Indeed, the social and cultural dislocations of modernity seem to have preceded the thing itself—if that "thing" is to be understood in the way it originally was by the Nahda.

If one can speak of an Arab modernist tendency at all, one can do so only, I think, in the context of some of the recent cultural and political transformations and fragmentations in the Arab world, a context of cultural crisis that this tendency has helped not only identify but *produce.* Moreover, such a modernism must be placed in opposition to the Nahda and to the literary or novelistic forms and styles associated with it. Such forms and styles are exemplified by a range of Arabic novels, from the earliest ones in the late nineteenth and early twentieth centuries (such as the romantic and historical novels of Jurji Zaydan, Muhammad Muwaihili, and Muhammad Haykal, including *The Conquest of Andalusia, A Period of Time,* and *Zaynab*), to those of the early independence period, and even to those following the Second World War (e.g., novels and stories by Yahya Haqqi, or the early Naguib Mahfouz, or the early Tayeb Salih).[16] These early works more or less share a straightforward realistic narrative, an omniscient narrative voice, and a relatively uncomplicated temporal and chronological framework; moreover, they were often very heavily inspired by (not to say imitative of) the various European literatures—which should come as no surprise since, as Anis Makdisi points out, "most of what was available to the reading public from the end of the last century to the second third of the present one took the form of translations of or adaptations from [Western cultural production]."[17]

Now, the works of what I am calling here—by way of opposition to the Nahda and its styles—*Arabic modernism* were all produced during or after what these texts themselves helped define and understand as a series of calamitous ruptures or breaks with the past.[18] These ruptures have in part to do with certain localized crises (including revolutions and civil wars) that are not generalizable across the different Arab states. But they also have very much to do with the shared Arab experience of imperialism—including its recent reconfigurations—and with other shared Arab crises, including the ongoing confrontations with Israel, Europe, and the United States.[19] These ruptures have also signaled the persistence of certain neocolonial relations of power and domination, relations that have locked the independent Arab states into a subalternity reminiscent of, but not identical to, that of the nineteenth century. This subalternity, indeed, has been defined and enabled simultaneously by the neocolonial situation that the Arabs still find themselves in and by the bitter divisions and lines of demarcation by which each Arab state separates itself from the others. The tendency that I am calling here *Arab modernism* contests the *political* as well as the narrative strategies hitherto put into practice in the Arab world, strategies based on narrowly conceived nationalism, on teleology, on a unilinear sense of history, and on modernity as defined either by capitalist institutions or by socialist revolutions that *both* hold open the promise of what turns out to be a perpetually deferred future happiness. And, hence, it stakes its claims in opposition both to the West and to the various Arab states as they actually exist.

This tendency is, in other words, a literature of crisis. By this, however, I do not mean that it merely *reacts* to certain historical or sociopolitical circumstances but rather that it contributes to the production of a sense of crisis in the Arab world. And it does so largely by historicizing that sense of crisis—that is, *by producing the very historical categories and concepts, including those of rupture and discontinuity, that enable the critical understanding or interrogation of the contemporary and by defining the historical conditions that allow the contemporary to take place or to make sense.* In other words, this literary and nonliterary trend, in cinematic and nonfictional texts as much as in properly fictional ones, helps produce not merely the expression or the articulation of crisis but the reality of crisis itself; it does not replicate reality but rather contributes to the production of the real in the Arab world.

In this sense, the brilliant self-erasures and rewritings of a novel such as Mahfouz's *Miramar* (1967) pose not only a challenge to the standardized and state-enforced histories and narratives of the Egyptian Revolution of 1952 (which are worked into the novel at various levels and registers) but also a direct attack on the unilinear temporality of the Nahda as well as the associated unilinear temporality of modernization itself, with its uncomplicated flow toward a completed state of modernity. While much of the uncertainty of one of Mahfouz's previous novels, *The Thief and the Dogs* (1961), is generated by threading the narrator's voice through the principal protagonist's, in *Miramar*, Mahfouz removes the fixed and omniscient narrator altogether, leaving us with the confused and contradictory narratives of the characters themselves. The novel unfolds, in fact, as the telling and retelling of the same story by each of the characters, and each narrative takes on the idiosyncratic style and perspective of the person whose viewpoint it represents. Thus, each narration not only brings a new perspective to all the other narratives and characters but also includes flashbacks, inner thoughts, and other less central narratives that are specific to each character, many of which are shrouded in half-spoken secrets and thus remain inaccessible to the reader. The overall effect is to undermine and, finally, to remove the possibility of any stable narrative voice or any stable reference point for the reader; without these fixed truths, *Miramar* keeps erasing itself and never moves toward a neat or conclusive resolution, repeatedly returning to a troubled and less and less certain present.

Partly because of the ways in which it integrates historical and contemporary narratives and themes into the various characters' narrations and rewrites or erases them along with other less significant details, *Miramar*'s subtle decomposition of the temporal structure of the romantic and realist novels of the Nahda is also a decomposition of the epistemological basis of linear or evolutionary history itself. That is, *Miramar*'s radical departure from previous narrative forms is *at one and the same time* a radical departure from earlier novelistic or literary styles and a departure from earlier historicizing operations, earlier understandings and formulations of Egyptian history or even of the situation of contemporary Egypt itself.

In their searing critiques of blind traditionalism, but also, hence, of the representatives of a supposedly revolutionary or nationalist future, such modernist novels as *Miramar* reject all unproblematic or univocal relationships to either past or future, whether in terms of narrative or of history, for these issues are inextricably related in such novels whose temporal structures are not only historically conditioned, or reflective of historical considerations and conditions, but themselves historicizing formulations, historicizing operations and hypotheses, in which, for example, the possibility of a return to a mythic past is rejected along with the alternative possibility of an uncompromised and perpetually deferred great leap forward to development. All that is left is, indeed, a highly unstable and contradictory present, one that defies the convenient and false reassurances of new and old political, religious, and literary dogmatisms. Whereas the advocates of the Nahda and of modernization stressed the potential of some future moment, and whereas various traditionalists called for the reinvention of some vanished moment of past glory, these texts that I am calling *modernist* point only to an uncompromising and inescapable present, a historical present that can be modified and changed only when Eurocentric constructions and understandings of modernity and tradition are dropped forever and when alternative constructions and formulations of history, a history in which Arabs are not merely added or included as subordinate or underdeveloped elements, have come to replace them.

There are, of course, differences among the participants in this tendency, particularly when it comes to defining a final break with the past, a break that enables the critical understanding and interrogation of the present. In certain of these works (e.g., *Cities of Salt, Season of Migration*), the past refers to the period preceding the arrival of Euro/American imperialism; but certain Egyptian novels and films, for example, posit, in addition, a significant successive rupture (one that, in effect, confirms the first break figured by imperialism), that is, the 1952 revolution (e.g., *Miramar* or *The Thief and the Dogs* or Yussef Chahine's film *The Land*). Other significant successive ruptures posited by recent Arabic fiction are similarly localized: the eruption of the civil war in Lebanon in 1975, for instance, appears in postwar Lebanese fiction (e.g., *Little Mountain*) as marking the same sort of irrevocable fall that 1952 signified for Mahfouz and other Egyptian writers, a fall that has enabled new critical interrogations of Lebanese history as well as of contemporary Lebanon; similarly, the Palestinian director Michel Khleifi's recent films (*Wedding in Galilee* and *Canticle of the Stone*), situating themselves in the wake of the *intifada*, have presented compelling experiments not only in cinematic style but also in historical formulation and narration that open up new ways of situating the intifada itself in Palestinian and, more generally, Arabic cultural forms and production. Aside from imperialism, moreover, there are other major breaks that are registered as shared experiences across the Arab world: the violent eruption in 1948 of the state of Israel in what had, until then, been Palestine still haunts the Arabs (it is particularly haunting for the Palestinians, of course); and the crushing defeat of 1967, the mutual pathetic betrayals of 1973, and the debacles of the so-called new world order (which seems to have lost its novelty) are similarly shared and experienced as crises throughout the Arab world.

Now, each of these ruptures is shown, in these modernist texts, to have brought about a total and sweeping change in realities, even in the rules through which reality is composed — again, both in historical terms and in the terms of narrative production, which are closely integrated — so that, as I have already suggested, the establishment of a modernist novel's temporal and chronological framework *involves and implies a project of historical periodization at one and the same time.* Such epistemological reorderings are especially clear in the cultural production emerging from, and contributing to, two fatefully related situations, which I briefly point to as emblematic or representative examples of my larger argument about Arab modernism. These two situations are those of the Lebanese and the Palestinians, for the questions of Lebanon and of Palestine have not only become inextricable from one another but have been, all along, fundamentally *Arab* questions that transcend the European-drawn border lines now so carefully policed and regulated by the various Arab states. That is, Lebanon and Palestine are each signs not only of a catastrophic failure to modernize as independent nation-states (along the lines proposed either by the Arab "renaissance" or by the General Syrian Congress) but also of the inability, or unwillingness, of the established Arab states to address these two Arab crises that lie *at the very heart* of the neocolonial problems confronting the Arab world — and even at the historical point of origin of intense European colonial involvement in the region (i.e., the years around the First World War, which I have already discussed), when Lebanon and Palestine were in some sense created anew by being violently torn from the "greater" Syria that that early anticolonial movement, the General Syrian Congress, had seen as the Arabs' only hope of resisting European encroachment. Indeed, the tragic and violent recent histories of Lebanon and Palestine *must* be understood in terms of that early Arab attempt to resist division as well as the subsequent European reterritorializations of Southwest Asia and, more recently still, the Arab-state acceptance of the borders drawn up by the European empires. For these borders, which had never existed previously (or at least not as defining states or nations), suddenly, and almost magically, became the very bases for the creation of the putatively independent Arab states — at the expense, above all, of the Lebanese and Palestinians, whose fates were handed over to the civilizing missions and false promises of the two greatest European empires.

Until the climactic paroxysm of violence that signaled the end of the Lebanese war in 1990, the civilians of Lebanon had seen their state collapse around them, and with it went many of Lebanon's prewar traditions as well as virtually all the meaning-generating structures of society. The war generated its own rules and orders, over which no one seemed to have any control, and, indeed, each new theory of the war saw its predictions and assumptions shattered in the next stage of the fighting. Most unsettling was a situation in which, on the one hand, there were people going to work and trying to lead lives as normal as possible and, on the other hand, there was the on-again, off-again war, which violently intruded every now and then on this normalcy, often with little or no apparent causality. As a result, the people of Lebanon (including, of course, the Palestinians, who had been displaced from Palestine in 1948 and 1967 and from Jordan in 1970) had to try to carry on their daily lives and social interactions while at the same time following each new development in that other reality called *the war* — and, between these two parallel realities, meaning and signification got cut off.

In such a situation, every memory of prewar life called attention to itself as a relic from what seemed to be a different world. At the same time, however, each such memory was faced with annihilation, as the physical or material world to which it corresponded was gradually and inexorably destroyed. What remained, then, as the everyday world of the war, was necessarily fragmented, and any engagement (fictional or nonfictional) with these realities was compelled to adopt new forms, different from the ones typical of prewar cultural production (indeed, the cultural aftermath of the First World War may be familiar to readers in Europe and the United States as a similar experience).[20] For both the fictional and the nonfictional narratives of the war are laid out in confusing and incoherent — schizophrenic — disorder, with incidents or memories from the various protagonists' prewar lives mixing in with other characters' stories, emotions, and thoughts as well as the terrifying flux of the war itself. As the narrator of *Little Mountain* says, sardonically, "Even surprises occurred in an orderly fashion before this war. My dreams were comprehensible. As for now, everything's changed, and even football images have faded from my mind."[21] Thus, Lebanese writers, who have been forced to confront not only the war itself but its *retroactive* schizophrenic dissolution of what turns out to have been merely the *illusion* of prewar stability, have been engaging in the creation of new literary styles and forms, which, like the later novels of Mahfouz, al-Tayyeb Saleh, and others, are radically opposed to the elevated styles and forms of the Nahda and have vastly different concerns and structures of feeling, in which both the war *and what went before it* have been radically reimagined, reconfigured, and understood in new ways that were not possible before the destruction of the war and before the schizophrenic flux of postwar cultural narratives.

I must at least mention in this regard the Palestinian novelist Emile Habibi's *The Secret Life of Said, the Ill-Fated Pessoptimist* (1974), which, like many other Palestinian texts (e.g., those by Ghassan Kanafani, Mahmoud Darwish, and, more recently, the film director Michel Khleifi), ranges through a number of different modes and styles, partly as an exploration of new ways of coming to terms with the dilemmas faced by the Palestinians, and partly as a way of investigating the contradictions of the question of Palestine in new historical configurations. As another example, Khleifi's *Canticle of the Stone* narrates the intifada through interweaving carefully selected documentary footage of the uprising, and especially of the horrific toll in human lives and suffering that the Israeli occupation forces have exacted from it, with the highly stylized dual cinematic narrative of two Palestinian exiles, whose dialogue takes place in classical Arabic and whose motions are rigorously overdramatized as they try to retrieve a lost past and imagine a distant future. One of the effects of the contrast is to highlight the immediacy of the intifada and the occupation as against much of what Khleifi presents (as he did very strongly in *Wedding in Galilee*) as increasingly ossified and out-of-touch classical cultures, values, and styles.

Another Palestinian text that is in some ways more emblematic not only of the question of Palestine but of that question's centrality to the contemporary Arab world is Ghassan Kanafani's *Men in the Sun* (1963). *Men in the Sun* presents conflicting narrations of the story of several Palestinian workers trying to make their way to Kuwait in order to find work there and hence to participate in the promises of instant wealth that oil-rich and independent Kuwait represents. Traveling, of course, without the luxury of passports and visas, the workers find an Iraqi driver who regularly smuggles Palestinians into Kuwait by putting them in the empty tank of his tanker truck for the final stretch over the Iraqi-Kuwaiti frontier. At the border post, the customs officials sufficiently delay the driver that, by the time he returns to his truck and gets over the border, the Palestinians inside have suffocated. The bleak and grimly allegorical ending of *Men in the Sun* anticipates that of *Season of Migration*, and it shares with the other novels that I have been discussing here a rejection of any easy solutions or fantastic alternatives to the present. Indeed, as Mary Layoun has forcefully argued, for Kanafani's novel, "Without the reappropriation and understanding of a collective past that continues to shape a shared present, both of which must be commandeered in the creation of an alternative future, there will be no real future. The future is the unceremonious 'grave' of the final chapter." Thus, Layoun goes on to say, the novel "implicitly pre-dicts or pre-figures the future in its demonstration of the limitations of individual memories and personal dreams that are an impetus for, but alone cannot 'speak' or 'figure,' a future different from the present." [22] In addition to this implicit insistence on the historical significance of collective rather than individual memories and practices, *Men in the Sun* relentlessly returns to the multiple narratives of an uneasy present, which it simultaneously recodes as *historical* narratives superimposed on a map of the frontier between two presently existing Arab states. Kanafani thereby shifts the question of Palestine to a broader question of Arab borders and frontiers (which, from our present perspective, is all the more compelling given what has happened on the particular frontier that he selected for his story as well as the consequences of the Gulf War for the Palestinians in Kuwait and elsewhere) and figuratively generalizes the question of Palestine to a question of Arab statehood and independence, a question that *Men in the Sun* addresses in very bleak terms.

In positioning themselves after a rupture (or, rather, after a series of ruptures that are all related), *Men in the Sun, Season of Migration,* and the other works that I have been gathering here under the loose rubric *Arab modernism* demand entirely new ways of conceptualizing the present.[23] What brings these works together across the boundaries dividing the Arab world — what allows me to configure them as *Arab* rather than merely as Lebanese, Egyptian, or Palestinian — is, indeed, their simultaneous implicit rejection of those boundaries (including the underlying conceptual and political systems that go with them, above all, that of the independent nation-state) and of the teleological formulation of modernity as a perpetually deferred future condition. What such an Arab modernism offers instead of either (Eurocentric) modernization or (Islamic) traditionalism is an insistence on the historical present and on the need to confront problems in and for the present, rather than by the endless invocation of impossible and temporal alternatives ("posts" or "pasts"). Modernity itself is challenged but also redefined as an undesirable present condition rather than as an ambiguous future one. *This,* in other words, *this* is modernity — we're already there, and this is it. The great goals of the early nationalist movements of the so-called Arab renaissance, including the prospect of national economic development in the form of independent states, are implicitly rejected as phantasmatic impossibilities. Arab modernism emerges from the current crisis in the Arab world — the crisis of a modernity apprehended as an immediate present experience rather than as a utopian (or dystopian) future condition. And, in this regard, among others, it bears a certain resemblance to the modernism that emerged in Europe during the crisis of modernity and revolution there, particularly following the First World War. This is *by no means* to suggest that Arab modernism simply recapitulates an earlier European modernism; but there are certain similarities between these two politicocultural tendencies that suggest the existence of continuities as much as discontinuities between these radically different experiences of modernity as a crisis, continuities mediated through the violent dialogic process of imperialism itself (although, in this case, insofar as the various European modernisms were, as Raymond Williams has argued, constructed along a certain metropolitan/imperial axis and, hence, to a certain extent, narrated the projects of European imperialism, Arab modernism needs to be understood in part as a counternarrative of those same projects as well as their aftereffects).[24]

As I have already indicated, however, the crisis of modernity in the Arab world is the product partly of the Arab experience of colonialism in the nineteenth century and the early twentieth but also of the neocolonial conditions that exist in — and, indeed, help define — the Arab world today. Hence, the Arab confrontation with Israel and with the neocolonial policies of the West has supplanted the older (and related, although distinct) confrontation with nineteenth-century colonialism as one of the catalysts for the contemporary cultural and political crisis. And, if the advocates of a European-defined modernization in the Arab world stressed the importance of the nation-state as the fundamental unit of such modernization, Arab modernism challenges the finality and the desirability of that unit.

Here, once again, the question of Palestine plays a central role, for the Palestinian cause has been one of the most important factors in the consolidation of popular aspirations toward Arab unity, both in terms of the confrontation with Israel and in terms of the broader confrontation with Europe and the United States. And it is not coincidental that these popular aspirations (which have also been voiced by various intellectuals) have repeatedly challenged not only the borders separating Arab states from each other but also the institutions of those states themselves.[25] Indeed, a great deal of contemporary Arabic literary or critical production has as its major concern not only the broad and global *neocolonial* relations of power that I have already mentioned but also the specifically *colonial* situation that lies at the heart of the question of Palestine (namely, the continued Israeli occupation and/or colonization of the West Bank, Gaza Strip, east Jerusalem, southern Lebanon, and the Golan Heights). At the same time, the need to resolve the question of Palestine and, hence, to address the colonial and neocolonial networks of power out of which Israel was born and by which it is still sustained (but from which it will ultimately have to disengage itself if it is to be integrated into the region) points toward a further, and perhaps utopian, component of Arab modernism: namely, the need to devise new strategies to address today's crises, strategies that are no longer derived from either the Nahda or the West. Here, too, the question of *Lebanon* assumes great importance, for what the Lebanese crisis and war point to primarily is not so much the inability of the Lebanese people and the Lebanese state to adapt to difficult circumstances, or the artificiality of Lebanon as a nation-state (*all* nation-states and *all* nationalisms are artificial constructions in any case, and Lebanon is no more or less artificial than any other state), or the inability of Lebanon as a nation-state to adapt to its circumstances and to modernize and develop; they point, rather, *to the impossibility of those goals themselves* and to the dangers and contradictions inherent in trying to make nation-states work where *other* units of formation or analysis—including, above all, units that have not yet been invented—might have been, and might still be, more useful.[26] In other words, the histories of Lebanon and of Palestine, both torn away from (a nonexistent, utopian) greater Syria, which was itself torn away from the (nonexistent, utopian) Arab nation, have increasingly forced Arabs to question not only the ability of the various bits and pieces of greater Syria (as formulated by the General Syrian Congress), or even the bits and pieces of the Arab world, to survive and develop as modern nation-states but also the very concept of the nation-state, of nationalism, of development, of modernization itself and to question not only the history of these categories and their relation to the history of colonialism in the region but also their contemporary meanings and possibilities as well as the contemporary neocolonial situation in which the Arabs find themselves today.[27] After all, virtually all the Arab states that exist today were brought into being—as states, as ensembles of state apparatuses—as a result of the clash between Arab aspirations and European colonial policies or, rather, as a result of the victory of the latter over the former some seventy or eighty years ago. The effects of colonialism and of neocolonialism thus live on *in the very shapes of the Arab states themselves* so that, just as there can be no separation of the questions of modernization and the state, there can, in turn, be no separation of the questions of colonialism and the state in the Arab world; and this holds as much for the states that do exist and thrive (notably, the rich little states of the Gulf) as it does for the states that are today faced with grave danger (Egypt, Algeria), as it does for the states that either have had a difficult time coming into being (Lebanon) or have not *yet* come into being (Palestine).

Thus, to confront the question of the state in the Arab world is to confront the question of colonialism itself, and not merely its contemporary revitalizations. This brings me back to what I (briefly) suggest is a powerful utopian impulse in Arab modernism, an impulse that is inseparable from other cultural and political movements and aspirations (especially those at the popular level) in the Arab world today, an impulse that goes by the name *Arab unity*. This impulse develops out of a rejection of the boundaries imposed by, and on, the particular Arab states (including, as I have already mentioned, the conceptual and political systems that are coextensive with them). Such a rejection implies an affirmation of an Arab unity of some sort (i.e., an affirmation of an Arab commonality that underlies the various state forms that would otherwise fragment it), but it specifically suggests a form of Arab unity that defies and transfigures inherited European concepts, including that of nationalism as we have come to understand it today.[28] In other words, it expresses an alternative notion of Arab unity to that proposed by the early Arab nationalists, one that is, indeed, a nonnationalist form of pan-Arabism, which cannot be based on any narrowly defined concept of the nation inherited uncritically from Europe. This utopian impulse, therefore, contests not only the Nahda's teleological narrative of nationalist modernization (which aims at a future condition) but also the pan-Islamicist or traditionalist narratives of the various so-called fundamentalist movements (which, to a considerable extent, rely on claims of a past, prenationalist, unity based on Islam).[29] Moreover, this secular utopian impulse relies on language instead of religion as a unifying factor among Arabs; and it is, above all, in this particular regard that it may be taken as a nonnationalist impulse because, in certain of its forms (and I am thinking here of various experiments with language in narrative and dialogue, as in Munif's *Cities of Salt* and Khoury's *Little Ghandi*, both of which make use of local or regional dialect in addition to standard written classical Arabic), it linguistically produces what are *simultaneously* and fluidly local and pan-Arab identities (very much in opposition to traditional forms of Arab nationalism, which, based on the opposition of local and pan-Arab, stressed the latter over the former in an attempt to produce a static Arab subject).[30] Even if Arabic is not unique among the world's languages in this respect, it enables to a very great extent the *linguistic* production in narrative of *multiple and simultaneous* identities produced in, and figured through, language itself (i.e., language of class, district, city, locality, region, and pan-Arab). If this impulse does represent a number of experiments with new forms of pan-Arab identity, then it does so in a way that allows for the production of an interlinked or layered series of identities rather than a stiff or dualistic opposition between local identity and a pan-Arabism that claims to override difference in the construction of a unitary and illusory Arab subject, as some properly nationalist versions of pan-Arabism have attempted to do in the name of a greater national unity, all of which have failed in large part precisely because of the illusory nature of the subject whose construction they (episte-mologically and ideologically) relied on. Once again, in other words, this is no longer an expression of nationalism or a production of a national subject—and certainly not as we have come to understand these terms today—but rather the imagination—at moments, the utopian imagination—of a number of new forms of pan-Arabism and of pan-Arab identities that are based on, rather than defined against, the complex dynamics of the contemporary Arab world and are hence much more politically ambitious and epistemologically fluid and related to a range of new literary, historical, and political strategies that are developing in the Arab world.

In order to transcend the Nahda, such strategies (and, here, I am try-ing to point to modes of thought that are still coming into being and hence are difficult to pin down) must also transcend the conceptual categories and units of thought that nineteenth-century movement articulated and, to some extent, helped bring into being. Clearly, the very notion not merely of narrowly con-ceived nationalism but especially of national economic development—which may have made sense or seemed possible, even as a distant goal or objective, at the historical moment of the Nahda itself—looks increasingly doubtful and less feasible in the current configuration of global capitalism. For the nation-state has *already* been outstripped or outmoded as the unit of contemporary economic development, a kind of development that is today articulated either on a much smaller scale than that of the state or through the transient and un-stable transnational flows and movements of commodity chains and of capital itself, movements and flows that no longer offer the necessity, or even the pos-sibility, of a more equitable distribution of wealth and resources (if they ever did) and that, precisely because they can no longer be tapped into at the scale or level of the nation-state, certainly no longer allow for development on a national scale anywhere in the world, let alone in areas of the world that were formerly considered underdeveloped.[31] What this implies, of course, is that the old goals or projects of national economic development and modernization are no longer possible as such, or at least not in the terms in which they were originally pro-posed. And, hence, the great drive to modernize into the status or the level of the modern—that is, to move along the great stream of evolutionary time toward the bountiful waterfalls of modernity—must now be seen as a failure, not be-cause the goal at the end of the river could not be reached, but because the river of time itself never existed as anything other than a lure, a conceptual analogue to the notion of unilinear and universal history itself, which promised to its be-lievers salvation and fulfillment at the end of the day, or at the end of time.

Certain proclamations to the contrary, of course, neither time nor his-tory have come to an end. The collapse of modernization does not mean that modernity cannot be achieved but rather that what modernity was originally defined as—a completed state or process, a situation of completed modernization—is no longer conceivable or attainable as such. Indeed, in contesting the very notions of unilinear or universal history, the Arab modernism to which I have pointed resituates modernity as a contemporary condition rather than as a future goal; in so doing, it invalidates the possibility of an uncomplicated flow toward the modern (and hence away from tradition) and instead insists on the immanence of modernity in the Arab world today, as a forever incomplete mixture of various scales and stages of development, as a forever incomplete mixture of styles, forms, narratives, and tropes, as a process whose completion implies and involves a continuous lack of completion.[32] At the same time, and for reasons that I have already touched on, this modernism relentlessly draws our attention back both to the region's colonial history and to its troubled status in the neocolonial world of today as well as to the consequences of both colonialism and neocolonialism for cultural production and activity—not to mention political and economic development. This modernism, then, stands in a mutually determining relation to European and American postmodernisms as their simultaneous and necessary counterpart, for, if, as Fredric Jameson has argued, postmodernism appears as the First World cultural logic of late capitalism, then this Arab modernism can be apprehended, in a sense, as one of postmodernism's Third World symbiotic and antagonistic opposites (although to point this out is not by any means to exhaust its significance). Understood in this way, the distinction between modernism and postmodernism ceases to be a question of temporality and of stages of development, for, just as this Arab modernism does not follow in the footsteps of the various European modernisms, it will not follow their transformations into a postmodernism that, in Jameson's terms, arises out of a situation of completed modernization.[33] What we are dealing with here, then, is no longer the evolutionary temporal logic of modernity but, rather, one of the structural limits of capitalist economic development and, indeed, of late capitalism itself. Any theorization of global culture must, therefore, take into account the (contradictory) coexistence of modernity and postmodernity, a coexistence that is nevertheless situated within, and to a certain extent defined by, global postmodernism, a cultural-political system that, as Jameson has argued, itself involves the coexistence of contradictory modes of cultural (and economic) production, the synchronism of the nonsyncronous (to use Ernst Bloch's famous phrase). What this suggests, then, is that arguments over the modern or postmodern status of this or that text are somewhat worse than misleading because texts can be simultaneously modern and postmodern (consider, e.g., Rushdie's *The Satanic Verses,* which may be said to coextensively inhabit at least two antagonistic forms, modern and postmodern, allowing us to theorize its reception in the streets of the modern Third World in one way and its reception in the postmodern literary marketplace of the First World in quite another).

What I am also suggesting here, moreover, is that it is *much* worse than misleading to contrast a First World postmodernism with a Third World post-colonialism, for this theoretically simplistic and politically hazardous opposition can serve only to replicate or to reinscribe the evolutionary logic of modernity and even of the nineteenth-century European sense of historicism that I touched on in the introduction to these pages. In any case, as Ella Shohat and Anne McClintock (among others) have powerfully argued, the term *postcolonialism* is theoretically misleading and politically suspect for other reasons.[34] To Shohat's and McClintock's forceful arguments I would add only one or two minor observations. First, the *postcolonial* has, indeed, come to replace the *Third World*, although it does so specifically by substituting a spurious temporal logic ("after" colonialism) for an admittedly also problematic spatial logic (worlding). This substitution is particularly spurious and politically dangerous, and not only because it has done nothing to correct the limitations of the term *Third World*. For it has also — as I have been arguing — redefined the very same Third World according to the political temporality of modernity itself, merely adding the hint or suggestion that somehow colonialism was all along a Third World problem and of no concern to the First World and that now, while the First World basks in the wonders of a high-tech postmodernity, the Third World is still defined by the dilemmas first encountered in the old European colonialism, from which the First World has escaped any taint, let alone guilt by (historic) association.[35] After all, just as we were all involved in colonialism together, we are now, it seems to me, either all postcolonial, or we are not (and I, for one, find it hard to believe that colonialism is over and done with; in fact, if there was any lesson to be learned from the Gulf War, it was that, even in a neocolonial world, it is still very much possible to witness the full-scale deployment of a properly colonial exercise in power and political-military-economic domination). Thus, what the term *postcolonial* also covers up is the notion that the world is still defined — globally — by the persistence of certain forms of colonialism as well as neocolonial networks of power and domination. As I have already mentioned, what gets effaced in the experience of colonialism is the present and the very possibility of grasping the present, and announcing a "post" is no more historically or politically enabling than resurrecting a "past." The very suggestion, implicit in the term *postcolonial,* that somehow colonialism is over and done with presents severe problems for theoretical analysis and political action.

Granting this, it would seem that the problem facing the Third World — a term that I will use, even guardedly, because it seems to me that it grants certain kinds of political and epistemological possibilities — is to devise entirely new concepts with which to come to terms with a range of cultural, social, economic, and political crises. In this sense, Arab modernism is one configuration, one constellation, within a larger effort throughout the Third World (and indeed the First, as well) to invent new codes of understanding, an effort that some critics and theorists have identified too hastily as one, unified postcolonial endeavor. Frantz Fanon once said, "If we want to turn Africa into a new Europe, and America into a new Europe, then let us leave the destiny of our countries to Europeans. They will know how to do it better than the most gifted among us. But if we want humanity to advance a step further, if we want to bring it up to a different level than that which Europe has shown it, then we must invent and we must make discoveries."[36] I would agree with Fanon, but I would also suggest that the production of such new concepts does not involve further steps along the path of a unilinear history, which implies further deferral, but rather an intervention in this present with which, as Fanon said, "we feel from time to time immeasurably sickened."

Notes

Earlier versions were presented in a lecture delivered at the Département d'Études Anglaises at the Université de Montréal (January 1993) and in a paper presented at the Commonwealth Studies Conference held at Georgia Southern University, April 1993. I am grateful to Cesare Casarino, Richard Dienst, Fredric Jameson, Ronald Abdel-moutaleb Judy, Rebecca Karl, Muhammad Ali Khalidi, Fawzia Afzal-Khan, and Kalpana Seshadri-Crooks for invaluable comments on, and criticisms of, earlier drafts.

1 Al-Tayyeb Saleh, *Mawsim al-hijra ila al-shimal* (Beirut: Dar al-awdah, 1969), 168–69. Translations from the Arabic are mine unless otherwise noted.

2 I have written extensively about this novel elsewhere (see my "The Empire Renarrated: *Season of Migration to the North* and the Reinvention of the Present," *Critical Inquiry* 18, no. 4 [summer 1992]: 804–20, reprinted in *Colonial Discourse and Post-Colonial Theory*, ed. Patrick Williams and Laura Chrisman [New York: Columbia University Press, 1994], 535–50).

3 On progress, see Robert M. Young, *Darwin's Metaphor: Nature's Place in Victorian Culture* (Cambridge: Cambridge University Press, 1988), 164–247; and Robert Richards, *Darwin and the Emergence of Evolutionary Theories of Mind and Behavior* (Chicago: University of Chicago Press, 1989), 243–330.

4 On a new version of colonialism, see my *Romantic Imperialism: Universal Empire and the Culture of Modernity* (Cambridge: Cambridge UP, 1998). I examine the complex transition from older, Enlightenment versions of colonialism to the later and more properly modern colonial and imperial missions and projects.

   See Johannes Fabian, *Time and the Other: How Anthropology Makes Its Object* (New York: Columbia University Press, 1983). The formation of this stream of time owes a great deal to Charles Lyell's work on geology and geological time in the 1820s and 1830s (see Stephen Jay Gould, *Time's Arrow, Time's Cycle: Myth and Metaphor in the Discovery of Geological Time* [Cambridge, Mass.: Harvard University Press, 1987], 99–179).

   Hence, e.g., Jamal al-Din al-Afghani (1839–97) argued that Arabs and Muslims should counteract the drive to modernize by a revitalization of a traditionalism understood as the polar opposite of such modernity, while his student Muhammad Abduh (1849–1905) insisted that modernity and traditionalism lie on the same axis. But, while both Afghani and Abduh were arguing against the perceived need to modernize along European lines, each in turn argues his case along the same dualistic lines (modernity vs. tradition) that form many or even all of the epistemological foundations of modernity itself, conceived as a force or a stream pointing in one direction (while tradition lay in the opposite direction, farther upstream).

5   On al-Afghani, Abduh, and similar writers, see Albert Hourani, *A History of the Arab Peoples* (New York: Warner, 1991), 263–314, and *Arabic Thought in the Liberal Age, 1798–1939* (Cambridge: Cambridge University Press, 1988), 103–92. Here, I believe that it is important to add that the experience of modernity altered Arab perceptions of Arabic tradition so that there were two conceptions of it—one expressed by people such as Abduh, the other expressed by those such as Tahtawi, who regarded tradition as something to move beyond rather than return to. In other words, the very concept of tradition in the Arab world had to be substantially reinvented in the course of its clash with, and opposition to, modernity.

    On the proponents of progress, see Hourani, *Arabic Thought*, 260–340; and George Antonius, *The Arab Awakening: The Story of the Arab National Movement* (Philadelphia: Lippincott, 1939), 79–125.

6   Hourani, *A History of the Arab Peoples*, 343–44.

7   But Egypt had been under British occupation since 1882; the Arab lands to the east had fallen under occupation only during and after the First World War. There was, e.g., an Egyptian nationalist revolt in 1919 whose goals were independence for Egypt alone.

8   The British and the French had been busy even before coming into possession of these Arab territories and had already made agreements with each other (e.g., the secret Sykes-Picot agreement of 1916, in which the British and the French divided the region south of Turkey, east of Iran, north of Arabia, and west of the Mediterranean into zones of control between themselves) and with the infant European Zionist movement (e.g.,) the Balfour Declaration of 1917, in which the British government declared its support for the creation in Palestine of a "national home for the Jewish people") regarding the disposition of Arab lands and peoples following the war. Britain had, in addition to all this, pledged its support for the formation of a unified independent Arab state following the withdrawal of the Ottomans from southwest Asia (in the Sharif Hussein–Henry McMahon correspondence of 1915–16). (See Antonius, *The Arab Awakening*, 164–83, 243–75; and Zeine Zeine, *The Struggle for Arab Independence* [Beirut: Kha-yat's, 1960], 1–24. The text of the Sykes-Picot agreement is reproduced in app. B of *The Arab Awakening*, 428–30. See also Hourani, *A History of the Arab Peoples*, 315–32; and Edward W. Said, *The Question of Palestine* [New York: Times Books, 1979]. The text of the McMahon-Hussein correspondence is reproduced as app. A of *The Arab Awakening*, 413–28.)

9   Hourani, *Arabic Thought*, 293. Hourani refers to the mandatory system set up shortly after the war, when southwest Asia was parceled up into mandates—not coincidentally along the lines devised by the Sykes-Picot agreement—to be controlled indefinitely by the British and the French: the French got Syria (including Lebanon), and the British got Jordan and Palestine.

10   "By its very structure," Fanon once argued, "colonialism is separatist and regionalist. Colonialism does not simply state the existence of tribes; it also reinforces it and separates them" (Frantz Fanon, *The Wretched of the Earth*, trans. Constance Farrington [1961; reprint, New York: Grove, 1991], 94).

11   Lloyd George himself referred to the mandate system as "a substitute for old Imperialism" (quoted in Zeine, *The Struggle for Arab Independence*, 153).

12   Article 3 of the "Resolutions of the General Syrian Congress (Damascus, July 2, 1919)," in Antonius, *The Arab Awakening*, app. G, pp. 440–42.

13   See Samir Makdisi, "Economic Interdependence and National Sovereignty," in *The Arab State*, ed. Giacomo Luciani (Berkeley and Los Angeles: University of California Press, 1990), 319–48. See also Antoine Zahlan, *Technology Transfer and Change in the Arab World* (Oxford: Pergamon, 1978). Capital outflows, particularly toward the United States, have increased tremendously as a result of the Gulf War; consider the recent (1994) Saudi decisions

to award a multibillion-dollar telecommunications contract to AT&T over lower bids from French and Swedish companies and the $6 billion decision to update the fleet of Saudia Airlines with commercial airliners from Boeing and other American companies over competing bids from Europe's Airbus Industrie (which received no orders for its new and highly advanced A330 and A340 aircraft, which compete with Boeing's 747 and 777 and the McDonnell Douglas MD-11, for all of which orders were placed by Saudia).

14   See Giacomo Luciani and George Salameh, *The Politics of Arab Integration* (London: Croom Helm, 1988). Consider how different this picture might have been had there been one Arab economy instead of twenty or thirty competing Arab economies, with the revenues from the oil resources of the little Gulf emirates more evenly and, above all, more *productively* distributed within and throughout the Arab world, instead of being squandered on investments in the North (including a recent $100 million investment in the financially disastrous Euro-Disney park) and on all-too-often cosmetic projects in the Gulf itself!

15   See Abdallah Laroui, *The Crisis of the Arab Intellectual: Traditionalism or Historicism?* trans. Diarmid Cammell (Berkeley: University of California Press, 1977); and Adu-nis, *Al-Thabit wa al-mutahawwil: Sadmat al-hadatha* (Continuity and tranformation: The shock of modernity) (Beirut: Dar al-awdah, 1979), esp. 255–78. This split is still maintained at educational institutions in Southwest Asia; despite an early experiment for using Arabic as the medium of instruction at the American University of Beirut, as Anis Makdisi has pointed out, there took place, relatively quickly, a shift toward using English as the language of instruction for the hard sciences, medicine, engineering, and so on and using Arabic for courses in culture and history (see Anis Makdisi, *Al-itijahat al-adabiyya fi al-alam al-arabi al-hadith* [Literary trends in the modern Arab world] [Beirut: Dar al-ilm li al-malayin, 1988], 370).

16   For an excellent discussion of the late-nineteenth- and early-twentieth-century Arabic literary scene, with an emphasis on Haqqi, see Mary Layoun, *Travels of a Genre: The Modern Novel and Ideology* (Princeton, N.J.: Princeton University Press, 1990), 56–104.

17   Makdisi, *Al-itijahat al-adabiyya*, 371.

18   Here, perhaps inevitably, I find myself torn between a need to present textual evidence of what I mean and a strong wish not to condense rich and complex novels into nuggets centered on plot summaries merely because they are not widely read in the United States. In any case, let me say by way of example, at least, that the works of which I am thinking include the following: Naguib Mahfouz's *Miramar*, Saleh's *Season of Migration*, Ghassan Kanafani's *Men in the Sun*, Elias Khoury's *Little Mountain* and *Little Ghandi*, Abdel-Rahman Munif's *Cities of Salt*, Nawal el-Saadawi's *Woman at Point Zero*, Sahar Khalifa's *Wild Thorns*, Hanan al-Sheikh's *Scent of the Gazelle*, Emile Habiby's *The Secret Life of Said*, and Sherif Hetata's *The Net*. I am aware that grouping together these and other texts in the way that I am doing in this essay may elide certain important differences (in terms of politics, history, form, narrative, class, dialect, and gender, not to mention readership) among them, but an elaboration of their differences, or even further textual elaboration of their similarities, lies outside the scope of this essay; in any case, I would argue that, such discontinuities notwithstanding, it is still possible and, indeed, useful to group them together, if only provisionally, in order to recognize the extent of the continuity of their cultural, political, and historical projects with regard to modernity and the extent of the challenges that they *collectively* pose with regard to the project of the Nahda as well as various proponents of traditionalism.

19   See Samir Amin, "U.S. Militarism in the New World Order," *Polygraph* 5 (1992): 1–35.

20   For attempts to engage these new realities, see not only the fictional work of Elias Khoury but also his essays: *Zaman al-ihtilal* (The time of occupation) (Beirut: Institute for Arab Studies, 1985). And see also Jean Said Makdisi, *Beirut Fragments: A War Memoir* (New

York: Persea, 1990); and Etel Adnan, *Sitt Marie Rose*, trans. Georgina Kleege (Sausalito: Post-Apollo, 1982).

    On the Euro-American response to World War I, see, e.g., Paul Fussel, *The Great War and Modern Memory* (Oxford: Oxford University Press, 1975).

21 Elias Khoury, *Little Mountain*, trans. Maia Tabet (Minneapolis: University of Minnesota Press, 1989), 92.

22 Layoun, *Travels of a Genre*, 204. For a rich, and very thorough, reading of *Men in the Sun* in its multiple historical and political contexts, see the chapter "Deserts of Memory," 175–208.

23 Once again, it is important to bear in mind that what I am referring to tentatively as *Arab modernism* is not a movement as such but rather a *tendency* that includes various significant differences and discontinuities (see n. 18 above).

24 See Raymond Williams, *The Politics of Modernism* (London: Verso, 1989).

25 There is, however, irony here: although the Palestinian revolution is, of course, a struggle for national liberation—a struggle for an independent state—it has also helped inspire the creation of what might be regarded as a nonnationalist Arab unity based on the transcendence of states as they have been hitherto defined and institutionalized. It is too early to try to determine what effects the Gaza/Jericho self-policing agreement reached between Israel and the Palestine Liberation Organization will have in these terms. Many Palestinians and other Arabs regard the agreement as a capitulation. Indeed, it is, I would argue, no coincidence that the PLO has been most effective as a catalyst for promising political change, both with regard to the question of Palestine, when it was operated as a dispersed and fluid revolutionary organization with tremendous popular backing and that it has been at its least effective—in fact, disastrously so—when it has attempted either to seize state power (as in Jordan in 1970) or to assume the form of a quasi state (as in much of Lebanon in the mid- and late 1970s). The Gaza/Jericho self-policing agreement with Israel, whereby the PLO will assume certain overt functions of a state (so far this has been restricted to collecting garbage and deploying a disproportionately large police force in these "autonomous" areas), may thus lead to another catastrophic attempt to compress the politics of Palestine into a modern state form. In other words, it may very well be that the question of Palestine has much more to do with a generalized Arab transfiguration of state forms than with the Palestinian people's struggle for self-determination within the narrow confines of yet another independent Arab state. In this sense, it would hardly be surprising if, the more Gaza and Jericho take on the shape of a state, the more the Palestinians—or at least the relatively few Palestinians living in Gaza and Jericho—feel themselves to be more confined by their so-called independent state (if that is what it turns out to be) than liberated by it. ("The apotheosis of independence," as Fanon taught us in a similar context, "is transformed into the curse of independence, and the colonial power through its immense resources of coercion condemns the young nation to regression. In plain words, the colonial power says: 'Since you want independence, take it and starve'" [Fanon, *The Wretched of the Earth*, 97].)

26 The current situation in Lebanon, the product of what I am tempted to call *Harirism* (in reference to the country's multibillionaire prime minister Rafiq Hariri), signals, I believe, not so much an attempt to reintroduce and reinforce the Lebanese state and its state apparatuses as an attempt to do so in a uniquely self-effacing and arguably postnationalist manner. The reconstruction of the old commercial and cultural center of Beirut, which I take to be the crowning project of Harirism, is particularly interesting in this regard, as it involves the papering over of various political community differences among the Lebanese and the development of a new city center characterized by a newly engineered Lebanese flavor seemingly harking back to the good old days of religious and political tolerance, when Lebanon was not only the most important regional financial center but also the region's entertainment and intellec-

tual center—the Levantine entrepôt par excellence. But this is not in any meaningful sense nationalism or even cultural nationalism; it amounts, instead, to an attempt to mobilize a rhetoric of national development to describe a project that would, in fact, ensure greater local integration into the global (international) economy: integration would then take place not on the scale of the national economy (or in the unit of the nation-state) but in other more fluid forms and at a subnational level. I have written on this topic elsewhere (see my "Letter from Beirut" in *Architecture New York* 5 [March/April 1994]: 56–59, and "Laying Claim to Beirut: Urban Narrative and Spatial Identity in the Age of Solidere," *Critical Inquiry* 23, no. 3 (spring): 661–705.

27 In this sense, the utopian and nonexistent identities of greater Syria and the Arab nation function here not as regulating identities in a Hegelian sense, which is arguably what the existing Arab states and the brand of (Hegelian) nationalism that they represent have become.

28 As Giacomo Luciani and Ghassan Salamé have recently pointed out, the "demise" of pan-Arabism "is recorded time and again, as if some found pleasure in constantly writing its obituary. Yet somehow the ideal and call of the Arab nation refuses to die," so that, "while obituaries are being written, new, intense forms of Arab interaction are emerging" (Giacomo Luciani and Ghassan Salamé, "The Politics of Arab Integration," in *The Arab State*, ed. Giacomo Luciani [Berkeley and Los Angeles: University of California Press, 1990], 394).

29 Such pan-Islamicist claims are themselves arguably nonnationalist in nature (see ibid., 404–7).

30 Here, it is essential to recognize the differences between written, classical Arabic, which is standardized throughout the Arab world, and spoken Arabic, which differs very markedly from one locale or region to another in terms of vocabulary, syntax, and grammar. Such differences are increasingly being worked into literature and cinema by way of, e.g., using local dialect for dialogue and classical Arabic for narration. The first volume of Munif's *Cities of Salt*, in addition, very subtly marks the development of a local dialect into a more standardized modern form. In this sense, in fact, the differences between written and spoken Arabic subvert the usual distinction between modern and traditional since local dialects used to be considered more traditional (backward, isolated, etc.) but are now being used in literature to signify a transcendence of modern standard (written) Arabic.

31 Here, I am referring very broadly to the work of Samir Amin, *Unequal Development* (New York: Monthly Review Press, 1976), and *Imperialism and Unequal Development* (New York: Monthly Review Press, 1977); Ernest Mandel, *Late Capitalism* (London: Verso, 1987); Fredric Jameson, *Postmodernism; or, The Cultural Logic of Late Capitalism* (Durham, N.C.: Duke University Press, 1992); and others.

32 In fact, and virtually as a matter of definition, modernity can never exist in a pure form, for it always implies a certain degree of hybridization, a certain degree of mixture with the pre- or the antimodern. Thus, the true annihilation of the anti- or the premodern would imply nothing less than the end of modernity itself and the development of some new episteme or cultural logic, which Fredric Jameson has identified as the postmodern.

33 See Jameson, *Postmodernism*, 297–418.

34 There is no need to recapitulate here Shohat's and McClintock's very thorough arguments, which stand for themselves. What I am trying to do, however, is elaborate concerns that run parallel to, and complement, theirs. (See Ella Shohat, "Notes on the 'Post-Colonial,'" *Social Text* 10, no. 2 [1992]: 84–98; and Anne McClintock, "The Angel of Progress: Pitfalls of the Term 'Post-Colonialism,'" *Social Text* 10, no. 3 [1992]: 99–113.)

35 In this context, the following account in a recent survey of the global economy in the *Economist* would be amusing for its astonishing historical blindness were it not for the fact that,

today, many of us would accept such (self-inflicted) blindness as the truth: "Before the steam engine and the power loom gave Britain its industrial lead, the countries that we now call the third world dominated world manufacturing output. The admittedly shaky historical statistics suggest that in 1750, the third world (principally China and India) accounted for 73% of world manufacturing output; as late as 1830 its share was still over 60%. . . . By 1913 it had plummeted to just 8%, as *China and India were left far behind by Europe's technological revolution*" (*Economist*, 1 October 1994; my emphasis). Here, in fact, we have a convenient capsule version of the First World's myth about itself—as though the fact that Europeans came to outproduce the Third World could be accounted for by the magical effect of some mysterious (internal) "revolution"! As though imperialism had nothing to do with this strange transformation! As though the European empires did not systematically deindustrialize their Third World victims! As though all these *historical and political* changes could be explained by reference only to the mysteries of the invisible hand of the free market, the doctrine of comparative advantage, and so on and so forth! As though the First World owed nothing— nothing at all—to the Indians, Chinese, Arabs, Filipinos, Africans, and Native Americans that it plundered and marauded for three hundred years before it could begin at last its own takeoff into sustained growth, leaving the rest of us far behind! *In a word, as though the market had by its own mysteries produced this effect so that we must now look to the market— heralded by the IMF and the World Bank—to equally mysteriously solve the problems besetting Ruanda, Haiti, Palestine, India, Bangladesh, Iraq, and Peru.* Thus, in such flashes, has the First World repeatedly tried to absolve itself of any historical guilt or complicity, by reference to some magical power—the market—that allowed its own miraculous development just as it, sadly, unfortunately, and alas! produced the sad underdevelopment of the Third World. Alas! indeed.

36 Fanon, *The Wretched of the Earth*, 315.

Self-Othering: A Postcolonial Discourse
on Cinematic First Contacts

HAMID NAFICY

On 1 February 1979, an Air France jet carrying a grand ayatollah, who had been exiled to Iraq and France for fifteen years, landed at Tehran's Mehrabad Airport. A tumultuous crowd exceeding 1 million people greeted him as he deplaned. The Ayatollah Ruhollah Khomeini's triumphant return to Iran occurred only two weeks after a revolution had driven his opponent, Shah Mohammad Reza Pahlavi, into permanent and terminal exile. The historical irony is that it was the shah who had exiled Khomeini in 1963. With this shift in political power came also a shift in cultural and ideological paradigms. During the revolution, the institutions that had become associated with Pahlavi culture and its putative subservience to a secular, Western-style imperialism — liquor stores, banks, and movie houses — were destroyed in unprecedented manner and numbers. In August 1978, over three hundred spectators were burned to death in an arson fire set in Rex Cinema in the city of Abadan, radicalizing the antishah movement. By the time he was overthrown less than a year later, 180 of the 436 cinemas nationwide had been burned or destroyed for the symbolic value they had acquired.[1] However, it became evident very quickly that the new regime was not opposed to cinema per se. Inching through jubilant and boiling crowds, Khomeini was taken from the airport to his first destination: Zahra's Paradise, the massive main cemetery of the Iranian capital. There, in his first speech after his return, he moved to decouple cinema from the condemned Pahlavi regime. He said: "We are not opposed to cinema, to radio, or to television. . . . The cinema is a modern invention that ought to be used for the sake of educating the people, but as you know, it was used instead to corrupt our youth. It is the misuse of cinema that we are opposed to, a misuse caused by the treacherous policies of our rulers."[2] Less than a year later, he clarified what he meant by *misuse*: "By means of the eyes they corrupted our youths. They showed such and such women on television and thereby corrupted our youth. Their whole objective was to make sure that no active force would remain in the country that could withstand the enemies of Islam."[3]

For a long time, the colonial and neocolonial discourses posited that the colonizers impose their direct and full economic, political, and military dominance over the hapless and helpless colonized, who, as though by mere injection of ideology, are transformed from authentic, sovereign people into alienated, dependent subjects. Khomeini's criticism of Pahlavi-era cinema and television falls within this view. Much of "image studies" scholarship, too, has been informed by such a hypodermic theory that overemphasizes vision, domination, and hailing (in the Althusserian sense). This conception has been and must continue to be problematized, for power relations are rarely unidirectional and unproblematic, involving only hailing. Most often, they are multidirectional and complex, encompassing haggling, slippage, resistance, and accommodations of all sorts. Moreover, not all nations are colonized equally or in the same manner. And some that were not colonized have nevertheless suffered from neocolonial relations and imaginings. With the globalization of capital, colonial and neocolonial relations have given way to the modern imperialist mode of production and influence. This essay examines the effects of cross-cultural cinema spectatorship during the infancy of cinema in a neocolonial situation in Iran.

In such a situation, the knowledge of, influence over, and resistance against the colonizing power are based less on the immediate, direct, coercive colonial experience than on the generally one-way flow of mediations provided by the ideological, consciousness-shaping, and marketing institutions of the emporium — among them, religion, tourism, banking, education, journalism, and the media, entertainment, and mass-merchandising industries. What makes the ideological and mediating work of these institutions and industries unusually slippery and captivating is not only their attractive packaging and alluring messages but also their multinational and transcultural flow across geographic and cultural boundaries. As such, their economic and representational practices are less available to corroboration, attenuation, or contestation by those who are subjected to them than are those practices that involve direct, physical, and local contact (as is the case with colonialism). Their very long-distance, global reach tends to render the neocolonial relations of forces invisible and inevitable, thereby encouraging certain resistive or accomodating practices among the subject people, such as rumormongering, tattling, mimicry, evasiveness, conspiracy thinking, and paranoia.

Overdetermination of Westernization and Cinema

Film has been a powerful agent of neocolonial Westernization in many Third World countries, especially during the first few decades of its existence, when these countries were mainly consumers of Western cinematic imports, not producers of their own indigenous films.[4] In the movie houses, spectators were exposed to narratives that were defining anew the European and American concepts of national and Western identities. If, in the centuries past, the imaginative literature and journalism had been instrumental in constructing — even justifying — the ideas of nation, nationalism, and colonialism, the modern imperialism needed to recruit cinema and other mass media to consolidate and sustain the new, evolving imperial and late modern identities and power relations.[5] Although international travel and tourism preceded Westernization and Westernization itself came to many Third World countries before the advent of cinema, it was on the movie screens that the Third World populations came face to face with the people in the West in their own settings. Through early silent films, they encountered in an immediate manner, unimpeded by language differences, the modern lifestyle, the abundant material possessions, and the technological accomplishments of the West. Lacking a significant local film industry, the Third World people could not narrate their own stories in the new medium — stories in which they could explore, find, and assert their own identities. As a result, they tended to define themselves vis-à-vis the way the West was defining itself and imagining them by means of the new medium. This first-contact self-othering encounter at the dawn of the twentieth century was of paramount psychological and political significance, and its effect on the subjectivity of both the West and the Third World continues to be felt even today.

To examine this encounter, I turn to the introduction of cinema in Iran as an agent of Westernization, limiting myself to the first decade of the century, in which the "constitutional revolution" (1906–11) replaced a despotic monarchy with a parliamentary monarchy. This revolution and the periods immediately preceding and following it were characterized by a confluence of momentous and contradictory social forces. Despite the religious reformists' support of the revolution, the intermingling of these competing forces resulted in a seriously weakened religious establishment. However, although the emergent secularization and Westernization were Western in character, they were not colonization projects engineered by the West or by its local agents. Iran was not colonized, but the bitter rivalry between the two superpowers of the day, czarist Russia and imperial England, who vied with each other either to force or to fascinate it into their own sphere of influence, made for a ripe neocolonial situation. Westernization was not so much imposed or injected from the outside as it became structured in dominance. Much of the new constitution and many of the laws and legislative, judicial, and executive bodies for the parliamentary monarchy were adapted from European models. Likewise, modern education, the telegraph, electric lights, printing, photography, journalism, new literary forms, cinema, and many other technological innovations — some of which predated the revolution — were all imported or adapted from American and European models. In this way, Westernization won over the traditional systems of thought and became overdetermined, that is, dispersed throughout the emerging modern but oppressive apparatuses and ideological institutions.

Self-Othering and Spectatorship

There are several dimensions to constructing oneself as the other, the first of which involves the contact situation itself. Recent studies by anthropologists, historians, literary critics, and filmmakers have focused on the highly charged, shocking, and often dangerous experiences of the first contacts between peoples of different civilizations.[6] The first-contact situations themselves are usually transitory. Their consequences, however, are rarely temporary or shallow, for they tend to define the character of the relationship of the contacting peoples as well as their individual and group identities.

The neocolonial relation between Iran and the West at the turn of the century meant that, in their initial contact with the West and its institutions, Iranians suffered not so much from direct colonial violence or from the kind of excess and access that characterizes conquests and invasions but from what Gayatri Spivak has called *epistemic violence.* This includes the Orientalist production of the East through commerce, literature, travelogue, and photography as well as the overdetermination of Westernization, which brought in foreign laws, values, and human sciences and established the so-called native as "self-consolidating other" of the West.[7] No physical violence need be involved in this othering process, yet there is rupture in that this new episteme will now "mean" (for others) and "know" (for the self) that the self is othered. Specifically, contact with the West brought Iranians face to face with a knowledge so dynamic and superior as to threaten the indigenous ways of knowing. Early European and American movies caused a further epistemic violence by creating what Michael Chanan calls a *crisis of confidence in the eye,* which stemmed from the film's ability to manipulate and distort reality.[8]

However, cinematic self-othering does not stop with epistemic violence and representation crisis; it begins with them. If, as Jacqueline Rose has stated, the unity of the culture and the psychic unity of the subject go hand in hand with the latter a precondition of the former, then self-othering requires that the unity of the subject and the culture both be imperiled.[9] Epistemic violence threatens this unity, and encounter with cinema splits the subject through what Lacan has called *alienating identification.* Psychoanalytically, subject formation is a life-long process, one whose primordial scene may be located in the mirror-phase imprinting that occurs in early childhood. According to Lacan, the prelanguage infant, who experiences his own body as fragmented and uncoordinated and himself as lacking both individuality and subjectivity, recognizes with jubilation his own reflection in the mirror as a unitary and complete ideal image —

that of his primary caretaker, his (m)other.[10] The child's smile at the mirror, however, is based not so much on the recognition of his own image as on the misrecognition of himself as the other. This misrecognition becomes a key moment in self-othering. Because of it, the fusion of self with other (or with the Imaginary) is neither complete nor constant. It is not complete because, simultaneous with identification with the other, there is alienation from the self. It is not constant because the favored unity of the Imaginary is challenged by the child's entry into the Symbolic, that is, language acquisition and socialization. The resulting alienating identification sets into motion a split subjectivity that wavers between unity with (hailing) and differentiation from (haggling) the other. Like fusion, ambivalence becomes a key to knowledge and to identity as human beings will forever after "anticipate their own images in the images of others." [11] This is where the relevance of the mirror phase to cinema becomes evident.

Christian Metz has noted that, "at the cinema, it is always the other who is on the screen." [12] The exposure of Iranians at the turn of the century to Western films can metaphorically be regarded as constituting their first cross-cultural mirror-phase encounter with the other, which must have profoundly affected their sense of self both as individuals and as members of a nation. What were the images that these spectators saw on the screen? Early film programs were silent, a deficiency that was often compensated for by live music or narration provided on site by local exhibitors. Typically, programs contained four types of film.[13] Trick films highlighted cinema's ability to manipulate reality. Actualities, precursors to newsreel, documentary, and ethnographic films, featured news events, daily activities, ordinary scenery, and picturesque "natives" from all over the world.[14] Performance films showcased sports events, dances, magic acts, and other scenes arranged for the camera. Gradually, a fourth category, the so-called primitive narratives, evolved that told a story that was acted out for the camera.

The self-othering theory proposed here uses Lacan's alienating identification paradigm to speculate about the manner in which early Iranian audiences were hailed by and haggled with Western films. Although these films contained scenes from colonized and noncolonized countries, the bulk of them were taken in the West, offering for identification purposes the far richer and superior economic and technological lifestyle of the West. In the same manner that in the mirror stage the infant jubilantly fuses with the specular (m)other, the Third World spectators' first contact with cinema can be assumed to have engendered celebratory identification with the foreigners projected on the screen. As a result, the specular Western other would have been introjected as the ideal and idealized ego—worth imitating, possessing, or becoming. Compared to the self, it would have appeared whole and complete. At this point, the spectators could be said to have been happily "hailed" by cinema.[15]

The dynamics of the paradigm, however, lead us to expect alienating tension on the onset of identification. The introjection of the idealized other as superior coincides with projection of the self as inferior, resulting in constructing the self as the subaltern other of the West — deficient and lacking. Such an othered view of the self must have been encouraged by the racism, ethnocentrism, and caricaturing that characterized much of the early documentary and fiction films involving Third World populations.[16] The ensuing split subjectivity may have encouraged haggling, that is, resisting the othering trajectory by returning to the self in order to confirm the native Symbolic or to contest Westernization.

It must be emphasized that this conception of self-othering as a cross-cultural theory of spectatorship and identity formation is based only on a metaphoric and heuristic interpretation of Lacanian alienating identification theory. The cinema screen is not regarded as a literal mirror, and the Third World spectators (Iranians in this case) are not considered homologous to children. An unproblematic application of the mirror analogy would infantalize the Third World peoples more than they are already by some mainline media and ethnographic documentaries. More important, this formulation of self-othering in some ways reverses the Lacanian model by placing the Symbolic within and the Imaginary outside the self. This means that, while the symbolic is not operative in the infant's encounter with the mirror, it is very much engaged during cinematic spectatorship. Consequently, while the mirror phase occurs in individual, prelanguage infants within the Imaginary, film viewing unfolds in individuals who have already passed through the mirror phase, who experience the film in a public setting. Inside the theater, the socially constructed features of difference such as language, culture, religion, ethnicity, race, class, gender, and nationality are continually invoked, interfering with unproblematic identification with the diegetic characters. Some critics have commented on the similarities in the infant facing the mirror and the spectator viewing the film, both of whom are said to be in a state of relative immobility, passivity, trance — even regression — and overcathexes of vision.[17] By considering the theater as an active social space involving the Symbolic as well as the Imaginary, however, self-othering seriously questions these notions. Indeed, it is this possibility of engaging the extrapsychic forces that turns film viewing from a passive, private process involving the taking up of a subject position that is already carved out by the film (i.e., being hailed by the film) to an active and semipublic process that also involves political, ideological, and social negotiations and contestation to create a new positionality (i.e., haggling).[18] What destabilizes the state of tension in the movie house between self and other, tipping the balance in favor of constructing the self predominantly as the other, is the manner in which self-othering is inscribed and overdetermined socially — by means of Westernization, for example. As will be borne out by the ethnographic and biographical material presented below, from its very inception in 1900, cinema in Iran as a Westernizing agent got caught in a cross-cultural contestation over individual subjectivity and national identity in which opposing social forces each cast cinema as belonging to either the self or the other — to be embraced or to be ejected. In what follows, I explore, first, hailing by means of film and, then, haggling over cinema.

Hailing: Facing the Other

To examine the cinematic self-othering set into motion so long ago, one must rely not only on theory but also on filmic and historical records. Unfortunately, there is a dearth of such records. For nearly three decades, from the earliest Iranian documentary footage in 1900 to the first fiction feature made in 1929, Iranians were consumers of European, Russian, and American films (with the exception of occasional local documentaries). As a result, there are no locally produced fiction films in which the tensions of the initial self-othering can be read.[19] Research into the history of early cinema, too, is uneven and often suspect. For this analysis, I will draw primarily on eyewitness accounts of early spectators.

The first account is that of Muzaffar-ed Din Shah, the fifth shah of the Qajar dynasty, who saw films for the first time when he attended the 1900 World Exposition in Paris, whereupon he wrote the following entry in his diary: "We sat down, and they dimmed the lights. We watched the two apparatuses [magic lantern and film projector]; both are very good novelties. They picture and incarnate most of the sites of the exposition in such a manner that causes utmost astonishment and surprise. We saw many panoramas and the exposition buildings and the way the rain falls and the river Seine flows in the city of Paris, and we ordered Akkasbashi [the court photographer] to purchase all those apparatuses." In another entry, a few weeks later, he wrote,

> At nine o'clock in the evening we went to the hall of celebration, where they show films, moving and incarnated pictures. . . . When we first entered the hall of celebration we were very impressed; it is a truly magnificent place, twice as large as *tekkiyeh-ye dowlat* [the giant passion-play theater in Tehran], and, similar to the *tekkiyeh*, it is round in shape and adorned with cut-crystal ceilings. All around it are two levels of seats covered with red velvet on which people sit. In this hall, they show films. They raised a large screen in the middle of the hall and turned off all the electric lights and projected many films on that giant screen. Among them they showed travelers riding camels in the deserts of Africa and Arabia, which were very interesting to see. We also saw films of the exposition

itself, the moving alley, the river Seine with ships floating on it, people swimming and playing in the water, and many other things that were a pleasure to watch. We ordered Akkasbashi to purchase all kinds of them [both projector and films?] to bring to Tehran so that we could make a few [films] there to show to our own servants. We viewed about thirty films.[20]

The second account comes from Ebrahim Khan Sahhafbashi Tehrani (hereafter called Sahhafbashi), the constitutionalist antique dealer who opened the first commercial cinema in Iran in November 1904. He saw films, perhaps for the first time, in May 1897, just over a year after the first public exhibition ever of moving pictures by the Lumière brothers in Paris. He had attended the Palace Theatre in London, which showed films as well as live entertainment acts. Subsequently, he noted in his travel diary the following: "Another feature was an invention that worked with electric power that shows everything in the same state and with the same speed as the original. For example, it shows the falls [Niagara] in America exactly as it is, or it shows a regiment of soldiers marching or a line of railway cars moving at the same speed as the original. And this is an American invention."[21]

The third account is by the aged writer Mohammad Ali Djamalzadeh (still alive in 1997 at the age of 105), who, in personal correspondence with me from Geneva, reported his first encounter with cinema in November 1904. From his description of the location of the theater, its interior space, and the films he saw, we can deduce with some certainty that he must have attended, at age twelve, Sahhafbashi's short-lived theater in Tehran. This is part of Djamal-zadeh's description of what he saw there:

A *sayyed* [descendant of the prophet Mohammad] wearing a turban on his head was sitting at a table outside the theater, selling tickets for two *qerans*. I knew him, he was from Isfahan, and his name was Saifol Za-kerin. . . . Inside, the hall was sunk in utter darkness . . . [but] the screen was lit and could be seen well. It was the first time I had seen film, and I was overwhelmed with astonishment. It showed a street and a man who was paving it with a large and heavy steamroller. Suddenly, a pedestrian fell under it and was turned into a flat cardboard figure like this [a draw-ing of the flat figure is attached]. Then another person arrived and with his ax lifted the cardboard figure off the ground and stood him up, and he was alive again. . . . When the [film] session was over, I ran home non-stop (our house was far away) and breathlessly told my father and mother about what I had seen. I swore to them that I was telling them the truth, that I had seen the story with my very own eyes. My mother was very surprised, but my father smiled knowingly and tried to comfort me by showing me how it could have been done like a shadow play.

Djamalzadeh provides another tale of his childhood film viewing:

> Another time I viewed film with my father [Sayyed Jamal, the well-known constitutionalist clergyman] in a newly opened modern school called Aqdassiyeh. The principal, who was friends with my father, had invited him and a number of the intellectuals to view a film, and I was taken along. It was a short, educational film that showed a child who did not know proper table manners as he kept sticking his finger in his nose and chewing his food badly. While the film was being shown, Mr. Sa'idol Ulama, the school principal, stood in darkness and told the students in the class how improper it was for a child to stick his finger in his nose.[22]

What do we learn from these eyewitness accounts of the first contact with this Western novelty? Much of them are similar to the tales of spectators from other countries, a dominant theme of which is astonishment. What are the sources of astonishment among Iranians? First, it is the technology and the apparatus of projecting moving images that impressed them. For example, Muzzafar-ed Din Shah calls both film and slide projectors "very good novelties" and describes the process of film screening with some awe. Second is the manner in which film reproduced not only movement but also an exact replica of the original. The shah refers to the film's ability to "incarnate" life, and Sahhafbashi insists on its ability to show things "in the same state and with the same speed as the original." Third is the manner in which daily activities are singled out by framing and invested with meaning and beauty. The shah is struck by the way the rain falls, the river flows, and people play in the water. Djamalzadeh, on the other hand, is astonished, even panicked, by the film's power to manipulate and undermine reality by trick cinematography. Film for him created a crisis of confidence in the eye. It not only astonished and disturbed him by the alien world that it pictured but also shook his belief in the integrity of reality, causing an epistemic violence. That is why he breathlessly took refuge in his home to be comforted by his traditional authority figures. Finally, through its voyeuristic regime of vicarious tourism, film evoked the sense of wonder and curiosity about peoples and customs of other lands. All these responses are natural enough since film historiography has recorded similar accounts from early spectators of cinema elsewhere.[23] But what do we learn from these narratives about the production of othering and hailing by means of cinema?

All the texts cited are from the male elite, that is, a ruling king, a world-traveled antique dealer, the son of a modernist clerical leader (who would become a famous writer). These are in a way representatives of those social strata that, during the 1906–11 constitutional revolution, favored Westernization and cinema, that is, the court, secular constitutionalists, and religious constitutionalists. As the elite of society, they occupied a middle position between the West and the native masses, and, as such, they were implicated both as subjects and as subjectifiers.

What makes their reactions to cinema different from those of Western spectators is the neocolonial context in which film entered the country. That viewing films and contact with the West caused epistemic violence has been noted. The alienating repercussions of hailing may be discerned in the way in which the authors appear to construct themselves as the inferior other of the West at the same time as they seem to consolidate Europe as the ideal master self. The shah is impressed by his viewing experience and overwhelmed by the size and grandeur of the theater, which he notes is twice as large as the Dowlat passion-play theater, the pride of the Qajar court.

Even the shah (one of whose titles at this time was *shadow of God*) appears to have suffered from a degree of inferiority in the face of the Western other, resulting in two immediate responses predicted by the self-othering model. He wants to own his own apparatus because, by possessing the machines of the other, he can become like the other and the possessor of its power. He also wants to impress his subaltern courtiers by showing them astonishing scenes of the other(s). Thus, he will do to them what the West has done to him: held him astonished, in awe, in envy, and constructed as a subaltern. Imitating the other during hailing may trigger empowerment because it connotes the triumph of the other as the basis for forming a new, stable self-identity. This identity may be further validated by the triumph of secularization, Westernization, and modernity over traditional values and institutions. Ironically, empowerment can also be obtained by mimicry if *mimicry* is defined as the subversion and critiquing of that which is being imitated.[24] Although mimicry is a strategy of ambivalence, even resistance, the dynamics of self-othering is such that both imitation and mimicry can turn into their opposites under certain circumstances. Both are part of self-othering's multiplying effect.

That inferiority becomes productive when it is displaced with imitation is also evident in the film of the child with bad table manners. The showing of this silent film is organized to maximize its functioning as a model of propriety and imitation. The principal's live narration supplies the students with clues as to the lessons they should be drawing from the film. Such prompting was perhaps necessary since the table manners that the film depicted were so different from the ones practiced in Iran. The principal's narration may have helped the students read the film *with* the grain, not oppositionally — as they might have been prone to do by, for example, mocking the unruly boy or finding fault with Western upbringing. The idea was to cause imitation of the West among students, not its mimicry or mockery. The gathering of dignitaries at the screening may support this contention. We can speculate that they had been invited to witness an unusual affair (film showing in class), note the new school's modern methods (visual teaching), and validate using film as a moral teacher.[25]

The shah, of course, was not the only one who may have (mis)recognized himself as a self-othered Oriental subject. The secular and some of the religious elite also shared this cognition. Although Sahhafbashi's account of his film viewing is purely descriptive, emphasizing the film's ability to duplicate reality, there are many passages in his travel diary in which he hammers on this theme of the idealization of the West and the inferiority of the Iranians. In England, he writes: "You must see and envy." In the United States, he declares America a "paradise" and offers the following assessment, which demonstrates the deep ambivalence and the injured pride that accompanies self-othering: "How lucky are those who do not know and have not seen anything because they will sleep with ease of mind and will not suffer from envy." Later, while passing through Victoria, Canada, he writes passionately about his revulsion of the self and attraction to the other:

> Today was the Sabbath for these people, and I went to their church. When I thought well, I realized that everything they have, we have its opposite. For example, they have electric lights in their place of worship, and we have oil lamps. Their metal instruments are always clean and shiny; ours are dirty and rusted. They quietly listen in their churches, while we talk and shout in ours. Their preacher talks in a language everyone can understand; ours talks in such a dense Arabic language that he himself cannot understand. They pass the donation plate quietly, and people drop money in it for a certain cause without anyone making a special appeal; we insist on donations for our own personal play and pleasure. They sit on velvet-covered benches; we sleep on dusty wicker mats. They attract people to the church with beautiful and varied songs; we sing only with reluctance. The differences are enormous. The only thing that we do better is washing our anus [a reference to Iranian custom of cleansing with water after defecating rather than using tissue paper, as is the custom in the West].[26]

In these passages, we witness a cultural O.K. Corral, where the self squarely faces its other. Significantly, the location of the face-off is the place of worship, the institution that was perhaps closest to Iranian self-perception prior to the constitutional revolution. In this face-off, Iranian culture is condemned and its Western nemesis embraced. Sahhafbashi's abject hailing appears to be complete.

Sahhafbashi's insistence on the film's ability to duplicate reality is also significant in a postcolonial discussion of cinema. The film's "reality effect" has been one of the enduring topics in film studies. French film critic Andre Bazin spoke about it when he pointed to the film's power to create a "fingerprint," a "mummy," or a "deathmask" of reality.[27] The Frankfurt school critic Siegfried

Kracauer saw in this exact duplication of the physical world the film's ability to "redeem" the reality that had become reified and abstracted by modernity.[28] Sahhafbashi's insistence on exact duplication may well have had something to do with the film's redemptive power to preserve the physical reality or at least its aura (in the Benjaminian sense) — a reality that for Iranians was undergoing deep transformation and fragmentation under Westernization.

Haggling: Returning to the Self

By turn jubilantly and mournfully, proponents of Westernization were hailed by early cinema and by other attributes of Westernization that were becoming socially overdetermined, for in social situations hailing is always accompanied by alienating tensions and haggling. In Iran, haggling energized the desire to want to return to the native symbolic order, especially among traditionalists, who considered Westernization a grave threat to their dominance over ideology, culture, and power. It must be emphasized, however, that, despite all nativistic attempts, return is never to the same, or to a predefined, state of purity. All returns involve acts of reimagination and reconstruction of the same or of the previous. As such, returns are inherently syncretistic and already polluted. Return, thus, remains an unrealizable dream for the realization of which humans will forever strive.

The contestation between Iranian reformists and traditionalists to shape the cultural discourse and to influence the return process becomes evident if the emergence of cinema is contextualized. Muzzafar-ed Din Shah is credited with introducing film to Iran via his official photographer, Akkasbashi, who along with other exhibitors showed films in both the royal palace and the homes of the elite. It is thus that Iranian cinema, unlike American cinema, which began as a mass medium, started as a private elite enterprise. Lest the social overdetermination of cinema appear unproblematic, however, it is necessary to examine the microphysics of the kind of haggling that ensued within a few years when it moved out of the private and into the public arena. The concept of the microphysics of power, as formulated by Michel Foucault, presupposes that power is not univocal, monolithic, or unidirectional. Accordingly, its exercise and effects can be attributed to "dispositions, maneuvers, tactics, techniques, functionings . . . a network of relations, constantly in tension, in activity, rather than a privilege that one might possess." [29] This microphysical study of early cinema shows the multifaceted manner in which film became part of the ad hoc network of dispositions and relations that eventually overdetermined Western-style modernization and cinema in Iran.

On the one hand, the dispersion of procinema tendencies in the reformist strata (secular and religious) worked to structure it in dominance. The background of pioneers of cinema reveals a great diversity (in training, ethnicity, class, national origin, religious beliefs, and politics) as well as similarities (in desire for Westernized reforms). Professionally, the majority of the early cameramen who filmed local scenes or projected films were educated in Russia (e.g., Russi Khan Ivanov) or France (e.g., Akkasbashi, Khan Baba Mo'tazedi); ideologically, most were secular and desired Western-style modernization (e.g., Akkasbashi, Sahhafbashi); ethnically, a number of them were immigrants or of mixed nationality (e.g., Russi Khan Ivanov, Aqayev, and George Esmailiev); and national and religious minorities were also among them, such as Armenians (e.g., Artashes Patmangerian, Avanes Oganians) and Baha'is (e.g., Akkasbashi's father). In terms of political and class affiliation, some of them were attached to the Qajar court through marriage (e.g., Akkasbashi) or sponsorship (e.g., Russi Khan Ivanov).

On the other hand, the overdetermination of cinema in such varied social strata did not ensure its monolithic institutionalization. This is because the factors that favored its overdetermination also injected a measure of tension and haggling into the discourse and practice of cinema. As long as cinema was held within the private circles it was shielded. The moment it went public, however, the full force of these as well as of larger sociopolitical conflicts was unleashed on it, enmeshing it in the "two-cultures" debate and the power play between the religious traditionalists and the secular elite. The former cast cinema as other and the corrupter of traditional values, and the latter regarded it as the other of traditionalism and a mark of progress and technological transformation. In short, the power and the reach of cinema as a self-othering instrument reached beyond the psychic and the private to encompass the social and the public spheres, as well.

Two case studies demonstrate the complexities of these public tensions and social haggling over cinema. The first is the case of the first commercial public cinema established by Ebrahim Khan Sahhafbashi Tehrani. He was a proponent of parliamentary, not despotic, monarchy. During the revolution, he joined one of the secret societies that worked for progressive reforms. In one of the society's meetings, he apparently urged that black clothing be worn to show mourning for "our mother country, [which] is in the throes of death." On another occasion, he is said to have written an anonymous letter delivered to Muzzafar-ed Din Shah in which he threatened the king: "O, you who are wearing the royal crown and holding the royal staff, be fearful of the time when we shall remove the crown and the staff from you." [30] In addition to political reforms, Sahhafbashi imported many stern scientific instruments and consumer products (the X-ray machine, the steam-driven automobile, the phonograph, the Kinetoscope, and the film projector), and, in November 1904, he set up the first public commercial cinema in Tehran on Cheraq Gaz Street. [31] It is in this theater that the twelve-year-old Djamalzadeh saw his first film. Sahhafbashi's opposition to despotic monarchy brought him face to face with the court, and his establishment of a movie house (especially during the holy month of Ramadan, when abstinence from worldly pleasures is the rule) brought him into conflict with traditional Muslim clerics, especially the powerful Shaikh Fazlollah Nuri. However, both the early religious opposition to cinema and the shah's displeasure with Sahhafbashi were complex. Nuri proscribed cinema apparently because he had heard that Sahhafbashi was showing images of women without veils in his theater. But this was perhaps not the whole reason. Nuri seems to have objected to cinema altogether on the ground that it is a "Western agent for penetration into Iranian religious tradition," one that "stupefies" people.[32] This view is corroborated by his general conception of Westernization as a "drug" and a "disease," which he spelled out in his political tracts in 1907. According to him, Western democracy, as imported by means of the new constitution, was either a "sleeping potion" or contagion of a "fatal, killer disease."[33] He seems to have grasped the significance of Westernization and of cinema by proxy as alienating agents that can challenge the authority of the tradition and the near monopoly of the clerics to shape the minds of Iranians. It would be congruent with such a position for Nuri to attempt a "cure" by withholding the drug or by eradicating the source of the disease, which in the case of cinema meant its prohibition.

Apparently taking a cue from the powerful Muslim leader, the court moved to close down Sahhafbashi's cinema after only one month of operation.[34] The reasons for the court's banning of his cinema were also multifaceted. It is possible that Muzzafar-ed Din Shah wanted to put Sahhafbashi out of the film exhibition business because of his antiroyal and proconstitution activities. It is equally possible that, cognizant of the power of the clerical establishment, the shah did not want to alienate it further by supporting a Western novelty when not only his own rule but also that of the two-centuries-old Qajar dynasty was threatened. In the case of Sahhafbashi, the two forces that had opposed each other in the constitutional struggles came together against a common threat, cinema. The shah soon died of an illness, and the clerical leader, Nuri, was hanged in a public square in Tehran.

The second case, that of Russi Khan Ivanov's cinema, illustrates the complex manner in which the ethnicity and national origin of filmmakers can challenge cinema's overdetermination. It is said that Russi Khan Ivanov (hereafter called Russi Khan) was born to an English father and a Russian mother and that he was an ardent royalist, supporting Mohammad Ali Shah (Muzzafar-ed Din Shah's successor), who opposed parliamentary monarchy and bombed the parliament building.[35] In 1908, Russi Khan's Farus Cinema apparently became an arena for political struggle. One night, the proconstitution Mojahedin and another night the Proshah Russian Cossak Brigade seized the theater at gunpoint to view films. This state of tension finally caused Russi Khan to close his theater. When the Mojahedin finally defeated Mohammad Ali Shah in 1909, the public ransacked Russi Khan's photographic shop and destroyed his films and equipment.[36] This action foreshadowed the revolutionary destruction of cinemas some seventy years later when Khomeini came to power.

The reasons for the public's outrage against Russi Khan are not fully known, but the following points provide relevant circumstantial evidence to support the idea that it was his ethnicity, national origin, and politics that caused the outrage, not his establishment of movie houses. Russi Khan was an émigré with roots in both foreign powers that dominated Iranian politics; as a result, he was not fully trusted by the constitutionalists. Indeed, it appears that he was an anticonstitutionalist. He was closely linked to Mohammad Ali Shah's court and, in fact, accompanied the deposed monarch into exile in France. Moreover, he was on friendly terms with Colonel Liakhoff, the commander of the Russian Cossack brigade, who on a number of occasions saved Russi Khan from punishment by the local police. Finally, it is said that, during private screenings in his theater, he permitted the Russian and English diplomats to engage in prohibited acts, such as drinking alcohol.[37]

Even foreign Christian missionaries were part of the microphysical dispositions and relations that contributed to the overdetermination of Westernization and cinema. The first public noncommercial cinema in Iran, Soleil, was set up in 1900 by Catholic missionaries in the city of Tabriz.[38] There is no information as to what they showed in this cinema. During the constitutional revolution period, American Presbyterian missionaries frequently showed magic lantern slides to villagers in northeast Iran as part of their evangelical itinerancy. These hand-colored slides illustrating the life of Jesus Christ and other biblical stories were accompanied by live music and narration, apparently leaving powerful impressions on the villagers, who had never seen such shows. One missionary, Loretta C. Van Hook, reports that, on one mission in 1905 that took her to the village of Khoi, "certainly more than a thousand" villagers attended her eight or nine slide presentations, which they watched with fascination:

> I gave a number of stereopticon exhibitions which attracted people by the hundreds. I was surprised to find how much more they cared for the Bible pictures than for the few other pictures I had with me, which I had brought for diversion and to give an idea of the world outside of Persia. At one village we had the screen fastened on the wall of the court[yard] and showed the pictures out of doors. When they were finished not a person moved a muscle to go, although they were sitting on the ground, many of them with nothing under them. I said, "Are you not satisfied?" "No." The khan, one of the masters of the village, replied with emphasis, and so they were all run through again. It was the treat of their lives, while the pictures, appealing to the eye, helped to strengthen the impression of the story told.[39]

In addition to "lantern services," the Presbyterian missionaries, whose telegraphic address printed on their letterhead was "inculcate," integrated into their evangelicalism such innovations as live music, singing lessons, student performances, printed Bibles, illustrated religious tracts, gramophone recordings, and motion pictures.[40] Going through their extensive archives in Philadelphia, one realizes that the impressions that these new narrative technologies strengthened were not just those of the biblical tales. They also inculcated and inscribed the stories of Western domination and superiority over the Orient as well as the story of the encounter experience itself.[41] In short, during this period, while Muslim clerics by and large shunned audiovisual narrative technologies, the Christian missionaries were employing them in their proselytizing and civilizing missions.

The three eyewitness accounts by early film spectators, the case studies of Sahhafbashi's and Russi Khan's movie house experiences, and the reaction of Christian missionaries and Muslim clerics demonstrate that the introduction of cinema into Iran involved engagement in neocolonial, microphysical relations of power, dispositions, maneuvers, tactics, knowledge, and identity that themselves involved several sets of binary opposites, among them self and other, Iran and the West, Muslim clerics and the court, secular modernists and religious traditionalists, and Christians and Muslims. Other factors that considerably complicated these sets of relations were the politics, class affiliation, ethnicity, and national origin of the men who actively participated in the cultural politics and the politics of culture of the country. Women and gender became significant players and issues later on, when indigenous fiction films needed to recruit women as actors.

Notes

I thank the following people who commented on earlier versions of this essay: Teshome H. Gabriel, Afsaneh Najmabadi, Phil Rosen, Kaveh Safa, Michael Walsh, and Esther Yau.

1   Hamid Naficy, "Islamizing Cinema in Iran," in *Iran: Political Culture in the Islamic Republic*, ed. Samih K. Farsoun and Mehrdad Mashayekhi (London: Routledge, 1992).

2   Ruhollah Khomeini, *Islam and Revolution: Writings and Declarations of Imam Khomeini*, trans. Hamid Algar (Berkeley, Calif.: Mizan, 1981), 258.

3   Ruhollah Khomeini, *Seda va sima dar kalam-e emam khomeini* (Tehran: Sorush, 1363/1984), 147.

4   Hamid Naficy, "Recurrent Themes in the Middle Eastern Cinemas of Diaspora," in *The Cinema of Displacement: Middle Eastern Identities in Transition*, ed. Jonathan Friedlander (Los Angeles: UCLA Center for Near Eastern Studies, 1995).

5   See Benedict Anderson, *Imagined Communities: Reflections on the Origin and Spread of Nationalism* (London: Verso, 1983); Eric Hobsbawm, ed., *The Invention of Tradition* (Cambridge: Cambridge University Press, 1983); and Edward Said, *Orientalism* (New York: Vintage, 1979), and *Culture and Imperialism* (New York: Knopf, 1993).

6   For examples of anthropological work, see, e.g., Marshall Sahlins, *Islands of History* (Chicago: University of Chicago Press, 1985); Edward L. Schieffelin, Robert Crittenden, et al., *Like People You See in a Dream: First Contact in Six Papuan Societies* (Stanford, Calif.: Stanford University Press, 1991); and David Tomas, "Transcultural Space," *Visual Anthropology Review* 9, no. 2 (fall 1993): 60–78. For an example of historical work, see Greg Dening, *Islands and Beaches: Discourse on a Silent Land-Marquesas, 1774–1880* (Honolulu: University of Hawaii Press, 1980). For a literary critical example, see Tzvetan Todorov, *The Conquest of America: The Question of the Other*, trans. Richard Howard (New York: Harper and Row, 1982). And, for example of work by filmmakers, see Bob Connolly and Robin Anderson, *Black Harvest*, 16 millimeter, 90 minutes (Australia: Arundel Productions PL, 1992); *First Contact*, 16 millimeters, 60 minutes (Australia: Filmmakers Library, 1983); and *First Contact: New Guinea's Highlanders Encounter the Outside World* (New York: Viking Penguin, 1987).

7   On the Orientalist production of the East, see Edward Said, *Orientalism*. On the overdetermination of Westernization, see Gayatri Chakravorty Spivak, "The Rani of Sirmur," in *Europe and Its Others*, ed. Francis Barker, Peter Hulme, Margaret Iversen, and Diana Loxley (Colchester: University of Essex, 1985), 1:130.

8   See Michael Chanan, *The Dream That Kicks: The Prehistory and Early Years of Cinema in Britain* (London: Routledge and Kegan Paul, 1980).

9   See Jacqueline Rose, *Sexuality in the Field of Vision* (London: Verso, 1986), 142.

10 See Jacques Lacan, *Écrits: A Selection* (New York: Norton, 1977), 128–29, 1–7.

11 Ellie Ragland-Sullivan, *Jacques Lacan and the Philosophy of Psychoanalysis* (Urbana: University of Illinois Press, 1987), 25.

12 Christian Metz, *The Imaginary Signifier: Psychoanalysis and Cinema*, trans. Celia Britton, Annwyl Williams, Ben Brewster, and Alfred Guzzetti (Bloomington: Indiana University Press, 1982), 48.

13 See Thomas Guillaudeau, "Les productions Pathé et Mélièse en 1905–1906 (notes préliminaires)," *Iris* 2, no. 1 (1984): 33–46.

14 This category includes travel films, a genre that formed a high percentage of the early film programs and was popular with audiences interested in exotic sights/sites. On this genre, see Charles Musser, "The Travel Genre in 1903–1904: Moving toward Fictional Narrative," *Iris* 2, no. 1 (1984): 47–60.

15 It is this kind of hailing that would cause an Iranian intellectual in exile, Sayyed Hasan Taqizadeh, to declare in a 1920 exile periodical, *Kaveh*, that "Iran must externally and internally and physically and spiritually become Westernized" (quoted in Nader Entekhabi, "Nasionalism va Tajjadod dar Farhang-e Siasi-ye Ba'd az Mashruttiat" [Nationalism and Modernity in the Political Culture of the Post-Constitutional Revolution], *Iran Nameh* 21, no. 2: 192).

16 For recent analyses of such ethnocentric views of Middle Eastern societies in American films and mass media, see Hamid Naficy, *Iran Media Index* (Westport, Conn.: Greenwood, 1984), and "Mediating the Other: American Pop Culture Representation of Postrevolutionary Iran," in *U.S. Media and the Middle East: Image and Perception*, ed. Yahya R. Kamalipour (Westport, Conn.: Greenwood, 1995). See also Edward W. Said, *Covering Islam: How the Media and the Experts Determine How We See the Rest of the World* (New York: Pantheon, 1981); and Ella Shohat, "Gender and Culture of Empire: Toward a Feminist Ethnography of the Cinema," in *Otherness and the Media: The Ethnography of the Imagined and the Imaged*, ed. Hamid Naficy and Teshome H. Gabriel (Chur: Harwood Academic, 1993), 45–84.

17 See Jean-Louis Baudry, "The Apparatus," in *Apparatus*, ed. Theresa Hak Kyung Cha, trans.

Jean Andrew and Bertrand Auhst (New York: Tanam, 1980); and also Metz, *The Imaginary Signifier.*

18 For an elaboration of cinematic viewing by Third World spectators as an interactive and a socially constituted activity that involves both hailing and haggling, see Hamid Naficy, "Theorizing 'Third World' Film Spectatorship," *Wide Angle,* special issue, 18, no. 4 (October 1996): 3–26.

19 For the history of Iranian cinema, see Mohammad Ali Issari, *Cinema in Iran, 1900–1979* (New York: Metuchen, 1989); Farrokh Gaffary, "Cinema i: History of Cinema in Persia," in *Encyclopedia Iranica,* ed. Ehsan Yarshater (Costa Mesa, Calif.: Mazda, 1991), vol. 5, fasc. 6; and Hamid Naficy, "Iranian Feature Films: A Brief Critical History," *Quarterly Review of Film Studies* 4 (1979): 443–64, "Islamizing Cinema in Iran," in *Iran: Political Culture in the Islamic Republic,* ed. Samih K. Farsoun and Mehrdad Mashayekhi (London: Routledge, 1992), 173–208, and "Iranian Cinema," in *The Oxford History of World Cinema,* ed. Geoffrey Nowell-Smith (London: Oxford University Press, 1996), 672–78.

20 Muzzafar-ed Din Qajar, *Safarnameh-ye Mozaffar-ed Din Shah beh farang beh tahri-re mirza mehdi kashani* (Tehran: Foruzan, 1982), 100–101, 146–47.

For an analysis of the films shown at the 1900 Paris Exposition, see Emmanuelle Toulet, "Cinema at the Universal Exposition, Paris, 1900," *Persistence of Vision,* no. 9 (1991): 10–36.

21 Ebrahim Sahhafbashi Tehrani, *Safarnameh-ye Ebrahim Sahhafbashi-e Tehrani,* ed. Mohammad Moshiri (Tehran: Sherkat-e Mo'alefan va Mottarjeman-e Iran, 1357/1978), 39.

22 Mohammad Ali Djamalzadeh to Hamid Naficy, Geneva, 20 June 1984, 28 January 1987.

23 For eyewitness accounts of early film viewing by Maxim Gorky and Leo Tolstoi, see Jay Leyda, *Kino: A History of the Russian and Soviet Film,* 3d ed. (Princeton, N.J.: Princeton University Press, 1983). For an African account of first film viewing, see Amadou Hampate Ba, "The African Tale of Cinema," *Discourse* 11, no. 2 (spring–summer 1983): 106. For two documentary films about first-contact experiences and their repercussions, involving Papua New Guinean Highlanders and white Australian prospectors, see Connolly and Anderson's films *Black Harvest* and *First Contact* and also their book *First Contact.*

24 See Homi Bhabha, *The Location of Culture* (London: Routledge, 1994); and Hamid Naficy, *The Making of Exile Cultures: Iranian Television in Los Angeles* (Minneapolis: University of Minnesota Press, 1993).

25 This moral and civilizing use of cinema was not unprecedented, secular intellectuals from the mid-nineteenth century on having resorted to Western-style theater and to translations of the works of Molière and Voltaire to teach civilized moral and ethical manners to Iranians. Such a link was perceived to be so direct that, in the first issue of his *Ruznameh-ye Te'atr* (Theater newspaper), dated 5 May 1908, Mirza Reza Khan Tabataba'i Na'ini declared that there are three "principles of progress and civilization": schools, newspapers, and theater (see Mirza Reza Khan Tabataba'i Na'ini, *Ruznameh-ye te'atr,* ed. Mohammad Golbon and Faramarz Talebi [Tehran: Nashr-e Chesmeh, 1366/1987], 20–21). Sahhafbashi, the first commercial film exhibitor in Iran, too, considered moral teaching to be a chief function of theater (*Safarnameh-ye,* 52). It would be natural for him to regard cinema in the same light, as a medium of education.

26 Sahhafbashi, *Safarnameh-ye,* 38, 73, 76, 79–80.

27 See Andre Bazin, *What is Cinema?* trans. Hugh Gray (Los Angeles: University of California Press, 1967), 1:13–15. See also Dudley Andrew, *Andre Bazin* (New York: Oxford University Press, 1978), 79.

28 Siegfried Kracauer, *Theory of Film: The Redemption of Physical Reality* (New York: Oxford University Press, 1960).

29 Michel Foucault, *Discipline and Punish: The Birth of the Prison*, trans. Alan Sheridan (New York: Vintage, 1979), 26.

30 Nezamoleslam Kermani, *Tarikh-e bidari-ye iranian* (Tehran: Boniad-e Farhang-e Iran, 1347/1976), 1:51.

31 Gholam Haidari, *Sinema-ye Iran: Bardasht-e natamam* (Tehran: Chekameh, 1370/1991), 216.

32 Mohammad Tahaminezhad, "Risheh yabi-ye ya's — 2," *Vizheh-ye sinema va te'atr*, nos. 5–6 (1352/1973): 14, 17.

33 Fazlollah Nuri, *Lavayeh-e aqa Shaikh Fazlollah Nuri* (Tehran: Nashr-e Tarikh-e Iran, 1362/1983), 49, 27.

34 Jamal Omid, *Tarikh-e sinemay-e Iran — 1: Paydayesh va bahreh bardari* (Tehran: Faryab, 1363/1984), 51–52.

35 Haidari, *Sinema-ye Iran*, 223.

36 See Gaffary, "Cinema i."

37 See Omid, *Tarikh-e sinemay-e Iran*, 63.

38 Jamshid Malekpur, *Adabiyat-e namayeshi dar Iran: Dowran-e enqelab-e mashruteh* (Tehran: Entesharat-e Tus, 1363/1984), 2:61.

39 Loretta C. Van Hook, "Report of Evangelical Work," Board of Foreign Missions, microfilm reel 274, MF10, F7619, Presbyterian Historical Association, Philadelphia, 1 October 1905–1 October 1906, p. 3.

40 See *Woman's Work for Woman* (New York Woman's Foreign Missionary Societies of the Presbyterian Church) 16, no. 10 (October 1901): 285–86; *Woman's Work for Woman* 19, no. 10 (1904): 229; Mission of the Board of Foreign Missions of the Presbyterian Church in the U.S.A., *A Century of Mission Work in Iran (Persia), 1834–1934* (Beirut: American Press, 1934); and Reverend J. N. Hoare, *Something New in Iran* (London: Church Missionary Society, 1937), 54–55. The Presbyterian Church's *Catalog of Lantern Slides and Motion Pictures* (New York: Central Distribution Department, 1932–33) contains a list of "stereopticon lectures," 16- and 35-millimeter motion pictures, cue sheets, and music that were available for rental by the missionaries. The latter two items were designed to augment the experience of the silent films by providing narration and music.

41 Women played an influential part in the church's civilizing projects, from which they obtained a measure of independence vis-à-vis their own patriarchal systems (Frederick J. Heuser, "Women's Work for Women: Bell Sherwood Hawkes and the East Persia Presbyterian Mission," *American Presbyterians* 65, no. 1 [1987]: 7–17).

The "Post-Colonial" Colony: Time, Space, and Bodies in Palestine/Israel

JOSEPH MASSAD

C*olonial* and *postcolonial* are terms that are generally used to designate a historical trajectory of the beginning and end of the process of colonialism and the ushering in of a new era. A territory that is and a people who are colonized and inhabit a colonial order transform themselves and are transformed into inhabiting a postcolonial order, both spatially and temporally. The diachronic aspect of this process is guaranteed by the logical imperative of the process of colonialism itself: in order to decolonize oneself, one must have been colonized first. Consequently, colonialism's end, it is said, brings about postcolonialism. Aside from ignoring the material relations of colonial and postcolonial rule and rendering these terms limited to the discursive realm, this diachronic presentation of the history of colonialism has ignored the potential, if not the actual synchronicity, of these "two" eras in different contexts. Settler colonialism, being a variant of colonialism, presents us with different spatialities and temporalities as regards a diachronic schema of colonialism, then postcolonialism. The Rhodesian Unilateral Declaration of Independence in 1965, the formation of the Union of South Africa in 1910, the American Revolution in 1776, or the Declaration of the Establishment of the State of Israel in 1948 are some examples where settler-colonists declared themselves independent while maintaining colonial privileges for themselves over the conquered populations. The United States, Rhodesia, South Africa, and Israel, for example, instituted themselves as postcolonial states, territories, and spaces and instituted their political status as independent in order to render their present a postcolonial era. Yet the conquered peoples of these territories continue (including the people of Zimbabwe following independence and South Africa following the end of apartheid) to inhabit these spaces as colonial spaces and to live in eras that are thoroughly colonial.[1]

Given such a situation, how can one determine the coloniality and/or postcoloniality of these spaces or times? The answers to such questions ignore the commonality of these particular spaces and histories. Whereas after May 1948 Ashkenazic Jews would view themselves as living in a postcolonial space and era, Palestinians would view themselves as still living in a colonized space and in a colonial era. Mizrahic Jews would have a more difficult task characterizing the nature of the space and time they inhabit owing to their dual status of being (internally) colonized vis-à-vis the Ashkenazim with colonizer privileges vis-à-vis the Palestinians. The commonality of this space and time, then, at least in its abstract appellation, *Palestine* or *Israel*, renders its status a combinational one. The very naming of this space is, in fact, a process of historicizing it. To call it *Palestine* is to refer to it as a colonized space in both the pre-1948 and the post-1948 periods and to signal its continued appellation as such for a postcolonial period still to come. To call it *Israel* is to refer to it in the post-1948 period after the coming to fruition of the Zionist project forestalled any notion of a post-Israel Palestine.[2] Naming, therefore, functions as locating in history, as temporalizing, and, ultimately, as asserting power as colonial domination or as anticolonial resistance.

The synchronicity of the colonial and the postcolonial (as discursive and material relations) in Palestine/Israel as one era is a situation, however, that exists in reference not only to the different national groups and their relation to this common space and time but also to the same national group. The Zionist movement presented its project of creating a Jewish state through colonization as part of the European colonizing world, while socialist variants of it were presenting the Zionist project as one assisting in combating imperialism and the capitalist world order. Later, the Zionist establishment itself, which had initially presented its project as colonial, was presenting itself as a movement of national liberation, constituting its project as anticolonial in nature, albeit one established through colonization but not colonialism![3] The synchronic presentation of the Zionist project as colonial and anticolonial, coupled with the diachronic process of transforming its explicitly colonial heritage as anticolonial, shows the palimpsestic nature of current Zionist historiography. Moreover, the dual status of Mizrahi Jews as colonizer and colonized renders the national space and time within and during which they live as colonial/postcolonial synchronically. What is, then, this space and time called *Israel*? What constitutes the difficulty in naming it in relation to colonialism? Can one determine the coloniality of Palestine/Israel without noting its postcoloniality for Ashkenazic Jews? Can one determine the postcoloniality of Palestine/Israel without noting its coloniality for Palestinians? Can one determine both or either without noting the simultaneous colonizer/colonized status of Mizrahic Jews? How can all these people inhabit a colonial/postcolonial space in a world that declares itself living in a postcolonial time?[4] This essay will chart the ideological history of the Zionist movement with an emphasis on its epistemological underpinnings and how it was/is conceived by its agents in an attempt to begin to answer the questions outlined above.

Colonial Zionism, Jewish and Gentile

Since its prehistory, Zionism, in both its Jewish and its gentile versions, was incorporated within colonial thought. Non-Jewish Zionism was propagated for the first time within European colonial projects by Napoleon Bonaparte during his Egyptian campaign. By the closing years of the nineteenth century, French and British colonial officials were explicitly advancing the idea of the European Jewish colonization of Palestine as part of the construction of a permanent imperial order in the region. Sharing a colonial project, the interests of European Jewish proponents of Zionism and its gentile advocates converged, leading to collaboration among them.[5] The convergence of interests between Jewish and non-Jewish Zionists was a result of their shared views on anti-Semitism. Like European anti-Semites, Zionism viewed the presence of Jews among gentiles as the main cause for gentile anti-Semitism. Whereas Theodor Herzl had initially considered the option of converting Jews to Christianity as a solution to anti-Semitism, he, and his disciples after him, opted for a second solution, namely, the removal of Jews from gentile societies, that is, from Europe (a solution long advocated by anti-Semitic Christian Zionists). Removing Jews from gentile societies and normalizing them by creating a state for them would be, the Zionists argued, the only way to end anti-Semitism. Thus, Zionism and anti-Semitism had a unified goal — that of the removal of Jews from Europe — that became the basis for their shared imperial vision.

In France, Ernest Laharanne, private secretary of Napoleon III, wrote in 1860 *La nouvelle question d'Orient: Reconstruction de la nationalité Juive.* In his book, Laharanne emphasized the economic gains that could accrue to Europe if European Jews were to settle Palestine. He spoke highly of the Jewish people, who were "to open new highways and byways to European civilization."[6] Such views of Jews as transmitters of European civilization to the uncivilized were also espoused by the father of Jewish Zionism, Theodor Herzl. In his *Der Judenstaat* (which means "The State of the Jews," not "The Jewish State" [which in German is *Der Jüdische Staat*], as it is commonly translated), Herzl saw his proposed state as "the portion of the rampart of Europe against Asia, an outpost of civilization as opposed to barbarism."[7] Laharanne's work also influenced one of the earliest Jewish Zionists, Moses Hess, who used Laharanne's book extensively while writing his *Rome and Jerusalem* in 1862. The collusion with European imperialism was so central to the Zionist project that Hess asks of those unpersuaded of the practicality of Zionist aims: "Do you still doubt that France will help the Jews to found colonies which may extend from Suez to Jerusalem and from the banks of the Jordan to the coast of the Mediterranean?"[8]

On the British front, Lord Palmerston, who became Britain's foreign minister in 1830, was an advocate of Jewish "restoration" to Palestine. The context of Palmerston's Zionism was to provide support to a teetering Ottoman Empire against Muhammad Ali's defiance of the Ottoman sultan. For Palmerston, a Jewish presence in Palestine was a key element in supporting the sultan against "any future evil designs of Mahomet Ali or his successor."[9] British Zionist designs, like their French counterparts, were to coincide later with the rise of Jewish Zionism. Meeting with the kings and leaders of European empires (from the Italian king to the German kaiser, Czarist Russian ministers, the Ottoman sultan, etc.), Herzl finally settled on Britain as the "Archimidean point where the lever can be applied."[10] In his opening address to the Fourth Zionist Congress, taking place in London in 1900, Herzl proclaimed: "From this place the Zionist movement will take a higher and higher flight.... England the great, England the free, England with her eyes on the seven seas, will understand us."[11] In his negotiations with the British, the quid pro quo that Herzl had offered Joseph Chamberlain and Lord Lansdowne, the foreign secretary, in return for British imperial sponsorship of Jewish colonization was that Jews will

> wear England in their hearts if through such a deed it becomes the protective power of the Jewish people. *At one stroke England will get ten million secret but loyal subjects* active in all walks of life all over the world ... As at a signal, all of them will place themselves at the service of the magnanimous nation that brings long-desired help. England will get ten million agents for her greatness and her influence. And the spread of this sort of thing usually spreads from the political to the economic. It is surely no exaggeration to say that a Jew would rather purchase and propagate the products of a country that has rendered the Jewish people a benefaction than those of a country in which the Jews are badly off ... May the English government recognize what value there is in gaining the Jewish people. (emphasis added)[12]

Chamberlain offered the Zionists El Arish in Sinai, which they readily accepted. The project, however, did not materialize, Zionist envoys to the region concluding that settlement there was unpractical, owing to the arid conditions in the area and the lack of water resources. Chamberlain immediately located another possible territory for Jewish colonization, Uganda. He reassured Herzl that, although "it's hot on the coast, ... farther inland the climate becomes excellent, *even for Europeans*" (emphasis added). The offer was to be later rejected at the Sixth Zionist Congress in 1903 in favor of Palestine. The priority of Palestine, however, did not prevent Herzl from asserting that "our base must be in or near Palestine. Later we could also settle in Uganda, for we have masses of people ready to emigrate." Whereas, by 1903, Palestine was the primary candidate for the Jewish settler colony, this was not always the case. Herzl himself spoke of Argentina in his *Der Judenstaat* as a possible location for the Jewish colony. He even pursued other African locations as late as 1903, namely, Mozambique. He had met with the Portuguese ambassador, Count Paraty, requesting of him that he "inquire of his government whether it was willing to give us a Charter for an adequate territory." In a follow-up letter to the ambassador, Herzl explained to him that "the preliminary question to submit to the Minister is the following: Is there a territory *sufficiently habitable and cultivable by Europeans?*" (emphasis added). Other solicited territories included Herzl's request during a meeting with the Italian king for Tripolitania (Libya) as a territory for Jewish colonization. But, as in the case of Uganda, Tripolitania was not intended to be the primary territory for the Jewish state; rather, its function was "de déverser le trop plein de l'immigration juive en Tripolitaine sous les lois et institutions libérales de l'Italie." The king responded with surprise, owing to Herzl's earlier declaration that the Zionist movement did not want to send many Jews to Palestine before ensuring that the country would be theirs. For "our project means investments and improvements, and I don't want them undertaken as long as the country isn't ours." Seeing the parallel with Palestine, the king responded to the Tripolitania proposal by saying "Ma é ancora casa di altri" (but it is also the home of others). Herzl assured the king that "the partition of Turkey is bound to come, Your Majesty." [13]

Herzl's requested territorial concessions for his state of the Jews, it is important to stress, were always located in the colonized world. It was never suggested by Jewish or gentile Zionists that a state for the Jews be located in Europe — in the Pale of Settlement, for example.[14] Such a proposal would never have been considered by the European empires, who would never have agreed to the displacement of gentile Europeans for the purposes of erecting a Jewish state. Similarly, Stalin's Birobidzhan project of an autonomous Jewish region was located in the far reaches of Asia, far, that is, from Soviet Europe. What is interesting, however, is that such a proposal was never entertained by the Zionist movement at any time in its history. This was the result, not of an implicit understanding of the impracticality of a Zionist project that would require displacing white people, but, rather, of an understanding of European race politics that was quite explicit in the minds of Zionist leaders. In the context of his negotiations with Joseph Chamberlain (in which Herzl suggested Cyprus, El Arish, and the Sinai Peninsula as possible territories in the vicinity of Palestine), Theodor Herzl commented in his diaries, "In fact, if I could show him a spot in the English possessions *where there were no white people as yet*, we could talk about that" (emphasis added).[15]

Other Zionist thinkers who preceded and succeeded Herzl had a similar understanding of Zionist goals. Leo Pinsker, an assimilationist who was converted to Zionism by the pogroms of 1881, wrote in his famous 1882 book *Auto-Emancipation* that the "auto-emancipation of the Jewish people as a nation [would take place through] the foundation of a colonial community belonging to the Jews, which is some day to become our inalienable home, our fatherland." He understood that, "of course, the establishment of a Jewish refuge cannot come about without the support of [European] governments."[16] A similar sentiment was expressed by Herzl when, in a conversation with Chamberlain in which Chamberlain wondered whether the Jewish state could survive in the absence of Britain and in the presence of European rivalry over the Ottoman Empire, he stated, "I believe that our chances then would be even better. For we shall be used as small *buffer-state*. We shall get it not from the good will, but from the jealousy of the powers! And once we are at El Arish under the Union Jack, then Palestine too will fall into the British sphere of influence" (emphasis added).[17] Such a sentiment was to be echoed fifteen years later by the British War Office: "The Creation of a buffer Jewish State in Palestine, though this state will be weak in itself, is strategically desirable for Britain."[18]

As the references cited above to Jews as colonists indicate, European Jews and gentiles alike viewed European Jews as Europeans (only) insofar as they were/are undertaking a colonial venture. In his opening address to the First Zionist Congress, Theodor Herzl asserts this self-perception of Jews qua Europeans in stating, "It is more and more to the interest of the civilised nations and of civilisation in general that a cultural station be established on the shortest road to Asia. Palestine is this station and we Jews are the bearers of culture who are ready to give our property and our lives to bring about its creation."[19] Such sentiments were already characteristic of the early directors of Jewish agricultural settlements in Palestine as they were "in the mould of the French *service colonial* and imbued with their share of *la mission civilisartrice.*"[20] Asserting the coloniality of the European Jewish presence in Palestine, Chaim Weizmann stated in 1930, "We wish to spare the Arabs as much as we can of the sufferings which every backward race has gone through on the coming of another, more advanced nation."[21] Even self-styled socialist Zionists like Ber Borochov, who had to deal with the presence of the Palestinian people, advocated solidarity with them while stressing the practical tasks of Jewish colonization, which were being carried out at the Palestinians' expense. Embarrassed by the argument that Zionism oppresses the Palestinians, Borochov responded in 1917 by stating that, thanks to the new working methods, "there will be sufficient land to accommodate both the Jews and the Arabs. *Normal* relations between the Jews and Arabs will and must prevail" (emphasis added).[22]

Anticolonial Zionism: A New Strategy

Beginning in the 1930s, some Zionists were beginning to suggest a change in the ideological vocabulary of their colonial settler project. F. H. Kisch, the chairman of the Zionist Executive, noted in his diary in 1931 that he was "striving to eliminate the word 'colonization' in this connection [Jewish agricultural settlement in Palestine] from our phraseology. The word is not appropriate from our point of view since one does not set up colonies in a homeland but abroad: e.g. German colonies on the Volga or Jewish colonies in the Argentine, while from the point of view of Arab opinion the verb to 'colonize' is associated with imperialism and aggressiveness." [23] This was not only an expression of political shrewdness but also a reflection of the real ambivalence characteristic of Zionist thinking in relation to Palestine. On the one hand, Zionists claimed that Jews were a Semitic people who originated in Palestine, while, on the other hand, they viewed Jews as modern Europeans participating in colonial endeavors.

This trend was consolidated after the Zionists could no longer rely fully on British support. This transformation in Zionist-British relations was a result of the 1939 British-issued white paper restricting Jewish immigration to Palestine, a response to the anticolonial Palestinian Revolt of 1936–39. Many of the British-armed Zionists, whose weapons until then were used against Palestinian resistance to Jewish colonization, were now turning their weapons against their British sponsors. Many anti-British terrorist attacks took place throughout the 1940s, culminating in the assassination of the British high commissioner for the Middle East, Lord Moyne, in 1944. [24] Other terrorist attacks and massacres were to be committed against the Palestinians in the mid- and late 1940s as the date for British withdrawal from the country neared. The 1946 bombing of the King David Hotel by Menachem Begin's Irgun Zvai Leumi, killing a hundred Palestinians, Jews, and Britons; the assassination of the UN envoy Count Bernadotte by Yitzhak Shamir's Lehi; and the savage 1948 massacres of hundreds of Palestinian civilians, including children, at Al-Dawayimah by the mainstream Zionist army, the Haganah, and at Dayr Yasin by Begin's Irgun — all became features of either Zionist anticolonial resistance or the Zionist struggle for independence, depending on the ideological preference. [25]

Following the Zionists' unilateral Declaration of the Establishment of the State of Israel on 14 May 1948, five Arab armies intervened to reverse the establishment of the Jewish settler colony. The Israeli victory in the war that gave the Israelis control over 77 percent of Palestine resulted in the Zionist expulsion of close to 1 million Palestinians and the subsequent destruction of 385 Palestinian villages (of a total of 480). This war became known in Israeli ideological pronouncements as the War of Independence, and the officially named Declaration of the Establishment of the State of Israel was to be renamed in popular discourse (although never officially) the Declaration of Independence.

It must be noted that the declaration did not proclaim Israel a sovereign independent state; rather, it proclaimed it a Jewish state.[26] This was done not as an oversight, but as an explicit rejection of adding the words *sovereign independent* when an amendment to that effect was proposed. Thus, Israel was declared the state of Jews worldwide and not of its citizens (165,000 Palestinians remained in the territories of the state of Israel). Nevertheless, *the Declaration of Independence* and its derivative correlate, *the War of Independence*, became the operative terminology in popular parlance as well as in the ideological discourse of apologist politicians and academics. Independence from whom, however, remains unclear. After all, the British had already left voluntarily without being party to the war. The Arab armies had not been in occupation of any Palestinian land prior to the Zionist declaration. The Palestinian people had no regular army and were being bombarded by the mainstream Zionist forces leading to their expulsion beginning as early as December 1947. From whom, then, were the Zionists declaring their independence?

They could not have declared independence from imperial sponsorship as they had continued to be supported by the European empires, including Britain. Such sponsorship and alliance, it may be recalled, was to lead to the tripartite Israeli, French, and British invasion of Egypt in 1956 and the Israeli occupation of the Sinai Peninsula following Gamal 'Abd al Nasir's nationalization of the Suez Canal. Therefore, renaming the Declaration of the Establishment of the State of Israel the Declaration of Independence had a more important meaning in the ideological, not the practical, realm. Israel's establishment in 1948 followed and coincided with the independence of many formerly colonial territories. Renaming the Declaration of the Establishment of the State of Israel is then to be seen as an attempt to recontextualize the new Zionist territorial entity as one established *against*, not *via*, colonialism. Also, given the waning of the European empires, this renaming was equally an attempt *to rehistoricize the new Zionist era as a postcolonial one.* New arguments had to be amassed for the new line of Zionist apologia.

Although there is no need to rehash here all the Zionist arguments and the anti-Zionist responses, the following is important to point out in this context.[27] Self-styled Zionist socialists and their friends in the West were deploying the ideological weight of the slogan of socialism as a defense against the Zionism-is-colonialism argument. As Maxime Rodinson has argued, however,

> this socialist outlook can neither logically nor sociologically be used as an argument to deny the colonial character of the Yishuv. Those who do use it this way are, whether they are aware of it or not, following the traditional line of thinking in European socialism that the only kind of relations a socialist society can possibly have with other societies are those motivated by the most deeply-rooted altruism. This is ideological jug-

gling of the worst kind. . . . This approach [which followed from a certain interpretation of the young Marx] . . . acquired more or less theoretical shape from Stalinism. The theoreticians of Jewish nationalist socialism paid very little attention to the societies their project threatened to hurt or destroy . . . they naively thought that a renewal of the Jewish community could have only a beneficial effect on these societies and that as a result it was pointless to deal concretely with the question of what relations should be established with them. The analogy with the mental attitude of the French colonizers, imbued with the democratic ideology of the French Revolution, is obvious. It was for their own good that the Algerians and the Tonkinese were subjugated. In this way they would be prepared little by little for the day when later — much later — they would understand the Declaration of the Rights of Man and when, still later, it could be applied to them too.

Responding to the Zionist argument that, unlike colonial conquests, Zionism did not seek to exploit the native population thanks to its doctrine of pure *Avodah Ivrit* (Hebrew labor), Rodinson answers that, "if direct exploitation of the native population occurs frequently in the colonial world, it is not necessarily always a characteristic of it. It was an exception to the rule for the English colonists settling the territory that was to become the United States to have native Indians working for them. The English in the East Indies were not land-owners who exploited peasants, any more than they were in Australia or New Zealand. . . . Are there those who would, as a result, entertain the idea that British expansion into all these territories was not colonial in nature?[28] Moreover, whereas the Zionist ideology of Hebrew labor did not seek to exploit native Palestinians, it had no qualms about importing cheap Arab Jewish labor from Yemen in 1910 (and later the rest of the Middle East and North Africa) since their Jewishness did not compromise the Hebrewness of the ideology.[29]

Many, however, continue to defend the creation (independence, in Zionist speak) of Israel as no different than the independence of India. Isaac Deutscher, for example — one of the most important luminaries among Marxist historians, who had been an anti-Zionist "based on a confidence in the European labour movement, or more broadly in European society and civilization, which that society and civilization have not justified" — decided to abandon his anti-Zionism. In his defense of Israel's raison d'être, he still says, "Even now . . . I am not a Zionist." Not being a Zionist, however, did not prevent Deutscher from asserting that what happened to the Palestinian people as a result of Zionist colonialism cannot "in fairness" be blamed on the Jews. "People pursued by a monster and running to save their lives cannot help injuring those who are in the way and cannot help trampling over their property."[30]

Deutscher, it would seem, never stopped to consider that European Jews could still have fled the monster as refugees without becoming colonists.[31] He never investigated the en route (from Europe to Palestine) transformation of the status of European Jews from refugees to colonists. The Palestinians resisted the European Jewish presence in Palestine on account of their arrival as invading colonists. Had European Jews arrived as refugees, no national threat would have been perceived by the Palestinians, who had accommodated other refugee populations, like the Armenians, before. In another piece that he wrote on Israel's tenth anniversary, Deutscher describes how Israelis are celebrating the creation of their state by "recollect[ing] with intense pride the heroism with which, in the spring of 1948, their men and women took up arms and wrested independence and statehood from the Arabs, the British, and the hesitant and intriguing diplomacies of the Great Powers. . . . The emergence of Israel is indeed . . . a phenomenon unique in its kind, a marvel and a prodigy of history, before which Jew and non-Jew alike stand in awe and amazement, wondering over its significance. This is the stuff of which in earlier epochs the great heroic myths and legends were created, such as the legends of Thermopylae and of the Maccabees."[32] A legend it indeed was in the minds of Zionist leaders. This "heroic" legend was described by Chaim Weizmann, Israel's first president, in the context of the Palestinian anticolonial revolt of 1936–39, as follows: "On one side, the forces of destruction, the forces of the desert, have arisen, and on the other side stand firm the forces of civilization and building. It is the old war of the desert against civilization, but we will not be stopped."[33]

Although Deutscher proceeds to criticize Israel in its conceit over its neighbors, he continues to portray the colonizer and the colonized with a kind of liberal parity uncharacteristic of his Marxist thinking on other issues. In his classic essay "The Non-Jewish Jew," Deutscher concludes by lamenting that, in a world of nation-states, the Jews were forced to establish one. Marxist antinationalist that he is, however, Deutscher views the development of nation-states as a stage in world history and is aware of how the progressive nature of national liberation becomes regressive after liberation takes place:

> Even those young nation-states that have come into being as the result of a necessary and progressive struggle waged by colonial and semi-colonial peoples for emancipation — India, Burma, Ghana, Algeria, and others — cannot preserve their progressive character for long. They form a necessary stage in the history of some peoples; but it is a stage that those peoples too will have to overcome in order to find wider frameworks for their existence. In our epoch any new nation-state, soon after its constitution, begins to be affected by the general decline of this form of political organization; and this is already showing itself in the short experience of India, Ghana, and Israel.[34]

Note that Israel is not compared to South Africa, the United States, Rhodesia, or Australia, lest it be mistaken for a settler colony. It is "appropriately" listed with India and Ghana, which several lines earlier had been identified as countries who "have come into being as a result of a necessary and progressive struggle waged by colonial and semi-colonial peoples for emancipation." Nevertheless, even Deutscher, his ideological acrobatics aside, could not help but refer to Israel's kibbutzniks approvingly as "Israel's Pilgrim Fathers."[35]

Unlike many of Israel's apologists, however, the self-declared non-Zionist Deutscher was to continue his critiques of what he termed *Zionist nationalist conceit*. His mild critiques of 1958 multiplied in the light of the 1967 Arab/Israeli War. It was in that context that he shifted away from liberal notions of parity between the two contending sides. He states,

> On the face of it, the Arab-Israeli conflict is only a clash of two rival nationalisms, each moving within the vicious circle of its self-righteous and inflated ambitions. From the viewpoint of an abstract internationalism nothing would be easier than to dismiss both as equally worthless and reactionary. However, such a view would ignore the social and political realities of the situation. The nationalism of the people in semi-colonial or colonial countries, fighting for their independence, must not be put on at the same moral-political level as the nationalism of conquerors and oppressors. The former has its historic justification and progressive aspect which the latter has not. Clearly Arab nationalism, unlike the Israeli, still belongs to the former category.[36]

The implication is that Israeli nationalism, at some point, had also belonged to the former category. Whereas until the 1960s and 1970s Zionist apologia had to defend its new claim of being anticolonial, by the 1980s it needed only to assert its claim as incontestable fact.

A recent example where Israel is grouped with former colonies and where its colonial settler project is presented as anticolonial is Joel Migdal's *Strong Societies and Weak States*. Migdal, a mainstream political scientist in the U.S. academy, wrote his book as part of the 1980s political science research agenda exploring state-society relations, with an emphasis on the state. His book, which critiques the state-centered approach in studying the Third World, is considered to be one of the seminal contributions to the field in recent years. In discussing the effect of colonialism on the strength and/or weakness of the postcolonial state, Migdal begins with a theoretical framework that he applies to Egypt, Sierra Leone, and Israel. In his narrative, Israel's alleged anticolonial and postcolonial character is stated in a matter-of-fact way, presenting it to be as uncontroversial as the anticolonial and postcolonial character of India. For example, he would casually state that, compared to Sierra Leone, a "far less demure sort of excitement gripped India and Israel upon their independence in 1947 and 1948. . . . Also, mutual admiration was much less the order of the day between the British and their former subjects. Both Israelis and Indians felt they had realized their dreams despite the British, not because of them, and the long bitter struggles were not easily put aside." In describing the events leading to Israel's creation, Migdal, in the tradition of other pro-Israeli apologists, refers to the official Declaration of the Establishment of the State of Israel as the "declaration of independence." Furthermore, in discussing the Zionist movement and its efforts to recruit European Jews to settle in Palestine, Migdal, in a typically colonial fashion, states, "Probably close to 100,000 Jews immigrated to Palestine in those years [by World War I], but more than half left shortly after their arrival in that *desolate Asian outpost*" (emphasis added).[37]

Migdal is proceeding in an Israeli propagandistic tradition that, as we saw earlier, extends back to the 1930s. Unlike earlier pro-Israeli apologists, however, which include among them the conservative American social scientist Seymour Martin Lipset and the left-wing Tunisian Sephardi Jew Albert Memmi, Migdal no longer has to come up, as they did, with arguments to refute the Zionism-is-colonialism claim.[38] That argument, for Migdal, has been settled. He and many in the Israeli and Western academies need only assert that Israel was indeed established through anticolonial struggle for that to become fact.

Zionist speak has become so hegemonic that even scholars from the formerly colonized world who are associated with critiques of colonialism participate in its discourse. Kwame Anthony Appiah's *In My Father's House* is a case in point. In discussing the racialist basis of some strands of African and African American nationalist thought, Appiah compares Pan-Africanism and Zionism:

> The two major uses of race as a basis for moral solidarity that are most familiar both in Africa and in Europe and America are varieties of Pan-Africanism and Zionism. In each case it is presupposed that a "people," Negroes or Jews, has the basis for a shared political life in their being of a single race. There are varieties of each form of "nationalism" that make the basis lie in shared traditions, *but however plausible this may be in the case of Zionism, which has in Judaism, the religion, a realistic candidate for a common and nonracial focus for nationality,* the peoples of Africa have a good deal less culturally in common than is usually assumed. (emphasis added)

Appiah adds, "Judaism — the religion — and the wider body of Jewish practice through which the various communities of the Diaspora have defined themselves allow for a cultural conception of Jewish identity that cannot be made plausible in the case of Pan-Africanism. As evidence of this fact, I would simply cite the way the fifty or so rather disparate African nationalities in our present world seem to have met the nationalist impulses of many Africans, while Zionism has, of necessity, been satisfied by the creation of a single state."[39]

Note the matter-of-fact way in which pan-Africanism, a movement that calls for the unification of Africa and does so as a nationalist anticolonial movement, is rendered similar to Zionism, which calls for the unification of world Jewry in a colonial-settler state in Palestine. Moreover, the fact that West European Jews differed markedly in their cultures and traditions (including religious traditions and practice) from East European Jews (the *Ostjuden*) and that both groups were traditionally, culturally, and religiously different from Asian and African Jews, who also differed among themselves, is not factored into Appiah's analysis. For him, the Jew is the universal European Jew invented by Zionism. Appiah proceeds to voice his concern by noting that the fact that there were "Jewish racialists in the early story of modern Zionism . . . is important in the practical world of politics because a racialized Zionism continues to be one of the threats to the moral stability of Israeli nationalism; as witness the politics of the late Rabbi Meir Kahane."[40] In the tradition of Zionist liberalism, Kahane, who in fact has never advocated a practice against Palestinians that had not already been committed or advocated by the different variants of the Zionist movement and successive Israeli governments, is portrayed by Appiah as an exceptional threat to an as-yet-uncontaminated morality of Israeli nationalism. The racist colonial history of Zionism is thus obliterated by Appiah, whose central concern is the preservation of the alleged morality of Israeli nationalism.

The portrayal of Israel as anticolonial is not limited to political debates and academic polemics but can be found in all realms of Western culture. An illustrative example of this is the political thinking of the actor and pop culture figure Marlon Brando. Brando, a known human rights activist and defender of Native American rights, states, when pressed by a journalist about "what is it the Indians want from the [U.S.] government," "They want nothing more and nothing less than what the Jews have in Israel."[41] Brando's financial support for Begin's Irgun in the 1940s and his continued defense of the European Jewish settler colony were never in contradiction with his championing of Native American rights in the United States.[42] For him, the two cases are the same. In this narrative, it is the Palestinians who are seen as the colonists who have taken over this ancient Jewish land. In an ironic twist of anti-Semitic logic, Brando, like many anti-Jewish racists who believe that Jews control all the governments of the world, believed in 1982 that "Palestinians ran the Middle East."[43] This belief is invoked as the Palestinians and Lebanese were being killed in the thousands under Israeli bombardment throughout the 1970s and early 1980s, leading to the June 1982 second Israeli invasion of Lebanon in four years.

This new line of propaganda portraying Palestinians as the actual colonizers of the Jewish homeland was ratified by the scurrilous *From Time Im-*

memorial by Joan Peters, which argued that the Palestinians had in fact immigrated to Palestine in the mid to late nineteenth century and in the first decades of the twentieth century seeking the better economic climate brought about by Jewish colonization.[44] The book went through at least ten printings as major U.S. Jewish and gentile scholars endorsed it.[45] What is important about these arguments, however, is not whether they are supported by doctored documents to prove them but the *subtext* that makes them credible. The subtext of these arguments is the stuff on which Zionist ideology had relied since its very inception, namely, the Zionist (il)logic that (a) modern European Jews are the direct descendants of the ancient Hebrews; (b) the ancient Hebrews had exclusive rights to Palestine; and (c) European Jews have the right to claim the homeland of their alleged ancestors two thousand years later. It is with these Zionist axioms as subtext that Palestinians become the colonizers of Jewish land and their expulsion becomes nothing but part of the European Jewish anticolonial struggle for the restoration of Palestine to its true inheritors. In this logic, Brando's likening European Jews to Native Americans is treated as an uncontroversial assertion that is never questioned by his interviewer, who himself referred to the Zionist project as the "Jewish struggle for independence."[46] In this regard, Benjamin Beit-Hallahmi asserts that Zionism as a colonialist movement offered the world the most original and unique defense for such an enterprise. The justification in this case was based neither on a civilizing mission nor on commercial interests (although, as we saw earlier, this was also the case). Unlike settlers anywhere else in the world, Zionist settlers claimed that they were not moving to a new country but simply coming home after an extended stay abroad; the apparent natives were actually the real foreigners. Theirs was an act of repatriation.[47] In describing how the Zionists related to Palestine, Edward Said concurs:

> The colonization of Palestine proceeded always as a fact of repetition: The Jews were not supplanting, destroying, breaking up a native society. That society was itself the oddity that had broken the pattern of a sixty-year Jewish sovereignty over Palestine which had lapsed for two millennia. In Jewish hearts, however, Israel had always been there, an actuality difficult for the natives to perceive. Zionism therefore reclaimed, redeemed, repeated, replanted, realized Palestine, and Jewish hegemony over it. Israel was a return to a previous state of affairs, even if the new facts bore a far greater resemblance to the methods and successes of nineteenth-century European colonialism than to some mysterious first-century forebears.[48]

Consequently, it is pre-Israel Palestine that represents a colonial era in Zionist discourse, with Israel being its postcolonial successor.

Having presented a history of the ideological acrobatics of the Zionist project, I explore at this point how this national/colonial project mapped out the bodies of European Jews whom it posited as its agents. Like all nationalist projects, colonial and anticolonial alike, Zionism's own *embodiment* as a project was to take place through a specific figuration of those European Jewish bodies that it recruited. The following section traces this transformation of European Jewish bodies from their diasporic condition to their new Zionist condition as this was/is conceived by Zionism.

Colonizing the Body; or, The Signifying Penis

Zionism, as a movement, did not seek only to transplant Jews into a new territory and usher them into a new period of history through establishing for them a state. Zionism was also going to make available to European Jewry a whole range of economic/physical activity denied it in Europe (especially in the agricultural realm). Hence, the objective of the Zionist movement was not simply to transplant European Jews into a new geographic area but also to transform the very nature of European Jewish society and identity as it had existed in the Diaspora until then. The locus of this transformation was the European Jew's body.

As early as 1903, Max Nordau, one of Herzl's closest associates, wrote his "Jewry of Muscle." Nordau sought a prediasporic model of Jewish male bodies to be emulated by Jewish men for a postdiasporic Jewish body type to emerge. He asserted at the 1901 Zionist Congress in Basle: "We must think of creating a Jewry of muscles." He was later to add, "History is our witness that such a Jewry had once existed. . . . For too long, all too long have we been engaged in the mortification of our own flesh. Or rather, to put is more precisely — others did the killing of our flesh for us. . . . But now, all coercion has become a memory of the past, and at least we are allowed space enough for our bodies to live again. Let us take up our oldest traditions; let us once more become deepchested, sturdy, sharp-eyed men."[49] Bar Kochba, the hero of the last Jewish revolt against the Romans, became the new model for Nordau, who, back in 1898, along with Max Mandelstamm, had established the Bar Kochba gymnastic club in Berlin to promote the physical fitness of Jewish youths.[50] Soon after, similar clubs were established throughout Europe. Nordau concludes his article with the following wish: "May the Jewish gymnastic club flourish and thrive and become an example to be imitated in all the centers of Jewish life!" The transformation of Jewish men from "Schlemiels" into what Paul Breines calls "tough Jews" had just begun.[51]

Unlike his "feminine" predecessor, the new postdiasporic Jewish man would engage in agriculture, war, and athletics. The first two, at least, were areas of activity denied most European Jews at varying times of their residence in Europe. As Breines has explained, "Statelessness, according to Zionism, is the cause of meekness, frailty, passivity, humiliation, pogroms, futile appeals to reason and dialogue — in short, Jewish weakness and gentleness."[52] These views characterizing European Jews as feminine are derived from the then-dominant anti-Semitic discourse that posited Jews as the racial/feminine other.[53] The Masada Jewish man (in reference to the anti-Roman Jewish revolt at Masada in 73 A.D.) thus becomes the Israeli colonist-explorer in touch with the land/nature and is able to defend himself—an image that is ubiquitous in early Israeli films.[54] The Masada Jewish man becomes, in fact, the model for the Mossad agent, the Israeli soldier, the very essence of the militarized and masculine Israeli Sabra, thus realizing Zionist plans of rendering postdiasporic Jews as settler-soldiers.[55]

The rewriting of the Jewish body and of Jewish history by Zionism has infiltrated all Western cultural productions, including films made outside Israel. *Europa Europa* is one such film. Although this film is only one document among many, it is emblematic of how Zionism rewrites Jewish bodies. An analysis of this film helps illustrate Zionism's interpretation of prediasporic Jewish bodies and its plans to transform them.

In her highly acclaimed *Europa Europa*, based on the *Memoirs of Solomon Perel*, the European director Agnieszka Holland tells the true story of a German Jewish boy, Solomon (Solek) Perel, played by Marco Hofschneider, and his tragic life under Nazi rule.[56] The film's focus is the Jewish adolescent's male body. In fact, the film begins and ends with his body. *Europa Europa* opens with Solomon's circumcision, his covenant of the flesh with God, with the camera soon moving to Solomon's nude adolescent body as he is beginning to take a bath. The story is of a German Jewish boy who is caught by the Nazis. Aided by his European features, he pretends to be a German gentile so well that he is accepted as such and is subsequently sent to a Nazi military school for education and training. The entire film revolves around Solomon's (now Josef Peters) success or failure in concealing his circumcised penis from public view. The circumcised penis functions in the film as the only signifying mark of the Jew. Although Nazi genealogies of family histories and physical and anatomical descriptions, including phrenological measurements, are mentioned in the film, they fall by the wayside, giving room to the circumcised penis as the only practical way of identifying Jews. (Solomon was able to circumvent the Nazi inquiry into his parentage by lying and presenting himself to be a gentile German from Grodnok whose papers had been lost, and Nazi facial profiles and phrenological measurements of Solomon concluded that he was an "authentic Aryan.") It would seem that, according to this narrative, Jewish women could not have been identified as Jews by the Nazis had they had Solomon's skill, luck, and, above all, his features.

Since the difference between the ability of European-looking Jews and Semitic-looking Jews to pass as gentiles is never explored in the film (since the nineteenth century, the "blackness" of Jewish skin has been one of the important constructed markers of Jews posited by the scientific racialist discourse of anti-Semitism), the only practical way of identifying Jews, in the film, becomes one of identifying only the males among them by inspecting their penises.[57] Through this construction, the Jew, for Holland and Perel, is always already the male Jew. In fact, an Armenian man accused of being Jewish by the Nazis exposes his uncircumcised penis as proof of his innocence (one wonders what an Albanian or a Bosnian Muslim man, let alone woman, accused of being Jewish would have done in a similar situation). Although the film begins with an anti-Jewish attack by Nazi youth in which Solomon's sister, Bertha, is killed, during the attack, the camera, ignoring Bertha, is too busy following Solek's nude body as he jumps out of the bathroom window covering his penis with his hands. He remains in hiding in a back-alley barrel until the pogrom is over. A gentile neighbor provides him with her brother's Nazi military coat marked by the swastika to cover himself as he makes his way back to the house. In the coat, Solek looks indistinguishable from Aryan Nazis, thus rendering Nazi symbols as a pharmakon—responsible both for marking Jews out, *revealing* them, and for hiding/erasing their identity, *concealing* them, simultaneously. In fact, Nazi symbology is presented as a pharmakon throughout the film. What the narrative of *Europa Europa* enacts is precisely this tension between the two opposite/complementary functions of Nazism as pharmakon. Bertha's death, which is the only Jewish death on the hands of the Nazis that the film portrays close up, remains an unexplained phenomenon since she has none of the explicit Jewish markings allowed by the film. Her only possible marking as a Jew may have been, perhaps, her spatial proximity to Jewish men and/or, as Solek himself affirms, her "jealousy" of him, for "she wanted to be the boy." It would seem that Solek's own self-hatred and identification with the Nazis are unconsciously projected onto his sister.

However, Holland is at pains to show that, despite the fact that Jewish men are marked by the Jewish penis, this does not make them less desirable to German women and men. In fact, Solek's penis is the object of desire of German gentile women as well as of German gentile men. However, Solek's penis, the film asserts, is a heterosexual one. The pleasure that it gave a German Nazi woman, who had seduced the adolescent Solek, is evidence by her orgasmic expression in the darkness of a train car. Of course, the Nazi woman's excitement is over her assumption that it was a Nazi German gentile penis that gave her that pleasure. Her excitement was made even greater when she found out that Solek was born on the same day as the führer, 20 April. Solek's excitement over the loss of his virginity with her drives him to put his head out of the train window and yell with triumphant pleasure, with the wind caressing his hair and his newly acquired manly smile. At the military school, where Solek meets a German gentile civilian woman who adheres to Nazi ideology and hates Jews (a sentiment that landed her a powerful slap from Solek), Solek is scared of sleeping with her lest he be discovered. The young woman's impatience with

Solek's insistent celibacy (for she wanted to bear Aryan babies for the Third Reich), which was exacerbated by his slapping her, pushes her to call him "limp dick" — a castrating comment that distresses him greatly.

Other women, a Polish woman and a Soviet Russian Komsomol leader, also desired the young Solek, as did a homosexual German soldier, who discovers Solek's Jewishness while in hot sexual pursuit of his nude, bathing body. As a result of the discovery, the two become allies and platonic friends until the soldier's death in battle. The film makes clear that, while Solek's penis is available for the penetration of gentile women who desire it (except when self-preservation is at stake), his heterosexual penis is unavailable to other men, although he is flattered by the attention. The bathing motif (which, as we saw earlier, recorded Solek's first direct experience with the Nazis), with its attendant risks of vulnerability to Nazi discovery, would seem to be unconsciously related by Perel to the anti-Semitic image of the dirty Jew. Owing to Solek's identification with the Nazis, his recounting of the bathing scenes indicates, as it were, his obsessive compulsion with bodily cleanliness in order that he not be confused with dirty Jews.

While serving with Nazi soldiers under the guise of his gentile identity, Solek was confused by their kindness to him. He exclaims about what separates him from them: "A simple foreskin?" Like Hellenized Jewish circus fighters who used to undergo surgical procedures to hide their circumcision owing to their sense of shame when fighting in the nude with the Romans, Solek, in his Nazi school, out of terror of being discovered, attempts to push his foreskin by tying it with a thread in a desperate attempt to reverse his circumcision. His attempt fails. In disappointment, Solek despairingly states, "I couldn't escape my own body" — wherein his body is standing in metonymically for the circumcised penis.

Solek had many nightmares at the Nazi school in which he is pursued by the Nazis and is trying to hide from them. In one such dream, Solek's sister, Bertha, pushes him in the closet to hide him from the Nazis. In the closet, Solek finds the führer with both hands on his crotch in an attempt to hide his penis. Bertha tells Solek that the führer is also Jewish. This conflation of identities, in Solek's dream, between himself and the führer, with whom he shares the same birthday, the same closet, and the same circumcised penis, is brought to the fore with their success in passing as Nazis. Solek's ambivalent Jewishness (he tells us earlier how he hated Passover because eating eggs dipped in saltwater made him nauseous) and his ambivalent identification with the Nazis resolves itself in this context, wherein all Nazis, including the führer himself, are, like him, closet Jewish men who pass as Aryans. This fantastic move not only consolidates Solek's political choices in rendering Jews the real Nazis, thus alleviating his sense of guilt about betraying his family and his Jewishness, but also consolidates his newfound Aryan manhood. In fact, Solek is so manly that he excels in his military training at school, coming out first in competitions with his authentic Aryan classmates.

The final act of liberation by the Soviets brings with it the climactic moment of the film. In it, Solek and his long lost brother, the less European-looking (where European is always already gentile) Isaac, whose inability to pass caused him to be confined to one of Hitler's death camps, whip out their penises and urinate in full view of their surroundings (although with their backs to the camera). This scene is to be contrasted with an earlier scene in which Solek was attempting to urinate away from German Nazi soldiers but was almost discovered by them. Liberation from the Nazis has finally allowed the Jew, as man, to whip his circumcised penis out of the closet (this reduction of the horrific experience of European Jews under genocidal Nazi rule is certainly appalling). This staging of the circumcised penis as spectacle is engineered to meet the gentile gaze head-on as an assertion of a recovered Jewish masculinity. The real Solek narrating the story tells us that he moved to Palestine after the war. He states, "When I had boys, I barely hesitated to circumcise them." The film ends with the real Solomon Perel, now an old man, appearing with the caption: "Solomon Perel is now living in Israel."

The shame of the circumcised penis had occupied the thoughts of Max Nordau. In his "Jewry of Muscle," Nordau stresses,

> Our new muscle-Jews have not yet regained the heroism of our forefathers who in large numbers eagerly entered the sport arenas in order to take part in competition and to pit themselves against the highly trained Hellenistic athletes and the powerful Nordic barbarians. But morally, even now the new muscle-Jews surpass their ancestors, for the ancient Jewish circus fighters were ashamed of their Judaism and tried to conceal the sign of the Covenant by means of a surgical operation, . . . while the members of the "Bar Kochba" club loudly and proudly *affirm their national loyalty.* (emphasis added) [58]

The memoirs of Perel on which *Europa Europa* is based are, it must be remembered, written from Perel's new geographic and ideological location, that of Israel and Zionism. His new positionality seems to be quite influential in his reinterpretation of his unique Jewish experience under the Nazis. Like Nordau's muscle Jews, Solomon Perel was able to affirm his national loyalty by urinating in public, thus showing the mark of his Jewishness, his *brit mila* or covenant of the flesh, a mark that, he makes certain, is passed on to his Israeli sons.

Given this Zionist rewriting of the Holocaust experience, it is not surprising that Israel and the Zionist American Jewish establishment welcomed the film, lavishing it with praise and prizes. Agnieszka Holland (born to a Catholic Polish mother and a Jewish Polish father), however, had a harder time in Europe. Claude Lanzman, the director of the Holocaust documentary *Shoah,* called her an "anti-Semite." Lanzman stated: "It's no coincidence if Agnieszka Holland . . . chose this one Jew as the hero of 'Europa Europa' a movie that would make anyone vomit." His conclusion was based not only on *Europa Europa* but also on Holland's previous film, *Korczak*, which tells yet another real story, this time of a Jewish doctor, Janusz Korczak, who struggled in vain to save two hundred Jewish children living in his Warsaw ghetto orphanage. The final scene of the film shows a cattle car crammed with Jewish children heading for a concentration camp. In slow motion, the car uncouples from the train and comes to a stop. The children and Korczak then come out of the car skipping away happily under a flag emblazoned with the Star of David. As they recede, a caption appears on the screen: "Korczak and the children were gassed at Treblinka in 1942." In Israel, the film's final scene was hailed as symbolizing the birth of the Jewish state. In France, Jewish intellectuals condemned it as anti-Semitic since the real children whom it depicted were killed in the Holocaust, a fate quite different from those Jews who survived and colonized Palestine. Holland's response to these charges was simply that these Jewish intellectuals, along with Lanzman, are "viscerally anti-Polish."[59]

Europa Europa, however, is no more guided by anti-Semitic views of European Jews than Zionist thought itself is. The film participates in the discursive construction of Jews as indistinguishable from gentile Europeans except by their circumcised penises, in an attempt to preempt the civilizing mission that European Jews were undertaking in Palestine. Consonant with predominant anti-Semitic and Zionist views, this reduction of European Jews to phallic men who are always already marked by the sign of the covenant is the prerequisite for Holland's presenting of the Jewish penis as the only site/mark of Jewish identity that led Jews to the death camps. Based on this privileging, Holland posits the same Jewish-marked penis as the necessary mark for Jewish liberation. In that, her anti-Semitism is no more horrific than the overall Zionist discursive construction of Jews as responsible for their own victimization owing to their insistence on remaining in the Diaspora with their Jewish markings intact, rather than transforming these Jewish markings into new ones in the context of a colonial-settler nation-state. In line with this denigration of Diaspora Jews qua victims is the popular modern Hebrew term for *sissy,* the word *sabon,* or "soap." The term appeared in the wake of World War II when stories circulated about Jews being made into soap by the Nazis.[60] Like Zionism, Holland presents the solution of the colonial-settler nation-state as the only way to Jewish liberation that can preserve the Jewish-marked penis without fear of annihilation/castration (the two being the same thing in Holland's symbolic order). This is made clear in *Korczak,* where Polish Jews (including assimilating Jewish children who were being taught to speak Polish by Dr. Korczak) were to perish in the death camps, in contrast with Zionist Jews, who, at the beginning of the film, were portrayed as free, evidenced by the products of their agricultural labor — Dr. Korczak's assistant Stefa brought Jewish-grown oranges from her trip to Palestine to demonstrate to non-Zionist Jews, Korczak included, Jewish freedom. In Holland's *Korczak* narrative, unlike non-Zionist Polish Jews, Zionist Jewish colonial settlers, assimilated and unassimilated alike, survived the Holocaust because of the liberating Zionist project.

The image of castrated Jewish manhood was part of the European anti-Semitic arsenal against which Zionism responded by asserting its own cult of Sabra masculinity. The Jew as castrated man represented the terror of castration for anti-Semitic gentile men. According to Freud, the "castration complex is the deepest unconscious root of anti-Semitism; for even in the nursery little [gentile] boys hear that a Jew has something cut off his penis — a piece of his penis they think — and this gives them a right to despise Jews. And there is no stronger unconscious root for the sense of superiority over women . . . and from that standpoint what is common to Jews and women is their relation to the castration complex."[61] Hence, the Jewish penis becomes the site of reinterpretation of Jewish masculinity by Zionism. The only way in which Jewish men can rejoin the world of (gentile) men after the Nazi annihilation, the film suggests, is through a spectacular exposure of their circumcised penises as a visual assertion of phallicity against a discursively and materially castrating order.

The new Israeli Sabra is by Zionist design nothing like the pre-Israel European Jew. "He" and his penis are "normalized" by Zionist achievements (the Jewish penis could be the norm only in an exclusively Jewish nation-state). The Israeli clinical psychologist Benjamin Beit-Hallahmi states that the "Israeli ethos, like the dominant American one, is one of identifying with winners, and showing no feeling for the losers. Never identify with the weak, because you don't want to be like them. . . . So Israelis have two reasons for not identifying with victims: first, victimhood isn't part of their experience; second, it is contrary to the ideal of being tough."[62]

By returning Jewish men's bodies to their prediasporic selves and improving on them through the creation of the Israeli Sabra, Zionism has sought to decolonize European Jewish men's bodies from gentile control, to which these bodies had been subjected since the beginning of the Jewish Diaspora. Different Jewish experiences that contradict Zionist accounts of diasporic experience are quickly rewritten within the Zionist narrative. A major example of such rewriting is Zionism's attempt to reinscribe the death of 200,000 Soviet Jewish soldiers who fell in World War II as having fallen in the struggle for the Jewish state. Israel erected a monument for these soldiers in its central military cemetery in Jerusalem. In commenting about the monument, Tom Segev states that a "memorial to them here, among the graves of Israeli soldiers, seems to appropriate them posthumously into the Israeli army and into the Zionist movement. It proclaims, in a way, that they fell not in defense of the Soviet Union in its war against the Nazis but in defense of the Jewish people and for the establishment of the state of Israel. For this reason, they are worth being remembered among Israel's heroes, on the memorial mountain, alongside the fathers of Zionism and national leaders."[63]

Like its European gentile counterparts, Zionist colonial discourse viewed Palestine as the motherland to which European Jews were returning and a virgin land that the postdiasporic masculinized Jew will deflower and refecundate with postdiasporic Jewish seed.[64] The image of the land as mother is linked inherently to the sexual and reproductive project of colonial-settler nationalism. As Melanie Klein points out:

> In the explorer's unconscious mind, a new territory stands for a new mother. He [sic] is seeking the "promised land"—the "land flowing with milk and honey." . . . The child's early aggression [against its mother] stimulated the drive to restore and to make good, to put back into his [sic] mother the good things he had robbed her of in phantasy, and these wishes to make good merge into the later drive to explore, for by finding new [sic] land the explorer gives something to the world at large and to a number of people in particular. In his pursuit the explorer actually gives expression to both aggression and the drive to reparation. We know that in discovering a new country aggression is made use of in the struggle with the elements, and in overcoming difficulties of all kinds. But sometimes aggression is shown more openly; especially was this so in the former times when ruthless cruelty against native populations was displayed by people who not only explored, but conquered and colonized. . . . The wished-for restoration, however, found full expression in repopulating the country with people of their own nationality.[65]

Like the American Adam, the new Sabra, proud of his covenant, will be the deflowerer and inseminator of this mother/virgin land.[66] (In this vein, note the oranges that resulted from the reproductive union of Zionist settler-soldiers and the mother/virgin land portrayed in Holland's *Korczak*.) When, on returning from Palestine in 1920, a Polish Jew reported that "the bride is beautiful, but she has got a bridegroom already," Golda Meir retorted by saying: "And I thank God every night that the bridegroom was so weak, and the bride could be taken away from him."[67] The fact that, in modern Hebrew, the word *zayin* is the root for both *weapon* and *penis* simply lends more credibility to this Zionist weltanschauung, whose views of Jewish bodies are almost entirely borrowed from anti-Semitism.[68] (It must be noted that Hebrew is not alone in deploying patriarchal and militaristic notions in its vocabulary. This is a tradition that pervades most languages. Note, e.g., the vernacular use in English of a man "shooting his load" to signify ejaculation. This is also consistent with the infamous U.S. Marine training song in which, while grabbing their rifles in one hand and their penises in the other, Marines sing: "This is my rifle, this is my gun, this is for killing, and this is for fun.")[69]

The penis as a sign of liberation is transformed by Zionist atrocities into one of oppression. As in all colonizing and oppressive societies, the penis is used literally and metaphorically as a weapon of oppression. From the colonial conquests of the Americas, in which the rape of Native American women by European conquerors was ubiquitous, to the institution of black women in the United States being raped by their white masters from the time of slavery and beyond, to the U.S. military strategy for its soldiers to rape Vietnamese women by "searching" them with their penises as an anti-Communist weapon, the penis as a colonial instrument is institutionalized in international relations.[70] The coincidence of the Zionist reinterpretation of the diasporic Jewish experience with a postdiasporic Israeli colonial discourse and the fact that the latter is part of European colonial discourse more generally introduce a new dimension to this signifying penis. As part of a universal patriarchal tradition, it would seem that the rape of Palestinian women by Israeli soldiers in 1948 and today's Israeli soldiers' (perhaps Perel's sons are among them) not-so-uncommon practice of exposing their genitalia to Palestinian women on the streets of the *still* Occupied West Bank and Gaza Strip are giving new meaning to Nordau's vision of the affirmation of European Jewish national loyalty in the specular economy of Israel's occupation.[71]

This Zionist penis pride (to borrow Melanie Klein's term) was interestingly shared by none other than Zionism's "father," Theodor Herzl. When in law school, the twenty-year-old Herzl had contracted a veneral disease (possibly gonorrhea). We know of the story through a letter that Herzl had written to a close male friend, Heinrich Kana. In the letter, Herzl tells Kama that he has put the syringe aside and that his next attack of "xxx" will be cured by zinc sulphate. He proceeds to inform Kana how he had commissioned a penis linen sheath from a high-class ladies' fancy goods shop, making up all kinds of lies to the seamstresses to avoid embarrassment:

> Unfortunately, the said sheath is a little too tight for my penis. . . . I can only get him in when he is being quite quiet, like a peaceful trouser-burgher. But that is extremely seldom, for bold German-Austrian as he is . . . he rebels against my sheath regulation. So I got them to make a second underpants pocket for me . . . however, this second apparatus also has its defects. It is true that I can get the [young] candidate for knighthood into the linen shaft, but either he feels himself confined or he is now slipping out—you see what erection dilemma fills my mind—Should I perhaps strip him of the whole hair shirt?—All right, but you must not forget, much dripping liquid flows down. What would the washerwoman think?! Perhaps she would despise me. Should I risk it?[72]

As Peter Lowenberg notes, Herzl's exhibitionist penis pride is manifested through his recounting to his friend "the size of his organ, its erective power, [and] the wide experience of his 'young knight' in the pursuit of women."[73] In identifying his penis as a German-Austrian, Herzl is asserting the masculine characteristics of such a nationality. He could not have identified it/him as Jewish since that would have signified something feminine, or at least effeminate, and certainly not bold. Sharing the predominant anti-Semitic views of the time, which characterized Jewish men as effeminate, Herzl's assimilation of his penis into gentile Austro-Germanness ensures for him that such a fate will not befall him. His apparent fear of discovery by the seamstresses and by the washerwoman, moreover, seems to be an expression of an exhibitionist fantasy projected onto these women.

Exposing the penis, which according to Zionist reading signified Jewish (men's) liberation from the Nazis, now functions as an assertion of Israeli European Jewish power and authority. In Zionist discourse, however, since *all* Jews are conceived as always already survivors of the Holocaust living in an anti-Semitic world, the exhibitionism of Israeli male soldiers remains part and parcel of a Zionist discourse that defines such an action as "liberation." In this vein, the fact that many Israelis refer to the Occupied Territories as "liberated territories" is not incidental. As for Jewish women (Ashkenazim and Mizrahim alike), the Israeli state has relegated their bodies to the important task of national reproduction of new *de*colonized Jewish male bodies.[74]

Zionist plans for Mizrahic Jewish and Palestinian bodies were quite different from those for European Jewish bodies. While the utility or lack of utility of Mizrahic Jewish women's and men's bodies was discussed as early as the first decade of this century with Zionism's attempt to bring to Palestine Yemeni Jews to replace Palestinian workers, the utility and dispensability of Palestinian women's and men's bodies have been constant hallmarks of Zionist thinking throughout. While idealistic concepts, like Avodah Ivrit (Hebrew labor), had kept Palestinian workers out of some kibbutzin and other colonial settlements for a while, Zionism had to rely on their bodies for different periods in its history, including its present. Kibbutzim, however, have kept their ideals — they employ Palestinian workers as cheap labor while denying them membership in the exclusively Jewish (and mostly Ashkenazic) collectives. The reproduction of Palestinian bodies had become such a concern for Israel in the 1960s and 1970s that former Israeli prime minister Golda Meir could not sleep, worrying about how many Palestinians were being conceived or were born every night.[75] In order to feel better about this appalling situation, Meir had to repress the existence of Palestinian bodies. In 1969, she informed the *London Sunday Times,* "It was not as though there was a Palestinian people in Palestine considering itself as a Palestinian people and we came and threw them out and took their country away from them. They did not exist."[76] As for those, like

Moshe Dayan, who still acknowledged the existence of the Palestinians to the Israeli public, they emphasized the new toughness of Jews:

> Let us not today fling accusations at the murderers. Who are we that we should argue against their hatred? For eight years now they sit in their refugee camps in Gaza, and before their very eyes, we turn into our homestead the land and the villages in which they and their forefathers have lived. *We are a generation of settlers, and without the steel helmet and the cannon we cannot plant a tree and build a home.* Let us not shrink back when we see the hatred fermenting and filling the lives of hundreds of thousands of Arabs, who sit all around us. Let us not avert our gaze, so that our hand shall not slip. This is the fate of our generation, the choice of our life — *to be prepared and armed, strong and tough* — or otherwise, the sword will slip from our fist, and our life will be snuffed out. (emphasis added)[77]

Dayan's emphasis on the complementarity of war and agriculture in the context of the Jewish state is important to stress in the light of the initial Zionist goals of making these activities available to postdiasporic Jews. It is these activities that, as Zionism contended in its prestate era, would transform the feeble bodies of Jewish men into tough Sabras.

Naming as Geography

The renaming of Palestine as Israel was part of the spatial reorganization of the people who would inhabit it. It is important to remember here that, in the pre-Zionist period, *Israel* referred to the Jewish people, not to a state (*Bnei Yisrael*, or the "Children of Israel," *Israel* being the name given to Jacob, who fought the angel of God, hence the literal meaning of *Israel* as "the struggler with God"). Israel was how the Jewish God addressed his people. The conflation/collapse of the Jewish people into a Jewish state is by Zionist design an attempt to render the Jewish people nonexistent except in the confines of a Zionist time/space called *the Jewish state.*

Moreover, the renaming of Palestine as Israel by the European Jewish settler colonists was not only of symbolic value; it also involved (and still involves) a geographic overhauling of the entire country. Archaeology became the guiding principle of Israel's transformation of Palestine. The spatial regeneration of the ancient Hebrews' land was to go hand in hand with the transformation of Jewish and Palestinian histories and their rewriting according to Zionist dicta. In a reminder to the younger generation of Israelis, Moshe Dayan explained the process of creating geographic simulacra that informs Israeli state policies: "Jewish villages were built in the place of Arab villages. You don't even know the names of these Arab villages, and I don't blame you, because these geography books no longer exist. Not only do the books not exist, the Arab villages are not there either. Nahalal arose in the place of Mahlul, Gvat in the place of Jibta, Sarid in the place of Haneifa, and Kfar-Yehoshua in the place of Tel-Shaman. There is not one single place built in this country that did not have a former Arab population." [78]

This renaming process was not arbitrary; rather, it was institutionally organized from before Israel was founded. An important part of Zionist institutions in the pre-Israel era was the Jewish National Fund's Place-Names Committee. After 1948, it was replaced by the Israel Place-Names Committee.[79] Both committees suggested and/or approved all the new names given to streets, towns, cities, kibbutzim, moshavim, and other colonial settlements. Zionist renaming continued unabated on Israel's occupation of the West Bank and the Gaza Strip.[80] Whereas the West Bank was renamed (with the prediasporic names) Judea and Samaria, the Land of Israel Movement took it on itself to change the names of the streets in Palestinian East Jerusalem (not to mention Palestinian towns and cities). Expunging the Arabic signs, they renamed the streets with more appropriate names—Suleiman the Magnificent Street, for example, became Paratroop Street.[81]

Nationalist movements' attempt to retrieve the memory of the nation was analogized by Freud to a person's childhood memories: "This is often the way in which childhood memories originate. Quite unlike conscious memories from the time of maturity, they are not fixed at the moment of being experienced and afterwards repeated, but are only elicited at a later age when childhood is already past; in the process they are altered and falsified, and are put in the service of later trends, so that generally speaking they cannot be sharply distinguished from phantasies." Freud proceeds to explain how nations come to write their histories:

> Historical writing, which had begun to keep a continuous record of the present, now also cast a glance back to the past, gathered traditions and legends, interpreted the traces of antiquity that survived in customs and usages, and in this way created a history of the past. It was inevitable that this early history should have been an expression of present beliefs and wishes rather than a true picture of the past; for many things had been dropped from the nation's memory, while others were distorted, and some remains of the past were given the wrong interpretation in order to fit in with contemporary ideas. Moreover people's motive in writing history was not objective curiosity but a desire to influence their contemporaries, to encourage and inspire them, *or to hold a mirror up before them.* (emphasis added) [82]

The importance of this mirror was not missed by Jacques Lacan. Like the child whose fragmented self is unified in an inverted image represented by the child's reflection in the mirror, the reconstructed historical memory of the nation provides such a function. Lacan saw the mirror stage in a child "*as an identification.*"[83] This is exactly how historical memory as mirror *identifies* the nation's subject by unifying its fragmented self. It is through this Zionist identificatory mirror that *Jew* is imaged/imagined (on the basis of a specific figuration of *a* Jewish European experience) as a universal category that assimilates all other Jewish experiences into it as one and the same. It is through this mirror that a Yemeni Jew, a German Jew, a Polish Jew, a Libyan Jew, an Iraqi Jew, an Ethiopian Jew, etc. become the national subjects of the Zionist enterprise.

The very naming of the children of European Jewish immigrants who were born in Palestine *Sabras* is underwritten by Zionism's program of charting a new land-based Jewish identity. *Sabra* is the Arabic word for the native Palestinian cactus fruit or prickly pear (*tsabar* in Hebrew).[84] Zionists adopted it as the name of the new Palestine-born Jews of European parentage after World War I. According to Georges Friedmann, the term originated in the Tel Aviv school of Herzlia, where the immigrant European children did better academically than the Palestine-born children of European-Jewish immigrants. In order to make up for the feelings of inferiority that resulted, they would challenge the star pupils to peel a prickly pear and get to the sweet fruit under its thorny exterior without getting the thorns in their hands — something the Palestine-born Jews were able to do easily.[85] Thus, while having a tough exterior when fighting his enemies, the new Israeli is tender on the inside, especially with his loved ones.[86]

The naming of the new Jew (Beit-Hallahmi refers to the new Jew as the "anti-Jew") *Sabra* is consistent with Zionism's interest in nature and geography.[87] Not only is the new Jew a hard fruit to pick, but *he* also grows in the desert, the product of a new geography. *His* mother is nature and the land of Israel. *His* name is part and parcel of the geographic, historical, and cultural appropriation of Palestine by Zionism. That the very name of the new Jew is Arabic is no more of an inconsistency than the future Israeli cultural theft and appropriation of falafil and hummus (traditional Palestinian and Levantine Arab dishes) as Israeli Jewish dishes or *dabkah* (traditional Palestinian and Levantine Arab line dancing) as Israeli Jewish folk dancing.[88]

As Benjamin Beit-Hallahmi notes, this collective renaming of the children of European Jewish colonial settlers born in Palestine went hand in hand with the actual renaming of all European Jewish colonial settlers and their children individually. European Jewish last names such as Rosenthal, Goldstein, Schwartz, or Shapiro were changed to Galili and Golan (after the Galilee and the Golan Heights), Even (stone), Sella (rock), Sharmir (rock), Peled (steel), and Nir (furrow) to reflect the new relation to nature, political geography, and tough masculinity. Even ancient Jewish last names like Cohen (priest) and Levi (a Levite, member of the priesthood) were on many occasions changed to Keidan (spear) and Lavi (lion). First names were also changed according to the Zionist plan. Beit-Hallahmi asserts that, for the past two thousand years, "there was no Jewish Amos, no Yoram (the names of two Biblical kings who 'did evil in the sight of the Lord'). Only names rejected by the Jewish tradition now became acceptable, as the guiding principle became a rejection of that tradition."[89] In this vein, David Ben-Gurion, who was born in Plonsk in 1886 as David Green, on arriving in Palestine in 1906 found his new name in talmudic reports about the Great Rebellion against the Romans in A.D. 66.

Zionism's revival of Jewish history was in fact a revival of Hebrew geography. Jewish historical memory (Ber Borochov used to refer to Palestine as "the land of memories") was transfigured through Zionist hermeneutic filters into geographic memory. The Zionist celebration of the ancient Hebrew king rather than the Hebrew prophets was not accidental. It is, after all, the Hebrew kings, not the prophets, who conquered land and expanded the territory that Zionism now claims as its own. It is this collapse of Jewish history into Hebrew geography that prefigures Zionism's self-legitimating claims. In fact, some of the reconstructed figures of the ancient Hebrew past have acquired an opposite valuation from that given to them by the diasporic tradition. Bar Kochba (son of star) was actually called Bar Koziba (son of lie) by the pre-Zionist Jewish tradition in reference to his false claim as a messiah and as one who had forsaken God, leading to his defeat. In the Zionist tradition, he is the last Jewish "president" or *nasi'* (as Yigael Yadin, modern Israel's first military chief of staff and leading archaeologist in the 1950s, called him), nay the "last chief of staff of the historical armies of Israel."[90] Here, what is crucial to grasp is not only the shift of emphasis from what diasporic Jewishness and Judaism considered important in the Hebrew past to what modern Zionists excavate as important, but the very active invention of ancient Israel, an Israel that had never existed as such before Zionism's fantastic fabrications.[91]

For Palestine to become "the desert that European Jews would make bloom," the Israelis undertook the destruction of any signifying traces left by the expelled Palestinians, including 385 Palestinian villages of a total of 480.[92] In this regard, Israel Shahak wrote,

> The truth about Arab settlement which used to exist in the area of the State of Israel before 1948, is one of the most guarded secrets of Israeli life. No publication, book or pamphlet gives either [the] number [of Arab villages] or their location. This of course is done on purpose, so that the accepted official myth of 'an empty country' can be taught and accepted in the Israeli schools and told to visitors. . . . This falsification is specially grave in my opinion, as it is accepted almost universally, outside the Middle East, and because the destroyed villages were — in almost all cases — destroyed completely, with their houses, garden-walls,

and even cemeteries and tombstones, so that literally a stone does not remain standing, and visitors are passing and being told that 'it was all desert.' "[93]

To render their vision of Palestine ("a land without people for a people without land") a reality, the Israelis expelled the majority of the Palestinians.[94] As for the history of the Palestinians in Palestine, Zionism undertook its rewriting. As a result, the war between the European Jewish colonists and the colonized Palestinians extended to the realm of cartography and archaeology, with Israeli maps showing all historic Palestine as Israel and Palestinian maps showing all historic Palestine as an occupied country. As for archaeology, the Israelis, who have a monopoly on it, are engaged in a constant search for archeological "proofs" of prediasporic Hebrew settlement in all parts of historic Palestine in order further to authenticate European Jewish claims to Palestinian/Israeli space and time. One Israeli scholar characterizes archeology as a "national sport" for Israelis.[95] On many occasions, the military and archaeologists combine forces for important finds. On the occasion of uncovering letters written by Bar Kochba, the Israeli army's chief of staff called for "an all-out archeological offensive."[96]

Parallel to this geographic transformation of Palestine, juridical efforts were under way to delimit the nature of bodies with access to this newly transformed space. It is these efforts that resulted in the confiscation of the lands of both the expelled and the remaining Palestinians.[97] After the establishment of the Jewish state, Zionism required the exclusivity of Jewish accessibility to what that state encompassed, both spatially and temporally. Whereas, temporally, Israel's history became the history of European Jews, spatially, Israel had to create new faits accomplis. In that regard, 93 percent of the now Israeli land (Jews owned only 6.5 percent of the land before the establishment of Israel, the rest of the land being confiscated after 1948) was placed in the custody of the Jewish National Fund, with the legal stipulation that it could be leased to, lived on, and worked on only by Jews (although the best lands and resources went and still go to Ashkenazi Jews).[98]

The geographic transformation of Palestine was, in fact, an attempt to complete the epistemological transformation of how it is to be apprehended by European Jews, not only spatially and temporally, but also corporeally. The Zionist condition is characterized by what David Harvey has, in a different context, called a *space-time compression.*[99] The spatial-temporal Zionist condition is one inhabited by postdiasporic Jewish bodies. The corporeal self-perception of the Israeli Sabra is always already delimited within this space-time compression outside of which "he" cannot exist. Israel as a colonial/postcolonial space-time, however, allows the existence of new postdiasporic Jewish bodies only as holograms (virtual images, as in mirror reflections). If they exit (in the Zionist lexicon "descend from") the Israeli space-time continuum, these bodies lose their new corporeality and revert back to their pre-Israel diasporic condition—the mirror reflection as an organizing principle of national subjectivity shatters.[100] This occurrence results from the epistemological shattering of self-perception whose anchorage was lost with the changes in the material conditions of power and domination in which these bodies were embedded (as dominating and powerful, tough Sabras) in the Israeli space-time and that do not apply in the same way outside it. Like the *holodeck* on the starship Enterprise, which can be programmed to re-create any time, space, and body and which the programmer enters with an identity commensurate with the programming, Palestine was/is Zionism's holodeck. On the Enterprise, re-created bodies cannot exist outside the holodeck, even if they become conscious of their holodeck condition. In fact, they disappear into oblivion if they attempt to exit the holodeck's perimeter. Similarly, the Israeli Sabra with—almost always— "his" new body can exist only *within* the Israeli space-time, outside of which "he" reverts to being the "feminine schlemiel" that he was before. As such, the establishment of the Jewish settler colony makes it possible for postdiasporic Jewish male bodies to be *de*colonized *only* within it. These new Jewish bodies are actually imprisoned within this Zionist-created space-time—a space-time whose coloniality is rendered discursively postcolonial. *Israel, as a postcolonial colony, can exist only in this temporal-spatial-corporeal limitation.* Palestinian and Mizrahic bodies resisting this Zionist condition are simply attempting to chip away at its hegemony. The hegemony of Zionist discourse, however, is so pervasive that signs of Palestinian and Mizrahic agency are explained by Zionism—to continue with the "Star Trek" analogy—as simple program malfunctions and glitches that need only be corrected through Zionist reprogramming.

Notes

I would like to thank Fawzia Afzal-Khan, Neville Hoad, and Ella Shohat for their valuable comments on earlier versions of this essay. I would also like to extend my gratitude to Beth Kaimowitz, with whom I have had a fifteen year dialogue about Zionism from which I benefited significantly. Her insights contributed greatly to the way in which I understand Zionism today.

1 On the continuing colonial privileges of white colonial settlers in post-1980 independent Zimbabwe, see Andrew Astrow, *Zimbabwe: A Revolution That Lost Its Way?* (London: Zed, 1983).

2 On the (im)possibility of a post-Israel Palestine, see Joseph Massad, "Repentant Terrorists or Settler-Colonialism Revisited: The PLO-Israeli Agreement in Perspective," *Found Object* 3 (spring 1994): 81–90, and "Political Realists or Comprador Intelligentsia: Palestinian Intellectuals and the National Struggle," *Critique* (fall 1997): 21–35.

3 On Israeli academic apologia about the nature of Israel, see the discussion in Elia Zureik, *Palestinians in Israel: A Study in Internal Colonialism* (London: Routledge and Kegan Paul, 1979), 76–82.

4   For an elaboration of the problematic uses of the term *postcolonial*, see Ella Shohat, "Notes on the 'Post-Colonial,'" *Social Text* 31–32 (1992): 99–113; and Arif Dirlik, "The Post-Colonial Aura: Third World Criticism in the Age of Global Capitalism," *Critical Inquiry* 20 (winter 1994): 328–56.

5   See Richard Stevens, "Zionism as a Phase of Western Imperialism," in *The Transformation of Palestine*, ed. Ibrahim Abu-Lughod (Evanston, Ill.: Northwestern University Press, 1971).

6   Cited in Regina Sharif, *Non-Jewish Zionism: Its Roots in Western History* (London: Zed, 1983), 53.

7   Theodor Herzl, *The Jewish State: An Attempt at a Modern Solution to the Jewish Question* (London: H. Porders, 1972), 30. On the translation of *Der Judenstaat*, see Nathan Weinstock, *Zionism: False Messiah* (London: Ink Links, 1979), 39. It should be noted that Zionism was to adopt the slogan "a Jewish state" rather than "a state for the Jews" as its rallying cry.

8   Moses Hess, *Rome and Jerusalem: A Study in Jewish Nationalism*, trans. Meyer Waxman (New York: Bloch, 1918), 149.

9   Lord Palmerston to Ponsonby (British ambassador to Constantinople), PRO, FO 78/390, no. 34, 11 August 1840, cited in Sharif, *Non-Jewish Zionism*, 56.

10 Paul Goodman, *Zionism in England* (London, 1949), 18–19, cited in ibid., 74.

11 *Protocols of the Fourth Zionist Congress* (London, 1900), 5, cited in ibid.

12 *The Complete Diaries of Theodor Herzl*, ed. Raphael Patai, trans. Harry Zohn, vol. 4 (New York: Herzl, 1960), 1367.

13 Ibid., 1473, 1473, 1499, 1499, 1601, 1597, 1600, 1600.

14 The Pale of Settlement is the area covering those parts of Russia and Poland to which Jews were restricted. However, the area also included gentile Russians and Poles.

15 Ibid., 1361.

16 Leo Pinsker, *Auto-Emancipation*, reprinted in Pinsker's *Road to Freedom* (New York: Scopus, 1975), 104, 105.

17 *The Complete Diaries*, 1474.

18 "The Strategic Importance of Syria to the British Empire," 9 December 1918, General Staff, War Office, PRO, FO 371/4178, cited in *Zionism, Imperialism, and Racism*, ed. A. W. Kayyali (London: Croom Helm, 1979), 17.

19 Theodor Herzl quoted in Kayyali, ed., *Zionism, Imperialism, and Racism*, 16.

20 Shimon Shama, *Two Rothchilds and the Land of Israel* (London: Collins, 1978), 63, 68, 79–80, cited in Gideon Shafir, *Land, Labor, and the Origins of the Israeli-Palestinian Conflict, 1882–1914* (Cambridge: Cambridge University Press, 1989), 51.

21 Chaim Weizmann quoted in Simha Flapan, *Zionism and the Palestinians* (London: Croom Helm, 1979), 71.

22 Ber Borochov, "Eretz Israel in Our Program and Tactics," in *Class Struggle and the Jewish Nation: Selected Essays in Marxist Zionism*, ed. Mitchell Cohen (New Brunswick, N.J.: Transaction, 1984), 203.

23 F. H. Kisch, *Palestine Diary* (London: Victor Gollancz, 1938), entry for 28 May 1931, p. 420.

24 On the history of revisionist Zionism, see Lenni Brenner, *The Iron Wall: Zionist Revisionism from Jabotinsky to Shamir* (London: Zed, 1984).

25 On the assassination of Bernadotte, see ibid., 202–3. For details on the Al-Dawayimah massacre, see Benny Morris, *The Birth of the Palestinian Refugee Problem, 1947–1949* (Cambridge: Cambridge University Press, 1989), 222–23. On the details of Dayr Yasin, see David Hirst, *The Gun and the Olive Branch: The Roots of Conflict in the Middle East* (London: Faber and Faber, 1984), 124–29.

It must be noted, however, that the Haganah leadership condemned the Irgun massacre at Dayr Yasin mainly because of its enmity toward the Irgun leaders and its desire to discredit them.

26 On this point, see the discussion in Uri Davis and Walter Lehn, "And the Fund Still Lives: The Role of the Jewish National Fund in the Determination of Israel's Land Policies," *Journal of Palestine Studies* 7, no. 4 (summer 1978): 4–7.

27 See the important contribution of Maxime Rodinson on this question in his classic *Israel: A Colonial-Settler State?* (New York: Monad, 1973).

28 Ibid., 80–82, 88.

29 On the importing of Yemeni Jewish laborers by the Zionists, see Gideon Giladin, *Discord in Zion: Conflict between Ashkenazi and Sephardi Jews in Israel* (London: Scorpion, 1990), 41–48. See also Joseph Massad, "Zionism's Internal Others: Israel and the Oriental Jews," *Journal of Palestine Studies* 100 (summer 1996): 53–68.

30 Isaac Deutscher, "Israel's Spiritual Climate," in *The Non-Jewish Jew and Other Essays*, ed. Tamara Deutscher (New York: Hill and Wang, 1968), 111–12, 112, 116.

31 On the refugee-colonist status of European Jews, see Joseph Massad, "Palestinians and the Limits of Racialized Discourse," *Social Text* 34 (1993): 94–114.

32 Isaac Deutscher, "Israel's Tenth Birthday," in Deutscher, ed., *The Non-Jewish Jew*, 118.

33 Colonial Office 733/297/75156/II, app. A, extract from Chaim Weizmann's speech, 23 April 1936, Great Britain, Peel Commission Report, 96–97, cited in Philip Mattar, *The Mufti of Jerusalem: Al-Hajj Amin-al-Husayni and the Palestinian National Movement* (New York: Columbia University Press, 1988), 73.

34 Isaac Deutscher, "The Non-Jewish Jew," in Deutscher, ed., *The Non-Jewish Jew*, 40–41.

35 Deutscher, "Israel's Spiritual Climate," 103.

36 Isaac Deutscher, "The Israeli-Arab War, June 1967," in Deutscher, ed., *The Non-Jewish Jew*, 138.

37 Joel S. Migdal, *Strong States and Weak Societies: State-Society Relations and State Capabilities in the Third World* (Princeton, N.J.: Princeton University Press, 1988), 45, 46, 145.

38 On Lipset and Memmi, see Zureik's discussion of their views in *Palestinians in Israel*, 77–78.

39 Kwame Anthony Appiah, *In My Father's House: Africa in the Philosophy of Culture* (Oxford: Oxford University Press, 1992), 17, 43.

40 Ibid., 43.

41 Marlon Brando quoted in an interview with Lawrence Grobel in *Conversations with Brando* (New York: Hyperion, 1991), 109.

42 Brando's support for Begin's right-wing terrorist group (see ibid., 119–20) was a result of his disappointment with the Haganah and its leader, David Ben-Gurion, who were not "doing as they should have done."

43 Ibid., 175.

44 Joan Peters, *From Time Immemorial* (New York: Harper and Row, 1984).

45 See Edward Said and Christopher Hitchens, eds., *Blaming the Victims: Spurious Scholarship and the Palestinian Question* (London: Verso, 1988); and the following reviews of *From Time Immemorial:* Ian Gilmour and David Gilmour, "Pseudo-Travellers," *London Review of Books*, 7 February 1985, 8–10; Alexander Cockburn, *Nation*, 29 September 1984, 260–61, and (13 October 1984), 342–43. Cockburn renamed the book *From Lies Immemorial*; and Norman Finkelstein, "Disinformation and the Palestine Question: The Not-So-Strange Case of Joan Peter's *From Time Immemorial*," in Said and Hitchens, eds., *Blaming the Victims*, 33–69.

46 Grobel, *Conversations with Brando*, 105.

47 Benjamin Beit-Hallahmi, *Original Sins: Reflections of the History of Zionism and Israel* (London: Pluto, 1992), 82.

48 Edward Said, *The Question of Palestine* (New York: Vintage, 1980), 87.

49 Max Nordau, "Jewry of Muscle," in *The Jew in the Modern World: A Documentary History,* ed. Paul Mendes-Flohr and Jehuda Reinharz (Oxford: Oxford University Press, 1980), 434–35. For an overview of Nordau's political thought, see George Mosse, *Confronting the Nation: Jewish and Western Nationalism* (Hanover, N.H.: Brandeis University Press, 1993), 161–75.

50 Bar Kochba was defeated at Betar in A.D. 135.

51 Paul Breines, *Tough Jews: Political Fantasies and the Moral Dilemma of American Jewry* (New York: Basic, 1991).

52 Ibid., 47.

53 See Sander Gilman, *The Jew's Body* (New York: Routledge, 1991).

54 The importance of Masada is related to the fact that its Jewish defenders chose suicide rather than accept capture by the Romans. It should be pointed out that the women and children of Masada were actually killed by the husbands and fathers before the latter committed suicide. On the incorporation of Masada in Zionist national mythology, see Yael Zerubavel, *Recovered Roots: Collective Memory and the Making of an Israeli National Tradition* (Chicago: University of Chicago Press, 1995). See also Ella Shohat's discussion of the masculine Israeli colonial explorer in her *Israeli Cinema, East/West, and the Politics of Representation* (Austin: University of Texas Press, 1989).

55 On the Mossad agent, see Breines, *Tough Jews,* 75–167. On the Sabra, see Simona Sharoni, "Militarized Masculinity in Context: Cultural Politics and Social Constructions of Gender in Israel" (paper presented at the conference of the Middle East Studies Association, Portland, Oregon, October 1992).

56 *Europa Europa,* dir. Agnieszka Holland (Orion Pictures, 1991). The film became the second-highest-grossing German movie in the United States after *Das Boot.* It won a Golden Globe and a New York Film Critics award (see "Holland without a Country," *New York Times Magazine,* 8 August 1993, 28–32).

57 On the "blackness" of Jewish skin, see Gilman, *The Jew's Body,* 169–93.

58 Nordau, "Jewry of Muscle," 435.

59 Lanzman and Holland are quoted in "Holland without a Country," 32.

60 See Beit-Hallahmi, *Original Sins,* 128–29.

61 Sigmund Freud, "Analysis of a Phobia in a Five-Year-Old Boy," in *The Standard Edition of the Complete Psychological Works of Sigmund Freud,* ed. James Strachey (London: Hogarth, 1953–74), 10:36ff.

62 Benjamin Beit-Hallahmi, *The Israeli Connection: Who Israel Arms and Why* (New York: Pantheon, 1987), 238–39.

63 Tom Segev, *The Seventh Million: Israelis and the Holocaust* (New York: Hill and Wang, 1993), 421.

64 On Zionism's gendered agency and its relation to Palestine, see Ella Shohat, "Eurocentrism, Exile, and Zionist Discourse" (paper presented at the conference of the Middle East Studies Association, Washington, D.C., 1991), and "Imaging Terra Incognita: The Disciplinary Gaze of Empire," *Public Culture* 3, no. 2 (spring 1991): 41–70.

65 Melanie Klein, "Love, Guilt, and Reparation," in *Love, Guilt, and Reparation and Other Works, 1921–1945* (New York: Free Press, 1975), 334.

66 On the analogy between Israeli Sabras and the American Adam, see Ella Shohat, "Staging the Quincentenary, the Middle East, and the Americas," *Third Text* 21 (winter 1992–93): 102.

67 This story is told during a meeting in 1970 between Prime Minister Meir and a group of Israeli writers (cited in Beit-Hallahmi, *Original Sins,* 74).

68 On *zayin,* see Simona Sharoni, "To Be a Man in the Jewish State: The Sociopolitical Context of Violence and Oppression," *Challenge* 2, no. 5 (September/October 1991): 26–28.

69 See Susan Gubar, " 'This Is My Rifle, This Is My Gun': World War II and the Blitz on Women," in *Behind the Lines: Gender and the Two World Wars,* ed. Margaret Higonnet et al. (New Haven, Conn.: Yale University Press, 1987), 252.

70 On the rape of slaves, see Angela Davis, *Women, Race, and Class* (New York: Vintage, 1981), 172–201. Of course, other oppressive societies have used and continue to use the penis as a weapon; a prominent example of this is the Cossacks' rape of Jewish women in Czarist Russia.

On the rape of Vietnamese women, see Arlene Eisen-Bergman, *Women of Vietnam* (San Francisco: People's, 1975), 60–79.

On the penis in international relations, see Cynthia Enloe, *Bananas, Beaches, and Bases: Making Feminist Sense of International Politics* (Berkeley and Los Angeles: University of California Press, 1990).

71 For detailed descriptions of Israeli soldiers' (some of whom were Holocaust survivors) rape and murder of Palestinian women and children in 1948, especially at Al-Dawayimahh and Dayr Yasin, see Morris, *The Birth of the Palestinian Refugee Problem,* 222–23; and Hirst, *The Gun and the Olive Branch,* 124–29.

72 Theodor Herzl to Heinrich Kana, 8 June 1882, Herzl-Kana Correspondence, Central Zionist Archives, Jerusalem, cited in Desmond Stewart, *Theodor Herzl* (Garden City, N.Y.: Doubleday, 1974), 71–72. See also Peter Lowenberg, "Theodor Herzl: A Psychoanalytic Study in Charismatic Political Leadership," in *The Psychoanalytic Interpretation of History,* ed. Benjamin Wolman (New York: Basic, 1971), 152–53. I would like to thank Gadi Gofbarg for referring me to the Herzl story.

73 Lowenberg, "Theodor Herzl," 153.

74 See Nira Yuval-Davis, "National Reproduction and 'the Demographic Race' in Israel," in *Woman-Nation-State,* ed. Nira Yuval-Davis and Floya Anthias (London: Macmillan, 1989), 92–109.

75 See Hirst, *The Gun and the Olive Branch,* 242–43. For the reproductivist tendencies of Palestinian nationalism itself, see Joseph Massad, "Conceiving the Masculine: Gender and Palestinian Nationalism," *Middle East Journal* 49, no. 3 (summer 1995): 467–83.

76 Frank Giles, "Golda Meir: 'Who Can Blame Israel?' " an interview in *London Sunday Times,* 15 June 1969, p. 12.

77 Part of a funeral oration, delivered by Moshe Dayan, of a young Jewish settler killed by Palestinians as he was harvesting grain near the Egyptian border, cited in Uri Avneri, *Israel without Zionists: A Plea for Peace in the Middle East* (New York: Macmillan, 1968), 134. Dayan's speech was broadcast on Israeli radio, Kol Yisrael, on the eve of the 1967 Arab/Israel War, which coincided with the anniversary of the settler's death and Dayan's own birthday.

78 Moshe Dayan in *Ha'Aretz,* 4 April 1969, cited in Hirst, *The Gun and the Olive Branch,* 221.

79 See Saul Cohen and Nurit Kliot, "Israel's Place-Names as Reflection of Continuity and Change in Nation Building," *Names: Journal of the American Name Society* 29, no. 3 (September 1981): 227–48. The Jewish National Fund was/is the Zionist organization that owns all Jewish-"acquired" lands in Palestine.

80 See Saul Cohen and Nurit Kliot, "Place-Names in Israel's Ideological Struggle over the Administered Territories," *Annals of the Association of American Geographers* 82, no. 4 (1992): 653–80.

81 Hirst, *The Gun and the Olive Branch*, 240.

82 Sigmund Freud, *Leonardo da Vinci and a Memory of His Childhood*, in Strachey, ed., *Standard Edition*, 11:83-84.

83 Jacques Lacan, "The Mirror Stage as Formative of the Function of the I as Revealed in Psychoanalytic Experience," in *Écrits: A Selection* (New York: Norton, 1977), 2.

84 The Arabic words *sabrah, sabbar,* and *sabr* derive from the same root as the word *patience, sabr.* The Sabra cactus is a desert fruit characterized by its *patient* waiting for rain and water. It is a *patient* plant.

85 Georges Friedmann, *The End of the Jewish People?* (Garden City, N.Y.: Doubleday, 1967), 115.

86 The Sabra was the subject of Gadi Gofbarg's multimedia installation "Tough and Tender," exhibited at the Alternative Museum of New York from 29 September through 7 November 1992. See also Neery Melkonian, "Tough and Tender: An Interview with Gadi Gofbarg," *Afterimage* 20, no. 3 (October 1992): 8-10.

87 Beit-Hallahmi, *Original Sins*, 129.

88 I should note here that the standard Zionist response to these accusations is that these foods and dances are also shared by Arab Jews who immigrated to Israel and therefore are not appropriated from the Palestinians. This, however, flies in the face of the facts that there are very few Syrian, Palestinian, or Lebanese Jews in Israel (the majority of Syrian and Lebanese Jews immigrated to the United States and Latin America, especially Mexico, while there are very few Palestinian Arab Jews left anywhere). The vast majority of Arab Jews in Israel come from Morocco, Iraq, and Yemen, countries where hummus and falafil are not eaten and where *dabkah* line dancing is not practiced.

89 Ibid., 124. I should mention that Zionists also chose less violent names connected to nature, such as those of trees and birds (Ilana, Tamar, Ella, Alona, Oren), although, with a few exceptions, most of the "peaceful" names were women's first names.

90 Yigael Yadin, *Bar Kochba: The Rediscovery of the Legendary Hero of the Second Jewish Revolt against Rome* (Jerusalem: Weinfeld and Nicholson, 1971), 15. On Yadin and his discoveries, see G. W. Bowersock, "Palestine: Ancient History and Modern Politics," in Said and Hitchen, eds., *Blaming the Victims*, 181-91.

    Zerubavel, *Recovered Roots*, 58, quoting Yisrael Eldad (re "last chief of staff ").

91 See Keith Whitelam, *The Invention of Ancient Israel: The Silencing of Palestinian History* (New York: Routledge, 1996).

92 On the destroyed Palestinian villages, see Walid Khalidi, ed., *All That Remains: The Palestinian Villages Occupied and Depopulated by Israel in 1948* (Washington, D.C.: Institute for Palestine Studies, 1992).

93 Israel Shahak, "Arab Villages Destroyed in Israel," report dated 2 December 1973, in *Documents from Israel, 1967-1973,* ed. Uri Davis and Norton Mezvinsky (London: Ithaca, 1975), 43-44. See also Walid Khalidi, ed., *All That Remains: the Palestinian Villages Occupied and Depopulated by Israel in 1948* (Washington, D.C.: Institute for Palestine Studies, 1992).

94 See Nur Masalha, *Expulsion of the Palestinians* (Washington, D.C.: Institute of Palestine Studies, 1992); and Morris, *The Birth of the Palestinian Refugee Problem.*

95 Zerubavel, *Recovered Roots,* 57. See also the pioneering work of Nadia Abu El-Haj, *Excavating the Land, Creating the Homeland: Archaeology, the State, and the Making of History in Modern Jewish Nationalism* (Ph.D. diss., Duke University, 1995).

96 Zerubavel, *Recovered Roots,* 57-59.

97 See Sabri Jiryis, *The Arabs in Israel* (New York: Monthly Review Press, 1976).

98 On Jewish ownership of land before 1948, see Abraham Granott, *Agrarian Reform and the Record of Israel* (London: Eyre and Spottiswoode, 1956), 28. On the preference for Ashke-

nazi Jews, see G. N. Giladi, *Discord in Zion;* and Walter Lehn, *The Jewish National Fund* (London: Kegan Paul International, 1988).

99   David Harvey, *The Condition of Post-Modernity: An Inquiry into the Origins of Cultural Change* (Cambridge: Blackwell, 1990).

100   Israeli emigrants are labeled *yordim* or descenders, while Jewish immigrants to Israel are called *olim* or ascenders.

Postcolonial Theory in an American Context:

A Reading of Martin Delany's *Blake*

TIMOTHY POWELL

Postcolonial theory, whether explicitly acknowledged or not, has had a tremendous effect on American studies over the past decade, bringing to the fore important and often perplexing questions about the role of empire in forming America's national identity and the psychological anguish of the internally colonized. In 1984, in "Criticism in the Jungle," Henry Louis Gates Jr. utilized Frantz Fanon's theory that a colonial subject assumes the "weight of a civilization" in coming "face to face with the language of the [colonizing] nation" to make a meaningful connection between postcolonial writers and African American authors who face a similar dilemma in "attempt[ing] to posit a 'black self' in the very Western languages in which blackness itself is a figure of absence, a negation." [1] In the recent "Américo Paredes and Decolonization," José David Saldívar likewise uses postcolonial theory to argue that Paredes saw himself not as an "immigrant" but as a "postcolonial Chicano writer" whose homeland was appropriated in an imperial act of "U.S. military aggression [that] transformed the Rio Grande Valley from an organic class society . . . into a barbed wire and segregated society." [2] In the article "American Literary Emergence as a Post-Colonial Phenomenon," Lawrence Buell has even gone so far as to argue that canonical authors like Thoreau, Emerson, Whitman, and Melville suffer from the postcolonial trauma of writing in what Ashis Nandy describes as "a culture in which the ruled were constantly tempted to fight their rulers within the psychological limits set by the latter." [3]

This proliferation of postcolonial theory, however, creates any number of fundamental problems in terms of defining the historical and theoretical structure of colonialism in an American context. How, for example, can we even begin to define the basic binary of colonizer/colonized when all parties involved — in this case, African Americans, Chicanos, and Anglo-Americans — insist on seeing themselves as the colonized? This, in turn, raises the question of whether the historical and cultural complexities of American society are not far too intricate to captured in such simplistic, binary terms as colonizer and colonized? We need to ask, for example, whether we are blurring fundamental cultural distinctions between the historical plight of African Americans and that of Chicanos by placing them in the undifferentiated category *postcolonial subjects.*

If such fundamental questions of identity are essentially unclear, the temporal framework that defines the postcolonial moment is equally as mystifying. When, for example, can American colonization be said to begin? With the arrival of the first English settlers in Jamestown in 1607? With the arrival of the first black slaves in 1619? With the end of the Mexican-American War in 1848? Even less clear is when to posit the *post* that would mark the end of this initial period of colonization. Buell situates the moment in 1776, when the American colonies ruptured their political relation to Great Britain. But what of the postcolonial subjectivity of Chicanos and African Americans of which Saldívar and Gates write? Given the economic deprivation and entrenched segregation that keep contemporary Chicano barrios and black ghettos isolated outside the cultural quotation marks of "America" and the fact that, as Cornel West recently observed, 86 percent of white suburban Americans live in neighborhoods that are less than 1 percent black, can we conscionably speak of there having been a moment of liberation that marks the post of America's internal colonialism?[4] Moreover, in the face of the recent military, political, and economic intervention in Iraq and Somalia, can we presume to think that there has ever been an age of *post*colonialism in America?

This perplexing nexus of conflicting historical perspectives that refuses to resolve itself into clearly defined units of colonizer, colonized, and post should not, however, be seen as a critical quagmire that renders the proposition of transporting postcolonial theory to American studies completely absurd. Rather, I would argue that this nexus of contradictions offers us an extremely important point of entry into crucial issues, not only of American identity, but of the meaning(s) of *postcolonialism* as well. Important critical investigations have already begun in both these directions. In terms of American studies, as Amy Kaplan notes in her introduction to *Cultures of United States Imperialism,* "Imperialism has been simultaneously formative and disavowed in the foundational discourse of American studies."[5] As she goes on to suggest, the only way we can begin fully to understand the "foundational discourse" of American imperialism is first to come to critical terms with this disavowal. Likewise, Anne McClintock has recently made an important call for postcolonial theorists to try to engage "multiplicity" and to move away from thinking within "the single rubric of European time" that leads us to conceive of history in a "linear" fashion — " 'pre-colonial' to 'the colonial' to 'the post-colonial.' " Such rigid temporal and theoretical models, McClintock argues, lead us to see historically different situations in terms of "the singular category" of "*the* post-colonial condition," which, in turn, creates "a panoptic tendency to view the globe within generic abstractions voided of political nuance."[6]

In response to both Kaplan and McClintock, I want to try to translate postcolonial theory into a uniquely American and highly nuanced historical context. I will begin by delineating what Kaplan calls *the American inclination of disavowal*, which has historically cloaked the imperial impulse in a rhetoric of capitalist/democratic freedom. Having deconstructed the inner workings of this rhetorical disavowal, I will then try to hold open the self-cloaking mechanism of American imperialism in order to engage the multiplicity of meanings of *postcolonial subjectivity* in an American context. Finally, I will attempt to define *colonialism* in historically specific terms and to use this definition to give a postcolonial reading of Martin Delany's novel *Blake; or, The Huts of America* (1861).[7] I have chosen *Blake* because, in this text, Delany gives what I think is one of the most probing and insightful explanations of the inner workings of both internal and external colonialism in its uniquely American form. Moreover, Delany offers a culturally important glimpse into the complex sense of the national identity of America's internally colonized. Finally, Delany's text offers a significant theoretical alternative to what McClintock identifies as the "imperial idea of linear time," which has prevented postcolonial theory from realizing, in McClintock's words, the theory's "promise [of] a decentering of history in hybridity, syncreticism, [and] multi-dimensional time."[8]

The Self-Cloaking Mechanism of American Colonial Discourse

I begin by returning, for the moment, to Lawrence Buell's argument that the writers of the American Renaissance can be seen as postcolonial subjects. Buell's formulation raises important questions both about whether 1776 does in fact mark the post of American postcolonial consciousness and about how the mechanism of what Kaplan calls *disavowal* works in American studies. Historically, of course, Buell is not wrong to posit this moment as being the Revolution of 1776. White Americans were, after all, colonized by Great Britain and did free themselves through an act of revolutionary liberation into what could be called, in the strictest sense of the term, a postcolonial moment. Buell argues that, in this case, the colonizer/colonized dichotomy is mapped out, not along racial lines, but in terms of the cultural differences between Anglo-Americans and Anglos—more specifically, that writers like Melville, Whitman, and Thoreau were acutely conscious of England's cultural dominance in the United States and fashioned a uniquely American literature in response to what Buell calls Britain's *cultural colonization*.

In antithesis to Buell, and by way of trying to clarify the problematic binary colonizer/colonized, I argue that, by 1851, when Melville published *Moby-*

Dick, white Americans were no longer colonized — whether one defines *colonization* in cultural, economic, or military terms — but were fast on their way to becoming colonizers themselves, albeit in a uniquely American sense of the term ("Let America add Mexico to Texas, and pile Cuba upon Canada," cries Ishmael, in enthusiastic support of America's burgeoning sense of her own imperial power).[9] Because Buell is locked into a binary vision that sees the problem of postcolonial subjectivity solely in terms of Britain and (white) America, he misses what McClintock calls the *multiplicity* of colonial relations at work in antebellum American society. If we attempt to engage this multiplicity by not simply looking at the question exclusively in terms of white subjectivity, we will see that a very different view of colonizer and colonized begins to emerge. To take the point of view of Juan "Cheno" Cortina, for example, who led a successful revolt of twelve hundred Mexican Americans in Texas in 1859, Anglo-Americans were decidedly *not* the colonized but were instead constructed as being "our oppressors," "tyrants," or, in short, "the colonizers."[10] Likewise, in the first African American novel, *Clotel; or, The President's Daughter* (1853), William Wells Brown makes an impassioned plea for the right of blacks to revolt against slavery in the name of the Declaration of Independence — "Did not the American revolutionists violate the laws when they struck for liberty? They were revolters, but their success made them patriots" — thereby reversing the rhetoric of revolution and making white Americans into the colonizers who had to be overthrown in the name of liberty by *black* colonized subjects.[11] Finally, in relation to Native Americans, as early as 1823 Chief Justice John Marshall had been forced to concede, in *Johnson v. McIntosh,* that the legal validity of white entitlement to lands appropriated from Native American tribes could be justifed only by invoking the doctrine of discovery, a theory of entitlement by conquest dating back to the English colonization of the New World — thereby formally acknowledging the cultural (and imperial) continuity between white Americans and their British forefathers and unequivocally situating white Americans in the subject position of the colonizer relative to Native Americans.[12]

Buell is right, I believe, about recognizing 1776 as a fundamentally important moment of postcolonial rupture. His reluctance to acknowledge white Americans' identity as colonizers in relation to African Americans, Native Americans, and Chicanos is, however, somewhat surprising and can be taken, I think, as an informative point of entry into what Kaplan calls the *disavowal* that constitutes a fundamental cultural component of American imperialism. Committed to a worldview that sees the United States as a former colony that came into being as a nation through an act of revolutionary independence, Americans and Americanists have been historically hesitant to use the words *colonization* or *colonies* in connection with American expansionism or the treatment of culturally different groups within the United States. This anxiety and the

ability to conceal imperialist impulses in the guise of a commitment to anticolonial democratic freedom are fundamental aspects of what I will call the *self-
cloaking mechanism* of American colonialist discourse. This disavowal was so
strong that, even at the height of its colonial expansion at the turn of the century, when America intervened in Hawaii, Cuba, and Puerto Rico and even an-
nexed the Philippines in what was clearly a colonial relation, the United States
self-consciously avoided connecting itself to the history of European colonialism. The Supreme Court decision in *Dorr v. United States* (1904), for example,
concerning the restrictions of congressional legislation on Philippine territory,
studiously avoided the term *overseas colonies* in favor of *unincorporated territory*.[13] Likewise, half a century earlier, as America moved across the continent in
what was clearly an instance of imperial aggression disguised as Manifest Destiny, the lands occupied were never referred to as *colonies* but always *territories*.

The period in which this unique brand of American colonialism first really
began to take shape, in both its internal and its external forms, was during the
administration of James Monroe. What I will term America's *internal colonialism* was initiated by two historical movements — Indian removal, which Monroe instigated and Andrew Jackson saw through to completion, and the foundation of the American Colonization Society (dedicated to removing African
Americans to Liberia), which Monroe supported and financed in its earliest
stages. I come back to the question of internal colonialism in the next section.
For now, I focus on *external colonialism* in order to show how the Monroe Doctrine functions as the foundational document of the self-cloaking mechanism
of American colonialist discourse. Monroe first introduced the Monroe Doctrine (which, although it bore his name, was largely designed by his secretary
of state, John Quincy Adams) in his annual address to Congress in 1823. The
original intent, Adams wrote Benjamin Rush, was "that the American conti-
nents will no longer be subjects of *colonization*." Monroe asserted that, while
the United States did not have the grounds to interfere with "existing colonies," America maintained the "right" to protect "any Governments who have
declared their independence and maintained it" from the European powers.[14]

In a literal sense, the Monroe Doctrine thus defines a kind of *postcolonial colonialism* — *post*colonial in the sense that, as Monroe formulated the doctrine, it applied only to those nations in the Western Hemisphere that had "declared their independence" from the European colonial powers, yet still a form
of colonialism in that the doctrine gave the United States a loosely defined eco-
nomic/political sovereignty over the Western Hemisphere that would come to
be used, many times over, to justify America's imperial intervention. Monroe
defines the "right" of the United States to establish, not colonies (like those
of Britain, France, and Spain), but capitalist/imperialist spheres of influence.
These spheres of influence served the nation's conflicted sense of itself as a postcolonial superpower well in that they allowed America to intervene on foreign

soil without entitling the subjects of these "postcolonial colonies" to any democratic rights as American citizens or, more important, given the nation's deep-
seated nativist anxieties, to the right of return. This self-cloaking mechanism
outlined in the Monroe Doctrine would prove so effective that U.S. presidents
would use it to justify American imperial intervention everywhere from California in 1847, to the Philippines in 1899, to Kuwait in 1990. As it evolved, this
contradictory logic of anticolonialist colonialism came to turn on an essential
ambiguity inherent in America's ability to manipulate the term *freedom* such
that the Monroe Doctrine could be extended by President Bush to the Arabian
Peninsula in 1990, using the logic of protecting "free trade" to mask the fact that
we were defending a monarchical government in Kuwait where de facto slavery
continues to exist and democratic freedom is unknown.

It is important, in this sense, to try to understand more fully the way in
which capitalism and democracy have become intertwined in American colonialist discourse. What differentiates American imperialism from the Roman,
Napoleonic, Islamic, and British Empires (and what makes it exceedingly difficult to analyze even now) is that these empires reveled in the self-image of the
conqueror, erecting countless monuments to the glory and expanse of their empires. Americans, on the other hand, have self-consciously avoided any connotation of empire by consistently and disingenuously offering some sort of financial compensation for territories taken by imperialist conquest. We "bought"
Florida from Spain, "purchased" Louisiana from France, and offered Britain
money for Oregon.[15] After wresting away the Texas, New Mexico, and California Territories in the Mexican-American War, for example, the U.S. government
paid Mexico $15 million, prompting the *Whig Intelligencer* to conclude that "we
take nothing by conquest. . . . Thank God."[16] From the purchase of Manhat-
tan from the Indians to the acquisition of the Philippines from Spain, American
conquest has been *imperialism validated by receipt,* using the logic of capitalist
exchange to cloak its unique form of colonialism and thereby maintain its self-
identity as a former colony committed to the egalitarian ideals of democracy.

Colonization in an American Context

Having deconstructed the inner workings of the self-cloaking mechanism of
American colonial discourse, the challenge that lies ahead of us is to try to hold
open the inclination to disavowal and to come to a preliminary definition of
colonization that both engages multiplicity and is grounded in a historically
specified American context. Looking ahead to Delany, I turn the focus away
from American imperialism abroad to what McClintock calls *internal colonialism,* which occurs, she writes, "where the dominant part of a country treats a
group or region as it might a foreign colony."[17] As in the case of the external
colonialism defined by the Monroe Doctrine, internal colonialism in the United

States can also be seen as a form of postcolonial colonialism in that the post-colonial rhetoric of the 1776 American Revolution effectively cloaks another, more subtle form of colonialism at home. Again, this self-cloaking mechanism and the myriad of cultural contradictions that it invokes are the result of the entanglement of American capitalism and democracy. In this case, the capitalist need for cheap labor, which dictates socioeconomic inequalities, is masked by a democratic rhetoric that insists that all men are created equal. Yet, while this disavowal worked to facilitate the economic exploitation of America's internal colonialism, the complex interrelation of capitalism and democracy would also deeply aggravate the nativist anxieties of the dominant white society by necessitating the need for a constant influx of immigrants and ethnic minorities, who, in turn, would challenge these inherent economic inequalities in the name of America's democratic principles. I begin to try to unravel these conflicting and intimately intertwined social forces by undertaking a discursive archaeology of the way in which the terms *colonies* and *colonization* were used at the time Delany was writing.

The problem, as we will quickly see, with an analysis that sets out to engage multiplicity in a historical context as ethnically and racially complex as antebellum America is that familiar theoretical categories (e.g., the colonizer/colonized binary) must be radically revised. For the sake of clarity, I attempt to begin this process of revision by suggesting three types of internal colonization, with the understanding that these categories are neither definitive nor necessarily distinct. My purpose here is not to exhaust the subject of colonization in an American context, but rather to define some of the parameters of critical investigation and to open up the field for further analysis. With that caveat in mind, the three types that can be identified here, on the basis of the way the term was used in the nineteenth century, are *economically imposed internal colonies, self-imposed internal colonies,* and *externally imposed internal colonies.*

Economically imposed internal colonies can be defined as ethnic enclaves that were formed out of the tensions within American society between an economic need for cheap labor and a nativist commitment to keeping America socially white, male, and Protestant.[18] An example of this type of internal colony would be the "Paddy Camps" that formed in Lowell in the 1830s and 1840s when the Irish took over the mill jobs from young white, New England women. Whereas the Protestant women had lived in tightly controlled, pristine boardinghouses (which might, in an expanded study, be seen as an example of internal colonialism based on gender lines), the predominantly Catholic Irish lived in dilapidated, rough-hewn huts that were built within sight of the factories and boardinghouses but that were culturally outside the imagined community of Lowell's self-proclaimed Protestant "Native Americans." These *colonies* of Irish workers, as they were sometimes called, were kept self-contained by property laws that forbid the Irish from buying property outside the Paddy Camps. And, while the Irish were kept culturally separate by such social mechanisms, "Native Americans" nonetheless still reserved the right to intervene within these economically imposed colonies, as in May 1831, when white Protestants in Lowell responded to the attempt of the Irish to build a Catholic church with nativist riots.[19] Other examples of economically imposed internal colonies would include Mexican American *colonias* such as the one established on the great King Ranch in Texas in the 1850s, where Chicano laborers lived within the borders yet outside the cultural quotation marks of "America." Another example would be the liminal enclaves of the slave quarters on Southern plantations, which were economically integrated into the American economy but which were socially and culturally segregated by racist persecution and the nativist contention that "ours is a government of the white race."

Self-imposed internal colonies were established in response to the exclusionary and discriminatory forces of white nativism. The Catholic enclave of St. Mary's, for example, which was identified by its founding members as a colony, was established in 1842 in response to the persecution of Catholics by the Native American Party in Philadelphia and a series of violent riots in which nativist mobs burned several Catholic churches to the ground. St. Mary's would constitute a self-imposed colony in the sense that it was formed by the German Catholic Brotherhood, which raised the funds, bought the land, and maintained autonomous control of the social, political, and religious workings of the colony. The purpose of self-imposed internal colonies such as St. Mary's was the preservation of cultural integrity, in this case, the right to worship and educate their children in the German language and the Catholic faith.[20] African American enclaves like Canada West, which was established in the 1840s, can also be conceived of as self-imposed colonies in that they were organized, operated, and controlled by black Americans as refuges from white persecution and, later, the Fugitive Slave Law. The founders of Canada West, Henry Bibb, James Theodore Holly, and Mary Ann Shadd, were known in nineteenth-century parlance as *black colonizationists* because they advocated an agenda of black separatism that held that African Americans would be better off living away from whites, even if it meant having to leave the country.[21] The fact, then, that these African-American colonies were established in Canada (and not, say, in Pennsylvania, like St. Mary's) raises the critical need to address the historical specificity and multiplicity within the category *internally colonized subjects* so as not to blur together the experiences of Catholics and African Americans by essentializing the term *colonized*. The difference in location here should signal a fundamental difference in the degree of white nativist antipathy and resistance that the two groups had to confront. In the case of black Americans, the realization, in the words of Delany (who lived for a time at Canada West and who later advocated black colonization of Haiti and West Africa), that "we love our country, dearly love her, but she does not love us—she despises us, and bids us begone, driving us from her embraces," explains the linguistic and cultural contradictions of why these African-American *internal* colonies would be established *outside* the United States.[22]

What I am calling *externally imposed colonies* represent probably the single most important category in terms of understanding the nature of internal colonization in an American context. For, in a sense, every one of the examples at which we have looked thus far was externally imposed in that all these colonies were formed, directly or indirectly, in response to exclusionary forces of white nativism. Perhaps the purest form of externally imposed internal colonies would be Indian removal as carried out under the auspices of the Indian Removal Act of 1830, which gave the federal government the power to relocate Eastern Indian tribes west of the Mississippi in exchange for new territories, and the Indian Appropriation Act of 1851, which authorized Congress to establish what the commissioner of Indian affairs initially referred to as *colonies* but what later became more commonly known as *Indian reservations*.[23] This form of externally imposed colonization was carried out against the colonized subjects' volition and can be distinguished from self-imposed internal colonization in the sense that Native Americans lost political, social, and religious control over these colonies. Once again, the importance of race and the fact that Native Americans were not integrated into the burgeoning antebellum capitalist economy should not be overlooked as determinate factors of the degree and distance of Native Americans' internal exile from the dominant white culture.

Like the other two forms of internal colonialism, externally imposed colonization is a kind of cultural exile designed, in the words of the Senate Committee on Indian Affairs, to move Native Americans "outside of us."[24] As with America's postcolonial colonialism abroad, this form of internal colonialism was cloaked in a rhetoric carefully designed to preserve the illusion of America's devotion to its anticolonial principles of democracy. Thus, as one critic wrote, Monroe would carry out the terms of the Indian Removal Act "breathing the language of the purest benevolence."[25] The internal self-cloaking mechanism of America's commitment to a democratically conceived policy of social benevolence would, in turn, allow one federal agent to describe the Trail of Tears, on which forty-five hundred Cherokees died, as a "generous and enlightened policy . . . [that] was ably and judiciously carried into effect" with the Cherokees' best interests in mind—the argument being that white nativist hostility in Georgia was so thoroughly intractable that the Cherokees would be better off on internal colonies west of the Mississippi.[26]

This unique form of American colonization as internal cultural exile was not always externally imposed solely on the basis of race or ethnicity. The practices of Charles Loring Brace and the New York Children's Aid Society (CAS) demonstrate that similar forces of cultural exile could be carried out according to class differences as well. The CAS's "placing out" system, for example, was set up to send the children of what Brace called the "ignorant, debased, permanently *poor class*" to towns and settlements in the West. Between 1853 and 1895, the CAS transported more than ninety thousand boys to the West (often without first consulting their parents—Brace recalls in his diary that one boy was picked up while the train stopped briefly in Albany on the way west) to live with families who had no legal commitment to protect the children and who often turned them out with no compensation. Once again, however, this postcolonial colonialism was carried out in a self-cloaking rhetoric that allowed one New York minister to herald the CAS's efforts as "a great triumph of philanthropy." [27]

The single most important form of internal colonization with regard to Delany's novel, however, is undoubtedly the type practiced by the American Colonization Society (ACS). Founded in 1817, the society's stated goal was to "promote and execute a plan for colonizing (with their consent) the free people of color residing in our country [to] Africa." [28] Although falling well short of their proposed goal of relocating the entire black population of the United States to Africa, the ACS did manage to establish the "colony" of Liberia and, over time, to send between twelve and fifteen thousand African Americans "back" to the west coast of Africa. [29] The ACS was wildly controversial in antebellum America in part because it was founded by slaveholders who, in the words of one ACS supporter, were devoted to making America "a white man's country." [30] Delany himself would write that the ACS "originated in a deep laid scheme of the slaveholders of the country, to *exterminate* the free colored people of this continent." [31] It is therefore of the utmost importance to bear in mind a distinction here between the kind of self-imposed colonization that Delany favored ("What is the remedy? . . . emigration of the colored people") and the externally imposed colonization advocated by the ACS ("to confer a benefit on ourselves by ridding us of a population for the most part idle and useless"). [32]

What I hope these examples demonstrate is a form of colonization unique to American history—a postcolonial colonialism distinguished by its democratic self-cloaking mechanism and dedicated, externally, to establishing spheres of economic influence and, internally, to a form of cultural segregation that would keep the imagined community of America white, male, and Protestant. The multiplicity of both different conceptions of the colonizer/colonized binary and of the historical circumstances of the colonized should, however, deter us from attempting to reduce this multiplicity to any singular category of postcolonial subjectivity. Rather, I hope to move toward a fuller understanding of what Homi Bhabha calls *the perplexity of the living* and the multiplicity of various relations between colonizer and colonized by focusing my analysis on the historical circumstances of African Americans as described in Martin Delany's *Blake*.[33]

A Postcolonial Reading of Martin Delany's Blake

Martin Delany's *Blake* is an exemplary novel for our purposes both because it deconstructs the disavowal of American colonialist discourse and, moreover, because it meticulously maps out the internal and external components of America's unique form of postcolonial colonialism. Delany's protagonist, Henry Blake, is a liminal figure able to cross state lines in the deep South, to cross national boundary lines into Canada and back, and even to cross and recross the Atlantic to Africa—changing names, languages, and identities as need be. Wherever he goes, he "impart[s] the secret" of a "war upon the whites," and his movements from the plantations of the South, to Indian reservations, to free black colonies in Canada, to the maroon communities of fugitive slaves in the Dismal Swamps, to the west coast of Africa, and, finally, to Cuba define the borders of an imagined community of the diasporic black nation. In this sense, Delany's novel enacts what Homi Bhabha calls the *performative time* of postcolonial nation building such that Delany comes to be seen as being engaged in the project of "writing the nation" of the black Diaspora into being.[34]

Born Carolus Henrico Blacus, a free black in the West Indies, Blake is enslaved in the United States when he is kidnapped off a ship in Key West and spirited away to Natchez, Mississippi. After his wife is sold and taken to Cuba, Blake declares, "I never intend to serve any white man again" (p. 29) and sets off on a self-proclaimed mission to "complete an organization in every slave state before I return" (p. 42). Travelling at night, and fighting off "Nigger dogs" with his wits and bare hands as weapons, Blake travels from Texas, where he plants "a deep laid scheme for a terrible insurrection" (p. 85), through Georgia, Virginia, North Carolina, and South Carolina—"sowing the seeds of future devastation and ruin to the master and redemption to the slave" (p. 83). With each stop, Blake establishes "one good man or woman" who serves as "organizer for their own plantation" (p. 41) and whom Blake instructs to watch for his signal for the impending revolution to begin.

Blake's extensive travels can be thought of as a performative enactment that inscribes both the geographic and the cultural boundaries of Delany's conception of the not-yet-postcolonial black nation. Joining together the internally colonized subjects throughout the United States, Delany's syncretic view of this secret "organization" includes not just blacks but Indians as well. After visiting the plantations of Texas, Blake moves north to Arkansas, where he stops to consult the chief of the Choctaw Nation, which had been relocated from Mississippi to Arkansas as part of the Indian Removal Act of 1830. Blake tells the elders of the tribe, "What I now most wish to learn is, whether in case that the blacks should rise, they may have hope or fear from the Indian?" To this, the Choctaw chief responds, "The squaws of the great men among the Indians in Florida were black women, and the squaws of the black men were Indian women. You see the vine that winds around and holds us together" (p. 87). What "holds . . . together" blacks and Indians in Delany's vision is a shared sense of internal colonization externally imposed on them by the dominant white culture, which disavows its colonialist tendencies in an anticolonial rhetoric of democratic freedom.

Delany, however, effectively deconstructs this self-cloaking mechanism by reversing the terms of America's colonialist discourse such that whites can no longer claim to be the formerly colonized but must acknowledge instead that they have become colonizers. As Blake notes after leaving the Choctaw reservation in Arkansas: "Neither the robes of state nor gown of authority is sufficient to check the vengeance of awakened wrath in Arkansas. Law is but a fable, its ministration a farce, and the pillars of justice but as stubble before the approach of these legal invaders" (p. 88).

Delany is here able to pull aside the "robes of state" and the "gown of authority" that were used to cloak America's imperial conquest of the Southwest in the Mexican-American War and its internal colonization of the Indians on those lands by exposing the "awakened wrath" of America's internally colonized subjects. Recognizing "law" as a kind of "fable," Delany deconstructs the invented traditions put in place by the American legal system that obscure the reality that whites are but "legal invaders" who disavow the internal colonization of Mexicans, blacks, and Native Americans by using the "pillars of justice" to hide the naked imperial aggression of Indian removal and the Mexican-American War.

The diasporic nation that Blake's narrative movements inscribe comes to include all three forms of what I earlier identified as America's internal colonialism from the economically imposed plantations in the South, to the externally imposed Indian reservations in Arkansas, to the internally imposed colony that he establishes for fugitive slaves in Canada. The spiritual capital of this nation would, to Delany's mind, be the "mystical, antiquated, and almost fabulous" Dismal Swamp, where Blake goes to consult with "the old confederates of the noted Nat Turner" (p. 112). Blake is "anointed . . . priest of the order of High Conjurors" (p. 114) and instructed in the oral history of the black diasporic nation. Delany here experiments with what Edward Brathwaite calls *nation language* or what one character in the novel refers to simply as "good black talk"—"Dis many a day I been prayin' dat de Laud sen' a nudder Denmark 'mong us" (p. 112). Brathwaite defines *nation language* as the kind of English spoken by "the people," a creolization of the colonizer's imposed language that is "influenced by the underground language, the submerged language that the slaves had brought." [35] Delany brings this "submerged language" to the surface of his text in much the same way that he brings the submerged history of America's internally colonized to the surface of cultural consciousness in an act of what Bhabha calls *writing the nation*.

Blake's venture into what Delany describes as the "fearful abode" of "much-dreaded runaways . . . who continually seek the lives of their masters" (p. 110) offers us an important insight into the constitution of his imagined community of the black diasporic nation and how it is situated in relation to America. As Houston Baker has noted, these maroon societies existed on the "margins of *all* American promise, profit, and modes of production" and served an important function as cultural repositories of the "talents, sounds, images, [and] rhythms" of the marooned African nation.[36] Blake is welcomed into this society as a "nudder Denmark [Vesey]," initiated as a high conjurer, and situated historically in relation to other black revolutionaries like Nat Turner and General Gabriel. It is interesting to note that these keepers of the submerged history of the diasporic black nation include within that revolutionary legacy the American War for Independence of 1776. Delany notes that "some of the narrators" who recite to Blake the oral history of the black diasporic nation "claim to have been patriots in the American Revolution," and one old soul named Maudy Ghamus tells Henry, "I a' Gennel Gabel fit in de Malution wah, an' da want no sich fightin' dare as dat in Gabel wah!" (p. 113).

As we saw earlier, just as William Wells Brown would draw on the revolutionary rhetoric of America's War of Independence in the first African American novel, so, too, does Delany invoke the "Malution wah" as a formative part of the history and consciousness out of which the black diasporic nation is to spring. The meaning of 1776 is, however, entirely different for black and white patriots. As we saw earlier, whites would use the democratic, anticolonial rhetoric of American independence as a self-cloaking mechanism to disguise the internal colonialism of minorities at home as well as their imperial impulses abroad. For Delany's "bold, courageous and fearless adventurers" living in the self-imposed internal colony of the Dismal Swamp, the "Malution wah" is a historical precedent for the coming "war against the whites" that Henry Blake is to lead.

Blake's revolution includes not only the internally colonized blacks and Indians in the United States but also Afro-Cubans, who were colonized in the uniquely American sense defined by the Monroe Doctrine. The island of Cuba had long been coveted by American expansionists, and, as early as 1823, John Quincy Adams, chief architect of the Monroe Doctrine, had proclaimed possession of Cuba to be "indispensable to the continuance and integrity of the Union itself."[37] Pressure to annex the island mounted again around the time Delany was writing *Blake* in the form of the Ostend Report, which called on the U.S. government to purchase Cuba for $120,000,000. A sterling example of the self-cloaking mechanism of America's colonialist discourse and the logic of how the nation sought to validate its imperialism by receipt, the Ostend Report contended that the annexation of Cuba was justified by the "extreme oppression" of Spanish colonialism, which "justifies any people in endeavoring to relieve themselves from the yoke of their oppressors" while at the same time disavowing that American occupation would constitute a new "yoke" by boldly asserting that "the United States never acquired a foot of territory, except by fair purchase."[38] And, although the United States never did act on the recommendation of the Ostend Report, Delany's novel makes clear that Cuba was colonized in the manner defined by the Monroe Doctrine. For, although the United States never took political control of the island, Cuba was nevertheless manipulated by American slaveholders, who saw Cuba as within their economic sphere of influence.

Delany shrewdly incorporates into his novel the duplistic colonialist discourse that white proslavery expansionists employed in trying to make Cuba a postcolonial colony, in order to dismantle the disavowal and to make explicit the connection not only between Spanish and American colonialism but also between America's internal and external colonial policies. Delany embodies these American contradictions in the person of Judge Ballard, a Northerner who is already the proprietor of a large estate in Cuba and who is looking to buy a plantation in the South. Ballard says of Cuba: "I consider that colony as it now stands, a moral pestilence, a blighting curse, and it is useless to endeavor to disguise the fact; Cuba must cease to be a Spanish colony, and become American territory. Those mongrel Creoles are incapable of self-government and should be compelled to submit to the United States" (p. 62).

Typical of the duplicitous nature of American colonialist discourse, Ballard engages the self-cloaking mechanism by prefacing his call for imperial intervention in Cuba with the phrase "it is useless to endeavor to disguise the fact." Yet what follows is precisely that—a rhetorical "disguise" designed to disavow "the fact" that the United States intended to colonize Cuba. In making the distinction between colony and territory, Ballard attempts to mask the reality that control of Cuba is being shifted from one colonial power (Spain) to another (America).

Once in Cuba, Blake completely dismantles this self-cloaking mechanism of American colonialist discourse by reconfiguring the colonizer/colonized binary such that Creoles and blacks are clearly seen to be the colonized while Americans and Spaniards are grouped together as colonizers. As the Cuban poet Placido states in the text: "Since the advent of these Americans in the colony, our people have scarcely an hour of peaceful existence. Should we . . . strike for liberty, it must also be for independent self-government, because we have the prejudices of the mother-country and the white colonists alike to contend with" (p. 289).

Here, Cuban nationalism is configured in direct opposition to "the prejudices of the mother-country and the white colonists" from America. It is not just Cuban independence that Delany is concerned with here, however, but the independence of the diasporic black nation of which Cuba is but a small part. At the end of the novel, Delany inscribes a kind of culturally syncretic imagined community by bringing together elements from every corner of the diasporic black nation—the poet Placido from Cuba; Mendi from the Congo, who leads a slave uprising aboard ship; Abyssa, a Sudanese woman from East Africa whom Blake rescues from the slaver; Madame Cordora, a devout Roman Catholic mulatta from the upper reaches of Cuban society; and Blake's wife, born of a slave mother and a white American slavemaster. Delany consummates this black nationalist vision of pan-Africanism, which includes blacks of all shades, all classes, and from every corner of the black diasporic nation, with a double marriage, noting that "the consummation of conjugal union is the best security for political relations" (p. 276).

The connection between the first half of the novel and the second, between the internally colonized blacks on the slave plantations and the externally colonized Afro-Cubans, is explicitly established when Placido makes Blake the "General-in-Chief of the army of emancipation of the oppressed men and women of Cuba!" (p. 241) and Blake declares, "I am for war—war upon the whites. . . . Your destiny is my destiny. . . . Buckle on your armor then, and stand ready for the fight!" (p. 291). Yet, just as Blake is about to give the sign that will set in motion the revolutionary army of the diasporic black nation from Canada to Cuba and from Texas to the Dismal Swamps in Virginia, the novel breaks off. Originally published in serial form in the *Weekly Anglo-African*, the final chapters of Delany's novel have been lost, so the novel does not end in the usual sense of narrative closure. Instead, we are left hanging on the final words, "Woe be unto those devils of whites, I say!" (p. 313)—unsure whether the revolution that Henry Blake has so carefully planned succeeds, fails, or even occurs. *Blake*, in this sense, is a kind of uncanny (dis)embodiment of Abdul JanMohamed and David Lloyd's theory of minority discourse as "often-damaged, -fragmentary, -hampered, or -occluded."[39] Maddening in that the novel frustrates our longing for semantic closure (especially given that Delany seems poised here to overthrow the racial hierarchy on which America's internal colonialism is founded) the open-ended quality of Delany's novel, I would argue, makes it, however, an uncannily accurate depiction of the lived complexity of African Americans' internally colonized condition.[40]

It is not only the strangely fragmented form of Delany's novel that makes it a postcolonial American novel but Delany's ability imaginatively to escape the constraints of what McClintock calls the *imperial idea of linear time*. McClintock notes that, because the term *postcolonial* is still situated temporally in terms of the colonial period it is meant to escape, it "is haunted by the very figure of linear 'development' that it sets out to dismantle" such that we are left "gazing back, spellbound, at the epoch behind us, in a perpetual present marked only as 'post.'" Delany's novel, however, does not look back but instead takes us to the precipice of a black revolution such that, in the end, we are left looking forward to a postcolonial diasporic black nation that realizes what McClintock calls the "promise [of] . . . hybridity, syncretism, [and] multidimensional time."[41] Delany achieves this promise by, on the one hand, engaging a unique textual hybridity that incorporates a heteroglot array of voices from Maudy Ghamus's nation language to Placido's Spanish poetry to Judge Ballard's colonialist discourse. Moreover, Delany's syncretic vision embraces a cross-cultural community that extends from the Sudan to Texas and from Canada to Cuba. And, finally, Delany's novel can be said to occur in a multidimensional postcolonial temporality in that his protagonist moves in and out of so many different cultural dimensions that, as one character tell Blake, "it makes no difference when, nor where you are . . . as the scheme is adopted to all times and places" (p. 41). Having escaped the colonial order of chronology, Delany is thus able to have Blake move all across the South (traveling on foot and only at night) to Canada, Cuba, and even Africa without time ever seeming to move, keeping us always on the brink of the revolutionary moment.

Delany's novel, in this sense, seems to embody what Homi Bhabha calls, after Fanon, that moment of *occult instability* in which "the people" are caught in a "fluctuating movement" of nation building "*which they are just giving shape to.*"[42] Poignantly, the fragmented quality of Delany's text, poised on the precipice of a revolution that is doomed to be endlessly deferred, and the "fluctuating . . . just giving shape to" sense of temporality that the novel enacts depict with uncanny accuracy the painful plight of African Americans. For Delany's fragmented dream of a black revolution against the white colonizers modeled on the "Malution wah" captures with startling accuracy that historical tension within the African American community between an ever-present impulse to cultural independence and the disturbingly persistent plight of being contained as a nation within a nation by a form of internal colonization that the dominant white society refuses to acknowledge. And it is, finally, somewhere in this historical and psychological ambiguity of postless postcolonial subjectivity and anticolonial colonialism that the meaning of *postcolonial* in an American context can be said to lie.

Notes

1   Henry Louis Gates Jr., "Criticism in the Jungle," in *Black Literature and Literary Theory*, ed. Henry Louis Gates Jr. (New York: Methuen, 1984), 7.
2   José David Saldívar, "Américo Paredes and Decolonization," in *Cultures of United States Imperialism*, ed. Amy Kaplan and Donald E. Pease (Durham, N.C.: Duke University Press, 1993), 294.

3   Lawrence Buell, "American Literary Emergence as a Post-Colonial Phenomenon," *American Literary History* 4, no. 3 (spring 1992): 411–12.

4   Cornel West, *Race Matters* (New York: Vintage, 1993), 8.

5   Amy Kaplan, " 'Left Alone with America': The Absence of Empire in the Study of American Culture," in Kaplan and Pease, eds., *Cultures of United States Imperialism*, 5.

6   Anne McClintock, "The Angel of Progress: Pitfalls of the Term 'Post-Colonialism,' " *Social Text* 10, nos. 2–3 (1992): 85, 86.

7   Martin R. Delany, *Blake; or, The Huts of America* (Boston: Beacon, 1970); page numbers will be cited parenthetically in the text.

8   McClintock, "The Angel of Progress," 86.

9   Herman Melville, *Moby-Dick* (New York: Penguin, 1986), 158.

10   Rodolfo Acuña, *Occupied America: A History of the Chicanos* (New York: Harper and Row, 1981), 33–36.

11   William Wells Brown, *Clotel; or, The President's Daughter* (New York: Carol, 1969), 226.

12   For a fuller reading of the case and its consequences for America's national identity, see Robert A. Williams Jr., *The American Indian in Western Legal Thought: The Discourses of Conquest* (New York: Oxford University Press, 1990).

13   Frederick Merk, *Manifest Destiny and Mission in American History* (New York: Vintage, 1966). For more on historians' view of American imperialism in its various forms, see William Appleman Williams, ed., *From Colony to Empire* (New York: Wiley, 1972); Lewis Feuer, *Imperialism and the Anti-Imperialist Mind* (New York: Prometheus, 1986); Ernest May, *Imperial Democracy: The Emergence of America as a Great Power* (New York: Harcourt, Brace, and World, 1961); Rubin Francis Weston, *Racism in U.S. Imperialism: The Influence of Racial Assumptions on American Foreign Policy, 1893–1946* (Columbia: University of South Carolina Press, 1972); William Appleman Williams, *Empire as a Way of Life* (New York: Oxford University Press, 1980).

14   "Documents Relating to the Origins of the Monroe Doctrine," in *Expansion and Reform, 1815–1850*, ed. Charles M. Wiltse (New York: Free Press, 1967), 52, 60.

15   Richard Van Alstyne argues, in fact, that a close reading of the treaty in which Spain ceded Florida to the United States reveals that America did not purchase the territory but that "historians have assumed and repeated [this] ad nauseaum . . . [because,] unlike other nations, the United States does not 'take' territory, it only 'buys it' " ("The American Empire Makes Its Bow on the World Stage," in Williams, eds., *From Colony to Empire*, 48).

16   Howard Zinn, *A People's History of the United States* (New York: Harper and Row, 1980), 166.

17   McClintock, "The Angel of Progress," 88.

18   I am using the term *nativism* here in a very particular sense. The historical origins of the word in antebellum America can be traced back to a political movement that began in the late 1840s and crested in 1854 when Nativists, or the Know Nothing Party, swept many state elections. (In 1854, Nativists in Massachusetts won the governorship and all but 2 of the 390 seats in the state House of Representatives.) These political activists proclaimed themselves "Native Americans" and were primarily concerned with extending the period of naturalization so as to minimize the political effect of Irish Catholics, who were pouring into New York harbor at the rate of ten thousand per day during the height of the potato famine in Ireland. For more on political Nativism, see Tyler Anbinder, *Nativism and Slavery: The Northern Know Nothings and the Politics of the 1850s* (New York: Oxford University Press, 1992).

I am, however, using the term *nativism* here in a broader sense than that in which it was used at the midpoint of the nineteenth century. I have expanded the term to refer to the sense of cultural anxiety that the dominant white society felt in relation to African Americans, Native Americans, Catholics, Chicanos, Asians, and Jews (once again, whites obviously did not necessarily respond to each group in the same way, and these differences must be theorized). This move is precipitated by my sense that the term *racism* is too narrowly limited to black-white relations and does not, therefore, capture the cultural breadth of internal colonialism.

In terms of the confusion surrounding the nineteenth- and twentieth-century meanings of *Native American*, I have continued to use the appellation to denote both Indians and white nativists with the difference between the two groups being signified by the use of quotation marks when used to denote white nativists. One final thought in passing—the ambiguity is instructive in that it indicates a deep-seated uncertainty regarding the question of just who is a "Native American" and suggests an important insight into why whites felt that they had to exile Native Americans culturally in order to appropriate the title for themselves.

19   See Brian C. Mitchell, *The Paddy Camps: The Irish of Lowell, 1821–61* (Urbana: University of Illinois Press, 1988).

20   See Mary Gilbert Kelly, *Catholic Immigrant Colonization Projects in the United States, 1815–1860* (New York: U.S. Catholic Historical Society, 1939).

21   See Floyd J. Miller, *The Search for a Black Nationality: Black Emigration and Colonization, 1787–1863* (Urbana: University of Illinois Press, 1975).

22   Martin R. Delany, *The Condition, Elevation, Emigration, and Destiny of the Colored People of the United States* (New York: Arno, 1968), 203.

23   See Robert A. Trennert Jr., *Alternative to Extinction: Federal Indian Policy and the Beginnings of the Reservation System, 1846–51* (Philadelphia: Temple University Press, 1975).

24   Michael Paul Rogin, *Fathers and Children: Andrew Jackson and the Subjugation of the American Indian* (New Brunswick, N.J.: Transaction, 1991), 244.

25   Brian W. Dippie, *The Vanishing American: White Attitudes and U.S. Indian Policy* (Middletown, Conn.: Wesleyan University Press, 1982).

26   Rogin, *Fathers and Children*, 247.

27   Paul Boyer, *Urban Masses and Moral Order in America, 1820–1920* (Cambridge, Mass.: Harvard University Press, 1978), 99.

28   Second Article of the ACS constitution, as quoted in *Thoughts on African Colonization*, ed. William Lloyd Garrison (New York: Arno, 1968), 42.

29   See P. J. Staudenraus, *The African Colonization Movement, 1816–1865* (New York: Columbia University Press, 1961).

30   From the *African Repository*, the publication of the ACS, quoted in Garrison, ed., *Thoughts on African Colonization*, 113.

31   Delany, *The Condition . . . of the Colored People of the United States*, 169.

32   Ibid., 159; First annual report of the ACS, quoted in Garrison, ed., *Thoughts on African Colonization*, 113.

33   Homi K. Bhabha, "DissemiNation: Time, Narrative, and the Margins of the Modern Nation," in *Nation and Narration*, ed. Homi K. Bhabha (London: Routledge, 1990), 307.

34   Ibid., 297.

35   Edward Kamau Brathwaite, "English in the Caribbean," in *English Literature: Opening Up the Canon*, ed. Leslie Fiedler and Houston A. Baker Jr. (Baltimore: Johns Hopkins University Press, 1981), 16, 18.

36   Houston A. Baker Jr., *Modernism and the Harlem Renaissance* (Chicago: University of Chicago Press, 1987), 77.

37   Merk, *Manifest Destiny*, 220.

38   The Ostend Report was written by James Buchanan, J. Y. Mason, and Pierre Soule in 1854. It

is quoted from *The Works of James Buchanan*, ed. John Bassett Moore (Philadelphia: Lippincott, 1909), 9:265.

39 Abdul R. JanMohamed and David Lloyd, "Introduction: Toward a Theory of Minority Discourse: What Is to Be Done?" in *The Nature and Context of Minority Discourse*, ed. Abdul R. JanMohamed and David Lloyd (New York: Oxford University Press, 1990), 8.

40 By *open-ended*, I mean that this condition of internal colonization continues up to the present day.

41 McClintock, "The Angel of Progress," 97.

42 Bhabha, "DissemiNation," 304.

POSTSCRIPT

Surviving Theory:

A Conversation with Homi K. Bhabha

KALPANA SESHADRI-CROOKS

K alpana Seshadri-Crooks: Could you tell us about your early academic training in India?
Homi K. Bhabha: The education I had at Elphinstone College, Bombay, was very traditional, a sort of reflection of the Oxford or Cambridge tradition, translated to India by my teachers, who were mainly products of a fairly orthodox British education. The pedagogical norm was based on the English literary canon. However, I also remember the emergence of a much more informal countercanon that preoccupied us as students outside the classroom. There was a great interest in American literature: some of it was offered to us in courses, some in visiting speakers sponsored by USIS [United States Information Services], but, for the most part, it was an interest fostered by reading groups, independent theater ensembles, and, I seem to remember, the younger members of the advertising elite, who seemed to organize much of the cultural life of the city. Whereas the advertising world in the West is associated with mindless consumerism, the avant-garde cultural life of the Bombay of the 1960s and the 1970s was largely dominated by copywriters who fostered the most radical cultural tastes. Many of the avant-garde poets, painters, and filmmakers came from that world. They were really at the center of the Left liberal public sphere. I have always been intrigued by that particular postcolonial quirk where the advertising demimonde seemed to represent what was at the foreground of the arts. It was a "controlled" rebellion against more conventional "Eurocentric" norms that was explicitly "Americanist" in style and tone — I say *Americanist* rather than *American* because, I believe, it was a much more indigenous movement, a more explicitly translational reality. It served our purposes in urban, metropolitan India; it was not just some pale shadow of what was happening in New York, Los Angeles, or Chicago. The identification with certain American arts was a way of distancing ourselves generationally from what we saw

to be English. Englishness had blended into an everyday Indianness for a certain kind of bilingual, bourgeois middle-class Indian living in Bombay. It's very interesting how we used avant-garde Americanism to shake up what we saw as a kind of Indian Englishness that was the inheritance we had.

My ambitions in those days were not in the least bit critical/theoretical. The last thing that interested me was critical or conceptual argument. I was absolutely convinced in those days that my great gift was to be a poet. My loving and supportive friends encouraged this illusion, which seemed to have a remarkable, unquestionable authority in those times. Most of my time was spent writing poetry, some of which was published. That was my great pleasure. It absorbed me in a way that nothing else did. It was my all-embracing, all-absorbing passion.

KSC: What kind of a poet did you want to be?

HKB: It was all within the spectrum of Anglo-American verse. I had only a brief encounter with modernist Marathi literature in translation. There was a very rich Marathi poetic and theatrical tradition, and I remember being fascinated by its cosmopolitanism. Marathi literature held its own in a conversation with various European avant-garde traditions, translating and transforming them with a range of allusions to which those Western traditions were quite deaf. A similar process was visible in the case of the Dalit Panther Poets, who named themselves after the Black Panthers. These were the experiences that much later on, probably unconsciously, convinced me that hybridization is not some happy, consensual mix of diverse cultures; it is the strategic, translational transfer of tone, value, signification, and position — a transfer of power — from an authoritative system of cultural hegemony to an emergent process of cultural relocation and reiteration that changes the very terms of interpretation and institutionalization, opening up contesting, opposing, innovative, "other" grounds of subject and object formation. It is this double consciousness that produces what I call the *vernacular cosmopolitanism* of the postcolonial or minoritarian subject. It is a mode of living, and a habit of mind, that seeks cultural translation, not to recover the norms of universality, autonomy, and sovereignty, but to assert that there is a positive, agential value in the whole process of surviving domination that can add an edge, a cutting edge, to the critiques — contra neoliberalism or retro-Marxist — that come from those who have been displaced or marginalized on the grounds of their cultural, civilizational, or, as it is often described, moral and spiritual backwardness. There are always, more or less, polite ways of saying these things that change with whatever is the prevailing, polite protocol of injury and disempowerment. It is this subaltern creativity and innovation against the odds — a political and poetic agency — that sustains my work and shapes its solidarity with that form of historical revision initiated by Ranajit Guha and South Asian subaltern historiography. These views have been seen to be either hypertheoretical or naively optimistic.

But, I suppose, I have an attachment to poetic justice, and I believe that there is an ethical responsibility to be vigilant for the merest signs of subaltern life, as best one can, whether or not they constitute, by some macho or messianic measure, a major political act or a significant school of art.

But, for my own self, my early model, my mentor was W. H. Auden. I was never as enchanted with Keats or the Romantics; that was the staple of reading in those days. I was stimulated by Eliot, but I think somewhat put off by the kind of piety of the great later works. Auden was really my favorite poet. I was utterly stunned by his formal brilliance and totally seduced by the prodigious pleasure and appetite that he attributed to poetry. Poetry could and should be able to engage with the full clamor of contemporary experience — he calls this *the democratic aspect of literary creation*. The voraciousness of that appetite: whatever he wanted to talk about appeared in verse, from peeling shrimps, to the death of Yeats, to homoerotic love, to the Spanish Civil War, to his adoration of opera. I was just astounded and turned hungry, deeply hungry, in imitation of the insatiable desire of his verse. I also responded to the great playfulness of his verse and his ability to translate the way in which something could be immensely tender at one moment and totally tendentious at the other — while keeping the tension of transition alive in the very tone of the line. This shift in tone registered a faultless ear for verse of all kinds. He revived archaic forms and English rhythms in very contemporary moments. Auden truly fascinates me. I remember reading Auden by the gallon when I could absorb only a thimblefull. But I was totally absorbed. For me, that was really the vocation — to be a poet.

KSC: It seems that your approach to poetry is responsible for your critical sensibility as well. Your narrative adumbrates so many of your critical, theoretical themes.

HKB: I think it does, in a way. For me, an idea, a concept, a theory that I am trying to work through, never gets articulated to my satisfaction at the level of content, illustration, exemplification. To apply a concept or a theory is to be owned by it, to be in thrall to it. Your relation to an idea or method is then descriptive. This can be extremely useful, but it does not allow for the kind of dislocation that I find productive and necessary. But, when I have grasped the figurality of a concept, which is also its fragility, then the thing catches fire. For to understand the concept as figure is to see not only its topical, spatial status in a world of concepts or in the structure of an argument; it is also to appreciate its tropic or metaphoric structure — the terms in which it may not be quite what it claims it is and why it may be something other than it knows itself to be. The figurality of an idea or concept is, to put it figuratively, the idea or concept on the move, in the process of practice or performance; opened up in this sense, one can work with it in a trans- or interdisciplinary way while respecting the specificity of any particular location of a body of thought or, for that matter, any unique representation of a body of experience.

KSC: That's very useful. To hear you say this is going to clarify a lot about how to read your work. But this leads me to ask an unfortunately prosaic question. How do you write in this way? Is there a process here in which you engage? One of the difficulties in reading or teaching your work is that, contrary to hegemonic freshman comp ideals, your arguments do not seem to have an obvious development or progression.

HKB: I don't spend, some people think, enough time describing the object or the objective of the process. I like to do it; I like to perform it. I like to have the concept emerge in a kind of catching fire rather than an unfolding illumination. I like to think that the reader can almost be moved into occupying that space of the concept or the language and be placed in media res. I would almost like it to be a theatricalization of theory so that the reader is a part of it and does not understand it sitting in her chair overlooking and judging the concept from a distance. The reader, for me, must feel engaged at all levels of witnessing, in the very midst of an unfolding of a theoretical idea. For me, writing is really a contingent and dramatic process. At various levels, it's really a great struggle with a sense of incompletion and innovation.

KSC: How does the reader enter your work, translate it, or redeploy it for other purposes if it is worked from a perspective of incompletion?

HKB: It is surprising how systematically people use my work, feeling that it has provided them with concepts—hybridization, the notion of interstitial agency, ambivalence, mimicry, the pedagogical and performative.

KSC: Is that ironic, then?

HKB: I think that the structure of the work is ironic. To develop a certain concept, I place it in very strange, unexpected, uncanny contexts. By doing that, I set up a continual tension in the application of a concept, its translatability, and demonstrate at the same time its untranslatability. That's not to say its limits. A concept that merely shows its limits, or is pressed to do so, can still develop a sense of its ontological completion or authenticity—au fond, "this is what it really is." By producing concepts of partial identification in a critical discourse or rhetoric that itself reflects this mode of thought, I encourage a partial translational of/identification with my own ideas. My ambition is that people will acknowledge the idea and use it but will then be thrust into a terrain of the untranslatable, which will be their moment of primary elaboration. In that moment, when they stake out their own terrain, my concept or idea is both extended and transformed. I hope that at no level is there any kind of masterful assertion of the possession of a concept but always a much more collaborative relocation of a concept. That's the ambition I have, and I think that I have been well served by my readers in that way.

KSC: Your description of your work is of course retrospective insofar as you did not decide beforehand that this was the kind of work you were going to do. Which leads me to guess that you must have had this experience of reading with some other work.

HKB: I suppose that you could say that, as a writer, or even as a person, I'm not a joiner. I am a survivor in solidarity with other ideas. I like to survive ideas and theories rather than be subservient to them or be a part of a system. I take the notion of surviving an idea very, very seriously. And it is a position that I would like to think about further. On the one hand, it means that you get into a body of work, or into a conceptual minefield, and expect to be hit by it with all its stunning brilliance and savagery. You do not maintain the skeptic's distance, which is often the way in which we are instructed to engage with ideas. The skeptic knows where his or her grounds are and then allows another idea or another text to come in. The skeptic measures distances, proximities, or some innovations that are then accepted, but only on given grounds. I am really of the school of reading as ravishment, reading as being ravished. So survival in that sense is a way, not of preserving the ballast in the reading, but of letting it go and seeing how and where, through the sweptness of the work, one will emerge. In another sense, I think of survival in the way that Derrida talked of it in relation to Walter Benjamin: survival is the way of living on, a living on after the event, after the original. It is not living in seclusion but a living on-ness and a living on the borderlines. Survival, in that sense, is the precariousness of living on the borderline and has been one of my ways of close reading and writing. And then there is the third sense, the ethical sense of survival, which is that, however alienating the experience may be, you stick with it. You don't abandon it for a safer ship or a safer soil. And, really, very often, just at the level of personal experience, I will be in the midst of writing something, feeling totally wrecked by the vessel I've built for myself, seeing parts of the work splinter, break off, float away, but Ahab-like I want to say, "I'm going to see this thing through even if it means that I'm going to rebuild the boat while I'm in midocean and risk everything." So survival is not only a sticking with something to the end; it's also, for me, an experience of how, in motion, in transition, in movement, you must continually build a habitation for your ideas, your thoughts, and yourself.

KSC: It's almost like you were describing an aesthetics of politics rather than, say, a politics of aesthetics. But, with reference to building a habitation for one's ideas, I'd like to ask you about your new home in the U.S. academy. If we were to translate this to the academic context, these are the issues at stake in the so-called culture wars in the United States, aren't they? You've addressed this issue in various places, mostly to emphasize the unsettled nature of culture itself as a category of debate and of the term's adequacy as a guarantor of national, racial, and ethnic identity as such. But can you speak for a moment about the particularities of academic cultures especially in relation to Britain and the United States and what you have observed in their differences with regard to the presence or absence of the culture wars that seems symptomatic to you about the national, liberal enterprises in these locations?

HKB: Let's make a quick distinction between two kinds of culture wars: there is a war waged around the canon and the curriculum, and the theater of that war is the academy, the intellectual, highbrow journals, the arts pages, museums, the quality press; the second kind of culture war is an event that has a wider social reach, often becoming a popular media event, sometime performed in the new prime time of our times, the glamorous superstar trial. It concerns some crisis or trauma in the public sphere around issues of discrimination or violation, often articulated across lines of race, gender, sexuality—the class element is a crucial determinant, but, when class issues are seen to be the foci of conflict, then the terrain of culture, as the problematic of conflict or contention, yields to the rhetoric of the economic or the political. In the States, both forms of culture wars are easily identifiable. If the Dinesh DeSouzas and the Roger Kimballs fuel the former, then the Rodney King beatings, the Clarence Thomas/Anita Hill debacle, and the O. J. Simpson affair are prominent examples of the latter. As far as the United Kingdom goes, the university is not the central site of cultural debate, and therefore it is much less symbolically charged as a symptom of the state of the nation. The Rushdie event is perhaps the most significant British culture war of our times — there have been riots before, racial and cultural discrimination of various kinds — but there has never been another event as severe and crucial for Britain's liberal culture than the issue of *The Satanic Verses*.

The first kind of culture war is much more prominent in the United States than in Britain. Yes, when Cambridge wanted to give Derrida an honorary degree, there were protests and much lobbying against the idea, but the objectors were easily trounced. This is a culture war quite different from the familiar U.S. narrative where the representation of some form of ethnic representation, community interest, or minority cultural practice is seen as the corruption of the canon or the subversion of national life "as we know it." It is interesting that culture wars in the United States focus so much on what is happening in universities and other elite institutions, whereas the public schools, where the real culture wars are being fought with drugs, violence, diminishing budgets, and disappearing facilities, are hardly part of the conversation. The professionalization of the American academy gives it a presence and a prestige that needs to be protected and regulated; that's one reason. The other is that the sphere of liberal public culture seems to exist largely in the university and its affiliated institutions and social forms. The university is often the most liberal territory in American public life. So the university becomes the space for dissent and discussion. In contrast, Britain has a more developed liberal public sphere, one that exists independently of scholarly institutions. Newspapers, the media, the BBC's annual Reith Lectures, various cultural associations, are really descendants of eighteenth-century coffeehouses and small magazines from which Habermas derived his notion of the bourgeois public sphere. The post-1945 welfare reforms in Britain, with the flagship program of comprehensive education, did much to create a much larger shared world of cultural communication than exists in America.

This brings me to the most significant difference between the United States and the United Kingdom on the matter of minorities and the culture wars waged in their name. It is the difference between being a postslavery society and a postcolonial society. The United States is a society of many migrations and minorities, but the primal scene of cultural displacement, social alienation, and minoritization is the event of slavery. My strong feeling is that to be a minority in the United States requires you to take a position in relation to the questions of African American society, slave history, and postslavery history. And I think that this gives being a minority an articulated, mediated structure—you are not simply a minority relative to a majority or the state. Your status as a migrant minority must also be negotiated in relation to the presence of the postslavery situation, although that may not be the history of your past or present. A similar argument could be made in relation to the nation's first peoples.

Britain, on the other hand, is a postcolonial society immigration into which followed on the granting of independence to the colonies. Emigration often occurred during a period of great economic and political instability in newly independent Third World countries. This gives the ontological presence of the migrant a very different kind of quality, even when she or he is the victim of institutionalized or individualized racism. However much the issue of the welfare state is contested or eroded by Thatcherism and New Labour, the ethical ideal that it introduced persists, however compromised or attenuated it is. It spectrality should not be underestimated. At the ethicopolitical level, there are certain threshold notions about the common good that underlie British liberalism and its social discourse even when it produces social inequality. This is not a justification of the British system at all; it is a brief attempt at understanding why, despite discrimination and inegalitarianism, there is a belief in the pastoral nature of the state and a strange quiet acceptance of issues around cultural representation and regulation that would ignite the social fabric in the United States.

KSC: I'd like to come back to your work in the context of the culture wars. How do we situate the broad eclecticism of your work? It seems to straddle several discourses: political theory, art criticism, psychoanalysis, critical historiography, etc. What kind of a pedagogy does it or should it engender? Does postcolonial theory (as a critique of the discourses of modernity) have a method?

HKB: The eclecticism to which you refer is partly a matter of my education and partly an effect of the theoretical/pedagogical status of the work itself.

Try to imagine what it was like when, in the mid-1970s, I started work on Naipaul as part of an (unconscious) encounter with the colonial and postcolonial text. I knew that these texts needed a new conceptual framing and staging; the Leavisite or Marxist frameworks, deployed in those days to define Commonwealth literature (Leavisite) or Third World literature (Marxist sociology of literature), were too predetermined in their engagement. The Leavisite aesthetic was committed to a close reading and the question of quality; the Marxist reading was focused on contextualism and the issue of class. I was unable to buy into either, although I was influenced by both. Somewhere in my bones, I knew that a psychoanalytic account of subjectivity was absolutely crucial to the work I wanted to do. The theory of ideology (largely Althusserian in those days) foregrounded structural contradiction but didn't adequately account for the ambivalent mode of social agency and affective identification that I found most baffling and challenging in those texts. The partial, the metonymic, the ambivalent, the interstitial — these figures of inscription and identification that inscribed the colonial and postcolonial text were left unelaborated in the prevalent critical traditions. Nor did the contextualist or historicist approach pay enough attention to the fantasmatic scene that seemed to occupy a large part of the narrative of colonial and postcolonial texts. I was, in a naive way, convinced that the issues of race, identity, sexuality, and class that were at play in postcolonial fictional and nonfictional writings were as much issues of desire and affect as they were part of a wider political and historical discussion of rights and representations. This finally led me to Fanon, who has since become a major influence on, and confluence for, my work. So, talking of eclecticism, then, I seem to have realized early on that a dense interdisciplinarity and intense intradiscursivity would be the fate of the work I was intent on doing.

Very early on in my researches in the field of colonial inscription, I became aware of the widely disparate and heterogeneous orders of discourse that constituted colonial knowledge. The collage or bricolage of the discourse — its disorder — fascinated me all the more because its ordering principle was often rigidly taxonomic, hierarchic, and fetishistic. It is this disjunctive moment, this splitting, as it initiates an ambivalent articulation of contradictory and compensatory knowledges, in the service of power and authority, that I tried to develop through my work on the hybrid enunciative modalities of colonial and postcolonial discourse.

Is this an eclectic pedagogy? Is it a pluralistic or relativistic pedagogy? Is it a dialogic pedagogy? I suppose that I pose these issues as questions (instead of propositions) because, once you talk of ambivalence as an articulatory structure, these various readings emerge. I don't believe that the method of my work is pluralist or relativist. I am interested in the translational move that opens up an interstitial space for the negotiation of meaning, value, judgment — how the "one" survives in/of the "other" as a kind of structure of doubling (not sublimation or sublation) — not pluralism, but excessive iteration, if you will allow me this shorthand.

KSC: Does *theoretical correctness* mean anything to you? For instance, to work with Lacanian concepts is to be always anxious about a certain fealty to the integrity of the system or the teaching. For many, this sounds offputting and authoritarian, but it also assures a certain coherence and clarity that seem unbending toward hegemonic politics and opinion making. How do you conceive of your function in the academy precisely? A cultural critic, a philosopher, a theorist? I guess I'm trying to sort out the appellation that accompanies your work so often: that it is "original." Can you reflect on that notion in the sense in which you have encountered it in your own intellectual biography? Is there a theory of knowledge production, of language, that is operative in your discourse?

HKB: You are too kind, Kalpana. . . . You ask about the appellation of originality that often attaches to my work — and gives me great pleasure, of course — but you graciously omit the charge that I am "too difficult," willfully obscure, etc. Your question sets off in many directions. Let me try and respond to one or two of them. In the domain of the natural sciences, where protocols of reading and knowing differ greatly, we must, of course, take very seriously the demand for a certain stability of knowledge. But, natural sciences aside, theoretical correctness seems subtly to defeat the process of conceptual work, which must entertain the possibility that any particular body of thought, despite its ruling paradigms and metaphors, has no sovereign mastery of control over its enunciation (inscription or interpretation). This seems to me both obvious and worth saying, especially when schools of thought become prisons of method, whether by the misplaced dogmatism of practitioners or in response to institutional and disciplinary hegemonies — the desire to control a particular space of knowledge production, to "authorize" it. Let this not be misunderstood as the excesses of free play or free markets in ideas. Commitments are crucial, both pedagogically and politically, but *correctness* is hardly the term to use. I believe in something more akin to Foucault's notion of *strategic elaboration*, Deleuze's *assemblage*, both of which suggest that we almost always begin in the middle: that establishing a particular theoretical position must contend with a certain temporal disjunction at the very point or moment in which the subject takes its stand by loosing its foothold because there is no conceptual space to lay foundations in an empty space (elsewhere I have developed this as the time lagged). One is always palimpsestically overelaborating, overwriting, overinscribing, which means that the limits of thought or theory are always showing through other borders of historical, conceptual, and ethical possibility. Theoretical thinking teaches us the nontransparency of ideas, the radical indeterminacy of signifying structures — and this must apply to the making and holding of theory itself, which demands a responsibility to the thinking of a problem as always in excess of, or in violation of, the tools for thinking it. That must be the starting point, which, ironically, can only ever be, all at once, a beginning, a middle, and an end.

I don't really ponder my place in the academy or anywhere else—and this is not to deflect your question. I see myself as responding to exigencies and demands—internal and external—with the best intelligence and ethicopolitical responsibility that I can muster. For me, it is a matter of survival rather than some calm self-reflection. I very much enjoy a camouflagelike presence where you attempt really to identify yourself with a problem or question that you think is significant—you try to understand its genealogy of emergence, why it presents a problem in this or that historical moment, why its presence comes through this or that language of expression or discourse of representation or regulation. Then I enjoy even more the moment at which you make your move: you appear altogether in another color and shape, the scene changes, you have made your intervention, and the issue of agency, transformation, responsibility, must be posed from a different place of locution or location. One is, once more, beginning in the middle. . . . Let not the figure of the camouflage stand for inconstancy or the continual reinvention of oneself or one's circumstances; that is not at all what I mean. Camouflage is not a spontaneist approach; it is a strategic mode of intervention. As I've said elsewhere, camouflage, like mimicry, is not a harmonization, a repression of difference. It inscribes itself in the present discourse where it appears as a stain, which dislocates and revalues normative knowledges of race, writing, history. In fact, what is so interesting about the strategy of camouflage is how it has to deal with a situation that is obdurate and obstinate in its presence but is not fixed in its re-presentation. Agency requires that you take seriously what is given even while you act and react to change its authority as the only way of seeing or being seen.

KSC: Your work is particularly unique in the field as it goes beyond theories of representation (as successful interpellations of the migrant, the minority, the other) to invoke the problematic of failure. There's much that is implicit therein about being and meaning. I wonder if you don't work largely against the grain of a certain postcolonial studies that has established itself as the antitheory theory in the academy?

HKB: Isn't beginning in the middle—having to accept responsibility for anteriority while oddly anticipating the emergence of futures past as a practice of present time—always to acknowledge a certain failure or, at least in Lacanian terms, a certain fading? You have touched on a founding moment of my work, quite literally so. I started working with one predicament at the very forefront of my concerns—it was the predicament of Mr. Biswas in V. S. Naipaul's *A House for Mr. Biswas*. In Biswas's failure, there was a profound and strong sense of survival, in his repeated humiliations a real sense of agency, in his homelessness a real possibility of accommodation, in his servility a real intimation of sovereignty. But *survival* here means living in the ambivalent movement in between both these seemingly contradictory or incommensurate moments. Biswas is always in the middle; he is able to grasp the iterative, and, without laying a foundation, he is able to establish a narrative and ethical presence. For all his civilizational certainties, with which I profoundly disagree, V. S. Naipaul as novelist has a subtle awareness of the partiality of life — of how to live with the bits and pieces, the debris and detritus that get thrown up against the shore of movement, migration, displacement, and forced eviction. You will remember that one of the recurrent, repeated moments of historical evocation in *The Mimic Men* is the driftwood forlorn on the beach in Isabella, as a sign of the ship of indentured laborers from India that ran aground on the coast of Trinidad in the 1850s. Naipaul would probably disagree with my reading entirely. For me, however, these almost unrecognizable shards of wood, stripped of any reality and therefore symbolically potent as signs to be read and reread and relocated, constitute the possibility of building a life from the origins of shipwreck. Survival continually haunts the dream of sovereignty with the possibility that failure is not the other side of success or mastery; it is its lining, an intimate and proximate mode of being or living in the midst of what we think needs to be done afresh or anew and what requires repeatedly to be repaired, revised, or reassembled. It is in this sense that I believe, or hope, that my work may continue to survive.

WORKS CITED

Acuna, Roldolfo. *Occupied America: A History of the Chicanos.* New York: Harper and Row, 1981.

Adam, Ian, and Helen Tiffin, eds. *Past the Last Post: Theorizing Post-Colonialism and Post-Modernism.* Hemel Hempstead: Harvester Wheatsheaf, 1991.

Adnan, Etel. *Sitt Marie Rose.* Translated by Georgina Kleege. Sausalito: Post-Apollo, 1982.

Adorno, Rolena, and W. D. Mignolo, eds. "Colonial Discourse." *Dispositio,* special issue, vols. 36–38 (1989).

Adunis. *Al-thabit wa al-mutahawwwil: Sadmat al-hadatha* (Continuity and transformation: The shock of modernity). Beirut: Dar al-awdah, 1979.

Agrawal, Bina. "The Gender and Environment Debate: Lessons from India." *Feminist Studies* 18, no. 1 (spring): 119–58.

Ahmad, Aijaz. "Jameson's Rhetoric of Otherness and the 'National Allegory.'" *Social Text* 17 (fall 1987): 3–25.

———. "'Third World Literature' and the Nationalist Ideology." *Journal of Arts and Ideas* 17–18 (June 1989): 117–36.

———. *In Theory: Classes, Nations, Literatures.* New York: Verso, 1992.

———. "The Politics of Literary Postcoloniality." *Race and Class* 36, no. 3 (1995): 1–20.

Alarcón, Norma. "The Theoretical Subject(s) of *This Bridge Called My Back* and Anglo-American Feminism." In *Making Face/Make Soul,* ed. Gloria Anzaldúa. San Francisco: Aunt Lute, 1990.

———. "Conjugating Subjects: The Heteroglossia of Essence and Resistance." In *Another Tongue: Nation and Ethnicity in the Linguistic Borderland,* ed. A. Artega. Durham, N.C.: Duke University Press, 1994.

Albó, Xavier. "And from Kataristas to MNRistas? The Surprising and Bold Alliance between Aymaras and Neoliberals in Bolivia." In *Indigenous Peoples and Democracy in Latin America,* ed. D. L. Van Cott. New York: St. Martin's, 1994.

Alloula, Malek. *The Colonial Harem.* Translated by Myrna Godzich and Wald Godzich. Minneapolis: University of Minnesota Press, 1986.

Althusser, Louis. "Ideology and Ideological State Apparatuses (Notes towards an Investigation)." In *Lenin and Philosophy and Other Essays by Louis Althusser,* trans. Ben Brewster. New York: Monthly Review Press, 1971.

———. *Essays on Ideology.* Translated by Ben Brewster. London: Verso, 1984.

Amin, Samir. *Unequal Development: An Essay on the Social Formations of Peripheral Capitalism.* Translated by Brian Pearce. New York: Monthly Review Press, 1976.

——. *Imperialism and Unequal Development.* New York: Monthly Review Press, 1977.

——. *Eurocentrism.* New York: Monthly Review Press, 1989.

——. "U.S. Militarism in the New World Order." *Polygraph* 5 (1992).

Anbinder, Tyler. *Nativism and Slavery: The Northern Know Nothings and the Politics of the 1850s.* New York: Oxford University Press, 1992.

Anderson, Benedict. *Imagined Communities: Reflections on the Origin and Spread of Nationalism.* London: Verso, 1983.

Anderson, Perry. *In the Tracks of Historical Materialism.* London: Verso, 1983.

Andrew, Dudley. *Andre Bazin.* New York: Oxford University Press, 1978.

Antonius, George. *The Arab Awakening: The Story of the Arab National Movement.* Philadelphia: Lippincott, 1939.

Anzaldúa, Gloria. *Borderlands/La frontera: The New Mestiza.* San Francisco: Spinster/Aunt Lute, 1987.

Anzaldúa, Gloria, and Cherry Moraga, eds. *This Bridge Called My Back: Writings by Radical Women of Color.* New York: Kitchen Table/Women of Color, 1983.

Appadurai, Arjun. "Disjuncture and Difference in the Global Cultural Economy." *Public Culture* 2, no. 2 (spring 1990): 1–29. Reprinted in *The Phantom Public Sphere,* ed. Bruce Robbins. Minneapolis: University of Minnesota Press, 1993.

——. "Patriotism and Its Futures." *Public Culture* 5, no. 3 (1993): 411–30.

Appiah, Kwame Anthony. "Is the *Post-* in Postmodernism the *Post-* in Postcolonial?" *Critical Inquiry* 17 (winter 1991).

——. *In My Father's House: Africa in the Philosophy of Culture.* Oxford: Oxford University Press, 1992.

——. "The Postcolonial and the Postmodern." In *In My Father's House: Africa in the Philosophy of Culture.* New York: Oxford University Press, 1992. 336–57.

Apter, Emily. "Ethnographic Travesties: Colonial Realism, French Feminism, and the Case of Elissa Rhais." In *After Colonialism: Imperial Histories and Postcolonial Displacements,* ed. Gyan Prakash. Princeton, N.J.: Princeton University Press, 1995.

Arnold, David. *Colonizing the Body: State Medicine and Epidemic Disease in Nineteenth-Century India.* Berkeley and Los Angeles: University of California Press, 1993.

Arth (The meaning). Directed by Mahesh Bhatt. Color, 140 minutes. Bombay: 1982. In Hindi.

Ashcroft, Bill, Gareth Griffiths, and Helen Tiffin, eds. *The Empire Writes Back: Theory and Practice in Post-Colonial Literatures.* London: Routledge, 1989.

——, eds. *The Post-Colonial Studies Reader.* London: Routledge, 1995.

Astrow, Andrew. *Zimbabwe: A Revolution That Lost Its Way?* London: Zed, 1983.

Baker, Houston A., Jr. *Modernism and the Harlem Renaissance.* Chicago: University of Chicago Press, 1987.

Baker, Randall. "Protecting the Environment against the Poor: The Historical Roots of Soil Erosion Orthodoxy in the Third World." *Ecologist* 14, no. 2 (1984).

Bakhtin, Mikhail. *Rabelais and His World.* Translated by Helene Iswolsky. Bloomington: Indiana University Press, 1984.

Balibar, Etienne. "The Nation Form: History and Ideology." In *Race, Nation, Class: Ambiguous Identities,* ed. Etienne Balibar and Immanuel Wallerstein. London: Verso, 1991.

——. "What Is a Politics of the Rights of Man?" In *Masses, Classes, Ideas.* New York: Routledge, 1994.

Balibar, Etienne, and Immanuel Wallerstein, eds. *Race, Nation, Class: Ambiguous Identities.* New York: Verso, 1991.

Banerjee, Sumanta. "Marginalization of Women's Popular Culture in Nineteenth Century Bengal." In *Recasting Women: Essays in Indian Colonial History,* ed. Kum Kum Sangari and Sudesh Vaid. New Brunswick, N.J.: Rutgers University Press, 1990.

Barker, Francis, Peter Hulme, and Margaret Iversen, eds. *Colonial Discourse/Postcolonial Theory.* Manchester: Manchester University Press, 1994.

Barragan, Rossana. "The Spirit of Bolivian Modernity: Citizenship, Infamy, and Patriarchal Hierarchy." *Economic and Political Weekly* 32, no. 30 (1997).

Barthelme, Donald. *The Dead Father.* New York: Farrar Straus Giroux, 1975.

Barton, C. A. *The Sorrows of the Ancient Romans: The Gladiator and the Monster.* Princeton, N.J.: Princeton University Press, 1993.

Baudry, Jean-Louis. "The Apparatus." In *Apparatus,* ed. Theresa Hak Kyung Cha, trans. Jean Andrew and Bertrand Auhst. New York: Tanam, 1980.

Bazin, Andre. *What Is Cinema?* Translated by Hugh Gray. Vol. 1. Los Angeles: University of California Press, 1967.

Behdad, Ali. "Traveling to Teach: Postcolonial Critics in the American Academy." In *Race, Identity, and Representation in Education,* ed. Cameron McCarthy and Warren Crichlow. New York: Routledge, 1993.

———. *Belated Travelers: Orientalism in the Age of Colonial Dissolution.* Durham, N.C.: Duke University Press, 1994.

Beit-Hallahmi, Benjamin. *The Israeli Connection: Who Israel Arms and Why.* New York: Pantheon, 1987.

———. *Original Sins: Reflections of the History of Zionism and Israel.* London: Pluto, 1992.

Bennett, Tony. "Putting Policy into Cultural Studies." In *Cultural Studies,* ed. Lawrence Grossberg, Cary Nelson, and Paula Treichler. New York: Routledge, 1992.

Bennington, Geoffrey. "Postal Politics and the Institution of the Nation." In *Nation and Narration,* ed. Homi K. Bhabha. London: Routledge, 1990.

Berkowitz, M. *Zionist Culture and West European Jewry before the First World War.* Cambridge: Cambridge University Press, 1993.

Bernal, Martin. *Black Athena: The Afroasiatic Roots of Classical Civilization.* Vol. 1. New Brunswick, N.J.: Rutgers University Press, 1987.

Bhabha, Homi K. "The Commitment to Theory." In *Questions of Third Cinema,* ed. Jim Pines and Paul Willemen. London: British Film Institute, 1989.

———. "DissemiNation: Time, Narrative, and the Margins of the Modern Nation." In *Nation and Narration,* ed. Homi K. Bhabha. London: Routledge, 1990.

———. "Interrogating Identity: The Post-Colonial Prerogative." In *The Anatomy of Racism,* ed. David Theo Goldberg. Minneapolis: University of Minnesota Press, 1990.

———. *The Location of Culture.* New York: Routledge, 1994.

———. "Of Mimicry and Man: The Ambivalence of Colonial Discourse." In *The Location of Culture.* London: Routledge, 1994.

Bhagat, Rasheeda. "Agony in the Asylum." *Indian Express,* 20 February 1994.

Bharucha, Rustom. *Rehearsals of Revolution: The Political Theatre of Bengal.* Honolulu: University of Hawaii Press, 1983.

Bhaskar, Roy. "What Is Critical Realism?" In *Reclaiming Reality.* London: Verso, 1989.

Bhattacharya, Lopamudra. "Home Sickness." *Sunday,* 26 November–2 December 1995.

Biale, D. *Eros and the Jews: From Biblical Israel to Contemporary America.* New York: Basic, 1992.

Bidwai, Praful. "India's Passage to Washington." *Nation,* 20 January 1992. 47–50.

———. "North vs. South on Pollution." *Nation,* 22 June 1992. 853–54.

Black Harvest. Directed by Bob Connolly and Robin Anderson. 16 millimeter, 90 minutes. Australia: Arundel Productions PL, 1992.

Black Law, White Lies. Report of the People's Union for Democratic Rights (PUDR). *Economic and Political Weekly* 30, no. 18/19 (May 6, 1995): 977–80.

Blum, H. P. "The Prototype of Preoedipal Reconstruction." In *Freud and His Self-Analysis,* ed. M. Kanzer and J. Glenn. New York: Jason Aronson, 1979.

Boal, Augusto. *Theatre of the Oppressed.* Translated by Charles McBride and Maria McBride. New York: Theatre Communications Group, 1985.

Borochov, Ber. "Eretz Israel in Our Program and Tactics." In *Class Struggle and the Jewish Nation: Selected Essays in Marxist Zionism,* ed. Mitchell Cohen. New Brunswick, N.J.: Transaction, 1984.

Boschetti, Anna. *The Intellectual Enterprise: Sartre and "Les temps modernes."* Translated by Richard McCleary. Evanston, Ill.: Northwestern University Press, 1988.

Bourdieu, Pierre. *Homo academicus.* Translated by Peter Collier. Stanford, Calif.: Stanford University Press, 1988.

Bowersock, G.W. "Palestine: Ancient History and Modern Politics." In *Blaming the Victims: Spurious Scholarship and the Palestinian Question,* ed. Edward Said and Christopher Hitchens. London: Verso, 1988.

Boyarin, D. "*Épater l'embourgeoisement:* Freud, Gender, and the (De)Colonized Psyche." *Diacritics* 24, no. 1 (spring 1994): 17–42.

———. "Freud's Baby; Fliess's Maybe: Male Hysteria, Homophobia, and the Invention of the Jewish Man." *GLQ* 2, no. 1 (1994): 1–33.

———. *Unheroic Conduct: The Rise of Heterosexuality and the Invention of the Jewish Man.* Berkeley and Los Angeles: University of California Press, 1997.

———. "Bitextuality, Psychoanalysis, Zionism: On the Ambivalence of the Jewish Phallus." In *Queer Diasporas,* ed. C. Patton and B. Sánchez-Eppler. Durham, N.C.: Duke University Press, in press.

Boyarin, J., and D. Boyarin. "Self-Exposure as Theory: The Double Mark of the Male Jew." In *Rhetorics of Self-Making,* ed. D. Battaglia. Berkeley and Los Angeles: University of California Press, 1995.

Boyer, Paul. *Urban Masses and Moral Order in America, 1820–1920.* Cambridge, Mass.: Harvard University Press, 1978.

Brando, Marlon. Interview by Lawrence Grobel. In *Conversations with Brando.* New York: Hyperion, 1991.

Brathwaite, Edward Kamau. "English in the Caribbean." In *English Literature: Opening Up the Canon,* ed. Leslie Fiedler and Houston A. Baker Jr. Baltimore: Johns Hopkins University Press, 1981.

Breines, Paul. *Tough Jews, Political Fantasies, and the Moral Dilemma of American Jewry.* New York: Basic, 1991.

Brenner, Lenni. *The Iron Wall: Zionist Revisionism from Jabotinsky to Shamir.* London: Zed, 1984.

Brown, William Wells. *Clotel; or, The President's Daughter.* New York: Carol, 1969.

Bruce, Babbitt. "Free Trade and Environmental Isolationism." *New Perspectives Quarterly* 9, no. 3 (1992): 35–37.

Buchanan, James, J. Y. Mason, and Pierre Soule. *The Ostend Report.* 1854. In *The Works of James Buchanan,* vol. 9, ed. John Bassett Moore. Philadelphia: Lippincott, 1909.

Buell, Lawrence. "American Literary Emergence as a Post-Colonial Phenomenon." *American Literary History* 4, no. 3 (spring 1992): 411–42.

Butler, Judith. *Gender Trouble: Feminism and the Subversion of Identity.* London: Routledge, 1990.

Calás, Marta B. "An/Other Silent Voice? Representing 'Hispanic Woman' in Organizational Text." In *Gendering Organizational Analysis*, ed. A.J. Mills and P. Tancred. Newbury Park, Calif.: Sage, 1992.

Calhoun, Craig. *Critical Social Theory*. New York: Blackwell, 1995.

Canclini, Néstor García. "Cultural Reconversion." In *On Edge: The Crisis of Contemporary Latin American Literature*, ed. George Yúdice, Jean Franco, and Juan Flores. Minneapolis: University of Minnesota Press, 1992.

Chakrabarty, Dipesh. "The Death of History? Historical Consciousness and the Culture of Late Capitalism." *Public Culture* 4, no. 2 (spring 1992): 47–68.

———. "Postcoloniality and the Artifice of History: Who Speaks for 'Indian' Pasts?" *Representations* 37 (winter 1992): 1–26.

Chamberlain, H. S. *Foundations of the Nineteenth Century*. Translated by J. Lees. New York: Howard Fertig, 1968.

Chambers, Iain. *Migrancy, Culture, Identity*. London: Routledge, 1994.

Chanan, Michael. *The Dream That Kicks: The Prehistory and Early Years of Cinema in Britain*. London: Routledge and Kegan Paul, 1980.

Chatterjee, Partha. *The Nation and Its Fragments*. Princeton, N.J.: Princeton University Press, 1993.

Chinua, Achebe. *Things Fall Apart*. London: Heinemann, 1958.

Cixous, Hélène, and Catherine Clement. *The Newly Born Woman*. Translated by Betsy Wing. Minneapolis: University of Minnesota Press, 1986.

Clifford, James. "Notes on Theory and Travel." *Inscriptions* 5 (1989).

———. "Travelling Theories." In *Cultural Studies*, ed. Lawrence Grossberg, Cary Nelson, and Paula Treichler. New York: Routledge, 1992.

Clifford, James, and George Marcus. *Writing Culture: The Poetics and Politics of Ethnography*. Berkeley and Los Angeles: University of California Press, 1986.

Clingman, Stephen. *The Essential Gesture: Writing, Politics and Places*. New York: Knopf, 1988.

Cockburn, Alexander. "Beat the Devil." *Nation*, 29 September 1984, pp. 260–61, and 13 October 1984, pp. 342–43.

———. "Socialist Ecology: What It Means, Why No Other Kind Will Do." *Zeta*, February 1989.

———. "Beat the Devil." *Nation*, March 28, 1994.

Cohen, Saul, and Nurit Kliot. "Israel's Place-Names as Reflection of Continuity and Change in Nation Building." *Names: Journal of the American Name Society* 29, no. 3 (September 1981): 227–48.

———. "Place-Names in Israel's Ideological Struggle over the Administered Territories." *Annals of the Association of American Geographers* 82, no. 4 (1992): 653–80.

Cohen, Stanley, and Andrew Scull. Introduction to *Social Control and the State: Historical and Comparative Essays*. Oxford: Martin Robertson, 1983.

Colonial Office (CO) 733/297/75156/II, app. A. Extract from Weizmann's speech, 23 April 1936, Peel Commission Report.

Connolly, Bob, and Robin Anderson. *First Contact: New Guinea's Highlanders Encounter the Outside World*. New York: Viking Penguin, 1987.

Connolly, William. *Identity/Difference: Democratic Negotiations of Political Paradox*. Ithaca, N.Y.: Cornell University Press, 1991.

Conrad. *Heart of Darkness*. Oxford: Oxford University Press, 1984.

Cornell, Drucilla. *The Philosophy of the Limit*. New York: Routledge, 1992.

Cuddihy, J. M. *The Ordeal of Civility: Freud, Marx, Lévi-Strauss, and the Jewish Struggle with Modernity*. Boston: Beacon, 1987.

Damini. Directed by Raj Kumar Santoshi. Color, 140 minutes. India: 1993. In Hindi.

Daniels, Norman. *Just Health Care*. Cambridge: Cambridge University Press, 1985.

Davis, Angela. *Women, Race, and Class*. New York: Vintage, 1981.

Davis, Uri, and Walter Lehn. "And the Fund Still Lives: The Role of the Jewish National Fund in the Determination of Israel's Land Policies." *Journal of Palestine Studies* 7, no. 4 (summer 1978).

Debray, Régis. *Teachers, Writers, Celebrities: The Intellectuals of Modern France*. Translated by David Macey. London: Verso, 1981.

Delany, Martin R. *The Condition, Elevation, Emigration, and Destiny of the Colored People of the United States*. New York: Arno, 1968.

———. *Blake; or, The Huts of America*. Boston: Beacon, 1970.

Deleuze, Gilles, and Michel Foucault. *The Foucault Phenomenon: The Problematics of Style*. Translated by Sean Hand. Minneapolis: University of Minnesota Press, 1986.

Deleuze, Gilles, and Felix Guattari. *Anti-Oedipus: Capitalism and Schizophrenia*. Translated by Robert Hurley, Mark Seem, and Helen R. Lane. New York: Richard Seaver, 1977.

Dening, Greg. *Islands and Beaches: Discourse on a Silent Land-Marquesas, 1774-1880*. Honolulu: University of Hawaii Press, 1980.

Derrida, Jacques. "Structure, Sign, and Play." In *Writing and Difference*, trans. Alan Bass. Chicago: University of Chicago Press, 1978.

———. *Dissemination*. Translated by Barbara Johnson. Chicago: University of Chicago Press, 1981.

Deutscher, Isaac. "Israel's Spiritual Climate." In *The Non-Jewish Jew and Other Essays*, ed. Tamara Deutscher. New York: Hill and Wang, 1968.

Devji, Faisal Fatehali. "Hindu/Muslim/Indian." *Public Culture* 5, no. 1 (fall 1992): 1–18.

Dews, Peter. *Logics of Disintegration: Poststructuralist Thought and the Claims of Critical Theory*. London: Verso, 1987.

Dey, J. "Prostitutes Oppose Khairnar's Rescue Bid." *Indian Express*, 13 January 1996.

Dhanda, Amita. "Law, Psychiatry, and Human Rights." *Seminar* 430 (June 1995).

Dhareshwar, Vivek, P. Sudhir, and Tejaswini Niranjana. *Interrogating Modernity: Culture and Colonialism in India*. Calcutta: Seagull, 1993.

Diawara, Manthia. "The Nature of Mother in Dreaming Rivers." *Third Text* 13 (winter 1990/91): 73–84.

Dingwaney-Needham, Anuradha. "Inhabiting the Metropole: C.L.R. James and the Postcolonial Intellectual of the African Diaspora." *Diaspora* 2, no. 3 (1993): 281–304.

Dippie, Brian W. *The Vanishing American: White Attitudes and U.S. Indian Policy*. Middletown, Conn.: Wesleyan University Press, 1982.

Dirlik, Arif. "The Postcolonial Aura: Third World Criticism in the Age of Global Capitalism." *Critical Inquiry* 20, no. 2 (1994): 328–56.

Dostoevsky, Fyodor. *Notes from Underground*. Translated by Mirra Ginsberg. New York: Bantam, 1974.

Dussel, Enrique. "Eurocentrism and Modernity." *Boundary 2* 20, no. 3 (1993): 65–76.

Dworkin, Dennis L., and Leslie H. Roman, eds. *Views from the Border Country: Raymond Williams and Cultural Politics*. New York: Routledge, 1993.

Eagleton, Terry. "From *Polis* to Postmodernism." In *The Ideology of the Aesthetic*. Oxford: Blackwell, 1990.

Eisen-Bergman, Arlene. *Women of Vietnam*. San Francisco: People's Press, 1975.

Eisenstadt, S.N., and Oha Ahimar. *The Welfare State and Its Aftermath*. London: Croom Helm, 1985.

El-Haj, Nadia Abu. "Excavating the Land, Creating the Homeland: Archaeology, the State, and the Making of History in Modern Jewish Nationalism." Ph.D. diss., Duke University, 1995.

Ellison, Ralph. *Invisible Man*. New York: Random House, 1952.

Elon, A. *Herzl*. New York: Schocken, 1986.

Enloe, Cynthia. *Bananas, Beaches, and Bases: Making Feminist Sense of International Politics*. Berkeley and Los Angeles: University of California Press, 1990.

Entekhabi, Nader. "Nasionalism va tajjadod dar farhang-e siasi-ye ba'd az mashruttiat" [Nationalism and Modernity in the Political Culture of the Post-Constitutional Revolution]. *Iran Nameh* 21, no. 2 (1993): 185–208.

Europa Europa. Directed by Agnieszka Holland. Produced by Artur Brauner and Margaret Menegoz. Orion Pictures, 1991.

Fabian, Johannes. *Time and the Other: How Anthropology Makes Its Objects*. New York: Columbia University Press, 1983.

Fanon, Frantz. *Les damnés de la terre*. Paris: Masper, 1961. Translated as *The Wretched of the Earth* by Constance Farrington (1961; reprint, New York: Grove, 1991).

Feuer, Lewis. *Imperialism and the Anti-Imperialist Mind*. New York: Prometheus, 1986.

First Contact. Directed by Bob Connolly and Robin Anderson. 16 millimeter, 60 minutes. Australia: Filmmakers Library, 1985.

Flapan, Simha. *Zionism and the Palestinians*. London: Croom Helm, 1979.

Folktales from India. Selected and edited by A.K. Ramanujan. New Delhi, India: Viking Penguin, 1993.

Foucault, Michel. *Les mots et les choses: Une archéologie des sciences humaines*. Paris: Gallimard, 1966.

———. *L'archéologie du savoir*. Paris: Gallimard, 1969.

———. *Power/Knowledge*. Edited by Colin Gordon. New York: Pantheon, 1972.

———. *The Order of Things: An Archaeology of the Human Sciences*. New York: Vintage, 1973.

———. "Nietzsche, Genealogy, History." In *Language, Counter-Memory, Practice*, trans. Donald F. Bouchard and Shery Simon. Ithaca, N.Y.: Cornell University Press, 1977.

———. "Theatrum philosophicum." In *Language, Counter-Memory, Practice*, trans. Donald F. Bouchard and Shery Simon. Ithaca, N.Y.: Cornell University Press, 1977.

———. *Discipline and Punish: The Birth of the Prison*. Translated by Alan Sheridan. New York: Vintage, 1979.

———. "Governmentality." 1979. Reprinted in *The Foucault Effect: Studies in Governmentality*, ed. Colin Gordon and Peter Miller. London: Harvester, 1991.

———. "Heterotopias." *Diacritics* (Spring 1986).

Frank, Andre Gunder, and Marta Fuentes. "Nine Theses on Social Movements." *Economic and Political Weekly*, 29 August 1987.

Frankenberg, Ruth, and Lata Mani. "Crosscurrents, Crosstalk: Race, 'Postcoloniality,' and the Politics of Location." *Cultural Studies* 7, no. 2 (1993): 292–310.

Fraser, Nancy. *Unruly Practices: Power, Discourse, and Gender in Contemporary Social Theory*. Minneapolis: University of Minnesota Press, 1989.

———. *Justice Interruptus: Critical Reflections on the Postsocialist Condition*. New York: Routledge, 1997.

Fraser, Nancy, and Linda Gordon. "A Genealogy of Dependency: Tracing a Keyword of the U.S. Welfare State." *Signs: A Journal of Women and Culture* (winter 1994): 309–36.

Freud, Sigmund. "Analysis of a Phobia in a Five-Year-Old Boy." In *The Standard Edition of the Complete Psychological Works of Sigmund Freud*, vol. 10, ed. and trans. J. Strachey. London: Hogarth, 1953–74.

———. *The Interpretation of Dreams*, pt. 1. In *The Standard Edition of the Complete Psychological Works of Sigmund Freud*, vol. 4, ed. and trans. J. Strachey and A. Freud. London: Hogarth, 1955.

Friedmann, Georges. *The End of the Jewish People?* Garden City, N.Y.: Doubleday, 1967.

Fuchs, Martin. Introduction to "India and Modernity: Decentering Western Perspectives." *Thesis Eleven,* special issue, no. 39 (1994): v–xiii.

Fuss, Diana. "Interior Colonies: Frantz Fanon and the Politics of Identification." *Diacritics* 24, nos. 2–3 (summer–fall 1994): 20–42.

Fussel, Paul. *The Great War and Modern Memory.* Oxford: Oxford University Press, 1975.

Gaffary, Farrokh. "Cinema i: History of Cinema in Persia." *Encyclopedia Iranica,* vol. 5, fasc. 6, ed. Ehsan Yarshater. Costa Mesa, Calif.: Mazda, 1991.

Garland, David. *Punishment and Modern Society: A Study in Social Theory.* Oxford: Clarendon, 1990.

Garrison, William Lloyd, ed. *Thoughts on African Colonization.* New York: Arno, 1968.

Gates, Henry Louis, Jr. "Criticism in the Jungle." In *Black Literature and Literary Theory,* ed. Henry Louis Gates Jr. New York: Methuen, 1984.

Gauhar, Madeeha, and Shahid Nadeem. *Preface to Program Copy of Jaloos.* Lahore: Ajoka Theatre Workshop, 1987.

Gay, Peter. *The Bourgeois Experience, Victoria to Freud.* Vol. 3, *The Cultivation of Hatred.* New York: Norton, 1993.

Geller, Jay. "A Paleontological View of Freud's Study of Religion: Unearthing the *Leitfossil* Circumcision." *Modern Judaism* 13, no. 1 (2 January 1993): 49–70.

———. "Of Mice and Mensa: Anti-Semitism and the Jewish Genius." *Centennial Review* 38, no. 2 (spring 1994): 361–86.

Gellner, Ernest. *Nations and Nationalism.* Oxford: Blackwell, 1983.

George, Vic, and Paul Wilding. *Ideology and Social Welfare.* London: Routledge and Kegan Paul, 1985.

Ghosh, Amitav. *The Shadow Lines.* London: Bloomsbury, 1988.

Ghosh, Arun. "Health Care and Globalisation: Case for a Selective Approach." *Economic and Political Weekly,* 24 February 1996.

Giladin, Gideon. *Discord in Zion: Conflict between Ashkenazi and Sephardi Jews in Israel.* London: Scorpion, 1990.

Gilman, Sander L. "Black Bodies, White Bodies: Toward an Iconography of Female Sexuality in Late Nineteenth-Century Art, Medicine, and Literature." In *"Race," Writing, and Difference,* ed. Henry Louis Gates Jr. Chicago: University of Chicago Press, 1985. 223–61.

———. *Jewish Self-Hatred: Anti-Semitism and the Hidden Language of the Jews.* Baltimore: Johns Hopkins University Press, 1986.

———. *The Jew's Body.* New York: Routledge, 1991.

———. *Freud, Race, and Gender.* Princeton, N.J.: Princeton University Press, 1993.

Gilmour, Ian, and David Gilmour. "Pseudo-Travellers." *London Review of Books,* 7 February 1985.

Gilroy, Paul. "It Ain't Where You're From, It's Where You're At . . . : The Dialectics of Diasporic Identification." *Third Text* 13 (1990/91): 3–16.

———. *The Black Atlantic: Modernity and Double Consciousness.* Cambridge, Mass.: Harvard University Press, 1993.

Giroux, Henry. "Consuming Social Change: The 'United Colors of Benetton.'" *Cultural Critique* 26 (winter 1993/94): 5–32.

Gofbarg, Gadi. "Tough and Tender: An Interview with Gadi Gofbarg." By Neery Melkonian. *Afterimage* 20, no. 3 (October 1992): 8–10.

Goldstein, B. *Reinscribing Moses: Heine, Kafka, Freud, and Schoenberg in a European Wilderness.* Cambridge, Mass.: Harvard University Press, 1992.

Goldstein, J. "The Wandering Jew and the Problem of Psychiatric Anti-Semitism in *Fin-de-Siècle* France." *Journal of Contemporary History* 20 (1985).

González Casanova, Pablo. "Internal Colonialism and National Development." *Studies in Comparative International Development* 1, no. 4 (1965).

Goodman, Paul. *Zionism in England*. London, 1949.

Gordimer, Nadine. *The Essential Gesture: Writing, Politics, and Places*. New York: Knopf, 1988.

Gould, Stephen Jay. *Time's Arrow, Time's Cycle: Myth and Metaphor in the Discovery of Geological Time*. Cambridge, Mass.: Harvard University Press, 1987.

Gramsci, Antonio. *Selections from the Prison Notebooks*. Translated by Quintin Hoare and Geoffrey Nowell Smith. New York: International, 1971.

Granott, Abraham. *Agrarian Reform and the Record of Israel*. London: Eyre and Spottiswoode, 1956.

Grewal, Inderpal, and Caren Kaplan. *Scattered Hegemonies: Postmodernity and Transnational Feminist Practices*. Minneapolis: University of Minnesota Press, 1994.

Gubar, Susan. " 'This Is My Rifle, This Is My Gun': World War II and the Blitz on Women." In *Behind the Lines: Gender and the Two World Wars*, ed. Margaret Higonnet et al. New Haven, Conn.: Yale University Press, 1987.

Guha, Ranajit. "The Prose of Counter-Insurgency." In *Selected Subaltern Studies*, ed. Ranajit Guha and Gayatri Chakravorty Spivak. New York: Oxford University Press, 1988.

———. "Dominance without Hegemony and Its Historiography." In *Subaltern Studies*, vol. 6, ed. Ranajit Guha. Delhi: Oxford University Press, 1989.

Guillaudeau, Thomas. "Les productions Pathé et Mélièse en 1905–1906 (notes préliminaires)." *Iris* 2, no. 1 (1984): 33–46.

Gupta, Akhil. "The Song of the Nonaligned World: Trans-National Identities and the Reinscription of Space in Late Capitalism." *Cultural Anthropology* 7, no. 1 (1992): 63–79.

———. "Peasants and Global Environmentalism: Safe-Guarding the Future of 'Our World' or Initiating a New Form of Governmentality." Paper presented to the Agrarian Studies Seminar, Yale University, 25 March 1994.

Gupta, Reeta Dutta. "Juvenile Homes Are Like Jails." *Times of India*, 11 January 1996.

Habermas, Jürgen. "Modernity—an Incomplete Project." In *The Anti-Aesthetic: Essays on Postmodern Culture*, ed. Hal Foster. Seattle: Bay, 1983.

———. *The Philosophical Discourse of Modernity: Twelve Lectures*. Translated by Frederick G. Lawrence. Cambridge, Mass.: MIT Press, 1987.

Haidari, Gholam. *Sinema-ye Iran: Bardasht-e natamam* (Iranian Cinema: An Unfinished Take). Tehran: Chekameh, 1370/1991.

Hall, Stuart. "New Ethnicities." In *Black Film, British Cinema*, ed. Kobena Mercer. London, ICA, 1988.

Hampate Ba, Amadou. "The African Tale of Cinema." *Discourse* 11, no. 2 (spring–summer 1983).

Hansen, Kathryn. *Grounds for Play: The Nautanki Theatre of North India*. Berkeley and Los Angeles: University of California Press, 1992.

Haraway, Donna. "A Manifesto for Cyborgs: Science, Technology, and Socialist Feminism in the 1980s." *Socialist Review* 15, no. 80 (1985): 65–107.

Harriss-White, Barbara. "Onto a Loser: Disability in India." In *Illfare in India: Essays on India's Social Sector in Honour of S. Guhan*, eds. Barbara Harriss-White & S. Subramanian. New Delhi: Thousand Oaks California: Sage Publications, 1999.

Hartog, François. *The Mirror of Herodotus: The Representation of the Other in the Writing of History*. Translated by J. Lloyd. Berkeley and Los Angeles: University of California Press, 1988.

Harvey, David. *The Condition of Post-Modernity: An Inquiry into the Origins of Cultural Change*. Cambridge, Mass.: Blackwell, 1990.

Herzl, Theodor. Letter to Heinrich Kana, 8 June 1882. Herzl-Kana Correspondence, Central Zionist Archives, Jerusalem.

———. *Old-Newland (Altneuland)*. Translated by L. Levensohn. New York: Bloch, 1941.

———. "The Jewish State." In *Theodor Herzl: A Portrait for This Age*, ed. L. Lewisohn. Cleveland: World, 1955.

———. *The New Ghetto: A Play in Four Acts*. Abridged in *Theodor Herzl: A Portrait for This Age*, ed. L. Lewisohn. Cleveland: World, 1955.

———. *The Complete Diaries of Theodor Herzl*. Edited by R. Patai. Translated by H. Zohn. New York: Herzl Press, 1960.

———. *The Jewish State: An Attempt at a Modern Solution to the Jewish Question*. London: H. Porders, 1972.

———. *Zionist Writings: Essays and Addresses*. Translated by H. Zohn. New York: Herzl Press, 1973.

Hess, Moses. *Rome and Jerusalem: A Study in Jewish Nationalism*. Translated by Meyer Waxman. New York: Bloch, 1918.

Heuser, Frederick J. "Women's Work for Women: Bell Sherwood Hawkes and the East Persia Presbyterian Mission." *American Presbyterians* 65, no. 1 (1987).

Hirst, David. *The Gun and the Olive Branch: The Roots of Conflict in the Middle East*. London: Faber and Faber, 1984.

Hitchens, Christopher. *The Missionary Position*. London: Verso, 1995.

Hoare, Reverend J.N. *Something New in Iran*. London: Church Missionary Society, 1937.

Hobsbawm, Eric, and Terence Ranger, eds. *The Invention of Tradition*. Cambridge: Cambridge University Press, 1983.

"Holland without a Country." *New York Times Magazine*, 8 August 1993.

hooks, bell. *Black Looks: Race and Representation*. Boston: South End, 1992.

Horkheimer, Max, and Theodor W. Adorno. "Elements of Anti-Semitism: Limits of Enlightenment." In *Dialectic of Enlightenment*, trans. John Cumming. New York: Continuum, 1994.

Hossain, Rokeya Sakhawat. *Sultana's Dream*. Edited and translated by Roushan Jahan and Hanna Papanek. 1905. Reprint, New York: Feminist, 1988.

Hourani, Albert. *Arabic Thought in the Liberal Age, 1798–1939*. Cambridge: Cambridge University Press, 1988.

———. *A History of the Arab Peoples*. New York: Warner, 1991.

Hutcheon, Linda. *A Poetics of Postmodernism: History, Theory, Fiction*. New York: Routledge, 1988.

Huyssen, Andreas. "Mapping the Postmodern." *New German Critique* 33 (1984): 5–52.

Ignatieff, Michael. "State, Civil Society, and Total Institutions: A Critique of Recent Social Histories of Punishment." In *Social Control and the State: Historical and Comparative Essays*. Oxford: Martin Robertson, 1983.

Irele, Abiola. "Dimensions of African Discourse." *College Literature* 19, no. 3/20, no. 1 (1992/93): 45–59.

Issari, Mohammad Ali. *Cinema in Iran, 1900–1979*. New York: Metuchen, 1989.

Iyer, Krishna. *Justice and Beyond*. New Delhi: Deep and Deep, 1980.

Iyer, Lakshmi. "Pune Operations: Some Ethical Questions." *Hindustan Times*, 14 February 1994.

Jacob, Nitya. "Ethics of Hysterectomy for the Retarded." *Pioneer*, 23 February 1994.

Jain, Kalpana. "The Mindless Matter." *Times of India*, 20 February 1994.

Jalal, Ayesha. "The Convenience of Subservience: Women and the State of Pakistan." In *Women, Islam, and the State*, ed. Deniz Kandiyoti. Philadelphia: Temple University Press, 1991.

Jameson, Frederic. "Third World Literature in the Era of Multinational Capital." *Social Text* (fall 1986): 65–88.

———. *Postmodernism; or, The Cultural Logic of Late Capitalism.* Durham, N.C.: Duke University Press, 1991.

JanMohamed, Abdul. "Worldliness-without-World, Homelessness-as-Home." In *Edward W. Said: A Critical Reader,* ed. Michael Sprinker. Oxford: Blackwell, 1992.

JanMohamed, Abdul R., and David Lloyd. "Introduction: Toward a Theory of Minority Discourse: What Is to Be Done?" In *The Nature and Context of Minority Discourse,* ed. Abdul R. JanMohamed and David Lloyd. New York: Oxford University Press, 1990.

Jardine, Alice. *Gynesis: Configurations of Woman and Modernity.* Ithaca, N.Y.: Cornell University Press, 1986.

Jehangir, Asma. *Legal Literacy Pamphlets: Violence against Women.* Lahore: AGHS Legal Aid Cell, n.d.

Jiryis, Sabri. *The Arabs in Israel.* New York: Monthly Review Press, 1976.

John, Mary E. *Discrepant Dislocations: Feminism, Theory, and Postcolonial Histories.* Berkeley and Los Angeles: University of California Press, 1996.

Johnson, Barbara. "Nothing Fails Like Success." In *A World of Difference.* Baltimore: Johns Hopkins University Press, 1987.

Jones, E. *The Life and Work of Sigmund Freud.* New York: Basic, 1953.

Kakar, Sanjiv. "Medical Developments and Patient Unrest in the Leprosy Asylum, 1860–1940." *Social Scientist* 24 (April–June 1996): 62–81.

Kaplan, Amy. " 'Left Alone with America': The Absence of Empire in the Study of American Culture." In *Cultures of United States Imperialism,* ed. Amy Kaplan and Donald E. Pease. Durham, N.C.: Duke University Press, 1993.

Karl, Marx. *Grundrisse: Foundations of the Critique of Political Economy.* Translated by Martin Nicolaus. New York: Random House, 1973.

Kaufman, Linda, ed. *Gender and Theory.* Oxford: Blackwell, 1989.

———, ed. *Feminism and Institutions.* Oxford: Blackwell, 1989.

Kaviraj, Sudipta. "The Imaginary Institution of India." In *Subaltern Studies,* vol. 7, ed. Partha Chatterjee and Gyanendra Pandey. Delhi: Oxford, 1992.

Kayyali, A. W., ed. *Zionism, Imperialism, and Racism.* London: Croom Helm, 1979.

Kelly, Mary Gilbert. *Catholic Immigrant Colonization Projects in the United States, 1815–1860.* New York: U.S. Catholic Historical Society, 1939.

Kermani, Nezamoleslam. *Tarikh-e bidari-ye iranian* (The History of Iranian Awakening). Vol. 1. Tehran: Boniad-e Farhang-e Iran, 1347/1976.

Khalidi, Walid, ed. *All That Remains: The Palestinian Villages Occupied and Depopulated by Israel in 1948.* Washington, D.C.: Institute for Palestine Studies, 1992.

Khomeini, Ruhollah. *Islam and Revolution: Writings and Declarations of Imam Khomeini.* Translated by Hamid Algar. Berkeley, Calif.: Mizan, 1981.

———. *Seda va sima dar kalam-e Emam Khomeini* (Voice and Vision in the Words of Imam Khomeini). Tehran: Sorush, 1363/1984.

Khoury, Elias. *Zaman al-ihtilal* (The time of occupation). Beirut: Institute for Arab Studies, 1985.

———. *Little Mountain.* Translated by Maia Tabet. Minneapolis: University of Minnesota Press, 1989.

Kisch, F. H. *Palestine Diary.* London: Victor Gollancz, 1938.

Kishwar, Madhu. "Why I Do Not Call Myself a Feminist." *Manushi* 62 (1990): 2–8.

Klein, Melanie. "Love, Guilt, and Reparation." In *Love, Guilt, and Reparation and Other Works, 1921–1945.* New York: Free Press, 1975.

Kor de Alva, Jorge J. "The Postcolonization of (Latin) American Experience: A Reconsideration of 'Colonialism,' 'Postcolonialism,' and 'Mestizaja.' " In *After Colonialism: Imperial Histo-*

ries and Postcolonial Displacements, ed. G. Prakash. Princeton, N.J.: Princeton University Press, 1995.

Kornberg, J. Theodor Herzl: From Assimilation to Zionism. Bloomington: Indiana University Press, 1993. Originally published as Die Körperliche Renaissance der Juden: Festschrift zum 10 Jährigen des "Bar Kochba" Berlin (Berlin, 1909).

Kracauer, Siegfried. Theory of Film: The Redemption of Physical Reality. New York: Oxford University Press, 1960.

Kshirsagar, Alka. "No Method in the Madness." Times of India, 20 February 1994.

Kumar, Krishna. "Market Economy and Mass Literacy." Economic and Political Weekly, 11 December 1993: 2727–34.

Lacan, Jacques. Écrits: A Selection. Translated by Alan Sheridan. New York: Norton, 1977.

———. "The Mirror Stage as Formative of the Function of the I as Revealed in Psychoanalytic Experience." In Écrits: A Selection, trans. Alan Sheridan. New York: Norton, 1977.

Laclau, Ernesto. New Reflections on the Revolution of Our Time. London: Verso, 1990.

Laroui, Abdallah. The Crisis of the Arab Intellectual: Traditionalism or Historicism? Translated by Diarmid Cammell. Berkeley and Los Angeles: University of California Press, 1977.

Larsen, Neil. "Postmodernism and Imperialism: Theory and Politics in Latin America." In Reading North by South: On Latin American Literature, Culture, and Politics. Minneapolis: University of Minnesota Press, 1995.

———. "Shades of Althusser; or, The Logic of Theoretical Retreat in Contemporary Radical Criticism." Socialism and Democracy 9, no. 2 (fall 1995).

Layoun, Mary. Travels of a Genre: The Modern Novel and Ideology. Princeton, N.J.: Princeton University Press, 1990.

Lee, Phil, and Colin Raban. Welfare Theory and Social Policy: Reform or Revolution? London: Sage, 1988.

Lehn, Walter. The Jewish National Fund. London: Kegan Paul International, 1988.

Lewisohn, L., ed. Theodor Herzl: A Portrait for This Age. Cleveland: World, 1955.

Leyda, Jay. Kino: A History of the Russian and Soviet Film. 3d ed. Princeton, N.J.: Princeton University Press, 1983.

Lloyd, David. Anomalous States: Irish Writing and the Post-Colonial Moment. Durham, N.C.: Duke University Press, 1993.

Lockman, Zachary, and Joel Benin, eds. Intifada: The Palestinian Uprising against Israeli Occupation. Boston: South End, 1989.

Loewenberg, P. "Theodor Herzl: Nationalism and Politics." Decoding the Past: The Psychohistorical Approach. Berkeley and Los Angeles: University of California Press, 1985.

Lomasky, Loren E. "Justice to Charity." Social Philosophy and Policy 12, no. 2 (summer 1995): 32–53.

Lowenberg, Peter. "Theodor Herzl: A Psychoanalytic Study in Charismatic Political Leadership." In The Psychoanalytic Interpretation of History, ed. Benjamin Wolman. New York: Basic, 1971.

Luciani, Giacomo, and George Salameh. The Politics of Arab Integration. London: Croom Helm, 1988.

Luciani, Giacomo, and Ghassan Salame. "The Politics of Arab Integration." In The Arab State, ed. Giacomo Luciani. Berkeley and Los Angeles: University of California Press, 1990.

Lyotard, Jean François. The Postmodern Condition. Translated by Geoff Bennington and Brian Massumi. Minneapolis: University of Minnesota Press, 1984.

Lyotard, Jean François, and Jean-Loup Thébaud. Just Gaming. Translated by Wlad Godzich. Minneapolis: University of Minnesota Press, 1985.

Macleod, Roy, and Milton Lewis, eds. *Imperial Health in British India, 1857–1900*. London: Routledge, 1988.

Makdisi, Anis. *Al-itijahat al-adabiyya fi al-alam al-arabi al-hadith* (Literary trends in the modern Arab world). Beirut: Dar al-ilm li al-malayin, 1988.

Makdisi, Jean Said. *Beirut Fragments: A War Memoir*. New York: Persea, 1990.

Makdisi, Samir. "Economic Interdependence and National Sovereignty." In *The Arab State*, ed. Giacomo Luciani. Berkeley and Los Angeles: University of California Press, 1990.

Makdisi, Saree. "The Empire Renarrated: *Season of Migration to the North* and the Reinvention of the Present." *Critical Inquiry* 18, no. 4 (summer 1992). Reprinted in *Colonial Discourse and Post-Colonial Theory*, ed. Patrick Williams and Laura Chrisman (New York: Columbia University Press, 1994).

———. "Letter from Beirut." *Architecture New York* 5 (March/April 1994): 56–59.

———. *Romantic Imperialism: Universal Empire and the Culture of Modernity*. Cambridge: Cambridge University Press, 1998.

Malekpur, Jamshid. *Adabiyat-e namayeshi dar Iran: Dowran-e enqelab-e mashruteh*. Vol. 2. Tehran: Entesharat-e Tus, 1984.

Malhotra, Vinay Kumar. *Welfare State and Supreme Court in India*. New Delhi: Deep and Deep, 1986.

Malkki, Liisa. "Citizens of Humanity: Internationalism and the Imagined Community of Nations." *Diaspora* 3, no. 1 (1994).

Mandel, Ernest. *Late Capitalism*. London: Verso, 1987.

Mandi (The marketplace). Directed by Shyam Benegal. Color, 130 minutes. India: 1983. In Hindi.

Mani, Lata. "Multiple Mediations: Feminist Scholarship in the Age of Multinational Reception." In *Feminist Review* 35 (summer 1990): 24–41.

Marglin, Fredrique Apffel, and Stephen Marglin, eds. *Dominating Knowledge: A Development, Culture, and Resistance*. Oxford: Clarendon, 1990.

Mariátegui, Jose Carlos. *Textos Basicos: Selección, Pr'ologo y Nota Introductorias de Anibal Quijano*. Mexico: Fondo de Cultura Economica, 1996.

Masalha, Nur. *Expulsion of the Palestinians*. Washington, D.C.: Institute of Palestine Studies, 1992.

Massad, Joseph. "Palestinians and the Limits of Racialized Discourse." *Social Text* 34 (1993): 94–114.

———. "Repentant Terrorists or Settler-Colonialism Revisited: The PLO-Israeli Agreement in Perspective." *Found Object* (spring 1994): 81–90.

———. "Conceiving the Masculine: Gender and Palestinian Nationalism." *Middle East Journal* 49, no. 3 (summer 1995). 467.

———. "Zionism's Internal Others: Israel and the Oriental Jews." *Journal of Palestine Studies* 100 (summer 1996): 53–68.

———. "Political Realists or Comprador Intelligentsia: Palestinian Intellectuals and the National Struggle." *Critique* (fall 1997).

Masson, Jeffrey M., ed. and trans. *The Complete Letters of Sigmund Freud to Wilhelm Fliess, 1887–1904*. Cambridge, Mass.: Harvard University Press, 1985.

May, Ernest. *Imperial Democracy: The Emergence of America as a Great Power*. New York: Harcourt, Brace, and World, 1961.

McClintock, Anne. "The Angel of Progress: Pitfalls of the Term *Post-Colonialism*." *Social Text* 31/32 (1992): 84–98.

McGrath, W. J. *Freud's Discovery of Psychoanalysis: The Politics of Hysteria*. Ithaca, N.Y.: Cornell University Press, 1986.

Meese, Elizabeth, and Alice Parker, eds. *The Difference Within: Feminism and Critical Theory.* Philadelphia: John Benjamins, 1989.

Melville, Herman. *Moby-Dick.* New York: Penguin, 1986.

Merk, Frederick. *Manifest Destiny and Mission.* New York: Vintage, 1966.

Metz, Christian. *The Imaginary Signifier: Psychoanalysis and Cinema.* Translated by Celia Britton, Annwyl Williams, Ben Brewster, and Alfred Guzzetti. Bloomington: Indiana University Press, 1982.

Migdal, Joel S. *Strong States and Weak Societies: State-Society Relations and State Capabilities in the Third World.* Princeton, N.J.: Princeton University Press, 1988.

Mignolo, Walter D. "Colonial and Postcolonial Discourse: Cultural Critique or Academic Colonialism?" *Latin American Research Review* 28, no. 3 (1993).

——. "Misunderstanding and Colonization: The Reconfiguration of Memory and Space." *SAQ* 92, no. 2 (1993).

——. "Afterword: Human Understanding and (Latin) American Interests: The Politics and Sensibilities of Geocultural Locations." *Poetics Today* 16, no. 1 (1995).

——. *The Darker Side of the Renaissance: Literacy, Territoriality, and Colonization.* Ann Arbor: University of Michigan Press, 1995.

——. "Globalizacao, Processos de civilicão, linguas e culturas." *Centro de recursos humanos* 22 (1995).

——. "Globalization, Civilization Processes, and the Relocation of Languages and Cultures." In *Cultures of Globalization,* ed. Frederic Jameson and M. Miyoshi. Durham, N.C.: Duke University Press, 1998.

——. "Are Subaltern Studies Postmodern or Postcolonial? The Politics and Sensibilities of Geocultural Locations." *Disposition* (in press).

Miller, Floyd J. *The Search for a Black Nationality: Black Emigration and Colonization, 1787–1863.* Urbana: University of Illinois Press, 1975.

Mishra, Ramesh. *The Welfare State in Crisis: Social Thought and Social Change.* Brighton: Wheatsheaf, 1984.

Mission of the Board of Foreign Missions of the Presbyterian Church in the U.S.A. *A Century of Mission Work in Iran (Persia), 1834–1934.* Beirut: American Press, 1934.

Mitchell, Brian C. *The Paddy Camps: The Irish of Lowell, 1821–61.* Urbana: University of Illinois Press, 1988.

Mohanty, Chandra Talpade. "Under Western Eyes: Feminist Scholarship and Colonial Discourse." *Feminist Review* 30 (1988): 61–88.

——. "Cartographies of Struggle: Third World Women and the Politics of Feminism." In *Third World Women and the Politics of Feminism,* ed. Chandra Talpade Mohanty, Ann Russo, and Lourdes Torres. Bloomington: Indiana University Press, 1991.

Mohanty, Chandra, and M. Jacqui Alexander, eds. *Feminist Genealogies, Colonial Legacies, Democratic Futures.* New York: Routledge, 1997.

Mohanty, Chandra, Ann Russo, and Lourdes Torres, eds. *Third World Women and the Politics of Feminism.* Bloomington: Indiana University Press, 1991.

Mohanty, Satya P. "Us and Them: On the Philosophical Basis of Political Criticism." *Yale Journal of Criticism* 2, no. 2 (spring 1989): 1–31.

——. "The Epistemic Status of Cultural Identity: On *Beloved* and the Postcolonial Condition." *Cultural Critique* 24 (spring 1993): 41–80.

Morris, Benny. *The Birth of the Palestinian Refugee Problem, 1947–1949.* Cambridge: Cambridge University Press, 1989.

Mosse, George L. *Nationalism and Sexuality: Middle-Class Morality and Sexual Norms in Modern Europe.* Madison: University of Wisconsin Press, 1985.

———. *Confronting the Nation: Jewish and Western Nationalism*. Hanover, N.H.: University Press of New England, 1993.

Mumtaz, Khawar, and Farida Shaheed, eds. *Women of Pakistan: Two Steps Forward, One Step Back?* London: Zed, 1987.

Musser, Charles. "The Travel Genre in 1903–1904: Moving toward Fictional Narrative." *Iris* 2, no. 1 (1984).

Mutman, Mahmut, and Meyda Yegenoglu, eds. "Orientalism and Cultural Differences." *Inscriptions*, special issue, vol. 6 (1992).

Nadeem, Shahid. *Khasman khanian* (The husband-eaters). Lahore: Maktaba Fiqr-o-Danish, 1992.

Naficy, Hamid. "Iranian Feature Films: A Brief Critical History." *Quarterly Review of Film Studies* 4 (1979). 443–64.

———. *Iran Media Index*. Westport, Conn.: Greenwood, 1984.

———. "Islamizing Cinema in Iran." In *Iran: Political Culture in the Islamic Republic*, ed. Samih K. Farsoun and Mehrdad Mashayekhi. London: Routledge, 1992. 173–208.

———. *The Making of Exile Cultures: Iranian Television in Los Angeles*. Minneapolis: University of Minnesota Press, 1993.

———. "Mediating the Other: American Pop Culture Representation of Postrevolutionary Iran." In *U.S. Media and the Middle East: Image and Perception*, ed. Yahya R. Kamalipour. Westport, Conn.: Greenwood, 1995. 73–90.

———. "Recurrent Themes in the Middle Eastern Cinemas of Diaspora." In *The Cinema of Displacement: Middle Eastern Identities in Transition*, ed. Jonathan Friedlander. Los Angeles: UCLA Center for Near Eastern Studies, 1995. 3–63.

———. "Iranian Cinema." In *The Oxford History of World Cinema*, ed. Geoffrey Nowell-Smith. London: Oxford University Press, 1996.

———. "Theorizing 'Third World' Film Spectatorship." *Wide Angle*, special issue, 18, no. 4 (October 1996): 3–26.

Nancy, Jean-Luc. "Cut Throat Sun." In *In Other Tongue: Nation and Ethnicity in the Linguistic Borderland*, ed. A. Artega. Durham, N.C.: Duke University Press, 1994.

Nandy, Ashis, ed. *Science, Hegemony, and Violence: A Requiem for Modernity*. Tokyo: UN University; Delhi: Oxford University Press, 1990.

Nicholson, Linda J., ed. *Feminism/Postmodernism*. New York: Routledge, 1990.

Nordau, Max. "Jewry of Muscle." In *The Jew in the Modern World: A Documentary History*, ed. Paul Mendes-Flohr and Jehuda Reinharz. Oxford: Oxford University Press, 1980. Originally published as "Muskeljudentum," *Juedische Turnzeitung* (June 1903).

Nuri, Fazlollah. *Lavayeh-e aqa Shaikh Fazlollah Nuri* (Edicts of Mr. Shaikh Fazlollah Nuri). Tehran: Nashr-e Tarikh-e Iran, 1362/1983.

O'Gorman, Edmundo. *The Invention of America*. Bloomington: Indiana University Press, 1961.

Olaniyan, Tejumola, ed. "Post-Colonial Discourse." *Callaloo*, special issue, vol. 16, no. 4 (fall 1993).

Omid, Jamal. *Tarikh-e sinemay-e Iran—1: Paydayesh va bahreh bardari* (Iranian Film History: Emergence and Utilization). Tehran: Faryab, 1363/1984.

Padmanabhan, Manjula. "The Stain." In *Hot Death, Cold Soup*. New Delhi: Kali for Women, 1996.

Palmerston. Letter to Ponsonby, 1840. PRO, FO 78/390, no. 34.

Parker, Andrew, ed. *Nationalisms and Sexualities*. New York: Routledge, 1992.

Parry, Benita. "A Mishandled Critique." *Social Text* 35 (summer 1993): 121–33.

Partha, Chatterjee. *Nationalist Thought and the Colonial World: A Derivative Discourse*. London: Zed, 1986.

Peters, Joan. *From Time Immemorial*. New York: Harper and Row, 1984.

Pinsker, Leo. *Auto-Emancipation*. Reprinted in Leo Pinsker, *Road to Freedom* (New York: Scopus, 1975).

Pletsch, Carl E. "The Three Worlds; or, The Division of Social Scientific Labor, circa 1950–1975." *Comparative Study of Society and History* 23, no. 4 (1981).

"Postcoloniality." *Social Text*, special issue, vols. 31/32 (1992).

Postmodernism/Jameson/Critique. Edited by Douglas Kellner. Washington, D.C.: Maisonneuve, 1989.

Prakash, Gyan. "Postcolonial Criticism and Indian Historiography." *Social Text* 31/32 (1992): 8–19.

———. "Subaltern Studies as Postcolonial Criticism." *American Historical Review* 99, no. 5 (1994): 1475–90.

———. *After Colonialism: Imperial Histories and Postcolonial Displacements*. Princeton, N.J.: Princeton University Press, 1995.

Prasad, M. "A Theory of Third World Literature." *Social Text* 31/32 (1992): 57–83.

Pratt, Mary Louise. *Imperial Eyes: Travel Writing and Transculturation*. New York: Routledge, 1992.

Presbyterian Church. *Catalog of Lantern Slides and Motion Pictures*. New York: Central Distribution Department, 1932–33.

Protocols of the Fourth Zionist Congress. London, 1900.

Qajar, Muzzafar-ed Din. *Safarnameh-ye mozaffar-ed din shah beh farang beh tahri-re mirza mehdi kashani* (Travelog of Mozaffar-ed Din Shah to Europe, Written by Mirza Mehdi Kashani). Tehran: Foruzan, 1982.

Rabinow, Paul. "Representations Are Social Facts: Modernity and Post-Modernity in Anthropology." In *Writing Culture*, ed. James Clifford and George Marcus. Berkeley and Los Angeles: University of California Press, 1986.

Radhakrishnan, R. "The Postmodern Event and the End of Logocentrism." *Boundary 2* 12, no. 1 (fall 1983).

———. "The Changing Subject and the Politics of Theory." *Differences* 2, no. 2 (1990).

———. "Towards an Effective Intellectual." In *Intellectuals: Aesthetics/Politics/Academics*, ed. Bruce Robbins. Minneapolis: University of Minnesota Press, 1990. Reprinted in *Diasporic Mediations: Between Home and Location* (Minneapolis: University of Minnesota Press, 1996).

———. "Cultural Theory and the Politics of Location." In *Views from the Border Country: Raymond Williams and Cultural Politics*, ed. Dennis L. Dworkin and Leslie G. Roman. New York: Routledge, 1993.

———. "Postcoloniality and the Boundaries of Identity." *Callaloo*, special issue, 16, no. 4 (fall 1993): 750–71.

———. "The Changing Subject and the Politics of Theory." In *Diasporic Mediations: Between Home and Location*. Minneapolis: University of Minnesota Press, 1996.

Ragland-Sullivan, Ellie. *Jacques Lacan and the Philosophy of Psychoanalysis*. Urbana: University of Illinois Press, 1987.

Rajan, Rajeswari Sunder. *Real and Imagined Women: Gender, Culture, and Postcolonialism*. London: Routledge, 1993.

———. "Ameena: Gender, Crisis, and National Identity." *Oxford Literary Review* 16 (1994): 147–76.

Ramanathan, Usha. "Women, Law, and Institutionalisation: A Manifestation of State Power." *Indian Journal of Gender Studies* 3, no. 2 (July–December 1996).

Ramaseshan, Geethá. "What about Their Rights?" *Hindu*, 16 April 1994.

Ranger, Terence, and Eric Hobsbawm, eds. *The Invention of Tradition*. Cambridge: Cambridge University Press, 1983.

Rathenau, W. Letter to Wilhelm Schwaner, 23 January 1916. In *Schriften*, ed. A. Harttung. Berlin: Berlin, 1965.

Rawls, John. *Theory of Justice*. Cambridge, Mass.: Harvard University Press, 1971.

Raz-Krakotzkin, A. "Exile within Sovereignty: Toward a Critique of the 'Negation of Exile' in Israeli Culture." *Theory and Criticism: An Israeli Forum* 4 (autumn 1993). An English summary is provided.

Retamar, Fernandez Roberto. "Nuestra América y Occidente." *Casa de las Americas* 98 (1976).

Rich, Adrienne. "Notes towards a Politics of Location." In *Blood, Bread, and Poetry — Selected Prose, 1979–1985*. New York: Norton, 1986.

Richards, Robert. *Darwin and the Emergence of Evolutionary Theories of Mind and Behavior*. Chicago: University of Chicago Press, 1989.

Rivera Cusicanqui, Silvia. *Oprimidos pero no vencidos: Luchas del campesinado aymara y qhechwa de Bolivia, 1990–1980*. La Paz: CSUTCB, 1984.

———. "Sendas y senderos de la ciencia social andina." *Autodeterminación: Análisis histórico político y teoría social* 10 (1992).

———. "La raiz: Colonizadores y colonizados." In *Violencias encubiertas en Bolivia*, vol. 1, *Cultura y política*, ed. X. Albó et al. La Paz: CIPCA-Aruwiyiri, 1993.

———. "Los desaf'ios para una demoracia e'tnica en los alnores del tercer milenio." In *Ser mujer ind'igena: Chola o birlocha en la Bolivia postcolonial de los años 90*, ed. S. Rivera Cusicanqui. La Paz: Ministerio de Desarrollo Humano, 1996.

———. "La nocion de 'derecho' o las paradojas de la modernindad postcolonial: Indigenas y mujeres en Bolivia." *Temas Sociales* 19 (1997).

Rivera Cusicanqui, Silvia, and Rossana Barragan. "Presentacion" to *Debates post-coloniales: Una introduccion a los estudios de la subalternidad*. La Paz: Spehis/Aruwiri, 1997.

Robbins, Bruce. Review of Edward Said's *Culture and Imperialism*. *Nineteenth-Century Contexts* 18 (1994).

———. "Upward Mobility in the Postcolonial Era: Kincaid, Mukherjee, and the Cosmopolitan Au Pair." *Modernism/Modernity* 1, no. 2 (April 1994).

Robert, M. *From Oedipus to Moses: Freud's Jewish Identity*. Translated by R. Manheim. Garden City, N.Y.: Anchor Doubleday, 1976.

Rodinson, Maxime. *Israel: A Colonial-Settler State?* New York: Monad, 1973.

Rogin, Michael Paul. *Fathers and Children: Andrew Jackson and the Subjugation of the American Indian*. New Brunswick, N.J.: Transaction, 1991.

Rorty, Richard. *Achieving Our Country: Leftist Thought in Twentieth-Century America*. Cambridge: Harvard University Press, 1998.

Rose, Jacqueline. *Sexuality in the Field of Vision*. London: Verso, 1986.

Rouse, Roger. "Mexican Migration and the Social Space of Postmodernism." *Diaspora* 1, no. 1 (spring 1991): 8–23.

———. "Thinking through Transnationalism: Notes on the Cultural Politics of Class Relations in the Contemporary United States." *Public Culture* 7, no. 2 (winter 1995): 353–402.

Rushdie, Salman. *The Satanic Verses*. New York: Viking, 1988.

Sahhafbashi Tehrani, Ebrahim. *Safarnameh-ye Ebrahim Sahhafbashi-e Tehrani* (Travelog of Ebrahim Sahhafbashi-e Tehrani). Edited by Mohammad Moshiri. Tehran: Sherkat-e Mo'alefan va Mottarjeman-e Iran, 1357/1978.

Sahlins, Marshall. *Islands of History*. Chicago: University of Chicago Press, 1985.

Said, Edward W. *Beginnings: Intention and Method*. New York: Basic, 1975.

———. Interview. *Diacritics* 6, no. 3 (fall 1976).

———. *Orientalism*. New York: Vintage, 1979.

———. *The Question of Palestine*. New York: Vintage, 1980.

———. *Covering Islam: How the Media and the Experts Determine How We See the Rest of the World*. New York: Pantheon, 1981.

———. *The World, the Text, and the Critic*. Cambridge, Mass.: Harvard University Press, 1983.

———. "Intifada and Independence." In *After the Last Sky*. Boston: Pantheon, 1985.

———. "Intellectuals in the Post-Colonial World." *Salmagundi* 70–71 (spring–summer 1986): 44–81.

———. "Orientalism Reconsidered." In *Literature, Politics, and Theory*, ed. Francis Barker et al. London: Methuen, 1986.

———. "Representing the Colonized: Anthropology's Interlocutors." *Critical Inquiry* 15, no. 2 (winter 1989).

———. "Narrative, Geography, and Interpretation." *New Left Review* 180 (1990).

———. "Third World Intellectuals and Metropolitan Culture." *Raritan* (winter 1990).

———. "The Politics of Knowledge." *Raritan* 11, no. 1 (summer 1991): 17–31.

———. *Culture and Imperialism*. New York: Knopf, 1993.

———. "Gods That Always Fail." *Raritan* 13, no. 4 (spring 1994).

———. *Representations of the Intellectual*. New York: Pantheon, 1994.

———. *Peace and Its Discontents: Essays on Palestine in the Middle East Peace Process*. New York: Vintage, 1996.

Said, Edward, and Christopher Hitchens, eds. *Blaming the Victims: Spurious Scholarship and the Palestinian Question*. London: Verso, 1988.

Saldivar, José David. *The Dialectics of Our America*. Durham, N.C.: Duke University Press, 1992.

———. "Americo Paredes and Decolonization." In *Cultures of United States Imperialism*, ed. Amy Kaplan and Donald E. Pease. Durham, N.C.: Duke University Press, 1993.

Salih, A Tayeb. *Mawsim al-hijra ila al-shimal*. Beirut: Dar al-awdah, 1969.

Sangari, Kumkum. "The Politics of the Possible." In *The Nature and Context of Minority Discourse*, ed. David Lloyd and Abdul Jan Mohamed. Oxford: Oxford University Press, 1990.

Sangari, Kumkum, and Sudesh Vaid. Introduction to *Recasting Women: Essays in Indian Colonial History*. New Brunswick, N.J.: Rutgers University Press, 1989.

Sartre, Jean-Paul. *Being and Nothingness*. Translated by Hazel E. Barnes. New York: Philosophical Library, 1956.

Sattar, Arshia. "The Blood of Others." *Times of India Sunday Review*, 20 February 1994.

Schieffelin, Edward L., Robert Crittenden, et al. *Like People You See in a Dream: First Contact in Six Papuan Societies*. Stanford, Calif.: Stanford University Press, 1991.

Schnitzler, A. *My Youth in Vienna*. Translated by C. Hutter. New York: Holt, Rinehart, and Winston, 1970.

Schor, Naomi. "The Righting of French Studies: Homosociality and the Killing of 'La pensée 68.' " *MLA Professions* (1992).

Schorske, C. *Fin-de-Siècle Vienna: Politics and Culture*. New York: Knopf, 1980.

Schwarz, Roberto. "Nationalism by Elimination." In *Misplaced Ideas: Essays on Brazilian Culture*, trans. John Gledson et al. London: Verso, 1992.

Seed, Patricia. "Colonial and Postcolonial Discourse." *Latin American Research Review* 26, no. 3 (1991): 181–200.

Segev, Tom. *The Seventh Million: Israelis and the Holocaust*. New York: Hill and Wang, 1993.

Seshadri-Crooks, Kalpana. "The Primitive as Analyst: Postcolonial Feminism's Access to Psychoanalysis." *Cultural Critique*, no. 28 (fall 1994): 175–218.

Shafir, Gideon. *Land, Labor, and the Origins of the Israeli-Palestinian Conflict, 1882–1914.* Cambridge: Cambridge University Press, 1989.

Shahak, Israel. "Arab Villages Destroyed in Israel." In *Documents from Israel, 1967–1973,* ed. Uri Davis and Norton Mezvinsky. London: Ithaca, 1975.

Shama, Shimon. *Two Rothchilds and the Land of Israel.* London: Collins, 1978.

Shanmugaratnam, N. "Development and Environment: A View from the South." *Race and Class* 30, no. 3 (1989).

Sharif, Regina. *Non-Jewish Zionism: Its Roots in Western History.* London: Zed, 1983.

Sharoni, Simona. "To Be a Man in the Jewish State: The Sociopolitical Context of Violence and Oppression." *Challenge* 2, no. 5 (September/October 1991).

———. "Militarized Masculinity in Context: Cultural Politics and Social Constructions of Gender in Israel." Paper presented at the conference of the Middle East Studies Association, Portland, October 1992.

Sharpe, Jennifer. *Allegories of Empire: The Figure of Woman in the Colonial Text.* Minneapolis: University of Minnesota Press, 1993.

———. "Is the United States Postcolonial? Transnationalism, Immigration, and Race." *Diaspora* 4, no. 2 (1995): 181–200.

Shiva, Vandana. *Staying Alive: Women, Ecology, and Development.* London: Zed, 1989.

Shohat, Ella. *Israeli Cinema, East/West, and the Politics of Representation.* Austin: University of Texas Press, 1989.

———. "Eurocentrism, Exile, and Zionist Discourse." Paper presented at the annual conference of the Middle East Studies Association, Washington, D.C., 1991.

———. "Imaging Terra Incognita: The Disciplinary Gaze of Empire." *Public Culture* 3, no. 2 (spring 1991).

———. "Notes on the 'Post-Colonial.' " *Social Text* 31/32 (1992): 99–113.

———. "Staging the Quincentenary, the Middle East, and the Americas." *Third Text* 21 (winter 1992–93): 95–106.

———. "Gender and Culture of Empire: Toward a Feminist Ethnography of the Cinema." In *Otherness and the Media: The Ethnography of the Imagined and the Imaged,* ed. Hamid Naficy and Teshome H. Gabriel. Chur: Harwood Academic, 1993.

Sinfield, Alan. *Literature, Politics, and Culture in Postwar Britain.* Berkeley and Los Angeles: University of California Press, 1989.

Slemon, Stephen, and Helen Tiffin, eds. *After Europe: Critical Theory and Postcolonial Writing.* Mundelstrup: Dangaroo, 1989.

Soja, Edward W. *Postmodern Geographies.* London: Verso, 1989.

Spinoza, B. de. *The Political Works.* Translated by A. G. Wernham. Oxford: Oxford University Press, 1958.

Spivak, Gayatri Chakravorty. "The Rani of Sirmur." In *Europe and Its Others,* vol. 1, ed. Francis Barker, Peter Hulme, Margaret Iversen, and Diana Loxley. Colchester: University of Essex Press, 1985.

———. "Feminism and Critical Theory." In *In Other Worlds: Essays in Cultural Politics.* London: Methuen, 1987.

———. "Can the Subaltern Speak?" In *Marxism and the Interpretation of Culture,* ed. Cary Nelson and Lawrence Grossberg. Urbana: University of Illinois Press, 1988.

———. "Who Claims Alterity?" In *Remaking History,* ed. Barbara Kruger and Phil Mariani. Seattle: Bay, 1989.

———. *The Post-Colonial Critic.* Edited by Sarah Harasym. New York: Routledge, 1990.

———. "Poststructuralism, Marginality, Postcoloniality, and Value." In *Literary Theory Today,* ed. Peter Collier and Helga Geyer-Ryan. London: Polity, 1990.

——. *Outside in the Teaching Machine*. New York: Routledge, 1993.

——. "Scattered Speculations on the Question of Cultural Studies." In *Outside in the Teaching Machine*. New York: Routledge, 1993.

——. *Imaginary Maps: Three Stories by Mahasweta Devi*. New York: Routledge, 1995.

Sridhar, G. R. "A Beginning Must Be Made." *Hindu*, 20 March 1994.

Stam, Robert. *Subversive Pleasures: Bakhtin, Cultural Criticism, and Film*. Baltimore: Johns Hopkins University Press, 1989.

——. "Eurocentrism, Afrocentrism, Polycentrism: Theories of Third Cinema." *Quarterly Review of Film and Video* 13, nos. 1–3 (spring 1991).

Staudenraus, P. J. *The African Colonization Movement, 1816–1865*. New York: Columbia University Press, 1961.

Stavenhagen, Rodolfo. "Classes, Colonialism, and Acculturation." *Studies in Comparative International Development* 1, no. 7 (1965).

Steele, Shelby. *The Content of Our Character: A New Vision of Race in America*. New York: St. Martin's, 1990.

Stephens, Julie. " 'Feminist Fictions': A Critique of the Category 'Non-Western Woman in Feminist Writings on India.' " In *Subaltern Studies*, vol. 6, ed. Ranajit Guha. Delhi: Oxford University Press, 1989.

Stevens, Richard. "Zionism as a Phase of Western Imperialism." In *The Transformation of Palestine*, ed. Ibrahim Abu-Lughod. Evanston, Ill.: Northwestern University Press, 1971.

Stewart, Desmond. *Theodor Herzl*. New York: Doubleday, 1974.

"The Strategic Importance of Syria to the British Empire." General Staff, War Office, 9 December 1918. PRO, FO 371/4178.

Suleri, Sara. *The Rhetoric of English India*. Chicago: University of Chicago Press, 1992.

——. "Women Skin Deep: Feminism and the Postcolonial Condition." *Critical Inquiry* 18 (1992): 756–69.

Suresh, V., and D. Nagasila. "In Public Interest." *Seminar* 430 (June 1995).

Surin, Kenneth. "On Producing the Concept of a Global Culture." *South Atlantic Quarterly* 94, no. 4 (fall 1995).

Tabataba'i Na'ini, Mirza Reza Khan. *Ruznameh-ye te'atr* (Theater Newspaper). Edited by Mohammad Golbon and Faramarz Talebi. Tehran: Nashr-e Chesmeh, 1366/1987.

Tahaminezhad, Mohammad. "Risheh yabi-ye ya's — 2" (Diagnosing the Roots of Despair — 2). *Vizheh-ye sinema va te'atr*, nos. 5 and 6 (1973).

Tamir, J. "The March of the Co-opted Historians." *Ha'aretz*, 20 May 1994.

Taylor, Charles. *Sources of the Self: The Making of Modern Identity*. Cambridge, Mass.: Harvard University Press, 1989.

——. "The Politics of Recognition." In *Multiculturalism: Examining the Politics of Recognition*, ed. Amy Gutmann. New York: Routledge, 1994.

Taylor, Ronald, trans. and ed. *Aesthetics and Politics*. London: New Left, 1977.

Tharu, Susie. "Response to Julie Stephens." *Subaltern Studies*, vol. 6, ed. Ranajit Guha. Delhi: Oxford University Press, 1989.

Thomas, Nicholas. *Colonialism's Culture: Anthropology, Travel, Government*. Princeton, N.J.: Princeton University Press, 1994.

Tiffin, Chris, and Alan Lawson, eds. *De-Scribing Empire: Post-Coloniality and Textuality*. New York: Routledge, 1994.

Todorov, Tzvetan. *The Conquest of America: The Question of the Other*. Translated by Richard Howard. New York: Harper and Row, 1982.

Tomas, David. "Transcultural Space." *Visual Anthropology Review* 9, no. 2 (fall 1993): 60–78.

Toulet, Emmanuelle. "Cinema at the Universal Exposition, Paris, 1900." *Persistence of Vision*, no. 9 (1991): 10–36.

Trennert, Robert A., Jr. *Alternative to Extinction: Federal Indian Policy and the Beginnings of the Reservation System, 1846–51.* Philadelphia: Temple University Press, 1975.

Trinh T. Minh-ha. *Women, Native, Other: Writing Postcoloniality and Feminism.* Bloomington: Indiana University Press, 1989.

Umbartha (Threshhold). Directed by Jabbar Patel. Color, 135 minutes. India: Sujatha Chitra, 1982. In Marathi; also appeared in Hindi under the title *Subah.*

van der Veer, Peter. "The Foreign Hand: Orientalist Discourse in Sociology and Communalism." In *Orientalism and the Postcolonial Predicament: Perspectives on South Asia,* ed. Carol A. Breckenridge and Peter van der Veer. Philadelphia: University of Pennsylvania Press, 1993.

Van Erven, Eugene. *The Playful Revolution: Theatre and Liberation in Asia.* Bloomington: Indiana University Press, 1992.

Van Hook, Loretta C. "Report of Evangelical Work." Board of Foreign Missions, 1 October 1905–1 October 1906. Microfilm reel 274, MF10, F7619, Presbyterian Historical Association, Philadelphia.

Vanita, Ruth. "Thinking beyond Gender in India." *Seminar* 446 (October 1996).

Viswanathan, Gauri. *The Masks of Conquest.* New York: Columbia University Press, 1989.

———. "Raymond Williams and British Colonialism: The Limits of Metropolitan Cultural Theory." In *Views from the Border Country: Raymond Williams and Cultural Politics,* ed. Dennis L. Dworkin and Leslie H. Roman. New York: Routledge, 1993.

Weed, Elizabeth, ed. *Coming to Terms: Feminism, Theory, Politics.* London: Routledge, 1989.

Weinstock, Nathan. *Zionism: False Messiah.* London: Ink Links, 1979.

West, Cornel. "Interview with Cornel West." In *Universal Abandon: The Politics of Postmodernism,* ed. Andrew Ross. Minneapolis: University of Minnesota Press, 1988.

———. *The American Evasion of Philosophy: A Genealogy of Pragmatism.* Madison: University of Wisconsin Press, 1989.

———. *Race Matters.* New York: Vintage, 1993.

West, Morris. *Keeping Faith: Philosophy and Race in America.* New York: Routledge, 1993.

Weston, Rubin Francis. *Racism in U.S. Imperialism: The Influence of Racial Assumptions on American Foreign Policy, 1893–1946.* Columbia: University of South Carolina Press, 1972.

White, Jonathan, ed. *Recasting the World: Writing after Colonialism.* Baltimore: Johns Hopkins University Press, 1993.

White, Lucie E. "Subordination, Rhetorical Survival Skills, and Sunday Shoes: Notes on the Hearing of Mrs. G." In *Feminist Legal Theory,* ed. Katherine T. Bartlett and Rosanne Kennedy. Boulder, Colo.: Westview, 1991.

Whitelam, Keith. *The Invention of Ancient Israel: The Silencing of Palestinian History.* New York: Routledge, 1996.

Whitlock, Gillian, and Helen Tiffin, eds. *Re-Siting the Queen's English: Text and Tradition in Post-Colonial Literatures.* Atlanta: Rodopi, 1992.

Whitman, Walt. "Birds of Passage: Song of the Universal." In *Walt Whitman: The Complete Poems,* ed. Francis Murphy. London: Penguin, 1975.

Williams, Patrick, and Laura Chrisman, eds. *Colonial Discourse and Postcolonial Theory.* New York: Columbia University Press, 1993.

Williams, Raymond. *The Politics of Modernism.* London: Verso, 1989.

Williams, Robert A., Jr. *The American Indian in Western Legal Thought: The Discourses of Conquest.* New York: Oxford University Press, 1990.

Williams, William Appleman, ed. *From Colony to Empire.* New York: Wiley, 1972.

———. *Empire as a Way of Life.* New York: Oxford University Press, 1980.

Wiltse, Charles M., ed. "Documents Relating to the Origins of the Monroe Doctrine." In *Expansion and Reform, 1815–1850.* New York: Free Press, 1967.

Woman's Work for Woman (New York Woman's Foreign Missionary Societies of the Presbyterian Church), vol. 16, no. 10 (October 1901), and vol. 19, no. 10 (October 1904).

"Women: Towards Beijing." *Lokayan Bulletin* (Joint Women's Programme) 12, nos. 1–2 (July–October 1995).

Wood, Ellen Meiksins. *The Retreat from Class: A New 'True' Socialism.* London: Verso, 1986.

Yadav, Alok. "Nationalism and Contemporaneity: Political Economy of a Discourse." *Cultural Critique* 26 (winter 1993–94): 191–229.

Yadin, Yigael. *Bar Kochba: The Rediscovery of the Legendary Hero of the Second Jewish Revolt against Rome.* Jerusalem: Weinfeld and Nicholson, 1971.

Yerushalmi, Y. H. *Freud's Moses: Judaism Terminable and Interminable.* New Haven, Conn.: Yale University Press, 1991.

Yoshikawa, Yoko. "The Heat Is on Miss Saigon Coalition: Organizing across Race and Sexuality." In *The State of Asian America: Activism and Resistance in the 1990s,* ed. Karin Aguilar-San Juan. Boston: South End, 1994.

Young, Robert. "Poststructuralism: The End of Theory." *Oxford Literary Review* 5, nos. 1–2 (1982).

———. *Darwin's Metaphor: Nature's Place in Victorian Culture.* Cambridge: Cambridge University Press, 1988.

Yudice, George. "Marginality and the Ethics of Survival." In *Universal Abandon? The Politics of Postmodernism.* Minneapolis: University of Minnesota Press, 1988.

Yuval-Davis, Nira. "National Reproduction and 'the Demographic Race' in Israel." In *Woman-Nation-State,* ed. Nira Yuval-Davis and Floya Anthias. London: Macmillan, 1989.

Zahlan, Antoine. *Technology Transfer and Change in the Arab World.* Oxford: Pergamon, 1978.

Zea, Leopoldo. *Discurso desde la marginación y la barbarie.* Barcelona: Anthrops, 1988.

———, ed. *Ser mujer indigena, chola o birlocha, en la Bolivia postcolonial de los años 90.* La Paz: Ministerio de Desarrollo Humano, 1997.

Zeine, Zeine. *The Struggle for Arab Independence.* Beirut: Khayat's, 1960.

Zertal, I. "The Sacrificed and the Sanctified: The Construction of a National Martyrology." *Zemanim* 12, no. 48 (spring 1994).

Zerubavel, Yael. *Recovered Roots: Collective Memory and the Making of an Israeli National Tradition.* Chicago: University of Chicago Press, 1995.

Zinn, Howard. *A People's History of the United States.* New York: Harper and Row, 1980.

Žižek, Slavoj. *Enjoy Your Symptom: Jacques Lacan in Hollywood and Out.* New York: Routledge, 1992.

———. "An Interview with Slavoj Žižek." *Found Object* 2 (1993).

Zureik, Elia. *Palestinians in Israel: A Study in Internal Colonialism.* London: Routledge and Kegan Paul, 1979.

CONTRIBUTORS

FAWZIA AFZAL-KHAN is Professor of English at Montclair State University. She is the author of *Cultural Imperialism and the Indo-English Novel* (Penn State University Press, 1993) and of many articles on postcolonial and feminist theory and criticism published in *NWSA Journal, TDR, Womanist Theory and Research, Conradiana, Journal of Indian Writing in English, Journal of South Asian Literature, World Literature Written in English, Wasafiri, Reviews in Anthropology,* etc. She is currently on the Advisory Board of *RAWI (Radius of Arab American Writers)*, performing and publishing poetry, and working on a book of memoirs tentatively entitled *Sahelian: Growing Up Pakistani Style.* She is also finishing up her book on Pakistani alternative theater and the women's movement and working as an actress and singer for an avant-garde theater company in New York called Faim de Siècle. She will be a Fulbright Fellow to Pakistan in 2000–01.

ALI BEHDAD is Associate Professor of English and comparative literature at the University of California, Los Angeles. He is the author of *Belated Travelers: Orientalism in the Age of Colonial Dissolution* (Duke University Press, 1994) and is currently working on a manuscript on U.S. nationalism and immigration.

HOMI K. BHABHA is Chester Tripp Professor in the Humanities at the University of Chicago. He is the author of *The Location of Culture* (Routledge, 1994) and the editor of *Nation and Narration* (Routledge, 1990).

DANIEL BOYARIN is Taubman Professor of Talmudic Studies at the University of California, Berkeley. Selected publications include *Unheroic Conduct: The Rise of Heterosexuality and the Invention of the Jewish Man* (University of California Press, 1997); *Carnal Israel: Reading Sex in Talmudic Culture* (University of California Press, 1995); *A Radical Jew: Paul and the Politics of Identity* (University of California Press, 1994); and several edited collections, including *Jews and Other Differences* (University of Minnesota Press, 1997).

NEIL LARSEN teaches in the Department of Spanish and Classics and in the Programs in Critical Theory and Comparative Literature at the University of California, Davis. He is the author of *Modernism and Hegemony* (University of Minnesota Press, 1990), *Reading North by South* (University of Minnesota Press, 1995), and *Nations, Narratives, History: Questions of Theory and the "Postcolonial"* (Verso, forthcoming).

SAREE MAKDISI is Associate Professor of English at the University of Chicago. He is the author of numerous articles on contemporary Arab culture and of *Romantic Imperialism: Universal Empire and the Culture of Imperialism* (Cambridge University Press, 1998).

JOSEPH MASSAD is Assistant Professor of Modern Arab Politics and Intellectual History at Columbia University. He has published many articles on the Palestinian struggle and on Israeli society. His work has appeared in a number of journals, including *Social Text, Middle East Journal, Journal of Palestine Studies,* and *Critique.*

WALTER MIGNOLO is William Hanes Wannamaker Professor of Romance Studies at Duke University. His recent publications include *The Darker Side of the Renaissance: Literacy, Territoriality, Colonization* (University of Michigan Press, 1995) and an edited collection, *Writing without Words: Alternative Literacies in Mesoamerica and the Andes* (Duke University Press, 1994).

HAMID NAFICY is Associate Professor of film and media studies, Department of Art and Art History, Rice University, Houston. He has published extensively about theories of exile and diasporic cultures and media as well as about Iranian, Middle Eastern, and Third World cinema. His English-language books include *The Making of Exile Cultures: Iranian Television in Los Angeles* (University of Minnesota Press, 1993), *Otherness and the Media: The Ethnography of the Imagined and the Imaged* (coedited with Teshome Gabriel, Harwood Academic, 1993), *Iran Media Index* (Greenwood, 1984), and *Home, Exile, Homeland* (Routledge, 1998).

NGUGI WA THIONGO is Erich Maria Remarque Professor of Languages at New York University. Educated in Kenya, Uganda, and the United Kingdom, Professor Ngugi is a major voice of African literature and scholarship. A playwright, novelist, and essayist, his work has been translated into more than thirty languages and recognized by many national and international awards, including the Paul Robeson Award for Artistic Excellence, Political Conscience, and Integrity (1992); the Gwendolyn Brooks Center Contributors Award for Significant Contribution to the Black Literary Arts (1994); the Fonlon-Nichols Prize (1996), and the Distinguished Africanist Award by the New York African Studies Association (1996). In *Decolonizing the Mind: The Politics of Language in African Literature,* he set out his program for the development of an African literary and critical discourse based on African languages. At present, he publishes *Mutiiri,* a journal of literature and culture entirely in the Gikuyu language.

TIMOTHY B. POWELL is Assistant Professor of English at the University of Georgia, Athens. His publications include articles on Toni Morrison and Martin R. Delany, with essays in progress treating the work of Henry David Thoreau, Harriet Beecher Stowe, and the ghost dance movement. He is the editor of a collection of essays titled *Beyond the Binary: A Multicultural Reconstruction of "American" Identity* (Rutgers University Press, 1999) and the author of *Ruthless Democracy: A Multicultural Interpretation of the American Renaissance* (Princeton University Press, forthcoming).

R. RADHAKRISHNAN teaches critical theory and postcoloniality in the Department of English at the University of Massachusetts, Amherst. He has published extensively in collections of essays and in journals such as *MELUS, Boundary 2, Callaloo, Differences, Cultural Critique, Social Text, Transition,* and *Rethinking Marxism.* He is the author of two books, *Theory in an Uneven World* (Blackwell, forthcoming) and *Diasporic Mediations: Between Home and Location* (University of Minnesota Press, 1996).

BRUCE ROBBINS is Professor of English at Rutgers University. Selected publications include *Feeling Global: Internationalism in Distress* (New York University Press, 1999) and *The Servant's Hand: English Fiction from Below* (Columbia University Press, 1986). He has edited *Cosmopolitics* (with Pheng Cheah, University of Minnesota Press, 1998) and *Secular Vocations: Intellectuals, Professionalism, Culture* (Verso, 1993).

KALPANA SESHADRI-CROOKS is Assistant Professor of English at Boston College. She is the author of *Desiring Whiteness: A Lacanian Analysis of Race* (forthcoming).

ELLA SHOHAT is Professor of cultural and women's studies at the City University of New York (CUNY) Graduate Center and of cinema studies, CUNY, Staten Island. Her publications include *Israeli Cinema: East/West and the Politics of Representation* (University of Texas Press, 1989) and *Unthinking Eurocentrism: Multiculturalism and the Media* (with Robert Stam, Routledge, 1994). She has edited *Talking Visions: Multicultural Feminism in a Transnational Age* (MIT Press, 1999) and *Dangerous Liaisons: Gender, Race, and Postcolonial Perspectives* (University of Minnesota Press, 1997).

RAJESWARI SUNDER RAJAN is a Fellow at the Nehru Memorial Museum and Library, New Delhi, and a visiting professor of English at George Washington University. She is the author of *Real and Imagined Women: Gender, Culture, and Postcolonialism* (Routledge, 1994) and has edited *The Lie of the Land: English Literary Studies in India* (Oxford University Press, 1992) and *Signposts: Gender Issues in Post-Independence India* (Kali for Women, 1999).

INDEX

PERMISSIONS

Kalpana Seshadri-Crooks's "At the Margins of Postcolonial Studies" appeared originally in *Ariel* 26, no. 3 (July 1995): 47-71.

R. Radhakrishnan's "Postmodernism and the Rest of the World" appeared originally in *Organization* 1, no. 2 (October 1994): 305-40.

Sections of Ali Behdad's "*Une Pratique Sauvage:* Postcolonial Belatedness and Cultural Politics" have appeared in *Belated Travelers: Orientalism in the Age of Colonial Dissolution* (Durham, N.C.: Duke University Press, 1994) and in "Traveling to Teach: Postcolonial Critics in the American Academy," in *Race, Identity, and Representation in Education,* ed. Cameron McCarthy and Warren Crichlow (New York: Routledge, 1993), 40-49.

Ngugi Wa Thingo's "Borders and Bridges: Seeking Connections between Things" was published earlier as "Literature and Politics: Transcending Borders," in *In-Between: Essays and Studies in Literary Criticism* 5, no. 2 (September 1996): 115-22.

Ella Shohat's "Notes on the Postcolonial" appeared originally in *Social Text,* special issue, 31/32 (1992): 99-113.

An earlier version of Neil Larsen's "DetermiNation: Postcolonialism, Poststructuralism, and the Problem of Ideology" appeared in *Dispositio/n,* special issue, 20, no. 47 (1995): 1-16.

Bruce Robbins's "Secularism, Elitism, Progress, and Other Transgressions: On Edward Said's 'Voyage In'" appeared originally in *Social Text,* 40 (fall 1994): 25-37.

Fawzia Afzal-Khan's "Street Theater in Pakistani Punjab: The Case of Ajoka, Lok Rehs, and the (So-Called) Woman Question" appeared originally in *TDR* 41, no. 3 (fall 1997): 39-62.

Daniel Boyarin's "The Colonial Drag: Zionism, Gender, and Mimicry" appeared originally in *Unheroic Conduct: The Rise of Heterosexuality and the Invention of the Jewish Man,* Contraversions: Studies in Jewish Literature, Culture, and Society (Berkeley and Los Angeles: University of California Press, 1997).

Saree Makdisi's "Postcolonial Literature in a Neocolonial World: Modern Arabic Culture and the End of Modernity" appeared originally in *Boundary 2* 22, no. 1 (spring 1995): 85-116.

Library of Congress Cataloging-in-Publication Data
The pre-occupation of postcolonial studies / edited by
Fawzia Afzal-Khan and Kalpana Seshadri-Crooks.
Includes bibliographical references and index.
ISBN 0-8223-2486-5 (cloth : alk. paper)
ISBN 0-8223-2521-7 (paper : alk. paper)
1. Postcolonialism.   I. Afzal-Khan, Fawzia, 1958–
II. Seshadri-Crooks, Kalpana, 1960–
JV51 .P74   2000   325'.3–dc21   99-053103